GREAT COMPOSERS

1300-1900

GREAT COMPOSERS

1300–1900

A Biographical and Critical Guide

Compiled and Edited by
DAVID EWEN

THE H. W. WILSON COMPANY
NEW YORK   1966

INTRODUCTION

GREAT COMPOSERS: *1300-1900* is a replacement for *Composers of Yesterday,* published in 1937. The word "replacement" is used advisedly. The present volume is in no sense a revision of the 1937 publication. It is a completely new book.

Many factors were involved in the decision of editor and publisher to prepare a new work rather than embark upon a revision or enlargement of the earlier volume. Since 1937, a considerable amount of musicological research has helped to unearth new or corrected materials on the composers of the past. In addition, the editor himself, during the past quarter of a century, has been involved in his own researches, studies, and listening experiences throughout the world of music—and has done a considerable amount of work in European music libraries. Both the newly discovered data and the editor's continuing studies have led to new approaches and new evaluations on his part. These demanded a radical revision in his treatment of many composers, and of many of their compositions. Another significant factor was also involved. Since 1937, the recording industry—through the development of the long-playing record, high fidelity, and stereophonic sound—has made remarkable progress. More remarkable still is the way in which the catalog of recorded music has been extended and enriched. Many compositions and composers, virtually if not completely unknown in 1937, have since become everyday experiences to music lovers through recordings. These composers and these compositions, ignored in the 1937 book, must be discussed in any volume intended for an audience that has become knowledgeable and highly sophisticated.

GREAT COMPOSERS: *1300-1900* is designed to fill a vital need. Like the earlier book, it is the only one-volume work on composers of the past that tries to discuss so many creative figures (almost two hundred in number) with such completeness. All other one-volume collective biographies are devoted to the thirty or so supreme masters; the lesser figures are generally ignored. One-volume music dictionaries, though they touch on all the composers found in the present book, necessarily give only a brief treatment. The music lover today, in search of material on a specific composer, wants complete and detailed information—biographical, historical, analytical, critical, personal. And he wants that information not only on such giants as Beethoven, Bach, Mozart, Wagner, and Brahms. He wants information too on lesser masters whose works are basic to the repertory, as well as on composers whose works may be heard seldom, if at all, but whose careers deserve exploration because of their significance in the development of music.

Each sketch in this volume includes the principal works of the composer and a bibliography. Appendixes provide a chronological listing of the composers in the book and a listing by nationality.

DAVID EWEN

Miami, Florida

CONTENTS

GREAT COMPOSERS

1300-1900

Adolphe Adam *1803-1856*

ADOLPHE-CHARLES ADAM was the youngest member of a triumvirate that ruled over French *opéra-comique* during the mid-nineteenth century; the other two were Auber and Boieldieu. Adam was born in Paris on July 24, 1803, the son of a distinguished Parisian pianist, teacher, and originator of several piano methods. Although his father did all he could to keep Adolphe from music, the boy managed to study secretly while attending school. In the end he overcame his father's objections and obtained permission to pursue the study of music intensively—on the condition that he remain an amateur and never try to write for the stage. Consequently, he had his father's blessing when he entered the Paris Conservatory in 1817. There his teachers included Benoist, for organ, and Boieldieu for piano. The latter was a particularly strong influence on the young composer. As Jacques Halévy noted in *Souvenirs et portraits*, Boieldieu became Adam's "master, his guide, and his friend. . . . He disengaged him from the labyrinth in which he had until now been enmeshed, and brought him to melody which until now he had ignored. . . . Certainly Adam had an instinct for the theater, and would ultimately have discovered the road of which, at first, he lost sight; but Boieldieu avoided for him a long and circuitous route."

Once out of the Conservatory, Adam forgot his promise to his father and started to write for the stage. One of his earliest efforts was an overture for Boieldieu's *opéra-comique La Dame blanche*, based on melodies from the opera. Then Adam made his official bow as stage composer with a one-act *opéra-comique*, *Pierre et Catherine*, introduced at the Opéra-Comique in Paris on February 9, 1829. This was followed by a three-act opera, *Danilowa*, in 1830, and in 1834 by his first success, a one-act light opera, *Le Chalet*. The last retained its popularity through the years; before the end of

ADOLPHE ADAM

the century it had been given almost fifteen hundred performances in Paris.

Adam's eminence as a composer of *opéra-comique*, and his international fame, came with *Le Postillon de Longjumeau*, produced with great success at the Opéra-Comique on October 13, 1836. *Le Postillon* was first performed in the United States in New York on March 30, 1840, and in the same year it was acclaimed in London. Performances of *Le Postillon* were frequent in the United States after its première, often with Theodor Wachtel in the title part, a role in which he scored his greatest success and in which he appeared over a thousand times. The most famous vocal excerpt from this tuneful opera is the first act postillion song, *"Mes amis, écoutez l'histoire."* Wachtel used to elicit ovations for his rendition of this aria by cracking a whip, whose rhythm would provide an exciting background to the refrain "Ho, Ho."

When Adam was next acclaimed throughout the world of music it was not for an opera but for a ballet, the classic of French romantic ballet, *Giselle*. The text was a

Adam: à-dän'

work of Théophile Gautier, written in collaboration with Vernoy de Saint-Georges and Jean Coralli; the choreography was by Jules Perrot and Coralli. *Giselle* had a triumphant première at the Paris Opéra on June 28, 1841, with Carlotta Grisi appearing as the peasant girl, Giselle. In later years this part was danced by some of the world's most celebrated ballerinas, including Pavlova, Karsavina, Markova, and Moira Shearer.

In 1847 Adam founded the Théâtre National in Paris, an opera house planned to provide hearings for young, unrecognized composers, but the revolution of 1848 proved a death blow to this laudable enterprise. The collapse of his company involved Adam in enormous debts which he himself repaid within the next few years from the royalties of his operas. Of these the most successful was *Si j'étais roi*, produced by the Théâtre Lyrique on September 4, 1852. Its tuneful overture is still a favorite with salon orchestras. Equally successful was his serious opera *Richard en Palestine*, whose première took place at the Paris Opéra on October 7, 1854. In all, Adam wrote over fifty operas, light and serious, as well as ballets, incidental music for about thirty plays, songs, church music, and piano pieces.

He was at his best in the *opéra-comique* and ballet. His most significant traits as a composer were a fresh, expressive lyricism, a graceful style, a charming manner; what he lacked most were dramatic power, emotional depth, and genuine creative originality. "The misfortune about me," Adam once confessed, "is that I write with too much facility, far too much facility."

"If he failed completely in grand lyric drama," wrote Arthur Pougin in his biography of Adam, "in spite of his desires and ambitions, . . . he knew . . . how to bring into the field of *opéra-comique* a truly personal style, touched at the same time with grace and coquetry, with sentiment of emotion, and gaiety and comic verve."

Sterling MacKinlay comments: "Sometimes his melodies are trivial in the extreme; his structure of concerted pieces is of the flimsiest kind; his dance rhythms used without moderation." Nevertheless, MacKinlay adds, Adam's music was appealing for its "flowing melodiousness, rhythmic piquancy of style, precision of declamatory phrasing,

and charming effects of graceful, though sketchy, instrumentation."

In 1844 Adam was elected a member of the French Institute. Five years later he was made professor of composition at the Paris Conservatory. He died in Paris on May 3, 1856.

All his life Adam was a hard worker, devoting many hours of day and night to composition, for he seemed to require little sleep. He once said, "It is the fever of creation and hard work that prolongs my youth and succors me." But this passion for work did not keep him from enjoying the good life. A true Parisian, he was a gourmet, a lover of fine wines, and a *bon vivant*.

PRINCIPAL WORKS

Ballets—Faust; La Fille du Danube; Giselle; La Jolie fille de Gand.

Choral Music—Le Crépuscule.

Operas—Over 50 opéra-comiques and operas including: Le Chalet; Le Postillon de Longjumeau; Le Roi d'Yvetot; Richard en Palestine; Le Toréador; La Poupée de Nuremberg; Si j'étais roi; Le Bijou perdu; Le Muletier de Tolède; Les Pantins de Violette.

Vocal Music—Numerous songs for voice and piano including Noël (Minuit, Chrétiens).

ABOUT

Pougin, A., *Adolphe Adam*.

Isaac Albéniz *1860-1909*

ISAAC MANUEL FRANCISCO ALBÉNIZ, the first improtant member of the Spanish nationalist school, was born in Camprodón, Gerona, on May 29, 1860. He was exceptionally gifted at the piano, and made a public appearance in Barcelona when he was only four. Two years later his mother brought him to Paris to enter him in the Conservatory. Denied admission because he was too young, Albéniz took piano lessons privately with Marmontel. Upon returning to Spain he gave several concerts, then in 1868 entered the Madrid Conservatory. Unfortunately he was a boy of ungovernable moods and restless temperament, impatient with any kind of discipline. At thirteen he ran away from home, stowed away on board the *España* at Cádiz, and set sail for the New World. For a few years he supported himself by playing the piano in South America, Puerto Rico, and Cuba. His father—who happened to be in Cuba at the time as

Albéniz: äl-bā′nēth

customs inspector—came upon him accidentally and had him arrested as a disobedient child. But he soon had a change of heart and allowed the boy to continue his travels and concerts in the United States.

After performing in England, Albéniz went to Germany in 1874 and enrolled in the Leipzig Conservatory; his teachers included Reinecke and Jadassohn. Two years later he was back in his native land. Through the intercession of Count Morphy, he obtained a royal stipend for further music study at the Brussels Conservatory. His crowning ambition at the time, however, was to study piano with Liszt, and he soon deserted the Conservatory to travel in Austria and Hungary. He finally succeeded in meeting Liszt; but the belief, so long encouraged by Albéniz's biographers, that he actually studied with Liszt has no basis in fact.

He was in Spain again in 1880. In 1883 he married Rosita Jordana and in 1885 settled in Madrid. For a while he earned his living by giving concerts and teaching.

From 1890 to 1893 Albéniz lived mainly in London, where his first major work—a comic opera, *The Magic Opal*—was produced on January 18, 1893. By the end of 1894 he had moved to Paris to stay for several years. There he became a friend of Debussy and, during the winter of 1897-1898, taught a piano course at the Schola Cantorum.

A turning point in Albéniz's life was his meeting and friendship with Felipe Pedrell, whom he met for the first time in Barcelona in 1883. Sometimes described as "the father of Spanish music," Pedrell was a scholar who had done considerable and valuable research in old Spanish folk and art music. It was Pedrell's conviction that Spanish composers must write *Spanish* music, deriving its ideas and inspiration from Spanish geography, history, and culture, acquiring its idiom and techniques from native folk songs and dances.

Pedrell's ideas made a deep impression on Albéniz. Until that time he had written some operas, none particularly significant. He regarded himself, and was considered by others, as a pianist who wrote music, rather than a composer who gave piano recitals. But, once fired with the ambition to become a nationalist composer, he found his purpose and direction, and formed a style and personality uniquely his own.

ISAAC ALBÉNIZ

His first national efforts included two works for the piano, *Rapsodie espagnole* and *Seguidillas*. His first opera with a pronounced Spanish character, *Pepita Jiménez*, was introduced in Barcelona on January 5, 1896; it was the only one of his operatic works to become successful. He also completed a large work for piano and orchestra, *Catalonia*, which was introduced in Paris by the Société Nationale in 1899.

After 1900 misfortune dogged his steps. He was frequently ill and in pain, suffering the ravages of Bright's disease, which eventually took his life. His wife was a chronic invalid, too; and a daughter died suddenly. Despite all the domestic tragedy engulfing him, and despite his own poor health, Albéniz was able, between 1906 and 1909, to complete his masterpiece, *Iberia,* a suite of twelve Spanish pieces collected in four books. Today it is the work by which he is most often represented in the concert hall and on recordings. Among the most famous pieces in this suite are "El Puerto," "Triana," "El Corpus en Sevilla" (sometimes also known as "Fête Dieu à Seville"), "Evocación," and "El Albaicín," all made popular in the symphonic repertory through orchestral transcriptions by Fernandez Arbós.

"Iberia," wrote Georges Jean-Aubry, "marks the summit of the art of Albéniz. . . . In music there are many excellent scholars but few poets. Albéniz has all the power of the poet—ease and richness of style,

beauty and originality of imagery, and a rare sense of suggestion. A list of themes alone . . . would suffice to show their richness in melody and the variety of their rhythm. But more wonderful than the beauty of the themes is their suppleness and fluidity; their languorous intonation, or their heat and energy. That in which Albéniz is inimitable is the atmosphere he creates around a theme, the scenery with which he surrounds the 'melodic personage'—a word, a song, or a murmured confession. The method of Albéniz, if one can use such a word in regard to him, is almost inscrutable. It obeys only subtle and personal laws. An expressive counterpoint, always ductile and full of movement, supports his themes, plays with them or crosses them. The parts seem at times inextricably intermingled and suddenly all is again resolved in lucidity.

When Albéniz completed the first book of *Iberia* he was seized by the fear that his music was too difficult to perform successfully. For a while he was tempted to destroy his manuscript. But when a twenty-two-year-old pianist, Blanche Selva, committed the pieces to memory and performed them fluently for Albéniz, the composer realized that his fear had been groundless and completed the remaining three books. Blanche Selva introduced *Iberia* to the public: she performed the first book in Paris on May 9, 1906, the second book in St. Jean de Luz on September 11, 1907, the first three (the third receiving here its world première) in Paris on January 2, 1908, and the fourth, again in Paris, on February 9, 1909.

By the winter of 1909 Albéniz—then living in Paris—was too ill to leave his apartment. Though virtually an invalid, he did manage to travel with his family to the French Pyrenees. He died there, in Cambo-les-Bains, on June 16, 1909. "The spring has been damp and chill," his daughter Laura recalled later in publication, "and the flowers refused to bloom. My father's room opened on a terrace filled with woodbine and rose trees, and every day he asked me would the roses never bloom. Two days before my father's death the sun shone in fullest radiance, and on the morning, as though by magic, we found that all the roses had opened. They were the purest pink in color. And that evening, my sister and I went out on the terrace and cut all the roses to cover our father with them."

Albéniz was buried in the Southwest Churchyard in Barcelona.

Albéniz was a mild-mannered and highly impractical man. He never learned the value of money, squandering it recklessly whenever he had it. He hated to face the problems of everyday living, preferring to shut himself off from them and muddle through as best he could. He had a rich sense of humor; one of his more lovable traits was a roguishness which led him to play all kinds of pranks on his friends. He was fond of travel, and loved nature passionately.

In June 1960 a three-day festival commemorating the centenary of Albéniz's birth took place in Granada, Spain.

PRINCIPAL WORKS

Operas—The Magic Opal; Enrico Clifford; San Antonio de la Florida; Pepita Jiménez.

Orchestral Music—Catalonia, for piano and orchestra.

Piano Music—12 Piezas características; Cantos de España; Recuerdos de viaje; Rumores de la caleta; Tango in A minor; Jota aragonesa; Malagueña (op. 165, no. 3); Serenade espagnole; Suite española; Iberia, four books; Navarra (completed by De Severac); Azulejos (completed by Granados).

ABOUT

Chase, Gilbert, The Music of Spain; Collet, H., Albéniz et Granados; Laplane, G., Albéniz: Sa vie, son œuvre; Sagardia, A., Isaac Albéniz; Trend, J. B., Manuel de Falla and Spanish Music; Van Vechten, Carl, In the Garret.

Musical Quarterly, January 1929; Musical Times, December 1917.

Jacob Arcadelt *1505-1560*

JACOB ARCADELT, a significant representative of the Flemish polyphonic school and one of the earliest composers of the madrigal was born probably in Liège in or about 1505. He went to Italy when he was thirty-three, visiting Florence before he settled in Rome. In 1539 he became *magister cappellae* of the Julian Chapel, and a year later he entered the Papal Chapel where from 1544 to 1549 he served as abbot.

During his stay in Rome he met Michelangelo, two of whose poems he set to music. In 1539 Arcadelt published his first book of madrigals, an extremely important work which became so popular that within thirty years it reached its sixteenth edition. In this volume Arcadelt helped establish the four-part madrigal form which was used, without

Arcadelt: är'kȧ-dĕlt

basic changes, during the next half century and more. Writers of madrigals everywhere were influenced by him, Palestrina not excluded. Arcadelt's madrigals were characterized by an expressive lyricism, a delicate adjustment of music to words, and the assignment of equal importance to each of the voices. C. Hubert Parry has described Arcadelt's madrigals as "singularly simple in their harmonic aspects, as the harmonies were allowed to move very much in blocks and to present the simple rhythms of the poems set, without the disguise of the familiar cross accents and the subtleties of choral counterpoint."

Arcadelt's most celebrated madrigal was "Il bianco e dolce cigno" ("The Dying Swan"), believed to be the first example in music history of sentimental song. It is often singled out as the most celebrated piece of unaccompanied vocal music ever written. "Voi ve n'andat' al cielo" and "Voi mi ponest' in foco" are two other Arcadelt madrigals remarkable for their lyricism.

Arcadelt paid a visit to France in 1546 or 1547. He returned in 1555, to stay for the rest of his life. During the latter period he worked for a while for Cardinal Charles of Lorraine, Duc de Guise. Two years later he became a member of the Royal Chapel in Paris. His compositions at this time included French *chansons,* to which he brought the same kind of heightened expressiveness that characterized his best madrigals, as well as a gift for pictorial writing and refinement of style.

Jacob Arcadelt died in Paris in or about 1560.

PRINCIPAL WORKS

Choral Music—200 madrigals; 120 French chansons; 20 motets; 3 books of Masses.

ABOUT

Einstein, Alfred, The Italian Madrigal; Klefisch, W., Arcadelt als Madrigalist.

Anton Arensky *1861-1906*

A NTON STEPANOVICH ARENSKY was born in Novgorod, Russia, on August 11, 1861. His father, a physician, was an accomplished amateur cellist, his mother an excellent pianist. As a boy Anton studied harmony at the Rousseau School of Music in St. Petersburg. He had completed a string quartet by the time he was nine.

In 1879 he entered the St. Petersburg Conservatory, later joining the class of Rimsky-Korsakov, who had a decided influence on him. Arensky was an exceptional student who soon revealed considerable promise as a composer. Tchaikovsky was so impressed by one of his student efforts that he prevailed on Rimsky-Korsakov to delete one of his own works (the *Romeo and Juliet* fantasy) from a program that Rimsky-Korsakov was conducting, in order to make room for an Arensky composition.

In 1882, upon his graduation from the Conservatory, Arensky won the gold medal in composition. Two of his major works were also performed that year: his first symphony, in St. Petersburg, and his piano concerto, in Moscow. After leaving the Conservatory he went to Moscow, where he was immediately appointed professor of harmony at the Moscow Conservatory, a post he retained for twelve years. During this period he completed the opera *A Dream on the Volga;* it was successfully introduced in Moscow on January 2, 1891.

From 1889 on, Arensky had served with the Council of the Synodal School of Church Music. He withdrew in 1893, and a year later, on the recommendation of Balakirev, was appointed conductor of the Imperial Chapel Choir. For seven years he led notable choral concerts with this group. In 1901 a generous government pension of six thousand rubles a year enabled him to resign this post to devote himself completely to composition. But declining health, and his moral deterioration, kept him from work. He had always suffered a weakness for gambling and alcohol, which was compounded, after 1901, by other dissipations. Suffering from tuberculosis, he was finally compelled to retire to a sanitarium in Finland. He died in that country, in Terioki, on February 25, 1906.

It is quite true, as his severest critics have long maintained, that Arensky's writing was imitative of Tchaikovsky and Rimsky-Korsakov—to such a degree that Rimsky-Korsakov once prophesied that Arensky "will soon be forgotten." But Arensky did possess a marked gift for ingratiating melody; his workmanship was always impressive; and his style, while eclectic and derivative, had charm and grace.

Only one of his orchestral works has retained its popularity to the present time.

This is the delightful *Variations on a Theme of Tchaikovsky,* for strings, which had originated as a movement of Arensky's A minor String Quartet, op. 35. The composer later rewrote his music for string orchestra and published it as a separate work. The Tchaikovsky melody used by Arensky is the song "Christ in His Garden," from the *Children's Songs,* op. 54; this melody undergoes seven variations before the concluding coda.

Arensky was not at ease with the larger forms of music, although he did complete several operas, symphonies, and concertos. He was at his best writing chamber music and music for the piano. Among his significant chamber music works are the Piano Quintet in D and the Piano Trio in D minor. Arensky's piano compositions include four excellent suites for two pianos, in one of which (op. 15) appears what is unquestionably his most famous melody, a waltz. Arensky also produced some effective études, preludes, and caprices for piano.

PRINCIPAL WORKS

Ballet—Egyptian Nights.
Chamber Music—2 string quartets; 2 piano trios (including Trio in D minor); Piano Quintet in D; Serenade in G major, for violin and piano.
Choral Music—Anchar; Coronation Cantata; The Fountain of Bakhchisarai; The Diver.
Operas—A Dream on the Volga; Raphael; Nal and Damayanti.
Orchestral Music—2 symphonies; Piano Concerto; Intermezzo, for strings; Variations on a Theme of Tchaikovsky, for strings; Marche solennelle; Fantasia on Russian Folk Songs, for piano and orchestra; Violin Concerto in A minor; The Wolves, for bass voice and orchestra.
Piano Music—Barcarolle, berceuse, caprices, études, preludes; 4 suites for two pianos (also for orchestra); Pieces, for piano duet.
Vocal Music—Songs for voice and piano including Autumn, Happiness, In Spring, On Wings of Dreams, Two Roses, and Valse.

ABOUT

Leonard, R. A., A History of Russian Music; Montagu-Nathan, M., History of Russian Music.

Daniel François Auber *1782-1871*

D ANIEL FRANÇOIS ESPRIT AUBER, a founding father of the *opéra-comique,* was born in Caen, Normandy, on January 29, 1782. His father was an officer of the Royal Hunt until the Revolution deprived him of his sinecure. He then set up an art-dealer's shop in the Rue Saint Lazare in Paris, which prospered. As a boy Daniel proved gifted in several areas. By the time he was sixteen he spoke Italian fluently, wrote graceful prose, was a competent performer on the violin and piano, and was the composer of several ballads, of which "Le Bonjour" became popular. His father wanted him to enter business, and for this purpose sent him to London to familiarize himself with English business methods and the English language. But Auber involved himself more deeply in music than in business. He wrote several instrumental quartets and vocal romances which were performed at entertainments. As a ghost writer, he composed a set of four cello concertos for a virtuoso who liked to pass off the works of others as his own. And, in his own right, Auber completed a violin concerto which was successfully introduced in London by Jacques-Féréol Mazas, a distinguished French virtuoso.

Political unrest brought on by the rupture of the Treaty of Amiens sent Auber back to Paris in 1804. By this time he had decided to devote his efforts entirely to music. In 1805 he completed his first work for the stage, *L'Erreur d'un moment,* a one-act comic opera produced by a group of amateurs. Its main significance in Auber's career rests on the fact that it impressed Cherubini, a renowned opera composer and the director of the Paris Conservatory, who offered his services as Auber's teacher. While studying under Cherubini during the next few years, Auber spent a few months annually working for the Comte de Carman (later Prince de Chamay), in whose employ he completed a Mass (parts of which he later appropriated for his opera *La Muette de Portici*), and an opera, *Couvin. Couvin,* and the two operas that followed it, were such disastrous failures that Auber lost heart completely and for several years refused to write for the stage. His return to the stage in 1819 met with failure; but in 1820 *La Bergère châtelaine,* produced by the Opéra-Comique, scored a brilliant success. And *Emma,* which followed in 1821, was also received most favorably.

In 1823 Auber met the brilliant dramatist Augustin-Eugène Scribe, with whom he formed a writing partnership. With Scribe as his librettist, Auber was destined to achieve his greatest popular and artistic success. Over the years Auber set thirty-

Auber: ō-bâr'

seven of Scribe's texts; among these were the four works that placed Auber with the foremost masters of French opera and *opéra-comique.*

The first crowning success of the Auber-Scribe collaboration was *La Muette de Portici* (sometimes called *Masaniello*), produced by the Paris Opéra on February 29, 1828. This is not an *opéra-comique*—the genre for which Auber is most celebrated—but a romantic opera of broad structural dimension and serious musical content. The text was derived from a historical incident: the 1647 revolt in Naples against Spanish oppressors. Because of its provocative political theme, *La Muette de Portici* had powerful repercussions. It was said to have stimulated the revolutionary spirit that infected Paris just before the July revolution of 1830, and in Brussels it provoked riots that contributed to the ejection of the Dutch from Belgium.

La Muette de Portici is a work of forceful and original invention. Richard Wagner extolled its "bold effects in instrumentation, particularly for strings; the drastic groupings of the choral masses which here take on an important role in the action; the original harmonies; and the happy strokes of dramatic characterizations." So vital is its dramatic impact, so rich are its musical resources, and so effective are its big scenes that *La Muette de Portici* is often regarded as the foundation of French grand opera. *La Muette* also became one of the most successful operas produced in France; in Paris alone, it had received over five hundred performances by 1880. The American première took place in New York on August 15, 1831.

After *La Muette de Portici,* Auber created three masterworks in the *opéra-comique* form. The first, *Fra Diavolo,* opened at the Opéra-Comique on January 28, 1830; next *Le Domino noir* was performed on December 2, 1837, and *Les Diamants de la couronne* on March 6, 1841, both at the Opéra-Comique. The first two are among the most successful *opéras-comiques* ever written. *Le Domino noir* had enjoyed over a thousand performances at the Opéra-Comique by 1882, and *Fra Diavolo* matched that record by 1914. All three helped to crystallize and perfect the form and style of the *opéra-comique* and to establish its traditions; to this day they have remained among the finest specimens of the genre. The first American performance of *Le Domino noir* took place in New Orleans in November

DANIEL FRANÇOIS AUBER

1839; that of *Fra Diavolo* in New York on October 17, 1831; and that of *Les Diamants de la couronne* in New York on July 13, 1843.

In a discussion of Auber's scores for these and other *opéras-comiques,* Henri Lavoix wrote: "One must expect from Auber neither a profound dramatic sentiment, nor poetical outbursts, nor powerful effects, nor sensibility, nor tenderness, nor especially passion. Wit in melody; wit in the general style; wit in the harmonies, which are ingenious and distinguished; wit in the orchestra, notwithstanding more *brio* than brilliancy, more sound than sonority; wit in the rhythms (although these are sometimes vulgar); wit especially in the disposition of the scenes; wit ever and always, even when the heart should be moved: this is the predominating trait of his talent."

Many world-famous musicians were numbered among his most ardent admirers. When someone once remarked to Rossini that Auber's music was "petty," Rossini answered quickly: "Petty music, perhaps, but nevertheless the music of a *great* musician." Wagner wrote: "His music at once elegant and popular, fluent and precise, graceful and bold, bending with marvelous facility to every turn of his caprice, had all the qualities to win and dominate public taste. He mastered vocal music with a keen vivacity, multiplied its rhythm to infinity, and gave the ensemble pieces an *entrain,* a characteristic briskness scarcely known before his time."

Honors came to him throughout his life. In 1829 he succeeded Gossec as a member of the French Academy; from 1842 until the end of his life he was the director of the Paris Conservatory; and in 1857, Napoleon III appointed him *maître de chapelle*.

Auber continued to write operas until his death. His last opera, *Rêve d'amour,* was completed when he was eighty-seven. He died in Paris on May 12, 1871, after witnessing the first riots of the Paris Commune.

Francis Grierson once said of Auber that "he might have passed for an old-clothes man." Yet despite his lack of personal dignity and his almost pathological shyness, he did possess wit to an extraordinary degree, and with that gift considerable charm. His great passions were women, the table, horses, the boulevards of Paris, and the Bois de Boulogne. His greatest fault, perhaps, was excessive humility. "I have," he once said, "no self-conceit. If I had any, I should have more talent." He avoided performances of his own works, and never conducted even a single performance of his operas. "If I were to assist at performances of one of my works," he said, "I would not thereafter write a note of music."

Auber spent most of his life at his house in the Rue Saint-Georges in Paris, where he was attended by domestics, some of whom he employed for forty years. He habitually rose early, usually before dawn. His custom as composer, according to Ralph W. Wood, was "to conceive his music independently, and very often in advance, of the words it was to accompany." And one of his contemporaries, Loménie, recalled: "It is said that M. Auber in general draws little inspiration from his subjects. His ideas most of the time come to him unpremeditatedly, while he is riding in the woods. He notes them down on bits of paper, and all find a place one day in some score."

Principal Works

Operas—Over 40 operas and *opéras-comiques,* including: La Bergère châtelaine; Emma; Le Concert à la cour; Le Maçon; Fiorella; La Muette de Portici, or Masaniello; Fra Diavolo; Le Philtre; Le Cheval de bronze; Zanetta; Le Domino noir; Les Diamants de la couronne; La Sirène; La Barcarolle; Haydée; Zerline; Manon Lescaut; La Fiancée du Roi de Garbe; Le Premier jour de bonheur; Rêve d'amour.

About

Bacharach, A. L. (ed.), The Music Masters, vol. 2; Kohut, A., Auber; Malherbe, C., Auber; Pougin, A., Auber.
English Review, August 1914.

Carl Philipp Emanuel Bach *1714-1788*

CARL PHILIPP EMANUEL BACH, also known as "the Berlin Bach" and "the Hamburg Bach," was born in Weimar, Germany, on March 8, 1714. He was the third (though second surviving) son of Johann Sebastian and Maria Barbara Bach and their fifth child; his godfather was Georg Philipp Telemann, the eminent *Kapellmeister* and composer.

Carl's only teacher in music was his father. As a child, Carl took part in the concerts of the Bach household and was often in attendance at rehearsals and performances at the St. Thomas Church and the Thomasschule. Because of his father's eminence, Carl had ample opportunity to meet the leading musicians of the day. He later recalled: "Although I was kept at home for many years, and therefore saw little of the world, yet no master of music passed through this place without coming to make himself known to my father and play before him."

Perhaps because he was left-handed, and thus might not be expected to become a virtuoso of the first order, Carl Philipp was directed by his father to law rather than music. For nine years, beginning in 1724, the boy attended the Thomasschule. He went on to study law for three years at the University at Frankfurt an der Oder. But music was always prominent in his everyday life. He worked assiduously at the clavier, and despite being left-handed managed to achieve a truly remarkable virtuosity through sheer power of will. He wrote music continuously, and in 1737 performed some of his compositions before a distinguished audience that included Frederick Wilhelm I, the Prussian king. In addition, he founded a choral society in Frankfurt.

By 1738 Bach had become convinced that music would be his profession and he went to Berlin. There his powers as a virtuoso made a strong impression on Crown Prince Frederick, who engaged Bach as his personal clavecinist and as chamber musician when he ascended the throne in 1740. Bach noted in his autobiography that the first flute solo Frederick played as king was to his accompaniment.

One of Bach's daily duties at court was to accompany Frederick the Great, an avid flautist, at the clavier. This was not a particularly pleasant assignment, since the king, otherwise a musician of conservative and even reactionary tastes, was rather liberal about his own tempo and phrasing. "The king might be an autocrat of his kingdom," Bach remarked, "but [he] enjoyed no prescriptive preeminence in the realm of his art." In addition to these personal services, Bach's duties required him to participate in, and write music for, the orchestral or chamber music concerts that were held in the palace five nights a week. His salary was three hundred thalers a year, hardly a munificent income; but it gave enough promise of security to permit him to marry Johanna Maria Dannemann, daughter of a wine merchant, in 1744. They had three children.

Between 1742 and 1744 Bach published two sets of piano sonatas, six sonatas in each set. The first was dedicated to the king of Prussia, the second to Duke Carl Eugen of Württemberg, one of his pupils. They were his first works in an art form which he was to endow with new order. Bach's greatest sonatas are the series entitled *For Connoisseurs and Amateurs (Für Kenner und Liebhaber)*, published between 1779 and 1787. By virtue of these compositions Bach has come to be recognized as "the father of the piano sonata." More than any single musician, he helped to perfect the aristocratic manner of writing for the keyboard known as the *galant* style, and to crystallize the form of the sonata. The art of homophony was carried in these works to an advanced stage of artistic development.

It is impossible to overestimate the historic and aesthetic importance of these compositions. Indeed, they rank Bach with the foremost composers of piano sonatas of his generation. His influence was extensive. As a young student Haydn memorized these works. Later on in life he confessed: "For what I know I have to thank Philipp Emanuel Bach." Mozart, also an ardent admirer, acknowledged, "He is the father and we his children. Those of us who know what is right learned it from him; and those who have not confessed it are scoundrels." Beethoven, too, was powerfully influenced by the Bach sonatas. In short, Bach was, as Ernest Hutcheson said of him, "the pathfinder of the classic sonata form, blazing a trail that was broadened by Haydn to a thoroughfare, and by Mozart and Beethoven to a highway."

CARL PHILIPP EMANUEL BACH

Bach was unhappy during his long stay at the court of Frederick the Great, and often sought an avenue of escape. In 1750 he applied for the post of cantor in Leipzig, and in 1753 he tried to obtain a position in Zittau. Both times he was turned down. Finally, in 1767, when his godfather Telemann died, Princess Amalia offered Bach the post of *Kapellmeister* in Hamburg. He accepted eagerly, and remained in this post until the end of his life. As *Kappellmeister* Bach directed the services in several Hamburg churches; the music he wrote for these and other performances won the admiration of his contemporaries. He was also recognized as one of the foremost clavier virtuosos of his time, and a master exponent of the new "expressiveness" *(Empfindsamkeit)* which was then beginning to assert itself in keyboard performance.

Carl Philipp Emanuel Bach died in Hamburg of pulmonary consumption on December 14, 1788.

The distinguished eighteenth century English musicologist Charles Burney visited Bach in Hamburg and recorded a detailed and highly revealing impression. "When I went to his house, I found with him three or four rational and well bred persons, his friends, besides his own family, consisting of Mrs. Bach, his eldest son, who practises the law, and his daughter. (He has two sons, the youngest of whom studies painting at the academies of Leipzig and Dresden.) The instant I entered, he conducted me up stairs into a large and elegant music room, furnished with pictures, drawings, and prints of more than a hundred and fifty eminent musicians; among whom, there are many Englishmen and original portraits in oil of his father and grandfather. After I had looked at these, M. Bach was so obliging as to sit down to his Silbermann clavichord, and favorite instrument, upon which he played three or four of his choicest and most difficult compositions, with the delicacy, precision and spirit for which he is so justly celebrated among his countrymen. In the pathetic and slow movements, whenever he had a long note to express, he absolutely contrived to produce from his instrument a cry of sorrow and complaint such as can only be effected upon the clavichord, and perhaps by himself.

"After dinner, which was elegantly served and cheerfully eaten, I prevailed upon him to sit down again to a clavichord, and he played, with little intermission, till nearly eleven o'clock at night. During this time, he grew so animated and possessed, that he not only played, but looked like one inspired. His eyes were fixed, his underlip fell, and drops of effervescence distilled from his countenance. He said if he were to be set to work frequently in this manner he should grow young again. He is now fifty-nine, rather short in stature, with black hair and eyes, and brown complexion, has a very animated countenance, and is of cheerful and lively disposition."

Bach was extraordinarily prolific. He wrote over seven hundred compositions, many of which grew so famous during his lifetime that when the name of Bach was mentioned it referred to Carl Philipp, rather than his now more celebrated father. He completed over fifty piano concertos, numerous concertos for other solo instruments and orchestra, eighteen symphonies, about one hundred trios, over seventy piano sonatas and many other works. In music history he represents the transition from the period of polyphonic music, which preceded him— and of which his father was the apex—to the great classical era of Haydn and Mozart.

"How he formed his style would be difficult to trace," said Burney. "He certainly never inherited it nor adopted it from his father who was his only master."

"The position of Carl Philipp Emanuel Bach was important," wrote C. Hubert Parry. "In his best symphonies he adopted a line of his own. . . . [His works] have an underlying basis of harmonic form. . . . His management of the various instruments shows considerable skill and clear perception of the effective uses to which they can be put; and he treats them with thorough independence and variety." Paul Henry Lang called Bach "the outstanding master of the late rococo, of preclassical times, a master who triumphed over the weakness of the art and atmosphere of his own period."

One of Bach's most frequently performed orchestral works today is a Concerto in D major for strings which Maximilian Steinberg transcribed in 1909 from a work scored exclusively for viols.

Bach was the author of one of the earliest important treatises on clavier playing: *Versuch über die wahre Art das Klavier zu spielen*, published between 1753 and 1762. It was issued in New York in 1948 in an English translation, by W. J. Mitchell, under the title *Essay on the True Art of Playing Keyboard Instruments*.

PRINCIPAL WORKS

Chamber Music—About 100 trios; many sonatas for solo instruments and accompaniment.
Choral Music—4 Easter Cantatas; 4 Michaelmas Cantatas; 2 oratorios, including Die Israeliten in der Wüste: 2 Litanies; Passion According to St. Matthew; Passion According to St. Luke; Magnificat, motets, psalms, secular cantatas.
Orchestral Music—18 symphonies; about 50 piano concertos; various other concertos for solo instruments and orchestra.
Piano Music—Over 70 sonatas; sonatinas; numerous shorter pieces including Solfeggietto, fantasias, rondos, minuets.
Vocal Music—Various song cycles and songs for solo voice and accompaniment including Die Biene, Bitten, Jesus in Gethsemane and Trinklied.

ABOUT

Bitter, C. H., Carl Philipp Emanuel Bach und W. F. Bach und deren Brüder; Burney, C., The Present State of Music in Germany; Cherbuliez, A. E., Carl Philipp Emanuel Bach; Geiringer, K., The Bach Family; Kahl, W. (editor), Selbstbiographien deutscher Musiker; Vrieslander, O., Carl Philipp Emanuel Bach.

Johann Sebastian Bach *1685-1750*

JOHANN SEBASTIAN BACH was born in Eisenach, Germany, on March 21, 1685. The youngest child of Johann Ambrosius Bach, a violinist, Johann Sebastian was destined to become the most illustrious member of a family that for seven generations had produced professional musicians. Johann Sebastian received his first lessons in music from his father. Upon the death of both parents in his tenth year, the boy was entrusted to the care of his older brother, Johann Christoph, an organist in Ohrdruf, who gave him a thorough education in keyboard instruments. It was not long before the pupil surprised his teacher in performing on the clavier.

The young Bach's precocity seems to have aroused Johann Christoph's envy, with the result that he became harsh and unreasonable in his treatment of his younger brother. When Johann Christoph discovered the boy's interest in a manuscript collection of clavier music reposing in the household library, he saw to it that the collection was kept under lock and key. Johann Sebastian somehow managed to obtain a duplicate key and for several months, while the rest of the family slept, he copied out the music by moonlight, almost ruining his eyesight. When his older brother discovered him at this task one night he ruthlessly confiscated the fruits of the boy's nocturnal labors.

Johann Sebastian lived with his brother for five years. In 1700 he became a chorister at St. Michael's Church in Lüneburg. The next three years were relatively happy for the boy. He could now devote himself to the passionate study of the clavier, organ, violin, and composition. He could memorize every musical score within reach. He could make trips on foot to attend concerts: thirty miles to Hamburg for the performances of Jan Adam Reinken, one of the foremost German organists of the period; sixty miles to Celle for concerts of court music in the French style.

In 1703 Bach was appointed organist at a church in Arnstadt. He was permitted a month's leave of absence to visit nearby Lübeck and make the acquaintance of Dietrich Buxtehude, one of the most distinguished musicians of the time. In Lübeck Buxtehude gave performances on the organ and led concerts of instrumental music which so fascinated Bach that he overstayed his leave by two months; only the threat of immediate dismissal brought him reluctantly back to Arnstadt. He further irritated his employers by following Buxtehude's example in filling his chorale performances with

JOHANN SEBASTIAN BACH

improvisations that disturbed and confused the churchgoers.

Neither he nor his employers were, therefore, reluctant to part company when in 1707 Bach became organist of the St. Blasius Church in Mühlhausen. His salary was eighty-five gulden a year, plus three measures of corn, two trusses of wood, and six trusses of faggots—apparently enough of a subsistence to permit him to marry a cousin, Maria Barbara Bach, on October 17, 1707.

Bach's first important appointment came a year later, when he was made court organist and chamber musician at the ducal chapel in Weimar. During his extremely productive nine years at Weimar Bach became not only one of the most brilliant and celebrated organists in Germany but also the greatest composer of organ music of his generation, if not of all time. The fantasias, passacaglias, toccatas, preludes, and fugues he produced in abundance brought these forms to their ultimate technical and structural perfection and enriched them with unparalleled poetic and dramatic thought.

"His work in this line," says C. Hubert Parry, "seems to comprise all the possibilities of pure organ music. Everything that has been written since is but a pale shadow of his splendid conceptions. He had complete mastery of all genuine organ devices which tell in the hearing—the effects of long sustained notes accompanied by wonderful ramifications of rapid passages; the effects of sequences of linked suspensions of great powerful chords; the contrast of whirling rapid notes with slow and stately march of pedals and harmonies. He knew how the pearly clearness of certain stops lent itself to passages of intricate rhythmic counterpoint, and what charm lay in the perfect management of several simultaneous melodies—especially when the accents came at different moments in different parts; and he designed his movements so well that he made all such and many other genuine organ effects exert their fullest impressions on the hearers. He rarely allows himself to break into a dramatic vein, though he sometimes appeals to the mind in phrases which are closely akin to the dramatic—as in the great Fantasia in G minor, the Toccata in D minor, and the Prelude in B minor. He occasionally touches on tender and pathetic strains, but for the most part adopts an attitude of great dignity which is at once generous in its warmth and vigor, and reserved in the matter of sentiment."

In describing Bach's virtuosity at the organ, Nikolaus Forkel wrote: "He played with so easy and small a motion of the fingers that it was hardly perceptible. Only the first joints of his fingers were in motion; his hand retained, even in the most difficult passages, its rounded form; his fingers rose very little from the keys, hardly more than in a shake, and when one was employed the others remained still in their position. Still less did the other parts of his body share in his playing." Philipp Spitta adds: "Friends and foes alike bowed to the irresistible force of an unheard-of power of execution, and could hardly comprehend how he could twist his fingers and his feet so wonderfully and so nimbly without hitting a single false note or displacing his body with violent swaying."

While employed in Weimar, Bach made several tours in Germany, establishing a prodigious reputation as an organ virtuoso. In Cassel in 1714 his performance so impressed the Prince of Hesse that the prince removed a diamond ring from his finger and presented it to Bach. In 1717 Bach won a competition under unusual circumstances. A contest had been planned in Dresden for Bach and Louis Marchand, the celebrated French organist. It was arranged that both men would perform the same music at sight before a discriminating jury. Marchand de-

faulted by leaving Dresden just before performance time, refusing to meet the severe test of comparison with Bach. An even more positive tribute to Bach's genius in playing the organ was given by Reinken, who heard Bach improvise on a chorale for a half hour. "I thought," said Reinken, "that this art was dead, but I see it still lives in you."

In 1717 Bach left Weimar to become *Kapellmeister* and director of chamber music for Prince Leopold of Anhalt at Cöthen. For the next six years he arranged and directed performances of instrumental music, writing many of his most celebrated orchestral and solo compositions: the *Brandenburg Concertos,* orchestral suites, concertos for solo instruments and orchestra, sonatas, suites and partitas for solo instruments, and the *Well-Tempered Clavier.*

Bach's wife died in 1720 after having borne him seven children, four of whom survived. A year later, on December 3, 1721, Bach married again. His second wife was Anna Magdalena Wuelcken, a cultivated musician in her own right, and the daughter of the town trumpeter. She bore him a family of thirteen children, and also inspired the writing of many important pedagogic pieces (gathered in *The Little Clavier Book of Anna Magdalena Bach*), the *Inventions* and the renowned *French Suites* and *English Suites* for clavier.

In May 1723 Bach assumed his last post, succeeding Kuhnau as cantor of the Thomasschule in Leipzig. To get the job he was required to pass several tests over a period of a few months; one entailed the writing of his *The Passion According to St. John.* His duties included teaching a boys' class in Latin and music, serving as organist and composing music, and directing performances for church services. His annual salary was about $2,500 a year, supplemented by fees earned from funerals, weddings, and other events. For the rest of his life, Bach held this post under many unhappy circumstances and dismal working conditions. He lived in cold, dark, dank, and unsanitary rooms. He was continually at odds with a rector who did everything he could to humiliate Bach with the church officials. The singers and performers who worked under him were grossly incompetent. And many of his pupils were undisciplined scoundrels.

Yet despite all the humiliations, discomforts, and petty annoyances of these twenty-seven years, and for all the varied duties that absorbed his time and energies, Bach was able to produce a library of choral music incomparable for its majesty and grandeur—innumerable cantatas, chorales, and motets, and two of the great peaks of choral music, the *Passion According to St. Matthew* and the B minor Mass.

The Passion According to St. Matthew was completed in 1729. It was introduced in Leipzig on April 15 that year, with the composer conducting. Where Bach's earlier *St. John* Passion had been dramatic, the *St. Matthew* Passion was at turns reflective and exalted. "Devotion, humility and adoration reach their highest intensity in this music," wrote W. G. Whittaker. "It is the most intensely personal document in the whole range of musical art; it stands above creeds and beliefs, and speaks from heart to heart in the most miraculous manner. Although it is cast in a colossal mold, lasting over three hours when performed fully, demanding a double orchestra and double choir . . . one forgets the elaborate means employed, and the story passes along in the simplest manner, viewed by a mind full of reverence, sympathy, and faith."

Two sections of the Mass in B minor (the "Kyrie" and the "Gloria") were completed in 1733 and submitted to King Augustus III of Saxony when Bach applied for a post at the Saxon Royal Chapel; the other parts of the Mass were written five years later. No complete performance took place in Bach's lifetime; its première was given in Berlin in two performances spaced a year apart— the first half on February 20, 1834, the second on February 12, 1835.

Leopold Stokowski, the distinguished conductor and Bach specialist, wrote of the Mass: "[It] is planned on a vast scale, and the texture of the music is complex and highly concentrated, revealing a slow and rich outwelling of his inspiration. . . . While it is cast in a form similar to the great masses preceding Bach, this form is greatly enlarged and extended. . . . It has cosmic vastness of expression and consciousness. . . . The parts which are in reality prayers, such as the beginning of the first 'Kyrie,' have the intensity and simple directness that probably is always one of the chief elements in prayer. . . . In many places, such as the great choruses of the 'Gloria,' the 'Credo,' the 'Sanctus,' the 'Osanna,'

there is a blazing jubilation like radiant sunlight. It is as if all Nature, man, the planets, the whole universe were singing together. . . . At certain moments in the Mass, such as the 'Qui tollis' and 'Et Incarnatus' and 'Crucifixus,' there is in the music profound mystical intensity that could only have come from the spirit of a man who was moved to the uttermost of his being."

In 1747 Bach visited his son Carl Philipp Emanuel, who at that time was in the employ of Frederick the Great in Potsdam. The old master was welcomed by the king with much honor and ceremony. Bach improvised a six-part fugue on a melody that the king provided. After returning to Leipzig, Bach completed a monumental collection of contrapuntal compositions, all based on the theme supplied by Frederick. Entitled *A Musical Offering (Das Musikalisches Opfer)*, this work, Bach's last chamber-music composition, consisted of two fugues, several canons, and a concluding trio.

Towards the end of his life, Bach suffered from failing eyesight. An operation by Dr. John Taylor (the physician who had attended Handel) was unsuccessful, and Bach went completely blind. Despite this infirmity, he worked feverishly on eighteen chorales for the organ and on *The Art of the Fugue*. The latter was a vast collection of sixteen fugues, four canons, two fugues for two clavecins, and an unfinished fugue in which the master seemed still to be testing his power in counterpoint.

Ten days before his death, Bach's sight returned. But he soon suffered a paralytic stroke, and died in Leipzig on July 28, 1750. He was buried in the churchyard of St. John in Leipzig. For some reason never adequately explained, his grave was allowed to go unmarked, and for a long time its precise location was not known. But in 1894, when excavations were made to extend the foundations of the church, Bach's remains were retrieved and identified; they were reburied beneath the church in a sarcophagus.

Bach was a simple man whose only explanation for his fabulous output and achievements was that "I worked hard." He read little, except on the subject of theology (he was a devout Lutheran); he knew little about the other arts; his travels were confined to Germany. His cultural attainments, it must be admitted, were not exalted. Even in his native German his diction was often confused and ungrammatical. That some of the noblest and most majestic music ever conceived by man should have come from one of such limited intelligence and experience—and from one continually burdened and harassed by taxing and ungratifying work schedules—is one of the great paradoxes of art. It has led Ernest Newman to describe Bach as "the miracle man of music." "Any modern composer of genius," wrote Newman, "would go mad in such an environment, committed day in and day out to such a round of routine hard labor. How then did this astonishing man succeed in doing what he did? . . . Here is Bach, a poor boy, self educated in music, with the minimum of culture even in his own domain, who never read a book on musical aesthetics or musical form in his life, for such things did not exist in his day, but who somehow managed, for all that, to demonstrate in his works all the architectonic possibilities of the flow and combination of any given set of musical sounds. Yet while achieving this wonder his mind was not merely working like a superlative machine; his genius for permutation and combination went hand in hand with an inexhaustible power of artistic creation of the most varied kind, each purely technical problem being solved not as it is in the books, by any means of a portmanteau formula, but in terms of the particular aesthetic case in hand. Are 'culture,' then, and a capacity for other than purely musical thinking of no actual use to the composer who has the real thing in him by the grace of God?. . . . Truly we have as yet barely the glimmer of an understanding of what 'the musical faculty' is, and how it works."

Albert Schweitzer has described Bach's appearance from the portraits that have come down to us. Bach's was "the face of a man who has tasted of the bitterness of life. There is something fascinating in the harsh expression of these features, which are painted in full face. Round the tightly compressed lips run the hard lines of an inflexible obstinacy. It is thus the cantor of St. Thomas's may have looked in his last years as he entered the school where some new vexation or another was waiting for him. In the two other portraits, the severity is often softened by a touch of easy good

nature. Even the short-sighted eyes look out upon the world from their half-closed lids with a certain friendliness that is not even negated by the heavy eyebrows arched above them. The face cannot be called beautiful. The nose is too massive for that, and the underjaw too prominent."

Neither his contemporaries nor most of his successors recognized the true range of Bach's genius. In his lifetime he was honored mainly as an organist; and upon his death he was regarded as a composer of old-fashioned music in the contrapuntal style that was now rapidly becoming obsolete. Because he wrote at a time when the era of polyphonic music was drawing to a close his art was believed to be dated, with no chance of survival. His own children looked upon him with condescension, since they belonged to the new age of homophony. And the world around them concurred with their appraisal: in the decades that followed the name of Bach invariably brought up the image of one of his sons and not that of Johann Sebastian.

A few discerning musicians—notably Mozart and Beethoven—did hold him in highest esteem; but even they were unable to guess the extent of his prodigious achievements, since so few of his works had been published. Then came the awakening. In 1829 Mendelssohn decided to do something tangible to lift Bach from his long obscurity by reviving in Berlin the *Passion According to St. Matthew,* for the first time this work had been heard since Bach's own day. Its impact was cataclysmic and led to a revival of other Bach compositions, notably the *Passion According to St. John* in 1833. In 1850 Robert Schumann helped to found in Leipzig the Bach Gesellschaft for the purpose of publishing a complete edition of Bach's works. It took almost a century to realize this project, and when it was completed, the Bach corpus comprised forty-six volumes. Thus the world came to the realization for the first time of how much Bach had produced and of the greatness of his art. Bach societies then began to spring up all over Europe to perform Bach's music.

Since then we have come to honor Bach as one of the great music masters of all time, possibly *the* greatest. He was not only the summit of the polyphonic age in music, and as such the final development of the older forms and styles. He was also a peak in the new world of homophony that followed him. When we listen to some of the slow movements of his concertos or sonatas what we hear is the new age and not the old, and we begin to understand what Charles Sanford Terry meant when he said that Bach "saw the heavens opened, and was prophetically oracular."

PRINCIPAL WORKS

Chamber Music—6 sonatas for violin and clavier; 3 sonatas for unaccompanied violin; 3 partitas for unaccompanied violin; 6 sonatas, or suites, for unaccompanied cello; 3 sonatas for cello and clavier; 3 sonatas for flute and clavier; 4 trio sonatas; The Musical Offering.

Choral Music—190 religious cantatas; secular cantatas including Phoebus and Pan, Coffee Cantata, and Peasant Cantata; Passion According to St. John; Passion According to St. Matthew; 2 Magnificats; Mass in B minor; Christmas Oratorio; Easter Oratorio; short masses; motets, etc.

Clavier Music—Chromatic Fantasy and Fugue; 6 English Suites; 6 French Suites; 6 partitas; Italian Concerto; Goldberg Variations; The Well-Tempered Clavier; The Art of the Fugue; The Little Clavier Book of Anna Magdalena; Inventions.

Orchestral Music—6 Brandenburg Concertos; 4 suites; concertos for various solo instruments and orchestra.

Organ Music—Little Organ Book; Passacaglia in C minor; Chorale preludes, toccatas, preludes, fugues, fantasias.

Vocal Music—Songs for voice and clavier including Bist du bei mir, Gedenke doch, mein Geist. Komm suesser Tod, O Jesulein süss, So oft ich meine Tabakspfeife, Wie wohl ist mir.

ABOUT

David, Hans T., and Mendel, A. (editors), The Bach Reader; Dickinson, A. E. F., The Art of Bach; Forkel, J. N., Johann Sebastian Bach: His Life, Art and Work; Parry, C. Hubert, Johann Sebastian Bach; Pirro, A., J. S. Bach; Schweitzer, A., Johann Sebastian Bach; Spitta, P., Johann Sebastian Bach; Terry, C. S., Bach: A Biography.

John Christian Bach *1735-1782*

JOHN (or JOHANN) CHRISTIAN BACH, often referred to as the "English Bach" because of his long residence in London, was born in Leipzig, Germany, on September 5, 1735, the youngest surviving son of Johann Sebastian and Anna Magdalena Bach. Little is known of John Christian's early music education; but it can be assumed that he received instruction from his father, who was presumably inspired to write the

JOHN CHRISTIAN BACH

second part of the *Well-Tempered Clavier* by John Christian's precocity at the keyboard.

When Johann Sebastian died in 1750, John Christian was sent to Berlin to live with his older brother Carl Philipp Emanuel. During his six years' stay in that household, the boy received a thorough grounding in composition and clavier performance. At several public performances he gave in Berlin, John Christian was able to introduce some of his earliest keyboard pieces.

When the Seven Years War erupted in 1756, John Christian went to Milan to be employed by Count Agostino Litta as *maestro di cappella*. Through the Count Bach became acquainted with Padre Martini, the eminent theorist and teacher, under whom he began a period of study in Bologna. Having recently been converted to the Catholic faith, Bach devoted himself assiduously to writing church music. Within the next few years he completed a mass, which had successful private and public performances in 1797; a Requiem; a Te Deum; a Pater Noster; and other church compositions. From 1760 to 1762 he also served as organist of the Milan Cathedral.

The theater soon caught Bach's interest. It was in Berlin that he had eagerly heard his first Italian operas, and this admiration was heightened in Italy. Before long Bach had begun to write opera. His first works, *Artaserse* and *Catone in Utica*, written to librettos by Metastasio, were introduced in

1761, in Turin and Naples respectively. *Alessandro nell' Indie,* performed in Naples in 1762, proved even more successful. Bach's fame spread throughout Italy.

In 1762, Colomba Mattei, director of the King's Theatre in Haymarket, London, invited Bach to England. Since Bach had for some time been severely criticized by the Milanese church authorities for leaving his post too frequently, he eagerly accepted the new offer. His first Italian opera for an English audience, *Orione,* was produced on February 19, 1763 with a spectacular success; the King and Queen were so delighted that they returned to the theater the following evening for a second performance. Later that year *Zanaida* was given, to be followed by a long series of successes from 1765 to April 1778, including the operas *Adriano in Siria, Carattaco,* and *La Clemenza di Scipione.* Toward the end of 1763 Bach was appointed music master to Queen Sophia. He held this position for the rest of his life.

Early in 1764 Bach met Karl Friedrich Abel, a gifted performer on the viola da gamba, and a former pupil of Johann Sebastian Bach. As chamber musician to the Queen, Abel frequently met Johann Christian at court, and a close friendship developed between the two men. They moved into the same house, and began, in 1764, a series of joint concerts at Carlisle House which continued for about seventeen years, representing a rich chapter in the history of eighteenth century English musical performances.

The year 1764 marked Bach's first meeting with Mozart, the wonder-child of music who had come to London to perform at Buckingham Palace. Bach devised a series of tests to measure Mozart's incredible musical powers. Amazed by the results, Bach took Mozart on his knee, and together they played an improvised fugue on the harpsichord.

In 1772 Carl Theodor, Elector of Mannheim, invited Bach to write a new opera for his theater. The result was *Temistocle,* a formidable success. In 1774, Bach received a second commission from the Elector and produced *Lucio Silla.* Four years later Bach wrote a new opera, *Amadis des Gaules,* for production in Paris. Visiting the French capital in 1779, he renewed his acquaintance with Mozart, who had also come to Paris. "I love him, as you know," young Mozart wrote back to his father about Bach, "and respect him with all my heart."

Bach married Cecilia Grassi, a singer, in 1773. A year later they established the home on Newman Street which they were to occupy for the rest of their lives. They had no children.

English society suited Bach well. Cutting an elegant figure, he was the "darling of the English ladies." He lived in the grand manner, entertained royally, and spent money so extravagantly that, despite a handsome income, he was often forced to borrow huge sums to pay his bills. When he died he left debts amounting to more than five thousand pounds.

Bach's most familiar portrait is the one painted by Gainsborough in 1778, which still hangs in the Liceo Musicale in Bologna. It reveals a strong and handsome face, expressive eyes, firm lips, and sensitive features.

"Johann Christian Bach," wrote Johann Reichardt, a contemporary, "was a very lighthearted and jovial person. When one of his more serious friends once reproached him for his carefree ways, both as an artist and as a man . . . and held up to him the example of his elder brother in Berlin [Carl Philipp Emanuel], who wrote large works and knew very well how to hold onto the money he earned, Bach said: 'Oh well, my brother lives to compose whereas I compose to live; he works for others, I work for myself.' "

Bach died in London on January 1, 1782. It was "a sad day for the world of music," as Mozart wrote upon hearing the news. Bach was buried at the St. Pancras Church in London. Though he had been one of England's most celebrated musicians, his name was misspelled twice in the church burial register.

Of the thirteen operas which Bach wrote, Rochlitz has said: "Literally it was true, as an English poet said of him, 'Bach stands on the summit of Olympus.' His operas, written for England, Italy and Germany, portray all the magnificence of the composer's art. This Bach could have accomplished anything. . . . An ever-ready invention, lovely melodies, rich instrumentation, surprising modulations, magnificent duets, masterly choruses and recitatives characterize his operas."

But Bach is remembered today not for his operas, but for the many symphonies and concertos in which he developed the principle of contrasting themes and helped further to crystallize the sonata structure. He was truly a master of the rococo style, and his influence on his immediate successors was far-reaching. "His work," said Alfred Einstein, "is, in sweetness, grace, and fineness of style, the elegant forerunner and the most influential force in Mozart."

PRINCIPAL WORKS

Chamber Music—36 violin (or flute) sonatas; 34 trios for various combinations; 29 quartets for various combinations; 13 duets for two violins; 9 quintets for various combinations; Sextet for oboe, two horns, violin, cello and piano.

Choral Music—Cantatas, Magnificat, Mass, Requiem, Te Deum.

Operas—Artaserse; Alessandro nell' Indie; Orione; Adriano in Siria; Carattaco; La Clemenza di Scipione; Temistocle; Lucio Silla; Amadis de Gaules; various pasticcios.

Orchestral Music—50 symphonies; 37 clavier concertos; 31 sinfonie concertante; 13 overtures; church music for voice and orchestra.

Piano (Clavier) Music—38 sonatas; 10 sonatas for four hands; various other pieces.

Vocal Music—Danish arias, English songs, Italian arias; Italian canzonette for vocal duet.

ABOUT

Bitter, C. H., Die Söhne Sebastian Bachs; Geiringer, K., The Bach Family; Schoekel, H., J. C. Bach und die Instrumentalmusik seiner Zeit; Terry, C. S., J. C. Bach.

Wilhelm Friedemann Bach *1710-1784*

WILHELM FRIEDEMANN BACH, known as the "Halle Bach," was the second child and oldest son of Johann Sebastian and Maria Barbara Bach. He was born in Weimar, Germany, on November 22, 1710. He did not receive any music instruction until his tenth year, when his father began teaching him to play the clavier. It was in order to further his son's musical training that Johann Sebastian Bach wrote the first part of the *Well-Tempered Clavier* and the *Inventions*. Between 1726 and 1727 Wilhelm Friedemann also studied violin with J. G. Graun in Meersburg.

When the Bach family went to Leipzig in 1723, following Johann Sebastian's appointment as cantor of the Thomasschule, Wilhelm Friedemann was enrolled in that school: he had previously attended high

WILHELM FRIEDEMANN BACH

school in Cöthen. He went on to the University of Leipzig, where his course of study included mathematics as well as music and composition, his most intensive pursuits. He graduated in 1729.

In 1733 Wilhelm Friedemann was appointed organist of the Sophienkirche in Dresden; he remained until 1746. His main function as organist was to perform at services on Sunday afternoons and Monday mornings. With considerable leisure at his disposal, Bach could pursue a number of musical activities and devote himself to teaching and the study of mathematics. He completed a number of ambitious and gifted works during this period, including most of his symphonies and clavier sonatas, as well as various concertos and trios.

Seeking a more promising and lucrative position, Bach left Dresden to become organist at the Liebfrauenkirche in Halle. He filled this post with considerable distinction, performing at church, officiating at elaborate musical ceremonies during the holidays and directing other performances of choral and instrumental music. In 1751 he married Dorothea Elisabeth Georgi, daughter of the town excise official. They had one child, a daughter.

Obsessed with the feeling that his musical gifts and achievements were not sufficiently appreciated, Bach suddenly resigned from his Halle post in 1764. It was a disastrous move. For years he earned a precarious living as an organist and teacher, or by dedicating his compositions to wealthy patrons. He could barely sustain himself and his family. On several occasions he applied for a permanent post, but was turned down each time because of his age.

In 1774 Bach settled in Berlin, where he supported himself by selling some of his clavier pieces for trifling sums; in desperation he even tried to sell some of his father's compositions as his own. He grew increasingly bitter, despondent, and frustrated with the years. On July 1, 1784, he died of a pulmonary disease in Berlin.

Bach's personality was the subject of many works by such writers as Marpurg, Reichardt, and Rochlitz. A romantic novel by Albert Emil Brachvogel took him for its central character. All these writers emphasized Bach's weakness for drink and for dissolute living. Although research has proved that much of his discreditable behavior was grossly exaggerated, there is no question that Wilhelm Friedemann was lazy, boorish in manner, extremely selfish, and eccentric.

In many ways Wilhelm Friedemann Bach was an outstanding composer; his eminent brother, Carl Philipp Emanuel, once said that "he could replace our father better than all the rest of us put together." As C. H. Bitter has written, Wilhelm Friedemann Bach left "distinguished work to posterity, and opened up new paths and ways which lead to higher completion and greater perfection. His position in the history of music lies in his unity of purpose as the son of a great father."

"Wilhelm Friedemann," said Nikolaus Forkel, Johann Sebastian Bach's first biographer, "approaches the nearest to his father in originality of all his thoughts. All his melodies have a different turn from those of other composers, and yet they are not only extremely natural, but, at the same time uncommonly ingenious and elegant."

Principal Works

Chamber Music—5 trios; duets for flute and violin.
Choral Music—21 cantatas; German Mass.
Orchestral Music—9 symphonies; 5 clavier concertos; Concerto for Two Claviers and Orchestra.
Organ Music—Canons, chorale preludes, fugues, studies.
Piano Music—13 preludes; 10 fantasies; 9 sonatas; 8 fugues; Suite in G minor; polonaises; 2 sonatas for two pianos.

About

Bitter, C. H., Carl Philipp Emanuel Bach und Wilhelm Friedemann Bach und deren Brüder; Falck, M., Wilhelm Friedemann Bach; Geiringer, K., The Bach Family; Stabenow, K., J. S. Bachs Sohn.

Mily Balakirev *1837-1910*

MILY ALEXEIVICH BALAKIREV, founder of the Russian national school of composers known as "The Mighty Five," was born in Nijny-Novgorod, Russia, on January 2, 1837. As a child he learned piano from his mother, then went to Moscow to study with Alexandre Dubuque, a pupil of John Field. Balakirev caught the interest of the distinguished musicologist Alexander Ulibishev, who invited the boy to live in his house and take advantage of its immense music library. Ulibishev also arranged for Balakirev to continue his formal study of music.

Despite his preoccupation with music, Balakirev did not neglect his academic education. In 1853 he entered the University of Kazan, specializing in mathematics. Two years later he accompanied Ulibishev to St. Petersburg, where he made his formal debut as a composer on February 24, 1856, performing a movement of his first piano concerto. In St. Petersburg Balakirev met Glinka, whose music Balakirev admired greatly, and whose ideas on musical nationalism made a lasting impression on the young composer. As a dedicated disciple, Balakirev was fired with the ideal of helping to create in Russia a national school of musical composition. He soon found a circle of sympathetic listeners: César Cui; Dargomizhsky, who had already made his own tentative efforts to compose national Russian operas; the distinguished critic Stassov; and, a little later, Rimsky-Korsakov, Mussorgsky, and Borodin. Drawn together at first by a common dedication to music, they soon responded to Balakirev's passionate arguments for the creation of a national musical idiom, and tried to root their composition in Russian folk songs and dances, imbue it with Russian subjects and characters, reflect in it their native culture and background.

Balakirev, Cui, Rimsky-Korsakov, Mussorgsky, and Borodin met often to discuss these ideals and ways of realizing them. As César Cui later recalled: "These informal

Balakirev: bä-lä′kĕ-rĕf

meetings . . . gave rise from that time on-
wards to most interesting and instructive
debates, which ranged conscientiously over
the whole of the then existing literature of
music. . . . In this way, the little brotherhood ended by acquiring fixed convictions
and by forming criteria, which they applied
to a number of questions in the realm of art
that frequently lay outside the current ideas
of the public and the press. While each
member of the group retained his own characteristics and capacity, an ideal common to
all soon began to be sharply defined, and an
effort was made to imprint it on their
compositions."

Balakirev's first work in this vein was the
1858 *Overture on Russian Themes* for piano
and orchestra. Four years later, immediately
upon returning from a trip to the Caucasus,
Balakirev used that region's haunting folk
songs and dances and lore to produce his
first masterwork, *Islamey*, a freely developed
fantasy for piano based on two Oriental
melodies. In 1864 Balakirev completed a second *Overture on Russian Themes;* revised
twenty years later and retitled *Russia*, this
work was an effective tone poem employing
three folk songs to symbolize three periods
in Russian history: paganism, the birth of
the Cossack regime, and the Muscovite
Empire.

In 1862 Balakirev helped to found, and
became assistant director of, the Free School
of Music in St. Petersburg. There, over the
years, he directed important orchestral concerts that emphasized the work of young,
often obscure, Russians. It was after one of
these performances that the Russian national
school established by Balakirev received its
popular name. At a concert held on May 24,
1867, the works of Balakirev, Mussorgsky,
Cui, Borodin, and Rimsky-Korsakov were
featured; the critic Stassov, in his review,
referred to these composers as "the mighty
five," a sobriquet that has stayed with them.

Nor did Balakirev limit himself to writing
national music. He made a contribution to
musicology through his valuable research on
old Russian music. In 1866 he published
a collection of forty folk songs, in 1898 a
second volume of thirty songs. These editions helped to uncover and popularize much
Russian musical folklore.

Never stable in his emotions, Balakirev
grew increasingly hypochondriac and capricious over the years. In 1869 he succumbed

MILY BALAKIREV

to a superstition that led him to desert all
musical activity for a long period of time.
He paid constant visits to numerous fortune
tellers, accepting their omens and prognosti-
cations with childish trust. In 1873, to support himself, he took a job as a stores superintendent for the Warsaw Railway. He began to drift from superstition to an excessive
religious piety, and from piety to mysticism.

Rimsky-Korsakov described Balakirev's
religious mania: "In every room in his home
were holy images with a little lamp burning
in front of each. He was ever attending services. He had given up wearing furs, smoking, and eating meat. He liked to eat fish,
provided it had not been knocked on the
head. His love for all living creatures had
become so great that if a noxious insect
found its way into his room he would catch
it with care and throw it out of the window,
wishing it Godspeed. At the end of his talks
on religion with people he was fond of, he
used to press them to cross themselves. And
if they demurred, he would insist: 'Please
do! For my sake, just this once! Why not
try?' He believed in the supernatural effi-
ciency of this symbolic gesture—believed
that it might help to turn the minds of ir-
religious people who made it."

Balakirev returned to music in 1879, re-
suming his former activities as conductor
and composer. In 1881 he completed another masterwork, the orchestral tone poem
Tamara. It was introduced in St. Petersburg

on March 19, 1883. Balakirev also composed a piano sonata, several songs, and a second symphony, and subjected many of his earlier works (including the first symphony and the second piano concerto) to extensive revision.

The last years of his life were lonely. By 1887 it had become clear to his friends that he was losing his powers of concentration. His memory was so poor that he was forced to give up conducting. Withdrawing into almost total isolation, he surrendered completely to religion, spending hour after hour in prayer or spiritual meditation.

He died suddenly of congestion of the lungs on May 29, 1910 in St. Petersburg and was buried in the Alexander Nevsky cemetery near the graves of Glinka and Dargomizhsky.

The familiar painting of Balakirev by Ilya Repin reveals a "semi-Oriental cast of countenance and a somewhat unkempt hirsute appendage," as M. Montagu-Nathan has written. Behind this surface "lay a decidedly peculiar and almost baffling personality." He was an eccentric, a despot, a man in a perpetual state of quivering nerves. He was difficult of temperament. In one of his letters Borodin described a typically volatile reaction by Balakirev. Piqued at something Borodin had said, Balakirev flew into a tantrum. A few moments later, Balakirev forgave him and as a token of forgiveness punched him on the nose, then kissed him on the cheek. Balakirev's relations with Rimsky-Korsakov fluctuated between excessive affection and heated attacks; it was a mere trifle that finally ruptured their friendship.

In addition to the compositions cited, Balakirev wrote some of the best songs in the Russian repertory. Rosa Newmarch says: "They are little gems, cut in innumerable facets, of which each reflects an exquisite and subtle emotion. The accompaniments to these songs resemble the setting of a jewel—they are independent, but they enhance, they complete the musical thought which glistens in the center. . . . Some of them recreate marvelously the very atmosphere of the Orient. Nearly all these songs are emotional to a high degree and replete with an ardent sentiment of the triumph of love."

There is a strong artistic bond between Balakirev and Glinka, the composer who influenced him most decisively. "Balakirev resembled Glinka," wrote M. D. Calvocoressi, "in the straightforward, simple warmth of his utterance, in his love for intensity of color, his dislike for glare, his lack of conscious artifice, and his disdain for the more obvious ways of formulism. . . . He owes to Glinka . . . the rare limpidity, the perfectly mellow quality of his scoring; and to Glinka alone—apart, of course, from Russian and Eastern folk music—the range of colors for which he evinces the most marked predilection."

Despite his distinction as a composer, conductor, and teacher, Balakirev made perhaps his greatest contribution to music in crystallizing and solidifying the national thinking of the Russian composers who were his friends. It is largely this achievement that led Stassov to write: "But for Balakirev the fate of Russian music might have been far different from what we actually have to register. Had there been no Balakirev to act as leader, educator, champion, and helpmate, what would have happened to Cui, Mussorgsky, Borodin, Rimsky-Korsakov . . . and many other Russian composers? Most of them, no doubt, would have made their way independently. We cannot tell how; but we can confidently assert that, but for him, there would have been no new Russian school, and many a page telling of live, fearless and joyous activity and progress would be missing from the history of Russia's musical life. . . . The importance of the part he played in the evolution of Russian music is so great as to preclude all possibilities of comparison and entitles him to the first place in the history of Russian music after Glinka."

PRINCIPAL WORKS

Chamber Music—Octet; Septet; String Quartet (Quatuor originale russe); Romance, for cello and piano.

Choral Music—6 anthems; Cradle Song; Two Legends; Cantata.

Orchestral Music—2 piano concertos (the second completed by Liapunov); Overture on Russian Themes; Russia; In Bohemia; Tamara; Suite on Pieces by Chopin.

Piano Music—Islamey; Sérénade espagnole; Berceuse, esquisses, Humoresque, mazurkas, nocturnes, polkas, Tarantella, waltzes, and other pieces; Suite, for piano duet; Russian Folksongs, for piano duet.

Vocal Music—Over 50 songs for voice and piano, including Berceuse, The Dream, Ecstasy, Hebrew Melody, Lead Me, O Night, O Come to Me, The Pine, and The Song of the Golden Fish.

ABOUT

Abraham, G., Studies in Russian Music; Abraham, G. and Calvocoressi, M. D., Masters of Russian Music; Leonard, R. A., History of Russian Music; Montagu-Nathan, M., History of Russian Music; Seroff, V., The Mighty Five; Zetlin, M., The Five.

Ludwig van Beethoven *1770-1827*

LUDWIG VAN BEETHOVEN

L UDWIG VAN BEETHOVEN, second child of Johann and Maria Magdalena van Beethoven, was born in Bonn, Germany, on December 16, 1770. His father, a singer in the Electoral choir, was a ruthless martinet who planned to turn his son into as profitable an investment as the child prodigy Mozart had been. With the help of some friends who were local musicians, Johann van Beethoven subjected Ludwig to ruthless discipline and occasionally to physical abuse. At times he would return home late at night from one of his drinking bouts, rouse the sleeping child, and force him to practice his exercises on the clavier. Beethoven's childhood was darkened by poverty and the merciless autocracy of his intemperate father; but his mother's tenderness and the affection and sympathy of his grandfather, Ludwig van Beethoven, brought some warmth into his somber life.

Beethoven's first important teacher was Christian Gottlob Neefe, court organist and former cantor of the Thomasschule in Leipzig (a post formerly held by Bach). Neefe was not only an extraordinary musician, but a teacher who thoroughly understood Beethoven's sensitivity and appreciated his astonishing gifts. Under Neefe's careful guidance Beethoven developed rapidly. He was only eleven when his first compositions, three piano sonatas, were published. At twelve, while his teacher was absent from Bonn, Ludwig took his place as court organist. And at thirteen he was appointed cembalist for the rehearsals of the court theater orchestra. "Beethoven, son of the court tenor singer of that name," reported Neefe in *Cramer's Magazine*, "possesses talent of great promise. . . . He plays the piano with wonderful execution, and reads very well at sight. . . . He will certainly be a second Wolfgang Amadeus Mozart if he continues as he has begun."

Though he was no Mozart, able to dazzle audiences with spectacular feats, Beethoven did prove to be a musician of extraordinary power, especially in improvisation. He gained the interest and support of several influential people in Bonn—the Elector Max Franz (who in 1784 appointed him assistant organist at court), Frau von Breuning, and Count Ferdinand von Waldstein. They became his friends and patrons. On the advice of Neefe, and with funds provided by the Elector, Beethoven made a brief visit to Vienna in 1787. There his improvisation for Mozart prompted the older composer to say, "This young man will leave his mark on the world." Beethoven's trip was cut short by news that his mother was seriously ill. He rushed back to Bonn, and was at her side when she died. "She was, indeed, a kind mother to me," Beethoven wrote soon after her death. "Ah, who was happier than I when I could still utter the sweet name of 'mother,' and it was heard? To whom can I now say it? Only to the silent form which my imagination pictures to me!"

After his mother's death Beethoven assumed the responsibility of supporting his family, for by this time the older Beethoven's intemperance had caused his dismissal from his court post. Beethoven gave lessons, performed at court, and devoted himself to composition. One of his Masses, performed in

1790 in the Bonn Cathedral, was heard by Haydn, who was passing through on his way to London. "He is a man of great talent," the master said of the young composer. When Haydn revisited Bonn en route back to Vienna, he urged Beethoven to study with him.

Beethoven went to Vienna in November 1792, finding lodgings at Alserstrasse 45. Determined to make his mark in the big city, he bought a wig, silk hose, and a fashionable coat—sartorial trimmings planned for his visits to the salons and palaces, but soon discarded. He looked older than his years. His face was pock-marked, florid, and of leonine strength. He was gruff, ill-mannered, awkward, self-conscious, and ungovernable in spirit. His unruly strength made him an intractable pupil. He had come to Vienna to study; but neither Joseph Haydn, nor Albrechtsberger of St. Stephen's, nor even the *Kapellmeister* Salieri could please him—or be satisfied with him. Haydn, admiring Beethoven's genius, could not understand or tolerate the young man's undisciplined ways and boorish manners. Albrechtsberger said, shaking his head sadly: "He has never learned anything, and he can do nothing in decent style."

Beethoven, soon impatient with instruction, began to establish himself in Vienna as a virtuoso. He performed in the palaces of some of Vienna's most highly placed noblemen—Prince Lichnowsky, Prince Lobkowitz, Baron von Swieten, and others. He taught clavier to the children of the rich. He introduced his own compositions in fashionable salons. Though he not only considered himself the equal of his high-born benefactors but was insulting, bumptious, and rude to them, his patrons tolerated his storms and moods for the sake of his undeniable brilliance. As early as 1793 he was acknowledged to be "beyond controversy one of the foremost pianoforte players," as a contemporary journalist described him. His powers of improvisation were said to be matchless. "Apart from the beauty and originality of the ideas," said Karl Czerny, Beethoven's contemporary, "there was something extraordinary in the expression."

At his first public concert in Vienna, on March 29, 1795, Beethoven overwhelmed his audience and critics with his improvisations and the B-flat major Piano Concerto. By the close of the century he had published

his first set of trios, several piano sonatas, and the song "Adelaide." "I have more orders than I can execute," he said at the time. "I have six or seven publishers for each one of my works, and could have more if I choose. No more bargaining! I can name my terms and they pay."

On April 2, 1800, at the Burgtheater, the première of Beethoven's First Symphony took place in a program with his Septet. It cannot be said that contemporaries recognized in that symphony the birth of a new age for orchestral music. The *Allgemeine Musikalische Zeitung* condemned the work for its excessive "use of wind instruments, so much so that the music sounded as if written for a military band rather than for an orchestra." Academicians denounced its shocking opening tonality, its heavy-footed minuet movement. When the First Symphony was heard in Leipzig soon after its Vienna première, one critic described it as "the confused explosions of the presumptuous effrontery of a young man."

By 1802 the first of Beethoven's three creative periods had drawn to a close. He had written two symphonies, three piano concertos, six string quartets (op. 18), three piano trios, three string trios, a septet, eighteen piano sonatas, seven violin sonatas, and many other compositions. Discussing the works of his first period, Daniel Gregory Mason wrote: "Beethoven had in the first place thoroughly assimilated the sonata form developed by his forerunners as the most convenient and natural medium for the expression of the free, direct, and widely electric secular spirit in music. He had, in the second place, raised this form to higher potencies of beauty and expressiveness by rigorous exclusion of what was superfluous and inorganic in it, by purification of its texture and strengthening of its essential structural features, and by introduction into it, through the power of genius for composition, of more subtle and more thoroughgoing contrasts of rhythm, harmony, and general expressive character."

In 1802 Beethoven wrote: "I am not satisfied with my works up to the present time. From today I mean to take a new road." He was fully conscious of his powers ("With whom need I be afraid of measuring my strength?"); proudly self-assured ("This much will I tell you, that you will see me again, when I am really great; not only greater as an artist but as a man you will find me better, more perfect"); certain of his destiny ("I *must* write—for what weighs on my heart I *must* express"). And so he embarked upon his second creative phase, to realize completely new powers and richer, deeper poetic thought. The *Eroica Symphony* and the *Kreutzer Sonata* for violin were completed in 1803, the *Waldstein* and *Appassionata* Piano Sonatas in 1804. With these works the old classical order was decisively abandoned. A new Romantic era began to unfold. Structure, design, and law now bent before the poetic idea in which, as Alfred Frankenstein said, "a new sense of scale to the classic forms of instrumental composition . . . [was] related to the most dynamic forces of the society in which he lived."

Across these years of immense creativity there passed also the shadow of tragedy. Early in 1801 Beethoven had begun to detect that his hearing was failing him. As this infirmity developed he became increasingly sensitive, and tried, pathetically, to keep his deafness from even his close friends. He refused to appear in public; he shunned the society of all except the few with whom he was most intimate. The overpowering despair which the loss of his hearing brought is expressed in the remarkable document "The Heiligenstadt Testament," written in 1802 while he was living in the Viennese suburb of that name. "For me," he wrote, "there can be no recreation in the society of my fellows, refined intercourse, mutual exchange of thought; only just as little as the greatest needs command may I mix with society. I must live like an exile. . . . O Providence—grant me at least but one day of pure joy—it is so long since real joy echoed in my heart—O when—O when, O divine One—shall I feel it again in the temple of nature and man—Never?—No—O, that would be too hard."

Despair gave way to resignation ("Sorrowful resignation, in this must I find refuge"); resignation to defiance ("I will seize fate by the throat; it shall certainly never overcome me!"). If his career as a pianist had been destroyed, he would now dedicate himself completely to composition, hammering the pattern of his thoughts into works of unimaginable scope, dimension, and expressiveness. He wrote the three *Rasou-*

movsky Quartets, op. 59, in 1806; the mighty Fifth Symphony in C minor and the *Pastoral Symphony,* between 1805 and 1808; the Violin Concerto and the fourth and *Emperor* piano concertos, between 1805 and 1809; his one opera, *Fidelio,* an eloquent paean to human freedom, in or about 1805; the *Coriolan Overture,* in 1807; the great Cello Sonata in A major, in 1808. In Beethoven's second phase, Paul Bekker wrote, "music is no longer sonority pure and simple. It contains abstract ideas. Beethoven did not write music to preconceived ideas, but the ideas and the music went inseparably together. With him the dynamic urge which is an organic part of all harmonic music goes far beyond the ordinary scope of dynamic impulses and becomes the means of interpreting the idea. . . . It is . . . impossible to dismiss the idea from Beethoven's music without misrepresenting the man. It is the idea which constitutes the constructive power, the dynamic principle of form in his compositions. It is the idea which determines the character of his work and which makes possible the further development of harmonic music. Beethoven's true relationship with Schiller and Kant lies in their being men who stood for ideas, though they worked along different creative lines. But in his particular type of ideas, Beethoven is the great child of a great imaginative era —an era in which the gods and heroes of idealism throve, an era which believed in man as a spiritual being, in freedom and brotherhood, in the joy of divine inspiration, in the everlasting peace and happiness of mankind."

As the years passed Beethoven grew increasingly irritable, volatile, and unreasonable. He subjected even close friends and patrons to violent abuse. On more than one occasion he magnified a minor incident or misunderstanding into a major crisis. In the summer of 1806 he broke with his lifelong patron, Prince Lichnowsky, because he had been asked to perform for some visiting French officers (since Napoleon had declared himself Emperor in 1804, Beethoven hated all things French); for five years Beethoven refused to speak to the most generous of his admirers. He became estranged from Hummel because he had misinterpreted a casual remark and would accept no explanation. Stephan von Breuning, who had solicitously nursed Beethoven through a serious illness, was driven away over a trifle. Beethoven excoriated Ferdinand Ries because he suspected his friend of seeking a conductor's post which he had been offered.

Still his friends and patrons clung to him, cognizant of his genius, sympathetic to his stormy nature and growing introversion. The highest-born nobility—the Archduke Rudolph, for example—tolerated even Beethoven's fervent republicanism. In 1809 his patrons arranged a generous annual pension for him.

Yet what he wanted most desperately, and vainly, was a woman's love and dedication. Beethoven was often enamored, but with women who were too young, who were inaccessible because of their social position: Giulietta Guicciardi, to whom he dedicated the *Moonlight Sonata;* her cousin Theresa von Brunswick, inspiration for his *Appassionata Sonata;* the fifteen-year-old Therese Malfatti; or Goethe's friend, Bettina Brentano.

After Beethoven's death a passionate love letter was found in a secret drawer of his desk. In an intense outburst the composer had written, "Your love has made me one of the happiest and at the same time, one of the unhappiest of men. . . . What tearful longing after you—you—my life—my all—farewell. Oh, continue to love me, never misjudge the faithful heart of Your Beloved L. — Ever yours — ever mine — ever each other's."

The identity of the woman who aroused this violent emotional upheaval has never been uncovered, though we know that the letter to the "Immortal Beloved," as it is called, was written in 1812. There is some conjecture that Beethoven was addressing not a particular woman but all womankind, or that he was speaking to a woman of his dreams who had no actual existence.

From 1812 to 1818 Beethoven produced little of significance. During these stagnant and difficult years Beethoven was involved in litigation over his nephew, Karl, whom he wished to adopt, and whose irresponsibility and shiftless ways caused the composer continual anguish. Then in 1818, with the *Hammerklavier Sonata* for piano, Beethoven entered what was in many respects the most majestic and awesome of his creative periods. In this final stage of development Beethoven brought to music new freedom of structure, presentation and development of thematic material, and "voice treatment." His poetic expression now achieved a transcendental radiance and spirituality that sharply distinguish these last compositions from his other masterpieces. It was in this new manner that he wrote the *Missa solemnis,* the Ninth Symphony, the last string quartets, the last piano sonatas, the *Grosse fugue* for string quartet.

J. W. N. Sullivan's description of one of the last string quartets, the Quartet in C-sharp minor, op. 131, may well describe the other monumental compositions of this period. "It is the completely unfaltering rendering into music of what we can only call the mystic vision. It has the serenity which, as Wagner said, speaking of these quartets, passes beauty. Nowhere else in music are we made so aware, as here, of a state of consciousness surpassing our own, where our problems do not exist, and to which even our highest aspirations, those that we can formulate, provide no key. . . ." This, Sullivan concludes, "is the last and greatest of Beethoven's spiritual discoveries, only to be grasped in the moments of his profoundest abstraction from the world."

Beethoven made his last public appearance on May 7, 1824, attending the première of his Ninth Symphony. At the end of the symphony, Beethoven, long stone deaf, continued to beat time to himself though the symphony had concluded. Gently, one of the soloists turned him to face the audience and accept its ovation.

In 1826 Beethoven contracted pneumonia, which was soon complicated by jaundice and dropsy. Confined to bed, he retained his good spirits, read Scott and Ovid with considerable pleasure, delighted in the gifts sent him from all parts of Europe. But he was fatally ill, and in time was forced to acknowledge the fact. He signed his will on March 23, 1827; a day later he submitted quietly to the Last Sacraments. On March 25 he slipped into unconsciousness. "The strong man lay," wrote Gerhard von Breuning, "completely unconscious, . . . breathing so stertorously that the rattle could be heard at a distance. His powerful frame, his weakened lungs, fought like giants with approaching death."

Beethoven died in Vienna on March 26, 1827. His funeral took place three days later. Schools were closed, and a military force was called out to keep the Viennese under control. The torchbearers included Schubert, Hummel, Czerny, and Kreutzer.

In his biography of the composer, Romain Rolland described Beethoven as "short and thick set, broad shouldered and of athletic build. A big face, ruddy in complexion—except towards the end of his life, when his color became sickly and yellow, especially in the winter after he had been remaining indoors far from the fields. He had a massive and rugged forehead, extremely black and extraordinarily thick hair through which it seemed the comb had never passed, for it was always very rumpled, veritable bristling 'serpents of Medusa.' His eyes shone with prodigious force. It was one of the chief things one noticed on first encountering him, but many were mistaken in their color. When they shone out in dark splendor from a sad and tragic visage, they generally appeared black; but they were really a bluish gray. Small and very deep set, they flashed fiercely in moments of passion or warmth, and dilated in a peculiar way under the influence of inspiration, reflecting his thoughts with a marvelous exactness. Often they inclined upwards with a melancholy expression. His nose was short and broad with the nostrils of a lion; the mouth refined, with the lower lip somewhat prominent. He had very strong jaws, which could easily break nuts; a large indentation in his chin imparted a curious irregularity to the face. 'He had a charming smile,' said Moscheles, 'and in conversation a manner often lovable and inviting confidence; on the other hand his laugh was most disagreeable, loud, discordant and strident'—the laugh of a man unused to happiness. His usual expression was one of melancholy. Rellstab in 1825 said that he had to summon up all his courage to prevent himself from breaking into tears when he looked into Beethoven's 'tender eyes with their speaking sadness.' Braun von Braunthal met him in an inn a year later. Beethoven was sitting in a corner with closed eyes, smoking a long pipe—a habit which grew on him more and more as he approached death. A friend spoke to him. He smiled sadly, drew from his pocket a little note tablet, and in a thin voice which frequently sounded cracked, asked him to write down his request. His face would frequently become suddenly transfigured, maybe in the access of sudden inspiration, which seized him at random, even in the street, filling the passers-by with amazement, or it might be when great thoughts came to him suddenly, when seated at the piano. 'The muscles of his face would stand out, his veins would swell; his wild eyes would become doubly terrible. His lips trembled, he had the manner of a wizard controlling the demons which he had invoked.' . . . A Shakespearean visage—'King Lear'—so Sir Julius Benedict described him."

Beethoven's method of composition was to jot down his ideas as they came to him, on scraps of paper or in a sketch book. These ideas he would continually polish and revise until they were fully crystallized in a shape and form that pleased him. "I carry my thoughts about with me long, often very long, before I write them down," he once explained. "In doing this my memory stands me in such good stead that even years afterwards I am sure not to forget a theme that I have once grasped. I alter some things, eliminate and try again until I am satisfied. Then begins the mental working out of this stuff in its breadth, its narrowness, its height and depth. And, as I know what I want, the fundamental idea never deserts me. It mounts, it grows in stature; I hear, see the picture in its whole extent, standing all of a piece before my spirit, and there remains for me only the labor of writing it down, which goes quickly whenever I have time for it. For many times I have several pieces in hand at once, but am perfectly sure not to confuse them. You will ask me where I get my ideas. I am not able to answer that question positively. They come directly, indirectly; I can grasp them with my hands. Out amid the freedom of nature, in the woods, on walks, in the silence of the night, early in the morning, called forth by such moods as in the minds of poets translate themselves into words, but in mine into tones which ring, roar, storm until at last they stand as notes before me."

Robert Haven Schauffler subtitled his biography of Beethoven "The Man Who Freed Music," describing in his book how that revolution took place: "By his choice of texts . . . [Beethoven] presented vocal music with the freedom of the world of great literature—a pioneer accomplishment. Through the accidental circumstances that . . . [Bach's] B minor Mass was not published until years after Beethoven's *Missa solemnis,* our hero became the Luther among composers, extricating the Mass from the bonds of convention and dogma. He released the dramatic overture from subservience to that hybrid thing, opera; and the concerto orchestra from its abject servility as a mere accompanist to the solo part. More than any previous composer he rid music of the exhibitionistic taint of virtuosity for virtuosity's sake, and the reproach of composing to the order of outer compulsion rather than from inner necessity. His ingenuity helped to throw open to the piano and the orchestra a new world of richness and sonority. The accident of deafness freed the art in another way, by decreeing a divorce between composer and virtuoso and smashing the harmful old convention that the creative musician must necessarily fritter away his energies in interpretative work.

"Perhaps his supreme achievement as emancipator was the exertion of a more potent influence than that of his greatest predecessors towards freeing music from the shackles of literature, whose servant it was in the beginning. By pouring into music a wealth of suggestive factors which made it so much more opulent and self-contained than ever before, he made it easier for the imagination of the ordinary listener at length to escape from the weakening incubus of cliché programs and, under the stimulus of this powerfully independent art, to fashion its own poetic interpretations.

"Beethoven found the art of music narrowed to the pastime of a special class. He made it broadly human. He left it superhuman. Of course, he was far from being the only man who ever freed music. In many ages and lands the art has been enslaved and has found its liberators. But the most potent of all was Beethoven."

Principal Works

Chamber Music—16 string quartets; 10 violin sonatas; 9 piano trios; 5 string trios; 5 cello sonatas; 4 piano quartets; 3 string quintets; 2 trios for clarinet (or violin), cello and piano; Octet in E-flat major, for winds; Septet in E-flat major; Sextet in E-flat major; Grosse fugue, for string quartet; Sonata in F, for horn and piano.

Choral Music—Mass in C; Piano Fantasy, for chorus, orchestra and piano; Christus am Oelberge (Christ on the Mount of Olives); Meerestille und glückliche Fahrt; Der glorreiche Augenblick; Missa solemnis.

Opera—Fidelio.

Orchestral Music—9 symphonies; 5 piano concertos; Concerto in D major, for violin and orchestra, Concerto in C major, for piano, violin, cello, and orchestra; 2 Romances, for violin and orchestra; Ah, perfido! for voice and orchestra; Fidelio Overture; Leonore Overtures, Nos. 1, 2, 3; Coriolan Overture; incidental music to Egmont (including overture); incidental music to Prometheus (including overture); incidental music to the Ruins of Athens, including Turkish March; Consecration of the House Overture; contredanses, German dances, Ländler, minuets.

Piano Music—32 sonatas (also 6 easy sonatas and sonatinas); Variations on a Waltz by Diabelli; Thirty-two variations; Andante Favori in F major; bagatelles, écossaises, rondos, waltzes.

Vocal Music—An die ferne Geliebte, song cycle; 6 Lieder von Gellert; numerous songs for voice and piano including Adelaide, Andenken, An die Hoffnung, Bitten, Die ehre Gottes, Das geheimnis, Ich liebe dich, In questa tomba obscura, Der Kuss, Nur wer die Sehnsucht kennt, Der Wachtelschlag, Wonne der Wehmut; arrangements of Irish, Scotch, Welsh and Italian songs; canons.

About

Bekker, P., Beethoven; Burk, J. N., The Life and Works of Beethoven; Grove, G., Beethoven and His Nine Symphonies; Hamburger, M. (editor), Beethoven: Letters, Journals, and Conversations; Mason, D. G., The Quartets of Beethoven; Nettl, P. (editor), Beethoven Encyclopedia; Newman, E., The Unconscious Beethoven; Rolland, R., Beethoven; Rolland, R., Beethoven the Creator; Schauffler, R. H., Beethoven: The Man Who Freed Music; Specht, R., Beethoven as He Lived; Steichen, D., Beethoven's Beloved; Sullivan, J. W. N. Beethoven: His Spiritual Development; Thayer, A. W., The Life of Ludwig van Beethoven; Tovey, D. F., Beethoven; Tovey, D. F., A Companion to Beethoven's Piano Sonatas; Turner, W. J., Beethoven: The Search for Reality; Wagner, R., Beethoven.

Vincenzo Bellini *1801-1835*

VINCENZO BELLINI, composer of *La Sonnambula* and *Norma,* was born in Catania, Sicily, on November 3, 1801. His father, the organist of the Catania Cathedral, belonged to a family which had for several generations produced professional musicians. He gave Vincenzo his first music lessons. The religious and secular music that the boy was soon writing attracted the interest of the Duchess of Sammartino, who provided funds for the boy to attend the San Sebastiano Conservatory in Naples. At the conservatory Bellini studied with Tritto and Zingarelli, among others, and supplemented his formal education by reading the published scores of Pergolesi, Paisiello, and Jommelli, works that awakened his love for opera.

While still at the Conservatory, Bellini completed several ambitious works: two Masses, a cantata, a symphony, and an opera. His first work to be performed, the cantata *Ismene,* was given at the Conservatory in 1825; it received the congratulations of the influential impresario Barbaja. His first opera, *Adelson e Salvina,* was also introduced at the Conservatory that year. Barbaja now commissioned the young Bellini to write an opera for one of his theaters. On May 30, 1826, *Bianca e Fernando,* performed at La Scala in Milan, played to an enthusiastic audience, and Barbaja asked Bellini to write another opera, for the famed Italian tenor Rubini. Rubini starred in *Il Pirata* at La Scala on October 27, 1827, winning accolades for himself and the composer.

Although *Il Pirata* is hardly a product of Bellini's full maturity, it foreshadows some of the characteristics of Bellini's developed style. "It has arias in which the melody flows easily," wrote F. Bonavia. "It has a tenderness that captivates. The writing shows understanding of what the human voice can do to express pathetic emotion."

Three years later Bellini scored another success with *I Capuletti ed i Montecchi,* based on Shakespeare's *Romeo and Juliet.* It was presented at La Fenice in Venice on March 11, 1830. Berlioz praised the opera highly, singling out the second-act finale for especially enthusiastic comment.

La Sonnambula, the first of Bellini's undisputed masterworks was presented on March 6, 1831 at the Teatro Carcano in Milan. From its première it was a triumph. Maria Malibran, who starred in the first performance, later appeared in an English-language version that helped to popularize the opera abroad. The American première took place only four and a half years after its introduction in Milan, at the Park Theatre in New York, on November 13, 1835. In 1850 it was given in Chicago, the first grand opera to be produced in that city.

The powerful libretto by Felice Romani had stimulated Bellini's dramatic vigor and lyric inventiveness. With arias like "Vi ravviso," "Ah! non credea mirarti," and "Ah! non giunge," Bellini presented himself as the aristocrat of *bel canto.* "*La Sonnambula,*" wrote Wallace Brockway and Herbert Weinstock, "is as Romantic as *Der Freischütz,* but its Romanticism is Italian, delicately tinted by what was doubtless a super-

VINCENZO BELLINI

ficial acquaintance with the current fashions in European literature." Brockway and Weinstock added that in this opera Bellini wrote "melodies such as had never been heard before."

The success of *La Sonnambula* brought Bellini a commission from La Scala for a new work. The result was his second masterpiece, *Norma,* given on December 26, 1831, with Giuditta Pasta in the title role. *Norma* was Bellini's own favorite. "If I were shipwrecked at sea," he once said, "I would leave all the rest of my operas and try to save *Norma.*" It is easy to see why. Nowhere else did he attain such majestic melodic expressiveness and elegant lyricism. Norma's unforgettable aria, "Casta diva," is a classic example of his achievement. "I would give all my music to have written 'Casta diva,'" said Jacques Halévy, composer of *La Juive.* Of the opera as a whole Wagner said: "This opera among all the creations of Bellini is the one which, with the most profound reality, joins to the richest vein of melody the most intimate passion. . . . The music is noble and great, simple and grandiose in style."

Norma was first heard in the United States at the Park Theatre in New York on February 25, 1841. When the Academy of Music opened its doors on October 2, 1854, its first attraction was *Norma,* with a cast that included Giulia Grisi in the title role and her husband Mario as Pollione.

In 1833 Bellini paid a brief visit to London, then proceeded to Paris, where Rossini encouraged him to write *I Puritani* for the Théâtre des Italiens. It was produced on January 25, 1835, with a magnificent cast including Grisi, Rubini, Tamburini, and Lablanche. Despite the confused and slow-moving libretto (the story is set in England, during the war of Cromwell against the Stuarts), Bellini again soared to peaks of melodic inspiration. Cecil Gray considered this opera to be on a level with *La Sonnambula* and *Norma*.

Bellini died of intestinal fever in Puteaux, near Paris, on September 23, 1835. On the eve of his funeral, the Théâtre des Italiens was inaugurating a new season with *I Puritani*. When the performance ended, the musicians joined at the Invalides church, in a requiem service directed by Cherubini and Rossini. Bellini was buried in Père Lachaise cemetery in Paris; forty years later his body was removed to Catania.

Heinrich Heine thus described Bellini: "Bellini had a tall, up-shooting, slender figure, which always moved gracefully, coquettish looking as if just emerged from a bandbox; a regular, but large, delicately rose-tinted face; light, almost golden hair, worn in wavy curls; a high, very high marble forehead, straight nose, light blue eyes, well-sized mouth, and round chin. His features had something vague in them, a want of character, something milk-like; and in this milk-like face flitted sometimes a painful-pleasing expression of sorrow. It was this shallow sorrow that the young *maestro* seemed most willing to represent in his whole appearance. His hair was dressed so fancifully sad; his clothes fitted so languishingly round his delicate body; he carried his cane so idyll-like, that he reminded me of the young shepherds we find in our pastorals, with their crooks decorated with ribbons. His whole walk was so innocent, so airy, so sentimental. The man looked like a sigh in pumps and silk stockings."

"With all his charms," comments George R. Marek, "Bellini possessed plenty of meanness, and would do almost anything for money. That *les femmes* should have been strongly attracted to such a man (and vice versa) is to be expected. Here again his life follows a scenario's pattern. All the elements are there: the seamstress who adored him, the wife whom he mistreated, the beauty who left her wealthy husband to follow the composer and even the woman whom Bellini loved and who broke his heart (temporarily) by marrying another. She was the legendary singer Maria Felicitas Malibran."

Bellini's greatest strength as a composer lay in his remarkable melodic gifts. "He who ignores Bellini," said Roger Allard, "ignores true melody." And Ildebrando Pizzetti, Italy's most distinguished twentieth-century opera composer, has written: "The lyricism of Bellini expresses itself in a song that gushes forth with the essence of an emotion that springs from the drama, that gushes forth especially at moments that bring the drama to a resolution, similar to a fire which is ignited after it emits hot sparks. And this song . . . becomes a stream, a river, finally an ocean that rolls away to the distance towards the immense horizon. . . . Bellini has created a song that is ample, marvelous and unique. Unique is the song of the final scene of *Norma,* unique is the one which accompanies the closing of the first act of *Sonnambula,* and unique is the song which can be found in the most important scenes of *Puritani.*"

Musicologists have frequently pointed an accusing finger at Bellini's shortcomings as an opera composer. As Vittorio Gui wrote in *High Fidelity*: "When . . . Bellini took over the operatic form of his day, he also silently accepted a host of concessions—the dominant position of the prima donna, the fascination for wildly ornamented vocal lines, a certain lack of interest of orchestral color, stereotyped accompaniments, and so on. The weaknesses in the creative work of Bellini are easy to point out. . . . It is clear why, to critics, Italian opera in general and the work of Bellini in particular seemed artistically inferior. Yet nineteenth-century audiences . . . were thirsting for melos, the 'divine' melody; and in Bellini, this melos is all-important—the life-giving force for which the composer was willing to sacrifice everything. Melodies flowed from Bellini in dazzling fecundity. It is the one feature of Bellini's art which is above criticism, and which has been the object of admiration and even envy from such disparate composers as Chopin, Wagner, and Stravinsky."

One of the criticisms often directed against Bellini is the weakness of his harmonic writing. Cecil Gray has provided the following rebuttal: "His vocal writing could only be impaired by such treatment. Like folk song, it instinctively rejects harmonic elaborateness as foreign to its nature. . . . In the same way that a jewel is displayed to better advantage in a simple setting than in none at all, but is overshadowed by the brilliance of an elaborate one, so a melody of Bellini requires a certain degree of accompaniment which must never be allowed to become so obtrusive as to distract our attention from the melody, or to impress itself too strongly on our consciousness."

But it must be emphasized that Bellini was not merely a composer of inspired melody. He was also a powerful dramatist who influenced the direction and evolution of opera. He worked conscientiously to create a stronger union between text and music; his recitatives and ensemble numbers are often rich with dramatic interest. Richard Wagner recognized Bellini's dramatic gifts. "Never," he wrote in his memoirs, "will I forget the impression which Bellini's operas made upon me at a time when I was perfectly weary of the eternally abstract complexity of our orchestrations, and when a simple and noble song manifested itself as something new to me." Elsewhere Wagner added: "People believe that I hate all the Italian school of music and specifically Bellini. No, no, a thousand times no! Bellini is one of my predilections, because his music is strongly felt and intimately bound up with the words."

Bellini summarized his method of work as follows: "I study attentively the dispositions of the characters, the passions which sway them, and the sentiments which they express. Possessed by the feelings of each of them, I imagine myself for the moment to have become the one who is speaking, and I make an effort to feel like him, and to express myself in his manner. Knowing that music results from the employment of a variety of sounds, and that the passions of mankind manifest themselves by means of utterance of diverse tones, I have reproduced the language of passion in my art through incessant observation.

"Then in the seclusion of my study I begin to declaim the parts of the different characters in the drama with the utmost warmth, observing in the meanwhile the inflexions of my voice, the degree of haste or languor in their delivery—the accent, in short

—and the tone of expression which nature gives to the man who is in the throes of emotion: and I find in this way the musical motives and tempi best adapted to their communication to others through the medium of sounds.

"I transfer the results to paper, try it over on the piano, and if I feel in it the corresponding emotion, I consider myself to have succeeded. If I do not, then I begin again."

PRINCIPAL WORKS

Operas—Bianca e Fernando; Il Pirata; La Straniera; I Capuletti ed i Montecchi; La Sonnambula; Norma; Beatrice di Tenda; I Puritani.

Vocal Music—Songs for voice and piano, including L'Abbandono, Dolente immagine di figlia mia.

ABOUT

Biancolli, L. (editor), The Opera Reader; Brockway, W., and Weinstock, H., The Opera; Fracaroli, A., Bellini; Lloyd, W., Bellini; Pougin, A. Bellini: sa vie et son œuvre; Tiby, O., Vincenzo Bellini; Wagner, Richard, Prose Works.

High Fidelity Magazine, June 1963; La Revue musicale, May 1935 (Bellini issue).

Hector Berlioz *1803-1869*

LOUIS-HECTOR BERLIOZ, the first of the great Romantic composers, was born in La Côte-Saint-André, Isère, France, on December 11, 1803. His father, a physician, was a cultivated man who instilled in his son a love of classic literature, a knowledge of Latin, and an understanding of the rudiments of music. Though Berlioz was proficient at guitar, flute, and piano, and made his first efforts at composition, while still a boy, he was firmly discouraged from contemplating a career in music. His mother, devoutly religious, regarded any preoccupation with music or the theater as a sin and exerted herself to keep Berlioz from becoming too deeply involved in his favorite art. Berlioz' father also opposed extensive musical activity, hoping that his son would be a doctor; to that end he began to teach the boy the elements of anatomy.

The emotional extravagance that would later characterize Berlioz' personality was apparent during his boyhood. He wept at certain episodes in Virgil, went into raptures at the beauty of a Catholic service, plunged into adolescent infatuations with complete abandon. He was only twelve when he experienced his first romantic attachment, for

Berlioz: bĕr-lyôz'

HECTOR BERLIOZ

a girl six years his senior. "I had no idea what was the matter with me," he later recalled in his memoirs, "but I suffered acutely, and spent my nights in sleepless anguish. In the daytime I crept away like a wounded bird and hid myself in the maize fields and orchards. I suffered agonies when any man approached my idol, and it makes me shudder even now when I recall the ring of my uncle's spurs as he danced with her."

In his early teens Berlioz studied music with two local teachers. He also took to memorizing theoretical tracts, including those by Catel and Rameau, and used his newly acquired technical knowledge to complete a flute quintet which was given a private performance in his native town. He later composed a *Potpourri concertant* for flute, horn and strings, and several songs.

Accompanied by a cousin, Berlioz left for Paris in 1821 to begin his medical studies. Although his first experience with dissection so disgusted him that he fled home, certain that medicine could never be his calling, he dutifully continued his studies in Paris. His intense preoccupation with music continued, however, and a performance of Gluck's *Iphigénie en Tauride* finally resolved his conflict. "I would rather be Gluck or Méhul dead than what I am in the flower of my youth," he informed his father. Then, without awaiting parental permission, he entered the Paris Conservatory, supporting himself by teaching guitar and serving as a chorister at the Théâtre des Nouveautés.

At the Conservatory Berlioz was a pupil of Lesueur and Reicha. "You will not be a doctor or a druggist," Lesueur told him firmly, "but a great composer. You have genius. I say it, because it is true." As if in confirmation, Berlioz completed a *Messe solennelle* for an orchestra of 150, and introduced it at the Église Saint-Roch on July 10, 1825. He also started to work on an opera (never completed) and composed several songs which he published at his own expense. In 1827 he competed for the Prix de Rome with the cantata *La Mort d'Orphée;* it was turned down as "unplayable."

In the fall of 1827 an English Shakespearean troupe performed at the Odéon in Paris. Berlioz attended *Hamlet,* and immediately fell in love with "Ophelia," the actress Harriet Constance Smithson. Since he knew not a word of English, he wrote her a feverish love letter in French; she ignored it. After a number of unsuccessful efforts to arrange a meeting with Harriet (or Henrietta, as he liked to call her), he decided to use his musical talents to court her. Having learned that the actress was Irish, he composed several songs to Irish texts of Thomas Moore and on May 26, 1828, conducted a program of his own works. Still failing to engage her interest, he rented a room near her apartment, hoping that their paths would cross. But he was again frustrated, for Harriet Smithson was about to leave Paris for London.

"I am again plunged in the anguish of an interminable and inextinguishable passion, without motive, without cause," he wrote to a friend. "She is always in London and yet I think I feel her near me: all my remembrances awaken and unite to wound me; I hear my heart beating, and its pulsations shake me as the piston strikes of a steam engine. Each muscle of my body shudders with pain. In vain! 'Tis terrible! Oh, unhappy one! If she could for one moment conceive all the poetry, . . . of a like love, she would fly to my arms, were she to die through my embrace."

To avenge himself for her aloofness, Berlioz in 1829 worked out a programmatic symphony, representing Harriet by a recurrent musical idea—*idée fixe,* as he called it —which dominated the entire work. Inspired by De Quincey's *Confessions of an English Opium Eater,* Berlioz' *Symphonie fantastique* (originally entitled *Épisode de la vie d'un artiste*) is one of the most remarkable symphonic works of the early nineteenth century. It was years ahead of its time in dramatic and psychological interest, in symphonic structure and style, in thematic presentation, in realism of programmatic depiction, and in the Romantic outpouring of turbulent emotion. "One may smile," wrote Philip Hale, "at the frantic love of Berlioz for the Irish actress; at the program of the *Fantastic Symphony*. . . . But there's no denying the genius in this work, the genius that has kept the music alive in spite of a few cheap or arid pages; for there is the imagination, the poetic sensitiveness that we rightly associate with genius. If one could gladly shorten the 'Scene in the Fields,' what is to be said against that masterpiece, 'The March to the Scaffold,' with its haunting, nightmarish rhythm, its ghostly chatter of the bassoons, its mocking shouts of brass? Or who does not find beauty in the first movement, brilliance in the second, and a demoniacal spirit in the finale?"

The first performance of the *Symphonie fantastique* took place in Paris on December 5, 1830. Despite his former disgust with and renunciation of Harriet Smithson, he had not forgotten her. Indeed, he was now as much excited by thoughts of her as he had once been. With Harriet now back in Paris (still avoiding him) Berlioz hoped that the première of his symphony would evoke in her some interest in him. To his intense disappointment, she failed to attend. There were other compensations, however. The symphony met with huge success. Liszt, one of many prominent musicians in the audience, was enraptured by the music and became one of Berlioz' devoted friends and admirers.

Meanwhile Berlioz had tried to forget Harriet, not without success. He fell in love with Camille Moke, a brilliant concert pianist, and they were soon engaged. But when in 1830 Berlioz finally won the Prix de Rome, on his third try, he was forced to separate, temporarily, from his betrothed for a sojourn in Rome. He was completely miserable in Italy. He disliked most things Italian; he was irritated by the strict regimen at the Villa Medici; he was tormented by rumors that his betrothed was unfaithful. One day he impetuously left Rome to determine the truth for himself, but before he reached Paris he received word that Camille had just married another man. Berlioz, enraged to fever pitch, continued on, planning to kill the young couple in Paris. But en route he had a sudden change of heart, turned around, and went back to Rome.

In 1832 Berlioz was back in Paris. Nostalgically, he decided to rent the apartment that had been occupied by Harriet Smithson. He had not forgotten the actress during his absence, and learned with delight that she was in Paris again. Once more he tried to win her admiration by arranging a concert of his works, including in it the *Symphonie fantastique* which she had inspired. The concert took place at the Conservatory on December 9, 1832. This time Harriet attended. Berlioz' plan had its desired effect. The actress was so moved by the music that she consented to meet the composer. Once introduced to her, Berlioz had little difficulty persuading her of his passion and devotion. The fact that Harriet Smithson was suffering a sharp decline in stage popularity and had suffered serious financial reverses made her all the more receptive to Berlioz' solicitous attentions. On October 3, 1833, overriding the violent objections of their families, Harriet and Berlioz were married at the British Embassy. "She was mine," Berlioz recalled in his autobiography, "and I defied the world."

He was married to a woman whose beauty had faded, whose career in the theater was virtually ended, who limped as a result of a recent accident, who was heavily in debt, who—worst of all—did not love him. The marriage was a disaster from the start, ruined by their conflicting and volatile temperaments. Not even the birth of their son, Louis, to whom they were both devoted, could ameliorate their relationship. After several years of almost incessant turbulence, they decided to live apart. They were never divorced, however, and it was many years before Berlioz was able to marry Marie Recio, a singer who became his mistress in 1841.

Despite the turmoil of his first years of marriage, Berlioz completed several masterpieces. One had been commissioned by Niccolò Paganini, the renowned violin virtuoso. Impressed with the *Symphonie fantastique,* Paganini had asked Berlioz to write a large work for viola and orchestra, the viola having recently engaged his interest. Inspired by Byron's *Childe Harold,* Berlioz completed *Harold en Italie* (*Harold in Italy*), a symphony with viola obbligato. Paganini had expected a dazzling virtuoso composition glorifying his fabulous technique; what Berlioz produced instead was a deeply poetic and dramatic expression of his own Byronic dreams and yearnings. Paganini lost interest in the symphony after seeing the sketches of the first movement. *Harold en Italie* was introduced in Paris on November 23, 1834. Hearing the work four years later, Paganini sent Berlioz a gift of twenty thousand francs, with the statement that "Beethoven is dead and Berlioz alone can revive him."

Harold en Italie was succeeded by two other highly ambitious compositions. The Requiem (*Messe des morts*), cast in a gigantic mold, requiring a chorus of several hundred voices, a Gargantuan orchestra, and four small brass bands, was introduced at the Church of the Invalides on December 5, 1837, with very great success. The opera *Benvenuto Cellini*, however, was a complete failure. It opened at the Paris Opéra on September 10, 1838. The audience, shocked by some of Berlioz' innovations, created a disturbance at the première. After it had been given three more times, to an empty house, it disappeared from the repertory. It still is seldom performed, but an orchestral interlude entitled *Le Carnaval romain* (*Roman Carnival Overture*), one of Berlioz' finest orchestral works, has acquired a permanent place in symphonic literature.

While busily engaged in composition Berlioz held several posts. In 1835 he was appointed music critic of the *Journal des débats,* and in 1839 became assistant librarian at the Conservatory. These minor activities, and Paganini's generous gift in 1838, relieved Berlioz of his acute financial difficulties, freeing him for more ambitious creations. The most important of these endeavors was the monumental dramatic symphony for soloists, chorus and orchestra, *Roméo et Juliette,* introduced at the Paris Conservatory on November 24, 1839. It was received with highest praise. Wagner, still unknown as a revolutionary in music, was in the first-night audience; he confessed that the music took him "by storm and impetuously fanned my personal feeling for music and poetry."

In the Requiem and *Roméo et Juliette* Berlioz, revealed an artistic scope and depth that had not been apparent in his earlier compositions. Ernest Newman said, "Berlioz has now an eye for something more in life than his own unshorn locks and his sultry amours. He no longer thinks himself the center of the universe; he no longer believes in the Berliozcentric theory, and does not write with one eye on the mirror half of the time. In place of all this we have a Berlioz who has sunk his aggressive subjectivity and learned to regard life objectively. His spirit touched to finer issues, he sings, not Berlioz, but humanity as a whole. He is now what every great artist is instinctively—a philosopher as well as a singer; by the Requiem he earns his right to stand among the serious, brooding spirits of the earth. So again in the final scene of *Romeo and Juliet,* where he rises to loftier heights than he could ever have attained while in the throes of egoistic Romanticism."

In 1842 Berlioz made the first of several concert tours of Belgium and Germany. He conducted concerts of his works in Stuttgart, Hamburg, Berlin, and Darmstadt with great success. In Leipzig he established personal contact with Mendelssohn, in Dresden with Wagner (who conducted two fine Berlioz programs in that city), and in Berlin with Meyerbeer. Early in 1844 he returned to Paris between tours, led several performances, and published his monumental theoretical treatise, *Traité d'instrumentation.*

While traveling in Austria, Hungary, Bohemia, and Silesia between 1845 and 1846, Berlioz worked on his "dramatic legend," *La Damnation de Faust* (*The Damnation of Faust*). Goethe's *Faust* had fascinated him since 1827, when a French translation had appeared in Paris. "I could not put it down. I read it constantly, at my meals, in the theater, in the street, everywhere." By the autumn of 1828 he had actually set eight scenes from *Faust* to music. "Some of the ideas were good," he later wrote, "but I knew also how hopelessly immature and badly written they were." Seventeen years later Berlioz returned to the Faust theme, radically revising the excerpts he had written earlier, and adding a large amount of new material.

The première of this work, in oratorio form, took place at the Opéra-Comique on December 6, 1846. It was a dismal failure. On June 19, 1847 it was again performed as an oratorio, in Berlin, with much more gratifying results, and repeated performances increased its popularity. On May 18, 1893, the work was first performed as an opera in Monte Carlo. Since then it has frequently been presented at concerts and in the opera house; three of its orchestral excerpts, "Rakóczy March," "Dance of the Sylphs," and "Minuet of the Will-o-the-Wisps," have become staples in the symphonic repertory.

Berlioz' most important subsequent works include the *Te Deum*, completed in 1849; the oratorio *L'Enfance du Christ* (*The Childhood of Christ*), introduced in Paris on December 10, 1854; the comic opera *Béatrice et Bénédict*, based on Shakespeare's *Much Ado About Nothing*, first performed in Baden-Baden, Germany, on August 9, 1862; and a two-part opera based on Virgil's *Aeneid, Les Troyens* (*The Trojans*), completed in 1859 and introduced at the Théâtre Lyrique in Paris on November 4, 1863.

The death of his wife, Harriet, in 1854 left Berlioz free to marry Marie Recio. But his second marriage proved no happier than the first, and his domestic unhappiness was soon coupled with the bitter realization that his best work as a composer had ended. Suffering constantly from physical and nervous ailments, Berlioz kept himself in almost monastic seclusion in his Paris apartment, particularly after the death of his second wife in 1862. Perhaps in a pathetic effort to recapture his lost youth, he suddenly began to write passionate letters to a sixty-five-year-old woman, the mother of four grown children, whom he had loved in his youth and had not seen in half a century. Her justifiable bewilderment, followed by easily comprehensible indifference, served to intensify his nervous disorders. Berlioz mustered the energy and enthusiasm to conduct *The Damnation of Faust* and *Harold in Italy* in Vienna in 1866, with an extraordinary response from the audience (the critics were cool) and to lead another concert of his own works, in Cologne that year. But he was physically and spiritually exhausted. When in 1867 he heard the tragic news of his son's sudden death in Havana, of yellow fever, he lost the will to live and proceeded to destroy most of his letters, personal papers, criticisms and mementos. In a last, brief effort, however, he accepted an invitation to direct six concerts in St. Petersburg, where he scored a personal triumph.

In March 1868 Berlioz went to Nice, trying to recover his strength. There he was stricken by cerebral congestion. He recovered sufficiently to return to Paris, and died a year later, on March 8, 1869. Gounod and Ambroise Thomas were among his pallbearers. Berlioz was buried in the cemetery in Montmartre, to the accompaniment of his own music.

Romain Rolland has given the following description of Berlioz' appearance and personality: "He was really very fair and had blue eyes, and Joseph d'Ortigue tells us they were deep-set and piercing, though sometimes clouded by melancholy and langor. He had a broad forehead, furrowed with wrinkles by the time he was thirty, and a thick mane of hair, or, as E. Legouvé puts it, 'a large umbrella of hair, projecting like a movable awning over the beak of a bird of prey.' His mouth was well cut, with lips compressed and puckered at the corners in a severe fold, and his chin was prominent. He had a deep voice, but his speech was halting, and often tremulous with emotion; he would speak passionately of what interested him, and at times be effusive in manner, but more often he was ungracious and reserved. He was of medium height, rather thin and angular in figure, and when seated seemed much taller than he really was. He was very restless, and inherited from his native land, Dauphiné, the mountaineer's passion for walking and climbing, and love of a vagabond life, which remained with him nearly to his death. He had an iron constitution, but he wrecked it by privation and excess, by his walks in the rain and by sleeping out of doors in all weather, even when snow was on the ground."

In his hypersensitivity, sentimentality, and excessive outpouring of emotion Berlioz was a true Romantic. "When I hear certain pieces of music," he wrote in his autobiography, "my vital forces at first seem doubled. I feel a delicious pleasure, in which reason has no part. The emotion increasing in proportion to the energy or the grandeur of the ideas of the composer, soon produces a strange agitation in the circulation of the blood; tears, which generally indicate the end of the paroxysm, often indicate only a progressive state of it, leading to something still more intense. In this case, I have a spasmodic contraction of the muscles, a trembling in all my limbs, a complete torpor of the feet and the hands, a partial paralysis of the nerves of sight and heart; I no longer see, I scarcely hear."

Berlioz was one of music's most daring innovators. According to Daniel Gregory Mason, "He helped to break down the bonds of a narrow conservatism which was in danger of confining all music to the forms of the symphony and the sonata, and to the type of expression perfected by the classicists. By his daring imagination he abashed pedantry and opened up vistas of new possibilities." He was a pioneer in the use of the leading motive, or *Leitmotiv*, which in the *Symphonie fantastiv* he identified as *idée fixe*. He was many years ahead of his time in programmatic writing and a forerunner in composition of the tone poem. He was a virtuoso in using unusual and unorthodox rhythms, a genius in the science of orchestration.

"He possessed," said W. H. Hadow, "in a high degree every quality which successful scoring implies, a complete knowledge of the strength and weakness of each instrument, great skill in treatment and combination, ready invention, and boundless audacity. Further, he displays in this department of his art that sense of economy and reticence which has been noticed as absent elsewhere. He can be light-handed as Mozart (witness the *Invitation to the Dance*, the opening of the 'Rakóczy March,' and the first number of the *Tempest* fantasy), and yet when the moment comes to be vigorous and impressive there is no one more strong to wield the thunderbolt or direct the whirlwind. Even the crude violence of his 'Brigands' Orgy' or his 'Witches' Sabbath' becomes almost humanized when we observe the marvelous, matchless skill with which its horrors are presented."

Thus in his music, as in his personality, Berlioz was a child of Romanticism. He was one of the first composers to carry to music the Romantic's passion for literary subjects and fantasy, for grandiose statement by mammoth orchestral forces within large and flexible structures. He was above all a musical poet and dramatist of extraordinary invention, power, and passion.

PRINCIPAL WORKS

Choral Music—Requiem (Messe des morts); Roméo et Juliette, symphony for chorus, soloists and orchestra; Symphonie funèbre et triomphale; La Damnation de Faust; Te Deum; L'Enfance du Christ.

Operas—Benvenuto Cellini; Les Troyens; Béatrice et Bénédict.

Orchestral Music—Waverley Overture; Les Francs-juges; Symphonie fantastique; Le Roi Lear; Rob Roy; Nuits d'été, for voice and orchestra; Rêverie et caprice, for violin and orchestra; La Captive, for voice and orchestra; Le Carnaval romain; Harold en Italie; Le Corsaire.

Vocal Music—Irlande (Irish songs); numerous songs for voice and piano including Les Champs, Je Crois en vous, Le Main, La Mort d'Ophélie, and Zaïde.

ABOUT

Barraud, H., Berlioz; Barzun, J., Berlioz and the Romantic Movement; Boschot, A., La Crépuscule d'un romantique; Elliott, J. H., Berlioz; Newman, E., Musical Studies; Newman, E. (editor), Memoirs of Hector Berlioz; Pourtalès, G. de, Berlioz et l'Europe romantique; Tiersot, J. (editor), Les Années romantiques; Correspondance de Hector Berlioz; Turner, W. J., Berlioz: The Man and His Work; Wotton, T. S., Hector Berlioz.

Georges Bizet *1838-1875*

ALEXANDRE CÉSAR LÉOPOLD GEORGES BIZET was born in Paris on October 25, 1838. His father was a voice instructor and composer, his mother an excellent pianist. Having revealed exceptional musical talent as a child, Georges was enrolled in the Paris Conservatory at the age of nine. He remained at the school for over a decade, winning many awards as a pupil of Marmontel, Benoist, Halévy, and Gounod.

At the age of seventeen, while still a student at the Conservatory, Bizet composed his remarkable Symphony in C within several weeks. This now familiar work was never performed during Bizet's lifetime. It had lain forgotten in the Conservatory library for almost a century when it was discovered in 1935. The world première, which took place on February 26, 1935, in Basel, Switzerland, with Felix Weingartner conducting, proved an exciting and eventful musical experience. The symphony's fresh and spontaneous lyricism, its ingratiating charm, made it a welcome addition to the symphonic repertory. But it is an extraordinary work for other reasons. In style, structure and material it bears a striking resemblance to Schubert's symphonies. Yet Schubert's symphonies were unknown, both to the world at large and to the young Conservatory student, when Bizet composed this work. In addition, the exotic main theme of

Bizet: bē-zā′

the second movement anticipated by many years the trend toward an Oriental melodic line that was apparent in many later French composers. In the twentieth century this little symphony has been the inspiration for two ballets: *Le Palais de cristal,* produced by the Paris Opéra Ballet in 1947, and *Symphony,* a production of the Ballet Society of New York in 1948.

Two important developments in Bizet's life took place in 1857. First, he shared first prize with Lecocq in a competition for a one-act comic opera setting of *Le Docteur Miracle;* his opera was introduced at the Bouffes-Parisiens on April 9, 1857. Then he won the Prix de Rome with the cantata *Clovis et Clotilde,* performed in Paris in October 1857. Bizet spent three happy years in Rome. Though his health was poor, he enjoyed the country, the people, and the music. During his stay in Italy he completed a Te Deum; a descriptive symphony, with chorus, entitled *Vasco da Gama;* and *Don Procopio,* an *opera buffa.*

Bizet's first major work to receive an important performance was the opera *Les Pêcheurs de perles (The Pearl Fishers),* produced at the Théâtre Lyrique in Paris on September 30, 1863. Though not an important work or a consistently gifted one, this opera demonstrated Bizet's natural bent for Oriental melodic and harmonic coloring. "The Oriental coloring so vividly imparted to the music constitutes an undeniable charm," says Arthur Hervey. "The languidly enervating melodies, full of luscious sweetness, are redolent of Eastern climes. The score is imbued with poetical sentiment, . . . a strong dramatic temperament." Nadir's romantic first-act air, "Je crois entendre encore," is a favorite of tenors and is often given at concerts.

Les Pêcheurs was not successful. Neither were *La Jolie Fille de Perth* and *Djamileh* —the former given at the Théâtre Lyrique on December 26, 1867, the latter at the Opéra-Comique on May 22, 1872.

On June 3, 1869, Bizet married Geneviève Halévy, daughter of his teacher at the Conservatory. Their only child, Jacques, who was to become a successful writer, was born in 1872. For a while Bizet knew the humble existence of the struggling, unrecognized composer. To support himself and his wife, he was reduced to orchestrating dance music, arranging orchestral scores for piano, com-

GEORGES BIZET

piling anthologies of popular melodies, teaching music. In 1872 he wrote the incidental music for Daudet's play *L'Arlésienne.* His score attracted little attention when the play was produced on October 1, 1872. But on November 10 a suite which the composer derived from the score was received with unqualified enthusiasm at a Pasdeloup concert in Paris. The suite has become one of Bizet's most popular orchestral compositions. A second, less popular, suite from this incidental music was arranged after Bizet's death by his friend Ernest Guiraud.

In June 1872 Bizet wrote to a friend: "I am asked to write three acts for the Opéra-Comique. Meilhac and Halévy will do the piece. It will be bright, but of a brightness that allows style." Thus did Bizet first announce that he had begun what was destined to become his masterwork—the opera *Carmen,* based on Prosper Mérimée's famous story. On March 3, 1875, less than three years later, *Carmen* was staged at the Opéra-Comique.

There was a good deal in this new opera to upset conventional opera-goers: the vivid characterization of Carmen; some of the less proper episodes; the sight of a heroine smoking on the stage. Others objected that Bizet's score was too Wagnerian in its orchestral coloring and its use of leitmotivs. A few (largely of Spanish origin) insisted that Bizet's attempt to write Spanish music was synthetic at best, and complained that the melody of the famous "Habanera" had been lifted from Sebastian Yradier.

Despite these objections *Carmen* was not a failure, by any means, though many of the composer's early biographers concluded otherwise. It was received most enthusiastically by a good segment of the public and by some leading Parisian critics. "Monsieur Bizet," wrote Ernest Reyer in the *Journal des débats,* "is a past master in orchestration, and no one knows better the secret of fine harmony and suitable scoring." *Le Courrier de Paris* reported: "The work is one of those which redounds to the credit of a musician." Vincent d'Indy did not hesitate to proclaim it a masterwork. Excellent box-office receipts enabled the opera to run for a respectable thirty-seven performances, despite the fact that the work had been introduced late in the season. *Carmen* returned to the Opéra-Comique repertory the following season. The publisher Choudens paid Bizet twenty-five thousand francs for the publication rights and the French government conferred on him the rank of Chevalier of the Legion of Honor.

Though *Carmen* was successful upon its first introduction, its reputation abroad was not established until after Bizet's death. In 1878 it was heard in Marseilles, Lyons, Bordeaux, St. Petersburg, Naples, Florence, Ghent, Hanover, Mayence and New York (the American première took place at New York's Academy of Music on October 23). A revival at the Opéra-Comique in Paris in 1883 was a sensation. Nietzsche, who heard the opera some twenty times, called it one of the crowning works of the entire operatic repertory. Tchaikovsky prophesied that by 1890 it would become the most popular opera in the world.

Few today would deny that *Carmen* is one of the supreme achievements of the French lyric theater, one of the most popular operas ever written. "*Carmen,*" said D. C. Parker, "is unique in two senses. It is unique in the realm of opera; there is no work quite like it. It is unique also in that it stands head and shoulders above anything else Bizet had produced. . . . I place *Carmen* high by reason of the quality of its inspiration, the attraction of its themes, the handling of its ideas, and the musicianship displayed throughout."

"Several things strike us throughout," wrote Herbert F. Peyser. "Bizet's virtually Mozartean gift of characterization, the faultless balance he maintains between voice and orchestra, the transparence, the sensitiveness and the color of instrumentation, the tingling rhythm, the ceaseless diversity of expression ranging from the sentimental, the blithe, mercurial, and humorous to the sensual, the vulgarly swaggering, the starkly shattering and tragic. The score is a microcosm of all this and more."

Since Bizet died suddenly only three months after the première of *Carmen,* a rumor circulated, and was long believed, that he had died of a broken heart because of the opera's "failure." History is much less dramatic: *Carmen* had been no failure as has already been pointed out, and Bizet did not die of a "broken heart." He had long been suffering from throat cancer, and soon after the première of *Carmen,* he went for a rest to Bougival, outside Paris. On two occasions he spoke of a sense of suffocation. He died on the midnight of June 3, 1875, of a heart attack. The funeral services took place at the Trinité Church in Paris, and he was buried in Père Lachaise.

Physically, Bizet's most remarkable feature was "a head of light curly hair," according to Martin Cooper. "He was slight and energetic, but never very strong. A picture of him by a fellow artist at the Villa Medici shows him with myopic but vivacious eyes, a good oval-shaped face, and a rather small, pursed mouth. Later in life he grew a thick beard, and bad eyesight forced him to wear spectacles."

He was a simple and straightforward man, said Frederick Niecks. "You could not meet a stauncher friend or a more honest enemy. Naturally and fundamentally gay and good-natured, he was easily roused. But along with these traits there seems to have been also, at least early in life, some phlegm and a good deal of love of ease about him. In short, his was a good-natured and hot-tempered character."

In one of his letters Bizet disclosed that Mozart and Rossini were to him "the two greatest musicians." To a student seeking advice about composition he said: "Think of Mozart and study him unceasingly. Provide yourself with *Don Giovanni, Figaro, The Magic Flute,* and *Così fan tutte.* Look at Weber, too."

Bizet's philosophy of life is hinted at in another letter. "A perfect society means no more injustice and therefore no more attacks on social contract, no more priests, no more policemen, no more crimes, no more adulteries, no more prostitution, no more feelings, no more passions. One moment— no more music, no more poetry, no more Legion of Honor, no press (that's a good thing), no theater at all, no error and so—no art! . . . As a musician I declare that if you suppress adultery, fanaticism, crime, error, the supernatural, it is impossible to write a single note more. . . . The imagination lives on chimeras and visions. Suppress the chimera and goodbye to the imagination. No more art, science everywhere. If you say 'what is the harm to that?' I give up and argue no more, because *you are right*."

JOHN BLOW

PRINCIPAL WORKS

Operas—Ivan le Terrible; Les Pêcheurs de perles; La Jolie Fille de Perth; Djamileh; Carmen.

Orchestral Music—Symphony in C; Roma; L'Arlésienne, 2 suites (the second arranged by Ernest Guiraud); La Patrie; Petite suite.

Piano Music—Chants du Rhin (also for orchestra); Trois esquisses musicales; Jeux d'enfants, for piano duet (also for orchestra); nocturnes, waltzes.

Vocal Music—Feuilles d'album; Chantes des Pyrénées; individual songs for voice and piano including Adieux de l'hôtesse arabe, Agnus Dei, and Chanson d'avril; vocal duets, vocalises.

ABOUT

Bellaigue, C., Georges Bizet: Sa vie et son œuvre; Cooper, M., Georges Bizet; Curtiss, M., Bizet and His World; Dean, W., Bizet; Landormy, P., Bizet; Parker, D. C., Georges Bizet: His Life and Works; Stefan, P., Georges Bizet.

John Blow *1649-1708*

JOHN BLOW, outstanding seventeenth-century composer of English church music, was born in Newark-on-Trent, Nottingham, in February 1649. He was only six when his father died. His mother, recognizing the child's musical talent, directed him to the study of music. It is believed that Blow took his first music lessons at the Magnus Song School in Newark. When he was about eleven he became a chorister of the Chapel Royal, the first royal chapel choir to be organized. As a chorister Blow wrote three anthems; the texts were reproduced in Clifford's *Divine Services and An-*thems. He wrote a fourth anthem in collaboration with Pelham Humfrey and William Turner.

Blow's career as a chorister ended in 1664, when his voice broke. An amusing entry in Samuel Pepys' diary, dated August 21, 1667, is believed to refer to Blow. It reads: "This morning came two of Capt. Cooke's boys, whose voices are broke, and are gone from the chapel but have extraordinary skill; and they and my boy, with broken voice, did sing three parts; their names ware Blaew [sic] and Loggins; but notwithstanding their skill, yet to hear them sing with their broken voices, which they could not command to keep in tune, would make a man mad—so bad it was."

On December 3, 1668, Blow was appointed organist of Westminster Abbey at a salary of ten pounds a year. A month later he entered the King's service as a "musician for the virginals"; in 1674 he became Gentleman and Master of the Children of the Chapel Royal. With this appointment his reputation as an organist and church composer grew rapidly. In 1677 a degree of doctor of music was conferred on him by the Dean and Chapter of Canterbury, and as a mark of royal favor he was granted valuable leases on several properties. One of these was in the Great Sanctuary at Westminster Abbey, where he lived from 1678 until the end of his life. In 1674 he married Elizabeth Braddock, daughter of a Gentleman of the Chapel Royal. She died ten years later, having borne him five children; three daughters survived.

In 1679 Blow resigned as organist at Westminster Abbey. He was succeeded by his pupil, Henry Purcell. (When Purcell died in 1695, Blow returned to the Abbey.) On September 19, 1687, Blow was appointed Master of the Children of St. Paul's Cathedral, a position he held until the end of his life. His last post was that of Composer for the Chapel Royal, a newly created post which drew a yearly salary of forty pounds.

Blow published his most important ode, the ode for St. Cecilia's Day entitled "Begin the Song," in 1684. A year later he wrote his only stage work, *Venus and Adonis* (described as a "masque for the entertainment of the King"), which Harold Watkins Shaw regards as "an important precursor of Purcell's *Dido and Aeneas.*" Mr. Shaw adds: "It not only constitutes the earliest extant example of genuine opera in English, but also evinces a certain directness of utterance, emotional quality, and power of characterization which still hold attention today." Blow also wrote three anthems for the coronation of James II: "God Spake Sometime in Visions," "Let Thy Hand Be Strengthened," and "Behold O God Our Defender." A fourth, "The Lord God Is a Sun and Shield" was composed in 1689 for the coronation of William and Mary.

In 1700 Blow published *Amphion Anglicus,* a volume of songs and vocal chamber music, together with a collection of "ayres" for harpsichord or spinet. A set of instrumental suites was issued in or about 1704, and a volume of psalms for organ and harpsichord some time after that.

John Blow died in London on October 1, 1708. He was buried in the north aisle of Westminster Abbey, near Purcell's grave. The inscription on Blow's monument reads in part: "His own musical compositions, especially his church music, are a far nobler monument to his memory than any other that can be raised for him."

Sir John Hawkins, the eminent eighteenth-century music historian, described Blow as "a very handsome man . . . remarkable for a gravity and decency in his deportment. He was a man of blameless morals and of a benevolent temper, but . . . not . . . totally free from the imputation of pride."

Jeffrey Pulver has called John Blow "certainly the most considerable musician of the period"— excepting, of course, Henry Purcell. "He has left a large quantity of music marked by a fresh nobility, depth of feeling and sincerity."

Heathcote D. Statham commented: "There is breadth, dignity, and sincerity about the best of his church music which will ensure its being sung as long as church music is sung at all. And it is beautifully singable; in the flowing grace of his interweaving melodies, he can meet and sometimes beat the Elizabethans on their own ground. Above all he was an experimenter. . . . He combines the characteristics of a church musician . . . with a gay bravado, which compels him to 'throw his notes about' at random."

Henry Purcell said of his teacher: "Blow is one of the greatest masters in the world."

PRINCIPAL WORKS

Chamber Music—Sonata, for two violins and accompaniment.

Choral Music—English and Latin services, anthems, hymns, odes.

Opera—Venus and Adonis.

Organ Music—Toccata in D minor.

Harpsichord Music—Suites, various pieces.

Vocal Music—Songs for voice and accompaniment including A Love Song and The Self Banished.

ABOUT

Barrett, W. A., English Church Composers; Bridge, F., Twelve Good Musicians; Fellowes, E. H., English Cathedral Music; Fuller-Maitland, J. A., The Contemporaries of Purcell, Vol. I; Shaw, H. W., John Blow, Doctor of Music.

Musical Quarterly, July 1949; Musical Times, February 1902, November 1926.

Luigi Boccherini *1743-1805*

L UIGI BOCCHERINI was born in Lucca, Italy, on February 19, 1743. His father, a professional double-bass player, gave him his first music instruction. Luigi then became a pupil of Abbate Vannucci, *maestro di cappella* to the Archbishop. In 1757 he went to Rome to continue his study of music; there he began to attract attention as a composer and cellist.

Returning to his native city in 1760, Boccherini played cello for several years in theater orchestras. During this period he completed several ambitious works, including two oratorios and an opera which were performed. He also gave a sonata recital with Filippo Manfredi, a violinist, in a program made up entirely of his own compositions. So successful was this concert that the two artists decided to go on tour. They performed in many cities in north Italy and southern France, arriving in Paris in 1768. There they met with great popular acclaim. It was at this time that Boccherini's first published works, a set of six string quartets and two sets of string trios, were issued in Paris.

The Spanish ambassador to France, entranced with the success of these two young men, urged Boccherini and Manfredi to visit Spain. He promised them a warm welcome and the generous patronage of the Prince of Asturias (later Charles IV). Early in 1769 Boccherini left for Spain with a new set of trios dedicated to the Prince. The reception of the royal house hardly met his expectations. The expected patronage was not forthcoming, nor was the appointment at court he had hoped for. In fact, the young man was treated almost with disdain. Fortunately, he gained the interest and support of the King's brother, the Infante Don Luis, who engaged him as chamber musician and virtuoso.

When Don Luis died in 1785, Boccherini found a new patron in Frederick William II of Prussia, who had been impressed by one of the works Boccherini had dedicated to him. Until Frederick's death in 1797 Boccherini served as his chamber composer in Berlin. During these years, Boccherini's affluence and good health made it possible for him to produce an extraordinary amount of music; but his fortunes eventually took a sharp reversal. First, his health suffered a severe decline, forcing him to give up playing cello. With Frederick's death he lost his lucrative post. Last, he was overwhelmed by the death of his second wife and two daughters.

Unable to find a post in Berlin, Boccherini returned to Madrid. He suffered appalling poverty. Although his situation improved temporarily in 1800, when Lucien Buonaparte, the French Ambassador to Spain, commissioned him to write some chamber music, this favorable state of affairs did not last long. Boccherini tried desperately to earn enough, through hack work, to support himself and his family in their single room,

LUIGI BOCCHERINI

but he could do little to ease their hunger and poverty. His death in Madrid, on May 28, 1805, seemed a release from privation. In 1927, more than a century after his death, his remains were transferred to Lucca.

Boccherini was an extraordinarily prolific composer. His works include twenty symphonies and over three hundred works of chamber music. Little of this corpus, however, is now heard, except for his excellent Cello Concerto in B-flat major, op. 34, and a popular little minuet which comes from his E major String Quintet, op. 13, no. 5. Still, every revival of a symphony, string quartet, or string quintet by Boccherini pleases immensely with its delightful lyricism and sound classical style. "So long as men take delight in pure melody," said W. H. Hadow, "in transparent style, and in a fancy alert, sensitive and sincere, so long is his place in the history of music assured."

A contemporary of Haydn and Mozart, Boccherini most certainly did not share their artistic stature. But his place in music history is important because, together with these masters, he helped establish the style and structure of the classic string quartet and concerto. Boccherini was also the first composer to write music for string quintets and sextets.

"Everything for which his predecessors worked," wrote Robert Sodenheimer, "singly and laboriously, was garnered and absorbed by him. Sammartini's beginning, Stamitz's radicalism, Pugnani's tentative efforts . . . all these had their experimental value for Boccherini, and the achievements of all these hot bloods of the new art are at last justified and brought to fulfillment. In his hands, the new style yields up its most secret properties and possibilities. . . . In Boccherini . . . a sensitive and exuberant spirit is seen inhabiting, as it were, a tropical world. Of this spirit, subtle melodies are first conceived. Boccherini then concentrates on the independent leading of the parts (based on a plurality of motifs) achieving at times truly plastic effects, which belong rather to the romantic epoch than to the severe linear art of the classics. . . . What constitutes an epoch-making characteristic of Boccherini's work is the skillful manner in which he continues to vary his forms of expression within the smallest framework. . . . In this respect none of Boccherini's contemporaries can compare with him."

The twentieth century French composer Jean Françaix adapted some of Boccherini's little-known melodies, from a Sinfonia and various quintets, for a successful ballet, *Scuola di ballo.* This work was introduced in Monte Carlo in 1933.

PRINCIPAL WORKS

Chamber Music—125 string quartets; 102 string quintets; 60 string trios; 27 violin sonatas; 16 sextets; 6 cello sonatas; 6 duets for two violins; 2 octets.

Choral Music—Stabat Mater; Christmas Cantata; Mass, motets.

Operas—La Confederazione; La Clementina.

Orchestral Music—20 symphonies; 4 cello concertos.

Vocal Music—14 concert arias and duets with orchestra.

ABOUT

Bacharach, A. L. (editor), The Music Masters, vol. 1; Bonaventura, A., Boccherini; Parodi, L., Boccherini.

La Revue de musicologie, November 1929, February 1930.

François Boieldieu *1775-1834*

FRANÇOIS-ADRIEN BOIELDIEU, who with Adam and Auber helped to establish the *opéra-comique,* was born in Rouen, France, on December 16, 1775. Since his father was secretary to an archbishop and his mother the owner of a prosperous millinery establishment, the Boieldieu family

Boieldieu: bô-ĕl-dyû'

was in comfortable financial circumstances. The French Revolution, however, stripped it of its possessions; and in 1794 the divorce of François's parents broke up the family.

A musical child, François became a member of the choir school of the Rouen Cathedral. He was still in his early boyhood when a performance of Grétry's comic opera, *Raoul Barbe-bleue,* determined his career. The boy decided then that he wanted to be a composer of comic opera.

In 1793 Boieldieu wrote several songs which met with such popular favor that he was commissioned to write a special hymn honoring the revolutionary fêtes in Paris. This work for chorus and orchestra, *Chant populaire pour la fête de la Raison,* was performed in the Rouen Cathedral on November 30, 1793. His first opera, *La Fille coupable,* had already been presented in Rouen on November 2 that year, and a second opera, *Rosalie et Myrza,* was performed in 1795.

After his parents' divorce in 1794, Boieldieu went to live with Charles Broche, organist of the Rouen Cathedral, who gave him a systematic musical education. In 1796 Boieldieu went to Paris. Through the influence of such powerful musicians as Grétry, Méhul, and Cherubini, he gained access to several important salons and arranged to have several of his works published, including several piano sonatas and songs. Within the next year and a half three of Boieldieu's operas were produced. He also embarked on a highly successful concert tour with the singer Garat. By 1798 Boieldieu was a musician with a fully established reputation in Paris. That year he was appointed professor of piano at the Conservatory.

Boieldieu's first triumph as a composer of *opéra-comique* was the one-act opera *Le Calife de Bagdad (The Caliph of Bagdad),* produced at the Théâtre Favart on September 16, 1801. The first-night audience gave the new work a rousing ovation unwarranted, in the opinion of the renowned Cherubini, by a work of such slight character. "Aren't you ashamed of such undeserved success?" Cherubini asked Boieldieu after the première. Modestly, Boieldieu conceded that the triumph was greater than the opera deserved and then humbly asked Cherubini to teach him counterpoint. The master consented. Despite Cherubini's unfavorable opinion of the opera, it has remained one of its composer's enduring successes. Its première in the United States took place at the Park Theater in New York on August 27, 1827. At that time it was given in the French language; a few years later it was presented in English in New York. The overture is a perennial favorite with salon and café house orchestras.

On March 19, 1802, Boieldieu married Clotilde Mafleuray, a woman with a questionable background and an even more dubious reputation. Their union was not a success, and the couple soon separated. In 1803 Boieldieu was invited to Russia by the Czar to become director of court music and to write operas for the imperial theater; for these duties he received a munificent salary of four thousand rubles a year. During the next eight years Boieldieu wrote half a dozen operas and the incidental music to several plays, but none of these works had particular merit.

Boieldieu returned to Paris in 1811. He tried now to obtain a divorce from his estranged wife, but was prevented by the French authorities; their marriage lasted until his wife died, late in 1826. On January 22, 1827, Boieldieu married the singer Jenny Philis-Berton, whom he had met in Russia.

The first successful opera Boieldieu wrote after returning from Russia was *Jean de Paris,* performed at the Opéra-Comique on April 4, 1812. For Schumann this was "one of the first three *opéra-comiques* of the world, placed together with Mozart's *Figaro* and Rossini's *Barber.*" With his succeeding operatic works, Boieldieu attained a prominent position among French composers. In 1817 he succeeded Méhul as a member of the Institut and was appointed professor of composition at the Conservatory. In 1821 he was made Chevalier of the Legion of Honor.

Boieldieu's greatest operatic success was *La Dame blanche;* the libretto, by Eugène Scribe, was based on two romances by Sir Walter Scott. When it was introduced at the Opéra-Comique in Paris on December 10, 1825, it was immediately acclaimed as a masterwork. So popular was this work that in 1826 and 1827 several amusing parodies on it were produced in Parisian theaters —while *La Dame blanche* itself continued to fill the Opéra-Comique at each per-

FRANÇOIS BOIELDIEU

formance. The opera also scored major successes outside Paris; the highly acclaimed American première took place in New York on August 24, 1827. When, in 1832, the opera was given in New York in English the translation was made by John Howard Payne, author of "Home Sweet Home."

Much of the score of *La Dame blanche* was reminiscent of Scottish folk tunes and old French *chansons,* but what stood out in bold relief was Boieldieu's own brand of lyricism. "Peculiar to Boieldieu," said Francis Hueffer, "is a certain homely sweetness of melody which proves its kinship to that source of all truly national music, the popular song. *La Dame blanche* might indeed be considered as the artistic continuation of the *chanson* in the same sense that Weber's *Der Freischütz* has been called a dramatized *Volkslied.*"

La Dame blanche marked the apex of Boieldieu's career. A rapid decline in his creative powers and personal fortunes soon followed. Boieldieu had for many years been the victim of a lung disease; now his health began to deteriorate so sharply that in 1826 he was forced to resign his professional post at the Conservatory. When the French monarchy fell in 1830 he lost his pension and was reduced to extreme penury. In 1833, however, a grant of six thousand francs, presented to him by Louis Philippe in the name of the French government, provided him a modest income for the rest of his life.

Deprived of speech by his illness, Boieldieu went into complete seclusion in a small country house in Jarcy, devoting himself to gardening and landscape painting. He died there on October 8, 1834. At his funeral services in Paris Cherubini's Requiem was performed. Boieldieu was buried in the Père Lachaise cemetery.

Of the forty operas Boieldieu wrote, only a scattered few have survived, but these are outstanding works. "His speech," wrote Arthur Pougin, "is supple, elegant, well-ordered; and the grace of his language, its clarity, and the amiable spirit with which it is endowed are constantly of a nature to satisfy the listener and to procure for him delicate and ever renewed pleasure. No great force, no audacious strains, . . . no sublime flashes of light arouse our enthusiasm; but an abundant and varied inspiration, an imagination that is always fertile, a truly poetic sentiment, a unity and perfection of style. . . . The qualities of Boieldieu were . . . melodic richness, the excellence and solidity of his plan, a warm instrumentation that was brilliant and colorful, possessing charm and taste and distinction. . . . From the dramatic point of view, we have tenderness and grace, on the one hand, and, on the other, a rare comic sentiment and profound intelligence of the resources and needs of the theater."

PRINCIPAL WORKS

Operas—40 operas and opéra-comiques including: La Fille coupable; Zoraïme et Zulnar; Le Calife de Bagdad; Ma Tante Aurore; Télémaque; Les Voitures versées; Jean de Paris; La Fête du village voisin; Le Petit Chaperon rouge; La Dame blanche; Les Deux nuits.

ABOUT

Fauré, G., Boieldieu; Sa vie, son œuvre; Hargreave, M., Earlier French Composers; Augé de Lassus, L., Boieldieu; Pougin, A., Boieldieu, Sa vie et son œuvre.

La Revue musicale, February 1926, January 1940.

Arrigo Boito *1842-1918*

A RRIGO BOITO, equally distinguished as an opera librettist and composer, was born in Padua, Italy, on February 24, 1842. His father, a gifted artist, was an irresponsible bohemian who abandoned his family when Arrigo was still a child, leaving to his wife the burden of supporting two sons and raising them as musicians. Since Arrigo quickly showed his superior talent, his mother soon centered on him her zeal and her ambitions. Arrigo was always composing, and his teacher, Giovanni Buzzolla, assured Boito's mother that the boy had the "making of a capital composer."

When Arrigo was fourteen his mother took her family to Milan to enroll the boy in the Conservatory. At first Boito was so shiftless and lackadaisical that he was threatened with expulsion. The directors held him on probation only because they knew the immense personal sacrifice his mother had made to keep him at the Conservatory. Placed under the careful guidance of such teachers as Alberto Mazzucato and Ronchetti-Monteviti, Boito suddenly flourished. By the time he graduated he had become one of the school's most brilliant pupils.

Between 1860 and 1862 Boito collaborated with Franco Faccio in writing *Il Quattro giugno* and *Le Sorelle d'Italia*, two cantatas that were performed and well received at the Conservatory. On the strength of the latter work, the Italian government endowed each composer with a gold medal and a traveling fellowship. Boito spent two years touring France, Poland, Germany, Belgium, and England. Profoundly influenced by the French Romantic movement in literature and music, and German Romantic music, Boito upon returning to Italy engaged in a passionate struggle to reform Italian music. Awakening the long dormant interest of his compatriots in symphonic music, he urged them to abandon the clichés and formulas of Italian opera for some of the new ideas and approaches that were prevalent in Germany. For several years he wrote pamphlets and contributed many articles to *Figaro* and the *Giornale della Società del Quartetto,* savagely attacking the status quo, expounding his ideas with a frankness that made him many enemies. On one occasion he was challenged to a duel by an outraged musician and was severely wounded in the right arm.

In 1862 Boito provided Verdi with the text for the cantata *Hymn of Nations*. Thus began a long friendship and artistic association climaxed by Verdi's last towering masterpieces, the Shakespearean operas *Otello* (in 1886) and *Falstaff* (in 1893), for both of which Boito wrote the librettos. Of the

Boito: bô′ē-tō

Verdi-Boito collaboration H. C. Colles said: "Theirs was a union of brain and creative impulses, intellect and genius."

Meanwhile Boito had written the text and music of his first opera, *Ero e Leandro*, but he later destroyed this work. He also created the text for Faccio's opera *Amleto* and, in 1876, for Ponchielli's masterpiece, *La Gioconda*.

Boito's achievements as a composer were hardly less impressive. In 1866 he started work on the opera *Mefistofele*, written to his own libretto. He interrupted this endeavor to become a Garibaldi volunteer in the war between Austria and Italy, but completed the opera soon after the war, in 1868. The world première at La Scala, on March 5, 1868, drew considerable attention throughout Italy. Boito himself conducted, and the house was filled with his many admirers— as well as his equally numerous enemies, who interrupted the performance with hisses, shouts, catcalls, and even fist fights. After the final curtain, the riot continued in the piazza outside. Similar demonstrations erupted at the next two performances, forcing the chief of police to demand immediate deletion of the opera from the repertory.

After *Mefistofele* was withdrawn Boito subjected it to drastic revision. He cut down its excessive length, edited the orchestration, introduced new vocal material to enhance its popular appeal. Revived in Bologna seven years after its première, *Mefistofele* became a major success; there were repeated ovations after the final curtain. *Mefistofele* became a staple of the Italian opera house, attaining such popularity that by the outbreak of World War II it had been performed over five thousand times in Italy. *Mefistofele* also entered the repertory of leading operatic theaters outside Italy. In 1880 it was acclaimed in London, and on November 24 that year had its American première at the New York Academy of Music. *Mefistofele* was also produced during the first season of the Metropolitan Opera Association, on December 5, 1883.

"Boito," wrote H. C. Colles of *Mefistofele*, "made a serious attempt to convey in his music something of the philosophy underlying the Faust drama of Goethe. He succeeded sufficiently, at any rate in his prologue, to be ranked with the German masters, Schumann, Wagner, and Liszt, who had essayed a similar task. As originally

ARRIGO BOITO

produced at La Scala in Milan, five acts followed the prologue, but Boito subsequently reduced them to four. It was a bewildering scheme of prodigious length, in which daring experiment and conventional operatic procedure jostled one another, and its immediate failure was inevitable, quite apart from the conflict of prejudice in which it was received by the audience. Boito lacked the first-rate creative musical power to enable him to weld together the divergent elements of music drama and to surmount all the difficulties which Wagner was presently to do in *Götterdämmerung*."

It would be a mistake, however, to undervalue *Mefistofele*, which for all its shortcomings remains a monumental achievement. As Arthur Elson pointed out: "Despite the composite style of Boito's music, there can be no doubt of its value to Italy. He was the pioneer in many things that were new and good, and not alone Verdi, but even Mascagni was forced to follow his lead in adopting the modern vein of polyphonic composition."

Boito wrote a second opera, *Nerone*, a task that consumed almost half his lifetime. He first outlined it in 1862, four years before he had started work on *Mefistofele*. Forty years later Boito was sufficiently pleased with its development to permit the announcement of its world première. But he suddenly changed his mind, maintaining that the opera still required too much work to permit early performance. Boito continued to work on

Nerone until 1916, when he managed to complete the fourth act. Even then the opera was not quite ready for production. Nor did Boito live to put the final touches on it. That task was assumed by Arturo Toscanini. At long last, on May 2, 1924, six years after Boito's death, *Nerone* was finally introduced at La Scala, with Toscanini conducting. The première attracted world interest. The grandeur of the text, the poetic and dramatic content of the score, made a deep impression. But there was general agreement that the new opera was no *Mefistofele. Nerone,* wrote F. Bonavia, "is the music of a poet rather than of a master musician. The lyrical impulse so evident in *Mefistofele* has been curbed, perhaps in obedience to a theory, until it has lost the power to carry the listener in its swing. The omission of the fifth act—which exists in text but not in the opera—is also regrettable, for it robs the action of its logical conclusion."

In 1892 Boito was appointed inspector general of all Italian conservatories, and two decades later he entered the political arena by becoming a senator. When World War I broke out, he paid a visit to the Italian front. The trip sapped his strength and energy. Soon after that, while attending religious services at Sant' Ambrogio, he caught a severe chill. Broken in health, he entered a nursing home in Milan, where he died on June 10, 1918. Just before his death a nurse heard him singing to himself; but when she entered his room he was no longer breathing.

In a vivid pen-portrait, Maryla Friedlander wrote of Boito: "His eyes had an expression which alternated between the wearily languid and the insinuatingly vivacious. His exquisite goodness of heart at times assumed the stamp of irony. In fact Boito shifted from skepticism and diffidence on the one hand to youthful outbursts of ardor on the other without the slightest effort. Endowed with the rare gift for winning affection, he was capable of inexplicable silence and sudden estrangements from his warmest friends. . . . Boito felt the need of complete solitude when at work. Only those who were very close to the artist had access to his austere study. He was rarely seen at plays and concerts. . . . In his studio in the Via Principe Amedeo, all Boito's chairs and tables were covered with books and papers. Large half-opened portfolios contained reproductions of masterpieces of the entire world. . . . Boito never discussed himself, his youth, or his work or successes; above all not a word as to suffering, although one sensed that he did suffer."

PRINCIPAL WORKS
Operas—Mefistofele; Nerone.

ABOUT
Ballo, F., Arrigo Boito; Hardi, P., Vita di Arrigo Boito; Rensis, R. de, (editor), Lettere; Rensis, R. de, Franco Faccio e Boito, Documento; Stanford, V., Studies and Memories; Vajro, M., Arrigo Boito; Walker, Frank, The Man Verdi.
Music and Letters, July 1926; Musical Quarterly, October 1920.

Giovanni Battista Bononcini
1670-1747

FOR ALMOST A CENTURY the family of Bononcini (sometimes spelled Buononcini) dominated Italian opera. Its most celebrated member was Giovanni Battista Bononcini, born in Modena, Italy, on July 18, 1670. Giovanni studied music first with his father, then with G. P. Colonna and Giorgio Buoni. He was only fifteen when his first publication, a string trio, appeared. In 1687 he became a cellist in the chapel of San Petronio in Bologna; later that year he assumed the office of *maestro di capella* at San Giovanni in Monte. During this period he published many compositions, including Masses, oratorios, *sinfonie,* and chamber concertos.

In 1691 Bononcini settled in Rome. There he wrote his first two operas, *Serse,* introduced on January 25, 1694, followed by *Tullo Ostilio,* which was performed the next month. In 1698 he moved to Vienna, where he stayed until 1711, holding the post of court composer from 1700 on. He took a leave of absence from 1702 to 1705, to serve at the court of Queen Sophie Charlotte in Berlin. From 1711 until 1720 he traveled a great deal, mainly in Italy. Sometime before 1719, Bononcini was married to Margherita Balletti.

During these years Bononcini's popularity as an opera composer was matched only by his output; over a dozen of his operas had proved major successes in Vienna, Berlin, and Rome. In 1720 he was invited to London to write operas for the Italian company directed by Handel. A bitter rivalry soon

Bononcini: bō-nôn-chē′nee

erupted between Handel and Bononcini—a feud encouraged and kept alive by Handel's numerous enemies, who hoped to destroy his career by supporting his increasingly popular competitor. It was in this spirited battle of operatic personalities that the now famous phrase "tweedledum and tweedledee" was coined. It appeared in the following verse:

Some say, compared to Bononcini,
That Mynheer Handel's but a ninny.
Others aver that he to Handel
Is scarcely fit to hold a candle.
Strange all this difference should be
'Twixt Tweedledum and Tweedledee.

Bononcini's first opera in England, *Astarto,* introduced on November 19, 1720, was so successful that it ran for thirty performances. It was followed by several other highly acclaimed operas, including *L'Odio e l'amore* in 1721, *Crispo* and *Griselda* in 1722, and *Farnace* in 1723. It seemed certain that the tide of public favor had turned toward Bononcini. But Handel's popularity soon returned, with the production of several highly successful operas, and Bononcini's reputation in England declined rapidly— though not because of Handel's new operatic successes. In 1731 the startling revelation was made that a popular madrigal credited to Bononcini had been stolen from Lotti. Why a composer so facile, prolific, and versatile should have found it necessary to plagiarize is a mystery defying explanation. Bononcini maintained a proud silence while the accusation was hurled at him, and by his silence incriminated himself. The composer later wasted his personal fortunes in a foolish scheme with an alchemist to produce gold from a philosopher's stone.

Having lost both fortune and reputation, Bononcini left England and resided for a while in Paris. He visited Lisbon in 1735. In 1737 he returned to Vienna, where he lived in extremely straitened circumstances until Maria Theresa, Empress of Austria, granted him a monthly stipend in 1742. Bononcini died in Vienna, on July 9, 1747.

The tragic decline of Bononcini's fame during the last years of his life and his subsequent neglect have obscured the fact that Bononcini was one of the foremost composers of Italian opera in his generation. Few were more highly regarded, few more frequently performed. But he was too subservient to the conventions of his time, and to the prevailing ritual of operatic writing.

GIOVANNI BATTISTA BONONCINI

In spite of a pronounced lyric gift and at times dramatic strength, Bononcini's operas soon went out of fashion.

Bononcini also composed a large number of church and instrumental works; in some of these he revealed genuine creative power.

PRINCIPAL WORKS
Chamber Music—12 sonatas for two violins and bass; chamber concertos, sinfonie.
Choral Music—7 oratorios; Te Deum; cantatas, Masses.
Harpsichord Music—Suites, divertimenti.
Operas—Almost 100 operas, serenatas and other dramatic works including: Serse; Tullo Ostilio; La Fede pubblica; Polifemo; Endimione; Mario fuggitivo; Erminia; Astarto; Muzio Scevola; Crispo; Griselda; Farnace; Calpurnia; Astianatte; Alessandro in Sidone.

ABOUT
Burney, C., A General History of Music.

Alexander Borodin *1833-1887*

A LEXANDER PORFIREVICH BORO- DIN, a member of the influential Russian nationalist school known as "The Five," was born in St. Petersburg on November 11, 1883. He was the illegitimate son of Prince Ghedeanov, descendant of a royal Georgian family. Since Russian law required that a prince's illegitimate child be registered as the son of one of his serfs, Alexander was given the name of Borodin.

Borodin: bô-rô-dēn'

ALEXANDER BORODIN

The child was raised by a doting and over-solicitous mother. Frail from birth, Borodin was not permitted to attend school and was educated at home by private tutors. He was extraordinarily gifted in many areas: he mastered several languages, including English, French, and German, at an early age; proved apt in the sciences; and wrote little dramatic pieces for a puppet theater which he built himself. His greatest talent, however, lay in music. Without formal instruction he learned to play the flute and cello, and acquired the rudiments of theory from textbooks. At ten he wrote his first piece of music, a piano polka, *Hélène*, inspired by and dedicated to his first love. His musical horizons soon expanded through his friendship with Michael Shtchiglev. Michael played four-hand arrangements of Haydn and Beethoven symphonies with the young Borodin, took him to concerts, and arranged chamber music recitals in which Borodin could participate.

Despite his passionate preoccupation with music, Borodin did not lose his fascination with science. He set up his own laboratory at home, where he spent tireless hours in experimentation. In 1850 he entered the Academy of Medicine in St. Petersburg to specialize in chemistry. After graduating with highest honors in 1856, he joined the Academy faculty as assistant professor. Two years later he received his doctorate in chemistry. He now began to write important studies for major Russian scientific journals. From 1859 to 1862 he went abroad on a scientific mission.

While in Heidelberg, Germany, Borodin met a remarkable young musician and pianist, Catherine Protopopova, perhaps the most important influence on his subsequent musical career. Catherine opened up for him the world of German Romantic music, persuaded him to travel to Mannheim to hear his first Wagner music dramas, and encouraged him to study music, especially composition, more systematically.

In 1863, after his return to Russia, Borodin married Catherine. While pursuing an active career as a scientist and a teacher of science, Borodin joined his wife in a variety of musical endeavors. He spent many of his free hours playing the piano and cello, or composing. "In winter," he explained at this time, "I can only compose when I am too unwell to give my lectures. So my friends, reversing the usual custom, never say to me 'I hope you are well,' but 'I hope you are ill.'" His colleague and former professor, the chemist Professor Zinin, regarded these activities with strong misgiving. "All roads are open to you," he told Borodin. "But you must spend less time writing songs. I count on you to succeed me, but you think of nothing but music. You make a mistake hunting two hares at once."

It was Mily Balakirev who, more than anyone else, finally gave meaning and direction to Borodin's creative efforts by urging him to join the nationalist school and compose truly Russian music, grounded in Russian folk songs and dances. For a while Borodin studied with Balakirev. Then he set to work on his most ambitious effort, his First Symphony. It was also his first composition with a pronounced national character, and his first work to be performed in public. The première took place at a concert of the Russian Musical Society on January 16, 1869, with Balakirev conducting. The work was well received.

Borodin now became an active and highly productive member of "The Russian Five," the school with which Russian nationalistic music came to full flower (see sketch on Balakirev). In conjunction with Mussorgsky, Balakirev, Rimsky-Korsakov, and César Cui, Borodin began to write major works, intensely Russian in style, spirit, and subject matter. His scientific activities did not permit him to spend as much time as he would have liked on music; as Borodin himself acknowledged, "I am a Sunday composer." Yet he did produce several works which are among the richest achievements of the nationalist school. His Second Symphony, completed in 1876, was introduced on March 10, 1877, under Nápravnik's direction. His First String Quartet followed in 1879, and in 1880 he completed his most celebrated short work for orchestra, the tone poem *On the Steppes of Central Asia.* His String Quartet No. 2, with the celebrated "Nocturne" movement, was completed in 1885. And his masterpiece, the folk opera *Prince Igor,* engaged him from 1869 until the end of his life.

"Prince Igor," the composer explained, "is essentially a national opera which can be of interest only to us Russians who like to refresh ourselves at the fountainhead of our history, and to see the origins of our nationality revived upon the stage." Borodin did not live to complete this opera; that task was done by Rimsky-Korsakov and Glazunov. Its première performance took place three years after the composer's death, on October 23, 1890, in St. Petersburg. Although the opera itself is rarely produced, the "Polovtsian Dances" (with which Prince Igor and his son are entertained by their captor, the Tartar Khan Konchak, at the close of the second act) are frequently performed at symphony concerts.

Borodin's Second Symphony in B minor is in a sense a by-product of *Prince Igor,* for it employs much of the material that the composer had planned for his opera. Like *Prince Igor,* the symphony has Oriental brilliance of orchestral color, power, and melodic subtlety. "Hearing his music," said Michael Ivanov, "you are reminded of the ancient Russian knights in all their awkwardness and also in all their greatness." The distinguished Russian critic Stassov wrote: "The old heroic Russian form dominates it. . . . Borodin was haunted when he wrote this symphony by the picture of feudal Russia, and tried to paint it in his music."

Tragedy darkened Borodin's last years. His wife became a chronic invalid, and in 1884 he contracted cholera, from which he never completely recovered. Frequently, he suffered severe fits of depression. Yet his industry both in science and music were unabated.

While celebrating the carnival of 1887, decked out in a national costume, Borodin suddenly collapsed. He died soon after that in St. Petersburg on February 27, 1887.

"Alexander," wrote Victor I. Seroff, "inherited from his father a pair of dark Oriental eyes that look, as someone said, like the round flat surface of a filled glass. He owed to his Georgian ancestors the Oriental quality of sleepiness in his whole manner." Rimsky-Korsakov once noted that Borodin "slept little, but could sleep on anything and anywhere. He could dine twice a day, or go dinnerless altogether, both of which happened frequently."

Borodin regarded science rather than music as his true field of endeavor. He wrote: "It should be understood that I do not seek recognition as a composer, for I am somehow ashamed of admitting to my composing activities. This is understandable since, while for others it is a straightforward matter, a duty, and their life's purpose, for me it is a relaxation, a pastime, and an indulgence which distracts me from my principal work."

Borodin and his wife lived in the building of the Medical Academy. "The flat," M. M. Kurbanoff wrote, "was pleasant, with big windows facing the river Neva. From a dark hall, the way led to a small drawing room, containing a piano, and then to a dining room. To the left of the drawing room was Borodin's study which, as a rule, was in a state of great disorder. They were at home chiefly in the evenings, although even then Borodin would often disappear on some pretext or other. . . . I usually found them in the dining room drinking tea; at one end of the big table sat Mrs. Borodin, at the other end he himself, drinking his tea out of a tiny, almost miniature coffee cup. Of such cups he drank an infinite number, passing his every time to his wife, who poured the tea, causing great discomfiture to those who sat between them. When I asked him why he did not drink out of a larger cup, he would reply: 'You see when I have drunk ten such thimbles as this with all the paraphernalia of passing them to and fro and pouring, I have the illusion of having drunk an immense quantity, yet, in reality, I have drunk very little, for tea has a bad effect on me.' In spite of great fatigue from his lectures and the work on innumerable committees, Borodin took a lively interest in the conversation. His sense of humor and happy disposition kept the whole company in a perpetual state of merriment."

Devoted to his wife, Borodin did all he could to adapt his own life to hers, which, because of her chronic illness, was quite irregular. As Seroff informs us: "She had long since turned day into night and, of course, completely prevented any normal schedule on her husband's part." Her every whim became his routine. "The day's timetable in the Borodin household," explained David Lloyd-Jones, "was at some five to six hours' variance with that of the rest of the world: Borodin found that he was unable to compose at the piano during the day because his wife chose to sleep then, or at night because he would disturb the neighbors and deny himself the sleep he needed. Furthermore . . . it seems that the flat was an ever buzzing hive of students, relatives and friends (many of whom contrived to stay with Borodin whenever they were in need of medical attention) and a host of stray cats who made a habit of walking over the dinner table and sticking their noses into people's plates."

As a composer, Borodin, according to Arthur Pougin, had "a complex, subtle mind. In his harmonies he was delicate, refined and bold, and was not afraid to assault the ears of the audience of his day; he was a skilful contrapuntist; and he handled his orchestra with distinction. His weakness, such as it was, lay in a certain absence of unity in conception and in a lack which is occasionally noticeable of calmness and simplicity in all the nervous vigor he had at his command."

Borodin, said Stassov, was an epic poet like Glinka. "He is not less national than Glinka, but the Oriental element plays with him as it plays for Glinka, Dargomizhsky, Mussorgsky, Rimsky-Korsakov. He belongs to composers of program music. He can say with Glinka, 'For my limitless imagination I must have a precise and given text.'"

PRINCIPAL WORKS

Chamber Music—2 string quartets; String Sextet in D minor; Piano Quintet in C minor; Piano Trio in D major; Fantasy on Russian Themes, for two violins and cello; Concerto in D major-minor for flute and piano; Flute Sonata; Cello Sonata.

Operas—The Bogatyrs; Prince Igor.

Orchestral Music—3 symphonies (third unfinished); On the Steppes of Central Asia.

Piano Music—Petite Suite; Scherzo in A-flat major; Tarantella for four hands.

Vocal Music—Songs for voice and piano including False Note, Full of Poison Are My Songs, The Sea, The Sleeping Princess, Sunset; Serenade for Four Cavaliers to One Lady, for vocal quartet.

ABOUT

Abraham, G., Studies in Russian Music; Brook, D., Six Great Russian Composers; Calvocoressi, M. D., and Abraham, G., Masters of Russian Music; Dianin, S., Borodin; Leonard, R. A., A History of Russian Music; Montagu-Nathan, M., History of Russian Music; Pougin, A., A Short History of Russian Music; Rimsky-Korsakov, N., My Musical Life; Seroff, V. I., The Mighty Five; Zetlin, M., The Five.

High Fidelity Magazine, June 1963.

William Boyce *1710-1779*

WILLIAM BOYCE was born, probably in London, in or about 1710; the exact place and date of his birth have never been authenticated. His father, a cabinetmaker with a keen appreciation for music, soon recognized his son's musical talent and placed him as a chorister at St. Paul's Cathedral, where Boyce received formal instruction from Charles King. When his voice broke, the boy left the choir to study organ with Maurice Greene. After his formal study of music was completed, Boyce worked for several years as a harpsichord tutor at various private schools. In 1734 he was appointed organist of Oxford Chapel in Cavendish Square.

When Boyce was still a young man, his hearing began to fail, but he did not permit this handicap to interfere with his career as a professional musician. In 1736 he became organist of St. Michael's Parish Church in Cornhill, remaining until 1768. From 1749 on he combined this office with a position as organist at the All Hallows Great and Less Church on Thames Street. In 1736 Boyce was also appointed composer to the Chapel Royal, for which he wrote anthems. A year later he became the principal conductor of the Three Choirs Festival, a position he held for several years. When Maurice Greene died in 1755, the Duke of Grafton named Boyce Master of the King's music and conductor of the annual festivals of the Sons of the Clergy. In 1758 he was also appointed organist of the Chapel Royal.

During his lifetime Boyce created a library of church and secular music which established him as one of the foremost English composers of his time. He produced oratorios, masques, serenatas, anthems, odes, hymns, and services. Most of this work was later collected by Philip Hayes and published in two volumes by Boyce's widow in 1780 and 1790. One of his earliest important works, the serenata *Solomon,* written in 1743 to a text by Edward Moore, includes the popular aria for tenor and bassoon obbligato, "Softly Rise, O Southern Breeze." Boyce also composed many instrumental works, including overtures and sonatas, as well as eight symphonies.

Boyce's symphonies, which he wrote between 1750 and 1761 (structurally, they resemble concerti grossi more than symphonies) lay dormant and forgotten for almost two centuries, until Constant Lambert edited and published them in 1928. They are delightful examples of eighteenth century orchestral music, and well deserve their present-day revival. These works, as Lambert explained in the preface to his publication, "are not only of great technical and historical interest but have a vigor and charm that are rarely found together."

Boyce also wrote for the stage. In 1749 he contributed several songs to Garrick's farce *Peleus and Thetis,* and some incidental music for an entertainment by Moses Mendez entitled *The Chaplet.* During the next decade he continued to write music for various plays produced at the Drury Lane.

His greatest achievements, however, were in church music, particularly in his compilation of *Cathedral Music,* a three-volume collection of morning and evening services, hymns, and other forms of English church music by such great English composers of religious music as Blow, Bull, Byrd, Gibbons, Lawes, Locke, Morley, Purcell and Tallis. The first volume of this edition was issued during his lifetime, in 1760, the latter part in 1780, after his death. "The influence of this collection," says Harold Watkins Shaw, "in determining the repertory of cathedral choirs for a century and a half after publication of the first volume cannot be overestimated."

In 1768 Boyce's deafness finally compelled him to give up all musical activity. He retired to Kensington to live in semi-seclusion, working on the last two volumes of *Cathedral Music.* In his last years he suffered severely from gout. He died in Kensington on February 7, 1779, and was buried under the center dome of St. Paul's Cathedral. The

WILLIAM BOYCE

combined choirs of St. Paul's, Westminster Abbey and the Chapel Royal performed several of his compositions at his funeral services. The following inscription appears on his tombstone: "Happy in his competition, much happier in a constant flow of harmony, through every Scene of Life, Relative or Domestic; the Husband, Father, Friend."

"A more modest man than Dr. Boyce, I have never known," wrote Charles Wesley. "I never heard him speak a vain or ill-natured word, either to exalt himself or depreciate another." The historian John Hawkins who also knew Boyce personally, said: "He was endowed with the qualities of truth, justice, and integrity, was mild and gentle in deportment, above all resentment against such as envied his reputation, communicative of knowledge, sedulous and punctual in the discharge of the duties of his several employments."

Of Boyce's music William Alexander Barrett said, "Boyce's style as expressed in his church music is massive, dignified, and impressive. In what is now called picturesque writing, he was probably without a rival. His anthems . . . are as good as anything in the whole repertory of cathedral music." The eminent music historian Charles Burney wrote: "There is an original and sterling merit in his productions that gives to all his works a peculiar stamp and character of his own strength, clearness, and facility, without any mixture of styles." And John Hawkins commented: "In musical erudition he emulated Tallis and Byrd; in harmony and various modulations, Orlando Gibbons; and in the sweetness of melody, Purcell. . . . In a word it may be said that in skill, in powers of invention, he was not surpassed by any of the most celebrated of his predecessors or contemporaries."

One of Boyce's melodies, "Heart of Oak" from *Harlequin's Invasion* (1759), was taken by John Dickinson as the melody for America's first important political song, "The Liberty Song," published in 1768.

Constant Lambert adapted melodies from Boyce's symphonies and sonatas for a ballet, *The Prospect Before Us*, introduced at Sadler's Wells, London, on July 4, 1940.

PRINCIPAL WORKS

Chamber Music—12 sonatas for two violins.

Choral Music—Noah; Solomon; anthems, cantatas, hymns, masques, odes, oratorios, serenatas.

Orchestral Music—8 symphonies; concerti grossi, overtures, incidental music to numerous plays.

Organ Music—10 voluntaries (also for harpsichord).

Vocal Music—Various songs for voice and piano including By thy Banks, Gentle Stour.

ABOUT

Barrett, W. A., English Church Composers.
Monthly Musical Record, November 1, 1913.

Johannes Brahms *1833-1897*

JOHANNES BRAHMS was born in Hamburg, Germany, on May 7, 1833. He was the second child and oldest son of Johann Jakob, a double-bass player in the orchestra of the Hamburg Opera; his mother, Johanna Henrika, was a needleworker. Brahms soon showed signs of exceptional musical interest and talent. At the age of six he invented his own musical notation in order to set down on paper the melodies he had composed. A year later he started to study piano with Otto Cossel. He soon acquired enough proficiency to earn money performing in local (and sometimes disreputable) taverns and inns.

When Brahms was ten he began to study piano with Eduard Marxsen, a sensitive musician who appreciated the boy's extraordinary gifts. Four years later the boy gave a concert in which he introduced a composition of his own, a set of variations on a folk melody.

For many years the young Brahms suffered extreme poverty. To help support his family he was forced to produce hundreds of trivial pieces and transcriptions which were published under a *nom de plume*. In addition he played piano in saloons and gave music lessons to children. So severely did he tax his physical resources that at one time he was on the brink of a nervous breakdown. A relative persuaded him to retire to the country for a period of rest.

By this time Brahms had already attempted serious composition. He completed several piano pieces and songs, as well as a piano trio, which was performed privately in 1851.

In 1853 Brahms' meeting with Eduard Reményi, the distinguished Hungarian violinist, gave new direction to the young man's career. Impressed by the Brahms' musical gifts and pronounced talent at the piano, Reményi hired him as his accompanist on a tour through Germany. Through Reményi Brahms came to know some of Germany's most influential musicians, a few to be numbered among his most devoted friends and admirers. Among them were the distinguished violinist Joseph Joachim, who was rhapsodic in his praise after hearing Brahms play his own piano sonata and the song "O versenk' dein Leid"; Liszt, who presented Brahms with a cigarette case as a token of his esteem for the young man's piano sonata; and, most important for Brahms' personal life and artistic career, Robert and Clara Schumann.

Brahms met the Schumanns in Düsseldorf. When he first performed some of his compositions for the older composer, Schumann cried, "Clara must hear this!" After Clara had joined her husband in the music room, he said, "Hear! my dear Clara. You will hear such music as you never heard before." From that day the Schumanns regarded Brahms as a relative, invited him to live for a while in their home, showered upon him their enthusiasm, love, and counsel. In an entry in his diary, dated September 30, 1853, Schumann described Brahms' first visit, calling him a "genius." And in the October 28, 1853 issue of his journal, the *Neue Zeitschrift für Musik*, Schumann wrote the now famous essay in which Brahms' genius received public notice for the first time. Schumann was also influential in persuading a publisher to accept Brahms' three piano sonatas and three groups of songs, and in arranging an engagement for Brahms as pianist at the Gewandhaus in Leipzig in a program that included Brahms' First Piano Sonata and a scherzo.

In return, Brahms brought to the Schumanns all the devotion of which he was capable. When in 1854 Schumann showed alarming symptoms of mental breakdown, Brahms rushed to Düsseldorf to help him and his family. After Schumann had been consigned to an asylum Brahms took an apartment above the Schumanns' to comfort Clara and help care for her children. He remained in Düsseldorf up to the time of Schumann's death, in the summer of 1856.

For the next forty years Brahms never wavered in his regard for Clara Schumann. There is good reason to believe that, despite many other attachments, Clara Schumann was the woman whom he loved most deeply. The fact that he never married her points up his strange and inexplicable relationships with all women. Brahms was many times in love—with Agathe von Siebold, Luise Dustmann, and Elisabeth Herzogenberg, among others. He also conducted flirtations with the singers Hermine Spies and Alice Barbi. When these relationships approached matrimony, however, he withdrew hastily. Upon breaking off with Agathe von Siebold, because marriage with her seemed inevitable, he exclaimed: "Fetters I cannot wear!" On another occasion he explained lamely that the reason he refused to marry was that he feared bringing his wife news of his "failures." "Failures, they did not hurt me," he said, "but if I had been obliged to meet the questioning eyes of a wife and to tell her that once again I had failed—that I could not have endured."

Many reasons have been adduced for Brahms' deliberate avoidance of marriage. Some conjecture that his childhood experiences in the disreputable inns where he performed produced the fear of a sustained relationship with a woman.

From 1856 to 1859 Brahms lived in his native Hamburg. For part of that time he was musical director for the household of the Prince of Lippe-Detmold. During this period he completed two orchestral serenades, those in D major and A major, the Sextet in B-flat major, and most important of all, the First Piano Concerto in D minor. The concerto was first performed in Han-

JOHANNES BRAHMS

over, on January 22, 1859, with Joachim as conductor and Brahms as soloist. It was a dismal failure. After its second performance in Leipzig, five days later, *Signale* described the composition as a "series of lacerating chords."

In 1859 Brahms became the conductor of a women's chorus in Hamburg, which he directed for several years. In 1862 he paid his first visit to Vienna, bringing with him the manuscripts of the Piano Quartets in G minor and A major. On November 16 three members of the Hellmesberger Quartet joined Brahms in presenting the première of the G minor Quartet. On this occasion Brahms' performance attracted far more interest than his music; the quartet was described as "gloomy, obscure, and ill developed." At a second concert in Vienna, the A major Piano Quartet was introduced, together with some of Brahms' *Lieder*, and his piano *Variations on a Theme by Handel*. Again it was Brahms' piano virtuosity rather than his creative imagination that impressed the critics. Only the leader of the Hellmesberger Quartet, Joseph Hellmesberger, seemed to recognize Brahms' genius. "This is Beethoven's heir," he said prophetically.

Between 1857 and 1868 Brahms labored on one of his unqualified masterworks—*A German Requiem (Ein deutsches Requiem)*, based on a German text adapted from the Lutheran Bible rather than the Latin liturgy traditional with requiems. When three portions of this work were first heard in Vienna on December 1, 1867, they were received with undisguised hostility, but this was due largely to a poor performance. On April 10, 1868, Brahms conducted the world première of the complete work in Bremen. It was a complete triumph, Brahms' first huge public success. "Never had the enthusiasm been so great," said Albert Dietrich, who was in the audience. "The effect . . . was simply overwhelming, and it became clear at once to the audience that *A German Requiem* ranked among the loftiest music ever given to the world."

A German Requiem—written after the death of the composer's mother, to whom he was unusually devoted—is the composer's greatest choral work. "The score," says Karl Geiringer, "is not only the most extensive which Brahms has left to us, it is also one of the most precious. . . . Here the master decisively strikes into new paths. . . The Latin Requiem is a prayer for the peace of the *dead*, threatened with the horrors of the Last Judgment. Brahms's Requiem, on the contrary, utters words of consolation, designed to reconcile the *living* with the idea of suffering and death. In the liturgical text whole sentences are filled with the darkest menace; in Brahms's Requiem, each of the seven sections closes in a mood of cheerful confidence or loving promise. . . . Unsurpassable is the resigned, emotional melancholy of the first, fifth, and seventh movements; the spectral gaiety at the opening of the second; and the calm transfiguration in which the jubilation of this movement closes."

Brahms wrote several other impressive choral compositions at this time. A cantata, *Rinaldo,* based on Goethe, was completed in 1868; the moving *Alto Rhapsody,* after Goethe's *Harzreise im Winter* followed in 1869; and the monumental *Song of Fate (Schicksalslied)* appeared in 1871.

Brahms long hoped to become music director of the Hamburg Philharmonic. When this dream was shattered, he decided to leave his native city and settle permanently in Vienna. There, from 1871 to 1875, he conducted the orchestral concerts of the Gesellschaft der Musikfreunde. His first important work for orchestra was performed in Vienna on November 2, 1873—the *Variations on a Theme by Haydn,* which he also wrote in a version for two unaccompanied pianos. Grat-

ified with the success of his composition, and convinced now that he could orchestrate to his complete satisfaction, Brahms at last decided to venture on a symphony, an ambitious form he had long been avoiding. "You will never know," he once confessed, "how the likes of us feel when we hear the tramp of a giant like Beethoven behind us."

It took Brahms a decade to work on the various sketches for his First Symphony in C minor. But when the work was completed at last in 1876, Brahms was at the peak of his technical mastery and creative maturity. This work has been justly described as the greatest first symphony ever written. "From the first notes," said Lawrence Gilman, "we are aware of a great voice, uttering superb poetic speech."

The First Symphony was introduced in Karlsruhe, on November 6, 1876, with Dessoff conducting. The reaction was described as a "great but not overwhelming success." After the performance, members of the orchestra thanked Brahms for having proved at last that the final word in the symphonic form had not been said by Beethoven. The symphony was introduced soon afterwards in Germany, Austria, and England, with varying degrees of success. In Vienna the powerful critic Eduard Hanslick said it was "difficult of comprehension," and in Munich the work was loudly hissed.

But any doubt that Brahms was truly Beethoven's heir in the symphonic form was completely dispelled with his next three symphonies, each a towering masterwork. The Second Symphony in D major, completed in 1877, was introduced in Vienna on December 30, 1877, Hans Richter conducting; the Third, in F major, was completed in 1883, and was first heard in Vienna on December 2 that year, under Richter; the Fourth, in E minor, the last he was to write, was completed in 1885 and introduced in Meiningen on October 25, the composer conducting.

In his biography of Brahms, Walter Niemann pointed up the emotional climate of each of the symphonies, calling the first "Brahms' *Pathetic Symphony*"; the second, his *"Pastoral";* the third, his *"Eroica";* the fourth, his *"Elegiac."* "Each of the four symphonies," explains H. C. Colles, "takes a different emotional course. The First triumphs over the spirit of heaviness; the Second lives in the light; the Third begins on the flood-tide of energy but the tide ebbs;

the Fourth sums up a lifetime of experience in musical thinking. The first three are synoptic, in their portrayal of the falling tides of feeling. The last stands apart from them; in it Brahms appears increasingly absorbed in tracing out a design for its own sake. In the synoptic symphonies the expression of feeling dictates the design, a different one in each case; in the Fourth, the design controls the feeling and this new outlook issues in the tremendous *chaconne*-like pattern of its finale."

Recognition of his giant stature in the post-Romantic movement in Germany was now universal. In 1877 Brahms was offered an honorary doctorate by Cambridge University; he declined because he was reluctant at the time to make the journey to England. A year later he accepted an honorary doctorate from Breslau University in Germany, for which occasion he wrote his popular *Academic Festival Overture,* based on several popular student songs including "Gaudeamus igitur." In 1886 Brahms became a Knight of the Prussian Order for Merit and was elected a member of the Berlin Academy of Arts. In 1889 his native city, Hamburg, presented him with the freedom of the city, and in 1890 the Emperor of Austria conferred on him the Order of Leopold.

During the last twenty-five years of his life, Brahms lived in a modest, three-room apartment on Karlsgasse in Vienna. Despite his comfortable financial situation, he lived very simply. He brewed his own coffee, avoided delicacies, wore the same inexpensive and ill-fitting clothes for years before discarding them. Though in his artistic life all was systematic and neatly ordered, his personal life was rather disorganized. His lodgings were cluttered and chaotic. He would keep bundles of uncounted banknotes haphazardly in his closet, never knowing how much he had at any time.

"At home," Philip Hale wrote, "he went about in a flannel shirt, trousers, a detachable white collar, no cravat, slippers. In the country he was happy in a flannel shirt and alpaca jacket, carrying a soft felt hat in his hand, and in bad weather wearing on his shoulders an old-fashioned bluish-green shawl, fastened in the front by a huge pin. . . . He preferred a modest restaurant to a hotel *table d'hôte.* In his music room were pictures of a few composers, engravings (the Sistine Madonna among them), the portrait

of Cherubini by Ingres, with a veiled Muse crowning the composer ('I cannot stand that female,' Brahms said to his landlady), a bronze relief of Bismarck, always crowned with a laurel. There was a square piano on which a volume of Bach was usually standing open. On the cover lay notebooks, writing tablets, calendars, keys, portfolios, recently published books and music, also souvenirs of his travels."

Sir George Henschel, who knew Brahms well, described the master as follows: "He was broad-chested, of rather short stature, with a tendency to stoutness. The healthy and rather ruddy color of his skin indicated a love of nature and a habit of being in the open air in all kinds of weather; his thick hair fell nearly down to his shoulders. His clothes and boots were not exactly of the latest pattern, nor did they fit particularly well, but his linen was spotless. What, however, struck me most was the kindliness of his eyes. They were of a light blue, wonderfully keen and bright, with now and then a roguish twinkle in them, and yet of almost childlike tenderness."

Brahms usually spent his winters in Vienna when he was not making guest appearances as pianist and conductor in Europe. Summers (the time of year when he was most actively engaged in composing) were spent in the mountain districts outside Vienna, or in such Austrian resorts as Bad Ischl.

Brahms did not long outlive his beloved friend, Clara Schumann. While attending her funeral, in the spring of 1896, Brahms caught cold. The infection aggravated a cancer of the liver from which he had long suffered. On March 7, 1897 he attended a performance of his Fourth Symphony in Vienna, conducted by Hans Richter. It was his last public appearance. As though aware that they were bidding their beloved master farewell, the listeners rose to their feet to give him a rousing ovation. "Tears ran down his cheeks as he stood there," recounted Florence May, "shrunken in form, with lined countenance, strained expression, white hair hanging lank; and throughout the audience there was a feeling of a stifled sob, for each knew he was saying farewell." He died in Vienna on April 3, 1897, at 8:30 A.M. Music centers all over Europe sent representatives to his funeral. The city of Vienna, the Gesellschaft der Musikfreunde, the foremost composers of Austria, all paid him special honors. "The funeral procession that passed through the streets of Vienna," wrote Karl Geiringer, "extended further than the eye could reach, and immense numbers of people lined the road on either side."

In Brahms, Romanticism and Classicism found a common ground. Although he admired Wagner, he was incapable of thinking musically within the grand, dramatic forms of the music drama and tone poem. Brahms worked best within the traditional classical molds of the symphony, concerto, sonata, and quartet—but in a Romantic style that was richly poetic and deeply emotional. "In him," says W. H. Hadow, "converge all previous streams of tendency not as into a pool, stagnant, passive, motionless, but as into a noble river that receives its tributary waters and bears them onward in larger and statelier volumes. . . . Are we to say, then, that Brahms is more consummate a master of his medium than Bach and Beethoven? By no means; but, in consequence of their work, his medium is more plastic than theirs. . . . To Brahms we may apply Dryden's famous epigram, in which the force of nature 'to make a third has joined the other two.' By his education, he learned to assimilate their separate methods; by his position, in the later days of romance, he found a new emotional language in established use; by his own genius he has made the forms wider and more flexible, and has shown once more that they are not artificial devices, but the organic embodiment of artistic life."

In his piano music, according to James Gibbons Huneker, "Brahms has an individual voice. . . . His Spartan simplicity sometimes unmasks the illusory and elusive qualities of the instrument. . . . His techniques are peculiar, but they make the keyboard sound beautifully. . . . His piano music is gay, is marmoreal in its repose, is humorous, jolly, sad, depressing, morbid, recondite, poetic, severe and fantastic. He pours into the elastic form of the sonata Romantic passion, and in the loosest texture of his little pieces he can be as immovable as bronze, as plastic as clay. . . . He is sometimes frozen by grief and submerged by the profundity of his thought, but he is ever interesting. . . . Above all, he is deeply human."

In the *Lied* Brahms may not "attain quite the heights which Schubert does in a small handful of unexcelled masterpieces," said Cecil Gray, "but with this one glorious exception it is difficult to see whom one could place above him. . . . A song of Brahms is not . . . a mere turgid flow of notes without any intrinsic value apart from the poem, but a delicately organized and articulated structure with a logic of its own. . . . Brahms was never content until he had created a vocal line of intrinsic melodic beauty and an accompaniment as full of musical subtlety as he could make it."

In Herbert Anticliffe's opinion, it is in the chamber works that Brahms achieved his most personal expression. "Brahms . . . was happier by far in this than in any other mode of composition. Great as is his symphonic music, truthful and dramatic though his choral works, sensuous and brilliant his piano pieces, none appeals to our finer feelings so forcibly and effectively as the concerted chamber works. In these he meets and discourses with his friends. Perfect in their workmanship, they never smell of the lamp or wear the scholar's gown. They are the intimate thoughts of a man spoken only to his friends. . . . They will always be musician's music."

Summing up the qualities that set Brahms apart from other masters of his age, Daniel Gregory Mason said: "He excels all his contemporaries in soundness and universality . . . a heroic and simple soul, who finds life acceptable, meets it genially, and utters his joy and his sorrow with the old classic sincerity. He is not blighted by any of the myriad forms of egotism—by sentimentality, by the itch to be effective at all costs, or to be 'original,' or to be Byronic, or Romantic, or unfathomable. He has no 'message' for an errant world; no anathema, either profoundly gloomy or insolently clever, to hurl at God. He has rather a deep and broad impersonal love of life; universal joy is the sum and substance of his expression."

PRINCIPAL WORKS

Chamber Music—3 string quartets; 3 piano quartets; 3 piano trios; 3 violin sonatas; 2 string sextets; 2 string quintets; 2 cello sonatas; 2 clarinet sonatas; Piano Quintet in F minor; Clarinet Quintet in B minor; Clarinet Trio in A minor.

Choral Music—Schicksalslied; Triumphlied; Rinaldo; Ein deutsches Requiem; Rhapsodie (Alto Rhapsody); Gesang der Parzen; canons, motets, part-songs, romances.

Organ Music—11 chorale preludes.

Orchestral Music—4 symphonies; 2 serenades; 2 piano concertos; Concerto in D minor for Violin and Orchestra; Concerto in A minor, for violin, cello and orchestra; Variations on a Theme by Haydn (also for two pianos unaccompanied); Academic Festival Overture; Tragic Overture; Hungarian Dances.

Piano Music—3 sonatas; Variations on a Theme by Paganini; ballades, capriccios, Hungarian dances, intermezzi, rhapsodies, waltzes.

Vocal Music—15 Romances from Magelone; 4 ernste Gesänge; Liebeslieder Waltzes, for vocal quartet; Neue Liebeslieder Waltzes, for vocal quartet; Zigeunerlieder, for vocal quartet; canons, vocal duets, arrangements of folk songs; over 200 songs for voice and piano including Am Sonntag Morgen, An die Nachtigall, Auf dem Kirchofe, Die Botschaft, Feldeinsamkeit, Der Gang zum Liebchen, Gestillte Sehnsucht, Immer leiser wird mein Schlummer, Der Jäger, Das Mädchen spricht, Die Mainacht, Minnelied III, Nicht mehr zu dir zu gehen, O wüsst' ich doch den Weg zurück, Sapphische Ode, Der Schmied, Sonntag, Ständchen, Der Tod das ist die kühle Nacht, Vergebliches Ständchen, Von weiger Liebe, Wie bist du, meine Königin, and Wiegenlied.

ABOUT

Anticliffe, H., Brahms; Colles, H. C., Brahms; Dieters, H., Johannes Brahms; Fuller-Maitland, J. A., Johannes Brahms; Gal, H., Johannes Brahms; Geiringer, K., Brahms: His Life and Works; Harrison, J., Brahms and His Four Symphonies; Henschel, G., Personal Recollections of Brahms; Hill, R., Brahms; Latham, P., Brahms; May, F., The Life of Brahms; Niemann, W., Brahms; Pulver, J., Johannes Brahms; Rostand, C., Brahms; Schauffler, R. H., The Unknown Brahms; Specht, R., Brahms.

Max Bruch *1838-1920*

MAX CHRISTIAN FRIEDRICH BRUCH was born in Cologne, Germany, on January 6, 1838. The fact that he composed *Kol Nidrei* and arranged some Hebrew songs for chorus has led many to the erroneous conclusion that he was Jewish. Bruch came from a clerical Protestant family; his grandfather was a pastor at a Cologne church.

Bruch's father was a government employee, his mother a fine singer who appeared at several of the Rhine Music Festivals in Cologne. She gave Bruch his first music lessons. These were soon supplemented with instruction in theory from K. Breidenstein. Exceptionally precocious in music, Bruch completed over seventy compositions by the time he was fifteen, including a symphony, performed publicly in Cologne in 1852.

MAX BRUCH

In 1852 he received the Mozart Foundation Scholarship in Frankfurt am Main, which enabled him to study for four years with Ferdinand Hiller and Karl Reinecke. Hiller used his influence to have some of Bruch's music published. During the winters of 1857 and 1858 Bruch resided in Leipzig, where he came to know such eminent teachers as Moscheles and Ferdinand David. In 1858 he returned to his native city, where for about three years he supported himself by teaching music. During this period he found many opportunities to travel, visiting Berlin, Dresden, and Munich, as well as other cities. Among the works he completed at this time were an opera, *Scherz, List und Rache* (to a text by Goethe), introduced in Cologne on January 14, 1858.

From 1861 to 1865 Bruch lived in Mannheim. There he met the poet Emanuel Geibel, who had written *Die Loreley,* an opera libretto which Mendelssohn was planning to set to music. When Mendelssohn died Geibel turned his text over to Bruch. Their opera was produced in Mannheim on April 14, 1863, with minor success.

A year later a more successful work by Bruch was introduced in Aix-la-Chapelle. It was *Frithjof,* a choral setting of six dramatic scenes from the Frithjof saga. The work was so well received at its première that it was soon performed in Vienna, Brussels, Paris, and several leading German cities.

In 1865 Bruch was appointed conductor of orchestral concerts in Coblenz. A year later, encouraged by his friend, the eminent violinist Joseph Joachim, he completed one of his most famous compositions, the First Violin Concerto in G minor. It was successfully presented in Coblenz on April 24, 1866, with Otto von Koenigslow as soloist and the composer conducting. "Grave and earnest," writes J. A. Fuller-Maitland, "from beginning to end, yet rising into passionate outbursts of intensity, this work acquired at once a place of its own among violin concertos. Its melodies have a character deeper, nobler, and more genuinely expressive than any former work of the composer."

From 1867 to 1870 Bruch was *Kapellmeister* for Prince Schwarzburg-Sondershausen. As conductor of the orchestra, he grew more interested in instrumental music. In 1870 Bruch went to live for two years in Berlin; there, on March 21, 1872, his opera *Hermione* (based on Shakespeare's *A Winter's Tale*) was produced. The opera was received poorly. But several of his large works for chorus, including *Odysseus* and *Achilleus*, were acclaimed, and were responsible for placing Bruch among the most successful German Romantic composers of his day.

"In *Odysseus* and *Achilleus*," writes Arno Kleffel, "Bruch had found a field of material which made a strong appeal to his instincts and aesthetic feelings, a field in which he found opportunity to develop to the highest degree both in the masterful treatment of choral masses and in his ever growing art of instrumentation. . . . Bruch's music not only brought the Homeric world nearer to us again, but more, the musical setting has revealed to us for the first time various poetic phrases in their entire depth and purity."

From 1873 to 1878 Bruch lived in Bonn. On two occasions he left to conduct performances of his works in London. One composition was his Violin Concerto in D minor, written for and introduced by Pablo de Sarasate. During a return visit to Berlin in 1878, Bruch assumed the post of conductor of the Stern Choral Society. He did not hold it long, however; in 1880 he was appointed principal conductor of the Liverpool Philharmonic.

In Liverpool, in 1880, Bruch completed two of the orchestral works by which he is most often represented today on concert programs. One is the *Kol Nidrei*, variations for solo cello and orchestra, which the Jewish community of Liverpool commissioned him to write. Its première took place in Leipzig on October 20, 1881, with A. Fischer as soloist. The basic melody is a synagogual chant sung on the Day of Atonement, the holiest day of the Hebrew calendar; but the second melody, more German Romantic in style than Hebraic, is Bruch's own.

The second orchestral work completed that year was the *Scottish Fantasy*, for violin and orchestra, inspired by his reading of Sir Walter Scott's novels. Bruch wrote the composition for Pablo de Sarasate and dedicated it to him; Sarasate introduced it in Hamburg in September 1880. Here Bruch made adroit use of several popular Scottish melodies including "Auld Rob Morris," "The Dusty Miller," "I'm A' Down for Lack of Johnnie," and "Scots Wha Hae."

Bruch married Clara Tuczek, a singer, in Liverpool in 1881. Two years later he gave up his post with the Liverpool Philharmonic and visited the United States. He led several singing societies in performances of his choral works.

From 1883 to 1890 Bruch was the principal conductor of the Breslau Symphony. In 1891 he went to live in Berlin for the rest of his life. Until 1910 he was head of the Master School of Composition at the Royal High School. He received many honors commensurate with his high station in German music, including honorary doctorates from Cambridge and the University of Breslau, the Prussian Order for Merit in 1898, and corresponding membership in the French Academy.

In 1910 he withdrew from all his professional duties and spent the rest of his life in semi-seclusion at his home in Friedenau, near Berlin. There was much to sadden him in those last years: the death of his only son, a gifted painter, during World War I; the passing of his beloved wife in 1919; the defeat of Germany in World War I; and the disappearance of the works he regarded most highly from concert programs. He died in Friedenau on October 2, 1920.

PRINCIPAL WORKS

Chamber Music—8 piano trios; 2 string quartets; Four Pieces, for violin and cello; Songs and Dances on Russian and Swedish Folk Tunes, for violin and piano.

Choral Music—Frithjof; Salamis; Rorate coeli; Flucht nach Ägypten; Normannenzug; Römische Leichenfeier; Odysseus; Arminius; Das Lied von der Glocke; Achilleus; Das Feuerkreuz; Leonidas; Moses; Der letzte Abschied des Volkes; Easter Cantata; Heldenfeier; Die Stimme der Mutter Erde; Christkinder-Lieder; Trauerfeier für Mignon; various other choruses, part songs.

Operas—Scherz, List und Rache; Die Loreley; Hermione.

Orchestral Music—3 symphonies; 3 violin concertos; 2 Romanzas, for violin and orchestra; Concerto for Two Pianos and Orchestra; Scottish Fantasy, for violin and orchestra; Kol Nidrei, for cello and orchestra; Adagio on Celtic Themes, for cello and orchestra; Adagio appassionato, for violin and orchestra; Ave Maria, for cello and orchestra; Conzertstück, for violin and orchestra.

Piano Music—8 Pieces; Capriccio, for four hands; Fantasy, for two pianos.

Vocal Music—39 songs for voice and piano; 4 duets for soprano and contralto.

ABOUT

Bacharach, A. L. (editor), The Music Masters, vol. 3; Gysi, F., Max Bruch; Pfitzner, H., Meine Beziehungen zu Max Bruch: Persönliche Erinnrungen.

Opera News, February 2, 1963.

Anton Bruckner *1824-1896*

A NTON BRUCKNER was born in Ansfelden, Austria, on September 4, 1824. His father, like many Bruckners of preceding generations, was a village schoolmaster, and Anton, too, was directed toward that profession. He showed remarkable musical gifts from earliest childhood. When he was only four, he could play the violin and compose original tunes. His pronounced talent attracted the interest of one of his cousins, a musician, who started to teach him organ, composition, and theory.

The elder Bruckner died when the boy was thirteen. Anton's mother enrolled him at the music school of St. Florian as choirboy. For the next four years Anton received a comprehensive training in music. After leaving St. Florian in 1840, he enrolled at a teachers' preparatory school in Linz, then held several minor teaching posts in small Austrian towns. In 1845 he received an appointment as a teacher at St. Florian and for a number of years combined teaching with organ playing. It was not long before Bruckner acquired an excellent reputation for his virtuosity at the organ and his gift for improvisation. He also drew attention as a

ANTON BRUCKNER

composer, particularly with the Requiem in D minor, which was heard at St. Florian on March 13, 1849.

By 1853 Bruckner had come to the decision to give up teaching school for a professional career in music. He went to Vienna and devoted himself there to the intensive study of counterpoint with Simeon Sechter. "I never had a more serious pupil than you," his teacher told him. He also studied composition with Kitzler while learning harmony, fugue, and thorough bass by memorizing texts. In time he acquired so complete a grasp of music theory that when he took an examination in Vienna judged by several of the city's leading musicians, Johann Herbeck remarked: "He knows more than all of us together."

In 1856 Bruckner entered a competition for an appointment as organist of the Linz Cathedral. He won, and held the post for about twelve years. During this time he made several visits to Vienna, where in 1860 he was appointed music director of a choral society. It was with this organization that he made his official bow in Vienna as a composer, by directing the première of his Ave Maria, for seven-part chorus, on May 12, 1861.

One of the greatest musical experiences of Bruckner's life, and certainly a turning point in his career as a composer, was his hearing of Wagner's *Tannhäuser* in 1863. An ardent Wagnerian from the start, Bruckner traveled to Munich two years later to hear the world première of *Tristan und Isolde.* Now his commitment to his new musical religion became absolute. His aims and ideals as a composer required radical transformation. No longer was he interested primarily in writing choral music, classic in design and style; instead he sought the unrestricted freedom of Romantic expression in large forms. Knowing that he was no opera composer, and could not therefore follow in the footsteps of his idol, Bruckner turned to the symphony, endowing it with the same dramatic utterance and theatricalism—and the same harmonic and orchestral devices—that had so impressed him in the music of Wagner.

He wrote and discarded two symphonies before completing one that satisfied him, the First Symphony in C minor, in 1866. Bruckner conducted its première performance in Linz on May 9, 1868. The work was received with aversion by public and critics.

In 1867 Bruckner had been appointed organist in Vienna, and on July 6, 1868 he became professor of organ and harmony at the Conservatory. His permanent home was now in Vienna, in a simple three-room apartment where he lived for the rest of his life, attended to solicitously by his faithful maid, Kathi.

The unfavorable reaction to his First Symphony was the first of many failures that Bruckner encountered before his innovations met with success. He was forced to pay to have his Mass in F and his Second Symphony in C minor performed in Vienna in 1872 and 1873, and each had a disastrous reception. An official at the Conservatory told him: "It is time for you to throw your symphonies in the trash-basket." But even worse misfortunes attended the première of his Symphony No. 3 in D minor, which he had dedicated reverently to Wagner. Accepted for performance by the Vienna Philharmonic, it was dropped from the program after a single rehearsal because the musicians of the orchestra objected to it so violently. Then, on December 16, 1877, Bruckner himself directed the première of this symphony with the Vienna Philharmonic. The anti-Wagner forces in Vienna combined their strength to destroy this man so unmistakably influenced by Wagner's style and artistic principles. Shouts, jeers, whistles disturbed the performance. Many

people in the audience made a noisy retreat out of the auditorium. When Bruckner finished conducting his work and turned around to bow to his audience, he found before him no more than a handful of listeners. Tears poured down his face as he stood frozen on the conductor's platform. Gustav Mahler, one of several young musicians who had stayed to the end, rushed up to Bruckner and congratulated him. But Bruckner pushed him aside rudely. "Let me go," he said gruffly, "the people don't want to know anything of me."

In addition to critical abuse and public rejection, Bruckner suffered appalling financial distress. "I have only my place at the Conservatory," he wrote to a friend in 1875, "on the income of which it is impossible to exist. I have been compelled to borrow money over and over again or accept the alternative of starvation. No one offers me any help."

His many problems undermined his health, and in 1880 he suffered a severe attack of nerves. However, an extended holiday in Switzerland and Oberammergau helped to revitalize him. He returned to Vienna to work on one of his greatest compositions, the Seventh Symphony in E major. Before it was completed, his fortunes as a composer suddenly turned. On February 20, 1881, the première of his Fourth Symphony in E-flat major, the *Romantic,* conducted by Hans Richter in Vienna, scored a major success—Bruckner's first taste of triumph. To this day the *Romantic* has remained one of Bruckner's most frequently performed symphonies.

Bruckner's success now continued to mount, reaching its peak with the monumental Symphony No. 7. When Artur Nikisch conducted its première performance in Leipzig on December 30, 1884, it was hailed almost extravagantly. "Having heard this work," wrote an unidentified Leipzig critic, "and now seeing him in person we asked ourselves in amazement, 'How is it possible that he could remain so long unknown to us?'" Within the next few years the Seventh Symphony was received enthusiastically in Munich, Karlsruhe and Graz, where it had been directed by such eminent conductors as Hermann Levi, Felix Mottl, and Karl Muck. Hermann Levi, the distinguished Wagnerian conductor, insisted that this was "the most significant symphonic work since 1827."

One of the most deeply moving and inspired sections of this symphony is the third-movement Adagio, an eloquent threnody. Wagner had died in 1883, and since it was common knowledge that he had been Bruckner's idol, the rumor circulated that Bruckner had been moved to write this movement by his grief over Wagner's death. Historic truth is less romantic: the Adagio movement was completed a year before Wagner's death. Yet Bruckner did regard this threnody as prophetic warning of the impending tragedy. He later explained: "At one time I came home and was very sad. I thought to myself, it is impossible that the Master can live long, and then the Adagio came to my head."

After the triumph of the Seventh Symphony, Bruckner's position in Austrian music was entrenched. In 1891 he received an honorary doctorate from the University of Vienna, and soon after that the Emperor of Austria presented him with an imperial decoration. Bruckner's seventieth birthday, in 1894, was celebrated throughout the Empire. Perhaps most indicative of his honored status in Vienna was the fact that at the première of his Eighth Symphony in C minor on December 18, 1892, the audience booed the critic Eduard Hanslick, who had formerly been a vitriolic critic of Bruckner's music.

While working intensely on his Ninth Symphony in D minor Bruckner, who was suffering from a serious heart condition and attacks of dropsy, suspected that he did not have long to live. "I have done my duty on earth," he told a visitor. "I have accomplished what I could, and my only wish is to be allowed to finish my Ninth Symphony. Three movements are almost complete. The Adagio is nearly finished. There remains only the Finale. I trust Death will not deprive me of my pen. . . . If He refuses, then He must take the responsibility for its incompleteness."

The work was to remain unfinished. At the première of the symphony in Vienna on February 11, 1903, the conductor, Ferdinand Loewe, used Bruckner's Te Deum as the concluding section, setting a precedent that was long followed by conductors. Willi Reich, however, considers the practice to be highly unwarranted, since "this final choral work shows no relationship to the thematic world unforgettably established in the three completed movements of the symphony."

Bruckner was laboring on the final sketches of his symphony on October 11, 1896, when he complained of a chill and asked for a cup of tea. A friend helped him to bed. He had barely straightened himself when he stopped breathing.

At Bruckner's funeral services, the Adagio of his Seventh Symphony was performed as an elegy. Bruckner, at his own request, was buried under the organ of St. Florian, which he had played for so many years.

This is Gabriel Engel's description of the composer: "He was a little above the average height; but an inclination to corpulency made him appear shorter. His physiognomy, huge-nosed and smooth-shaven as he was, was that of a Roman emperor; but from his blue eyes beamed only kindness and child-like faith. He wore unusually wide white collars, in order to leave his neck perfectly free; and his black loose-hanging clothes were obviously intended to be, above all, comfortable. He had even left instructions for a roomy coffin. The only thing about his attire suggestive of the artist was the loosely arranged bow tie he always wore. About the fit and shape of his shoes, he was, according to his shoemaker, more particular than the most exactingly elegant woman. As he would hurry along the street, swinging a soft black hat, which he hardly ever put on, a colored handkerchief could always be seen protruding from his coat pocket."

It must be added that a good deal of the hostility and contempt that Bruckner encountered for so many years was due to his own eccentric and crude personality. He was a rather pitiable, even ludicrous, character— a peasant lumbering about the city in somewhat ridiculous clothes, speaking with a rural accent, brusque and awkward in his mannerisms. He was as naïve as a child; worse still, he was obsequious toward those he regarded as his superiors. Those who demonstrated the least kindness to him received effusive gratitude as embarrassing as it was exaggerated—and often offensively ingenuous. On one occasion, moved to barely controlled tears by Hans Richter's première performance of his Seventh Symphony, Bruckner tried to compensate the great conductor by pressing a Viennese coin into his hand and urging him to use it for a pitcher of beer.

Bruckner never married, though he was often in love. Invariably his emotional involvements were with girls far younger than he. When he was forty-three he hoped to marry Josephine Lang, a seventeen-year-old girl; her parents refused to consider the match. At sixty-one he fell in love with Marie Barl, also seventeen, who regarded his passionate outpourings as the ravings of an eccentric genius. Still later he wooed a four-teen-year-old girl.

Bruckner believed devoutly and passionate-ly in three things: God, Wagner, and his own music. About the merits of his crea-tions he never had any doubt whatever, even when they had been most severely attacked. Once, toward the end of his life, he said: "When God calls me to Him and asks me: 'Where is the talent which I have given you?' Then I shall hold out the rolled-up manuscript of my Te Deum and I know He will be a compassionate judge." He always considered himself Beethoven's successor, and his music as a mystical outpouring to be accepted with humility.

In his inspired pages he revealed some-thing of Beethoven's greatness, which more than compensated for his garrulousness, bombast, and megalomania. In his best pages he was, as Lawrence Gilman once said of him, "both the poet and the seer, looking at us with fathomless grave eyes, speaking soberly of incredible things; or ut-tering magnificence like a Hebrew prophet; or rolling up heavens like a scroll. This is the treasurable Bruckner—the mystic, rhap-sodist, prophet, whose speech was transfig-ured, whose imaginings were penetrated (as Swinburne said of Baudelaire) with the sug-gestion of indescribable wonders, echoing with a strange murmur of revelation."

"Bruckner's particular significance," wrote Paul Bekker, "lies in his having made use of the most subjective elements of Roman-ticism in the expression of popular feeling and naïvely religious faith. For this reason also his music seems to many of us to possess a calm and tranquil beauty. He differs from Brahms in the first place by the inevitable grandeur of his form, for as a composer of the expansive type he strove for symphonic structure, while the concentration of cham-ber-music forms was foreign to his nature. The intellectual and psychological factors in Romanticism were equally alien to him. Here again he differs significantly from Brahms. Through the simplicity of his feel-ing, Bruckner is the first to return to the expression of an impersonal, a universal atti-tude. That it is which gives him his reli-gious trend and gives his music its tranquillity."

"Bruckner's symphonies," wrote Kurt Pah-len, "are like sounding cathedrals or gor-geous Baroque monuments, imperishable me-mentos of security, tranquillity, infinity, plenitude and unworldliness. His Leitmotifs were expressed in an upward soaring of the soul, in a peaceful overcoming of mundane things, and in a constant glorification of the divine. If he ever experienced the inward agony and the terrible and torturing doubts of Beethoven, the crushing melancholy of Schubert, the tormenting and never-satisfied search for the supreme ideal and ultimate truth of . . . Gustav Mahler, if he ever went through the cruel labor pains accompanying the birth of so many masterpieces, he had succeeded in overcoming it all without let-ting the world know about it."

Bruckner's symphonies were originally published (and for a long time performed) in extensively cut, revised adaptations by Ferdinand Loewe. These were considered the acceptable versions until 1932, when a defin-itive publication of Bruckner's works in their original form and orchestration began to appear. This complete edition now com-prises twenty-two volumes. Many present-day conductors are still partial to the Loewe editions; others maintain that Bruckner's original versions are preferable. "The ques-tion of these *Urfassungen* (original versions) is fundamentally not a philosophical but an artistic one," explains Hans F. Redlich. "The form of Bruckner's symphonies is cer-tainly more characteristic without the cuts, and his orchestration—without Wagnerian doubtings and subtleties of light and shade —has a far more personal and individual ring."

The presentation of Bruckner's sym-phonies in their original versions during the 1930's led to a reevaluation and upgrading of Bruckner's music in Austria and Germany. H. C. Robbins Landon explained in *High Fidelity Magazine* (February 1963) that Bruckner's popularity in Austria "has been rising steadily ever since the First World War. . . . Gradually, to many Austrian and German music lovers, Bruckner came to mean all things. As World War II pro-gressed, it was to Bruckner that they turned in times of bombing, darkness, and death. When Hitler's death was announced over Hamburg Radio in those final cataclysmic days of April 1945, it was the Adagio of the Seventh Symphony that followed. . . . Even more than Wagner, Bruckner came to mean the essence of German spiritual life; all that was *Dichter* and *Denker,* all that was mystic and philosophic, seemed to be summed up in the solemn grandeur of Bruckner's adagios. . . . An officer on leave in late 1944 wrote in his diary, 'The [Bruckner] Ninth with Hans Weisbach; now I know what we are fighting for; to return to the Front will be easier.' . . . A couple of years ago, Vienna's famous concert organization, the Gesellschaft der Musikfreunde, sent out to its subscribers a questionnaire asking them what kind of music they wanted to hear, which composers, which works. . . . As anyone familiar with postwar Vienna might surmise, Anton Bruckner came out on top by a comfortable margin [one hundred votes more than second-place Mozart]."

PRINCIPAL WORKS

Chamber Music—String Quintet in F major; Abendklänge, for violin and piano; Intermezzo, for string quintet.

Choral Music—3 Masses; Requiem in D minor; Germanenzug; Abendzauber; Helgoland; Te Deum; Ave Marias, cantatas, male choruses, graduals, hymns, offertories, psalms.

Orchestral Music—9 symphonies (the Ninth, unfinished); Overture in G minor; 4 Kleine Orchesterstücke; marches.

Organ Music—Fugue in D minor; pieces, preludes.

Piano Music—Three Pieces, for piano duet; Quadrille, for piano duet; Klavierstück in E-flat major; Stille Betrachtung an einem Herbstabend; Erinnerung Fantasy in E-flat major.

Vocal Music—Frühlingslied, Amaranths Waldeslieder, Im April, Mein Herz und deine Stimme, Herbstkummer.

ABOUT

Auer, M., Anton Bruckner, sein Leben und Werk; Bruckner, A., Gesammelte Briefe; Cardus, N., A Composer's Eleven; Carner, M., Of Men and Music; Engel, G., The Life of Anton Bruckner; Engel, G., The Symphonies of Bruckner; Furtwängler, W., Johannes Brahms, Anton Bruckner; Grüninger, F., Der Meister von Sankt Florian; Newlin, D., Bruckner, Mahler, Schoenberg; Redlich, H. F., Bruckner and Mahler; Wolff, W., Anton Bruckner: Rustic Genius.

John Bull *1562-1628*

JOHN BULL, an early master of English keyboard music, was born in Somersetshire, England, probably in 1562; the exact date is unknown. There is good reason to

JOHN BULL

believe that he was the son of a London goldsmith. When John was nine he entered the Chapel Royal, where he studied with William Blitheman, one of England's most eminent organists. He then concentrated on becoming an organist, soon acquiring an impressive reputation. On December 24, 1582 he was appointed organist of the Hereford Cathedral. Three years later he became a Gentleman of the Chapel Royal. He had not neglected formal study during these years, and received his baccalaureate in music from Oxford in 1586, his doctorate from Cambridge four years later.

In 1591 Bull became one of the two organists of the Chapel Royal. He soon came into high favor with Queen Elizabeth, who bestowed on him several land leases on several land properties and a sinecure as Keeper of the Enfield Chase. It was upon the Queen's personal recommendation that Bull was appointed in 1596 to the newly created chair in music at Gresham College. He held this post until 1607.

In 1601 Bull embarked on an extensive trip to the Continent, ostensibly for his health, actually as a spy for the Queen. During the trip an episode occurred that has often been described by his biographers. While in France, Bull entered the Cathedral of St. Omer incognito and was led into the vestry, where a highly complicated contrapuntal composition was shown to him. No musician in the world, he was told, could possibly contribute an additional voice to the composition. Bull accepted the challenge, locked himself in the vestry, and completed no fewer than forty additional voices for this piece of music. "Only the devil could have accomplished this," one musician is reported to have said. "Not the devil," replied Bull, "but your humble servant—John Bull."

When King James ascended the throne in 1603 Bull was appointed music teacher to the royal children; he filled this post for a decade. Then in 1613, he suddenly and inexplicably left England without permission, to enter the service of the Spanish Viceroy in Brussels. King James is believed to have dispatched a note to the British Minister in Brussels, expressing indignation that the Spanish Viceroy had shown so little courtesy to England by engaging Bull. The answer the King received has never been adequately interpreted or explained. It read that Bull did "steal out of England through the guilt of a corrupt conscience in order to escape punishment which notoriously he had deserved and was designated to have been inflicted on him by the hand of justice for his . . . grievous crimes."

In any event, Bull never returned to England. He remained in Belgium for the rest of his life, becoming organist of the Notre Dame Cathedral in Antwerp in 1617. He died in Antwerp on March 12 or 13, 1628, and was buried in the cathedral cemetery.

Bull's portrait, painted in 1589, when the composer was about twenty-six, is preserved in the music school at Oxford. It reveals him to be "dark and melancholy in aspect," in the description of Thurston Dart, "with a heavy-lidded, almost Spanish intensity to his gaze. In the background of the picture, the mortal emblems of skull and hourglass are an ironic commentary on the homely quatrain inscribed around its frame." The quatrain reads as follows:

> The Bull by force
> In field doth raigne
> But Bull by Skill
> Good will doth gaine.

Though Bull wrote several contrapuntal compositions for voices, his significance for English music lies primarily in his one hundred fifty-odd pieces for the keyboard (virginal or organ), an enduring monument in the early history of English instrumental music. To Wanda Landowska, his repertory represented some of the most important instrumental music produced during the Renaissance. Thurston Dart points out that Bull's music is "distinguished from that of his contemporaries above all by its prodigious difficulty." Dart adds: "Bull was the Liszt of his time, introducing into keyboard technique new-minted devices that remained current coin for centuries—long chains of parallel sixths and thirds, the full spectrum of chromaticism, intricate cross rhythms, agile skips and leaps, cross-handed harmonies."

Many of Bull's pieces for virginal exploit virtuosity for its own sake, as was the case with the famous *Walsingham Variations,* which Margaret H. Glyn describes as "a big virtuoso piece containing nearly all present piano technique, if allowance be made for the limited treble compass and the absence of octave passages." But in *The King's Hunt,* also a set of variations, Bull reveals a gift for pictorial writing by describing the events of a chase programmatically. And in one of his true masterpieces, *Queen Elizabeth's Pavan,* he demonstrates a pronounced gift for fresh lyricism.

Compositions by John Bull, together with pieces by William Byrd and Orlando Gibbons, were published in 1612 or 1613 in *Parthenia,* the first collection of music for the virginal issued in England.

PRINCIPAL WORKS
Chamber Music—About 50 pieces for viols.
Choral Music—Anthems, hymns, canons, madrigals.
Keyboard Music (virginal or organ)—Over 150 pieces including allemandes, courantes, fantasias, galliards, gigues, In Nomine's, pavanes, preludes, ricercari, variations.

ABOUT
Bridge, F., About Twelve Good Musicians; Glyn, M. H., About Elizabethan Virginal Music and Its Composers; Henry, L., Dr. John Bull; Reese, G., Music in the Renaissance.
Music and Letters, January 1947, April 1954, July 1959; Musical Times, February 1928; Musical Quarterly, July-October 1954.

Dietrich Buxtehude *1637-1707*

DIETRICH BUXTEHUDE, Swedish organ virtuoso and composer who influenced Johann Sebastian Bach so decisively, was born in Helsingör, then under Danish rule, in 1637. The details of his life are meager. It is probable that most, if not all,

Buxtehude: bŏŏks-tĕ-hŏŏ'dĕ

of his instruction in organ came from his father, Hans Jensen Buxtehude, who for almost thirty years was the organist of the Olai Church in Helsingör. In 1657 young Buxtehude was appointed organist in a church in Helsingborg, and three years later in Helsingör.

At the age of thirty Buxtehude settled in Lübeck, Germany, where he applied for the post of organist at St. Mary's. One of the conditions for obtaining the position was that the applicant marry his predecessor's daughter. Buxtehude assumed his new post on April 11, 1668, and on August 3, in fulfillment of this contract, married Anna Margreta Tunder.

Buxtehude held this position for forty years, acquiring a remarkable and widespread reputation as an organ virtuoso and composer. The young Johann Sebastian Bach walked two hundred miles to Lübeck to hear Buxtehude perform. Handel also made a pilgrimage to Lübeck in 1770, though more, apparently, in an effort to obtain Buxtehude's post than to hear his music.

Discussing Buxtehude's powers as a performer, A. Eaglefield Hull wrote: "There is no doubting that Buxtehude was a remarkable player who exploited all the possible effects of his magnificent, probably unique, instrument. His works prove it. To mention one point only, his music contains more directions than Bach's for rapid changes of keyboard; and whereas it is possible to play through Bach's pieces without changing manuals, it is not possible to do so with Buxtehude's organ music."

Besides achieving fame as an organist and composer, Buxtehude is noted for the concerts (*Abendmusiken*) which he arranged in Lübeck beginning in 1673. These performances, among the first public concerts ever given on the Continent, took place on five consecutive Sundays before Christmas and featured organ music, other forms of instrumental music, and music for chorus and orchestra, much of it of Buxtehude's own creation.

Dietrich Buxtehude died in Lübeck on May 9, 1707.

The greatest significance of Buxtehude in the development of instrumental music rests in his many remarkable compositions for organ. He wrote chaconnes, chorale preludes, fantasias, fugues, passacaglias, preludes, and toccatas in which these structures were developed and extended far beyond the limits previously established by his predecessors. At the same time he filled these molds with an unprecedented richness of thematic development, inventiveness in color and effect, emotional impact, and virtuosity in keyboard performance. C. Hubert Parry said: "Buxtehude's whole manipulation of detail, harmony, phraseology and structure is singularly mature and full of life. The breadth and scope of his works, his power of putting things in their right places, his daring invention, the brilliancy of his figuration, the beauty and strength of his harmony, and above all a strange tinge of Romanticism which permeated his disposition, as Spitta has justly observed, marked him as one of the greatest composers of organ music, except the one and only Johann Sebastian Bach. And in Johann Sebastian Bach's organ works the traces of the influence of Buxtehude are more plentiful than those of any other composer. It is not too much to say that unless Dietrich Buxtehude had gone before, the world would have had to do without some of the most lovable and interesting traits in the divinest and most exquisitely human of all composers."

It is the belief of Cecil Gray, among others, that the form in which Buxtehude produced some of his richest invention was the chorale prelude, of which pieces like *Ich dank dir, lieber Gott, In Dulci jubilo* and *Nun bitten wir dem heil'gen Geist* are notable examples. Buxtehude raised the chorale prelude "to an unexampled pitch of elaboration and enriched [it] with every conceivable device of contrapuntal and decorative resource at his disposal. In his hands, indeed, the theme is frequently so varied and adorned with arabesques as to become totally unrecognizable, and even when presented textually it is often hidden from sight altogether under the exuberant welter of ornamentation with which it is surrounded."

In addition to his organ music, Buxtehude's church cantatas were an important influence on Bach. A medium of limited artistic dimensions for his predecessors, Sweelinck and Scheidt, the church cantata gained with Buxtehude such profound religious feeling and exaltation, as for example in *Alles was ihr Tut,* that one can readily understand A. Eaglefield Hull's comment: "As John the Baptist was to Christ, so was . . . Buxtehude to Bach."

Explaining the immense appeal that Buxtehude's work had for his contemporaries, Romain Rolland said: "Writing for a concert public, and not for religious service, he felt the need of making his music a kind which would appeal to everyone. . . . Buxtehude avoided in his music the ornate and clustering polyphony which was really his métier. He sought nothing but clear, pleasing and striking designs, and even aimed at descriptive music. He willingly sacrificed himself by intensifying his expression, and what he lost in abundance he gained in power. The homophonic character of his writing, the neatness of his beautiful melodic designs of a popular clarity, the insistence of the rhythmic and repetition of phrases which sink down into the heart are all essentially Handelian traits. No less in the magnificent triumph of his ensembles, his manner of painting in bold masses of light and shade."

PRINCIPAL WORKS

Chamber Music—Sonatas for strings and continuo.

Choral Music—Missa Brevis; numerous cantatas.

Organ Music—Chaconnes, chorale preludes, fantasias, fugues, passacaglias, preludes, toccatas.

ABOUT

Hutchings, F., Dietrich Buxtehude: The Man, His Music, His Era; Moser, H. J., Dietrich Buxtehude: Der Mann und sein Werk; Pirro, A., Buxtehude.

Chesterian, January-February 1933; Monthly Musical Record, July 1920; Musical Quarterly, October 1937.

William Byrd *1543-1623*

WILLIAM BYRD, one of the earliest masters of English music and a major figure of the Tudor period, was born in 1543, probably in Lincolnshire. Nothing is known of his parents and little about his childhood and youth. It is known, however, that he attended the St. Paul's School for a while, and strongly believed that at least part of his music instruction came from Thomas Tallis.

The first authenticated date in Byrd's life is February 27, 1563, the day he was appointed organist of Lincoln Cathedral. In 1568 he married Juliana Birley, who bore him six children. From 1570 to the end of his life he was Gentleman of the Chapel Royal, sharing the post of organist with Tallis from 1572 on, and after Tallis' death in 1585 occupying it by himself.

On January 22, 1575, Byrd and Tallis received from Queen Elizabeth an exclusive patent for printing music and selling music paper. Their first publication was *Cantiones sacrae* in five and six voices, issued in 1575, and dedicated to the Queen; to this volume Byrd contributed eighteen motets and Tallis sixteen. They were the first Latin motets ever written and issued by English composers.

Byrd and Tallis fared so poorly with their exclusive patent that in 1577 they were forced to petition the Queen for an annuity to help them over a difficult financial period. The Queen's assistance enabled them to continue to operate their firm. When Tallis died Byrd became its sole proprietor, and issued several volumes of his works: *Psalmes, Sonnets and Songs of Sadnes and Pietie* in 1588; a volume of *Cantiones sacrae* and *Songs of Sundrie Natures* in 1589; a second set of *Cantiones sacrae* in 1591; two sets of *Gradualia,* in 1605 and 1607; and *Psalmes, Songs and Sonnets,* in 1611. He also completed, in or about 1591, a monumental collection of forty-two pieces for the virginal, entitled *My Lady Nevell's Booke* (Lady Nevell was probably one of Byrd's pupils).

Until about 1593, Byrd resided in or near London, for some time in the house owned by the Earl of Worcester. In 1593 he acquired a two-hundred-acre farm in Stondon Massey, near Ongar, Essex, and lived there for the rest of his life. Between 1593 and 1605 he was so completely involved in various litigations concerning the ownership of his farm that he wrote little music and published none. This long silence was broken at last with the appearance of his first volume of *Gradualia* in 1605.

William Byrd died in Stondon Massey, on July 4, 1623. Upon his death Byrd was reverently referred to in the Chapel Royal check book as "Father of Musicke." Contemporaries of Byrd, and the succeeding generation, often spoke of him as "the miracle man" and "the parent of British Music."

Few of the early masters of English music are more deserving of the latter sobriquet. With little or no precedent or tradition to guide him, Byrd helped to create, virtually alone, the first important Latin and English church music in England. His Latin church music includes over 250 motets, together with three Masses and one volume of Lamentations; for the English church he wrote anthems and services. W. H. Hadow regards the Masses as "the finest of their kind ever written by an English composer, and of the highest rank the world over. Not Lassus or Palestrina ever rose to a loftier and more serene eminence." E. H. Fellowes regards Byrd as the "supreme master" of the motet. "Every phase of religious sentiment is expressed, whether penitential, meditative, supplicatory, or laudatory; a great variety of style and treatment is also shown in the musical setting of the words, though of course the unaccompanied, or *a cappella*, principle is uniformly observed."

His achievement in English church music is hardly less remarkable; the *Short Service* is a characteristic product. Fellowes remarks: "The more we study this so-called *Short Service* of Byrd, the more we appreciate his outstanding genius; the melodic beauty and molding of each phrase, the perfection of treatment as regards verbal accentuation, and the well-balanced schemes of modulation by which the interest is sustained, call for the highest admiration. As a model for the more concise type of English Service, this little work is nearly perfect, and in its own line it has never yet been surpassed."

Today most music lovers know the composer best through his madrigals, songs, and keyboard music. Here, too, his importance as a pioneer and a creative force can hardly be exaggerated. His were the first madrigals and songs by an English composer. His pieces for the virginal were also the first in England to be written originally for an instrument; up to his time the only instrumental music in England consisted either of popular dances or adaptations of vocal polyphonic music.

Byrd's first piece of secular music was the madrigal "Though Amaryliss Dance in Green," which appeared in 1588 in his collection, *Psalms, Sonnets, and Songs of Sadnes and Pietie,* and is still regarded as one of his best. Several others are hardly less distinguished, notably "Come to Grief, Forever," "I Thought My Love Had Been a Boy," "Lullaby, My Sweet Little Baby," "This Sweet and Merry Month of May," and "Why Do I Use My Paper, Ink and Pen." They do not attain the style, manner, and

WILLIAM BYRD

idiom that were still to be perfected by such masters of the English madrigal as Morley, Wilbye, or Gibbons. They are rather severe in style; the melodic line is sustained rather than broken up in phrases, and is concentrated in one voice; the subsidiary voices are accompaniments rather than polyphonic threads. In fact, these madrigals, many of which were written for a principal voice, with the subsidiary voices assigned to viols, are more like art-songs than the madrigal as we know it today: Byrd himself emphasized the solo-vocal character of his madrigals by referring to the principal voice as "the first singing part." But they bear enough resemblance to the Italian secular madrigal for us to regard them as the beginnings of the English madrigal school.

In addition to these works, Byrd wrote several truly remarkable art songs, one of which, "My Little Sweet Darling," is an acknowledged masterpiece. "This song," said Fellowes, "is an example of the perfect balance of interest between the voice part and the accompaniment which distinguishes the highest class of song. . . . 'My Little Sweet Darling,' composed at least as early as 1583, shows us that Byrd could write the perfect art song in which he provided an accompaniment of independent interest and importance, though at the same time it never hampers or detracts from the supremacy of the singer as the senior partner in the joint enterprise."

Byrd's importance in the field of instrumental music is no less decisive than his influence on vocal music—in Fellowes' words he is "the father of all keyboard music." Of the more than 140 pieces he wrote for the virginal eight (including *The Earl of Salisbury*) are found in *Parthenia*, the historic volume published in 1612 or 1613. This joint effort of Byrd, Orlando Gibbons, and John Bull was the first collection of music for virginal to be issued in England, and one of the first English music books to be printed from engraved plates. Many of Byrd's other compositions for the virginal are found in his collection *My Lady Nevell's Booke*.

Discussing these works, Fellowes wrote: "He had practically nothing upon which to build in the way of form or style. Virginal music in his hands was something entirely new, the outcome of his amazing originality, imagination, and fertility of invention." Among Byrd's most celebrated virginal pieces are *The Bells, The Carman's Whistle, The Earl of Oxford's March, The Earl of Salisbury, The Queen's Alman, Sellinger's Round,* and *Wolsey's Wilde*. The twentieth-century English composer Gordon Jacob transcribed three of these pieces—*The Bells, Earl of Oxford's March,* and *Wolsey's Wilde*—as a suite for modern orchestra.

Whatever his medium, Byrd was a true poet of tones. "The curve of his melodic line," wrote Wanda Landowska, the distinguished harpsichordist, "which is both sinuous and ornamental, is full of sweetness with a content fresh and savory." Iconoclast and innovator, dreamer and poet, Byrd was one of the brightest lights of the Elizabethan era and one of the glories of its music.

PRINCIPAL WORKS

Chamber Music—Fantasias, In Nomine's and various other pieces for viols.

Choral Music—3 Masses; over 250 motets; anthems, English services, rounds.

Virginal Music—Allemandes, airs, fantasias, galliards, grounds, pavanes, preludes, variations and other pieces.

Vocal Music—Various songs for voice and accompaniment; vocal duets, trios.

ABOUT

Bacharach, A. L. (editor), The Music Masters, vol. 1; Fellowes, E. H., English Madrigal Composers; Fellowes, E. H., William Byrd: A Short Account of His Life and Works; Foss, J. H. (editor), The Heritage of Music, second series; Howes, F., William Byrd.

Giulio Caccini *1546-1618*

TOGETHER WITH Jacopo Peri, Giulio Caccini was one of the founding fathers of opera. Born in Rome (the reason for his sobriquet, "Romano"), in or about 1546, he received instruction in singing from Scipione della Palla. In 1564 he went to Florence and found employment as a singer and lutist at the court of the Grand Duke of Tuscany. Except for a brief return to Rome in 1592 and a visit to Paris in 1604, he lived in Florence for the rest of his life.

As a member of the *Camerata*, a group which met regularly at the palace of Giovanni Bardi to discuss art, Caccini shared the aspiration to create a new kind of music, dramatic in orientation, and based on the forms of Greek drama. He thus helped to bring about the new style of monody and with it the new form of *dramma per musica*, or opera. (For a more detailed account of the Camerata and the birth of opera see sketch on Emilio del Cavaliere.)

Caccini's early compositions consisted of madrigals in the prevailing polyphonic style. As a member of the Camerata, however, he started to write music in a new declamatory idiom. His first productions in this vein were several recitatives, which he would sing to his own accompaniments. He then used the monodic style to provide settings for several scenes by Bardi. There is good reason to believe that a few of his recitatives were interpolated into Peri's opera *Dafne;* it is known that he contributed several vocal pieces to Peri's second opera, *Euridice*, which was performed on October 6, 1600. Caccini also wrote his own musical settings to the texts of Rinuccini's *Dafne* and *Euridice,* which Peri had used before him. Since Caccini's *Euridice* was issued early in January 1601, he has won the distinction of having written the first opera to be *published*. However, the performance of his *Euridice,* at the Palazzo Pitti on December 5, 1602, postdates not only Peri's *Euridice,* but another opera, *Il Rapimento di Cefalo,* on which Caccini had collaborated with several others and which was performed at the Palazzo Vecchio on October 9, 1600.

The operas of Peri and Caccini were made up almost entirely of monodies or recitatives which carried the story line. Variety was introduced through the interpolation of choruses and ballet numbers—but hardly

Caccini: kät-chē′nē

enough to prevent monotony. A small ensemble of lutes, a lyre, and a harpsichord provided instrumental accompaniment.

Pietro della Valle has described the typical mode of performing opera for the general public in Caccini's day. A cart would bring the opera company to the public square, where the opera was given several times a day. So great was the appeal of this new art form that "there were some who even continued following our cart to ten or twelve different places where it stopped, and who never quitted us as long as we remained in the street, which was from four o'clock in the evening until after midnight."

In 1602 Caccini produced an important set of madrigals for solo voice and accompaniment, entitled *Le Nuove musiche (The New Musics)*. With this publication, the new style of recitative or monody was fully defined and identified. In his preface to this volume Caccini elucidated not only his aim in writing these madrigals in the new monodic style, but also the artistic goal of the *stilo rappresentativo*, the name by which the new monodic style came to be known. "These wise and noble personages have constantly strengthened me and with the most lucid reasons determined me to place no value upon that music which makes it impossible to understand the words and thus [destroys] the unity and meter and sometimes [lengthens] them in order to suit the counterpoint—a real mangling of the poetry. But they have influenced me to hold to the principle so greatly extolled by Plato and other philosophers: 'Let music be, first of all, language and rhythm, and secondly tone, but not vice-versa.' "

Caccini's *Nuove musiche* was an epoch-making work, in which the break with the older polyphonic style becomes complete, heralding the new age of homophony. "It must be confessed," said Giovanni Battista Doni, Caccini's contemporary, "that we owe to him in great measure the new and graceful manner of singing, which at that time spread itself all over Italy; for he composed a great number of airs which he taught to innumerable scholars." Other distinguished contemporaries were no less appreciative of Caccini's contributions. The *abbate* Angelo Grillo called him "the father of the new style of music," while Bardi of the Camerata went so far as to maintain that Caccini "attained the goal of perfect music."

But Robert Marchal is probably right in asking that "we permit the *Nuove musiche* and *Euridice* to rest quietly in their eternal sleep" and not do the composer "the evil service of awakening them." Marchal continues: "With a strong conscience he worked at the foundations of a structure which greater talents have built up. But let us remember that their author was a workman of first importance, and that he pointed out direction to those who followed him—the realm of Song—which worthier and stronger souls than he were to enrich and ennoble."

Caccini's daughter, Francesca, was a professional singer; she appeared as Euridice in Peri's opera when it was introduced. She also composed an opera, *La Liberazione di Ruggiero*, in 1625.

Giulio Caccini died in Florence, Italy, on December 10, 1618.

PRINCIPAL WORKS

Choral Music—Madrigals.

Operas—Dafne; Euridice; Il rapimento di Cefalo (in collaboration with others).

ABOUT

Ehrichs, A., Giulio Caccini; Henderson, W. J., Some Forerunners of Italian Opera; Walker, D. P., Les Fêtes de la Renaissance.

La Revue musicale, June 1925.

Giacomo Carissimi *1605-1674*

GIACOMO CARISSIMI, the first significant composer of oratorios, was born in Marino, near Rome, in 1605. Biographical information on him is very meager: We know that between 1624 and 1627 he was employed at the Cathedral of Tivoli, first as a singer, later as organist. For a short period thereafter he served as *maestro di cappella* in Assisi. From 1628 to the end of his life he was *maestro di cappella* at S. Apollinare in Rome. Through his work as a teacher, composer, and church musician he exerted a powerful influence on the music of his times. His many pupils included Alessandro Scarlatti, Marc-Antoine Charpentier, Bassani, and Bononcini. Carissimi died in Rome on January 12, 1674.

Carissimi is one of the important links between the polyphonic age that preceded him and the dawning period of homophonic music; in his works the old art and the new are skillfully fused. He had extraordinary ability as a contrapuntist, but he parted with the purely polyphonic style of masters like Palestrina by including in many of his works recitatives that ranged in style from the *secco* variety to the highly lyric and expressive, and by employing instrumental accompaniments.

"The impetuous reformers in the style of Galilei," wrote Karl Nef, "quite unreasonably desired to forget completely the old choral art. However, they soon found themselves compelled to borrow from it, and a complete amalgamation took place in the case of Carissimi, who treated the chorus in his oratorios in as masterly a manner as he did the solo, and with consummate skill allowed them to relieve and supplement one another. He stripped the realistic elements which had long cleaved to the new music. In his compositions, the new style confronts us in perfect clarity. Carissimi advances to a classical purity, and he was fully conscious of the fact, for he had achieved it only through struggle."

Carissimi's outstanding contributions to music are his oratorios, in which that art form was formalized for the first time. The term "oratorio" is derived from the church oratory (Italian *oratorio*) in which sermons were delivered by St. Philip Neri, the mid-sixteenth century founder of the Oratorians, or Fathers of the Oratory. St. Philip Neri prefaced and followed his sermons with musical dramatizations of episodes from the Scriptures—an innovation that encouraged several early polyphonic composers to write religious music in a similar vein. Among these were Kapsberger, who in 1622 wrote the *Apotheosis* for the canonization of St. Ignatius Loyola and St. Francis Xavier, and Vittorio Loreto and Domenico Mazzocchi. Although these early efforts produced settings to sacred texts, written for solo voices, chorus, and orchestra, they did not embody the techniques which later distinguished the oratorio form. It was Carissimi who established most of the conventions and procedures of the oratorio.

Carissimi wrote several oratorios, of which *Jepthe*. written in or about 1660, is the most important. Carissimi was one of the first composers to dispense with scenery and costumes in the presentation of his oratorios. He was one of the first to introduce the character of a Narrator (or Historicus), to maintain the story's pace. (In *Jepthe* the part is assigned not to a single person, as is the case with later oratorios, but to various male and female soloists.) Dramatic or lyrical recitatives, or monodies, alternate with stirring choruses to describe the various episodes in the story. Dissonances were employed to heighten tragic incidents. Because these essential features of the later oratorios are so clearly visible in *Jepthe,* the work is often singled out by the historian as the first modern oratorio.

Carissimi also wrote several notable chamber cantatas, of which *The Judgment of Solomon* is perhaps the best known.

To Cecil Gray the distinguishing traits of Carissimi's music are a "pathos and a sweetness which sometimes hover perilously on the verge of sentimentality and effeminacy."

PRINCIPAL WORKS

Choral Music—Oratorios, including Jepthe; cantatas, Masses, motets.

Opera—L'Amorose passioni di Fileno.

ABOUT

Massenkeil, G., Die Oratorische Kunst in de lateinischen Historien und Oratorien Giacomo Carissimis; Schering, A., Geschichte des Oratoriums; Vogel, E., Die Oratorientechnik G. Carissimis.

Archiv für Musikwissenschaft, January 1956; Musical Quarterly, April 1962.

Alfredo Catalani *1854-1893*

ALFREDO CATALANI, distinguished Italian opera composer, was born in Lucca on June 19, 1854. His father, the organist of the San Frediano Church in Lucca, gave him his first music lessons; the boy then studied with F. Magi, a local teacher. When Catalani was only fourteen, he wrote an ambitious four-part Mass which was performed in the Lucca Cathedral. On the basis of this composition he gained admission to the Paris Conservatory without the formality of an entrance examination. At the conservatory he studied composition with Bazin.

After returning to Italy in 1873, Catalani attended the Milan Conservatory for two years. His first stage work, *La Falce*, was a one-act opera with libretto by Arrigo Boito; it was performed in July 1875. This work was followed by a full-length opera, *Elda,* introduced in Turin on January 31,

1880. *Elda* failed to attract much interest, and Catalani revised it radically several years later, retitling it *Loreley.* The new version, seen for the first time in Turin on February 16, 1890, was a great success which helped to establish the composer's fame in Italy and abroad. *Loreley* had its American première in Chicago on January 17, 1919; on March 4, 1922 it entered the repertory of the Metropolitan Opera. The "Danza delle Ondine" from *Loreley* became extremely popular with European salon and café orchestras.

An even greater triumph attended Catalani with *La Wally,* whose première took place at La Scala in Milan on January 20, 1892. The text, by Luigi Illica, was based on a novel by Wilhelmine von Hillern. Set in Switzerland in the nineteenth century, it recounts a love triangle, ending violently in the death of the two principal characters in an avalanche. Like *Loreley,* the opera boasts an orchestral dance episode that is often performed alone, the famous "Valzer dei fiori." *La Wally* was frequently performed by Arturo Toscanini; the conductor regarded the work so highly that he named his son after the heroine, Wally. It was Toscanini who led the American première of this opera at the Metropolitan Opera on January 6, 1909.

Unsophisticated in his musical style, leaning heavily on flowing lyricism and full-hearted emotion, Catalani enjoyed a huge vogue until the *verismo* movement in Italian opera outdated his works. There is, nevertheless, much to admire in such operas as *Loreley* and *La Wally.* "His melodies," says Donald Jay Grout, "are refined and musical, nearly always free of exaggerated pathos, supported by interesting and original harmony in a varied texture and with excellent balance of interest between voice and orchestra. . . . Along with some curious traces of 'Tristan chromaticism' there are experiments in modern devices (parallelism, augmented triads) which anticipate many of the characteristics of Puccini. The robust and vital rhythms are notable, especially in the choruses and dances of *La Wally.*"

In 1886 Catalani succeeded Ponchielli as professor of composition at the Milan Conservatory. Catalani died in Milan on August 7, 1893.

ALFREDO CATALANI

PRINCIPAL WORKS
Operas—Loreley; Dejanire; Edmea; La Wally. *Orchestral Music*—Ero e Leandro.

ABOUT
Bonaccorsi, A., Alfredo Catalani; Gatti, C., Catalani: la vita e le opere; Pardini, D. L., Alfredo Catalani.

Music and Letters, January 1954; Musical Quarterly, July 1937.

Emilio del Cavalieri *1550-1602*

EMILIO DEL CAVALIERI, one of the first composers to use the monodic style that led to the emergence of homophony, was born in or about 1550; the place of his birth is unknown. He was the son of a nobleman. After completing his instruction in music, he served as organist of the Oratorio del Santissimo Crocifisso in Rome from 1578 to 1584. Then he went to Florence, where from 1588 to 1596 he was Inspector General of Arts and Artists at the Tuscan Court. In 1589 he wrote music for an intermezzo performed at the marriage ceremonies of Ferdinand I, Grand Duke of Tuscany, and Christine of Lorraine.

In Florence, Emilio del Cavalieri became a member of a group of dilettantes, comprising noblemen and leading representatives of the city's cultural life, who met regularly at the palace of Giovanni Bardi or Jacopo Corsi. This circle came to be known as the *Camerata,* or "the men who met in a

Cavalieri: kä-vä-lyâ´rē

chamber." Infected with the spirit of the Renaissance, its members hoped to revive the forms of the ancient Greek drama by combining music with plays on classical subjects. Since sixteenth-century polyphonic music was completely unsuitable for the purpose and demands of the stage, the Camerata concluded that a completely new kind of music was needed for dramatic purposes, a music which, as Giovanni Battista Doni explained a century later, would be "closer to that of classical times," and in which melody would be so prominent that "poetry could be clearly understandable." Turning for guidance to the Greeks—especially to Aristoxenus, who had said that song must be patterned after speech, and to Plato, who had maintained that music had to be "first of all language and rhythm, and secondly tone and not vice-versa,"—the Camerata devised a new style of music. It was modeled after speech patterns and inflections, and intended for a single voice with harmonic accompaniment rather than a group of simultaneous voices singing contrapuntally. This was the *stilo rappresentativo*, a monodic style that consisted of recitative or declamation.

The first to expound his theories on the *Nuove musiche*, or "New Music" as this style came to be called, was Vincenzo Galilei, a member of the Camerata, in a volume entitled *Dialogue of Ancient and Modern Music*, issued in 1581; this work has sometimes been described as the opening volley in the war against polyphony. It was Cavalieri, however, who first put this theory into practice. In 1590 he wrote music for two pastoral fables *(favole pastorali)* to texts by Laura Guidiccioni: *Il Satiro* and *La Disperazione di Fileno*. Another pastoral fable, *Il Giuoco della cieca*, was performed publicly in Florence in 1595. In both works the music consisted of declamations set against harmonic instrumental accompaniment. This *stilo rappresentativo* was soon used by Jacopo Peri for the first opera ever written, *Dafne* (see sketch of Peri).

Cavalieri's greatest work was *La Rappresentazione di anima e di corpo*, first performed in February 1600 in the Oratorio della Vallicella, St. Philip Neri's Church, in Rome. Because the première took place in the Oratorio, and because the musical term "oratorio" was derived from works performed there, Cavalieri's work was long designated by music historians as an oratorio, the first

of its kind. It is, however, nothing of the sort, but rather a three-act morality play or religious drama with music. The main characters are personifications of such concepts as Time, Life, Soul, Body, Pleasure, the Intellect, speaking in short recitatives which alternate occasionally with choral passages and four instrumental interludes. *La Rappresentazione* was as important in establishing the artistic validity of *Nuove musiche* as Peri's operas. It has historic interest in another way, too, as the first stage work to be divided into three acts.

The first stage performance of *La Rappresentazione* in modern times (possibly the first such performance since 1600) took place in Cambridge, England, on June 9, 1949. The text was translated into English by Professor Edward J. Dent.

PRINCIPAL WORKS

Choral Music—Il Satiro; La Disperazione di Fileno; Giuoco della cieca; La Rappresentazione di anima e di corpo; L'Ascensione del nostro signore.

ABOUT

Alaleona, D., Nuova musica; Guidiccioni-Nicastro, La Rappresentazione di anima e di corpo.

La Revue musicale, 1923; Rivista musicale italiana, 1929, 1951.

Francesco Cavalli *1602-1676*

P IER (PIETRO) FRANCESCO CAVALLI, who succeeded Monteverdi as the most significant figure in early Venetian opera, was born in Crema, Italy, on February 14, 1602. His father, Gian Battista Caletti-Bruni, was for forty years *maestro di cappella* at the Crema Cathedral. Francesco changed his name when the nobleman Cavalli became his patron and adopted him.

In 1617 Cavalli's patron brought the boy to Venice, where he was placed as chorister at St. Mark's Cathedral. Since Monteverdi was then the Cathedral's *maestro di cappella*, it is assumed that young Cavalli received some instruction from him. In 1627 Cavalli became a tenor at St. Mark's, and for several years after that followed a career as a church singer. But his personal contact with the great Monteverdi and Venice's importance as a center of operatic activity, with five theaters given over to operatic performance, inevitably turned Cavalli's interest to the stage. In 1639 he wrote his first opera, *Le Nozze di Teti e di Peleo.* It is with this work that the word "opera" was used for the first time: Cavalli called his stage work an *opera scenica,* rather than a *dramma per musica* as his predecessors had done.

Cavalli was an unusually prolific composer. Between 1639 and 1665 thirty-four of his operas were produced in Venice and elsewhere. The most important and successful were *Giasone,* given on January 5, 1649; *Serse,* presented on January 12, 1654, and four years later performed in France in connection with the marriage ceremonies of Louis XIV; and *Ercole amante,* written to inaugurate a new hall in the Tuileries in Paris, where it was introduced on February 7, 1662.

In 1640 Cavalli was appointed second organist of St. Mark's. He rose to the post of first organist in 1665, and in 1668 became *maestro di capella.* In 1660 and 1662 he visited France to attend performances of *Serse* and *Ercole amante.*

Cavalli died in Venice on January 14, 1676. Shortly before his death he wrote a Requiem to be performed at his own funeral; his wishes were respected. Cavalli was buried in S. Lorenzo in Venice.

Cavalli wrote over forty operas. His genius, says Romain Rolland, "dominated the whole of Italian opera writers in the seventeenth century." Cavalli introduced a new, unified dramatic concept, carried to his duets and choruses a heightened expressiveness, and was responsible for recitatives so lyrical that some are remarkably close to the aria in quality. Like Monteverdi, he paid great attention to the orchestra, often giving, as R. A. Streatfeild has written, "musical expression to the sights and sounds of Nature —the murmur of the sea, the rippling of the brook, and the tempestuous fury of the winds."

"Cavalli," wrote Henri Prunières, "speaks the language of his time and borrows from his master, Monteverdi, a part of his vocabulary. It is through the vigor, the freedom, the sparkle of his style, as well as by the richness of his speech, that he intrigues us. . . . If he is simple, if he pleases himself with consonant harmonies, it is not because of his incapacity to write a more complicated music . . . but because he has expressly chosen to do so."

PRINCIPAL WORKS

Choral Music—Requiem; Mass; antiphons, psalms, vespers.

Operas—Over 40 operas, including: Le Nozze di Teti e di Peleo; Giasone; Rosinda; Orione; Serse; Ciro; Erismena; Ercole amante; Scipione Africano; Mutio Scevola; Pompeo Magno; Coriolano; Eliogabalo.

ABOUT

La Laurencie, L. de, Les Créateurs de l'opéra français; Prunières, H., Cavalli et l'opéra vénitien au XVIIe siècle; Wiel, T., Francesco Cavalli.

Marc'Antonio Cesti *1623-1669*

LIKE CAVALLI, Cesti was a distinguished member of the early Venetian school of opera composers. He was born in Arezzo, Italy, on August 5, 1623. At his baptism he was christened Pietro Antonio Cesti, but throughout his life his publications identified him as Antonio Cesti, and that name was perpetuated for some time after his death. He is now known only as Marc'Antonio, probably a corruption of "Frate Antonio," as he called himself when he became a Minorite Friar.

As a choirboy at the Arezzo Cathedral, Cesti probably received instruction in music from the *maestro di capella,* Bartolomeo Ruscelli. After becoming a member of the Minorite Friars at fourteen, Cesti settled in Rome, where from 1640 to 1645 he studied with Carissimi and Abbatini. In 1645 Cesti established himself in Volterra as a teacher in the local seminary and *maestro di cappella* at the Cathedral. In 1648 he moved to Venice. There he wrote and produced his first opera, *Orontea,* in 1649. This highly successful work was revived in Venice in 1666 and 1683 and presented in Milan and Bologna between 1662 and 1669. After his second opera, *Cesare amante,* was acclaimed in 1651, Salvator Rosa, a contemporary, described Cesti as an "immortal . . . the leading composer of the day."

Sometime around 1650 Cesti was released from his religious vows. Apparently the authorities were quite willing to permit him to separate from the church, for his personal life was not above suspicion. Cesti proceeded to Florence where he was employed at the Medici court of Ferdinand II. He was summarily dismissed because of "reprehensible conduct," though the specific charge has never been explained. From

Cesti: chās'tē

Florence Cesti went on to Lucca, working as a singer there in the fall of 1650. In Lucca his third opera, *Alessandro il vincitor di se stesso,* was produced in 1654.

From 1659 to 1662 Cesti was a member of the papal choir in Rome. During this period he returned to Florence briefly to attend the première of one of his finest and most celebrated operas, *Dori,* introduced during the carnival of 1661. He was *Kapellmeister* to Archduke Ferdinand of Austria in Innsbruck from 1652 to 1668, his assignment in Innsbruck coinciding with his duties in Rome for the ten-year period between 1642 to 1662. Through the influence of Emperor Leopold I of Austria, Cesti was permitted to leave his post in Rome in order to concentrate on his work in Innsbruck. In 1669 he returned to Florence, where he died that year on October 14. His last opera, *Genserico,* had been produced in Venice ten months earlier, on January 31, 1669.

Cesti was esteemed by some of his contemporaries even more highly than were Monteverdi and Cavalli. A good deal of Cesti's popularity derived from his pleasing lyricism and sentiment. In comparing Cesti with Monteverdi and Cavalli, R. A. Streatfeild has said: "Those of his operas which remain to us show a far greater command of orchestral and vocal resources than Monteverdi or Cavalli could boast, but so far as real expression or sincerity are concerned, they are inferior to the less cultured efforts of the earlier musicians."

"In Cavalli," wrote Cecil Gray, "the balance between aria and recitative is more or less equal; in . . . Cesti, the arias definitely predominate in number, length, and significance. In the operas of the former the musical treatment generally coincides with the dramatic interest; in those of the latter, the situation is unfolded in dry and perfunctory recitative, and the musical development reserved for moments of dramatic repose. . . . In fact, he continually tends to sacrifice dramatic to lyrical expressiveness and . . . one finds in his work, to a far greater extent than in that of Cavalli an attempt to effect a compromise between the conflicting claims of monody and polyphony."

PRINCIPAL WORKS

Choral Music—Cantatas, canzonets, madrigals, motets.

Operas—Orontea; Cesare amante; Alessandro il vincitor di se stesso; L'Argia; Dori; Tito; Il Pomo d'oro; Le Disgrazie d'amore; Semiramide; La Germania esultante; Genserico.

ABOUT

Wellesz, E., Essays in Opera.

La Revue musicale, June 1928; Rivista musicale italiana, July 1923.

Emmanuel Chabrier *1841-1894*

A LEXIS-EMMANUEL CHABRIER was born in Ambert, Puy-de-Dôme, in the Auvergne region of France, on January 18, 1841. At six he started to take piano lessons. Four years later, while attending the *lycée* in Clermont-Ferrand, he also began to study violin. His father, however, had no intention of permitting Emmanuel to become a professional musician, insisting that the boy follow his own career in law. In 1856 the family settled in Paris, where Chabrier completed two years at the *lycée* before entering law school. He also continued to study piano with Édouard Wolff, and counterpoint and fugue with Semet and Hignard.

After completing his law studies in 1862, Chabrier was appointed to the Ministry of the Interior. During his eighteen years in the Ministry, he attempted to satisfy his urge to create music, writing little pieces for the piano and composing sketches for an opera. He also joined a musical circle that included such eminent French musicians as Vincent d'Indy, Gabriel Fauré, André Messager, and Henri Duparc. His interest in art was also nurtured through his close friendship with many distinguished French artists, including the Impressionist painter Édouard Manet.

On December 27, 1873, Chabrier married Marie Alice Dejean, the daughter of a theater manager; they had two sons. After his marriage Chabrier turned more earnestly to composition. He completed two operettas, *L'Étoile,* produced at the Bouffes-Parisiens in 1877, and *Une Éducation manquée,* which the Cercle de la Presse performed in 1879. Neither work was distinctive or successful.

In 1879 an overwhelming experience changed the course of Chabrier's life. On a visit to Munich, he heard a performance of Wagner's *Tristan und Isolde.* Its impact upon him was so overpowering that on leaving the opera house that night he vowed

Chabrier: shà-brē-ā′

to dedicate himself completely to music. The next year he gave up his post with the Ministry and directed his creative efforts toward works more serious than light opera. In 1881 he published an excellent suite of ten pieces for the piano, *Dix pièces pittoresques.* Four of these were later orchestrated by the composer and assembled into the symphonic *Suite pastorale.*

In 1883 Chabrier embarked on a three-month holiday in Spain. His fascinated impressions of the country, people, folk songs, and dances were embodied in a major orchestral work, the rhapsody *España,* which at last won him wide recognition. Introduced at the Château d'Eau in Paris on November 4, 1883, with Lamoureux conducting, *España* proved an immediate triumph.

España is a fantasia in which Spanish melodies and rhythms are developed with extraordinary effect. Two of the melodies which Chabrier used, a *jota* and a *malaguena,* were native to Spain; a third was his own. The result was a "musical tableau possessing an extraordinary intensity of life," as Julien Tiersot wrote. "Across the seductive and intriguing rhythms of its themes one seems to perceive the contortions of Spanish dancers carried away as by some frenetic whirlwind. Strange associations of sounds . . . accumulations of harmonies which are so overcharged and so voluntarily incomplete, chords with free combinations, rhythms either broken or badly superimposed—this is what one perceives in this work which is so different from anything one has heard in France, Germany, or anywhere else."

In 1884 and 1885 Chabrier served as chorus master for the Lamoureux Orchestra. His work here inspired him to complete several choral compositions, including *La Sulamite,* a *scène lyrique* for mezzo-soprano and women's chorus, introduced on March 15, 1885. As chorus master Chabrier assisted in a production of two acts of *Tristan und Isolde,* an enterprise that enhanced his admiration for Wagner. In frank emulation of the Wagnerian style, he soon completed the opera *Gwendoline,* to a libretto by Catulle Mendès. Introduced at the Théâtre de la Monnaie in Brussels on April 10, 1886, *Gwendoline* was performed only once, because the opera company that had produced it went bankrupt before a second perform-

EMMANUEL CHABRIER

ance could be scheduled. But it was performed successfully in several cities in Germany and France from 1889 to 1893, and on December 27, 1893 it was produced by the Paris Opéra.

Chabrier's next opera was completely different in style, mood, and artistic aim. *Le Roi malgré lui* (with a text by Najac and Burani, based on a comedy by F. Ancelot) was, by comparison with *Gwendoline,* a light opera. Structurally it was an *opéracomique,* gay and tuneful in style. Yet Chabrier brought to his writing such strikingly original harmonic schemes and orchestration, such bold inventiveness, that many critics regard it as one of his major productions.

Le Roi malgré lui was introduced at the Opéra-Comique in Paris on May 18, 1887. By a bad stroke of luck, the Opéra-Comique burned down after the third performance of the work, and it could not be given until new quarters had been found. But *Le Roi malgré lui* was often performed, however, in Germany, and occasionally given in French cities outside Paris, establishing itself in time as a classic of the *opéra-comique* repertory. The composer Maurice Ravel once said that he would have preferred writing *Le Roi malgré lui* to composing Wagner's *Nibelungen Ring!*

Two important works for the piano followed *Le Roi malgré lui: Joyeuse marche,* later orchestrated by Chabrier, which was introduced in its symphonic version in Angers in 1888; and in 1891 the *Bourrée fantasque,* the composer's tribute to Auvergne, where the bourrée is believed to have originated. The second piano piece is also famous today in an orchestral adaptation by Felix Mottl, first performed in Karlsruhe in 1897. Charles Koechlin also transcribed *Bourrée fantasque* for orchestra.

During the last two years of his life Chabrier suffered a form of paralysis that affected his mind as well as his body. In a poignant letter, Chabrier's son André describes the strange reactions of the composer to a performance of his opera *Gwendoline* at the Paris Opéra in 1893. "He was applauding as though the work of another was being played. 'Very good, very good . . . wait, that isn't bad!' he said at certain passages. He laughed without cause, childishly, the bravos rose towards us, people looked at us, and in the shadow sunk into a corner on a chair, our mother was sobbing, and we two boys wept seeing her tears. He did not concern himself with anything, he was without thought and without strength."

While working on an opera, *Briséis* (libretto by Catulle Mendès), Chabrier died in Paris, on September 13, 1894. The one act which he had been able to complete was given a concert performance in Paris on January 31, 1897; it was staged by the Paris Opéra on May 8, 1899.

Cécile Chaminade described Chabrier as "caustic, full of animal spirits, brusque, and a 'good fellow.' This brilliant musician . . . had a very mercurial temperament. Ambitious, enthusiastic, and good-hearted, he was a loyal friend to those whom he liked. . . . He was subject to fits of profound melancholy, irritability and nervousness, which were the forerunners of the terrible malady which later took him from our midst. In more exalted moments, he passed all bounds in this enthusiasm for artists and people with whom he was in sympathy."

Chabrier was known for his caustic tongue, especially in talking to or about musicians whose ability he dismissed. "There are three kinds of music," he once said, "the good, the bad, and that of Ambroise Thomas." When Benjamin Godard said to him, "What a pity you applied yourself to music so late in life," Chabrier responded, "And what a pity you applied yourself to music so early."

He had a severe conscience and absolute integrity in judging his own music. "It will be performed," he said, "when I am satisfied with it; when I shall have terminated it after a conscientious and unhurried labor —or else I'll send it flying to the devil and it will not be performed. It will be good or it will not be at all. Everything costs me a great deal of trouble. I haven't what is known as facility."

A French critic once referred to Chabrier's musical style as *"le rire musical,"* the "musical laugh." Chabrier's idiom was generally light in touch, good-humored and sunny. "It has an air of mirth," said G. Jean-Aubry, "a frank and somewhat boisterous manner of presenting itself. There are some who stop at that and say, 'How funny!' as one might of some artist's prank, and they seek no further. And yet—he is a man who endeavors to conceal his heart with a laugh, who loves life, and finds in it a manifold enjoyment. . . . He had . . . a sense of true life, a genius for comic music that none has surpassed, unremitting fancy in the handling of the orchestra, overflowing imagination, and above all these a taste that remained surest in his most ardent mirth."

"He was the direct precursor of Ravel and Debussy, whose most daring effects he anticipated," wrote Gilbert Chase. "By his harmonic sensitiveness, and his extremely subtle, and at times, daring feeling for tonal relationships, he showed himself to be very much in advance of his times."

In the twentieth century Chabrier's music was adapted for two ballets, to choreography by George Balanchine. The first, *Cotillon,* adapted from several piano pieces, was introduced in Monte Carlo on April 12, 1932; the second, a classical ballet based on the music of the *Bourrée fantasque,* was presented by the New York City Ballet in New York on December 1, 1949.

PRINCIPAL WORKS

Choral Music—La Sulamite; Ode à la musique.

Operas—L'Étoile; Une Éducation manquée; Gwendoline; Le Roi malgré lui; Briséis (unfinished).

Orchestral Music—España; Suite pastorale; Joyeuse marche.

Piano Music—Dix pièces pittoresques; Capriccio; Habanera; Bourreé fantasque; Pièces posthumes; Valses romantiques, for two pianos.

Vocal Music—Songs for voice and piano, including Ballade de gros dindons, L'Île heureuse, and Villanelle des petits canards.

ABOUT

Cortat, A., French Piano Music; Desaymard, J., Emmanuel Chabrier; Desaymard, J. (editor), Chabrier d'après ses lettres; Martineau, R., Emmanuel Chabrier; Servières, G., Emmanuel Chabrier.

Music and Letters, April 1923; Musical Quarterly, October 1935; La Revue musicale, October 1926.

Marc-Antoine Charpentier *1634-1704*

MARC-ANTOINE CHARPENTIER, the important seventeenth century composer of French church music and operas, was born in Paris in 1634. As a young man he went to Italy to study painting, but was so impressed by the music of Carissimi that he arranged to study with the older composer. The influence of Italian church music, and of Carissimi's style, are apparent in all of Charpentier's later works.

Upon returning to Paris after completion of his studies, Charpentier was appointed *maître de chapelle* to the Dauphin. But he soon incurred the antagonism of the most powerful figure in French music, Jean Baptiste Lully, who was responsible for having Charpentier removed from his post. It has been said that this incident so antagonized Charpentier that he refused to accept Lully's ideas and principles as a musician. It is quite probable, however, that even had no enmity existed between the two composers, Charpentier would have remained faithful to the methods and styles he had assimilated from Carissimi. In any event, as soon as Charpentier began to compose for the French stage he aligned himself with the school opposing Lully and the French classic opera. By this paradox Lully, an Italian, was set up as the proponent of French opera, whereas the Italian tradition was represented by a Frenchman, Charpentier.

When Molière and Lully parted as collaborators, the great French playwright invited Charpentier to write the incidental music for his plays produced at the Théâtre Français. Their first effort was *Le Mariage forcé* in 1672, followed by *Le Malade imaginaire* in 1673. After Molière's death in 1673, Charpentier continued to write incidental music (*intermèdes*) for the theater until about 1685. His music for Thomas Corneille's tragedy *Circé* was particularly well received in 1675.

From 1680 to 1686 Charpentier was *maître de chapelle* and music teacher to the Princesse de Guise. In or about 1684 he was also *maître de chapelle* of a Jesuit collegiate church and monastery, for which he wrote several *tragédies spirituels*. One of these, *Miserere des Jésuites,* has been recorded on a long-playing disc.

Of the approximately sixteen operas which Charpentier composed, the most important is *Médée,* written to a text by Thomas Corneille and introduced at the Paris Opéra on December 4, 1693. Although it made a profound impression on many leading musicians in Paris—some considering it the most important opera that had appeared since Lully's works—*Médée* was given only one performance. Its prompt removal from the Paris Opéra repertoire was due, doubtless, to the cabals and intrigues of the Lullists, and their objections to what they regarded as Italian procedures and methods. *Médée* reveals greater intellectual power and musical scholarship than Lully's operas, more talent in declamatory writing, and richer invention in orchestration. In all these respects it anticipates Rameau. However, *Médée* never rises to Lully's eloquence of lyricism and choral writing or his dramatic strength.

Despite his long preoccupation with the opera, Charpentier is most important as a writer of church music. He was the first composer to introduce the Latin oratorio, and the dramatic and expressive style of Carissimi, in France. By combining these Italian influences with native French refinement and sophistication, Charpentier evolved a style which produced some of the most forceful, original, and inventive religious choral music created in France up to his time. Charpentier completed about 150 such works, including oratorios, Masses, psalms, motets, Te Deums, and *Histoires sacrées* or dramatizations of episodes from the Bible. Among his most significant church compositions are the *Midnight Mass* (based on tunes from old French church carols); the Mass *Assumpta est Maria;* the oratorio *Le Reniement de Saint-Pierre* (successfully revived in Paris and recently recorded); and the motet *Oculi omnium.*

On June 28, 1698 Charpentier was appointed to the post which he held for the rest of his life, *maître de chapelle* of the Sainte-Chapelle Church in Paris. It was as a composer for these church performances that he wrote many of his finest and most

Charpentier: shȧr-päN-tyā′

ambitious religious works. Marc-Antoine Charpentier died in Paris on February 24, 1704.

PRINCIPAL WORKS

Chamber Music—Ballets des saisons; Concert; Caprice; minuets, Noëls, overtures, preludes.

Choral Music—Histoires sacrées; Tragédies spirituelles; Airs sérieux et à boire; Airs à boire sur des sujets plaisants; Salve Regina; Magnificat; Masses, motets, oratorios, psalms, Te Deums.

Operas—L'Inconnu; Les Amours d'Acis et de Galatée Endimion; Médée; Philomèle; pastorales; incidental music to various plays.

Vocal Music—Various songs and airs.

ABOUT

Brenet, M., Les Musiciens de la Sainte-Chapelle; Crussard, C., Un Musicien français oublié, Marc-Antoine Charpentier.

Musical Quarterly, January 1955; Zeitschrift der Internationalen Musikgesellschaft, May 1905.

Ernest Chausson *1855-1899*

ERNEST AMÉDÉE CHAUSSON was born in Paris on January 20, 1855. A banker's son, he was financially self-sufficient throughout his life. As a young man he was given ample opportunity to cultivate his natural interest in books, the arts, and travel. Directed initially to law, he became convinced at the age of twenty-five that he wanted to be a musician and entered the Paris Conservatory. For a short time he studied composition with Massenet, but he soon chafed at the formal and traditional curriculum of the Conservatory, and the academic restrictions imposed on him. Through Henri Duparc, Chausson met César Franck, was immediately impressed with the older composer's high-minded purpose, humility, and idealism, and left the Conservatory to study with Franck for three years. It was from Franck that Chausson drew his main inspiration and guidance as a man and as a composer. Franck introduced Chausson to abstract music, encouraged him to write compositions poetic in content, restrained in emotion, mystic in feeling, at times introspective, always written with complete integrity. Like Franck, Chausson accepted his obscurity and made no attempt to gain important performances or to court popularity. Although he composed relatively few works, they were musically significant.

Chausson's first important piece of music was *Viviane* (1882), a tone poem for orchestra based on an Arthurian legend. Guillaume Lekeu, another Franck disciple, described it as a "prolonged and delicious caress." Chausson's greatest works, and those by which he is best known today, were written between 1891 and 1898. The first, the Symphony in B-flat, completed in 1890, was performed in Paris at a concert of the Société Nationale on April 18, 1898. The music is often distinctly Wagnerian in its chromatic harmonies, dynamics, and orchestration. But its use of the cyclic form, the omission of a scherzo movement, and the brooding elegiac mood of the slow movement (*Très lent*) reveals also the influence of Franck.

Franckian, too, in nobility of thought, poetry of expression, and sensitivity of emotion are Chausson's next two works. The Concerto for Piano, Violin and String Quartet, introduced by Eugène Ysaÿe and his ensemble in Brussels on March 4, 1892, was described by G. Jean-Aubry as "one of the most important French chamber-music works of the end of the nineteenth century"; in any event it is the most significant of Chausson's works in a more intimate medium. The *Poème* for violin and orchestra was introduced in Paris by Eugène Ysaÿe with the Colonne Orchestra, on April 4, 1897.

In the monumental Symphony, the Concerto, and *Poème,* Chausson revealed, as Julien Tiersot wrote, "a greater sureness of touch, greater authority and mastery" than in any of his earlier works. "They are luminous, airy, full of joyous and vibrant power. . . . Here he had the soul of a poet; his melodies . . . are exquisite."

Vincent d'Indy, another of Franck's students, regarded Chausson's chamber music as his most outstanding achievement. In this category we find not only the Concerto, mentioned above, but also a piano trio, piano quartet, and violin sonata. Here, said d'Indy, "his art is revealed more completely than even in his dramatic or symphonic works. It is in this branch, especially, that his ascent towards the highest becomes assured, and it is here that the transformation is seen in continuous—one might almost say in gradual—fashion of the richly endowed scholar into the master called to tread the loftiest summits of music."

Chausson: shō-sôn′

During most of his mature life, Chausson lived in Limay, in the Seine-et-Oise region, with his wife and five children. His house was a virtual museum, designed by Henri Lerolle and filled with paintings by the French Romantics and Impressionists. Some of the furnishings in his home were adapted to meet his comforts and needs, as, for example, a table with a built-in miniature piano.

"His library," revealed Pierre de Bréville, "showed the breadth of his intelligence, the various subjects in which he was interested. He had collected memoirs, legends, the literature of all peoples, poets, philosophers. He had read these books, so that one could not see how in so short a life he had accomplished so much in so many ways."

In June 1899 Chausson, riding a bicycle near his home, lost control of the wheel and smashed into a wall. Internal injuries and a fractured skull proved fatal. He died in Limay on June 10, 1899.

In a memorial article published soon after Chausson's death, Pierre de Bréville wrote: "Chausson, like César Franck, was unknown during his lifetime. He did not occupy the public place to which he had a right. Directors of concerts thought little about him, managers of theaters were not curious about his opera, and the newspapers were as a rule unkind or silent. . . . He was interested in the music of his colleagues; their success brought him joy. He was ingenious in his methods of bringing young talent before the public; he was always ready to render them any service in a delicate manner. If he met with ingratitude, he did not mind it, for kindness was natural to him, and he was generous because he was in love with generosity."

This is the critical estimate of Chausson's music by G. Jean-Aubry: "When he is himself, Chausson is nearly unequaled. Others have more charm, more power, more refinement; others succeed better in investing our minds by all avenues of our curiosity, but none has greater purity than he. . . . Chausson's scrupulous soul is incapable of evasion. At every moment we see it face to face in its entirety. . . . When he is himself, his emotion is pure and noble, with nothing to make us feel that it claims to outrage us. On the contrary, it is there, at our side, in a discreet attitude, waiting gently medita-

ERNEST CHAUSSON

tive for us to pay attention to the simple, lasting word it utters. . . . Chausson's soul is revealed . . . diverse in its constant purity, passing from juvenile and serious freshness to the melancholy to which his mature mood was more conducive. . . . Where he is himself, one can only cherish him; and even when he is not himself, as in the Symphony, where the figures of Wagner and Franck are too closely indicated, he still succeeds in infusing a charm that is his only, and which makes bearable the avowal of discernible influences."

PRINCIPAL WORKS

Chamber Music—Piano Trio; Concerto in D major for Violin, Piano and String Quartet; Piano Quartet in A major; String Quartet (unfinished).

Choral Music—9 motets; Hymne védique; Chant nuptial; Chant funèbre; Ballata; Vêpres du Commun des vierges.

Operas—Les Caprices de Marianne; Hélène; Le Roi Arthur.

Orchestral Music—Viviane; Solitude dans les bois; Poème de l'amour et de la mer, for voice and orchestra; Symphony in B-flat major; Poème, for violin and orchestra; Soir de fête; Chanson perpétuelle, for voice and orchestra.

Piano Music—Cinq fantaisies; Quelques danses; Paysage.

Vocal Music—Chansons de Miarka; Serres chaudes; Chansons de Shakespeare; Deux poèmes; individual songs for voice and piano, including Ave Verum Corpus, Chanson perpétuelle, Le Colibri, La Nuit, Les Papillons, Les Temps des lilas.

ABOUT

Barricelli, J. P., and Weinstein, L., Ernest Chausson: The Composer's Life and Works; Cooper, M., French Music; Séré, O., Musiciens français d'aujourd'hui; Tiersot, J., Un demi siècle de la musique française; Weinstein, L. and Barricelli, J.-P., Ernest Chausson.

La Revue musicale, December 1925.

Luigi Cherubini *1760-1842*

MARIA LUIGI CARLO ZENOBIO SALVATORE CHERUBINI was born in Florence on September 14, 1760. He was the tenth of twelve children. At the age of six he began to study music, first with his father, cembalist of the Pergola Theater, then with various teachers, including Felici and Castrucci. Cherubini proved remarkably precocious. At twelve he wrote an ambitious Mass that was performed publicly. Between his thirteenth and seventeenth years he completed several more Masses, two cantatas, an oratorio, a magnificat, a Miserere, and a Te Deum. His talent attracted the interest of the Duke of Tuscany, who persuaded Emperor Leopold II to provide Cherubini with the funds to travel to Venice and study with Giuseppe Sarti.

At the age of nineteen Cherubini completed his first opera, *Quinto Fabio.* Introduced in Alessandria in fall 1780, it proved a failure. Despite this inauspicious beginning, Cherubini continued to write opera prolifically, and with greater success. Three works were performed in 1782, one in 1783, two in 1784, and three in 1785. The most successful, *Alessandro nell'Indie,* was introduced in Mantua in 1784. Cherubini's first operas were faithful to the formulas and traditions of the Italian school—its florid melodies, large-scale production, and stilted librettos (by Metastasio and others) based on history and legend.

A transitional period began for Cherubini in 1784 when he was invited to London. There four new operas were produced: *Demetrio,* on January 8, 1785; *La Finta principessa,* on April 2, 1785; *Artaserse,* on April 16, 1785; and *Giulio Sabino,* on March 30, 1786. Although none of these works was particularly successful. Cherubini was favored by the Prince of Wales, and for a year was given the honorary office of composer to King George III. The distinguished music historian Charles Burney, who became acquainted with Cherubini between 1785 and 1786, thought him "a young man of genius. . . . who . . . is now traveling fast to the Temple of Fame."

After a year in England, Cherubini lived in Paris for a year, then visited his native Italy briefly to attend the production of his thirteenth opera, *Ifigenia in Aulide,* in Turin in February 1788.

Upon his return to France Cherubini established permanent residence in Paris, and began to write the operas that demark a new creative phase. The first, *Démophon,* written to a libretto by Marmontel, was given by the Paris Opéra on December 5, 1788. Here Cherubini broke permanently with Italian tradition. Influenced by the works of Gluck and Rameau and having newly become acquainted with Haydn's symphonies, Cherubini began to enrich his harmonic and orchestral writing, emphasize its lyric qualities, and seek out dramatic values. *Lodoïska,* heard at the Théâtre Feydeau on July 18, 1791, opened new horizons for opera with its remarkably advanced harmonic thinking and startling orchestral effects. "The first performance of *Lodoïska,*" says Paul Henry Lang, "was an event in the history of the lyric stage that ranks with the presentation of Gluck's *Iphigénie* and Mozart's *Don Giovanni.*" It received two hundred performances in its first year.

Médée, one of the two operas by Cherubini that are most frequently revived, had its première at the Théâtre Feydeau on March 13, 1797. "The sternness of the characters, the mythological background and above all the passion of Medea herself," wrote Alfred Loewenberg, "must have seized his imagination and inspired him with those poignant accents of grief, jealousy, and hatred in which *Médée* abounds." Beethoven's admiration of *Médée* is well known; the overture to the Cherubini opera is believed to have been the inspiration for Beethoven's *Egmont Overture.* Brahms was once quoted as having said of *Médée,* "This is what we musicians among ourselves recognize as the highest dramatic music."

The American stage première of *Médée* took place as recently as 1958, in San Francisco, more than 160 years after the first performance. Prior to that the opera was heard only in concert performance in New York.

Cherubini: kā-roō-bē′nē

A second work that has enjoyed great popularity in recent years is *Les Deux journées*, or, as it is known in Germany, *Der Wasserträger*. Its first performance took place at the Théâtre Feydeau in Paris on January 16, 1800. Frederick Niecks described this work as "overwhelming in tragic passion and immense in constructive musicianship." *Les Deux journées* is a notable example of the type then so popular in France, the so-called "rescue opera" (Beethoven's *Fidelio* is another example.) Count Armand and his wife are rescued from the clutches of Mazarin, with whom they have lost favor. Their rescuer is Michele, a water carrier who conceals them in a water barrel and thus helps them to escape from Paris. "*Les Deux journées*," wrote Donald Jay Grout, "added still another emotional element in the form of frequent outbursts of the most exemplary sentiments of loyalty, kindness, and general devotion to the ideals of 'humanity,' with whom the 'good' characters of the libretto are fully identified. The music consists mostly of ensemble numbers which are developed usually at some length with more regard for musical than dramatic considerations." Among the finest of the ensemble passages are the popular chorus of the soldiers with which the second act opens, and the bridal chorus in the third act. The most famous aria is the first-act romance "Un Pauvre petit Savoyard," whose refrain is repeated several times throughout the opera.

Anacréon, which the Paris Opéra introduced on October 4, 1803, is remembered today only for its overture. At its first-night performance the opera was a fiasco, largely because of a preposterous libretto which provoked guffaws of laughter on the part of the audience, then shouts of disapproval. But the overture, music of rare nobility, is an orchestral work often represented on symphonic programs.

While writing operas Cherubini held a succession of important posts. For a while he was director of the Italian Opera in Paris. From 1789 to 1792 he was conductor of light opera at the Théâtre de Monsieur in the Tuileries. When the Conservatory was founded in 1795 Cherubini became one of its Inspectors. In his first year as Inspector, Cherubini married Cécile Tourette. They had a son and two daughters.

In July 1805 Cherubini was invited to Vienna to write an opera for the court the-

LUIGI CHERUBINI

ater. The result was *Faniska*, first performed at the Kärnthnerthor Theater on February 25, 1806. The composer and his opera were held in the highest esteem by the Viennese; one critic, discussing Beethoven's *Fidelio*, prophesied that some day *Fidelio* would rank as high as *Faniska*.

Les Deux journées was also performed in Vienna with great success. The troubled times, however, were not propitious for musical events. In November 1805 Napoleon and his French troops entered Vienna, throwing the city into turmoil. Cherubini was recruited by the invaders to arrange musical performances for Napoleon at Schönbrunn. Cherubini also had the opportunity during this period to meet Beethoven personally. His reaction to the master was simple: "He is always brusque."

After his return to France Cherubini continued to gather honors. During the Hundred Days he was elevated to the rank of Chevalier of the Legion of Honor. Though he had lost his post as Inspector of the Conservatory, he was compensated in 1816 with appointments as musician and superintendent of the King's Chapel and professor of composition at the Conservatory, as well as election to the Institut. In 1822 he rose to the post of director of the Conservatory, which he held with great distinction for about twenty years.

Though Cherubini wrote several operas after 1809, his most significant creative efforts were directed to sacred music. He produced several hundred works, including Masses, Kyries, the Requiem in D major, and numerous shorter works for various combinations of voices.

Cherubini's last years were spent in semiretirement in Paris, where he died on March 15, 1842. He was buried in the Père Lachaise cemetery.

The celebrated portrait of him by Ingres hangs in the Louvre. It shows him, as W. R. Anderson has written, "very handsome, even in old age, with . . . ascetic lips and waving silvery hair [reminding] us somewhat of the familiar pictures of Cardinal Newman."

His hobbies included drawing, botany, and billiards. He was notorious for his sharp tongue. When Napoleon confessed his preference for music that was neither loud nor complex, Cherubini replied quickly: "I see that Your Excellency prefers music that does not prevent him from thinking of matters of state." Asked by Halévy to express his reaction to one of Halévy's operas, Cherubini remained silent. "But master," pleaded Halévy, "you do not answer me." "Why should I answer you," retorted Cherubini, "if in your opera you have spoken to me for two hours and yet said nothing!"

J. Combarieu has pointed out the strong influence on Cherubini of his contemporaries. "He owes something to Gluck, to Haydn for his instrumentation, to Mozart for his treatment of voices. . . . He belongs between the old tradition of Italian music and the brilliant works of the nineteenth century, but more to the former than to the latter."

"Cherubini's finest works," said R. A. Streatfeild, "suffer from a frigidity and formality strangely in contrast with the grace of Grétry or the melody of Méhul, but the infinite resources of his musicianship make amends for the lack of inspiration, and Les Deux journées may still be listened to with pleasure, if not with enthusiasm. . . . The solidarity of his concert pieces and the picturesqueness of his orchestration go far to explain the enthusiasm which his works aroused in a society which as yet knew little, if anything, of Mozart."

What has been described as the first staged American performance of a Cherubini opera took place in San Francisco on September 25, 1954. On that occasion a long-forgotten Cherubini opera buffa was revived—The Portuguese Inn (L'Hôtellerie portugaise), originally presented in Paris in 1798. "The music as a whole," reported Alfred Frankenstein, "strongly recalls Mozart, with touches of Rossinian earthiness and irony." In the spring of 1960 the city of Florence celebrated the bicentenary of Cherubini's birth by reviving still another long forgotten work, Elisa (1794). "The sheer silliness of the libretto," commented Francis Toye, "makes it a thoroughly unsatisfactory opera, precluding any likelihood of restoration to the contemporary repertory. The libretto of Elisa is so silly that it hampers the effects of the music. No composer could have made anything of such trash." Yet in spite of this handicap, Toye went on to say, Cherubini's music is of exceptional interest. "No musician . . . could listen to this score without being moved to admiration. It is all so beautifully done; the composition is so masterly, and the scoring, and the writing for the chorus especially, are so effective. Curiously, too, this music seems to look forward rather than back. We are somehow reminded of things still to come rather than things that went before. What a lot Beethoven, Weber and Rossini took from him!" But it was not only those three whose work owed much to Cherubini. By virtue of his long affiliation with the Paris Conservatory, he also exerted a profound influence on an entire generation of French musicians.

PRINCIPAL WORKS

Ballet—Achille à Scyros.

Chamber Music—6 string quartets; String Quintet in E minor.

Choral Music—17 Cantatas; 14 choruses; 11 solemn Masses; 2 Requiems; antiphons, hymns, Lamentations, Litanies, motets.

Operas—La Finta principessa; Artaserse; Didone abbandonata; Ifigenia in Aulide; Démophon; Lodoïska; Elisa; Médée; L'Hôtellerie portugaise; Les Deux journées (or Der Wasserträger); Anacréon; Faniska; Les Abencérages; Bayard à Mézières; Blanche de Provence; La Cour des fées; Ali Baba.

Orchestral Music—11 marches; 11 dances; Symphony in D major; Overture.

Piano Music—6 Sonatas; Grand Fantasia; Chaconne.

Vocal Music—4 sets of solfeggi; airs, duets, nocturnes, romances.

ABOUT

Bellasis, E., Cherubini: Memorials Illustrative of His Life; Blom, E., Stepchildren of Music; Crowest, F. Cherubini.

Monthly Musical Record, January-June 1916; Music and Letters, July 1924.

Frédéric Chopin *1810-1849*

FRÉDÉRIC FRANÇOIS CHOPIN, the foremost composer of music for the piano, was born in Zelazowa Wola, near Warsaw in February 1810. His father, Nicolas, was an Alsatian who had moved to Poland to teach French. There he married Justine Kryzanowska, a lady-in-waiting to Countess Skarbeck. Frédéric was the second of their four children.

While he was still an infant his family moved to Warsaw proper, where his father had been engaged to teach in a secondary school.

As a child Chopin revealed so phenomenal a gift for music that comparison between him and the young Mozart was inevitable. He started taking piano lessons from Adalbert Zwyny before he could read or write. At the age of nine he made a remarkable public appearance as pianist. By then he had also been writing music for some time: his first published composition, a Polonaise in G minor, had already been issued in 1817, and in 1817, too, another of his pieces, a march, had been performed by a military band. Soon Chopin's impressive talent won him entry to the most select salons in Warsaw, where he was pampered and given his first taste of elegance.

Zwyny remained Chopin's teacher until 1822. While attending high school Chopin started to study harmony and counterpoint with Joseph Elsner, director of the Warsaw Conservatory. From 1826 to 1829 he continued to study music with Elsner full time, at the Conservatory. Elsner combined a respect for rules and tradition with a sympathetic appreciation of the boy's individuality; under him Chopin made remarkable progress. Among the compositions he completed between 1825 and 1828 were the Rondo in C minor, op. 1, his earliest mazurkas and nocturnes, the first Piano Sonata, and the *Variations on "Là ci darem"* for piano and orchestra. "Frederic Chopin, third year student, reveals amazing capabilities and musical genius," was the comment noted on his Conservatory report.

Upon graduating with highest honors from the Conservatory in July 1829, Chopin visited Vienna. On August 11 and 18 he gave two concerts, at which he introduced his *Variations on "Là ci darem"* among other works. He made a profound impression

FRÉDÉRIC CHOPIN

both as a pianist and a composer. The *Allgemeine musikalische Zeitung* spoke of the "indescribable dexterity of his technique, the subtle finish of his gradations of tone, reflecting a profoundly sensitive nature, the clearness of his interpretation and of his compositions, which bear the mark of great genius." A Viennese publisher issued his *Variations.* But Chopin was homesick for Warsaw and for Constantia Gladkowska, the Warsaw Conservatory pupil with whom he had (unbeknownst to her) fallen in love. "How often do I tell my piano all that I should like to tell you!" he confided to a friend. "Six months have passed and not yet have I exchanged a single syllable with her of whom I dream every night." His suffering is expressed in the slow movement of his Second Piano Concerto, and in the Waltz in D-flat major, op. 70, no. 3.

Disheartened and increasingly restless, Chopin decided to leave Poland again for another series of European concert performances. Just prior to his departure, his teacher, Elsner, performed in Zelazowa Wola a cantata that he had written in Chopin's honor. Elsner then presented Chopin with a silver urn containing some Polish earth. Chopin left Poland on November 2, 1830. He was never to see his native land again.

Chopin's first stop was Vienna, where he stayed until July 1831. He gave two concerts, on April 4 and June 11, and haunted the offices of publishers, but met with indifference to his compositions and performances. Disappointed, he continued on to Germany. On September 8 in Stuttgart, Chopin heard the electrifying news that the Russians had just captured Warsaw. His first impulse was to return home to join the battle, but he was finally dissuaded by the pleas and arguments of his mother and friends. His patriotic ardor found expression, instead, in his celebrated Étude in C minor, op. 10, no. 12, known as the *Revolutionary Étude*.

A week later Chopin arrived in Paris and established residence there. Though he had planned only a brief visit, Paris remained his home for the rest of his life. Chopin met some of France's most prominent musicians. On February 26, 1832 he made his Paris début as pianist with a performance that made a deep impression on Meyerbeer, Ferdinand Hiller, and Liszt, among others. Fétis, the distinguished French critic, wrote in *La Revue musicale*: "Here is a young man who, by giving himself up to his natural impressions, and following no model, has discovered, if not an absolute revolution in piano music, at least something of what composers have been seeking in vain for a long time past, namely an abundance of original ideas whose type is nowhere to be found."

Before long Chopin had become one of Paris's most eagerly sought-after musicians: as a teacher, for the children of the rich and of the aristocracy; as a composer, by publishers; as a guest, in the most fashionable salons. Leading French musicians paid him homage. "I move," he wrote to a friend in 1833, "in the highest circles among ambassadors, princes and ministers, and I know not how I got there, for I did not in any way thrust myself forward." He was composing a great deal: preludes, mazurkas, polonaises, études, and other pieces. "He is the Ariel of the piano," said one French critic.

Descriptions of Chopin during this period have been provided by contemporaries. "I found myself," wrote Legouvé, "face to face with a pale, melancholy, elegant young man with a slight foreign accent, brown eyes of incomparable softness and limpidity, chestnut hair almost as long as that of Berlioz, and falling in a wisp to his brow." Franz Liszt said: "His whole person was harmonious. His glance was intelligent rather than dreamy; his soft, shrewd smile had no touch of bitterness. The fineness and transparency of his complexion charmed the eye, his fair hair was silky, his nose slightly aquiline, his movements well-bred, and his manners bore such an aristocratic stamp that one involuntarily treated him like a prince. His gestures were frequent and graceful. His voice was always toneless, and often indistinct; he was not very tall, and was slight of build."

In 1834 Chopin fell in love with Maria Wodzinska, a beautiful, dark-haired girl of sixteen. Consumed with emotion, he wrote several compositions for her, including the *Valse d'adieu*, op. 69, no. 1. Maria's parents were sympathetic to the match. But when Chopin fell seriously ill in the winter of 1835, Maria's father and uncle conspired to end their relationship.

In the fall of 1836, Liszt introduced Chopin to the famous writer Aurore Dudevant, better known under her pseudonym George Sand. She was five years older than Chopin, his very opposite in temperament and personality. Where he was sensitive, refined and effeminate, she was coarse and masculine; where he was decorous and almost prudish, she was unconventional and amoral. "How repellent that woman is," Chopin is reported to have said to a friend after their first encounter. "Is she really a woman?" When, during the summer of 1837, George Sand invited him to her château in Nohant, he declined politely but firmly.

The loss of Maria in 1837 plunged Chopin into extreme melancholy, a mood perhaps best reflected in the "Funeral March," which he wrote that year and later included in his Second Piano Sonata. Possibly in order to escape his depression, Chopin soon began to court George Sand. By the summer of 1838 they were often together. Chopin was dazzled by her penetrating mind, dynamic personality, strength of character, vibrance, and fierce independence; George Sand was drawn by his musical genius as well as his charm and elegant manners.

To avoid the attentions of another suitor, George Sand decided to spend the winter of 1838 on the island of Majorca. Chopin went with her and her two children. They settled first in Palma, where the wretched weather played havoc with Chopin's always delicate health. He coughed incessantly.

The citizens, suspecting that he suffered from tuberculosis, avoided personal contact with him or his companion. Chopin and George Sand left Palma for Valdemosa, settling in a deserted monastery. But Chopin's health continued to decline, and his mind began to harbor many fantasies and nightmares. "He became utterly demoralized," wrote George Sand. "He could bear pain with a fair amount of courage, but he could not control his uneasy imagination. Even when he was well, the cloister was filled for him with terror and phantoms. He did not say so, and one had to divine it. On returning from my nocturnal explorations . . . I would find him at ten o'clock at night sitting at the piano, pale and with haggard eyes, and his hair almost standing on end. It took him some moments to recognize me."

With the return of good weather, Chopin and Sand went eagerly back to France. Though he had been practically an invalid when he left Majorca, Chopin was revitalized by the warm climate of southern France and an additional period of rest in Marseilles and Nohant. By the time he was back in Paris his former good spirits and physical vigor had been restored. The dismal holiday in Majorca, moreover, had not been a total loss, for Chopin had completed one of his masterworks, the twenty-four Preludes of Opus 28.

Apart from his creative efforts and several concert appearances, Chopin's life was fairly uneventful for the next seven years. He spent his winters mostly in Paris, his summers at Sand's home in Nohant. In 1847, however, his *liaison* with George Sand ended, largely because of the intrigues of Sand's son and daughter.

Chopin's health deteriorated rapidly; he seemed to lose interest even in his own music. On February 16, 1848 he gave what was to be his last public appearance in Paris, then left to tour England and Scotland. But throughout that busy round of concert performances and social engagements, Chopin was violently ill. When he returned to Paris on November 23, 1848, he was no longer able to give concerts or lessons, nor could he compose because of the ravages of tuberculosis. Living in seclusion, he was supported financially by his close friends.

Chopin died at his home on the Rue de Chaillot on October 17, 1848. Before his death he had left specific instructions that his unpublished manuscripts be destroyed, a request that was not carried out. He also insisted that his body be cut open after his death, in order to avert any possibility of his being buried alive; this request was fulfilled. At his behest, too, Mozart's Requiem was performed at his funeral services at the Madeleine Church. He was buried in the Père Lachaise cemetery, where a monument was unveiled on October 17, 1850; on that occasion Polish earth was scattered over his grave.

Few composers have been so meticulous in their workmanship as Chopin. He subjected his compositions to endless revision, holding many works from publication until he could test them in public performance. He once characterized himself as a "reviser par excellence," adding, "I am going to make changes until I die." On another occasion he explained: "During the work one thinks it [a composition] is good, otherwise one could not write at all. . . . It is not until later that reflection comes, rejecting or keeping the work. Time is the best censor and patience the best teacher."

"His creation was amazing," wrote George Sand. "He formed thoughts without seeking them or anticipating them. On the piano an idea suddenly occurred to him . . . and during a walk it was singing in him. Then he was in a hurry to play his new thoughts. . . . Then, however, began the most painstaking work that I have ever witnessed. There was no end of impatient and undecided essays to fix certain details of the theme as he had heard it inwardly. He analyzed very much when writing down what was conceived as a whole, and his regret that he could not represent it perfectly made him desperate. For days, he locked himself up in his room, running up and down, breaking pens, repeating, changing one single measure a hundred times, writing, scratching it out and the next morning starting all over again with painstaking and desperate efforts. He would work for six weeks on one single page, to write it finally exactly the way he had sketched it in the original draft."

Liszt gave the following account of his friend: "His manners in society possessed that serenity of mood which distinguishes those whom no ennui annoys, because they expect no interest. He was generally gay, his caustic spirit caught the ridiculous rapidly and far below the surface at which it usually strikes the eye. He displayed a rich vein of drollery in pantomime. He often amused himself by reproducing the musical formulas and peculiar tricks of certain virtuosos, in the most burlesque and comic improvisations, imitating their gestures, their movements, counterfeiting their faces with a talent which instantaneously depicted their whole personality. His own features would then become scarcely recognizable, he would force the strangest metamorphoses upon them, but while mimicking the ugly and the grotesque, he never lost his own native grace. Grimace was never carried far enough to disfigure him; his gaiety was so much the more piquant because he always restrained it within the limits of perfect good taste, holding at a careful distance all that could wound the most fastidious delicacy. He never made use of an inelegant word, even in moments of the greatest familiarity; an improper innuendo, a coarse jest would have been shocking to him. . . .

"On some occasions, although very rarely, we saw him deeply agitated. We saw him grow so pale and wan, that his appearance was actually corpse-like. But even in moments of the most intense emotion, he remained concentrated within himself. A single instant for self-recovery always enabled him to veil the secret of his first impression. . . .

"He could pardon in the most noble manner. No rancor in his heart toward those who had wounded him, though such wounds penetrated deeply into his soul, and festered there in vague pain and internal suffering, so that long after the exciting cause had been effaced from his memory, he still experienced the secret torture. By dint of constant effort, in spite of his acute and tormented sensibilities, he subjected his feelings to the rule rather of what ought to be than what is; thus he was grateful for services proceeding rather from good intentions than from a knowledge of what would have been agreeable to him. Nevertheless the wounds caused by such awkward miscomprehensions are, of all others, the most difficult for nervous temperaments to bear."

Chopin occupies a unique place in the history of music for several reasons. He is the only great composer who confined himself largely to piano composition: of his 169 works only a scattered handful are not for piano solo, and all the others employ the piano. He is one of the few masters who specialized in the smaller forms. And he is one of the minority of the world's great creators of music who maintained a consistently high level of artistic attainment. With only a few unimportant and random exceptions, everything he wrote is part of the living repertory and represents him at full maturity.

A basic element in some of Chopin's greatest works is strong national feeling, influenced by Polish folk song and dance. "I should like," he once said, "to be to my people what Uhland is to the Germans." J. Cuthbert Hadden goes on to explain: "It was an aspiration with him from the first to put Poland as it were into his music."

The nationalist influence is most obvious in the mazurkas and polonaises which elevate the Polish dance to an artistic form, ranging from fiery patriotism to nostalgia for the homeland, from irony to contemplation.

Besides the mazurkas and polonaises, Chopin's shorter works include ballades, études, fantasies, nocturnes, preludes, scherzos, and waltzes. In his four ballades, Chopin, inspired by the poems of Adam Mickiewicz, endowed a form that was comparatively free, improvisational, and narrative in quality with deep poetic feeling, perhaps more intense than in his other works. The ballade form had been used successfully before Chopin, but the concert étude and the piano prelude were forms which he helped to create and popularize. Although his études were exercises in various techniques of keyboard performance, Chopin brought to his lessons such inexhaustible invention and imagination that in his hands exercise became art. The prelude—a completely independent composition without set form in which a definite feeling or mood is projected—proved for Chopin one of the most graceful media for his finest inspiration. "Many of them call up to the mind's eye visions of dead monks," explained George Sand, "and the sound of their funeral chants which obsessed him; others are suave and melancholy; these would come to him in his hours of sunshine and health, amid the sound of children's laughter beneath his window, the distant thrum of the guitar, and the song of the birds among the damp leafage; or at the sight of pale little roses blooming above the snow. Others are dreary and sad, and wring the heart while charming the ear."

The nocturne, "a piece for the night," was a form of piano music developed by the Irish pianist and composer John Field. But as James Gibbons Huneker said, Chopin "ennobled the form . . . giving it dramatic breadth, passion, even grandeur. . . . Chopin loved the night and its starry mysteries; his nocturnes are truly night pieces, some wearing an agitated, remorseful countenance; others seen in profile only; while many are like whisperings at dusk—Verlaine moods."

Chopin's waltzes are salon music *in excelsis*, waltz music for listening rather than dancing. Whereas the waltzes of such Viennese composers as Schubert had an earthy lustiness reminiscent of the peasant origins of this dance form, Chopin's are elegant, beautifully mannered, refined, and sophisticated.

Chopin composed two piano concertos and three piano sonatas. He was not, however, at ease with larger structures, as he was with cameos. His concertos and sonatas are greater in their parts than in their entirety; they are often merely a series of short pieces, each brilliantly conceived but never really part of an organic whole. Typical is the famous Chopin Funeral March, undoubtedly the most celebrated funeral march ever written, which is a movement of his Second Piano Sonata in B-flat minor.

In all of Chopin's music, Liszt wrote, "we meet beauties of the highest kind, expressions entirely new, and harmonic material as original as it is thoughtful. In his compositions boldness is always justified; richness, often exuberance, never interferes with clearness; singularity never degenerates into the uncouth and the fantastic; the sculpturing is never disordered; the luxury of ornament never overloads the chaste tenderness of the principal lines. ⁒ . . Daring, brilliant and attractive, . . . [his compositions] disguise their profundity under so much grace, their science under so many charms, that it is with difficulty we free ourselves sufficiently from their magical enthrallment to judge coldly their theoretical value."

"He had no predecessor and no successor," said Ernest Hutcheson. "Chopin came and departed like a comet from remote space."

PRINCIPAL WORKS

Chamber Music—Piano Trio in G minor; Cello Sonata in G minor.

Orchestral Music—2 piano concertos; Variations on "Là ci darem," for piano and orchestra.

Piano Music—55 mazurkas; 24 études; 24 preludes; 15 waltzes; 11 polonaises; 6 ballades; 4 impromptus; 4 scherzos; 3 sonatas; Barcarolle in F-sharp minor; Berceuse in D-flat; Tarantelle in A-flat; écossaises, fantasies, rondos; Rondo in C major, for two pianos.

Vocal Music—17 Polish Songs.

ABOUT

Abraham, G., Chopin's Musical Style; Boucourechliev, A., Chopin: A Pictorial Biography; Bourniquel, C., Chopin; Cortot, A., Aspects of Chopin; Gide, A., Notes sur Chopin; Hadden, J. C., Chopin; Hadow, W. H., Studies in Modern Music; Hedley, A., Chopin; Holcman, J., The Legacy of Chopin; Huneker, J. G., Chopin: The Man and His Music; Hutcheson, E., The Literature of the Piano; Kobylanska, K. (editor), Chopin in His Own Land: Documents and Souvenirs; Liszt, F., Chopin; Mizwa, S. P. (editor), Frédéric Chopin; Murdoch, W., Chopin; Niecks, F., Frédéric Chopin as Man and Musician; Sand, G., Histoire de ma vie; Weinstock, H., Chopin: The Man and His Music.

Domenico Cimarosa *1749-1801*

D OMENICO CIMAROSA, composer of the *opera buffa Il Matrimonio segreto*—one of the most important to precede Rossini's works—was born in Aversa, near Naples, on December 17, 1749. His mother was a laundress. His father, a bricklayer, was killed in a fall from a high scaffold when Domenico was still a child. The monks for whom his mother laundered helped her supervise the boy's musical and academic education. When he was eleven Cimarosa entered a charity school maintained by the Minorites, where he was taught music and Latin. Cimarosa made such remarkable progress in music as a pupil of the monastery organist that in 1761 he was transferred to the Santa Maria di Loreto Conservatory in Naples for more intensive musical tuition. There, for over a decade, he studied under such masters as Sacchini, Fenaroli, and the foremost *opera buffa* composer of the period, Niccolò Piccini, a particularly forceful influence on Cimarosa.

In 1770 Cimarosa's first publicly performed work, the oratorio *Giuditta*, was well received in Rome. About two years later he wrote his first opera, *Le Stravaganze del*

Cimarosa: chē-mä-rô′zä

DOMENICO CIMAROSA

conte, a moderate success when produced in Naples through the patronage of a woman who soon afterwards became his mother-in-law. *La Finta Parigina,* performed in Naples in 1773, was highly acclaimed, and established Cimarosa's reputation in Italy.

During the next two decades Cimarosa lived alternately in Rome and Naples. An extremely prolific and popular composer, he completed about seventy serious as well as comic operas in twenty-nine years. In 1781 alone six of his operas were heard; *Giannina e Bernardone,* performed in Venice in November that year, spread his fame throughout Europe. His contemporaries considered him the foremost Italian opera composer of his time.

In 1787 Cimarosa was invited to Russia to succeed Paisiello as court composer to Catherine II. His trip through Florence, Vienna and Warsaw (en route to Russia) was a march of triumph. In St. Petersburg, his residence for several years, he wrote operas as well as music for a ballet, some cantatas, and a Mass.

In 1791 Cimarosa left Russia for Vienna, succeeding Salieri as court *Kapellmeister* to Leopold II. It was in the Austrian capital that he wrote his most celebrated composition, the *opera buffa Il Matrimonio segreto,* produced at the Burgtheater on February 7, 1792; its text, by Bertati, was based upon *The Clandestine Marriage,* an English play by George Colman and David Garrick.

Il Matrimonio segreto was a complete triumph, so delighting the Emperor that after the performance he invited the cast to a supper so that it could repeat the work in its entirety. The Viennese public was no less enchanted. In its subsequent performances throughout Europe, *Il Matrimonio segreto* proved to be one of the most popular of the genre written between Pergolesi's *Serva padrona* and Rossini's *Barber of Seville.* Verdi considered it the ideal *opera buffa.* Professor Edward J. Dent maintained that Mozart learned a good deal from Cimarosa's "back chat in *recitatives,* his charming tunes, his patter songs for the bass, his chattering ensembles."

"Cimarosa," wrote A. Maczewsky, "was the culminating point of genuine Italian opera. His invention is simple, but always natural; and in spite of his Italian love for melody, he is never monotonous; but both in form and melody is always in keeping with the situation. . . . His real talent lay in comedy—in his sparkling wit and unfailing good humor. His invention was inexhaustible in the representation of that overflowing and yet naïve liveliness, that merry teasing loquacity which is the distinguishing feature of the genuine Italian *buffa* style. His chief strength lies in the vocal parts, but the orchestra is delicately and effectively handled, and his ensembles are masterpieces, with a vein of humor which is undeniably akin to Mozart."

The American première of *Il Matrimonio segreto* took place in New York on January 4, 1834. Its first performance, at the Metropolitan Opera, took place on February 25, 1937, in an English translation.

After leaving Vienna in 1794, Cimarosa visited Venice, then Rome in 1796. In 1798 he returned at last to Naples. There he was appointed *maestro di cappella* and music instructor to the royal family. When French republican troops invaded Naples and sent the Bourbons in flight to Sicily, Cimarosa endeared himself to the new regime by writing music for a political poem, *A Neapolitan Carmagnole.* The Bourbons did not forget this defection when they regained power in Naples. The author of the poem was condemned to death and Cimarosa was imprisoned for a short time. His prison sentence had disastrous effects on his health and spirit.

Upon his release, Cimarosa left Naples and went to live in Venice. While working on his last opera, *Artemisia*, he succumbed to a gangrenous abdominal tumor, and died on January 11, 1801. Upon his death the rumor that he had been poisoned by order of Queen Caroline spread through Venice and gained such credence that the court was forced to issue an official denial, and the Pope's personal physician was dispatched to Venice to investigate the matter.

Cimarosa married twice; both his wives died in childbirth. He was a suave, charming, extremely cultured man, with a ready wit. Highly gregarious, he enjoyed having people around him, even when he was at work. He had a very high opinion of his own talent, often referring to himself as the greatest Italian composer of his generation. Despite his involvement in Neapolitan republicanism, he was not especially interested in politics. "He was in essence," sums up Francis Toye, "a jolly man, very good natured, enormously fat, who loved the good things of life."

A prolific composer of over seventy-five operas, as well as many choral and instrumental compositions, Cimarosa survives in contemporary performance through only a handful of works, mainly *Il Matrimonio segreto* and a few delightful concertos and sonatas for harpsichord. A Concerto for Oboe and Strings, occasionally performed today, is Arthur Benjamin's arrangement of material from four Cimarosa sonatas. Another contemporary composer, Gian Francesco Malipiero, adapted five pieces by Cimarosa into a symphonic work entitled *La Cimarosiana*. The ballet *Cimarosiana*, which was produced by Diaghilev's Ballet Russe de Monte Carlo in the early 1920's, was based on music from Cimarosa's opera *Le Astuzie femminili* (1794).

Cimarosa's touch was essentially light, and there can be little question that his best music was for the stage. "He was," says George T. Ferris, "the finest example of the school perfected by Piccini, and was, indeed, the link between the old Italian opera and the new development." R. A. Streatfeild has written: "His talent is thoroughly Italian, untouched by German influence, and he excels in portraying the gay superficiality of the Italian character without attempting to dive far below the surface."

PRINCIPAL WORKS

Choral Music—3 oratorios; cantatas, Masses, motets, psalms, Requiems.

Harpsichord Music—Sonatas.

Operas—76 comic and serious operas including: La Finta Parigina; L'Italiana in Londra; L'Infedeltà fedele; Giannina e Bernardone; Il Convito; La Ballerina amante; Artaserse; L'Impresario in angustie; Le Vergine del sole; Il Matrimonio segreto; Le Astuzie femminili; Penelope; Gli Orazi e Curiazi.

Orchestral Music—7 symphonies.

Vocal Music—Arias, cavatinas, solfeggi.

ABOUT

Ferris, G. T., Great Italian and French Masters; Tibaldi Chiesa, M., Cimarosa ed il suo tempo; Vitale, R., Domenico Cimarosa: la vita e le opere.

Musical Quarterly, April 1947.

Muzio Clementi *1752-1832*

MUZIO CLEMENTI was born in Rome on January 23, 1752. His father, a silversmith who specialized in ecclesiastical vessels, soon became aware of his son's musical potential and placed him under the tutelage of Buroni, a church choirmaster. After that the boy studied thorough bass with Cordicelli, composition with Carpini, and voice with Santarelli. At the age of nine he was appointed church organist. At twelve he wrote an oratorio and at fourteen a Mass, both of which were performed successfully in Rome.

In 1766 Clementi gave a piano recital that was attended by Peter Beckford, an English Member of Parliament. Beckford was so impressed with the boy that he prevailed upon his father to permit him to take Muzio back to England in order to supervise his musical training. In Wiltshire Beckford led Muzio to study the works of such masters as Corelli and Alessandro Scarlatti, besides getting cultural background.

In 1773 Clementi first became known in England as a pianist and composer. That year he gave a remarkable piano recital, drawing wide attention to his extraordinary powers at the keyboard, especially in improvisation. He also published his first set of piano sonatas, works that caused Carl Philipp Emmanuel Bach to take special notice of him. Clementi was soon busily occupied in performing at concerts and in teaching; from 1777 to 1780 he was the conductor of the Italian Opera in London.

MUZIO CLEMENTI

In 1781 Clementi made an extensive tour of Europe. In Vienna Emperor Joseph II arranged for Clementi to appear in a piano-playing match with Mozart, since the two masters were then regarded as rivals for first place among living virtuosos of the keyboard. On December 24, 1781, Clementi played one of his own sonatas and Mozart extemporized a set of variations; each was so gifted that the Emperor declared the contest a draw.

While in Lyons in 1782, Clementi fell in love with Victoire Imbert-Colomès, the daughter of a banker, and one of his pupils. Since Victoire's father objected violently to Clementi as a son-in-law, the lovers eloped, but they were apprehended in Chambéry before they could marry. Although they were soon separated, Clementi's devotion to Victoire lasted for years, and he dedicated several compositions to her.

In 1782, Clementi returned to England, and spent most of his time conducting, composing, teaching, and performing on the piano. He achieved fame in all endeavors. As a composer he produced his first symphony in 1786. As a teacher of piano his influence was far-reaching; his many pupils included John Field, J. B. Cramer, Moscheles, and Kalkbrenner, who were all to become renowned pianists.

Clementi was also engaged in business enterprises. In 1798 he joined a firm that sold music and manufactured musical instruments. The venture soon went into bankruptcy. In 1802, however, Clementi founded a music publishing and piano manufacturing company that became highly successful, despite a disastrous fire in 1807. Originally called Clementi & Company, and later Clementi, Collard and Collard, the firm is still in existence as Collard and Collard.

In 1802 Clementi accompanied his pupil John Field to St. Petersburg. En route he gave several triumphant concerts in Paris and other European capitals. When he felt that Field had established himself solidly as a piano teacher in Russia, Clementi left for Berlin and stayed there a year. On September 15, 1804, he married Caroline Lehmann, daughter of the cantor of the St. Nicholas Church. Caroline died less than a year later in childbirth.

By 1810 Clementi had given up concert work and teaching to divide his energies between his exacting business venture and composition. On July 3, 1811 he married Emma Gisburne; they had four children. Their spacious and attractive house off Bedford Square in London was for many years a meeting place for the leading literary and musical figures of the day.

In 1813 Clementi helped found the Royal Philharmonic Orchestra. Over a period of years he wrote several delightful symphonies for the orchestra, serving also as conductor on occasion. In 1817 he published one of his most important works, the *Gradus ad Parnassum*, on which, it is sometimes said, the science of modern piano playing rests. The distinguished pianist Karl Tausig called the études of Clementi and Chopin "the only . . . works in musical literature which are entirely indispensable to the pianist." Certainly there are few pianists or piano pupils anywhere in the world who have not been trained on these important Clementi exercises.

Hardly less valuable for piano technique —and even more important in crystallizing the form of the classic sonata—are Clementi's more than one hundred sonatas for piano. To Frederick Niecks they represent Clementi's "most important poetic achievements, the works in which he has incorporated the greatest emotional intensity possible to him, and where the virtuoso contents himself with being the servant of the idea."

"His divination of the treatment most appropriate to the instrument," wrote C. Hubert Parry, "marks his sonatas as among the very first in which the genuine qualities of modern piano music on a large scale are shown."

Clementi's symphonies are only occasionally revived today, usually in the editions and restored versions of Alfredo Casella. Yet Clementi regarded his later symphonies as his "testament to posterity." Here, we learn from Casella, "the style is that of a musician whose life spans the gap from the death of Johann Sebastian Bach to the bloom of Romanticism. A fundamentally classic spirit, severely trained and the possessor of a truly exceptional constructive technique, Clementi in these symphonies aims visibly to renew the great classic heredity with the new aspirations of the century. And his profoundly Italian genius happily achieves this synthesis. In these works we find a new and more potent assertion of the music, at once grandiose and witty, tragic but more often serene, of the best piano sonatas."

The last years of Clementi's life were spent quietly on his estate in Evesham, where he died on March 10, 1832. He was buried in Westminster Abbey.

A man of great personal charm and attractive bearing, Clementi moved gracefully among the social and intellectual élite that formed his milieu. He was cultured and well-read, an excellent linguist, and a classical scholar. One of his favorite diversions was billiards. Although a wealthy man, he was parsimonious; a paragraph in the autobiography of Louis Spohr, the German violinist and composer, describes Clementi, with upturned sleeves, washing his stockings and linen in a tub.

PRINCIPAL WORKS

Chamber Music—Various sonatas for piano with violin or flute and cello.
Orchestral Music—Overtures, symphonies.
Piano Music—Over 100 sonatas and sonatinas; 6 duos for four hands; 2 duos for two pianos; Gradus ad Parnassum; canons, caprices, fugues, preludes, toccatas, variations, waltzes.

ABOUT

Bacharach, A. L. (editor), The Music Masters, vol. 1; Froio, G., Muzio Clementi: la sua vita, le sue opere; Schonberg, Harold C., The Great Pianists; Unger, M., Muzio Clementis Leben.

Musical Quarterly, July 1923, January 1931, January 1942; Music and Letters, July 1932; La Revue musicale, March 1936.

Arcangelo Corelli *1653-1713*

ARCANGELO CORELLI, one of the great pioneers in establishing a modern style and technique of violin playing and in creating the sonata and concerto forms, was born in Fusignano, near Imola, Italy, on February 17, 1653. He took his first violin lessons from Giovanni Benvenuti in Bologna, where he had gone to live at the age of thirteen. Later he studied counterpoint with Simonelli, and continued his study of violin with Leonardo Bragnoli. Even as a youth he gained so imposing a reputation as a violin virtuoso that at seventeen he was elected to the renowned Accademia Filarmonica in Bologna.

Corelli settled in Rome in 1671; several years later he became a violinist in the orchestra of the St. Louis of France Church and directed the orchestra at the Teatro Capranica. Except for brief visits to Modena and Naples (and possibly to Paris and Germany), Corelli stayed in Rome all his life. His unusually high position in the city's musical life is indicated by the fact that he won the powerful patronage of Cardinal Benedetto Panifili, in whose household he lived until 1690 and who later endowed him with a lifetime pension; of Queen Christina of Sweden while she resided in Rome; and, last, of Cardinal Pietro Ottoboni. Cardinal Ottoboni appointed Corelli *maestro di cappella* at his palace. Each Monday evening Corelli directed concerts which became outstanding cultural events.

Corelli was acclaimed throughout Italy as one of the greatest violin virtuosos of his age, "the prince of all musicians," as George Mattheson called him, "the virtuoso of virtuosos of the violin and a veritable Orpheus of our time," in the words of one compatriot. His performance possessed an overwhelming beauty of tone, resiliency of technique, fire and brilliance in interpretation. One eyewitness said that when Corelli played "his countenance was distorted," his eyes "were red as fire," and his "eyeballs rolled in agony." But there was elegance as well as vehemence in his playing. In his skillful use of double and triple stops, arpeggios and chords, trills and appoggiaturi, Corelli helped to establish a modern technique of violin performance. He was also a pioneer in his method of bowing, which was adopted by many of his contemporaries and successors.

ARCANGELO CORELLI

Corelli's achievements as a performer were matched by his excellence as a teacher of the violin. A generation of performers came under his influence, particularly Geminiani and Locatelli, who, with Corelli at their head, helped to found the first important era of violin playing.

Geminiani was of the opinion that Corelli's merit as a composer lay not in his "depth of learning like that of Alessandro Scarlatti, nor great fancy or rich invention in melody or harmony," but in "a nice ear and most delicate taste which led him to select the most pleasing harmonies and melodies, and to construct the parts so as to produce the most delightful effect on the ear."

Geminiani's reserved evaluation does not take into account Corelli's historic importance. As one of the first composers to crystallize an instrumental as opposed to vocal style of music, Corelli gave powerful impetus to the homophonic movement already in progress at the time. In addition, he helped to develop and popularize two of the most important structures of instrumental music—the sonata and the concerto. Between 1681 and 1694 he published in Rome four volumes of trio sonatas (sonatas for two instruments and figured bass). And in 1700 he issued his monumental opus 5: the volume of sonatas for solo violin and figured bass, with which the violin sonata emerged as a distinct musical genre.

The term "sonata" had been used before Corelli's time, as a counterpart to "cantata"

(a composition to be "sounded" or played). Indeed, two kinds of sonatas were in existence by the time Corelli issued his first opus: *sonata da chiesa* (church sonata), a four-movement composition alternating fast and slow movements in a dignified style, which was the direct antecedent of the later instrumental sonata for solo instrument and accompaniment; and the *sonata da camera* (chamber sonata), lighter in style and consisting of a series of dances, the forerunner of the later suite. Both kinds are found in Corelli's five volumes. But in opus 5, Corelli put the technique of playing and writing for violin on a sound basis for the first time. He was also one of the first innovators of the two-theme, or binary form which in later years would become a major feature of the classic sonata form.

The most popular work in opus 5 is the concluding sonata in D minor, known as *La Folia.* The "folia" was a popular melody, probably of Portuguese origin, dating from the early sixteenth century. Many composers liked to use it for variations—and so did Corelli. His *Folia* departs sharply from both the *chiesa* and *camera* forms of the other works in opus 5 in taking on the "theme-and-variations" form. The theme is the "folia," which is followed by twenty-three variations.

C. Hubert Parry described Corelli's style as follows: "Corelli's methods are ostensibly contrapuntal, but it is noteworthy that his is not the old kind of counterpoint but rather an artistic treatment of part-writing, which is assimilated into chords whose progressions are adapted to the principles of modern tonality. He uses sequences for the purposes of form, and modulations for the purposes of contrast and balance, and cadences to define periods and sections, and other characteristic devices of modern art; and though the traces of the old church modes are occasionally apparent, they are felt to be getting more and more slight. There is more of art than human feeling in his work, as is inevitable at such a stage of development; but his art as far as it goes is very good, and the style of expression refined and pleasant."

Equally epoch-making was its successor, opus 6, a set of twelve concerti grossi published posthumously in 1714. Here were formalized the conventions which would govern the composition of the concerto grosso for the next half century and more: the use of a group of soloists (called the *concertino*) in combination with, or set off against, the rest of the orchestra (called the *ripieno* or *concerto grosso*); and the use of light and shade for contrast in the presentation of melodic ideas. In *Music in the Baroque Era,* Manfred F. Bukofzer emphasizes the "decisive step in the development of the concerto proper" taken by Corelli in opus 6. To Corelli, says Bukofzer, belongs "the credit for the full realization of tonality in the field of instrumental music. His works auspiciously inaugurate the period of the late baroque music." Corelli's concerti grossi, Bukofzer adds, "represent in fact the earliest known examples" of that form, an "innovation that was instantly successful and widely imitated. . . . Although closely bound to the contrapuntal tradition of the early Bologna school, Corelli handled the new idiom with amazing assuredness."

One of the concerti grossi still often represented on symphony programs is the eighth in G minor, known as the *Christmas Concerto* because, as Corelli wrote, it was "composed for the night of the Nativity." Except for the concluding movement, there is really nothing in the music that is topical. But the last movement, a "Pastorale," is deeply religious, describing Christ's cradle in Bethlehem. As a devout melody in thirds with a gently swaying Sicilian rhythm, the "Pastorale" became a model for similar pieces by such later composers as Handel (in the *Messiah*) and Johann Sebastian Bach (in the *Christmas Oratorio*).

Arcangelo Corelli died in Rome on January 8, 1713. He was buried in the Pantheon near Raphael's tomb; his grave is marked by a marble monument donated by Cardinal Ottoboni, the patron to whom Corelli bequeathed his art treasures and entire fortune. The Cardinal kept the art works, but gave the money to Corelli's relatives. It is legend, not fact, that Corelli died bitter at seeing younger musicians usurp his prestige. To the end of his days Corelli was esteemed most highly by his contemporaries, and for many years the anniversary of his death was commemorated with performances near his grave.

Despite his wealth, Corelli was miserly to a fault. He lived frugally and watched his expenses with mathematical exactitude. One of his contemporaries noted that he was usually "shabbily dressed," and that he always went "on foot instead of taking a carriage. He loved art passionately, and amassed a magnificent collection of paintings and sculpture. Yet he never allowed himself the luxury of visiting an art gallery on days when admission was charged.

Several eminent twentieth-century musicians have adapted the melodic material from Corelli's volume of violin sonatas, opus 5, into orchestral suites. John Barbirolli prepared a Concerto in F major for oboe and strings, and a Concerto Grosso, and Fernández Arbós produced a three-movement Suite for Strings, comprising a "Sarabande," "Gigue," and "Badinerie."

PRINCIPAL WORKS

Chamber Music—48 sonatas for two instruments and figured bass; 12 sonatas for violin and figured bass.
Orchestral Music—12 concerti grossi.

ABOUT

Foss, H. J. (editor), The Heritage of Music, third series; Pincherle, M., Corelli; Rinaldi, N. Arcangelo Corelli.

Peter Cornelius *1824-1874*

CARL AUGUST PETER CORNELIUS, composer of *The Barber of Bagdad,* was born in Mayence, Germany, on December 24, 1824. He was the son of a professional actor, and the nephew and godson of Peter von Cornelius, the celebrated German painter, for whom Mendelssohn wrote the *Cornelius March.*

Peter's father would have liked him to become an actor, but the boy's talent lay in music. He made rapid progress with his school lessons in singing, violin, and theory. He also studied music with the director of a local choral group and with Heinrich Esser. Then, as a violinist in the Mayence Orchestra, Cornelius visited London in 1840. There he tried to fulfill his father's ambition for him by becoming an actor. But his first attempt was such a dismal failure that he abandoned the stage.

After the death of his father in 1844, Cornelius taught music to support himself and his mother. A year or so later he settled in Berlin, residing a while at the home of his famous uncle and godfather. Here he met some of the city's foremost literary and artistic figures. While earning

PETER CORNELIUS

his living as a music teacher, Cornelius spent five years studying theory with W. S. Dehn, and working out problems in counterpoint. He also wrote poetry, essays on music for newspapers, two libretti for comic operas, and some translations from the French into German. In addition he composed a great deal of choral, instrumental, and chamber music.

He brought several of his compositions to two distinguished Berlin musicians. One was Taubert, the conductor of the Berlin Royal Opera, who advised him to abandon the larger structures and concentrate on songs. "I had come with plans for palaces," remarked Cornelius bitterly at this advice, "and he said 'go build pig-sties.'" The verdict of Otto Nicolai, composer of *The Merry Wives of Windsor*, was even harsher. Cornelius later recalled, "He says I know nothing, can't write a note correctly. . . . In fact, he kicked me!"

His interest in the "music of the future" as promoted by Wagner and Liszt was aroused after reading some of Liszt's essays. This impelled him in 1852 to make a pilgrimage to Weimar, where Liszt was then music director to the Grand Duke. He soon became Liszt's friend and disciple. He also moved with fascination and admiration among some of the other Liszt devotees then in Weimar, including Berlioz, whose personality and music made an overwhelming impact on him. Berlioz helped support Cor-

nelius during this period by providing him with minor assignments. Before long, Cornelius was able to supplement his income by teaching, writing articles for the papers, and translating Liszt's lectures from French into German.

While working for Liszt as a secretary and translator, Cornelius came upon a tale in *A Thousand and One Nights* that seemed ideal not only for comic opera but also a text to which Wagnerian aesthetics and musical principles could be applied. Although Liszt was far from enthusiastic about the project, Cornelius went to work on both libretto and score. When he performed the completed opera for Liszt, the older composer's doubts were dispelled, and he proclaimed the work a masterpiece.

The comic opera was *The Barber of Bagdad (Der Barbier von Bagdad)*. Its première took place in Weimar, December 15, 1858, Liszt conducting. That first performance was an outright fiasco, though through no fault of Cornelius or the opera. It was provoked by an anti-Liszt faction, a group that had for some time been gathering in Weimar, determined to overthrow Liszt's rule. Some objected to his private life, others to his continued espousal of new music; still others resented his dictatorial control over musical style. This clique came out in full force to create a scandal at the première of *The Barber*, with such effect that Cornelius' opera had no repeat performance. Liszt, outraged, resigned his post.

Cornelius did not live to see another performance of his opera. About three years after his death, it was revived in Hanover, again encountering unfavorable reaction. Felix Mottl conducted still another revival in 1884 in Karlsruhe, with only slightly better results. It was not until the opera was performed in Munich, on October 15, 1885, that it scored a triumph. From Munich it went on to acclaim in virtually all opera centers of the world. Today it is regarded as one of the undisputed classics in German comic opera.

When *The Barber of Bagdad* was introduced in the United States, at the New York Metropolitan Opera on January 5, 1890, W. J. Henderson wrote: "The score is full of the most characteristic and fluent melody, admirably written and distributed among the various voices and instruments." A. Maczewsky described *The Barber* as "one of the most elegant and refined comic operas ever composed by a German."

With Liszt gone from Weimar, Cornelius had no reason to remain; and in 1858 he settled in Vienna. There he met Richard Wagner for the first time. In 1865 Wagner induced Cornelius to join him in Munich where some of the music dramas were being projected. Cornelius was engaged there as "reader" to King Ludwig II, who was Wagner's patron, and as professor of harmony and rhetoric at the Conservatory.

Cornelius' second opera, *Der Cid*, was successfully introduced in Weimar on May 21, 1865. Two years later Cornelius had achieved enough financial security to marry Bertha Jung, his fiancée of several years. They were married in September 1867 and had four children, three sons and a daughter. An intensely pious Catholic, Cornelius led a happy marital life with a woman of the Protestant faith.

While holding his well-paying teaching post in Munich, Cornelius did literary work (including an autobiography and several essays on Wagner, as well as translations) and composed choral and vocal works. He also started a third opera, *Gunlöd,* but did not live to complete it. (The opera was finished by Eduard Lassen and introduced in Weimar on May 6, 1891.)

In his closing years Cornelius suffered from diabetes. He died in Mayence, Germany, on October 26, 1874, two months short of his fiftieth birthday.

Cornelius has been described as a man of singular kindness, modesty, gentleness, generosity and good humor. "Who could approach Peter Cornelius without at once loving him?" asked Karl Goldmark. "His spirit was of such childlike naïveté, and yet such depth; his true, warm-hearted open nature, his highly cultivated, clear mind could not fail to take everyone captive at once. . . . I often went to his room; we drank black coffee, and over our cigars chatted agreeably on music and musical development; and naturally we spoke much about Richard Wagner."

In a letter to a friend, written in 1849, Cornelius evaluated himself: "If I were to pass judgment on myself, it would be in these terms: I have a fair talent for composition, in spite of the fact that nature has not endowed me with the inexhaustible invention of a Mozart or a Rossini. . . . I can quietly lay claim to one good thing— what little I have is my own property. I do not dig in other people's fields, or adorn myself with others' feathers; so I may hope that when I come to my years of discretion I shall have, God willing, a certain individuality to display."

Cornelius wrote several remarkable songs. The most famous is the cycle *Christmas Songs,* in which as Lawrence Gilman wrote of Cornelius' songs, "his world . . . is a world of ineffable and melancholy twilight. There are moments when he seems immeasurably distant, wrapped in a shimmering, impenetrable mist of dreams, but even as you would strain your senses to follow him, he is standing beside you again, smiling that infinitely winsome smile of his and talking to you. . . . Those songs which most justly represent him—such as "Angedenken," "Trauer," "Ein Ton," "An der Traum," "Nachts," "Auftrag" . . . are the articulate and surviving documents of one to whom 'upon the public ways life came.' He has not told us all that, perhaps, he might have told us; but it is something to have borne witness, as he indubitably has, to so much that is of enduring validity and beauty."

PRINCIPAL WORKS

Choral Music—Requiem; Trost in Tränen; Liebe; Die Vätergruft; Blaue Augen; Freund Hein; Reiterlied; O Venus; various choruses.

Operas—Der Barbier von Bagdad; Der Cid; Gunlöd (completed by Eduard Lassen).

Vocal Music—Vater unser; Trauer und Trost; Rheinische Lieder; Weihnachtslieder (Christmas Songs); various individual songs for voice and piano, including Andenken, An der Traum, Auftrag, Ave Maria, Ein Ton, Ich und Du, Nachts; vocal duets; Der Tod des Verräters, vocal trio.

ABOUT

Cherbuliez, A. E., Peter Cornelius; Cornelius, C. M., Peter Cornelius, Der Wort- und Tondichter; Egert, P., Peter Cornelius; Gilman, L., Phases of Modern Music.

Musical America, December 20, 1924; Musical Quarterly, July 1934; Musical Times, September 1906.

François Couperin *1668-1733*

FRANÇOIS COUPERIN, known as Couperin le Grand (Couperin the Great), was born in Paris on November 10, 1668, into a family which for two centuries had produced professional musicians. "Le

Couperin: kōō-prăN′

FRANÇOIS COUPERIN

first two movements of *La Sultane,* the Introduction and the Allegro; they are occasionally performed at symphony concerts.

When Thomelin, chapel organist to Louis XIV, died in 1693, the King sponsored a competition to fill the vacancy. Couperin won easily and on December 26, 1693 was officially designated *organiste du roi.* In addition to his functions as organist, Couperin was teacher to the royal princes and princesses, and to the Duke of Burgundy. In 1701 he was appointed clavecinist to the King. He also wrote chamber music—the first important works of this kind in France—for performance at the Sunday evening concerts for the King that were held in the royal apartments at Versailles. These compositions, called *Concerts royaux,* written to lighten the mood of the King, were tuneful and easily assimilable. They consisted of dance movements, were scored for harpsichord and various unspecified instruments and maintained uniform tonality throughout. Couperin published four such works in 1722. Three years later he published a set of ten more *Concert royaux* under the collective title *Les Goûts Réunis.*

In 1713, Couperin published the first volume of his *Pièces de clavecin,* following it with three more volumes in 1716-1717, 1722, and 1730. The work is a landmark in the early history of French keyboard music, embracing some 230 pieces of music gathered into twenty-seven suites, or, as Couperin called them, *Ordres.* In these suites he brought a new flexibility and variety of expression to the rather formal dance movements that made up the suite. He expanded the technique of keyboard writing and performance, established a modern system of fingering, and perfected the art of embellishment or ornamentation. Most important, Couperin gave powerful impetus to the development of program music through his use of fanciful and picturesque titles for his pieces, and through his deliberate creation of vividly descriptive compositions.

As Couperin himself explained, "I have always had an object in composing all these pieces inspired by various events. The titles correspond to the ideas I had in mind." Accordingly, some of the *Pièces de clavecin* are satirical, some picturesque, some impressionistic, some highly realistic. They describe jugglers, people at court, reapers, grape gatherers. They mimic gossip, the sights and

Grand" was affixed to François's name to single him out as the most distinguished of the Couperins, as the earliest important composer of French instrumental music, and as a giant figure in the early development of music for the keyboard. His father, Charles, organist of the St. Gervais Church, lived in an apartment adjoining the church which was traditionally turned over rent free to its organists; it was here that François was born.

Until his death in 1679, Couperin *père* taught François organ. Then the boy studied with Jacques Thomelin, the eminent organist of the Saint-Jacques-la-Boucherie. At seventeen François Couperin was appointed to the organ post at St. Gervais that his father had held and that since 1679 had been filled by Lalande. Four years later, on April 26, 1689, Couperin married Marie-Anne Ansault. They had two daughters, both excellent musicians—one a church organist, the other the only woman ever to serve as clavecinist to the King.

In 1692 Couperin wrote four sonatas for two violins and bass. This marks the first important use of the *sonata da chiesa* form in French instrumental music. Couperin's indebtedness to Corelli is unmistakable, but by 1695 he had developed, in the sonatas *La Sultane* and *La Superbe,* a style that was recognizably French in its refinement, purity, and grace. The twentieth century French modernist Darius Milhaud orchestrated the sounds of Paris, a prude, a seductress, the sounds of bells, windmills, hurdy-gurdy players, popular tunes and dances of the time. Some project a mood picture, "describing" the weather and the atmosphere of court life, attempting to give musical equivalents for emotions and even colors. Indeed, it has been said that one can construct a vivid picture of French society in the late seventeenth and early eighteenth centuries by studying Couperin's four volumes of clavecin pieces.

Two of the *ordres* have particular fascination. *Les Fastes de la grande et ancienne Ménestrandise,* in the second volume, is a miniature five-act play for harpsichord, written in protest against the attempt of the musicians' guild to enroll court musicians. The program music describes the march of guild officers and jury members into the meeting room, then recreates tonally the complaints of barrel-organ players and musical beggars; the sport of jugglers, tumblers, and clowns with their animals; musicians crippled in the service of their profession; and, in the last part, the routing of the entire assemblage in confusion. An especially interesting innovation, in addition to the satiric treatment of his material, is Couperin's interpolation of the popular music of his day.

In the third volume, the *ordre* entitled *Les Folies françoises ou les Dominos* is a fascinating effort to draw a parallel between a mood and a color: jealousy with dark gray, loyalty with blue, despair with black, and so forth. Couperin gives a musical equivalent to the colors and moods.

Other pieces of special interest are "La Favorite," a reflection of court life in Versailles, and the mood pictures "La Ténébreuse" and "La Lugubre" in the first book. The second book includes "Les Moissonneurs," a peasant gavotte; the highly expressive and emotional "Les Langueurs tendres"; and, in the opinion of Wanda Landowska and other authorities, the most important single piece in all four volumes, the Passacaille, one of the most eloquent pieces of music ever written for harpsichord. The third volume contains "Le Carillon de Cithère," "Les Petits moulins à Vent," "Le Toc-Toc-Choc," and the highly impressionistic "Les Vergers fleuris." The fourth book is noteworthy for a portrait of Harlequin in "L'Arlequine"; satires on court society in

"Les vieux seigneurs" and "Les jeunes seigneurs"; and two atmospheric pieces, "Mistérieuse" and "Les Pavots."

In those harpsichord pieces, writes Wanda Landowska, "Couperin created a style and technique of his own. Like Chopin, Couperin is great not only for what he brings to his instrument by way of creative gifts, but also in what he draws from it. The resources of the instrument are wonderfully extended and immeasurably enriched by this early French master, who must be considered one of the earliest great masters of the keyboard. . . . One finds in his pieces for the harpsichord that sustained and full lyric line, those strong and appealing harmonies, that intensity of expression, that richness of atmosphere, all of which are qualities uniquely his."

In the years 1714-1715 Couperin completed the three *Leçons de Ténèbres,* which many musicologists regard as Couperin's most significant compositions for the church. The text, in Latin, is adapted from the words of the prophet Jeremiah, and Couperin's musical style is a union of French tradition with Italian techniques in the writing of arias. In describing this work, Harold C. Schonberg wrote in the New York *Times:* "Couperin's music is highly ornamented, as was all the music of the period, but these are Gothic-like ornamentations, full of mood and meaning, and anything but vocal or instrumental display. . . . One does not need to be a scholar to recognize the intensity of the music, its clarity and passion hidden under an emotional reserve."

When Louis XIV died in 1715, Couperin restricted his activities at court. He lived in a comfortable apartment in the Palais Royal section of Paris, where he often gave harpsichord and chamber music concerts for friends. In 1730 he withdrew completely from his post as the court clavecinist and was succeeded by his daughter, Marguerite-Antoinette. At the same time his cousin, Nicholas Couperin, took over his position at St. Gervais. For the next three years Couperin lived in virtual seclusion in the Rue Neuve des Bons Enfants in Paris. He died on September 12, 1733.

Couperin's theoretical treatise on the art of playing the harpsichord, *L'Art de toucher le clavecin,* published in 1716, exerted a far-reaching influence on many of his contemporaries everywhere, including Johann Sebastian Bach.

The twentieth century composer Richard Strauss developed some melodies from Couperin's *Pièces de clavecin* into a delightful *Divertimento* for small orchestra (op. 86).

PRINCIPAL WORKS

Chamber Music—Concerts royaux, for harpsichord and various unspecified instruments; trio-sonatas including La Sultane, L'Apothéose de Corelli and L'Apothéose de Lulli.
Choral Music—Leçons de Ténèbres; Élévations; Magnificat; hymns, psalms.
Harpsichord (Clavecin) Music—Pièces de clavecin, four volumes; appendix to L'Art de toucher le clavecin.
Organ Music—42 pieces for organ assembled into two masses.
Vocal Music—Songs for voice and continuo; vocal duets and vocal trios.

ABOUT

Brunold, P., François Couperin; Citron, P., Couperin; Mellers, W., François Couperin and the French Classical Tradition; Tessier, A., Les Couperins; Tiersot, J., Les Couperins.
Monthly Musical Record, February-August 1889; Musical Quarterly, July 1926; Revue de musicologie, December 1952.

César Cui *1835-1918*

CÉSAR ANTONOVICH CUI was a member of the renowned Russian nationalist school "The Five" (see sketch on Balakirev). Although he composed many works in all the major forms, his greatest contribution to the nationalist cause was rather as a propagandist. He was born in Vilna on January 18, 1835. His father was a French officer, part of the Napoleonic forces that had invaded Russia in 1812. Wounded in Smolensk, he was left on the battlefield as dead. After his recovery he decided to remain in Poland. He married a Lithuanian noblewoman, and became an instructor of French at the Vilna high school.

César's early music education was largely self-acquired. He learned notation by copying out portions of Italian operas and Chopin mazurkas. At fourteen he received formal instruction in theory from Moniuszko, the famous Polish composer. Despite his obvious gift for music, he was directed by his parents to engineering. In 1850, after graduating from the Vilna high school, Cui entered the School of Military Engineering at St. Petersburg. Immediately upon graduation in 1857 with the rank of lieutenant, he was appointed subprofessor at the school,

specializing in fortifications. He became a respected authority in the field, wrote several major treatises, held the rank of Lieutenant General of Engineers, and served as instructor of seven grand dukes, including the future Czar Nicholas II.

Meeting with Balakirev in 1857 revived Cui's early passion for music. For two years Cui was Balakirev's pupil, absorbing the older composer's ideals for Russian nationalist music. Before long he joined Balakirev and three other progressive Russian musicians, Mussorgsky, Borodin, and Rimsky-Korsakov, to form a new school of composers known as "The Five," dedicated to the creation of a musical art deeply rooted in Russian folklore, folk music, and culture. With this aim Cui completed, in 1857, two acts of an opera, *The Captive in the Caucasus;* the libretto, by Krilov, was based on a poem by Pushkin. Twenty-five years later Cui added the third act, and the complete opera was finally given in St. Petersburg on February 16, 1883.

In 1858 Cui married Malvina Bamberg, a gifted music student. To support his wife he established a preparatory school for potential engineering students. He did not, however, neglect composition. Cui's first published work was a Scherzo for four-hand piano whose main theme was derived from letters in his wife's name. In 1859 he completed the score for an operetta, *The Mandarin's Son*, which was given a private performance; here Cui digressed temporarily from his national aims to write music that was markedly influenced by the French *opéra-comique* school, notably the work of Auber.

Cui's most important opera was *William Ratcliff*, its text based on a drama by Heine. Introduced in St. Petersburg on February 26, 1869, it was the first large-scale work by a member of "The Five" to receive a major performance. His colleagues in "The Five" were delighted with it. "*Ratcliff* is not only yours but ours," exclaimed Mussorgsky. Rimsky-Korsakov regarded the third-act love duet as "the finest . . . in all contemporary musical literature." Other critics and musicians, however, were less effusive. Tchaikovsky wrote, "It contains charming things, but unfortunately it suffers from a certain insipidity. . . . By nature Cui is more drawn towards light and piquantly rhythmic French music; but demands of 'the invincible band' which he has joined compel him to do violence to his natural gifts and to follow those paths of would-be original harmony which do not suit him." *William Ratcliff* received only seven performances, then was dropped from the repertory. It was revived in Moscow in 1900 with little more success, then lapsed into oblivion.

In 1864 Cui began a successful career as a music critic, writing for Russian, French, and Belgian publications. He used his pen zealously to spread the gospel of the new Russian national school, and was no less passionate in denouncing Italian opera. His prolific writing did much to popularize the music of "The Five," in Russia and throughout Europe.

As a composer Cui was far less successful. Among his later operas were *Angelo* in 1876, based on the drama by Victor Hugo which had also provided the libretto for Ponchielli's *La Gioconda; Le Filibustier* in 1894; *The Saracen,* derived from a play by Dumas *père,* in 1899; *A Feast in Time of Plague,* based on Pushkin, in 1901; and *Mam'zelle Fifi,* after the celebrated story of Maupassant, in 1903. He also wrote orchestral suites, various choruses and songs, and many compositions for piano and for violin and piano. Paradoxically, of this abundance, only one or two songs and a trifle for violin and piano have survived; the latter is the popular "Orientale," from the suite *Kaleidoscope,* op. 50. In fact, most of Cui's work has been almost completely forgotten. As M. D. Calvocoressi has written, "His operas are no longer produced, and, though he possessed creative talent, his music no longer affords aesthetic pleasure or exerts an influence. Cui's name is kept alive in musical history not because of his compositions, which are practically dead, but by virtue of the fact that he was a leader in an all-important musical movement."

In Hermann Laroche's opinion, "Cui's gift for melody is not abundant. His tunes cannot exactly be called common; one merely feels that they lack individuality. One cannot point at any particular place to plagiarism, or indicate the source from which such and such a motive had been taken, for they have not been stolen from anywhere; they have simply been suggested; and these suggested ideas, which are adapted with such taste and sense of beauty in Cui's writing, take the place in Cui's music, as in that of so many others, of original melodic invention."

CÉSAR CUI

During his lifetime, nevertheless, Cui was an honored figure in Russia. Some of the foremost Russian artists, including Repin and Serov, painted his portrait. In 1910 on the occasion of his fiftieth anniversary as a composer, a gala concert of his works, directed by Ippolitov-Ivanov was given at the Conservatory, and the Belaev Prize was awarded to him for one of his orchestral pieces. The première of his ninth opera, *The Captain's Daughter,* in St. Petersburg in 1911, was attended by the Czar and the Czarina. And in 1915 his eightieth birthday was celebrated with festivities in leading Russian cities.

César Cui died in St. Petersburg on March 24, 1918.

Victor I. Seroff has provided the following description of Cui: "[He] was of medium height, and seemed to have nothing seductive about him at first glance. His brownish hair, parted correctly on one side, the well-trimmed beard and whiskers that framed his delicate features, and his grayish blue eyes which blinked as he looked through his glasses, all made him seem to be just what his uniform indicated—an Army Corps Engineer. But as one heard his voice, soft but penetrating, dominated by gentle authority, one could discern a double personality. Outwardly cold, peaceful, patient, a man who could control his emotions, and with a measure of wisdom in his philosophy, methodical, positive and precise. Cui was capable of very simple, intimate, warm relationships. Ready with confidence, he was given to a gaiety that bordered on the infantile, was the enemy of banality and fond of all sorts of dreams and fantasies. His was the imagination of a poet."

PRINCIPAL WORKS

Choral Music—Mystic Chorus; Ave Maria; Les Oiseaux d'Argenteau; various other choruses.

Chamber Music—Twelve Miniatures, for violin and piano (also for violin and orchestra); Seven Miniatures, for violin and piano (also for piano solo); String Quartet in C minor; Kaleidoscope, for violin and piano; Six Bagatelles, for violin and piano; Five Little Duets for flute and violin.

Operas—The Captive in the Caucasus; William Ratcliffe; Angelo; Le Filibustier; The Saracen; A Feast in Time of Plague; Mam'zelle Fifi; Matteo Falcone; The Captain's Daughter.

Orchestral Music—4 suites; 2 scherzos; Tarantella; Marche solennelle; Two Pieces, for cello and orchestra.

Piano Music—Suite; Valse-Caprice; Deux Bluettes; À Argenteau; Three Waltz Movements; Theme and Variations; impromptus, pieces, polonaises, waltzes.

Vocal Music—13 Vignettes musicales; Six mélodies; 3 German Songs; Les Deux ménetriers; Vingt poèmes; individual songs for voice and piano, including Hunger, Romance, and The Statue of Czarskoë Selo.

ABOUT

Bacharach, A. L. (editor), The Music Masters, vol. 3; Calvocoressi, M. D., and Abraham, G., Masters of Russian Music; Leonard, R. A., A History of Russian Music; Montagu-Nathan, M., History of Russian Music; Seroff, V. I., The Mighty Five.

Karl Czerny *1791-1857*

THOUGH Karl Czerny wrote over a thousand compositions, he is remembered today exclusively for his remarkable books of piano exercises on which young pianists everywhere are nurtured. Karl Czerny was born in Vienna on February 20, 1791. His father, a piano teacher, gave Karl piano lessons for four years. Karl was remarkably precocious. "I was able to play little pieces on the piano to my parents when I was three years old," he recalled in his autobiography, and by the time he was ten he had acquired an imposing repertoire. A friend of the family, the violinist Krumpholz, introduced the prodigy to Beethoven, who immediately accepted the boy as a pupil. Czerny studied intensively with Beethoven between 1800 and 1803, more intermittently for another decade. From 1804 to 1806 he also studied

KARL CZERNY

with Hummel and in 1810 gained valuable guidance from Clementi. Displaying remarkable progress, Czerny soon won the support of such notables in Vienna as Prince Lichnowsky and Archduke Rudolph, to whom he had been introduced by Beethoven.

In 1804 Czerny planned an extensive concert tour of Europe, but political unrest prevented him from realizing this project. After several appearances in Vienna, Czerny decided to devote himself to teaching and composition rather than to concert work. Except for brief trips to Leipzig in 1836, Paris and London in 1837, and Italy in 1846, he remained in Vienna until his death. He became one of the most esteemed teachers in Europe; among his many pupils were Liszt, Thalberg, and Leschetizky. The celebrated Sunday afternoon musicales at his home were attended by Beethoven, Hummel, Clementi and Liszt, among many other renowned musicians. Czerny's first published composition appeared in 1805, when he was only fourteen. It was the *Variations concertantes* for violin and piano, a series of variations on a theme by his friend and benefactor, Krumpholz. Although it was thirteen years before the publication of his second composition, a *Rondo brilliante* for four-hand piano, he subsequently became an extremely prolific composer, creating huge choral works, as well as compositions of every variety for piano. Many of his works had a great vogue in the early nineteenth century and realized a fortune for his publishers, Cappi and Diabelli.

"His writings," said Leschetizky, "lacked depth, but no one can deny that they show a great knowledge of form, of the resources of the instrument, and of all the pianistic effects."

Except for the occasional revival of a piano composition (Vladimir Horowitz has recorded the *Variations on La Ricordanza,* op. 33), virtually none of Czerny's works have survived beyond the several volumes of piano studies and exercises which Clementi encouraged him to prepare. "I practice Czerny exercises for half an hour every day," Liszt once said. There is hardly a pianist since that time who has not profited from these studies. "Czerny understood better than anyone else the simple, primitive form from which all piano passage writing is evolved," said Hugo Riemann. "His studies, therefore are of immense help in the earlier stages of development." The most celebrated of his pedagogical volumes were *Die Schule der Geläufigkeit,* op. 299, and *Die Schule der Fingerfertigkeit,* op. 740. His most valuable studies and exercises were assembled in three volumes and issued under the collective title *Complete Theoretical and Practical Piano School.*

Czerny's nervous system and physical resources were severely taxed by his active life. In or about 1850 he was forced to give up most of his activities. He died in Vienna on July 15, 1857. He never married, and was survived by no immediate relatives. His large fortune was distributed among many charities and benevolent institutions, including the Vienna Conservatory.

C. F. Pohl described Czerny as "modest and simple in manner of life, courteous and friendly in his behavior, just and kindly in his judgment on matters of art, and helpful to all young artists who came his way. His disposition was so gentle that he shrank from a harsh or coarse word even spoken in jest."

Principal Works
Chamber Music—Quartets, trios.
Choral Music—300 Graduals and Offertories; 24 Masses; 4 Requiems.
Orchestral Music—Concertos, overtures, symphonies.
Piano Music—Hundreds of compositions for the piano including études, sonatas, variations, and so forth.

About
Bacharach, A. L. (editor), The Music Masters, vol. 2; Schonberg, H. C., The Great Pianists.
Etude, June 1909; Musical Quarterly, July 1956.

Léo Delibes *1836-1891*

CLÉMENT PHILIBERT LÉO DELIBES, the first great composer of ballet music, was born in Saint-Germain-du-Val, in the Sarthe district of France, on February 21, 1836. Soon after the death of his father, his mother took him to Paris. As a boy Delibes sang in the choir of the Madeleine Church. Aware of his great musical talent, his mother entered him in 1848 in the Paris Conservatory, where he studied under Bazin, Benoist, Le Couppey, and Adolphe Adam. Adam was influential in helping the young Delibes obtain his first professional positions in 1853, as accompanist at the Théâtre Lyrique and as organist of the Church of St. Pierre de Chaillot. Soon Delibes began to write music for the popular theater. His first operetta to be performed was *Deux sous de charbon,* presented at the Folies Nouvelles in 1855. *Maître Griffard* was introduced two years later. About twelve of his operettas were produced in the next few years at the Folies Nouvelles, the Bouffes-Parisiens, and the Variétés.

From 1862 to 1871 Delibes was principal organist at St. Jean-St. François. In 1863 he became accompanist and second chorusmaster of the Paris Opéra. The director of the Opéra commissioned him to write the music for a ballet, *La Source,* which the Opéra presented on November 12, 1866. "One easily recognized here originality and distinction of style," wrote Ernest Guiraud. In 1867 Delibes was commissioned to write additional music for a revival of Adolphe Adam's opera *Le Corsaire.* One piece was the orchestral intermezzo "Pas des fleurs," which has since become popular as the *Naila Waltz.* It acquired that name when it was interpolated into a Viennese production of Delibes's ballet *La Source,* which was then renamed *Naila.*

In 1870 Delibes was commissioned to write the music for a new ballet, *Coppélia.* It was presented for the first time at the Paris Opéra on May 25, 1870, with complete success. The historic importance of *Coppélia* is now universally acknowledged. It is one of the

Delibes: duh-lēb'

LÉO DELIBES

earliest ballets to use the subject of the doll become human, to use such folk dances as the czardas effectively, and to attain so consistent a level of artistic excellence that it can also be enjoyed as a concert piece. "Before *Coppélia*," explains George Balanchine, "no one listened to ballet music except in the theater; ballet music was simply a pretext for dancing and, in itself, valuable only for sentimental reasons. The composer was the servant of the choreographer. But with Delibes's masterful score . . . music and dance became unified; collaboration between choreographer and composer was necessary. Tchaikovsky was directly inspired by Delibes's ballet music to write his own. Delibes is the first great ballet composer."

The most memorable portions of the score of *Coppélia*, often assembled into a semiclassical suite for concert performance recording, include the Prelude, Swalinda's Waltz (*Valse lente*), the villagers' Mazurka and the fiery Czardas immediately following, Intermezzo, Bolero, Gigue, and what is perhaps the most popular single piece, the elegant *Valse de la poupée*.

Having firmly established his reputation with *Coppélia*, and assured of a livelihood, Delibes married Mlle. Denain of the Comédie-Française in 1872. A year later his first important operatic success, the *opéra-comique Le Roi l'a dit*, was introduced at the Opéra-Comique on May 24, 1873. It was followed on June 14, 1876, by Delibes's second important ballet, *Sylvia*, which has become,

like *Coppélia*, a classic. "M. Delibes," said the critic of *L'Opinion*, "has written a score which reveals the hand of a master symphonist. The picturesque choice of themes, the expressive variety of melodies, the attractive improvisation of harmonies, and the highly colored orchestration make this ballet an exquisite work." The score contains another highly popular orchestral piece, the *Pizzicato Polka*. Other episodes, sometimes assembled into a suite for concert performance, include the *Les Chasseresses*, Intermezzo, *Valse lente*, and *Cortège de Bacchus*.

On the basis of these successes, Delibes became one of the most prominent musicians in France. He was showered with honors. In 1877 he became Chevalier of the Legion of Honor, in 1881 was appointed professor of composition at the Paris Conservatory, and in 1884 was elected to the Institut.

On April 14, 1883, Delibes's greatest opera, *Lakmé*, was produced at the Opéra-Comique. Inspired by Pierre Loti's autobiographical *Le Mariage de Loti*, the story of his romance with a native girl, Rarahu, in Tahiti, *Lakmé* is a work in the grand Romantic tradition, an adornment of the French lyric theater. "The music of *Lakmé*," said Julien Tiersot, "resembles one of those exotic jewels with which women love to adorn themselves. It is beautifully wrought." Set in India, and exotic in subject, the opera is most notable for the fascinating Orientalism of its score, best typified in the famous coloratura aria "The Bell Song," the Hindu dances, Lakmé's prayer to Dourga, and the background music to several of the Hindu ceremonials. These, as Herbert F. Peyser has explained, "derive their Oriental quality from the composer's use of scale formations and of certain raised intervals or lowered which . . . establish such a feeling in at least a general manner. The scale consisting of B-flat, C, D-flat, E, F, G-flat, A-flat and B-flat enables him to simulate an Indian idiom even if he does not adopt the subtler details and division of Oriental tonalities. Rhythmic and melodic repetitions and instrumental details like the nasal sounds of the oboe are other obvious effects enabling Delibes to attain the colors he has aimed at."

Lakmé has been a favorite of coloratura sopranos ever since the performance of Marie van Zandt, who created the title role. The American première took place at the Academy of Music in New York on March 1,

1886. Adelina Patti appeared as Lakmé when the opera entered the repertory of the Metropolitan Opera in 1891.

Delibes died of lung congestion in Paris on January 16, 1891. His unfinished opera *Kassya* was completed by Massenet.

Despite the poetic beauty and undeniable charm of *Lakmé,* and the wit and originality of *Le Roi l'a dit,* Delibes's greatest significance in music rests unquestionably in his ballets. "It is especially because he wrote *Coppélia,* and even more *Sylvia,*" said Jean Poueigh, "that Léo Delibes deserves to figure among the precursors of the modern school. In a class of composition which, until then, had been neglected, he brought an elevation and vigor of style, a fullness of form and a richness of instrumentation unknown before him. . . . He introduced symphonic music into the ballet, at the same time remaining truly French and preserving in choreographic music that nimble elegance, that caressing grace, that spiritual vivacity, which are like wings of the dance."

"His elegance," summed up Émile Vuillermoz, "has been decisive on the musicians of our time. Delibes is the great forerunner of the 'artist writer' from which our modern school has evolved."

Principal Works
Ballets—La Source; Coppélia; Sylvia.
Choral Music—O Salutaris; Alger; Messe brève; various choruses for men's and women's voices.
Operas—Le Roi l'a dit; Jean de Nivelle; Lakmé; Kassya (finished by Jules Massenet); numerous operettas.
Vocal Music—Songs for voice and piano, including Arioso, Bonjour, Suzon, and Les Filles de Cadiz.

About
Curzon, H. de, Léo Delibes; Guiraud, E., Notice sur la vie et les œuvres de Léo Delibes; Seré, O., Musiciens français d'aujourd'hui.

Josquin des Prés

See Josquin

Karl von Dittersdorf *1739-1799*

KARL DITTERS VON DITTERSDORF was born Karl Ditters in Vienna on November 2, 1739. "My father," he wrote in his autobiography, "held the office of

KARL VON DITTERSDORF

costumier at court and at the theater in the days of Charles VI. He was a good draughtsman, too." Ditters' father was also a lover of good music, quick to appreciate and encourage his son's talent. When Karl was seven he started to study music with Joseph Ziegler, soon progressing enough to play violin in the orchestra of a local church. A horn player employed by Prince Joseph Friedrich von Hildburghausen recommended the boy to the Prince, who immediately took a fancy to him. The Prince not only engaged Karl to play in his court orchestra but also saw to it that the boy obtained a thorough academic and musical education. Among Ditters' music teachers were Trani for violin and Bonno for composition.

In 1759 financial difficulties compelled the Prince to disband his orchestra. For a while Ditters was employed at the court theater. In 1761 he embarked on a concert tour of Italy with Gluck, drawing much admiration for his violin playing. Upon his return to Vienna, however, Ditters was disconcerted to learn that a new violinist, Lolli, had stolen the limelight. He challenged Lolli to a competition in which he established his superiority. Encouraged, Ditters asked for an increase in salary as court musician. Upon being refused he resigned, and in 1765 went to work at the estate of the Bishop of Grosswardein, in Pressburg, as *Kapellmeister.* For the weekly concerts, which he directed, Ditters composed a substantial library of instrumental and choral music. Since the palace boasted an excellent theater, he also wrote for it his first comic opera, *Amore in musica*, in 1767. Another ambitious work, an oratorio, *Isacco*, was successfully performed in Vienna.

In 1769, Ditters left the Bishop's employ to become *Kapellmeister* for the Count Schafgotsch, the Bishop of Breslau, at his estate in Johannisberg. A close bond of friendship developed between the two men, so strong, indeed, that the Count arranged for Ditters to receive the Order of the Golden Spur from the Pope in 1770. This honor had previously been conferred on Gluck and Mozart. A year later Ditters married the singer Nicolini, whom he had brought from Vienna to assist in opera performances.

In 1773 the post of overseer of forests fell vacant at the Count's estate, and this improbable position was offered to Dittersdorf since his employer was aware of the musician's uncommon knowledge of hunting and forestry. This was actually an honorary appointment: the Count had specified that the duties of overseer be handled by a subordinate so that Ditters might not be deflected from his activities as *Kapellmeister*. The tangible benefit of the appointment was that Ditters could be raised to the nobility by the Emperor, Joseph II. At this time he assumed the name Karl Ditters von Dittersdorf.

While in Johannisberg, Dittersdorf was able to visit Vienna frequently. There he became acquainted with Haydn, and on several occasions joined him in performances of chamber music at Mozart's home. Several of his own compositions also were highly successful in the Austrian capital. One was the oratorio *Esther*, which in 1773 was extremely well received by a select audience that included the Emperor himself.

The Emperor now offered Dittersdorf the lucrative post of court *Kapellmeister*. The composer turned it down because he was reluctant to leave Johannisberg. He did, however, accept many important commissions from Vienna. In 1785 he wrote a remarkable set of twelve symphonies based on incidents in Ovid's *Metamorphoses;* they were highly acclaimed. Unfortunately, only six of these have survived. In 1786 an oratorio, *Job,* further enhanced his reputation. And on July 11, 1786, his masterwork, the

"Singspiel" *Doktor und Apotheker (The Doctor and the Apothecary)*, was introduced in Vienna. The work, one of the most brilliant examples of early German comic opera, proved an immediate sensation. Soon after the première Dittersdorf was commissioned to write three comic operas in a similar vein. And in 1789 King Frederick William II of Prussia invited Dittersdorf to Berlin to conduct a special performance of *Doktor und Apotheker*. The American performances of this classic took place early in this country's history: the première was held in 1796, in Charleston, South Carolina and was followed by performances later that year in Philadelphia, and in 1798 in New York.

Of the twenty-eight operas which Dittersdorf wrote, only his *Doktor und Apotheker* is still revived on occasion. "Combined with his fresh flow of easy melody, humor, and sense of color," says Francis O. Souper, "he produced a living thing. His crescendos and his finales are two devices in which he shows his dramatic power most markedly."

Upon the death of the Count in 1795, Dittersdorf lost his comfortable post. He now fell upon evil days, darkened by poverty, illness, and the total eclipse of his erstwhile popularity. People had lost interest in his music. Breitkopf and Härtel, the publishers, informed him that they had ceased to issue his works because musicians everywhere neglected them.

Dittersdorf finally found a patron in Baron von Stillfried, who provided him with lodgings in his Bohemian estate, Rothlhotta, near Neuhof. He lived there for the last years of his life in complete obscurity, crippled by gout, absorbed only in his autobiography, which he dictated to his son. He died in Neuhof on October 24, 1799.

In addition to the programmatic orchestral compositions based on Ovid, Dittersdorf completed about fifty symphonies. These were so highly regarded when the composer was still at the height of his fame that some contemporaries considered them the equal of certain works by Haydn and Mozart. Discussing these symphonies, Friedrick Niecks explained that "there is a great deal of tone-painting, but extremely little of what is popularly so called, namely, imitation of nature. The object of the composer's painting is moods and feelings, and scenes and actions in their brightness or darkness, their rest or movement, their swiftness or slowness, their

precipitance or reluctance, their vigor or languor, their roughness or smoothness. . . . The
style of the symphonies is that of a facile,
but not of a careless or insipid, writer. Dittersdorf had not the powerful genius of a
Haydn, a Mozart, or a Beethoven, but the
freshness and abundance of his ideas and his
dexterous handling of the form prove that he
was more than a mere man of talent; that,
in fact, he too was a genius, only much less
exalted than the three sublimities."

Dittersdorf was also the composer of many
string quartets, some of which are still heard
today and have been recorded. These, too,
were esteemed in their day almost as highly
as the chamber music of Haydn and Mozart.

PRINCIPAL WORKS

Chamber Music—String quartets; 12 divertissements for two violins and cello.

Choral Music—Oratorios including Isacco,
Davidde, Ester, Job; cantatas.

Operas—28 operas including Doktor und
Apotheker, Betrug durch Aberglauben, Democrito
corretto, Die Liebe im Narrenhaus, Hieronymus
Knicker.

Orchestral Music—About 60 symphonies, including twelve based on Ovid's Metamorphoses;
12 violin concertos; Concerto Grosso; Il Combattimento dell'umane passioni.

Piano Music—12 sonatas for four hands; 72
preludes.

ABOUT

Dittersdorf, Karl Ditters von, Autobiography;
Krebs, C., Dittersdorfiana; Nettl, P., Forgotten
Musicians.

Monthly Musical Record, February 1929; Music
and Letters, November 1930.

Gaetano Donizetti *1797-1848*

D OMENICO GAETANO MARIA DONI-
ZETTI, the composer of *Don Pasquale*
and *Lucia di Lammermoor*, was born in Bergamo, Italy, on November 29, 1797. He was
the youngest of four sons. Two of his
brothers played in military bands. His
father, a weaver who became a pawnbroker
three years after Gaetano's birth, apprenticed
Gaetano to an architect, but the boy proved
so listless and apathetic that his master summarily dismissed him. His father next hoped
to direct Gaetano to law. But Gaetano
showed interest only in the arts, particularly
in music, and his father finally permitted
him to enter the Bergamo School of Music.
At school Donizetti studied music with passionate intensity. Upon the recommendation
of one of his teachers, Johann Simon Mayr,

GAETANO DONIZETTI

he was sent in 1815 to the Liceo Filarmonico
in Bologna, to become a pupil of Padre Mattei. Mattei, who had been one of Rossini's
teachers, stirred Donizetti's interest in the
operas of Rossini, some of which he had
already studied at the Bergamo School. They
were to remain an enduring influence.

When Donizetti's studies at the Liceo
were completed, his father insisted that he
turn to teaching for his livelihood. This
prospect was so disagreeable to the youth
that he enlisted in the Austrian army instead. Happily, his superiors permitted him
to pursue a career in music. In 1818 he completed the opera *Enrico di Borgogna,* introduced that year in Venice. (This was not,
as is sometimes claimed, his first opera; between 1816 and 1817 he had written three
others which were not performed.) *Enrico
di Borgogna* was modeled after Rossini's
works, as were its immediate successors. The
triumph of another early opera, *Zoraide di
Granata,* had unexpected consequences. Introduced at the Teatro Argentina in Rome
on January 28, 1822, it met with wild acclaim: after the première Donizetti was carried on the shoulders of opera-lovers to the
Capitol, to be "crowned" king of opera. In
further cognizance of his success, the government released him from all further military
duty.

Once he could devote himself to composition, Donizetti became remarkably prolific.
Between 1822 and 1829 he wrote and produced over twenty operas, four in 1828

alone. All were strongly influenced by Rossini. In 1824, he married Virginia Vasselli, a girl of sixteen, with whom he was idyllically happy. They had three children, but none survived: two were stillborn, and the third died two weeks after birth. Virginia died of cholera fourteen years after their marriage.

The second period of Donizetti's creative development began with *Anna Bolena*, which he wrote for the celebrated Italian opera stars Pasta and Rubini. Introduced at the Teatro Carcano in Milan on December 26, 1830, *Anna Bolena* was a success of the first magnitude. Moreover, it showed a new freedom from the influence of Rossini. With this work Donizetti began to evolve an individual dramatic style and a personal lyricism. Performed throughout Europe, *Anna Bolena* gave its composer international renown for the first time. Donizetti was already hailed by many as Rossini's successor, though it can hardly have been realized at the time that in 1829, with *William Tell,* Rossini had written his last opera.

During the next five years, Donizetti wrote fifteen operas, two of which reveal his fullest creative powers. One was an *opera buffa*, *L'Elisir d'amore*, based on a libretto by Eugène Scribe, and introduced in Milan on May 12, 1832. A remarkable gift for *bel canto,* combined with deft characterization and a ready wit, made *L'Elisir* an immediate favorite with audiences; an extraordinary demand required that it be given thirty-two consecutive evenings in Milan.

"Fresh, graceful and occasionally tender," wrote R. A. Streatfeild, "it forms the happiest contrast to the grandiose nonsense which the composer was in the habit of turning out to suit the vitiated taste of the day, and is a convincing proof that if he had been permitted to exercise his talent in a congenial sphere, Donizetti would be entitled to rank with the most successful followers of Cimarosa and Paisiello."

L'Elisir d'amore—first performed in the United States at the Park Theatre in New York on June 18, 1838—was a particular favorite of Enrico Caruso. He never failed to win ovations for his performances of its most memorable aria, "Una furtiva lagrima." It was for Caruso that the Metropolitan Opera revived *L'Elisir* in 1904; and it was while appearing in this opera in Brooklyn, in 1920, that Caruso was stricken on stage with the throat hemorrhage that soon afterwards took his life.

On September 26, 1835, three and a half years after the world première of *L'Elisir,* Donizetti's most celebrated *opera seria,* *Lucia di Lammermoor,* was introduced in Naples. *Lucia,* based on Sir Walter Scott's *Bride of Lammermoor,* is the opera by which Donizetti is most often represented today in the world's leading opera houses. Stark in its tragedy where *L'Elisir* had been vivacious and light of heart, *Lucia* is nevertheless as fresh and spontaneous in its lyricism as the *opera buffa* that had preceded it. But beyond the beauty of its arias, *Lucia* is outstanding for the brilliance of its coloratura writing, for the intensity of its emotions, for its stirring dramatic values. The unforgettable drama of the famous "Mad Scene," and the skillful ensemble writing and penetrating characterization of the second act sextet, "Chi mi frena" (one of the most famous ensembles in all opera), are only two of its many outstanding portions. There are many other passages, as Herbert F. Peyser pointed out, "in which the genius of Donizetti reveals itself at its most characteristic. The first two choruses of the opening scene . . . and a little later the lilting 'Come vinti da stanchezza,' are typical of their composer. . . . More important is Henry Ashton's vigorous expression of his intention to avenge his wrongs upon Edgardo Ravenswood . . . ('La pietade in suo favore') which concludes in a spirited chorus of his retainers. . . . The . . . music from this point [the Sextet] to the close of the act, with Edgardo's maledictions and vows of vengeance, is among the great episodes of Italian opera."

His fame enhanced by the success of *Lucia* throughout Europe, Donizetti was invited to Paris in 1835 to help produce several of his operas. In 1837 he was appointed director of the Collegio di Musica in Naples, where he had been professor of counterpoint and composition since 1834.

When in 1839 his opera *Poliuto* (based on Corneille's *Polyeucte*) was censored, Donizetti resigned as director of the Conservatory and went to live in Paris. There the third of his creative periods unfolded, the era of his French operas. The first work belonging to this period was an *opéra-comique* *La Fille du régiment (The Daughter of the Regiment),* introduced at the Opéra-

Comique on February 11, 1840. Despite a rather cool reception, it went on to become a strong favorite with French audiences. By 1914 it had enjoyed over a thousand performances at the Opéra-Comique. It was also highly successful in Italy and Germany. In America the opera was first performed in New Orleans on March 6, 1843.

Stirringly martial and patriotic in spirit, *La Fille* had an especially powerful impact in the United States during both World Wars. When it was revived at the Metropolitan Opera during World War I, Frieda Hempel, in the title role, interpolated into the score the popular song "Keep the Home Fires Burning." And, during World War II, soon after the Nazis had occupied France, Lily Pons appeared in one of the scenes draped in a French flag.

La Favorita, which the Paris Opéra presented on December 2, 1840, was a tragic opera in the grand tradition, with vast scenes, ballets, and stirring climaxes *à la* Meyerbeer. But Donizetti's rare melodic gift was not sacrificed for extravaganza. It is found at its best in the first-act romance of Fernando, "Una vergine," and in Leonora's stirring third-act aria, "O mio Fernando." The last act of *La Favorita,* which rises to dramatic heights, took Donizetti only a few hours to write.

After a brief return to Italy for the production of two new operas, Donizetti visited Vienna for the première of *Linda di Chamounix* at the Kärnthnerthor Theater on May 19, 1842. In recognition of its spectacular triumph the Emperor, Ferdinand I, appointed Donizetti court composer and Master of the Imperial Chapel.

After his return to Paris late in 1842, Donizetti wrote for the Opéra-Comique his greatest work in the *buffa* style and one of the finest Italian comic operas, *Don Pasquale,* presented by the Théâtre des Italiens on January 3, 1843, with a remarkable cast that featured Lablache as Pasquale and included Tamburini, Norina, and Mario. With the help of Ruffini, Donizetti had prepared his own libretto, based on a play by Anelli, and it is said that he completed the entire opera in about two weeks. For all its speed of execution, *Don Pasquale* remains a model of the ideal *opera buffa.* It is consistently melodious and witty; and the music extracts, as Ernest Newman said, "the last ounce of . . . humorous expression out of each situation."

"One of the most remarkable things about *Don Pasquale,*" wrote Wallace Brockway and Herbert Weinstock in *The Opera,* "is its unspoiled freshness. . . . There is springtime in *Don Pasquale. . . .* The chattery, saucy overture, a potpourri of good things from the opera, is Donizetti's most tolerable. . . . The barefaced nonsense of the plot is matched by the high-spirited, often farcical, numbers, reaching their most delicious absurdity in the prolonged quartet at the end of Act II."

Donizetti's last opera was *Catarina Cornaro,* introduced in Naples on January 12, 1844. By then the composer had begun to suffer severely from intense headaches, melancholia, and hallucinations—a possible consequence of a cerebro-spinal disease that had long afflicted him. In 1845 he was found stretched out on the floor of his room, the victim of a paralytic stroke. His mind then began to wander, and for about a year and a half, during 1846 and 1847, Donizetti was confined to an insane asylum in Ivry, where he muttered to himself incessantly. He was released in October 1847 and permitted to return to the city of his birth, to be cared for by his brother. Donizetti died there on April 8, 1848. "More than four thousand persons were present at the funeral," recalled Donizetti's valet. "The procession was composed of the numerous clergy of Bergamo, the most illustrious members of the community and its environs and of the civic guard of the town and suburbs. The discharge of musketry, mingled with the light of three or four thousand torches, presented a fine effect; the whole was enhanced by the presence of three military bands. . . . Never hitherto had such great honors been bestowed on any member of that city." Donizetti was buried outside the town; in 1875 his remains were moved to the S. Maria Maggiore Church in Bergamo.

Donizetti was one of a triumvirate that ruled Italian opera in the first half of the nineteenth century, the other two being Bellini and Rossini. He had serious creative faults. He was too facile, too prolific, too careless. Much of his writing is superficial and trite. But a half dozen of his more than sixty operas enjoy a high rank in the repertory. Donizetti knew the theater and his audiences, and he catered to both with an extraordinarily versatile lyricism that could be charming, charged with emotion, or highly dramatic.

Il Duca d'Alba, an opera on which Donizetti was engaged in 1840 but which he did not live to complete, was performed for the first time in Rome, thirty-four years after the composer's death. It had a belated American première on October 20, 1959. Howard Taubman said of it in the New York *Times:* "At its best *Il Duca d'Alba* has the authentic flair of the Italian lyric theater. . . . The music is molded ingratiatingly for the voices. It has lyricism; it is touching in its handling of the personal destinies of some of its people; it treats the chorus with impressive individuality. . . . Some of the arias are empty in their sentimentality. But suddenly the temperature changes. An aria or a duet takes on intensity. Donizetti rises to the challenge of a fine dramatic moment and writes music that has urgency for today."

PRINCIPAL WORKS

Chamber Music—12 string quartets.

Choral Music—6 Masses; Requiem; Ave Maria; cantatas, motets, psalms, Vespers.

Operas—Anna Bolena; L'Elisir d'amore; Parisina; Lucrezia Borgia; Gemma di Vergy; Lucia di Lammermoor; Il Campanello di notte; Maria di Rudenz; Il Duca d'Alba; La Fille du régiment; Poliuto (or Les Martyres); La Favorita; Linda di Chamounix; Don Pasquale; Maria di Rohan; Dom Sébastien.

Vocal Music—Ariettas, canzonets, duets, songs.

ABOUT

Bossi, L., Donizetti; Fraccaroli, A., Donizetti; Geddo, A., Donizetti, l'uomo, le musiche; Monaldi, G., Gaetano Donizetti; Weinstock, H., Donizetti; Zavadini G., Donizetti: Vita, musiche, epistolario.

John Dowland *1563-1626*

JOHN DOWLAND, distinguished Elizabethan lutenist-composer and the first important composer of songs in England, was born in Ireland, probably in Dalkey in County Dublin, in or about 1563. At fifteen he went to London, finding employment as a page in the household of Sir Henry Cobham. When Sir Henry was appointed English Ambassador to France in 1579, he took Dowland to Paris with him. Dowland remained in Sir Henry's service until 1583; in 1582, while thus employed, Dowland became a convert to Catholicism.

Dowland next joined the staff of Sir Edward Stafford, Cobham's successor as English Ambassador to France, with whom he made several trips to France. Little is known of Dowland's activities during the next few years. About 1585 he returned to England and was married. In 1588 he received a degree in music from Christ Church, Oxford, and, sometime before 1597, a similar degree from Cambridge. In 1588 his first piece of music to be published, a galliard, appeared; in 1592 he contributed several harmonized melodies to a book of psalms by Este.

In or about 1593 Dowland tried to obtain a position as court lutenist and was rejected, probably because of his religion. Embittered by his failure, he left England and for several years traveled on the Continent. In Cassel he was patronized by the Duke of Brunswick; in Italy he studied for a while with Marenzio, the famous madrigalist.

When he returned to England in 1595, Dowland went back to the Protestant faith, perhaps in the hope that this would pave his way to a court position. Although he did not obtain such a position, he soon established an impressive reputation as a performer on the lute, and as a composer. In 1596 several of his compositions for lute appeared in Barley's *New Book of Tableture.* A year later he published the monumental first volume of his *Songs and Airs of Four Parts with Tableture for the Lute,* the first collection of its kind by a major English composer. Here he departed from some of the traditions of madrigal writing to produce the first important art songs in England, by emphasizing a single melody and its accompaniment, and by successfully rendering into music the spirit and mood of his text. This major pioneer work in song literature enjoyed both immediate and enduring success. In sixteen years it was published in five editions and it helped to spread Dowland's fame throughout Europe.

By 1598 Dowland was generally acknowledged to be the foremost living lutenist. Richard Barnfield extolled his performance in a famous sonnet (sometimes erroneously attributed to Shakespeare), telling of his "heavenly touch upon the lute," which "doth ravish human sense." On the strength of his fame as a virtuoso, as well as his success as a composer, Dowland received an appointment as court lutenist to King Christian IV of Denmark on November 11, 1598. His generous salary of five hundred thalers a year was supplemented in 1600 and 1601 by additional gifts of six hundred additional thalers. Dowland resided at Elsinore for several years, a fact which probably accounts for the legend that he gave Shakespeare the plot for *Hamlet.* While employed in Denmark, Dowland published two additional volumes of *Songs and Airs,* in 1600 and 1603. The second volume contains his most celebrated song, "Flow, My Tears" (or "Lachrymae"), as well as "Sorrow Stay" and "I Saw My Lady Weep"; the third includes the excellent pieces "Say, Love" and "Weep No More You Sad Fountains." In 1605, Dowland took an extended leave of absence from the Danish court. In London, he issued his only collection of instrumental music, *Lachrymae, or Seven Tears;* the first composition was based on the melody of his song "Flow, My Tears." He also revisited his birthplace near Dublin in 1605. On this occasion he was given an honorary degree from the University of Dublin.

When Dowland returned to Denmark after a somewhat longer period of time than had been anticipated, he was summarily dismissed from the Danish court for having extended his leave beyond reasonable limits. There were also suspicions that he had engaged in some irresponsible financial activities. In 1609 Dowland returned to England, making his home in London's Fetter Lane. There he completed and published a theoretical treatise on singing. He also found occasional employment as a lutenist in divers homes of the English nobility. In 1612, while employed by Lord Walden, son of the Earl of Suffolk, he published his last collection of songs, *The Pilgrim's Solace.* Despite these intermittent activities, however, Dowland suffered dire financial need. The neglect of Dowland by those who had once honored him was lamented by Henry Peacham in 1612, in the famous poem *Minerva Britanna,* which contains the following lines:

So since (old friend), thy years have made
    thee white,
And thou for others, hath consum'd thy
    spring,
How few regard thee, whom thou didst de-
    light,
And far and near, came once to hear thee
    sing:
Ingrateful times, and worthless age of ours,
That lets us pine, when it hath cropped our
    flowers.

Dowland's last important appointment, in 1615, was as a lutenist to the court of Charles I. He died in London on January 21, 1626.

"His songs," wrote E. H. Fellowes, "show no signs of old age, and indeed some of them sound amazingly modern both as regard form and harmonic effect even in the company of twentieth-century music. . . . The art songs or *Lieder* of Schubert, Schumann and Brahms with piano accompaniment are the lineal descendants of Dowland's 'ayres' with lute accompaniment."

Philip Heseltine considers *A Pilgrim's Solace* as the summit of Dowland's art in song. "Taken as a whole, [it] must be regarded as his masterpiece and the crown of his life and achievement. In every number in this amazing book we see his genius displayed in full maturity. It is a remarkable fact that this book, appearing at a time when polyphonic tradition was fast giving way before the figured bass and its attendant harmonic developments, is at once the most contrapuntal of Dowland's works and the one in which the widest range of purely harmonic combinations may be found. This was, indeed, 'new music,' but it bore little resemblance to the 'new music' of the Italians who were bent on making music subservient to diction. Careful as he was in setting words with the just note and accent . . . Dowland was not the man to sacrifice any element of musical expression to mere verbal exigencies."

PRINCIPAL WORKS

Chamber Music—Lachrymae, or Seven Tears, for viols and lute.
Vocal Music—3 volumes of Songs or Airs; A Pilgrim's Solace.

ABOUT

Fellowes, E. H., The English Madrigal Composers; Flood, W. H., Late Tudor Composers; Warlock, P., The English Ayre.

Guillaume Dufay *1400-1474*

G UILLAUME DUFAY, an outstanding figure in the Flemish school of polyphony, was born in Hainaut in the Low Countries, in or about 1400. As a boy chorister at the Cathedral of Cambrai he studied music with Grenon and Loqueville. At sixteen he wrote a song that was performed at the marriage ceremonies of Charles Malatesti and Vittoria di Lorenzo Colonna, niece of Pope Martin V.

Between 1419 and 1426, Dufay traveled a great deal. He resided in several Italian cities, including Rimini and Pesaro, and in 1427 seems to have attended the University of Bologna. For a two-year period, between 1426 and 1428, he was *maître de chapelle* in Cambrai. From 1428 to 1433, and again from 1434 to 1437, he sang in the papal choir. During that period he was also patronized by Louis, Duke of Savoy, with whom he resided. On March 21, 1437, he entered the priesthood, becoming a canon at Cambrai. (Later that year he was in Paris, attending the Sorbonne.) In 1438 he was appointed canon of Saint-Donatien in Bruges.

From 1438 to 1444 Dufay resided in Savoy. In or about 1445 he received a law degree from the University of Turin, and appears to have established permanent residence in Cambrai that year, again becoming a canon. Since the clerical post allowed him extended leaves of absence, he was also able to serve as canon at Sainte-Waudru in Mons in 1446, and as cantor for the Duke of Burgundy in 1450. In 1450 the town of Cambrai presented Dufay, by then a highly esteemed musician, with an honorarium of sixty gold pieces "because of the quality and merit of our master . . . who has enriched our church with musical songs."

During his lifetime Dufay helped to make Cambrai one of the foremost centers of polyphonic music of the day. He had many disciples, one of the most distinguished of whom was Gilles Binchois (1400-1460).

Dufay died in Cambrai on November 27, 1474. A few months before his death, on July 8, he prepared his last will and testament, asking that a group of Cathedral choristers sing to him on his deathbed one of his own hymns, "Magno salutis gaudio," and the motet (Ave Regina), one of his most deeply moving compositions, which he had written ten years earlier for this very purpose. His wish was not fulfilled exactly as he had requested; the Ave Regina was instead sung at his funeral services.

Dufay wrote about one hundred and fifty compositions, including French *chansons*, a Magnificat, Masses and motets. An important early influence on his music was the French Gothic school of the fourteenth century; later Dufay was influenced even more strongly by the music of John Dunstable. "There can be no doubt," says Charles van den Borren, "that Dufay would not have

been what he was if the English master had not shown him the way. He owes much to Dunstable. . . . [But] it is precisely because he knew how to emancipate himself from this influence that he won the eminent position which he occupies in the history of music."

Dufay's seven Masses, of which the *Missa Caput* is perhaps the greatest, were long regarded as his chief contribution to the polyphonic music of his day. But Julien Tiersot, recognizing their artistic merit and historic importance, feels that "they are not, in any case, the vast and complete monuments like those which Palestrina, Bach, and Beethoven erected later on. This inferiority explains itself: the material, in the time of Dufay, was hardly assembled. . . . After all, the architect does not create the stone; he merely assembles it and gives it shape."

Paul Henry Lang points out that Dufay and his Flemish contemporaries and immediate successors "cultivated the song (in the modern sense of the word), the song which gives a perfect picture of the poem and its content. . . . Quiet, profound, transcendent feelings are their domain and self-restraint and tasteful expression is their ideal."

PRINCIPAL WORKS

Choral Music—7 Masses including L'Homme armé and Missa Caput; hymns, Magnificat, motets.

Vocal Music—59 French chansons.

ABOUT

Borren, C. van den, Guillaume Dufay, son importance dans l'évolution de la musique au XVe siècle; Bukofzer, M., Studies in Medieval and Renaissance Music; Reese, G., Music in the Renaissance; Sollitt E. N., From Dufay to Sweelinck; Stainer, J., Dufay and His Contemporaries.

Musical Quarterly, July 1935; The Score, January 1950.

John Dunstable *1370-1453*

JOHN DUNSTABLE, England's first important composer, was born in or about 1370, probably in Dunstable, Bedfordshire, England. Biographical material about him is meager. Recent research has revealed that various members of his family had been highly successful skinners and landowners. Nothing is known about his early years or musical training. It is known that from 1419 to 1440 he served as canon of Hereford

Cathedral and prebendary of Putson Manor, and was for several years in the service of the Duke of Bedford. He died in London on December 24, 1453, and was buried in St. Stephen's Church in the Walbrook district of London. His gravestone describes him as "astrologer, mathematician, and musician." "Thus in our time," said Johannes Tinctoris of Dunstable in the fifteenth century, "music took a wonderful flight because it seemed to be a new art which originated with the English under the leadership of Dunstable."

The manuscripts of about fifty choral and vocal works by Dunstable have survived, mainly in collections in Trent, Modena, and the British Museum. With Machaut, Dunstable is one of the earliest composers in the history of Western music who, as Ernest Walker remarks, "can really be said, archaic though his method inevitably is, to have something like artistic style. His feeling for melodiousness of parts is often very remarkable, and occasionally he rises to sheer beauty, as in the delicate little Alleluia at the end of his motet, *Quam pulcra es.*"

Martin le Franc has singled out "sweetness of tone and firmness of outline" as two distinguishing features of Dunstable's music. Of the first quality H. E. Wooldridge wrote: "In beauty, in sweetness and purity of sound . . . [Dunstable's music] by far exceeded that of the foreign schools to whom, indeed, as they themselves confessed, it came as a revelation, and the prospect of a new art; but its texture was equal with that of the foreign music lacking in respect of variety, and was not at all adaptable to the special sentiment of words. The eminence of Dunstable . . . consisted not so much in a finer and more expressive style than theirs, as in more effective varieties of plan and contrivance in the presentation of this somewhat monotonously beautiful material."

Yet expressiveness is precisely the trait which Charles van den Borren finds in all of Dunstable's works. "Expression—that is the right term to use in speaking of Dunstable. . . . There can be no doubt that in this respect Dunstable has realized works which are more and better than beautiful sonorous compositions. The sacred motets have not only a character essentially different from the secular *chansons* of the time, but one may go so far as to say that the

English master often inspired the generalized expression of his melody with a romantic subjectivity, of which no trace is to be found in his Franco-Netherlandish successors in the second half of the fifteenth century."

In reviewing an album of Dunstable's sacred secular music issued by Expériences Anonymes, Alan Rich emphasized the English character of Dunstable's harmonic language. "The English musical traditions behind Dunstable were quite different from those in other parts of Europe. Especially notable was the English love for rich, euphonious harmonies based on the intervals of thirds and sixths. These intervals were considered dissonant and banned elsewhere in the Middle Ages. . . . Dunstable's rich harmonies became the turning point in the development of the fifteenth-century Flemish style, out of which grew such later masters as Josquin des Prés. But Dunstable's music is worthy for more than merely historical considerations. He can be rightly regarded as the first 'modern' composer, whose approach to melody and harmony sired a line of musical thinking that comes right down to our own time."

PRINCIPAL WORKS
Choral Music—Masses, motets, part songs.
Vocal Music—chansons.

ABOUT
Davey, H., A History of English Music; Harvey, J., Gothic England.

Musical Quarterly, July 1954; Proceedings of the Musical Association (London), 1921, 1938.

Henri Duparc *1848-1933*

MARIE EUGÈNE HENRI FOUQUES DUPARC, outstanding French composer of art songs, was born in Paris on January 21, 1848. He showed little interest in music during his boyhood. Nor did he object to the career in law planned for him when he was sent to the Jesuit school at Vaugirard for his academic education. But César Franck gave piano lessons at Vaugirard and Duparc became one of Franck's pupils and, as Franck himself later maintained, one of his best. Under Franck's influence Duparc started to attend concerts, study harmony, and begin composition. His first large-scale work was a cello sonata, in 1867, his first publication a set of piano

HENRI DUPARC

pieces, *Feuilles volantes,* in 1869. Several orchestral works followed: *Poème nocturne* in 1873; *Aux étoiles,* performed in Paris on April 11, 1874; *Ländler,* introduced at a concert of the Société Nationale on June 24, 1874; and *Lénore,* a tone poem presented at a Concert Populaire directed by Pasdeloup on October 28, 1877. Later in life, Duparc destroyed most of his adolescent compositions as unworthy of survival. The only exceptions were *Aux étoiles,* which he allowed to be published in 1910, and *Lénore.* The latter is Duparc's most celebrated orchestral work, its popularity enhanced by a transcription for two pianos by Saint-Saëns and for duet piano by Franck.

It is in the art song that Duparc achieved his greatest and most enduring work. His first five songs, which appeared in 1868, already included two masterpieces, "Soupir" and "Chanson triste." He wrote only twelve songs after 1868 (the last in 1884), most with orchestral accompaniment. Thus the total of Duparc's lifetime of achievement in the song form amounts to a mere handful of pieces. But the power of his invention, the sensitivity of his blending of music and words, and the subtlety of his art have assured him, with a paltry seventeen songs, an unquestioned place in French music as a leader in the renaissance of French song and have given him stature among the greatest song composers of all time.

In discussing Duparc's songs, Georges Jean-Aubry wrote: "There is perhaps no expression more apt to throw light on the nature of Henri Duparc's work than the sentence in which Baudelaire says, 'I have found the definition of the beautiful, of that which, to me, is beauty; it is something ardent and sad, something a little vague, leaving scope for conjecture.' For Henri Duparc, beauty is of the same nature. It is something ardent and sad, but this ardor is not set free, this sadness is not spoken, but is exhaled with poignant simplicity. The art of these works is not complex, although the substance of the musical dream contained in them is rich. This art is not complex if the writing is considered in general. From the first moment, a line is revealed that is noble and of wholly classical purity. It is not until afterwards that we are struck with the delicate undulation of this line, in which is discovered a power of expression that cannot be surpassed by methods of refinement. . . . It is nearly always . . . by means of nuances that Henri Duparc gives accents to his dreams. Nothing is further from Romanticism and from verbal lyricism, but perhaps nothing is nearer to the modern soul, whose deepest anxieties are betrayed, outwardly, only by almost imperceptible waves."

Since Franck exerted so powerful an influence on Duparc, it is interesting to compare the style of the two composers. "Duparc's pupilage is unmistakable," said Sydney Northcote. "It may be discerned in such general tendencies as enharmonic modulations and characteristic chromaticisms, a fondness for the two-bar phrase unit, and here and there a typical melodic motive. But there is a manifest, a subtle and sure sense of dramatic expression, and a more positive melodic eloquence than the master ever achieved. His harmonic texture lacks the depth and infallibility of Franck, and now and then it succumbs to the limitations of the idiom. But it is always fluid and expressive, with a sincere impressionism that is at once restrained and natural. There is a quality of originality in the flexibility and amplitude of phrases and development, and the sincerity and balance of the declamation are undeniable."

Though Duparc lived until 1933, he produced little creative work for the last fifty years of his life, after the composition of "La vie antérieure" in 1884. All his life he had been afflicted by agonizing anxieties and nervous disturbances; after 1884 these tensions made it completely impossible for him to compose. "It is frightful," he wrote to a friend in 1888, "to be so neurotic as I certainly am. The least little thing finishes me." He contemplated writing an opera, *Russalka*, based on Pushkin, and from time to time he toyed with other operatic projects, including *King Lear*. But he seemed incapable of actually undertaking a project, burdened as he was by a relentlessly severe artistic conscience, overwhelmed by inexplicable fears, arrested by inhibitions that stifled further activity.

In 1885 Duparc left Paris and settled for a while in Switzerland with the hope of regaining his mental equilibrium, attended to solicitously by his patient wife and devoted children. A few years later he returned to France, residing first in Pau, then at Tarbes. His mental and physical health continued to deteriorate. His eyesight began to fail him, and then paralysis set in. He visited the shrine at Lourdes in hope of finding a miraculous cure; it never came. Then he sought refuge in religious ecstasy, a development he described in an extended prayer in prose. Beyond his religious preoccupation, his main diversion was painting. But to music, to his fellow musicians, to his past compositions he seemed completely indifferent.

Henri Duparc died at Mont de Marsan, France, on February 12, 1933.

Duparc was one of the founding fathers of a society organized in Paris in 1871, the renowned Société Nationale de Musique, which provided hearings for the works of new French composers.

César Franck dedicated his celebrated Symphony in D minor to Duparc.

PRINCIPAL WORKS
Orchestral Music—Aux étoiles; Lénore.

Piano Music—Feuilles volantes.

Vocal Music—Sérénade; Romance de Mignon; Galop; Chanson triste; Soupir; L'Invitation au voyage; La Vague et la cloche; Extase; Sérénade florentine; Le Manoir de Rosemonde; Testament; Phydilé; Lamento; Élégie; La Vie antérieure; Au pays où se fait la guerre; La Fuite, vocal duet.

ABOUT
Bacharach, A. L. (editor), The Music Masters, vol. 3; Coeuroy, A., La Musique française; Ferchault, G., Henri Duparc; Northcote, S., The Songs of Henri Duparc; Séré, O., Musiciens français d'aujourd'hui.

Music and Letters, October 1932.

Francesco Durante *1684-1755*

THOUGH the music of Francesco Durante is no longer performed, he was in the eighteenth century one of the most successful, influential, and highly esteemed Italian church composers. He was born in Frattamaggiore, near Naples, on March 31, 1684. As a boy he attended the Conservatory di Sant' Onofrio, where his uncle, Angelo Durante, held a teaching post. Francesco left the Conservatory to go to Rome, continuing his studies with Pitoni and Pasquini. It was there that his lifelong preoccupation with church music began.

In July 1710 Durante became instructor at the Sant' Onofrio Conservatory in Naples, but he remained only six months. Little is known of his activities for the next seventeen years; however, there is good reason to believe that he spent some of that time in Germany. In 1728 he was appointed *maestro di cappella* at the Conservatory dei Poveri di Gesu Cristo. He left this post in 1739, then in 1742 returned to it, remaining for the rest of his life. After 1742 he also served as *primo maestro,* and later as teacher, at Sant' Onofrio; he was also a faculty member of the Conservatory of Santa Maria di Loreto. Durante was one of the most distinguished teachers of his generation; his many pupils included some who would become eminent opera composers: Pergolesi, Piccini, Jommelli, Sacchini, and Paisiello.

Francesco Durante died in Naples on August 13, 1755.

Durante married three times. His first wife was a shrew and a passionate gambler, with little regard for his career or achievements. On one occasion she sold his manuscripts for a trifling sum so that she could indulge her vice; Durante was reduced to the laborious task of rewriting his music from memory. He worked through many nights to earn additional funds for defraying her debts. After her death, Durante married one of his servants, to whom he was tenderly devoted until her untimely death. His third wife was also one of his servants.

"Durante," writes Frederick Westlake, "seems to have been a man of the utmost integrity, at once simple and profoundly wise. We find him in the records of the Neapolitan conservatories, called in to compose the differences between his more excitable colleagues. He was a great 'character,' who bore the sorrows and afflictions of his life with a positively superhuman equanimity. . . . His simple manners were endearing. Always rather slovenly dressed, he nevertheless attached considerable importance to his wig, on which a good deal of his dignity depended. In order not to disarrange it he would carry his three-cornered hat under his right arm and would often be seen to stop in the streets and purchase some fresh figs, which he put in his hand and consumed on the way to the Conservatory. He seems to have been fond of fruit: Paisiello records that he died 'of a diarrhea brought on by a feed of melons.' "

Durante was one of the leading creative figures in the Neapolitan school. Though he composed some instrumental music, his immense reputation in his own time rested almost exclusively on his sacred works. His many oratorios, motets, psalms, cantatas and hymns were so widely performed throughout Europe that Jean-Jacques Rousseau once called him "the greatest harmonist of Italy, that is to say, of the world."

Edward J. Dent wrote of Durante that he "is sentimental. . . . He has no great love for massive contrapuntal effects. His parts weave in and out on purely conventional lines; the same sequences and imitations are perpetually recurring, and his most individual moments are to be found in his somewhat sugary solos. When he is at his very best, he is most touchingly beautiful, and seems to foreshadow Mozart."

PRINCIPAL WORKS

Chamber Music—12 duetti da camera for two violins; divertimenti.

Choral Music—50 motets; 14 Masses; 3 oratorios; antiphons, hymns, madrigals, psalms.

Harpsichord Music—6 sonatas; fugues, partitas, toccatas.

Vocal Music—18 duets for soprano and contralto; 6 secular solo cantatas.

ABOUT

Musica d'oggi, August-September 1936.

Jan Dussek *1760-1812*

JAN LADISLAV DUSSEK, the first important Bohemian composer for the piano, was born in Čáslav on February 12, 1760. He was the eldest of three brothers who all became professional musicians; their father

was the town choirmaster and organist. Jan was only five when his father started to give him piano lessons and nine when he began to study organ. As a boy, he was sent to Iglau as a chorister at the Minorite Church. There his music study continued with Father Ladislav Špinar. At the College of Jesuits, he began his study of the humanities. Soon fired with the ambition to enter the Church, he proceeded to Prague, where for two years he studied theology, receiving a bachelor's degree. An Austrian artillery officer, Count Männer, became his patron and brought him to Malines. There Dussek gave his first professional piano recital, on December 16, 1779. For a short period he was organist of St. Rombaut Church in Malines. Then, feeling the need for a new setting, he went on to Berg-op-Zoom, serving as organist in one of its main churches. It was the last time he was to be employed in this capacity.

In 1782 Dussek moved to Amsterdam, the city where his first works were published: three clavier concertos and twelve violin sonatas. As a result of his success, Dussek was invited to The Hague to give music lessons to the children of the Stadtholder. After a year, despite his growing eminence as a composer and pianist, Dussek felt he needed further musical education. He sought out Carl Philipp Emanuel Bach in Hamburg and for about a year studied assiduously with him. Dussek then made a sensational concert appearance in Paris, astonishing his audience with his amazing virtuosity on the piano and harmonica.

For several years thereafter Dussek toured Europe extensively, giving concerts on the piano and the harmonica. In St. Petersburg Prince Radziwill invited him to become his house musician at his palace in Lithuania. Dussek remained a year, then continued to tour Germany and Poland. In 1786 he arrived in France, where Marie Antoinette, enchanted with his performances, made him generous offers to stay and work at Versailles. But Dussek had set his heart on Italy, and went on to that country to gather fresh accolades, especially for his harmonica performances. By 1788 he was back in France, but sensing the imminence of revolution, departed soon for England.

Dussek, as Harold C. Schonberg has pointed out, was the first of the great touring piano virtuosos. He was "constantly on the

Dussek: doo'shĕk

move. . . . He was a celebrity and a show-man, and a good musician and a great pian-ist to boot." What effect Dussek had on his audiences everywhere was proved by a state-ment from one of Dussek's noted contem-poraries, Johann Wenzel Tomaschek: "After the few opening bars of his first solo, the public uttered one general 'Ah!' There was, in fact, something magical about the way in which Dussek, with all his charming grace of manner, through his wonderful touch, extracted from the instrument deli-cious and at the same time emphatic tones. His fingers were like a company of ten sing-ers endowed with equal executive powers and able to produce with the utmost perfection whatever their director could require."

For the next twelve years Dussek lived in England, establishing an excellent reputation as a teacher of piano and winning the high regard of many famous musicians. Haydn himself, after his first visit to London in 1792, wrote to Dussek's father that he con-sidered himself "fortunate in being able to assure you that you have one of the most upright, moral and, in music, most eminent of men as a son."

In 1792 Dussek married Sophia Corri, a seventeen-year-old singer. They had one child, a daughter, born in 1801. Soon after his marriage Dussek entered into a business partnership with his father-in-law. Unfor-tunately, Dussek was no entrepreneur: he was extravagant, impractical, and completely uninterested in commerce. In 1800 he was compelled to flee London to avoid imprison-ment for debt. In Germany, where he re-mained for two years, he met Prince Louis Ferdinand of Prussia, who persuaded him to serve as a musician to his households in Ber-lin and Magdeburg. When the Prince died in the battle of Saalfeld in 1806, Dussek wrote one of his finest compositions as a memorial, the *Élégie harmonique* for piano, which James W. Davison considers "one of the most pathetic and beautiful in the repertory."

From 1806 to 1807 Dussek was in the serv-ice of the Prince of Isenburg. After resigning from this post, he became chamber musician and household music director for Talleyrand in Paris, a position that afforded him a great deal of freedom and leisure. Since demands on his time and effort were singularly spar-ing, Dussek grew fat and lazy, and drank too much. Finally, a severe attack of gout forced him to give up his sinecure and go into com-

JAN DUSSEK

plete retirement in St. Germain-en-Laye, outside Paris. He died there on March 20. 1812.

A. W. Thayer considered Dussek as "good, noble, and just, impartial and kindly, a real friend; sympathizing with all that was true and beautiful in those he knew . . . while his joyous disposition, liberal sentiments, and freedom from prejudice of any kind endeared him especially to musicians."

Although Dussek wrote a substantial amount of chamber music, his most impor-tant works are for piano. He not only had an extraordinary sense of classic form and an aristocratic style, but often anticipated the harmonic language and Romantic spirit of such later masters as Schubert and Brahms. Some of his piano sonatas contain remarkable canonic passages, and the influ-ence of his long career as an organist is clearly felt in some of the slow movements.

Time has tended to dwarf Dussek's artistic stature. He stood, after all, between two giants of piano music, Mozart and Beethoven. But C. Hubert Parry takes pains to point out that his proximity to these towering figures did not "suppress Dussek's personality or extinguish his individuality, which is still clear in his own line, and has exerted some influence both upon the modern style of playing, and also upon the style of musical thought of a few modern composers to whom the giants did not appeal strongly."

"If this artist with his numerous and rich melodic ideas," said Henri de Curzon, "had taken the pains of deepening and developing them musically, his compositions would have assumed a much stronger and more original character. They possessed improvisations of great beauty, amplitude and unrivaled poetry, and certain of his 'organ points' are celebrated."

Some of Dussek's most important piano sonatas are the C minor, op. 35, no. 3; the *Farewell,* in E-flat major, dedicated to Clementi, op. 44; the E-flat major, op. 75; and his last sonata, *L'Invocation,* in F minor, op. 77.

PRINCIPAL WORKS

Chamber Music—about 30 violin sonatas; 14 piano trios; 3 string quartets; flute sonatas; Piano Quartet in E-flat; Piano Quintet in F minor.

Choral Music—Grand Mass.

Harp Music—6 sonatinas.

Opera—The Captive.

Orchestral Music—12 piano concertos; Serenade in E-flat; Feudal Times.

Piano Music—40 sonatas; 9 sonatas for four hands; Sonata in E-flat for two pianos; dances, rondos, preludes, variations, and other pieces.

Vocal Music—Canzonets; various songs for voice and piano; Canons, for three and four voices.

ABOUT

Blom, E., Classics: Major and Minor; Schonberg, H. C., The Great Pianists.

Music Review, February 1955; Musical Opinion, December 1927.

Antonín Dvořák *1841-1904*

A NTONÍN DVOŘÁK, Bohemia's most celebrated composer, was born in Nelahozeves, near Prague, on September 8, 1841. He was the eldest of eight children. His father was an innkeeper and butcher who hoped to make Antonín a businessman. From childhood, however, Antonín displayed interest only in music. He received instruction in music from a local teacher; at eight he sang solos in church and sometimes played the violin in the town band. Later, in Zlonice, where he was sent at the age of twelve to learn German in preparation for a business career, he was taught organ, piano, and theory by Anton Liehmann.

For a while Dvořák worked for his father. Then in 1857 he received permission and assistance to attend the Organ School in Prague for comprehensive training in music. For about ten years after his graduation in

1859, he supported himself by giving music lessons and playing viola in the orchestra of the National Theater. He lived in abject poverty and complete obscurity. During this period, however, he wrote a good deal of music in the German Romantic style.

When Bedřich Smetana was appointed conductor of the National Theater, Dvořák came under his influence. It was through Smetana that Dvořák's interest in national Bohemian music was aroused, although it was some time before he actually wrote in a national style. His first opera, *Alfred,* was a frank imitation of Wagnerian opera; other works—symphonies, chamber music, Masses —were reminiscent of Beethoven, Mozart, or Liszt.

Dvořák's first work in a national idiom was *Hymnus,* a cantata for chorus and orchestra based on Hálek's poem *The Heirs of the White Mountain.* Introduced in Prague on March 9, 1873, it scored a major success. That year Dvořák became organist of the St. Ethelbert Church, where he remained for about three years. Assured of some measure of financial security, he married Anna Čermáková, a member of the chorus of the National Theater. She bore him six children, and died twenty-seven years after his death.

Dvořák now made impressive progress as a composer. His Symphony in E-flat was introduced in Prague in 1874, and in 1875 received the Austrian State Prize. *The King and the Collier,* a delightful comic opera, was acclaimed at its première at the National Theater on November 24, 1874. In 1876 Dvořák completed a group of vocal duets, *Airs from Moravia,* which received a prize from the Austrian State Commission.

Dvořák's first choral masterwork, the Stabat Mater, was completed in 1877, inspired by the tragic death of his first-born, a three-and-a-half-year-old son. "In his overwhelming sorrow," says Rosa Newmarch, "the composer turned to the Stabat Mater in which he found a vent for his grief and a source of consolation. . . . [He seems] suddenly to have matured. Nothing he achieved before it, and few of the works that immediately followed it, show such clear and definite lines, such finish in structural details." The Stabat Mater was heard for the first time in Prague, on Christmas Day of 1880. On March 19, 1883, it was given in London where it was such a triumph that the composer was invited to direct the work in England during the following season. Dvořák conducted a mammoth performance in London with an orchestra of one hundred and fifty and a chorus of nine hundred, and the work was repeated at the Worcester Festival.

Meanwhile, Dvořák was also beginning to attract interest in Bohemia and Austria. Johannes Brahms, then a member of the Austrian Commission, took a personal interest in Dvořák, and referred the younger composer to his publisher, Simrock. "I have recommended him to send you his *Moravian Duets*. If you play them through you will enjoy them as much as I have done. . . . Dvořák has written in all possible branches: operas, symphonies, quartets, piano pieces. Decidedly he is a very talented man. Besides, he is poor. Please take this into consideration."

Simrock published the *Moravian Duets,* then suggested that Dvořák write an album using Bohemian folk melodies and rhythms in the way that Brahms had used Hungarian material for the popular *Hungarian Dances.* Dvořák complied with his first set of eight *Slavonic Dances,* for piano duet, in 1878. Encouraged by their success, Simrock commissioned Dvořák to orchestrate them. In 1886 Dvořák wrote a second series of eight *Slavonic Dances,* again in two arrangements, for four-hand piano and for orchestra. With the *Dances,* Dvořák's reputation spread throughout Europe, bringing him commissions from other publishers and invitations to appear as guest conductor with major orchestras.

Although Dvořák made extensive use of folk rhythms and native melodic idioms in his *Dances,* the basic thematic material was always his own. Folk songs themselves are never borrowed in his work: it is rather in style and spirit that the *Dances* are so intensely nationalistic. As Karel Hoffmeister wrote: "Something of the Slavic character speaks in every phrase of them—the stormy high-spirited mood of the furiants; the whimsical merriment, the charm, the touch of coquetry, the ardent tenderness of the lyrical passages."

Nationalism was also a pronounced element in his other works of this period. He continually introduced such Bohemian dances as the polka and the furiant into his chamber music and orchestral works. In 1878 he completed three *Slavonic Rhapsodies* for orchestra, giving a musical representation

ANTONÍN DVOŘÁK

of old Bohemia—its sagas, knights, and tournaments. He again drew his inspiration from Bohemia of bygone days in *Legends,* in 1881, written originally as a piano duet, and later orchestrated. In 1882 he completed a folk opera, *Dimitrij,* introduced at the National Theater on October 8.

In 1884 Dvořák scored a personal triumph when he went to England for the first time to conduct his Stabat Mater. A welcome guest during the next few years, he continued to appear at leading English festivals, directing premières of his major choral works. One of the most exalted of these compositions was the Requiem, whose world première was directed by Dvořák at the Birmingham Festival in 1890. Long neglected, this masterwork has recently come into its own, particularly after a most successful revival in New York City on February 27, 1964, following an absence of some sixty years. "It is a shame," reported Harold C. Schonberg in the New York *Times,* "that we have had to wait so long for a performance of the noble Dvořák Requiem. It is a beautiful score. . . . Dignified, devout, full of calm and spacious melody, the Requiem is a testament to the composer's faith as well as to his inspiration." In 1891 Cambridge University conferred on him an honorary doctorate; and the Czech University in Prague accorded him a similar honor.

In 1892 Dvořák came to the United States to become director of the National Conservatory in New York, which had been founded in 1885 by Mrs. Jeanette Thurber. Upon arriving in the United States, Dvořák was welcomed at the pier by a chorus of three hundred voices and an orchestra of eighty and presented with a silver wreath. He occupied a five-room apartment at 327 East 17th Street, a stone's throw from the Conservatory. For the next three years his home was a favorite rendezvous for the city's leading musicians.

The critic James Gibbons Huneker and the Negro baritone H. T. Burleigh brought the folk music of the American Negro to Dvořák's attention. Negro spirituals fascinated him; he studied the music avidly and repeatedly asked Burleigh to sing for him now one song, now another. Later he wrote: "These beautiful and varied themes are the product of the soil. They are American. They are the folk songs of America, and your composers must turn to them. In the Negro melodies of America I discover all that is needed for a great and noble school."

Inspired by these melodies, Dvořák wrote several major works in which his thematic material, though always original, derived their character and style from spirituals. One of these was the Concerto in B minor for cello and orchestra; another was his most celebrated symphony, the E minor, entitled *From the New World,* which he completed in 1893. The beautiful elegiac melody of its second movement—which was made into the famous song "Goin' Home," to lyrics by William Arms Fisher—is so pronounced in its emulation of Negro music that it was long suspected to be an actual spiritual which Dvořák had "quoted." But this melody (like all the others in the symphony) is original. Harry Rowe Shelley, one of Dvořák's pupils at the Conservatory, was with Dvořák when he finished writing the slow movement. In shirt sleeves at the piano, Dvořák suddenly "sang out the great theme with passion and fervor. . . . His whole body vibrated." When he had played and sung the whole movement he asked Shelley simply: "Is it not beautiful music?"

The *Symphony from the New World* had its world première in New York on December 15, 1893, with Anton Seidl conducting the New York Philharmonic. It was an astonishing triumph. There was such "wild enthusiasm" after the second movement that the composer had to take bow after bow in his seat in the box. "The success of the symphony was magnificent," Dvořák reported.

"The newspapers say that never has a composer had such a triumph. . . . The public applauded so much that I felt like a king in my box."

Despite this honor and homage, Dvořák was homesick for his native land. For a while he appeased his nostalgia by spending his vacations in the little town of Spillville, Iowa, which had a sizable Bohemian colony. There he could hear the Bohemian language, eat Bohemian food, listen to Bohemian folk music, play the organ at the town church, exchange jokes and small talk with simple people. On his fifty-second birthday his compatriots in Spillville gave him a typically Bohemian feast which touched him deeply.

On one visit to Spillville, Dvořák was host to several Iroquois Indians who had come to play for him some of their tribal songs and dance music. Again Dvořák was impressed with native American art and decided to use it in his own compositions. In this case, too, he avoided using real Indian melodies. Instead he skillfully imitated their style, mood, and stylistic peculiarities. He developed these themes, as he himself explained, "with all the resources of modern rhythm, harmony, counterpoint, and orchestral color." Among the works to employ these themes were the String Quartet in F major, better known as the *American Quartet;* the String Quintet in E-flat major; and a sonatina for violin and piano, whose slow movement was transcribed by Fritz Kreisler as the popular *Indian Lament.*

Homesickness finally forced Dvořák to leave the National Conservatory and return to Prague in 1895. He served briefly as professor at the Prague Conservatory, then, from 1901 until his death, as its director. On his sixtieth birthday—which was celebrated throughout Bohemia, and which brought him honor, tribute, and congratulations from all parts of the world—Dvořák was made a member of the Austrian House of Lords. He was the first musician ever to be honored in this way.

During the last years of his life Dvořák was a victim of Bright's disease. He died in Prague on May 1, 1904. The day of his funeral was declared by government decree an occasion for mourning throughout Bohemia.

Dvořák was a man of utmost simplicity, passionate sincerity, and generosity. He lived without ostentation, rose and retired early, and enjoyed best spending an evening at home with friends. He liked to play cards, but was a bad loser. If he lost several games in sequence, he would throw the cards angrily on the floor. In this respect he behaved like a spoiled child. In other ways, too, he had much of the child in him, particularly in his passion for locomotives and boats. He would travel a great distance to be able to watch a train rush by; he habitually went down to the waterfront in New York once or twice a week to inspect a ship in harbor and, if possible, to discuss its features with the crew. On many evenings he would speculate at what exact point in the Atlantic a certain ship might be at that moment, and how fast it was traveling.

He ate heartily, drank strong coffee in great quantities, and smoked cigars profusely. He was a passionate lover of nature, and delighted in taking long quiet walks in the park. Hypersensitive, he abhorred thunderstorms—would bolt all windows, then play the piano as loudly as he could to drown out the noise of the storm. He was also nervous about crossing streets, and for this reason often induced a friend to accompany him on a walk.

"As a teacher," wrote Paul Stefan, "Dvořák was basically practical. He gave gifted pupils as free a hand as possible. In the less talented he attempted to inculcate at least the fundamentals of technique. And no matter how much irony he employed, he was always fair and intelligent. Joseph Suk used to say that Dvořák would almost drive you to tears, but you learned a good deal in the process. His pupils did not always immediately understand what he meant, but his very being and the intuition he took for granted and knew how to convey to others—all this bridged over every incompatability. If, for instance, he declared: 'I'm very fond of Chopin and Schumann, although I can't bear them,' they knew exactly what he meant."

Discussing the general traits of Dvořák's music, W. H. Hadow said: "His melody is often as simple and ingenuous as a folk song, but in polyphony, in thematic development, in all details of contrast and elaboration, his ideal is to organize the rudimentary life and to advance it into a fuller and more adult maturity. . . . He has little sense of economy, little of that fine reticence and control which underlie the most lavish moments of Brahms

and Beethoven; his use of wealth is so prodigal that his generosity is sometimes left with inadequate resources. . . . But for all this, he is a great genius, true in thought, fertile in imagination, warm and sympathetic in temper of mind."

Philip Hale summed up the strength and weakness of Dvořák's creativity as follows: "His music was best when it smacked of the soil, when he remembered his early days, the strains of vagabond musicians, the dances dear to his folk. One of a happily primitive folk, he delighted in rhythm and color. He was not a man to translate pictures, statues, poems, a system of metaphysics, a gospel of pessimism into music. He was least successful when he would be heroic, mystical, profound. . . . Dvořák had his faults, and they were tiresome and exasperating. His naïveté became a mannerism. Like a child he delighted in vain repetitions; he was at times too much pleased with rhythms and colors, so that he mistook the exterior dress for the substance and forgot that after all there was little or no substance behind the brilliant trappings. We believe that he will ultimately be ranked among the minor poets of music. His complete works may gather dust in libraries; but no carefully chosen anthology will be without examples of his piquancy, strength, and beauty in thought and expression."

Karel Hoffmeister draws the following comparison between Dvořák and Smetana, the Bohemian master who influenced him so decisively: "Both are melodists with a highly developed feeling for characteristic rhythm. But Smetana's melody and rhythm are restricted to his own personality and to the Bohemian character, whereas Dvořák with his wider outlook showed greater diversity in these respects. His music shows a more general Slavonic coloring, and an exclusively Bohemian style appears only from time to time, while here and there we discern his close affinity to his models, Beethoven and Schubert. Smetana works in a more restricted area, but his outline is always firm and original. Dvořák covers a wider ground, but his lines of demarcation are less definite, and occasionally admit an outside influence. . . . Smetana pays comparatively little attention to the externals of his art. . . . Smetana planned for himself a life task: to depict in music the soul of the Bohemian people in all its most significant features. . . . Not so Dvořák. The guiding factor in his creative work was not intellectual power but the gift of intuition. Intellect, which in Smetana balanced intuition, was of far less importance in the case of Dvořák."

PRINCIPAL WORKS

Chamber Music—13 string quartets; 4 piano trios; 3 string quintets; 2 piano quintets; String Sextet in A major; Violin Sonata in F major; Four Romantic Pieces, for violin and piano; Violin Sonatina in G major.

Choral Music—Hymnus; Song of Czechs; Stabat Mater; Amid Nature; The Spectre's Bride; St. Ludmilla; Mass in D major; Requiem; Te Deum; 7 choral songs for unaccompanied male voices; 5 choruses for unaccompanied male voices.

Operas—The King and the Collier; The Pigheaded Peasants; Vanda; The Cunning Peasant; Dimitrij; The Jacobin; The Devil and Kate; Rusalka; Armida.

Orchestral Music—7 published symphonies; 4 tone poems based on ballads by Erben (The Water Sprite, The Midday Witch, The Golden Spinning Wheel, The Wood Dove); 3 concert overtures (In Nature's Realm, Carnival, Othello); 3 Slavonic Rhapsodies; Slavonic Dances, two sets (also for piano four hands); Legends (also for piano duet); My Home; Scherzo capriccioso; Heroic Song; Piano Concerto in G minor; Violin Concerto in A minor; Cello Concerto in B minor.

Piano Music—Silhouettes; Theme and Variations in A-flat; From the Bohemian Forest, for piano duet; Poetic Pictures; Suite in A major, "American"; 8 Humoresques; dumky, waltzes, mazurkas.

Vocal Music—Evening Songs including Songs My Mother Taught Me; Gypsy Songs; 10 Biblical songs; individual songs for voice and piano including The Girl Mowed Grass, In So Great Anxiety of Heart, Leave Me Alone, A Lullaby, The Maiden's Lament, and My Darling, My Little Grass.

ABOUT

Fischl, V. (editor), Antonín Dvořák: His Achievement; Hadow, W. H., Studies in Modern Music; Hoffmeister, K., Antonín Dvořák; Hořejš, A., Antonín Dvořák: The Composer's Life in Pictures; Mason, D. G., From Grieg to Brahms; Robertson, A., Dvořák; Sirp, H., Antonín Dvořák; Sourek, O., Dvořák, Leben und Werk; Stefan, P., The Life and Work of Antonín Dvořák.

Zdeněk Fibich *1850-1900*

Z DENĚK FIBICH, an important member of the Bohemian national school, was born in Šebořice on December 21, 1850. His father, a forester on the estate of Count Auserburg, was in comfortable financial circumstances and encouraged the boy to develop his pronounced musical inclinations through systematic and comprehensive study.

Zdeněk took piano lessons in his native town, then at the age of ten enrolled in the Vienna Conservatory. In 1862 he entered Bedřich Smetana's music school in Prague. There he completed a symphony at the age of fourteen, and directed a public performance of one of its movements.

From 1865 to 1867 he attended the Leipzig Conservatory; his teachers included Moscheles, Richter, and Jadassohn. He wrote a few piano pieces, including *Le Printemps* and *Album Leaves*, his first published works. In 1868 he spent several months in Paris attending the Conservatory. Then for another few months he studied with Vincenz Lachner in Mannheim. In that city he heard his first Wagnerian music-drama, an influence that proved profound and permanent.

Fibich returned to Prague in 1870, married Ružena Hanušova, and settled down to a career as a piano teacher. In 1871 he completed his first opera, *Bukovin*, introduced at the National Theater on April 16, 1874. In 1873 he wrote a *Comedy Overture* for orchestra and his first two tone poems.

In 1873 Fibich also left Prague to accept a teaching position in Vilna. He remained for only a year, partly because of its restricted social life, but largely because his wife had fallen seriously ill there. His wife died in 1874, soon after their return to Prague.

In 1875 Fibich married his sister-in-law, Betty Hanušova, a singer at the National Theater; it seems to have been a marriage of convenience. From 1875 to 1878 he was second conductor of the National Theater, where his second opera, *Blanik*, was presented on November 25, 1881, then, from 1878 to 1881, director of the choir of the Russian Church in Prague.

In 1881 Fibich decided to devote himself completely to composition and resigned his post at the Russian Church. Living as a recluse, he avoided all social contact and rarely left his home, absorbed completely in writing. He composed a third opera, *The Bride of Messina*, his first symphony, two tone poems (*The Tempest* and *Spring*), and some songs.

His most ambitious project was the trilogy *Hippodamia*, a set of three melodramas with music created between 1889 and 1891. Following Wagner's lead, Fibich made such extensive use of the. leitmotiv technique that, at first hearing, one can hardly follow the diverse thematic subjects within the complex fabric. As a whole, says Richard Gorer, "*Hippodamia* can only be reckoned a brilliant *tour de force,* though it should be added that there are passages so effective as to justify the use of melodrama, for they could not be so poignant or effective if any other form were employed."

In or about 1893, Fibich fell in love with Anežka Schulzová, a poetess, and left his family to live with her. Emerging from his long period of withdrawal, Fibich again grew vitally interested in the world outside his home. Anežka wrote the librettos for his last two operas: *Šarka,* in 1897, and *The Fall of Arkun,* in 1898.

During the last years of his life Fibich suffered severely from a kidney disease. He died in Prague on October 15, 1900.

Fibich wrote over six hundred works. "Like Tchaikovsky," wrote Ralph Hill, "Fibich's idiom is more Western than national in style; he used folk song only when a particular tune interested him as such or when his literary text demanded an essentially national treatment. In this way, his musical outlook was the antithesis of his famous contemporaries, Smetana and Dvořák. . . . Most of Fibich's music was directly inspired by poetry and fairy tales of a fantastic nature. His love for poetry and mythology was second only to music. . . . The most interesting and individual part of his output are the piano music and the melodramas."

In his stage works Fibich remained faithful to the aesthetics, principles, and techniques of the Wagnerian music-drama—even when treating Bohemian subjects. In his various melodramas, however—melodramas for stage as well as melodramas with orchestra, or orchestra and piano—Fibich hewed new paths through his effective use of spoken text against musical background. "He completely subjected the music to the poetry," says Henri Hantich. "The spoken voice dominates the symphonic tonality of the orchestra, which makes abundant use of the leitmotiv and is bound by no other rules except those which the dramatic accent imposes. In this way, he went further than Wagner. . . . The ideal type of this new form created by Fibich is the trilogy *Hippodamia.* This work, composed of three dramas . . . abounds with dramatic scenes full of captivating effects, and assures for Fibich a prominent place."

"The importance of Fibich's operas," according to Vladimir Helfert, "lies in the fact that they represent the most faithful application of Wagner's theories in Bohemian opera. . . . Fibich may be called the creator of modern Bohemian melodrama. Following in the footsteps of . . . Schumann and Liszt, Fibich created a new form of melodrama on the basis of the Wagnerian leitmotiv idea. . . . Thereupon he made the bold attempt at creating a great scenic melodrama by means of continuous musical accompaniment to the spoken drama."

One of Fibich's most popular works today is the *Poem* for piano (op. 41, no. 4); it is familiar in numerous transcriptions—for orchestra, voice and orchestra, organ, cello and piano, and violin and piano, the last in an arrangement by Jan Kubelik.

PRINCIPAL WORKS

Chamber Music—2 string quartets; Piano Quartet in E minor; Romance for violin and piano; Idyll, for clarinet and piano; Quintet, for violin, clarinet, horn, cello and piano.

Choral Music—Melusina; The Romance of Spring; Missa brevis.

Operas—Bukovin; Blanik; The Bride of Messina; The Tempest; Hedy; Šárka; The Fall of Arkun.

Orchestral Music—7 tone poems; 4 overtures; 3 symphonies; 3 melodramas; Impressions of the Country; Festival Polonaise for violin and orchestra; In the Twilight; Spring.

Piano Music—Album Leaves; Scherzo; From the Mountains; Moods, Impressions and Reminiscences; Novella; Studies in Painting; Sonata, for four-hand piano; bagatelles and duets for four-hand piano.

Melodramas—Hippodamia (The Wooing of Pelops, The Atonement of Tantalus, Hippodamia's Death).

Vocal Music—Eternity (melodrama with piano); Gleams of Spring; My Sister's Songs; Five Songs for Children; various songs and ballads for voice and piano including Dreaming Lake and My Love Is Like a Red, Red Rose.

ABOUT

Hostinský, O., Erinnerungen an Fibich; Richter, C. L., Zdenko Fibich. Eine musikalische Silhouette.

Musical Opinion, March 1931.

John Field *1782-1837*

JOHN FIELD, the important predecessor of Chopin and innovator of the nocturne form for piano, was born in Dublin, on July 26, 1782. He came from a family of pro-

JOHN FIELD

fessional musicians: his grandfather was a church organist, his father a violinist in the orchestra of the Theatre Royal. Both conducted a musical academy at the home in which John Field was born.

Showing interest in piano when he was seven, John was given his first instruction by his grandfather. The old man was a martinet, so severe in his discipline that on one occasion the boy tried to run away from home to escape his tyranny.

In 1791 Field began study with Tommaso Giordani. A year later Giordani arranged a series of concerts at the Rotunda, and on March 24 Field made his concert debut as pianist. In 1793 Field wrote several piano compositions, and featured his Rondo at one of his concerts in Dublin.

Late in 1793 John Field's father was appointed concertmaster of the Haymarket Theatre orchestra in London. John Field was apprenticed to Muzio Clementi, the celebrated pianist who owned and ran a piano factory. In return for demonstrating and selling pianos Field received piano instruction from Clementi. When he made his London debut in April 1794, Field was billed as Clementi's pupil; and when he appeared in a joint recital with the violinist Barthélemon a month later, Field performed one of his teacher's sonatas. As a pianist Field aroused much interest in London. Some of the city's leading musicians honored him, as did Haydn, visiting England for the second time.

By 1799 Field had written his first piano concerto, which he introduced at a benefit concert at the Haymarket Theatre. Two years later he repeated the work at the Covent Garden Theatre, creating a sensation. His reputation as a composer grew rapidly. Late in 1801 his first volume of piano sonatas was published.

In the summer of 1802, Field left with Clementi on a European tour, to achieve extravagant success in Paris, then Germany, and finally St. Petersburg, where the two musicians arrived early in 1803. Field also demonstrated pianos for Clementi when the latter opened a showroom in St. Petersburg.

The impression that John Field left as a performer was recorded by the eminent violinist-composer Louis Spohr, who was in Russia at the time, in his autobiography: "When Field, who had outgrown his clothes, sat down at the piano and stretched out his arms over the keyboard, so that his sleeves shrank nearly up to his elbows, his whole figure appeared awkward and stiff in the highest degree; but as soon as he began to play, everything else was forgotten, and one became all ears."

Clementi left Russia in the summer of 1803, but Field stayed on. He taught piano to families of the aristocracy, and in a short while became quite wealthy. Affluence brought with it indolence and overindulgence—in food, drink, and love. In 1808 Field married Mlle. Percheron, a French actress, setting off on a turbulent marital life that endured just five years. The couple separated in 1813.

In 1814 Field wrote and published his first three nocturnes for piano. The "nocturne" was a form for piano which he devised, and to which he brought a new piano style. Both as the creator of the nocturne, and as the developer of a new technique, Field exerted a profound influence upon Chopin; Anton Rubinstein once went so far as to maintain that Field was the founder of "modern" piano music.

Each of Field's nocturnes is a gem. These pieces are sometimes sentimental, sometimes atmospheric, but always filled with sensitive lyrical ideas, expressive accompaniments, and an extraordinary range of mood. "The best of these exquisitely polished miniatures with their delicate melodies and their shy, fugitive gracefulness," wrote Ernest Walker, "will long serve to keep their name fragrant." And Eric Blom has said: "There is nothing else to take their place, not even Chopin's similarly named pieces. Here, he sings his heart out, and it is because he has learned to sing that he becomes so entirely himself. . . . His range of mood within the species of the nocturne is extraordinary—far greater than Chopin's. . . . [Here] John Field gave something to the world of music without which it would be as the world of flowers without the daisy; no worse for those who do not know what they miss, but not free from wistful regret for those who had once beheld the modest blossom."

In his edition of Field's nocturnes, Franz Liszt wrote: "Their first tones, already, transport us into those hours when the soul, freed from the burdens of the day and resting only in itself, soars upward to the mysterious regions of the starry heights. Here we see it, like Philomel of the ancients, ethereal and winged, hovering among the flowers and scents of the garden of a nature with whose essence it is lovingly permeated."

In all, Field wrote eighteen nocturnes. Among the most famous are Nocturnes No. 3 in A-flat major, No. 4 in A major, No. 5 in B-flat major, and No. 12 in G major.

In St. Petersburg Field taught piano to Glinka, who was to be one of Russia's foremost composers and the father of Russian musical nationalism. Glinka had the following impression of his teacher's piano playing: "Field's playing was at once sweet and strong and characterized by admirable precision. His fingers fell on the keys as large raindrops which spread themselves like iridescent pearls. . . . I do not share the opinion of Liszt, who told me once that he found Field's playing 'sleepy.' No, it was not sleepy; on the contrary, it was vigorous, capricious, and spontaneous. In particular, he never descended to charlatanism to produce his effects."

In 1822 Field moved from St. Petersburg to Moscow, where his success as pianist, teacher, and composer continued to mount. But he continued to lead an intemperate and dissipated life. As a consequence his creativity as a composer soon declined. Eventually he even neglected his teaching appointments, wasting not only his time and talents, but his health and fortune as well.

In an attempt to recover his fame and financial resources, Field accepted an invitation to appear as soloist with the Phil-harmonic Society of London. On February 27, 1832, he performed his own Concerto in E-flat, to enjoy resounding success as a pianist and composer. Less than a month later he was a mourner at the funeral of his former teacher, patron, and friend, Clementi.

In 1832 and 1833 Field gave concert performances in Paris. "As pianist," wrote Joseph d'Ortigue, "Field has no rival, whether as regards genre or method. . . . Field is Field—a school of his own. . . . His music is the music of the fairies." Field was acclaimed no less enthusiastically in the rest of Europe.

But by the time he reached Naples, in May of 1834, Field was completely broken in health. The strain of his numerous concert appearances, combined with the abuses to which his body had so long been subjected, finally took their toll. He was confined to a hospital for nine months. Then a Russian family in Naples (people he had once met in St. Petersburg) took him for a rest cure to Ischia and induced him to go back with them to Russia. In 1835 Field gave three concerts in Vienna, his farewell to the piano. He returned to Moscow toward the end of August 1835, and died there on January 23, 1837.

PRINCIPAL WORKS

Chamber Music—2 divertimenti for piano, flute and strings; Piano Quintet; Rondo, for piano and strings.
Orchestral Music—7 piano concertos.
Piano Music—18 nocturnes; 4 sonatas; 2 Airs anglais variés; 2 Airs en rondeau; fantaisies, polonaises, rondeaus, variations, waltzes.

ABOUT

Blom, E., Classics: Major and Minor; Flood, W. H. G., John Field of Dublin; Schonberg, H. C., The Great Pianists.

Friedrich von Flotow *1812-1883*

FRIEDRICH FREIHERR VON FLO-TOW, the composer of *Martha*, was born in Teutendorf, Mecklenburg-Schwerin, on April 26, 1812, descended from Prussian nobility who traced their genealogy back to the thirteenth century. Flotow's father, a cavalry captain, was an amateur flautist, his mother a gifted pianist and singer. When his mother detected Friedrich's musical gifts (he was hardly past his fourth birthday at the time) she began to teach him piano. Later he studied music in the nearby town of

Flotow: flō'tō

FRIEDRICH VON FLOTOW

Güstrow. There Friedrich made his first serious attempt at composition, completing a piano sonata when he was fourteen. Two years later he became a member of the church choir.

Friedrich's father had planned a diplomatic career for him. When the youth announced firmly that he intended to be a musician and nothing else, his father consulted one of his musician friends, who urged him to accede to his son's wishes. In 1827, Flotow was sent to Paris for intensive study of piano with Johann Peter Pixis, and of theory and composition with Anton Reicha.

When the 1830 July Revolution erupted in Paris, Flotow returned home. Through the support and influence of his uncle he gave a concert of his works which included a piano concerto and two orchestral overtures. Several years later he completed his first opera, *Pierre et Catherine*, produced in Ludwigslust and Schwerin in 1835. By 1835 he had returned to Paris, where he mingled with some of the city's most distinguished musicians — Meyerbeer, Halévy, Rossini, Auber, and Offenbach. Several of his new operas were given private performances; they include *Rob Roy*, based on Sir Walter Scott's novel, and *Sérafine*, produced in or about 1836. His first success, though a minor one, was *Le Comte de Saint-Mégrin,* completed in 1838. He also collaborated with Albert Grisar, a successful light opera composer, on *opéras-comiques* and *opéras*

bouffes; the most significant of these joint efforts was *Le Naufrage de la Méduse,* a huge success when performed at the Théâtre de la Renaissance on May 31, 1839.

Flotow's first important opera was *Alessandro Stradella*, a major success in Hamburg, where it was introduced on December 30, 1844. It was an operatic adaptation and expansion of a minor *pièce lyrique* which Flotow had written in 1837, and which had been performed that year at the Palais Royal in Paris. The libretto was based on a dramatic episode in the life of a famous seventeenth-century Italian composer. Flotow's melodic score, in which French elegance of style was admirably fused with the German Romantic element, included an outstanding tenor aria in "Jungfrau Maria," as well as a highly melodic overture that is still frequently played.

Flotow achieved an even greater triumph with his masterwork, *Martha*, first seen at the Kärnthnerthor Theater in Vienna on November 25, 1847. An operatic adaptation of the ballet *Lady Henriette*, which he had written in Paris in 1844, *Martha* is the one opera by which Flotow is generally represented today. The American première of the work was an English translation, given at Niblo Gardens in New York on November 1, 1852. *Martha* entered the repertory of the Metropolitan Opera on March 14, 1884, when it was given in Italian. On January 27, 1961 it enjoyed a highly successful revival at the Metropolitan in a fresh English translation. On this occasion Louis Biancolli wrote in the New York *World Telegram:* "Only a heart of stone could resist its bland charms."

It is interesting to note that the main aria of this tuneful and irresistibly charming opera score, "The Last Rose of Summer," was not Flotow's own melody but an old Irish air originally known as "The Groves of Blarney," a setting of a poem by Thomas Moore. Uniquely his own, however, is another unforgettable aria, the beautiful "M'Appari," a particular favorite of Enrico Caruso, who never failed to inspire a thunderous ovation whenever he appeared in the role of Lionel. Hector Berlioz, who disliked *Martha* upon first hearing it, still had nothing but the highest praise for "M'Appari." He wrote: "Its fragrance alone is sufficient to disinfect the rest of the work."

To other authorities, however, *Martha* is a work of surpassing appeal, filled with infectious melodies, delightful comic episodes, and touching sentimental interest. As Edgar Istel commented, Flotow "understood without subtlety and parade of learning how to spread over [the score] . . . melodies which take hold of one owing to their sincerity."

The death of his father and younger brother in 1847 and 1848, and his precarious position as a nobleman in the revolutionary atmosphere of Paris, led Flotow to leave France for his parental abode in Teutendorf. There he completed *Sophia Catharina,* which brought him the decoration of the Cross of St. John after its première at the Berlin Court Opera on November 19, 1850. In 1849 he married Elisa Sophie Philippine, but his marital happiness was short-lived: both his wife and their child died in 1851. Two years later Flotow married Anna Theen, and settled with her on an estate near Vienna. They had three children.

From 1856 to 1863 Flotow was Intendant of the Court Theater in Schwerin. Flotow continued writing operas for the remainder of his life, but none equaled *Martha* either in quality or popularity. Perhaps the most impressive of the later works is *L'Ombre,* whose première took place at the Opéra-Comique in Paris on July 7, 1870.

During the last decade of his life Flotow traveled about a great deal, making important visits to Paris, Vienna, and other European music centers in connection with performances of his operas. In 1880 he retired near Darmstadt. Despite failing eyesight and health, he visited Vienna in 1882 to attend the five hundredth performance of *Martha.* The tremendous ovation he received made the occasion one of the greatest triumphs of his career.

Flotow died soon afterwards in Darmstadt, on January 24, 1883, the victim of an apoplectic stroke.

PRINCIPAL WORKS

Ballets—Lady Henriette; Die Libelle; Die Gruppe der Thetis; Tannkönig; Der Königsschuss.

Operas—Rob Roy; L'Esclave de Camoëns; Alessandro Stradella; Martha; Rübezahl; Naida; Zilda; L'Ombre; Die Musikanten.

ABOUT

Bardi-Poswiansky, B. Flotow als Opernkomponist; Flotow, F. von, Erinnerungen aus meinem Leben; Flotow, R. R. von, Friedrich von Flotows Leben; Neumann, W. Friedrich Flotow.

César Franck *1822-1890*

CÉSAR-AUGUSTE FRANCK was born in Liège, Belgium, on December 10, 1822. Several of his ancestors had been famous Walloon painters. His father, a banker of German extraction, aspired to have his son become a celebrated virtuoso and enrolled him at the Liège Conservatory. The boy won first prize in singing at the age of nine, first prize in piano at twelve, and gave concerts throughout Belgium as a prodigy. Convinced of his son's genius, César's father moved the family to Paris in 1835 so that the youth might attend the renowned Conservatory. After some preliminary study with Anton Reicha, Franck entered the Conservatory in 1837; he stayed five years, winning prizes in fugue, piano, organ, and counterpoint. César's father was dissatisfied with what he regarded as slow progress. Impatient to have him launch his career as a virtuoso, he withdrew César from the Conservatory in 1842, returned with his family to Belgium, and had the youth give several concerts, none of which attracted much interest. During this period Franck wrote a set of three piano trios which were issued by subscription.

In 1843 the Franck family left Belgium again, to settle permanently in Paris. They lived first in the Rue Lafitte and afterwards in the Rue La Bruyère, where they invited guests to listen to César play the piano and to hear his compositions. On March 17, 1843 Franck gave his first public concert devoted entirely to his own music. It did little to further his career. To help support his family, which had by now depleted its financial resources, he gave music lessons; but what he earned could hardly pay for even the barest necessities.

In his composition, Franck was becoming increasingly ambitious. In 1845 he completed his first major work, *Ruth,* a biblical eclogue, his first departure from piano and chamber music toward works of larger dimension. *Ruth* was heard at the Conservatory on January 4, 1846 before a specially invited audience that included Meyerbeer and Liszt. Though "a simple work full of delicacy and charm," as Arthur Hervey described it, *Ruth* did not impress the critics or professional musicians, most of whom regarded it as an inferior imitation of Félicien David's *Le Désert,* which was then popular in Paris.

CÉSAR FRANCK

During the Paris revolution of 1848, Franck married Mlle. Desmousseaux, a young actress. To reach the church where they were married, the young couple had to surmount a barricade built by insurgents.

Long disappointed by his son's failure to achieve success on the concert stage, and further upset by his marriage to an actress, Franck's father broke completely with him. The breach was hardly a misfortune. Freed from parental domination, Franck was able to pursue the goals toward which his musical conscience and genius were leading him: toward organ playing, and toward composition of the highest artistic standards. After serving as an assistant organist at Notre Dame de Lorette, Franck became the principal organist of Saint-Jean-Saint-François au Marais in 1851. Seven years later he assumed the post which he occupied for the remainder of his life, and where his remarkable gifts as virtuoso achieved recognition: as organist of Sainte-Clotilde. "For thirty years, every Sunday," wrote Vincent d'Indy, "every festival day, towards the last every Friday morning, he came to stir up the fire of his genius on admirable improvisations." His admirers, disciples, and pupils would gather in or near the organ loft to hear his extraordinary performances. When Franz Liszt heard Franck in 1866, he remarked that Johann Sebastian Bach had just come back to life.

Franck's life had a simple, familiar pattern. The organist Tournemire recorded:

"From half past five in the morning until half past seven, Franck composed. At eight he left the house to 'comb' Paris. He dispensed solfeggio and piano lessons for the convenience of pupils in the Jesuit school at Vaugirard (lessons, one franc and eighty centimes an hour, from eleven to two). He had only a bite of fruit or cheese to sustain him. . . . He would go to Auteuil, to a fashionable institution for young ladies of society who often constrained him to teach them the impossible novelties of the hour."

Beyond working as organist at Sainte-Clotilde and giving private lessons, Franck served as professor of organ at the Conservatory from 1872 on. Though some of his colleagues disliked him for his candor and his stout refusal to become involved in their political battles at school—and though some pupils regarded him as an eccentric—Franck exerted a lasting influence on an entire generation of young French musicians. His classes became much more than mere formal lessons in organ performance. He passed on to his students his own high artistic standards—his idealism, humanity, and untainted integrity—as well as his ideas on composition. He filled his pupils with his own enthusiastic devotion to the contrapuntal technique of Bach, and to the principles of absolute, as opposed to dramatic, music. Those who profited most from his instruction became disciples only too willing to bear his torch when they entered the ranks of the professionals. They included men who were later to become distinguished French musicians—Debussy, d'Indy, Chausson, Pierné, Duparc, and Ropartz.

All the while Franck pursued composition with a high-minded purpose which never wavered. In 1872 he completed the first version of *Rédemption,* a tone poem for soprano, chorus, and orchestra. When first performed (at a Concert Spirituel on April 10, 1873) it was very poorly received, though largely because of a dismal performance. A year later he subjected the work to extensive revision.

For a decade, between 1869 and 1879, Franck labored on a monumental oratorio which he considered his best work thus far: *Les Béatitudes.* In 1879 he arranged a special performance of this work at his home, inviting some of Paris's influential musicians. Many failed to appear; some slipped away while the performance was still in progress; only two visitors stayed on to the end. *Les Béatitudes* was not performed publicly in its entirety until after Franck's death. Introduced at the Concert Colonne in 1893, it brought forth an ovation. Ernest Chausson said of this music that it "certainly surpassed all other French works in sublimity. One would be obliged indeed to go back to the very first classical masters to find so powerful an expression of the soul's despair, its appeal to divine justice, its striving after the ideal, after holiness."

The fiasco of the first private performance was only one of many disappointments Franck encountered before his genius was finally acknowledged. Harvey Grace notes: "Probably no composer of his rank met with so little recognition at the hands of his contemporaries. Almost until the end, the record is one of neglect, or of performances badly organized or technically inadequate." On May 1, 1885, Franck's pupils and friends, disturbed by the failure of French audiences and critics to give just measure to Franck's genius, arranged a concert of his works at the Cirque d'Hiver. The program (directed by Pasdeloup and the composer) included two parts of *Les Béatitudes;* the *Variations symphoniques* for piano and orchestra (which Franck had completed that year); and the tone poem *Le Chasseur maudit* (written in 1882, and performed for the first time on March 31, 1883 at a concert of the Société Nationale). This all-Franck program was deplorably performed and received just as poorly; it accomplished little to lift the composer from his undeserved obscurity.

On February 17, 1889, the première of Franck's now celebrated Symphony in D minor took place in Paris. This, too, was a terrible failure. The men in the orchestra, who disliked the work, gave a slovenly presentation. Academicians were horrified at Franck's use of an English horn in his orchestration, an instrument rarely encountered in a symphony until that time. Charles Gounod curtly described the work as "the affirmation of incompetence pushed to dogmatic lengths."

Franck's stoic reaction to these varied disasters was characteristic. What was all important to him was writing his music and hearing it performed. This was his sole victory. Bitter public or critical reaction seemed to make little impression on him. After the

contemptuous response to his symphony, his pupil de Bréville found him "radiant." De Bréville wrote: "He had heard his music played . . . he planned new compositions, he promised himself to write for the brass otherwise than he had done in the Finale." And when Franck returned home, he did not say a word to his wife of the frigid reception he had just encountered. Instead he said glowingly, "It sounded well, just as I thought it would."

Today the Symphony in D minor, Franck's only work in that form, is of course a favorite with audiences everywhere for its dramatic and emotional appeal, and for its irresistible eloquence. H. C. Colles has described it as "noble"; Vincent d'Indy called it "majestic, plastic and perfectly beautiful"; to Debussy it was "amazing."

The only real acclaim Franck himself enjoyed for his music came in the last year of his life. On April 19, 1890, the première of his String Quartet was given. The enthusiasm of audience and critics was so great that a second performance of the work was hurriedly arranged for the following month. A few days after the Quartet had been introduced, the Ysaÿe Quartet gave an all-Franck program in which the composer participated. Again the response was admirable. "There, you see," remarked the composer simply to a friend, "the public is beginning to understand me."

In May 1890, on his way to give a lesson, Franck was struck by an omnibus. At his pupil's home he fainted, but soon recovered sufficiently to give his lesson. Soon afterward, Franck suffered an attack of pleurisy complicated by the after-effects of his accident. Despite the seriousness of his condition, he insisted on leaving his sickbed to visit his organ loft and perform his last work, the *Three Chorales* for organ. It was the last time he would touch that beloved instrument. He died in Paris on November 8, 1890. Franck was buried in the Montrouge cemetery; several years later his remains were transferred to the cemetery in Montparnasse. Fourteen years after his death a monument to him was erected near Sainte-Clotilde, upon which occasion leading members of the Conservatory and the Ministry of Fine Arts delivered orations in his praise.

His pupil and disciple Vincent d'Indy described Franck as follows: "César Franck was short, with a fine forehead and a vivacious honest expression, although his eyes were almost concealed under his bushy eyebrows. His nose was rather large and his chin receded below a wide and extraordinarily expressive mouth. His face was round and thick, gray side-whiskers added to its width. . . . There was nothing in his appearance to reveal the conventional artist type. . . . Anyone who happened to meet this man in the street, invariably in a hurry, invariably absent-minded, and making grimaces, running rather than walking, dressed in an overcoat a size too large for him and in trousers a size too short, would never have suspected the transformation that took place when, placed at the piano, he explained or commented upon some fine composition."

Franck's humility, modesty, and simplicity have often been described. To Debussy, Franck was "a man without guile. The discovery of a beautiful harmony was sufficient to make him as happy as the day was long. . . . A great deal has been said about his genius without ever mentioning the unique quality of his ingenuousness. This man, who was unfortunate, unrecognized, possessed the soul of a child, and one so irradicably good that neither contradictory circumstances nor wickedness of others could ever make him feel bitter. . . . He wrote . . . so to speak, face to face with the spirit of music, before which he would kneel, uttering at the same time the most profoundly touching prayer that ever fell from human lips. César Franck served his art with steadfast devotion. . . . He served music without ever asking for renown."

In describing the essential qualities of Franck's music, Leland Hall wrote: "With the exception of a few early pieces for piano, all his work bears the stamp of his personality. Like Brahms, he has pronounced idiosyncrasies, among which his fondness for shifting harmonies is the most constantly obvious. The ceaseless alternation of chords, the almost unbroken gliding by half-steps, the lithe sinuousness of all the inner voices, seem to wrap his music in a veil, to render it intangible and mystical. Diatonic passages are rare, all is chromatic. Parallel to this is his use of short phrases, which alone are capable of being treated in this shifting manner. His melodies are almost invariably dissected, they seldom are built up in broad design. They are resolved into their finest motifs, and as such are woven and twisted

into the close iridescent harmonic fabric with bewildering skill. All is in subtle movement. Yet there is a complete absence of sensuousness, even, for the most part, of dramatic fire. The overpowering climaxes to which he builds are never a frenzy of emotion; they are superbly calm and exalted. The structure of his music is strangely inorganic. His material does not develop. He adds phrase upon phrase, detail upon detail, with astonishing power to knit and weave closely what comes with what went before. His extraordinary polyphonic skill seems inborn, native to the man. Arthur Coquard said of him that he thought the most complicated things in music quite naturally."

Guy Ropartz, another disciple of Franck, said: "He stands out from among his contemporaries like a man of some other age; they are skeptics, he was a believer; they are self-advertising, he worked in silence; they seek glory, he was content to await it; they aim at easily acquired reputations by daring improvisations, he built enduring monuments amid the calm of a retired life."

Franck introduced a structural method of his own invention known as the "cyclical form." Melodic ideas, termed "generative phrases," are built up into fully developed themes: thematic subjects, introduced in earlier parts of a work, are repeated and developed in later movements to give unity to the entire composition.

PRINCIPAL WORKS

Chamber Music—Piano Quintet in F minor; Violin Sonata in A major; String Quartet in D major.

Choral Music—Ave Maria; Trois offertoires; Ruth; Rédemption; Les Béatitudes; Rébecca; Hymne; Le Premier sourire du mai.

Operas—Le Valet de ferme; Hulda; Ghisèle (unfinished).

Orchestral Music—Les Éolides; Le Chasseur maudit; Les Djinns; Variations symphoniques, for piano and orchestra; Symphony in D minor; Psyché (with chorus).

Organ Music—Six Pièces pour grande orgue; 44 Petites pièces, for organ or harmonium; Offertory on a Breton Melody; L'Organiste, 55 pieces for harmonium; Trois chorales.

Piano Music—Trois petits riens; Prelude, Chorale and Fugue; Danse lente; Prelude, Aria and Finale.

Vocal Music—Songs for voice and piano including Ave Maria, Le Mariage des roses, Nocturne, Panis Angelicus, La Procession; 6 duos.

ABOUT

Demuth, N. César Franck; Dupourcq, N., César Franck: Le milieu, l'œuvre, l'art; Horton, J., César Franck; Indy, V. de, César Franck; Kunel, M., César Franck; Kunel, M. César Franck inconnu d'après des documents inédits; Vallas, L. César Franck.

Robert Franz *1815-1892*

R OBERT FRANZ, genius of the *Lied,* was born in Halle, Germany, on June 28, 1815. His name at birth was Robert Knauth. In 1843 his father changed "Knauth" to "Franz" to avoid confusion with his brother, who was engaged in a competitive business. When Robert Franz started to publish his *Lieder,* some critics maliciously accused him of having assumed his surname in order to encourage comparison with another who had enriched the world of song—Franz Schubert.

Music was important to Robert Franz from childhood on. He heard a great deal of it at home, where his father would sing hymns, and at church. The Lutheran chorale *Ein' feste Burg* made a particularly strong impression on him during his childhood. "As if in a dream," he later recalled, "I still hear the tones of the trombone choirs, wafted down upon us from the towers." At school he insisted on providing his own harmonic accompaniment to exercises in unison singing; for this he was frequently punished by the singing master. But later on, in secondary school, he found a sympathetic teacher in the cantor Karl Gottlieb Abela, who gave him instruction in piano and organ and introduced him to the choral music of Handel and Haydn. Before long Robert Franz was recruited as accompanist in performances of several choral masterworks.

His father grew concerned over Robert's increasing preoccupation with music, and for a while a bitter dispute raged between father and son over the boy's future. A distant relative, however, interceded for Robert and finally broke down his father's resistance to his study of music. In 1835 Robert Franz was permitted to go to Dessau, where he studied harmony and counterpoint with Friedrich Schneider.

After a two-year stay in Dessau Franz returned home. For a few years he was unable to find employment as a musician. He spent

ROBERT FRANZ

his time studying the works of Bach, Beethoven, and Schubert, in reading philosophy and literature, and in composition. It is believed that a love affair inspired the composition of his first songs. He completed them in or about 1840, and dispatched several to Robert Schumann in Leipzig. Schumann wrote a glowing article about Franz in the *Neue Zeitschrift für Musik,* and found a publisher for Franz's songs. In 1843, Franz's first opus, a set of twelve *Lieder,* appeared, drawing high praise from such leading musicians as Gade, Mendelssohn, and Liszt.

In 1841 Franz was appointed organist of St. Ulrich Church in Halle. He next became conductor of the Singakademie in that city, and music director of the Halle University. His new economic security enabled him to devote himself more assiduously to song writing, and to make several trips throughout Europe. During a visit to Vienna in 1846 he met Liszt for the first time.

In 1848 Franz married Maria Hinrichs, also a song composer. Not long after his marriage Franz grew aware of his increasing deafness, signs of which had appeared as early as 1841. These symptoms were followed by visible manifestations of nervous disorders. Nevertheless, Franz continued to write songs. In addition, he assumed the ambitious assignment of editing the music of Bach and Beethoven, and providing polyphonic accompaniments for those compositions in which only a figured bass was indicated.

His reputation as a song composer spread throughout Germany. In 1856 he was rewarded with an annual royal stipend, and five years later the University of Halle conferred on him an honorary doctorate in music.

By 1868 Franz's deafness and nervous ailments finally compelled him to give up all his posts. Deprived of his income, Franz endured appalling poverty until a committee (which included Liszt and Joachim) was formed to arrive at some means of supporting him. Through its efforts, Robert Franz concerts were given throughout Europe to raise necessary funds. On June 28, 1873, Franz was presented with a gift equivalent to twenty-five thousand dollars, which made him financially self-sufficient for the remainder of his life.

Franz's physical deterioration continued until in his closing years he completely lost his hearing and mobility of hands. His voice was so weak it was barely audible. The death of his wife in 1891 added loneliness to his infirmity. Henry T. Finck, who visited Franz in the summer of 1891, described the pathos of seeing "the deaf old master, shut from the tone world he had helped to create, dwelling for fifteen minutes on the songs of his wife (of his own he seemed to have no thought) with tears repeatedly rolling down his cheeks. 'Her picture is in the other room —did you see it? No? Then I must get it!' Placing it in my wife's hands he exclaimed: 'There, take a good look at that! Such a face you will never see again.' "

Robert Franz died in Halle on October 24, 1892.

Theodor Held, Franz's contemporary, left the following description of the composer: "Lean, fairly tall and sinewy, he moved forward with a stoop and with nervous restlessness as if otherwise he might not reach his goal. His free and slightly receding forehead, his prominent eyebrows, and his long pointed nose made an impressive combination. The whole picture was framed by dark, closely brushed hair which did not turn gray until his very last years. Beardless, he went through the world. He spoke rapidly, but clearly, with a slight lisp."

Franz was one of the foremost composers of the *Lied* in the era following Schubert and Schumann. He completed about three hundred and fifty songs. A painstaking workman who continually revised his songs through the years, even the earliest ones, he brought to whatever he wrote a richness of thought and maturity of feeling. "My opus 1," he once remarked, "I consider no better and no worse than my opus 53."

His strength lay in his simplicity, directness, freshness, and forthright emotion. He avoided realistic writing, underplayed the dramatic element, often made no attempt to realize in melody the content of a poem. "Beauty is truth," he would say, "but a thing is not beautiful because it is true." He further explained that he aimed only to have his music bring its listeners "peace and reconciliation."

"In examining Franz's songs," wrote Henry T. Finck, "one is first of all impressed by the reticence, dignity and purity of their style. They are true lyrics—expressions of personal feeling in simple, well-balanced musical forms, undisfigured by dramatic episodes, obtrusive climaxes, or any of those other devices of less fastidious songwriters which are as abhorrent to true artistic feeling as they are grateful to the egotism of singers and the sentimentality of listeners. . . . He cared primarily, not for the luxuriance of decoration, but for structural symmetry and harmony; not for an emotion bordering on hysteria, but for the calm expression of sincere, simple feeling; not for utter self-revelation but for a dignified presentation of what was artistically worth presentation, against a background of reticence and reserve. . . . In simplicity and graciousness of melody, in musicianly part-writing, and in legitimately expressive harmony, Franz is preëminent."

As W. F. Apthorp pointed out, Franz holds an important place in the history of the *Lied*. "He carried . . . [it] to its highest known pitch of perfection. Uniting the purely lyric element one finds in such splendor in Schubert with the wondrously subtle and mobile expressiveness of every varying shade of emotion that characterized Schumann, fusing these two elements so that their union was absolutely . . . complete, Franz gave the finishing master touch to the plastic form of the *Lied*. Franz's songs are as truly lyrical, in the most exact sense of the word, as Schubert's; at the same time they are to the full as emotionally expressive, as picturesquely and poetically suggestive, as vivid pieces of tone-painting, as Schumann's. And more than this, he has given them the most stoutly organized, pure and concise form known in songwriting. To what Schubert and Schumann did before him, Franz brought the natural and logical completion; he crowned the edifice."

PRINCIPAL WORKS

Choral Music—Psalm 117; Choral Liturgy; chorales, part songs.

Vocal Music—About 350 songs for voice and piano including Es hat die Rose sich beklagt, Für Musik, Gute Nacht, Im Herbst, Im Rhein, im heiligen Strome, Die Lotosblume, Marie am Fenster, Mein Schatz ist auf der Wanderschaft, Mutter, O sing mich zur Ruh, O säh ich auf der Haide dort, Schlummerlied, Stille Sicherheit, Die Widmung, and Wonne der Wehmuth.

ABOUT

Barbak, S. E., Die Lieder von Robert Franz; Bethge, R., Robert Franz: ein Lebensbild; Liszt, F., Robert Franz; Pfordten, H. von der, Robert Franz.

Musical Quarterly, October 1915.

Girolamo Frescobaldi *1583-1643*

GIROLAMO FRESCOBALDI, one of the greatest organists of his generation and an important predecessor of Bach in writing organ music, was born in Ferrara, Italy, in 1583, probably in September. As a boy he studied organ with Luzzasco Luzzaschi, the eminent organist of the Ferrara Cathedral. Frescobaldi early demonstrated unusual powers both as an organist and a singer, and was acclaimed in many Italian cities as an outstanding prodigy.

In January 1607 he became organist of the Santa Maria Church in Rome. He held the post only a few weeks, leaving to travel in Flanders, and settled briefly in Brussels. In 1608 his first two publications appeared: a volume of five-part madrigals in Antwerp, and a collection of four-part fantasias in Milan.

On November 1, 1608 he became organist of St. Peter's Church in Rome. His reputation as an organ virtuoso was by then so widespread that, it has been reported, over thirty thousand music lovers went to St. Peter's to hear his first performance at the Church.

In 1615 and 1616 Frescobaldi issued several important volumes of ricercari, canzoni, toccatas, and other pieces for organ and for clavicembalo.

GIROLAMO FRESCOBALDI

After twenty years at St. Peter's, Frescobaldi, dissatisfied with his compensation, took an extended leave of absence. For about five years he lived in Florence, where he was court organist for the Grand Duke of Tuscany, Ferdinand II. He might have remained in Florence permanently had not the political and social upheavals in the city driven him back to Rome. There he returned in 1623 to his post as organist of St. Peter's, and remained for the rest of his life.

Frescobaldi was acknowledged throughout Europe to be one of the greatest organists of his generation. The eminent musicologist Ambros maintained that the great era of classical organ performance which reached an apex with Johann Sebastian Bach began with Frescobaldi. One of Frescobaldi's contemporaries referred to him as "the marvel of the age." In 1637 Johann Jakob Froberger traveled from Vienna to Rome to study with the master.

Frescobaldi's last publication, issued in 1635, was one of his most significant. He called it *Fiori musicali (Musical Flowers)*. It is a collection of various pieces for organ —including toccatas, canzoni, capriccios, ricercari, and so forth—intended for performance at mass. One of Frescobaldi's most celebrated organ compositions is included in this volume: the *Toccata per l'elevazione (Toccata for the Elevation)*.

Frescobaldi died in Rome on March 1, 1643.

Frescobaldi's many compositions for the organ are among the most important written before the age of Bach. He crystallized and amplified such organ forms as the toccata, ricercare, canzona, capriccio, fantasia, and fugue while endowing them with deeply personal feeling, nobility of thought, serenity of style, brilliant virtuosity, and dramatic effects that have led many to call him "the Italian Bach." He was able to realize, at last, a style that was indigenous to the organ, not transplanted from vocal music. "Both his subjects and the manner in which they are treated are more prominently instrumental in character than those of any of his predecessors," commented Cecil Gray. "His genius was essentially diatonic, the natural bent of his mind strongly traditional and adverse to innovations which, when they appear in his music, lack spontaneity and inevitability."

While Alfredo Casella also emphasizes the originality of Frescobaldi's instrumental style, "already free from vocal tyranny," he points out that no less significant an achievement was his success in endowing his writing with human value. The organ composers before Frescobaldi, explains Casella, wrote beautiful music which "never offers a real human interest," whereas with Frescobaldi "one feels music vitalized by the breadth of love—humble, but already like a vision of serenity."

PRINCIPAL WORKS

Choral Music—Madrigals.
Organ and Cembalo Music—Canzoni, capriccios, fantasias, fugues, toccatas, ricercari.

ABOUT

Machabey, A., Frescobaldi, la vie, l'œuvre; Machabey, A., Girolamo Frescobaldi Ferrarensis; Ronga, L., Girolamo Frescobaldi; Sostegni, A., L'Opera e il tempo di Girolamo Frescobaldi.

Musical Quarterly, October 1938.

Johann Froberger *1616-1667*

JOHANN JAKOB FROBERGER, pioneer in the development of early German keyboard music and one of the first creators of the keyboard suite, was born in Stuttgart on May 19, 1616. His father, a church cantor, was his first music teacher. In the early 1630's the boy was sent to Vienna, where he enrolled in the Institut Singer oder Cantorenknaben. Upon leaving this choir school,

he was appointed third organist at the Vienna court on January 1, 1637. He remained until the end of September of that year. Then a court stipend enabled him to spend three and a half years in Rome, studying organ with Frescobaldi. In this way Froberger was able to carry the great tradition of organ performance and composition established by Frescobaldi back to Vienna when he returned in March 1641. From 1641 to 1645, and again from 1653 to 1657, Froberger served as court organist.

Upon leaving his position in Vienna in 1657, Froberger visited France, where he became so engrossed with the lute performance of Galot and Gautier that he felt impelled to apply the techniques of lute performance to harpsichord music. Froberger thus was one of the first masters to abandon the techniques borrowed from organ performance which had characterized harpsichord playing, and to evolve a new method more suitable for that instrument.

In 1662 Froberger departed for England. His biographer Mattheson gives a dramatic and picaresque account of Froberger's adventures en route and of his first musical experiences in England; although these episodes were long accepted as historical fact, many historians today regard them as invention. According to Georg Mattheson, Froberger was attacked by highwaymen en route to Calais and robbed of all his possessions. Arriving in Calais, ragged and penniless, Froberger nevertheless gained passage aboard a ship bound for England. When this vessel was attacked by pirates Froberger jumped overboard and swam to the coast. He was found by a local fisherman, who fed, clothed, and housed him. From there Froberger made the journey to London on foot, feeding himself on the way as best he could.

By the time he arrived in London, according to the Mattheson account, he was half-starved and in rags. Passing Westminster Abbey, he entered to give thanks for his safe arrival. There he attracted the interest of the Abbey organist, Christopher Gibbons (son of the distinguished English composer Orlando Gibbons), who employed him as an organ-blower. During one of Gibbons' performances Froberger overblew, whereupon the infuriated Gibbons struck him. When Gibbons' temper subsided, Froberger managed to get to the organ, where he started to improvise. His performance made a profound impression on all those who heard him, including a noblewoman, who introduced Froberger to King Charles II. At court, Froberger's performances on the harpsichord won the enthusiasm of all. The King removed a gold chain from his neck and presented it to Froberger. From then on Froberger was the constant recipient of royal favor.

It is difficult to say how much fiction and how much fact lie in this story. All that is known is that Froberger did, in fact, enjoy prosperity and acclaim in England, and was a favorite at court.

Froberger's last years were spent in Héricourt, Haute-Saône, France, as house musician to the Duchess Sibylle. He died there of an apoplectic stroke on May 7, 1667. A day before his death he presented his patroness with "a piece of gold wrapped upon and sealed," in her words, with instructions that it be given to the pastor of the local parish "where he had chosen a burial place, asking me to deliver it and let him be buried in the church of Bavilliers; also to distribute alms among the poor, and to give presents of money to the lower menials of the chateau."

Froberger's outstanding contribution to music was perhaps the establishment of the form of the harpsichord suite, beginning with an allemande, and continuing with a courante, sarabande, and gigue. This order of movements was followed by later composers, either strictly or with deviations. His greatest artistic distinction lies in his development of flexibility in organ and harpsichord keyboard performance, and his enrichment of instrumental style.

Froberger wrote for both organ and harpsichord; but it is for the former instrument that he created some of his finest compositions. "If, in style, generally, his organ music shows him to be a follower of Frescobaldi," says Cecil Gray, "his compositions for harpsichord, on the other hand, show him in the role of innovator and pioneer. . . . He was . . . the first to raise . . . [the suite] to a high standard of artistic excellence and even occasionally to make it the vehicle for the expression of profound emotions."

Edmund van der Straeten wrote: "As a composer, Froberger combined originality of thought with a perfect mastery over all the resources of his art, and daring spirit of innovation, particularly with regard to the use and treatment of discords."

PRINCIPAL WORKS
Harpsichord Music—Suites.
Organ Music—Canzoni, fantasias, fugues, ricercari, toccatas.

ABOUT
Beier, F., Über Johann Jakob Frobergers Leben; Seidler, K., Untersuchungen über Biographie und Klavierstil Johann Jakob Frobergers.
Monthly Musical Record, January 1, 1916.

Andrea Gabrieli *1520-1586*

ANDREA GABRIELI, a major figure in the Venetian school of polyphonic music, was born in Venice, in the district of Canareggio, in 1520. As a boy chorister at St. Mark's Cathedral he became a pupil of its *maestro di cappella,* Adrian Willaert, one of Venice's senior musicians. In 1558 Gabrieli became organist of the San Geremia Church and a member of the renowned Accademia della Fama. Extensive travel in subsequent years took him to Germany and Bohemia. As organist for Duke Albert V of Bavaria, he attended the Duke's coronation in Frankfurt am Main.

After his return to Venice, Gabrieli was appointed second organist of St. Mark's on January 1, 1585, acquiring in that position great prestige not only as organist but as a composer and teacher.

As a composer Gabrieli achieved renown in sacred and secular music. His works include madrigals, Masses, motets, and psalms for voices; ricercari, canzoni, capriccios, and other short pieces for organ. He was ahead of his time in many ways. He anticipated operatic writing in the dramatic impact of some of his cantatas; perfected a new concept in translating text to music in his madrigals and motets; and pioneered in the introduction of instruments into vocal music and the fusion of instrumental and vocal resources into a unified artistic concept. He was one of the first composers anywhere to write instrumental sonatas, and his organ music was an important predecessor of Frescobaldi's in realizing an instrumental as opposed to a vocal style and developing a virtuoso technique of organ performance. Last, Gabrieli was the worthy successor of both Willaert and Palestrina in perfecting an enduring polyphonic style in the pre-Baroque epoch. "The towering tone clusters of Gabrieli's double and multiple choirs," said Paul

Henry Lang, the "scintillating, orchestral accompaniments, the brilliant solo passages, and the sharp dynamic contrasts are already leading into the dramatic and monumental world of the Baroque."

"With Andrea Gabrieli," wrote Hermann Kretzschmar, "begins the golden age of a really solemn, elevated and noble style of orchestral music . . . rooted in the spirit of the time in which, during the sixteenth and seventeenth centuries, churches, states, cities, and corporations held grand festivals. The music is marked with the stamp of Venetian art: the splendor and sumptuousness, the loftiness and grandeur which stir and exalt us in the masterpiece of Montegna, of Paolo Veronese and Titian. These qualities characterize as well the canzoni and sonatas of this early master of the orchestra."

Andrea Gabrieli died in Venice in 1586.

PRINCIPAL WORKS

Choral Music—Madrigals, Masses, motets, psalms, and various other choruses.
Instrumental Music—Canzoni, Capriccios, ricercari, sonatas.

ABOUT

Reese, G., Music in the Renaissance; Zerr-Becking, I., Studien zu Andrea Gabrieli.

Giovanni Gabrieli *1557-1612*

GIOVANNI GABRIELI, nephew and pupil of Andrea Gabrieli (see above), was an important member of the Venetian polyphonic school. He was born in Venice, in or about 1557. His early instruction in music was provided by his uncle Andrea. From 1575 to 1579, Giovanni was attached to the court at Munich, as a pupil of, and assistant to, Orlando di Lasso.

On November 1, 1584, Giovanni Gabrieli substituted for Merulo as organist of St. Mark's Cathedral in Venice. On January 2, 1585 he assumed the post of second organist and upon the death of his uncle Andrea in 1586 became first organist. By that time his fame as an organist had spread throughout Italy.

Gabrieli's reputation as a composer, however, was not established until 1587, with the publication of a volume entitled *Concerti di Andrea et di Giovanni Gabrieli,* which included five madrigals and motets by the younger Gabrieli. This initial effort was succeeded by the publication, in 1593, of eleven Intonazioni for organ, and, in 1597, of the first volume of Giovanni's monumental *Sacrae Symphoniae,* consisting of forty-two motets, twelve instrumental canzoni, three sonatas, and a Mass. Another volume of *Sacrae Symphoniae,* consisting of fifty-two motets, three Magnificats and a Mass, was issued posthumously in 1615.

Giovanni Gabrieli advanced more boldly than any of his contemporaries in the directions that his famous uncle had first pointed out. He further emphasized the role of instruments in vocal music, gave the motet and Mass broader dimensions, solidified the instrumental forms of the canzone and suggested the sonata, and introduced to instrumental writing new dynamics, color, luster, and blending of timbres. As an instrumental composer he was so far in advance of his times that he is sometimes called the "father of orchestration." "By means of harmonic richness and blending of instrumental timbres," said Cecil Gray, "he attains a grandeur, brilliancy, and fiery energy which music has never before known."

Gabrieli's immense prestige as a composer is suggested in the statements of his contemporaries. Michael Praetorius, the distinguished sixteenth century theorist and composer, referred to him in *Syntagma musicum* as "the most eminent and most famous of us all." Heinrich Schütz, who studied with him and extended his influence to German music, wrote: "What a man is Gabrieli! If antiquity had known him it would have preferred him to Amphion. If the Muses would wish a spouse, Melpomene could not have chosen anyone but him, so great was his mastery in song. All this is confirmed by his certain reputation."

L. Finzenhagen has analyzed Gabrieli's contrapuntal art: "One recognized in his work the richest and fullest development of the Venetian school. This music possesses the fullness of harmonic colors and it also owns that sweet, and at the same time, lively play of nuances, which is the singular characteristic of the Venetian school of painting." Drawing a closer parallel between Gabrieli and the Venetian painters, the renowned historian Ambros remarked: "The church music of Gabrieli, with its answering choirs and its accompanying strings and trombones, is to music what an Assumption of Titian is to painting."

Gabrieli's later works are so revolutionary as to be almost startling. Here, as Manfred F. Bukofzer noted, one finds a "dissonant treatment, melodic design, rhythmic flow, the attitude towards the words, and the disposition of vocal and instrumental parts" that were unique for that period. "The composer now seized upon the words with a fervor and intensity of affection unprecedented in sacred music. . . . The fervor of word interpretation breathed the mystic and aggressive spirit of the Counter-Reformation which overwhelmed the faithful with gigantic structures, be it architecture, painting, or music."

Gabrieli was one of the most famous teachers of his generation; his pupils included Hassler, Sweelinck, and Schütz, among many others.

Giovanni Gabrieli died in Venice on August 21, 1612.

PRINCIPAL WORKS

Choral Music—Madrigals, Magnificats, Masses, motets.
Instrumental Music—Canzoni, fantasias, intonazioni, ricercari, sonatas, toccatas.

ABOUT

Bukofzer, M. F., Music in the Baroque Era; Reese, G., Music in the Renaissance; Winterfield, K. G. A., Johannes Gabrieli und sein Zeitalter.

Le Guide musical, March 30, 1913; Music Review, January 1947; Musical Quarterly, October 1962.

Niels Gade *1817-1890*

NIELS WILHELM GADE, one of the earliest national composers of Denmark, was born in Copenhagen on February 22, 1817. His father was a cabinet maker who later turned to the manufacture of musical instruments; he gave the child his first lessons on the guitar. Then Niels studied violin with a local teacher. In early boyhood he left school to become an apprentice in his father's shop, but after a year and a half he was certain that he wanted to be a musician. His father did not stand in his way but permitted Niels to study violin with one of Copenhagen's leading teachers, F. T. Wexschall, and counterpoint with A. P. Berggreen. Berggreen introduced the youth to Danish poetry and folk music,

NIELS GADE

arousing in him an interest in musical nationalism. It was also through Berggreen's influence that Gade's first published piece, the song "Lebt wohl, geliebte Bäume," based on a Goethe poem, appeared in 1836.

After giving a violin recital in Copenhagen in May 1833, Gade entered the music school of the Royal Orchestra. He remained with the orchestra for a short time, then embarked on a concert tour of Sweden and Norway. It proved so unsuccessful that Gade was forced to ask his father for funds to pay for his fare home. In Copenhagen he continued to study at the Royal Orchestra music school. He composed incidental music for a play, *Aladdin*, performed in 1839, and also some songs and a piano sonata.

In 1840 Gade won first prize in a competition conducted by the Copenhagen Musical Union for a concert overture. His winning work, *Nachklänge aus Ossian (Echoes from Ossian)*, was introduced on November 19, 1841, with immense success. It was one of the most important orchestral works by a Danish composer that had yet been written, and, though one of Gade's earliest creations, one of his most successful. Encouraged, Gade composed his First Symphony in C minor, which he dispatched to Mendelssohn in Leipzig immediately upon its completion. "I cannot resist the wish to address you in order to tell you what an extraordinary pleasure you have given me with your excellent work," Mendelssohn wrote the young

Gade: gä'duh

composer on January 13, 1843. "For a long time past no work has made a more vivid and beautiful impression upon me." Mendelssohn conducted the première of this symphony with the Gewandhaus Orchestra in Leipzig on March 2, 1843. It afforded, as Mendelssohn dutifully reported to Gade, "lively and unalloyed pleasure" to an audience which "after every one of the four movements, broke out into the loudest applause. After the Scherzo, the people were in a state of real excitement, and there was no end to the rejoicing and clapping of hands."

A royal stipend now enabled Gade to visit Leipzig and meet Mendelssohn and Schumann personally. Mendelssohn invited Gade to conduct several concerts of the Gewandhaus Orchestra and to join the faculty of the Leipzig Conservatory. Upon Mendelssohn's death in 1847, Gade took over the direction of the Gewandhaus Orchestra for about a year.

In 1848, Gade returned to his native country, soon establishing himself as one of its most energetic and influential musicians. In 1850 he was appointed director of the Copenhagen Musical Society, which he led in several notable concerts; these included performances of Beethoven's Ninth Symphony and Bach's *Passion According to St. Matthew,* which were rarely given in Denmark. In April 1852 he married Sophie Hartmann, daughter of an eminent Danish musician.

Until his return to Copenhagen, Gade's music was mostly a distillation of Mendelssohn's style. After 1848, however, Gade became increasingly interested in Danish folk music. He prepared arrangements of many folk songs and dances, used folk material in his compositions, and at times imitated in his melodies the basic stylistic elements of Danish folk music. One of his earliest and most important works in a national idiom was *Elverskud,* a cantata for solo voices, chorus and orchestra, completed in 1853, and based on an old Danish folk song.

Gade's wife died in childbirth in July 1855; the tragedy moved him to write his Sixth Symphony in G minor. Gade later married Mathilda Staeger.

In 1862 Gade conducted performances at the Royal Opera, and in 1866 became one of the directors of the Copenhagen Conservatory. From 1862 to 1882 he often toured Europe as a guest conductor. In recognition of his eminence as a musician, Gade received the Prussian Ordre Pour le Mérite in 1882. In his own country Gade was honored with an appointment as Commander of the Daneborg in 1872, and a life pension in 1876.

Gade died suddenly in Copenhagen on December 21, 1890. That morning he had been well enough to perform on the organ at church services.

Cornelius Rybner thus discusses Gade's nationalism: "During the *Ossian* period he composed those of his works that have contributed most to the national element in Scandinavian music, and have for all times secured him a place in the hearts of his own people. By his treatment of that very element he showed the world the beauty of that folklore of the North at the hands of a great sculptor. The splendid means of instrumentation at his command gives to his orchestral works a certain elusive beauty of coloring that seems to have its roots in the very heart of his country and which has ever since haunted the music of all Scandinavians."

William Saunders also pointed up the typically Danish character of Gade's best works. "The beautiful bizarreries of his orchestration give one many a passing mental glimpse of the field and the fjord, while with the charm and delicacy of line and color, so characteristic of his larger works, there is much that is reminiscent of the calm yet not unjoyous life of the villagers and peasantry of those northern climes."

PRINCIPAL WORKS

Ballets—Faedrelandets Muser; Napoli.

Chamber Music—3 violin sonatas; 2 string quintets; String Octet in F major; String Quartet in D major; Piano Trio in F major; Novelletten, for piano trio; Pictures of the Orient, for violin and piano; Fantasies, for clarinet and piano; Folk Dances for violin and piano.

Choral Music—Comala; Elverskud; Spring Message; The Holy Night; At Sunset; Kalanus; Zion; The Crusaders; Seasonal Pictures; The Mountain Thrall; Gefion; Psyche; Der Strom.

Orchestral Music—8 symphonies; 6 overtures; Violin Concerto; Novelletten, for string orchestra; Holbergiana.

Piano Music—Sonata in E minor; Spring Flowers; Aquarellen; Arabesque; Folk Dances; Idylls; Four Fantastic Pieces.

Organ Music—Three Pieces; choral preludes.

Vocal Music—Nine Songs in the Folk Manner; Horseman's Life, for male quartet; Six Songs, for male quartet; Five Songs, for quartet.

ABOUT

Bacharach, A. L. (editor), The Music Masters, vol. 2; Behrend, W., Niels Gade; Gade, N., Aufzeichnungen und Briefe.

Monthly Musical Record, January 1, 1883; Musical Quarterly, April 1917.

Baldassare Galuppi *1706-1785*

BALDASSARE GALUPPI was born on October 18, 1706, on the island of Burano near Venice. It was for this reason that he was called "Il Buranello" during his lifetime. His father, a barber, was a part-time violinist who occasionally performed in local theater orchestras; from him Baldassare received his first music instruction. For a while Galuppi earned his living as an organist in small churches. In 1722 he wrote his first opera, *La Fede nell'incostanza*, which was performed in Chioggia and Vincenza and hissed off both stages. This so discouraged Galuppi that he planned to give up music and become a barber, too. But the celebrated Venetian composer Benedetto Marcello urged him to persevere, and Galuppi continued for about three years to study music with Lotti, one of Marcello's highly esteemed pupils. When Galuppi began to write opera again, he collaborated with a fellow student; the result was a one-act opera produced in Venice in 1728. Then Galuppi completed *Dorinda*, performed with great success at the Teatro Sant'Angelo in Venice in 1729.

Galuppi now became extremely prolific as a composer of opera, writing as many as five operas a year. Some of his works used librettos by Metastasio; others were based on texts by Goldoni. By 1740 his fame had spread throughout Europe. In 1741 he was invited to London to assist in performances of several of his works.

In 1740 Galuppi became *maestro del coro* at the Ospizio dei Mendicanti in Venice. Eight years later he was appointed second *maestro di cappella* at St. Mark's Cathedral.

In 1749 Galuppi directed his creative gifts into *opera buffa*, the field in which he wrote his best and most successful works. The first effort in this genre was *L'Arcadia in Brenta*, written to a libretto by Goldoni and produced at the Teatro Sant'Angelo in Venice in 1749. Goldoni's masterwork— and the only one of his operas to survive—

BALDASSARE GALUPPI

was written five years later. It was *Il Filosofo di campagna*, presented at the Teatro San Samuele in Venice on October 26, 1754. The text concerns the futile efforts of a foolish old man to keep his daughter from marrying the man she loves. For this amusing tale Galuppi produced a score brimming with lively tunes. His music was vivacious and merry, yet at times gently touched with sentiment and tenderness. After its highly successful première, *Il Filosofo* became a favorite of opera audiences everywhere, one of the most frequently performed and widely admired of the genre until Rossini's *The Barber of Seville*. It was long, however, before the opera was heard in the United States. What is believed to be the first American presentation was broadcast on television on February 7, 1960.

In 1762 Galuppi became first *maestro di cappella* at St. Mark's and director of the Conservatorio degli Incurabili. Four years later he was invited to Russia by Catherine II to produce some of his famous operas as well as write new ones. Galuppi's opera *Didone abbandonata* so delighted the Empress that she sent the composer a golden snuffbox studded with diamonds.

In 1768 Galuppi returned to Venice and resumed his directorial post at the Conservatory. Under him the Conservatory became one of the finest institutions of its kind in Italy. Galuppi continued to write

Galuppi: gä-lōōp'pē

opera after opera (he completed over one hundred during his lifetime), as well as a large body of church music. He died in Venice on January 3, 1785. On the centenary of his death a monument was erected in his memory in his native town.

A contemporary writer described Galuppi as "very slender, with small face full of intelligence. His conversation sparkled with wit. His manners were distinguished, and he had a love of all the arts; he owned some magnificent canvases by Veronese. His character was esteemed no less than his talents; he had a large family and lived a quiet and respectable life."

"The music of Galuppi," wrote the eminent musicologist Fétis, "does not glisten with harmonic color, but with a sustained gaiety and indefatigable verve. The graceful forms of his song have brought him fame which, for a long time, resisted the caprices of fashion."

One of Robert Browning's famous poems is entitled "To a Toccata of Galuppi"; the specific composition which the poet referred to has never been identified.

PRINCIPAL WORKS

Choral Music—20 oratorios; cantatas.
Harpsichord Music—Sonatas.
Operas—Over 100 serious and comic operas including: Dorinda; Issipile; Adriano in Siria; La Calamità de' cuori; Scipione in Cartagine; Enrico; Didone abbandonata; Il Filosofo di campagna; Il Re pastore; Ifigenia in Tauride.

ABOUT

Blom, E., Stepchildren of Music; Corte, A. della, Baldassare Galuppi: Profilo critico.

Francesco Geminiani *1687-1762*

FRANCESCO GEMINIANI was born in Lucca, Italy, in 1687, probably in December. His first violin teacher was Carlo Ambrogio Lonati in Milan. He also studied with Corelli in Rome in his youth.

In 1707 Geminiani returned to Lucca, and for three years was violinist in the Signoria Orchestra. In 1711 he moved to Naples, where he studied composition with Alessandro Scarlatti. He then became the concertmaster and leader of a Neapolitan orchestra. A violinist of fiery temperament and robust style (Tartini once described him as "*Il furibondo Geminiani*"), he apparently

confused and disturbed his musicians with his "unexpected accelerations," as Charles Burney reported, "and relaxations of measure," as well as his frequent use of *tempo rubato*. He was soon relieved as conductor and assigned a place in the orchestra.

In 1714 Geminiani went to England. He soon gained powerful patrons and considerable prestige. He was invited to play at court, but in deference to the great Handel (then somewhat in disrepute with English royalty) he refused to appear unless Handel was his accompanist. For the next few years Geminiani prospered in England as a virtuoso and teacher of violin. He also published his first opus in 1716, a set of twelve violin sonatas. Burney remarked of this publication: "Though few could play them, yet all professors allowed them to be still more masterful and elaborate than those of Corelli."

While pursuing a successful and varied career as a musician, Geminiani, unfortunately, embarked upon a business venture as a dealer in paintings. Although Geminiani had once said that he loved art more than music, he was hardly equipped for art as a business, and incurred such heavy financial losses that he went into bankruptcy and was imprisoned. His patron and pupil, Lord Essex, eventually obtained his release.

In 1728 Geminiani was offered an important post as Master of Music and Composer for the State of Ireland. Some say he turned it down because he refused to renounce his Catholicism, as was demanded of him; others maintain that it was Sir Robert Walpole who stood in the way of the appointment because of Geminiani's religion. In any event, the composer never assumed that office. During this period, while engaged industriously in composition, Geminiani directed some of his efforts towards writing theoretical treatises. One of these, the *Art of Violin Playing* (written in English) is a pivotal work, the first instruction book of its kind ever to appear, preceding by several years even the pioneer effort of Leopold Mozart, father of Wolfgang Amadeus Mozart. Geminiani's treatise appeared anonymously in 1730; only some years later was it issued under his name. It handed down the principles and traditions of violin playing as established by Corelli; and it is surprisingly modern in its solution of many technical problems.

Geminiani: jȧ-mē-nyä′nē

In 1731 Geminiani gave a series of twenty highly successful concerts in London. A year later he issued in London the first set of his Concerti Grossi (op. 2). In 1733 he settled in Dublin, establishing residence in Spring Gardens, a court in Dame Street, where he opened a little auditorium called "The Geminiani Great Room," for the presentation of concerts. These performances continued until 1740, attracting large audiences. Geminiani published a second set of Concerti Grossi (op. 3), a set of twelve violin sonatas (op. 4), and six cello sonatas (op. 5).

After a brief visit to Paris in 1740 Geminiani returned to London, where for the next nine years he conducted concerts during Lent at Drury Lane. From 1749 to 1755 he lived in Paris, and in 1759 he was back in Dublin, working as a violin teacher for Count Bellamont.

Geminiani's most significant volume of concertos, his opus 7, appeared in 1746. These works, as A. B. Hutchings noted in *The Baroque Concerto,* "embrace no new principles of construction and make no new use of dance forms." Nevertheless, Hutchings continues, they are "his finest achievements. They include compact few-movement works like the No. 5 in C minor on a French overture plan, and spreading canzona-style works like No. 6 with thirteen changes of speed. Perhaps the best is No. 3, 'composti di tre stili differenti.' "

Francesco Geminiani died in Dublin on September 17, 1762. It has been said, on good authority, that his death was hastened by the loss of the manuscript of one of his theoretical treatises.

Edmund van der Straeten did not hesitate to call Geminiani "one of the greatest, if not the greatest, violinists of his time, who had enlarged in many ways the resources of his instruments, as his concertos and sonatas clearly show." Geminiani's place in the early history of Italian instrumental music, however, rests not only on his uncommon virtuosity but on his success in amplifying the concerto and sonata structure, and in enriching the style of composition as bequeathed to him by his teacher, Corelli. As van der Straeten said: "He also extended the sonata form, which is more developed and freer in form, even if that often lacks the clearness and beautiful symmetry of the work of his master, Corelli.

FRANCESCO GEMINIANI

Burney and many great musicians have pointed out his want of originality and weakness in harmonic treatment, but those who have the courage to judge for themselves will find many beautiful melodies in his slow movements, and the most delightful dance movements, while some of his Allegros are likewise attractive. He was a master of the instrumental fugue."

In addition to *The Art of Violin Playing* Geminiani produced several significant theoretical works, including *The Art of Accompaniament* [sic], *Guida armonica, The Art of Playing the Guitar,* and *Treatise of Good Taste.*

Principal Works

Chamber Music—24 violin sonatas; various other sonatas for solo instruments and accompaniment; trios.

Harpsichord Music—Pièces de clavecin.

Orchestral Music—18 violin concertos; concerti grossi.

About

Straeten, E. van der, The History of the Violin. Strad, November 1929; Westminster Magazine, April 1777.

Carlo Gesualdo *1560-1613*

C ARLO GESUALDO, Prince of Venosa, one of the foremost composers of the madrigal and a leading musical figure of the Renaissance, was born in Naples in or about 1560. He came from an old, distinguished,

Gesualdo: jä-zōō-äl'dō

CARLO GESUALDO

wealthy Neapolitan family that had included King Roger II. He was directed to the study of music at an early age. One of his earliest teachers was Pomponio Nenna, a famous madrigalist, who gave him instruction in composition, singing, and lute. The young Gesualdo was also influenced by the frequent musical performances at home, where his father maintained a musical establishment.

As a young man Gesualdo was made *maestro di cappella* of the Scuola Napoletana, where his pronounced musical gifts attracted notice. During this period he helped develop at his palace one of the most influential musical courts in Naples, equipped with a large staff of singers, instrumentalists, and composers. He also became one of the city's most generous patrons of music.

When Gesualdo was twenty-five, he married Donna Maria d'Avalos. A member of a powerful Neapolitan family, she had, despite her youth, already been twice married, and had acquired a dubious moral reputation. A few years after her marriage to Gesualdo she attracted the interest of Gesualdo's uncle, whose attentions she rejected. Turning against her and determined to bring about her destruction, he brought Gesualdo incontrovertible evidence that she was unfaithful. On October 16, 1590, Gesualdo discovered his wife and her lover, a young duke. He ordered that the guilty pair be killed and that their naked bodies be

flung on the steps of the palace and left there for several days as a warning to all unfaithful wives. He also ordered the murder of his infant child, now doubting its paternity. This episode has been romanticized by several notable authors, including Anatole France *(Les Puits de Sainte-Claire)* and Brantôme *(Les Vies des dames galantes)*.

Threatened with reprisal by his murdered wife's relatives Gesualdo went into hiding seventy miles from Naples, in a town that still bears his name. In 1591 his father died, and the title of Prince of Venosa passed on to him. A year later he returned to his court in Naples. On February 19, 1594 he married Leonora d'Este, daughter of the Duke of Ferrara, and set up a household at the Palazzo Marco Pio in that city. His second union proved no happier than the first. His wife objected continually to Gesualdo's numerous infidelities and on one occasion tried to induce her brother, the Cardinale Cesare d'Este of Modena, to persuade the Pope to grant her a divorce. Her effort was unsuccessful, however, and the marriage endured until Gesualdo's death.

During his several years' residence in Ferrara, Gesualdo published the first four volumes of his madrigals, two in 1594, a third in 1595, and a fourth a year later. Between 1595 and 1611 he issued two more such volumes, and a seventh appeared posthumously in 1626.

In or about 1597 Gesualdo returned to Naples, where he established a renowned musical academy. He died in that city on September 8, 1613.

Robert Craft has described Gesualdo's appearance in this manner: "His head was egg-shaped, his complexion was lifeless, his eyes were dark and narrow, his ears were the large ears common to all composers, and his fingers were the long, lithe digitals without which virtuosity of the lute would have been impossible."

In addition to his madrigals, which number about 120, Gesualdo composed three volumes of sacred music and two keyboard canzoni. It is in the madrigal form, however, that he was most important and most original. The "modernist" of his time, he brought to his writing startling progressions, discords, and modulations. His chromaticisms in some ways anticipate Wagner.

In his madrigals, Gesualdo's prime interest was not in melody for its own sake but in dramatic and emotional power. His intensity of feeling was original in his day. His works, wrote Philip Heseltine, are truly "vivid and passionate exclamations of the human soul. While Peri and Monteverdi were bringing to birth that new vehicle of expression which was to become opera, Gesualdo, without the aid of action and a theater, was dramatizing the emotions themselves, and his contribution to the first period of dramatic music was no less important than theirs."

Among Gesualdo's most celebrated madrigals are "Dolcissima mia vita," "Moro lasso," and "Resta di darmi noia." "The listener," said Robert Craft, "cannot imagine music of this period more emotionally charged." Of "Resta di darmi noia" Alfred Einstein wrote, "Tortured harmony and restless declamation have been transformed from mannerism into full-blown expression, and this expression is more affecting if one considers the piece as an autobiographical confession."

In 1960 Igor Stravinsky used material from some of Gesualdo's madrigals for a major choral work entitled *Gesualdo Monumentum.*

Principal Works

Choral Music—120 Madrigals; Sacrae Cantiones; Responsoria.

Instrumental Music—2 canzoni for keyboard.

About

Einstein, A., The Italian Madrigal; Gray, Cecil and Heseltine, P., Carlo Gesualdo, Prince of Venosa, Musician and Murderer.

High Fidelity Magazine, September 1961.

Orlando Gibbons *1583-1625*

ORLANDO GIBBONS, one of the most remarkable composers of the Tudor period, was born in Oxford in 1583, probably in December. His father, the town councillor, was a trained musician; he gave Orlando his first music lessons. While Gibbons was still young the family moved to Cambridge. There, in February 1596, he was placed in the choir of King's College, and two years later he matriculated.

On March 21, 1605, Gibbons was appointed organist of the Chapel Royal in London, a unique honor for one so young,

ORLANDO GIBBONS

and convincing indication of the high estate he had achieved as an organist. He held this post for the remainder of his life, but from time to time was called upon for other important performances.

Gibbons received his baccalaureate from Oxford in 1606 and in the same year he married Elizabeth Patten, daughter of the Keeper of the King's Closet.

Some time between 1605 and 1612 (the exact date is unknown), Gibbons published a set of nine fantasias for three viols. With this work, the fantasia—written in a fugal style anticipating a later technique of fugue-writing—became a significant instrumental form in English music. These pieces were also the first important works for stringed instruments produced by an English composer. They are distinguished, said Ernest Walker, "by real dignity and solidity of style; the workmanship is elevated and serious, and there is none of the sound for mere sound's sake that we find not infrequently in the other instrumental music of the period."

Between 1612 and 1613, Gibbons contributed six pieces to the monumental collection *Parthenia*, the first compilation in England devoted exclusively to virginal music. His contribution included a remarkable four-part fantasia, two galliards, a prelude, *The Queen's Command*, and a pavane which is probably his best known single piece of keyboard music, *The Earl of Salisbury*. Gibbons was also the composer of many other pieces for the virginal—fantasias and pavanes, as well as allemandes, airs, courantes, galliards and fancies—which rank with the finest keyboard music produced during this period.

The year 1614 witnessed still another publication by Gibbons of prime importance, *Madrigals and Motets in Five Parts*. It is here that we find such pieces as "The Silver Swan," "What Is Our Life?" "Dainty Fine Bird," "How Art Thou Thrall'd," "Ah, Dear Heart" and "Fair Is the Rose," through which Gibbons became one of the last great exponents of the madrigal. In the opinion of J. A. Fuller-Maitland they are "some of the finest specimens of that beautiful form in which the art of polyphonic vocal music seems to have reached its highest point."

A. E. F. Dickinson has said of Gibbons' best madrigals: " 'The Silver Swan' shows Gibbons' melodic sense as well as the tart harmony of the augmented fifth. . . . The gnomic manner persists through the book. A setting of Raleigh's 'What Is Our Life?' is the most elaborate essay in this manner, with the stage metaphors closely matched by the music. Elsewhere the satirical vein fetters the composer and he has to resort to formal sequences and imitations. As a set, these madrigals preserve a certain strain of ethical reflection in developed counterpoint."

In 1611, and again in 1615, Gibbons received munificent grants as marks of royal favor. In 1619 he was appointed chamber musician to the King, and in 1623 was made organist of Westminster Abbey. In 1622 he obtained a doctorate from Oxford.

In 1625 Gibbons officiated at the funeral of James II. Later that year, he was invited by Charles I to Canterbury for festivities honoring the arrival of the King's bride, the French princess Henrietta Maria. On this occasion Gibbons suffered an apoplectic stroke that proved fatal. He died on June 5, 1625 and was buried one day later in Canterbury Cathedral. The haste with which he was buried aroused the suspicion that he had been a victim of plague, but the rumor was proved false by a post mortem examination.

In addition to his madrigals, fantasias for viols, and keyboard music, Gibbons produced a library of English church music which some critics consider to be without equal in the religious music of this period. Henri Prunières remarks: "He was certainly the most representative master of the new church style—distinctively English in his austerity. One must be an Englishman to appreciate Gibbons, as one must be a Calvinist to appreciate Goudimel. . . . He was a composer who owed nothing to Rome, and he brought to perfection a primitive English type of mysticism, noble, dignified, and severe."

"There is in Gibbons," wrote E. H. Fellowes, "a variety of style, a diversity of character, a variableness of intention which distinguishes him from his forerunners."

"His prevailing tone is grave and solemn," comments W. H. Hadow, "as though with him the madrigal caught some echo from the Church service; he has keen feeling for expressive melody and harmonic beauty of sound."

Orlando Gibbons had seven children. The most celebrated was Christopher (1615-1676), who became the organist of Westminster Abbey and wrote some excellent church music.

PRINCIPAL WORKS

Chamber Music—Fantasias, for three viols.
Choral Music—Anthems, hymns, madrigals, motets, psalms, services.
Virginal Music—Allemandes, airs, courantes, galliards, fantasias, pavanes, In Nomine's.

ABOUT

Fellowes, E. H., Orlando Gibbons: A Short Account of His Life and Works; Fellowes, E. H., Orlando Gibbons and His Family: The Last of the Tudor School of Musicians; Glyn, M. H., About Elizabethan Virginal Music and Its Composers.
Chesterian, May 1925.

Mikhail Glinka *1804-1857*

MIKHAIL IVANOVICH GLINKA, the first great Russian composer, and the father of Russian nationalism in music, was born in Novospasskoi, in the government of Smolensk, on June 1, 1804. His father, a retired army captain, was a prosperous landowner. Music exerted a powerful fascination for the child Glinka; he was deeply—sometimes violently—affected by the concerts of a private orchestra at his uncle's home and by songs in church. In 1817 he entered a private school for children of the nobility in St. Petersburg, proving an exceptional student not only in music, but in languages and the sciences. While attending school, he studied piano with Carl Meyer and later with John Field, and violin with Böhm. In 1822, the year in which he graduated from school, he produced his first compositions, a set of five piano waltzes.

In 1823 Glinka suffered a nervous disorder and went to the Caucasus for a rest and vacation. Returning home, he began to study music more assiduously, memorizing textbooks on harmony and orchestration, studying masterpieces from the published scores in his uncle's library. Since a career in music had not been planned for him, however, he became a civil employee in the Ministry of Communications in 1824, and remained at that post for four years.

Glinka did not abandon his musical interests during this time. He joined a group of dilettantes, with whom he would spend hours discussing music and exchanging thoughts on the arts and aesthetics. In 1830, convinced that he wished to become a professional musician, he departed for Italy for further study. He spent about a year as a pupil of Basili, director of the Milan Conservatory. In Rome he met Donizetti and Bellini, and forthwith became a profound advocate of Italian opera. And in Berlin, in 1833, he studied composition and theory with Dehn.

It was in Berlin that Glinka first conceived the notion of writing *Russian* music; until then his works had been influenced primarily by the Italians. As he confided in his *Memoirs:* "Homesickness led me little by little to write Russian music." To a friend he explained his ambition: "My most earnest desire is to compose music which would make all my beloved countrymen feel quite at home and lead no one to allege that I strutted about in borrowed plumes."

When his father died in 1834, Glinka returned to Russia to supervise the estate. On May 8, 1835 he married Maria Petrovna Ivanova, an attractive young girl who soon after the marriage turned out to be a coquette and a shrew. The couple separated and were divorced in 1846.

In St. Petersburg Glinka became friendly with some of the city's leading poets and writers, including Pushkin, Gogol, and Zhukovsky. Their discussions of national poetry and literature led him to consider their im-

MIKHAIL GLINKA

plications for music, and fired the spark of musical nationalism he had nourished so long. Now Glinka set for himself the ambitious task of composing a national Russian opera. The poet Zhukovsky suggested the subject of Ivan Sussanin, the seventeenth-century peasant hero who saved the life of young Michael Feodorovich, the first of the Romanoffs, by sacrificing his own. Baron Rozen provided Glinka with the text. Glinka spent about two years writing his opera. Originally it was entitled *Ivan Sussanin.* After one of the rehearsals, which was attended by Czar Nicholas I, Glinka renamed it *A Life for the Czar,* in gratitude for the Czar's appreciation of the work.

The première took place on December 9, 1836. Many of the sophisticated noblemen in that brilliant first-night audience (which included the Czar and his court) disdained the work, regarding with snobbish condescension a national Russian opera, based on Russian history, written in the Russian language, and using popular folk material. They referred derisively to the score as "coachmen's music." The Czar, however, delighted with the opera, presented Glinka with a ring valued at four thousand rubles. And the general public reacted so favorably that the opera had a successful run of thirty-two performances in its first season.

With *A Life for the Czar,* opera came of age in Russia and musical nationalism emerged. Prosper Mérimée wrote in 1840, "Poetically as well as musically, it is a

faithful account of all that Russia has suffered and sung. In it are to be discovered
her love and her hate, her lamentations and
rejoicing, her gloomy nights and her radiant
dawns. It is more than an opera; it is a
national epic."

Stylistically, the opera blends Italian,
Polish, and Russian ingredients. Some of
the arias and ensembles are true to Italian
tradition and style. The Polish element is
pronounced in several dances, such as the
mazurka and the polonaise. And the Russian character is most pronounced in many
of the stirring choruses: the bridal chorus,
the choruses based on the old Russian
Slavsia (song of glory), the stirring hymn
to Russia which opens the final act, and the
remarkable song of glory to the Czar and
Ivan that concludes it. Russian, too, are
some of the principal melodies, which derive
their melodic and rhythmic patterns from
Russian folk songs, or their modal character
from old Russian church music.

Soon after the successful production of
A Life for the Czar, Glinka was appointed
choral director of the Imperial Chapel. In
this office he toured Finland and the
Ukraine searching for new singers. He was
also planning a new opera, even more intensely Russian in spirit, background, and
context—an opera that he hoped would be
thoroughly nationalistic in musical idiom,
that would fully embody his patriotic ideals.
That work was Ruslan and Ludmila, based
on a poem by Pushkin. Glinka sketched
the introduction and finale in 1839, but
poor health forced him to interrupt his work
until the winter of 1841. He completed the
opera the following April, and it was introduced at the Imperial Theater in St.
Petersburg on December 9, 1842.

It was not successful at first. To the general public it was too advanced in method
and style to be immediately appreciated.
Musical authorities were divided in their
opinion. Serov, one of Russia's most powerful critics, regarded it as "the last aberra-
tion of lamentably warped genius." On the
other hand, to Stassov the opera was the
"mature expression of Glinka's inspiration."
And César Cui regarded it as "the product
of a mature talent that has reached the
final stages of development. Regarded as
absolute music, Ruslan is a work of the first
rank; and from this point of view it will
bear comparison with the great operatic

masterpieces. In it Glinka marked out new
paths and opened up horizons undreamed
of before his time."

Success came to Ruslan too late for Glinka
to enjoy it. It was not acclaimed until its
revival two years after his death. In 1892,
a generation after his death, another revival achieved a complete triumph. But by
then, its influence had been felt by a generation of Russian composers who owed
much of their creative development to this
pioneer work.

In 1842, however, the failure of this advanced opera was a severe blow to Glinka,
who regarded it as his finest creation.
Broken in spirit, poor in health, he felt the
need for a change of scene, and spent much
of his time traveling. In 1843 he visited
Paris, where he was warmly welcomed by
Meyerbeer, Liszt, and Berlioz. In 1845 he
went to Spain, where his interest in Spanish folk songs and dances was aroused. His
delight in and fascination with Spanish folk
music led him in 1845 to write a caprice
brillant for orchestra, Jota aragonesa. It
was the first work by a Russian to make
successful use of Spanish folk idioms in a
serious concert work. Three years later
Glinka completed a second work for orchestra based on Spanish material, Night
in Madrid.

In 1848 Glinka produced the orchestral
work which today is regarded as his finest
symphonic composition. It was Kamarinskaya, a fantasy based on two Russian folk
songs which the composer had heard in
Warsaw: a marriage song, "Over the Hills,
the High Hills," and a dance song,
"Kamarinskaya." "He has left us a masterpiece," Tchaikovsky once wrote of this fantasy, "every measure of which is the outcome
of enormous creative power."

The outbreak of the Crimean War finally
brought Glinka back to St. Petersburg, where
he attempted to write a third opera, The
Bigamist, based on a drama by Kukolnik.
Unable to muster the enthusiasm to bring
this work to a final and successful resolution, he turned to the writing of church
music. In 1856 he paid a brief visit to Berlin in order to devote himself to the intensive study of Western church music.
During his stay he gave a concert of his
works on January 21, 1857; it included an
excerpt from A Life for the Czar. Soon after
the concert Glinka caught a cold which had

fatal consequences. He died suddenly in Berlin on February 15, 1857, and was buried in that city. A few months later his remains were transferred to St. Petersburg and re-interred in the cemetery of the Alexander Nevsky Monastery.

Glinka's sister, Mme. Ludmilla Shestakova, gave the following description of Glinka's personality: "My brother had an innocently childlike, tender, delicate, affectionate nature. He was certainly a little capricious, and was spoiled; he had to have everything his own way. Still if he had his faults, he made haste to recognize them and redress them. He never forgot a good turn or a good action. Nothing disturbed his good nature: neither family disputes nor the conversations at the clubs where he happened to be. One cannot exactly say that he was unmethodical, but he was unable to conduct his own affairs; anything in the nature of household matters was particularly distasteful to him. His faults were excessive susceptibility and distrust. He dreaded death to such an extent that he took the most ridiculous precautions against it, and avoided everything, no matter how trivial, which he thought might possibly be harmful. The slightest indisposition terrified him, as though it were a disaster. He treated himself on homeopathic lines, and always kept in the house a small medicine chest containing the most necessary remedies. He followed von Hahnemann's principles in avoiding scents and smells, more especially camphor, which he looked upon as a poison. Spices and aromatic articles were banished from the table; at least he imagined they were. As a matter of fact, the cook did not hesitate to use them in dishes which she sent up for family consumption. One day Glinka found a bay leaf in his soup. Putting it on the edge of the plate he remarked: 'I dislike bay leaves either on my head or in my soup.'"

Hector Berlioz wrote of Glinka's musical style, "Glinka's talent is essentially supple and varied. His style has the rare advantage of being able to adapt itself, at the desire of the composer, to the exigencies and character of the subject treated. Glinka can be simple and even naïve without ever condescending to employ a vulgar phrase. His melodies take unexpected turns, and are built on periods which charm by their very strangeness. He is a great harmonist, and uses the instruments with a care and an acquaintance with their intimate resources which make his orchestra one of the most novel and vivacious modern orchestras that one can hear."

"His claim to immortality," sums up M. Montagu-Nathan, "must rest upon having unified the experience and aims of earlier and lesser composers in the accomplishment of his single purpose, that of placing Russian musical nationality on a firm basis."

PRINCIPAL WORKS

Chamber Music—2 string quartets; Septet in E-flat major; Trio pathétique; Viola Sonata in D minor.
Choral Music—First Ekteniya; In Life's Hard Moments; various other choruses, hymns, and valedictory songs.
Operas—A Life for the Czar; Ruslan and Ludmila.
Orchestral Music—Symphony in B-flat major; Overture-Symphony on Russian Themes; Valse-Fantaisie; Jota aragonesa; Night in Madrid; Kamarinskaya; Festival Polonaise; overtures.
Piano Music—Fugues, impromptus, mazurkas, nocturnes, tarantella, variations, waltzes.
Vocal Music—Songs for voice and piano, including Doubt, The Lark, Midnight Review, The Northern Star; vocal quartets.

ABOUT

Brook, D., Six Great Russian Composers; Calvocoressi, M. D., Glinka; Calvocoressi, M. D., and Abraham, G., Glinka; Findeisen, N. F. (editor), Collected Letters of Glinka; Glinka, M. I., Autobiography and Notes on Instrumentation; Glinka, M. I., Memoirs; Leonard, R. A., A History of Russian Music; Montagu-Nathan, M., Glinka.

Christoph Willibald Gluck *1714-1787*

CHRISTOPH WILLIBALD RITTER VON GLUCK, who ushered in a new era in eighteenth-century opera with his musical dramas, was born in the town of Erasbach, in the Upper Palatinate, on July 2, 1714. His father, a forester on the estate of Prince Kaunitz, went to work for Prince Lobkowitz when Gluck was fifteen. As a child, Gluck often accompanied his father to the forests, carrying heavy tools on his back and going barefoot in winter through ice and snow. His earliest schooling, at various Catholic schools in Kamnitz and Albersdorf, included music instruction in singing, violin, and organ. Not much is known of Gluck's adolescence; the long-held belief of many biographers that he studied music in a Jesuit college is now sub-

CHRISTOPH WILLIBALD GLUCK

ject to serious doubt. In 1732, in any event, Gluck went to Prague, studied music for a while, then supported himself mainly by teaching music, singing in church choirs, and playing dance music.

In 1736 Gluck visited Vienna for the first time. He presented himself to Prince Lobkowitz, the son of his father's employer, who promptly engaged him as a chamber musician. Before long, however, the Italian Prince Melzi, impressed with the young man's talent, induced Gluck to leave his post to work for him in Italy. For a number of years Gluck studied the Italian style with Giovanni Battista Sammartini and absorbed the traditions of Italian opera. He also completed his first opera, *Artaserse.* His work, introduced in Milan on December 26, 1741, was so outstanding a success that it brought the young composer several commissions for new operas. From 1741 to 1745 Gluck wrote eight more operas in the Italian style, all of which were well received. But, as Martin Cooper pointed out, the scores for these first operas were "the conventional music of the Italian *opera seria.* . . . There is little individuality about any of those early works."

At the time, however, these conventional works suited popular taste and won Gluck great popularity in Italy and abroad. In 1745 London's Haymarket Theatre engaged him to write two operas. During his stay in England Gluck also made several appear-

ances in public concerts, in one of which he collaborated with Handel. In 1746 he left England to conduct a traveling Italian opera company touring Germany.

In 1748 Gluck returned to Vienna, no longer the petitioner of twelve years earlier, but a musician whose fame was established outside the Austrian capital. In Vienna he enhanced his reputation with the opera *Semiramide riconosciuta,* which the Prince of Hildburghausen had commissioned for the birthday of the Empress Maria Theresa. The opera, written to a text by Metastasio, reopened the historic Burgtheater on May 14, 1748. The Empress's pleasure and the audience's enthusiasm promised Gluck a bright future in Vienna. But he was not yet ready to plant his roots, and he left the city to travel abroad. During the next two years he visited Copenhagen, Hamburg, Prague, and other European cities where several new operas, all written to texts by Metastasio, were introduced.

In 1750 Gluck married Marianne Pergin, the daughter of a prosperous Viennese merchant. Four years later he was appointed court composer. In this capacity he continued to write opera as well as music for ballets and court entertainments, marching from success to success. "He has surprising fire, but he is somewhat mad," said Metastasio, mindful of Gluck's already pronounced tendency toward experimentation; Gluck's music, the librettist added, was full of "noise and extravagance." For Gluck, by this time, was already veering from the formal Italian opera for which Metastasio wrote librettos: its emphasis on pageantry and spectacle; its complete subservience to the demands of the singer; its fetish for vocal ornamentation and superficial musical effects.

A similar impatience with Italian ways marked the thinking of two influential people in Vienna: the Count Giacomo Durazzo, director of Vienna's theaters, whose literary sympathies were with the French; and Ranieri de' Calzabigi, a poet and man of letters as well as chamber councilor to the exchequer. From his conversations with these men, Gluck came to the conclusion that what the opera of his day needed most was a major reform in style.

Later, Gluck explained the nature of that reform in the historic document that appeared as a preface to *Alceste:* "I resolved to avoid all those abuses which had crept into Italian opera through the mistaken vanity of singers and the unwise compliance of composers, and which had rendered it wearisome and ridiculous, instead of being, as it once was, the grandest and most imposing stage work of modern times. I endeavored to reduce music to its proper function, that of seconding poetry by enforcing the expression of the sentiment, and the interest of the situations, without interrupting the action, or weakening it by superfluous ornament. My idea was that the relation of music to poetry was much the same as that of harmonious coloring and well-disposed light and shade to an accurate drawing, which animates the figures without altering their outlines. I have therefore been very careful never to interrupt a singer in the heat of a dialogue, in order to introduce a tedious ritornelle, nor to stop him in the middle of a piece either for the purpose of displaying the flexibility of his voice on some favorable vowel, or that the orchestra might give him time to take breath before a long sustained note. Furthermore, I have not thought it right to hurry through the second part of a song if the words happened to be the most important of the whole, in order to repeat the first part regularly four times over; or to finish the air where the sense does not end in order to allow the singer to exhibit his power of varying the passage at pleasure. In fact, my object was to put an end to abuses against which good taste and good sense have long protested in vain. My idea was that the overture ought to indicate the subject and prepare the spectators for the character of the piece they are about to see; that the instruments ought to be introduced in proportion to the degree of interest and passion in the words; and that it was necessary above all to avoid making too great a disparity between the recitative and the air of a dialogue, so as not to break the sense of a period or awkwardly interrupt the movement and animation of a scene. I also thought that my chief endeavor should be to attain a grand simplicity, and consequently I have avoided making a parade of difficulties at the cost of clearness; I have set no value on novelty as such, unless it was naturally suggested by the situation and suited to the expression; in short, there was no rule which I did not consider myself bound to sacrifice for the sake of effect."

This revolt against Italian opera and its methods and principles was initiated with *Orfeo ed Euridice,* the opera by which Gluck is still most often represented in the world's opera houses. It was introduced at the Burgtheater in Vienna on October 5, 1762, with the famous *castrato* Guadagni appearing as Orpheus. When first heard, *Orfeo* was severely criticized. Compared with the pageantry, vast scenes, and large vocal ensembles to which the Viennese had become accustomed through Italian opera, *Orfeo* appeared bare, even impoverished. There were only two principal characters and only four solo voices in the entire opera. Almost nothing happened. No huge climaxes carried the plot to a peak of audience interest. The airs were denuded of the kind of ornamentation that the Viennese so enjoyed in their opera melodies; nor did the opera give the performers an opportunity to display their technical powers. Finally, the orchestration seemed noisy and heavy-handed, for Gluck had dispensed with the harpsichord and had introduced into the orchestral ensemble such instruments as clarinets, trombones, and cymbals.

Time, of course, has reversed the initial appraisal. *Orfeo,* we know today, is a masterwork of compelling beauty and deep emotional content. "There is no opera," said Henry Chorley, "in the world's long list which, with merely three female voices and a chorus, can return to the stage in days like ours, to make the heart throb and the eyes water."

The American première of *Orfeo ed Euridice* took place in New York City on May 25, 1863. At the Metropolitan Opera it was first heard on December 30, 1891; and it had a distinguished revival on December 23, 1909, under the direction of Toscanini, with Louise Homer as Orfeo and Johanna Gadski as Euridice.

With repeated performances, the Viennese audiences of Gluck's day came to appreciate the majesty and eloquence of *Orfeo ed Euridice.* But before this reversal occurred, Gluck continued courageously along the path he had forged with *Orfeo.* On December 16, 1767, *Alceste* was given at the Burgtheater —the second masterpiece with the new simplicity, directness, and dramatic truth that Gluck was expounding. Once again, the opera was too original in style, too revolutionary in material, to be appreciated at first hearing. "If this is the sort of evening's entertainment the Court Opera is to provide," some said after the première, "then goodbye. We can go to church without paying two gulden."

What is generally accepted as the American première of *Alceste* took place at the Metropolitan Opera on January 24, 1941, with Marjorie Lawrence in the title role. Kirsten Flagstad's last appearance at the Metropolitan Opera, in 1952, was in the same role.

When his third operatic innovation, *Paride ed Elena,* introduced on November 3, 1770, aroused severe criticism and antagonism, Gluck decided at last to leave Vienna and carry his message to Paris, the city of Rameau. He arrived in the French capital in 1773 with a new opera, *Iphigénie en Aulide,* with text by du Roullet, the attaché to the French legation in Vienna. In Paris Gluck encountered even greater opposition, largely from the advocates of Italian opera. But there were others who disliked him simply because he was German, still others who objected to his revolutionary doctrine for opera. But for the personal intervention of Marie Antoinette—who had been Gluck's pupil in Vienna before her marriage—*Iphigénie en Aulide* might never have been performed. Finally given at the Opéra on April 19, 1774, the work made a profound impression upon many discriminating musicians. But Gluck's enemies still remained carping critics. First they maintained that Gluck did not have the gift of song; then they accused him of setting to music dramatic episodes and materials that simply did not lend themselves to melody.

Gluck's position in Paris was, nevertheless, much strengthened by the introduction of *Orfeo ed Euridice* in France, on August 2, 1774. This time the part of Orfeo was assumed by a true tenor. His success in Paris provoked bitter dispute between the two operatic factions. In Vienna, where Gluck had returned for a brief stay, news reached him that his enemies in Paris had imported the renowned Italian opera composer Niccolò Piccini to write works for the Opéra based on French texts, in direct opposition to Gluck's operas. Gluck's first act was to despatch a fiery letter to *L'Année littéraire,* propounding again his ideas and principles, and provoking even greater hostility in certain quarters. By the time Gluck

had returned to Paris in 1776 and presented *Alceste* at the Opéra on April 23, Paris was divided into two warring camps: those who were on Gluck's side and those who were out to destroy him. *Alceste* was received so badly that Gluck's enemies surely seemed to have the upper hand. A new Gluck opera, *Armide*—presented on September 23, 1777— fared somewhat better, however, and it was now the turn of his allies to feel encouraged.

The climactic battle in this operatic war occurred when both Piccini and Gluck were engaged to write an opera on the same subject—*Iphigénie en Tauride*—though to different librettos. Gluck's opera, performed first, on May 18, 1779, was a sensation. "I know not," said Grimm, "if what we have heard be melody. Perhaps it is something much better; I forget the opera and find myself in a Greek tragedy." Piccini now tried to have the performance of his own opera canceled, but without success. At its première it suffered severely in comparison with Gluck's work, not only because of its inherent inferiority but because of a shabby presentation: the prima donna who appeared as Iphigenia was drunk throughout the performance. Gluck's triumph was now complete, the defeat of Piccini decisive.

Gluck had one more opera performed in Paris—*Écho et Narcisse,* on September 24, 1779. Then he returned to Vienna permanently. He was now a wealthy man, a composer of international renown. He spent his last years quietly at Wiedner Hauptstrasse No. 22, rendered invalid for most of this period by paralysis brought on by apoplectic strokes. Gluck died of a stroke on November 15, 1787, and was buried in the cemetery of Matzleinsdorf. A simple inscription appeared on his tombstone: "Here lies an upright German man. A zealous Christian. A faithful spouse. Christoph Ritter Gluck, of the Noble Art of Music and a Great Master."

Romain Rolland has described Gluck as "tall, broad-shouldered, strong, moderately stout, and of compact and muscular frame. His head was round, and he had a large red face strongly pitted with the marks of smallpox. His hair was brown, and powdered. His eyes were gray, small and deepset but very bright; and his expression was intelligent but hard. He had raised eyebrows, a large nose, full cheeks and chin, and a thick neck. Some of his features rather recall those of Beethoven and Handel."

Of Gluck's personality, Rolland wrote: "In society, he often wore a stiff and solemn air, but he was quickly roused to anger. . . . Gluck lacked self-control, was irritable, and could not get used to the customs of society. He was plain-spoken to the verge of coarseness. . . . He was insensible to flattery, but was enthusiastic about his own works. . . . He liked few people—his wife, his niece, and some friends; but he was undemonstrative and without any of the sentimentality of the period; he also held all exaggeration in horror and never made much of his own people. He was a jolly fellow, nevertheless, especially after drinking—for he drank and ate heartily until apoplexy killed him. There was no idealism about him, and he had no illusion about either men or things. He loved money and did not conceal the fact. He was also very selfish."

To Ernest Newman, Gluck's personal character "shows itself both in his music and in his physical structure. To the last he was a hardy, virile peasant, trained to rough and sturdy habits of life. In his face can be clearly seen those qualities that appear again in his music and in his correspondence: the head is thrown back proudly and confidently, the large and mobile mouth has an air of quick intelligence, and the eyes look straight and fearlessly upon the beholder."

In a discussion of Gluck's innovations in opera, and the impact of his work on the evolution of musical drama, Lawrence Gilman wrote: "Gluck's reforms are more frequently mentioned than understood. He was not a revolutionary and he made no radical changes in the operatic form which he found in general favor. What he did was distinctly in line with the movement toward simplicity, begun while he was yet an explorer of new fields, in his own search after the path to artistic success. . . . To accomplish his ends, he stripped the opera of the pompous garb of artifice which had been gradually imposed upon it by a century of pseudo-classicism and a slavish adherence to accepted models. He sought to wed text to music plainly expressive of the thought, and to abolish all vocal device and meretricious ornament introduced as mere decoration and without dramatic purpose.

And he discerned with the swift comprehension of genius the rightful place of the ballet which had long been almost intrusive in French opera despite the fact that it was the principal ancestor of the lyric drama of the country."

PRINCIPAL WORKS

Ballets—Don Juan; Semiramide.

Chamber Music—6 sonatas for two violins and accompaniment.

Choral Music—Frühlingsfeier; De Profundis; other choruses.

Operas—Semiramide riconosciuta; Ezio; Il re pastore; L'Ivrogne corrigé; Tetide; Le Cadi dupé; Orfeo ed Euridice; Il Trionfo dì Clelia; La Rencontre imprévue; Il Telemacco; Alceste; Paride ed Elena; Iphigénie en Aulide; Armide; Iphigénie en Tauride; Écho et Narcisse.

Vocal Music—Oden und Lieder.

ABOUT

Berlioz, H., Gluck and His Operas; Cooper, M., Gluck; Einstein, A., Gluck; Landormy, P., Gluck; Newman, E., Gluck and the Opera; Rolland, R., Some Musicians of Former Days.

Karl Goldmark *1830-1915*

KARL GOLDMARK was born in Keszthely, Hungary, on May 18, 1830. The son of a synagogue cantor, he was a highly musical child, who liked to invent his own tunes. One day the town schoolmaster overheard some of his improvisations and discovering that the child was too poor to obtain instruction in music, persuaded a friend to teach him violin. Soon afterwards, hearing an organ in church, Karl determined to become a musician. "I had never heard anything like this before," he later wrote in his memoirs. "The church was quite a distance off, and besides we were never allowed to enter it. For the first time in my life I heard and experienced the overpowering force of harmony and of music in general. . . . At this moment my fate and future were decided upon and my career settled. I was to be a musician, and strangely enough it came about through the Catholic Church."

In 1842 Goldmark entered the Sopron Musical Society for lessons in violin and composition. A year later he gave a successful violin recital. In 1844 he went to Vienna. For about a year he studied violin with Jansa, then attended the Vienna Conservatory as a student of violin with Böhm, and of harmony with Preyer.

KARL GOLDMARK

During the revolutionary upheavals of 1848, when the Conservatory closed down temporarily, Goldmark's music education came to an abrupt end. He earned his living playing violin in theater orchestras. One day he was called out of the theater by a government official and led to the city prison, to receive the astonishing news that he was to be shot as a traitor. The officials, of course, had seized the wrong person; fortunately the error was rectified before the firing squad was summoned.

After the revolution, Goldmark was employed as a violinist in the orchestra of the Karlstheater. He returned to music study, memorizing texts on harmony and counterpoint, and embarked on serious composition, soon becoming so completely absorbed in writing that he gave up his theater job. The first concert devoted entirely to his music took place in Vienna on March 20, 1857; it included a piano quartet, an orchestral overture, and some vocal and choral music.

During a visit to Hungary in 1859, Goldmark presented another successful concert of his compositions in Budapest. He also completed a new chamber music work, the String Quartet in B-flat, which the Hellmesberger Quartet performed in Vienna. One day after this performance, two eminent Viennese musicians, Karl Tausig and Peter Cornelius, called on Goldmark to express their enthusiasm.

Goldmark's first major success was the orchestral overture *Sakuntala*, introduced in

Vienna on December 26, 1865. Eduard Hanslick, Vienna's most powerful critic, spoke highly of its gracious lyricism, romantic moods and vivid harmonic and orchestral colors. The work is still popular today.

During the next few years Goldmark supported himself by teaching piano and writing music criticism for the *Konstitutionelle Zeitung*. He espoused the cause of Wagner and the "music of the future." For about a decade a major artistic project was absorbing all his creative energies: it was the opera *The Queen of Sheba (Die Königin von Saba)*, with a libretto by Salomon Hermann Mosenthal, based on the Old Testament. Produced at the Vienna Royal Opera on March 10, 1875, it met with mixed reactions. Eduard Hanslick disliked it intensely, maintaining that only the "Festival March" was worth listening to. Richard Wagner expressed profound dismay, finding its theatricalism and pageantry a negation of his own artistic principles. Many others, however, were delighted with its effective fusion of German Romanticism with Oriental moods and color and its ingratiating lyricism spiced with exotic flavor. The opera met with such extreme public favor that within a few years it had been performed more than three hundred times in Vienna alone. By 1886 it had been seen in most of the world's leading opera houses, including the Metropolitan Opera in New York, where it was given for the first time on December 2, 1885. In reviewing the American première, Henry Krehbiel wrote in the New York *Times:* "Herr Goldmark's music is highly spiced. He is plainly an eclectic whose first aim was to give the drama an investiture which should be in keeping with its character externally and internally. At times his music rushes along like a lava-stream of passion; every bar pulsates with eager, excited and exciting life. He revels in instrumental color; the language of his orchestra is as glowing as the poetry attributed to the king whom his operatic story celebrates. Many other composers before him have made use of Oriental cadences and rhythms, but to none have they seemed to come so like native language as to Goldmark."

In 1876 the première of still another of Goldmark's important works, the programmatic symphony *Rustic Wedding (Ländliche Hochzeit)*, took place in Vienna. Hans Richter directed the performance with the

Vienna Philharmonic. The work consists of five tone pictures beginning with a wedding march (a theme and fifteen variations), and continuing with a bridal song, serenade, a garden scene, and a dance.

Another Goldmark composition to survive in the orchestral repertory is his melodious First Violin Concerto in A minor, which Johann Lauterbach introduced in Nuremberg on October 28, 1878.

Karl Goldmark died in Vienna on January 2, 1915.

"I have frequently been in Goldmark's company," the eminent conductor Felix Weingartner recalled, "but never without receiving mental stimulation. He was of astonishing freshness, not knowing what fatigue was. In jolly company he was sure to be the last one to go home. Infirmities of age and a conforming manner of living were strangers to him. His mind was as clear and bright as his eye. Frequently I met him in the Prater, and we walked together for a while. The talk at once soared from the commonplace to higher regions. Ordinary conversation he would never indulge in. He usually spoke of poetry or music. His opinions were acute, but amiable and never malicious, even when they were negative."

In a brief evaluation of Goldmark's music, J. A. Fuller-Maitland wrote: "Goldmark's main characteristics are his complete mastery of every kind of musical effect, his wealth of melodic invention, and skill in manipulating themes."

Principal Works

Chamber Music—2 string quartets; 2 piano trios; 2 violin suites; Piano Quintet in B-flat major; Violin Sonata in D major; Cello Sonata.

Choral Music—Meeresstille und glückliche Fahrt; Frühlingshymne; Im Fuschertal; Psalm CXIII; various choruses for unaccompanied men's voices.

Operas—Die Königin von Saba; Merlin; Das Heimchen am Herd (The Cricket on the Hearth); Goetz von Berlichingen; Ein Wintermärchen (A Winter's Tale).

Orchestral Music—2 symphonies; 2 violin concertos; Sakuntala; Im Frühling; Der gefesselte Prometheus; Sappho; In Italien; Aus Jugendtagen.

Piano Music—3 Pieces for piano duet; 2 Novelletten; Sturm und Drang; Prelude and Fugue; Georginen; Dances, for duet (also for orchestra).

Vocal Music—Various songs for voice and piano.

About

Goldmark, K., Notes from the Life of a Viennese Composer; Koch, L. (editor), Karl Goldmark: 1830-1930.

Monthly Musical Record, May 1, 1916.

Nicolas Gombert *1490-1556*

NICOLAS GOMBERT, an important member of the Netherlands polyphonic school, was born in south Flanders, probably in Bruges, in or about 1490. Virtually nothing is known of his boyhood or youth. It is believed, though not proved, that he studied with Josquin des Prés, and clearly the music of that composer exerted an important influence on the younger man.

In 1526 Gombert was a singer in the court chapel of Charles V, with whose entourage he traveled extensively through the Netherlands, Germany, and Spain. In 1529 he received another court appointment, as Master of the Boys of the Royal Chapel, and saw the first publication of his compositions, nine four-part chansons, which were included in a collection. Gombert remained in the employ of Charles V until about 1540; during this period he was also canon at the Cathedral of Tournai and at Notre Dame in Courtrai, in 1534 and 1537 respectively. Gombert died in Tournai in 1556.

Gombert was the agency through which the polyphonic art of the Netherland school, as developed by Josquin des Prés, was passed on to the rest of Europe. In his Masses and motets, Gombert developed the technique of imitation far beyond the achievements of his immediate predecessors. He demonstrated a concern for his texts not often encountered in the polyphonic composers of his day; and he revealed a remarkable gift for rhythm.

Heinrich Besseler, who describes Gombert as the founder of the "classical Netherland school," points out the warmth and refinement of both his structures and his style, "accordant with the general mystic purpose of the Netherland polyphony."

Donald N. Ferguson describes Gombert's art in this way: "He holds firmly to the ideal of a true polyphonic texture, keeping all the voices of equal interest (in contrast to the tendency in lighter songs to allow the upper voice to predominate). He uses almost no passages of plain harmony such as occasionally appear in Josquin; but he is no devotee of the more elaborate compositional devices. . . . Perfect texture . . . rather than expressiveness was Gombert's primary objective."

Choral Music—160 motets; 11 Masses; 8 Magnificats; Musae Jovis (dirge on the death of Josquin des Prés); chansons.

Eppstein, H., Nicolas Gombert also Mottetenkomponist; Schmidt-Georg, J., Nicolas Gombert, Leben und Werk.

François Gossec *1734-1829*

F RANÇOIS JOSEPH GOSSEC was born on January 17, 1734, in Vergnies, Hainaut (now in Belgium). He was a farmer's son. His interest in music revealed itself early. It is said that as a child, while herding cows, he constructed a fiddle from a *sabot* and horsehair and learned to play on it. As a boy he was a chorister in several churches in Walcourt, Maubeuge and finally at the Cathedral of Antwerp. During this period he undertook the systematic study of violin and harpsichord. In 1751 he went to Paris with a letter of introduction to Rameau, through whose influence he procured a job as conductor of the house orchestra of Rameau's patron, Le Riche de la Pouplinière. For La Pouplinière's concerts, Gossec started to write symphonies and a great deal of chamber music. A volume of his trio sonatas was published in 1752. One of his most ambitious compositions was the *Messe des morts*, performed in Paris in May 1760. Here Gossec anticipated Berlioz in sonority, orchestration, and tone colors. For the "Tuba mirum" section he used two orchestras, one comprising woodwinds backstage, and a string ensemble for the platform.

When La Pouplinière died in 1762, Gossec became a household musician for the Prince de Conti, eventually rising to the post of Intendant of Music. He now produced many excellent string quartets, some outstanding sacred music, and his first efforts for the stage. As early as 1757 he had written some airs for a revival of *Les Amours des dieux*, an opera by Jean Joseph Mouret. But Gossec's first opera was not written until after he had started to work for the Prince de Conti. It was *Le Périgourdin*, given a private performance at the Prince's palace.

The first public performance of one of his operas took place at the Comédie Italienne on June 27, 1765; the work was *Le Faux Lord*. His first successes were *Les Pêcheurs* in 1766 and *Toinon et Toinette* in 1767.

In 1770, soon after leaving the employ of Prince de Conti, Gossec founded the Concert des Amateurs, which he directed for several years in outstanding symphonic concerts; at these concerts he introduced Haydn symphonies in Paris. In 1773 he became director of the Concert Spirituel, which developed into a major musical organization. From 1780 to 1785 he was assistant director at the Paris Opéra. In addition to his immense contributions as a conductor, Gossec also distinguished himself in the field of pedagogy. In 1784 he founded and became director of the École Royale de Chant, established for the purpose of developing singers. It is from this school that the Paris Conservatory emerged in 1795.

With the outbreak of the French Revolution, Gossec allied himself wholeheartedly with the new regime as a citizen and as a composer. "He clung to new ideas without bigotry or self-seeking," explains Georges Jean-Aubry, "and found in them an opportunity for the exercise of his art. He saw in 'patriotic *fêtes*' a means of endowing music with a new and totally different meaning; he realized that music which up to the present had been a prerogative of a special class and in the service of religion, should now appeal to the public in general." In spirit with the times, he wrote numerous revolutionary marches (including funeral music for Mirabeau), and large compositions for various festivities, including *Peuple, réveille-toi*, *L'Offrande à la liberté*, *Le Chant du 14 juillet*, *Le Triomphe de la république*, *Hymne à l'Être suprème*, and a mighty Te Deum for a revolutionary *fête*, requiring twelve hundred singers and three hundred instrumentalists.

In 1795 Gossec was made a member of the newly founded Institut de France. When the Paris Conservatory was created that year, Gossec became one of its Inspectors and was appointed professor of composition; he held the latter post until 1815. In 1802 his eminent position in French music was officially recognized with his election as Chevalier of the Legion of Honor. He was also appointed to the Académie des Beaux-Arts.

After 1815 Gossec lived in virtual retirement in Passy (then a suburb of Paris), devoting himself primarily to composition. He died there on February 16, 1829. In 1877 a monument to his memory was erected in his native city.

One of Gossec's friends, never identified by name, left the following description of the composer: "His figure was small, heavily set, and solid. His face, tinted with red, breathed forth calmness and human goodness. His blue eyes became vividly animated when he spoke about his art, and were touched with gentle understanding when he praised his contemporaries. He carried his head slightly bent towards the left. He remained faithful to the dress and habit of former years. . . . He wore a highly powdered wig, a little three-cornered hat, a large, gray suit with a vest fringed in white, and trousers and stockings of black silk. Large silver buckles were attached to his slippers, and he held in his hand a large cane with an ivory head."

Today Gossec is probably remembered only for a trifling instrumental work, a popular gavotte which he wrote in 1786 for his opera *Rosine,* and which has entered the violin repertory by way of Willy Burmeister's transcription. Though little of his vast output is ever performed, he remains one of the most significant of eighteenth-century French instrumental composers. Just as he anticipated Berlioz in the use of orchestral forces, effects, sonorities, and colors, so, as a composer of symphonies and quartets, did he foreshadow Haydn in contrasts of dynamics, thematic development, and clarification of the classic sonata form. Gossec was, indeed, a founding father of the French symphony and string quartet.

He represents, as Paul Landormy pointed out, "an important phase of our musical history. He is, in the eyes of his contemporaries, the first French symphonist at the end of the eighteenth century. Then, under the Revolution, he was significant in organizing great demonstrations of popular art and musical instruction at the Conservatory. In this domain—as well as animator of crowds and creator of open-air music—he was an innovator. He anticipated the development of choral art, as well as that of 'fanfares,' and tone colors in which he was a pioneer."

PRINCIPAL WORKS

Chamber Music—String quartets; trios; duets.

Choral Music—Messe des morts; Messe des vivants; Saul; La Nativité; L'Arche d'alliancer; Te Deum; Hymne à la liberté; Hymne à la natur; Hymne à la victoire; Ronde nationale; motets.

Operas—Les Pêcheurs; Toinon et Toinette; Sabinus; La Fête de village; Thésée; Rosine; Les Sabots et le cerisier.

Orchestral Music—Over 30 symphonies; overtures, serenades.

ABOUT

Dufrane, L., Gossec: Sa vie et ses œuvres; Prod'homme, J. G. François Gossec; Tonnard, F., François Gossec, musicien hennuyer de la révolution française.

Chesterian, January 1934; Musique, December 15, 1927.

Claude Goudimel *1505-1572*

CLAUDE GOUDIMEL, significant musical voice of the Reformation in France, was born in Besançon in or about 1505. Nothing is known of his early life. The first definite piece of information about him is that his first publication, a volume of *chansons,* appeared in 1549 while he was residing in Paris. Between 1557 and 1568 he lived in Metz, where he associated himself with the Huguenots, though there is no proof that he ever became one. In any event, after the composition of a Magnificat and four Masses, between 1557 and 1558, Goudimel left writing for the Roman Catholic Church and turned his efforts to providing musical settings for the Huguenot psalter. His first volume of psalms, "in the form of motets," appeared in 1562; by 1566 he had issued seven more volumes.

In the Protestant setting of his psalms, Goudimel "did not content himself with . . . simple arrangements, but elaborated the psalm tunes . . . into works of consummate art," wrote Karl Nef. "At times the original melody was retained with circumambient counterpoint; at times, quite after the manner of the motet, the melody itself was dissipated into figuration."

As Goudimel explained in the preface to his second volume of psalms in 1565 (psalms that were simpler in structure than those in the first volume, with the melody persisting in tenor instead of being elaborated in all the voices), he did not intend his psalms for the church. He designed

Goudimel: goo-dē-mĕl'

them for use in the home in praise of God, and this was the way they were utilized not only by Huguenots but even by Catholics. "These richly polyphonic settings," explain Howard D. McKinney and W. R. Anderson, "seem to take on an added impulse of freedom and suggestion of artistry from their increased movement. One or another of the parts takes little flights around the voice which holds the melody. Nothing is overdone; and all is charming, simple, and seemly, as befitted the spirit of Calvinistic reform."

In 1568 Goudimel returned to his native city, but the last years of his life were spent in Lyons. There he was one of the victims in the St. Bartholomew massacre of Huguenots, which took place on August 27, 1572.

It was long believed that Goudimel lived for a time in Rome, where he was said to have founded a music school attended by Palestrina. This, however, has been completely disproved. Palestrina was, nevertheless, influenced by Goudimel, and used one of Goudimel's melodies for his *Missa Brevis* in 1570.

PRINCIPAL WORKS

Choral Music—Chansons, Magnificat, Masses, motets, psalms.

ABOUT

Becker, G., Goudimel et son œuvre.
Neue musikalische Zeitung, 1922; Proceedings of the Musical Association, 1918.

Charles Gounod *1818-1893*

CHARLES FRANÇOIS GOUNOD, composer of the opera *Faust*, was born in Paris on June 17, 1818. His father, a gifted painter who had received a second Prix de Rome, died when Charles was five. The boy was raised by his mother, a pianist, who gave him his first music instruction. "The life with a widowed mother," wrote Martin Cooper, "who was also his first guide and the one who formed his earliest musical taste, played . . . a considerable part in determining the complexion of his musical personality. His artistic inclinations never met any opposition at home, were indeed fostered in an atmosphere of emotional intimacy rather too exclusively feminine; so that it was only later, and so to speak as one removed from life as Gounod had come to know it, that he developed the

harder, more masculine qualities; and this lack—due partly, no doubt, to temperament, but certainly not corrected by circumstances and early environment—made itself permanently felt."

Gounod studied first in a boarding school, then at the Lycée St. Louis. From the beginning he was drawn ineluctably to music and composition. His first visit, as a child, to an opera performance left an unforgettable impression. "I felt as if I were in some temple, as if a heavenly vision might shortly rise before my sight," he explained later in his life. "Oh, what a night! What rapture! What Elysium!" One day, the boy went to his mother with a request that he be permitted to leave the Lycée and devote himself entirely to music. His mother consulted the director of the school who, in turn, called the young Gounod for an interview. When Gounod played one of his songs, the director said: "You *will* be a musician."

In 1836, after completing his studies at the Lycée, Gounod entered the Paris Conservatory. For three years he studied with Halévy, Paër, and Lesueur, proving a remarkably adept pupil. In 1837 his cantata *Marie Stuart et Rizzio* received the second Prix de Rome. A year later *Fernand* won the Grand Prix.

Deeply religious from boyhood on, Gounod was profoundly affected by Italian church music during his three-year stay in Rome. He studied the Italian masters, most significantly, Palestrina. He haunted the Sistine Chapel, at whose services great Italian church music was performed. Inspired by these experiences, he started to write church music, including two Masses. One of these was performed in 1841 at the Church of San Luigi dei Francesi.

In 1842 Gounod visited Vienna, where his Requiem and a Mass were performed successfully. After a brief stay at Berlin and Leipzig he returned to Paris in 1843 and became organist and precantor at the Missions Étrangères in the Rue du Bac. His daily associations with the Missionary Fathers further aroused his religious ardor—to the point where, in 1846, he decided to become a priest. For a while he studied theology at St. Sulpice. In the end, however, he realized that he could not abandon music for religion. Although he completed his theological studies, he never took holy

Gounod: goo-nō'

orders. Some of the religious music he wrote during this period identified its author as "Abbé Charles Gounod."

Until about 1850, Gounod's creative efforts were directed almost exclusively to church music. In 1850, however, he became a friend of Pauline Viardot, the celebrated opera singer, who urged him to write an opera for her. Gounod turned for the first time to the stage, completing *Sapho*. It was introduced at the Paris Opéra on April 16, 1851, with Pauline Viardot in the title role. *Sapho* enjoyed a modest success with the critics, if not with the audiences. Berlioz described its composer as "a young man richly endowed with noble aspirations; one to whom every encouragement should be given at a time when musical taste is so vitiated." *Sapho* may not have been an epoch-making work, and it is not numbered among Gounod's masterpieces, but there was a good deal in it to command respect. As R. A. Streatfeild remarked, it contains "the germs of much that afterwards became characteristic in Gounod's style. In the final scene of Sappho's suicide, the young composer surpassed himself, and struck a new note for opera."

In 1852 Gounod became conductor of the Orphéon Society in Paris. During the eight years that he held this post, he wrote numerous choral compositions. In 1852 he also wrote incidental music to *Ulysse*, a play by Ponsard, which was a failure. Nevertheless he felt secure enough in his profession to marry. His bride was Agnès Zimmermann, the daughter of a successful Parisian musician.

Gounod encountered failure again with his second opera, *La Nonne sanglante*, produced at the Opéra on October 18, 1854. Nor did *Le Médecin malgré lui*, a comic opera based on Molière, presented January 15, 1858, further his career in the theater. But hardly more than a year later Gounod completed the opera that made him world famous and that was to become one of the monuments of the French lyric theater: *Faust*.

When first performed at the Théâtre Lyrique on March 19, 1859, *Faust* gave very little indication of its future triumph in all parts of the world. A number of mishaps and difficulties attended its first performance. The principal tenor had fallen ill before the première, and was replaced by

CHARLES GOUNOD

a singer who had little time to learn his part. The title role thus was weakly projected, both vocally and histrionically. In addition, the censor objected to the cathedral scene, which he regarded as offensive to the Catholic Church. Further difficulties were encountered when admirers of Goethe felt that the libretto was an adulteration of a masterwork, and when critics denounced the juxtaposition of a love scene with an episode utilizing religious church music. As a result, *Faust* proved such a failure that no major publisher would accept it for publication. It was finally issued by the comparatively small house of Choudens, a newcomer in the publishing field; and the subsequent success and fame of Choudens was built solidly on *Faust*.

The renown of *Faust* can be said to have begun with its successful revival at the Paris Opéra on March 3, 1869, when the spoken dialogue of the 1858 première was replaced by recitatives and ballet episodes were introduced. So completely did the work captivate French operagoers that it became a staple in the repertory. During the next thirty-five years *Faust* was given at the Opéra on an average of once every nine days. In the next forty years it was performed there over a thousand times, and by 1934 it had been heard in two-thousand performances. The opera was introduced in London in 1863 by two rival companies, immediately establishing itself as a favorite with English opera audiences; Queen

Victoria regarded it so highly that she asked to hear parts of it just before her death. The American première is believed to have taken place in Philadelphia on November 18, 1863. When the Metropolitan Opera opened its doors for the first time, on October 22, 1883, its initial offering was *Faust,* with Christine Nilsson appearing in the role of Marguerite, which she had created. *Faust* has been given in over twenty-four different languages in more than forty-five countries. One can hardly exaggerate in calling it one of the most popular operas ever written.

"With few exceptions," say Wallace Brockway and Herbert Weinstock in *The Opera,* "the familiar numbers in *Faust* (and there are many) have the crushing sweetness of salon music. . . . Much of the popularity of *Faust* has always depended upon the ease with which many of its tunes touch emotions that are universal. These are sentimentality, religiosity, vague aspirations. . . . They pervade the score."

Herbert F. Peyser said: "*Faust* has an iron constitution. Even the poorest of performances cannot kill it. And if the description is at all permissible *Faust* might be characterized as the most operatic of operas. It contains about every feature, every specialty the average taste looks for in the entertainment furnished by the lyric theater. . . . It maintains an astonishing vitality."

Gounod subsequently wrote eight more operas. Two were successful, though neither enjoyed the triumph of *Faust. Mireille,* based on the Provençal poem of Mistral, was introduced on March 19, 1864. "The evocation of the Provençal landscape," wrote Martin Cooper, "the hint of folk song in the choruses and the famous "Chanson de Magali," the musette of the shepherd boy, and Mireille's "Heureux petit berger" show Gounod at his very best—simple, winning, genuinely naïve, and with an emotional spontaneity rare in operatic music of the sixties."

Roméo et Juliette—first seen on April 27, 1867—has proved second only to *Faust* as the most popular of Gounod's operas; certainly it is the most celebrated operatic version of this Shakespeare tragedy. While it is quite true, as Ernest Newman long contended, that Shakespeare's tragedy of frustrated love is not suitable for operatic treatment ("there is very little in the play,"

maintained Newman, "that lends itself to the purposes of opera"), Gounod created several instances of outstanding lyric theater. Herbert F. Peyser singled out some of the most memorable episodes of *Roméo et Juliette,* notably "Juliet's waltz song, Romeo's cavatina in the garden scene, the duets of the lovers, and the scene in the tomb." But the love music of *Roméo et Juliette* is "on a lower plane of invention, . . . in its general style disturbingly similar to that of *Faust.*" Peyser concluded: "But even at their best, pages emphasize the composer's weakness rather than his strength—the weakness of a lyricist who has said everything better once before."

With the outbreak of the Franco-Prussian War in 1870, Gounod left for London, and remained four years. He founded a choral society which he directed in outstanding concerts for several seasons; for some of these performances he wrote several impressive choral works. Not until he returned to Paris in 1874 did he try to write again for the stage. He completed three more operas, none successful: *Cinq-Mars* in 1877, *Polyeucte* in 1878, and *Le Tribut de Zamora* in 1881.

In the last decade of his life Gounod was drawn more than ever to religion and mysticism. He now devoted himself primarily to the composition of religious works. Between 1881 and 1884 he completed two choral trilogies, *La Rédemption* and *Mors et Vita.* A Mass in memory of Joan of Arc was performed in 1887; a Te Deum and a fourth Mass were published in 1888. His last work was a Requiem which he did not live to complete.

In 1888 Gounod was made Grand Officier of the Legion of Honor. He died in the Saint-Cloud suburb of Paris on October 18, 1893, the victim of a stroke. He was buried in the cemetery in Auteuil.

Ernest Newman once described Gounod as an amiable man effusive in his affections, a sometimes cloying flatterer, a gushing sentimentalist—in short, a man whose sincerity was not above suspicion even to good friends. Wagner spoke derisively of his "unflagging and nauseous garrulity."

"Gounod was always a late riser," Howard Paul remarked. "He protested he could do with a great deal of sleep. He dressed with scrupulous care, and at home wore a black velvet cap and very finely made patent leather shoes. When his toilet was over, he repaired to his sanctum, drank a glass of milk, and sat down to a table to work in an immense room with a vaulted ceiling suggesting a church, and principally furnished with an organ, two grand pianos, and a fine musical library. He sometimes smoked while he wrote, then he received visitors, and at twelve o'clock he breakfasted with his wife. His afternoons, four days a week, were devoted to work, and he was not a persistent diner out, though he received numerous invitations. He was fond of passing his evenings at the opera, occasionally the Boulevard theaters, and now and again, by way of what he termed a naughty spree, he went to the broad farces at the Palais Royal, for with his constitutional seriousness of character he liked an occasional laugh. He was not by any means an ascetic in temperament, but more like the monks of old who, if the French chansons are to be depended on, had a perfect appreciation of right good cheer. He was exceedingly fond of walking in the Bois, and most Saturdays he attended the meeting of the Académie des Beaux-Arts."

In a discussion of Gounod's musical style, Arthur Hervey wrote: "Gounod created a musical language of his own, one of extraordinary sweetness, of wondrous fascination, the soft eloquence of which seemed to penetrate into the innermost recesses of the heart. No asperities of style, no startling outbursts of ill-repressed passion were there to mar the exquisite suavity of melodies floating in a troublous atmosphere of intoxicating harmonies."

PRINCIPAL WORKS

Chamber Music—String Quartet in A minor; Petite symphonie; Hymne à Sainte-Cécile, for violin, piano and organ.

Choral Music—Gallia; La Contemplation de Saint François au pied de la croix; La Mort de Saint François; Pater Noster; La Redémption; Mors et Vita; cantatas, Masses, psalms, Requiems, Te Deums.

Operas—Sapho; La Nonne sanglante; Le Médecin malgré lui; Faust; Philémon et Baucis; La Colombe; La Reine de Saba; Mireille; Roméo et Juliette; Cinq-Mars; Polyeucte; Le Tribut de Zamora.

Orchestral Music—2 symphonies; Chant des compagnons; Saltarello; Marche romaine; Marche funèbre d'une marionnette (Funeral March of a Marionette); Marche religieuse; Les Rendezvous, waltzes for piano and orchestra.

Piano Music—Melodies, Pieces, Wedding Marches, valses.

Vocal Music—Over 200 songs for voice and piano including Au Printemps, Au Rossignol, Ave Maria (accompaniment, Bach's Prelude), Jésus de Nazareth, O ma belle rebelle, Où voulez-vous aller?, Repentir, Serenade, and There Is a Green Hill Far Away.

ABOUT

Bellaigue, C., Gounod; Bovet, A. M., Charles Gounod; Gounod, C., Autobiography; Landormy, P., Gounod; Tolhurst, H., Gounod.

Karl Heinrich Graun *1704-1759*

KARL HEINRICH GRAUN, prolific eighteenth century opera composer, was born in Wahrenbrück, Saxony, on May 7, 1704, the youngest of three sons of an excise collector; all became professional musicians. Karl Heinrich was educated at the Dresden Kreuzschule from 1713 to 1720; his instructors included Schmidt, Petzold, and Grundig. In 1713 he was also a treble singer to the town council. While attending the Kreuzschule Graun composed several motets and other choral works, the most important being the *Grosse-Passions Cantate,* completed when he was only fifteen. At the same time he devoted much of his leisure to studying the Italian operas of Antonio Lotti and Reinhard Keiser. They left a strong and permanent impression on him.

In 1725 Graun was appointed tenor at the court of Brunswick-Wolfenbüttel, where he occupied himself, outside his duties as a singer, with composition. After contributing several airs to operas by other composers he completed his first opera, *Sinilde,* which was produced in 1727. This was followed by *Iphigenia in Aulis* in 1728, *Polidorus* in 1731, and *Scipio Africanus* in 1732. In 1733 he wrote *Lo Specchio della fedeltà*, his first Italian opera, for the wedding of the Crown Prince of Prussia and Elisabeth Christina, the Princess of Brunswick-Lüneberg.

In 1735 Graun was appointed music director for Crown Prince Frederick at Rheinsberg, in which office he wrote about fifty cantatas in the Italian style, several German songs, flute concertos to be performed by Prince Frederick, and, in 1740, funeral music for the prince's father, King Frederick William I. When Crown Prince Frederick succeeded his father on the throne, he appointed Graun court *Kapellmeister* in Berlin. Determined to make his opera house one

Graun: groun

KARL HEINRICH GRAUN

of the finest in Europe, the new King despatched Graun to Italy to engage some of the best singers for his own opera company. Graun's first opera in his new post was *Rodelinda,* produced on December 13, 1741. For the opening of a new opera theater at court he wrote *Cleopatra e Cesare,* introduced on December 7, 1742. Graun subsequently wrote about thirty operas produced at court. He remained faithful to Italian traditions and conventions and, like so many Italian composers, emphasized lyric beauty, displaying skill in the writing of florid melodies for the voice. "Graun's music," says Donald Jay Prout in *A Short History of Opera,* "is in typical mid-eighteenth century style. The overture is of the Italian type, in three movements with homophonic texture. . . . The arias are well written and effective. . . . The *secco* recitatives show some harmonic variety and are enlivened by the use of deceptive cadences."

Though Graun was prolific as a composer for the stage, he did not neglect choral music. In 1755 he wrote a remarkable "Passion-Cantata," *Der Tod Jesu,* which became so popular in Germany that it was performed annually in that country until the mid-nineteenth century. In 1756 he wrote another outstanding choral composition, a Te Deum celebrating Frederick the Great's victory at Prague.

Graun remained in Berlin as *Kapellmeister* until the end of his life. He died in Berlin on August 8, 1759. "Never shall I find such a man again!" mourned the King when he heard that Graun had died.

"Graun was, without doubt, one of the most gifted classical composers of his generation," said a critic in the *Allgemeine Musik-Gesellschaft* of Zurich. "His composition, above all, was clean and neat, the harmony full, but at no time was the principal voice overburdened. His fugues and choruses are neither topheavy nor polished, neither affected nor frivolous. In all of his works there is apparent a genuine order of modulation. In this respect he was very sensitive to the slightest harshness. His melody is the most pleasant which one might hear and . . . although his Adagios were long, it was necessary—as Hiller said— for Graun to develop them for them to seem not long at all."

Marpurg, the eighteenth-century theorist and critic, called Graun "the greatest ornament of German music, the master of pleasing melody . . . tender, sweet, sympathetic, exalted, stately and terrible by turns. All the strokes of his pen were perfect. His genius was inexhaustible."

PRINCIPAL WORKS

Chamber Music—About 35 trio-sonatas; 3 harpsichord quintets; various duets.

Choral Music—Cantatas, oratorios, Passions, Te Deums.

Operas—Scipio Africanus; Pharao Tubaetes; Rodelinda; Cleopatra e Cesare; Catone in Utica; Adriano in Siria; Mitridate; Armida; Montezuma; Ezio.

Orchestral Music—About 30 harpsichord concertos; flute concertos; concerti grossi.

ABOUT

Mayer-Reinach, A. Karl Heinrich Graun als Opernkomponist; Mennicke, K. H. Hasse und die Brüder Graun als Sinfoniker.

Monthly Musical Record, July-September 1903; Musical Opinion, April 1931.

Christoph Graupner *1683-1760*

CHRISTOPH GRAUPNER, eminent German composer of eighteenth-century instrumental music, was born in Hartmannsdorf, Saxony, on January 13, 1683. While attending school Graupner studied singing with Mylius and organ with Küster. When the latter became organist in Reichenbach, Graupner joined him for two additional

Graupner: group'nĕr

years of organ study. Graupner then went on to Leipzig, where for nine years he attended the Thomasschule; his teachers included Schelle, Heinichen, and the renowned Kuhnau. He then turned to the study of law, but when Saxony was invaded by Sweden, he left Leipzig for Hamburg. Between 1706 and 1709, Graupner was harpsichordist at the Hamburg Opera, of which Keiser was at that time director. Since Hamburg was one of the great centers of operatic performance in Germany, the period proved a fruitful one for young Graupner, preparing him to write music for the stage. In 1707 he completed his first opera, *Dido, Königin von Carthago,* and also collaborated with Keiser in writing *Der angenehme Betrug* (revived in Hamburg in 1931). Graupner wrote six more operas in Hamburg, some in collaboration with Keiser.

For an undetermined reason, possibly emotional entanglements, Graupner was forced to leave Hamburg in 1710. He moved to Darmstadt, where he was appointed vice *Kapellmeister* to the Landgrave Ernst Ludwig of Hesse-Darmstadt. Two years later he rose to the rank of full *Kapellmeister,* a post he retained until the end of his life. In 1722 when the office of cantor of the Thomasschule in Leipzig was vacated, Graupner was recommended for the job. He was, however, too secure in and too satisfied with his station in Darmstadt to make a change, and so the post passed on to Johann Sebastian Bach.

In Darmstadt, between 1710 and 1719, Graupner completed three more operas. Then, from 1719 on, he devoted himself to the two areas in which he proved most significant: church music for the services at court and instrumental compositions. Between 1719 and 1745 he completed over thirteen hundred works for chorus. His output in the instrumental field proved no less vast, including numerous symphonies, concertos, overtures and sonatas. These played a historic role in establishing and crystallizing German instrumental style and structure in the era before Haydn and Mozart. Johann Sebastian Bach was known to have admired Graupner's instrumental music and was probably influenced by it.

PRINCIPAL WORKS

Chamber Music—Various trio-sonatas, and sonatas for various combinations of instruments and accompaniment.

Choral Music—Over 1300 sacred works including cantatas.

Harpsichord Music—Gigues, fugues, preludes, sonatas.

Operas—Dido, Königin von Carthago; Il Fido amico; L'amore ammalato; Der Fall des grossen Richters in Israel; Berenice e Lucilla; Telemach; La Costanza vince l'inganno; several other operas in collaboration with Keiser.

Orchestral Music—Over 100 symphonies; over 80 overtures; over 50 concertos for various solo instruments and orchestra.

ABOUT

Nagel, W., Christoph Graupner als Sinfoniker; Noack, F., Christoph Graupners Kirchenmusiken.

André Modeste Grétry *1741-1813*

A NDRÉ ERNEST MODESTE GRÉTRY, an important composer of *opéra-comique,* was born in Liège, Belgium, on February 10 or 11, 1741. He was of Walloon descent. His father, a violinist in a church in Liège, soon directed him to music. At nine Grétry became a chorister at the Saint-Denis Church, but his master there was so strict and demanding that the child refused to devote himself to his assigned tasks and was dismissed. At the same time, however, he was a proficient student of singing and organ at La Cigogne music school; and later he thrived under the sympathetic guidance and instruction of Rennekin and Leclerc.

In his memoirs Grétry recalled an episode revealing his profoundly religious and mystical nature while a child. On his way to Saint-Denis one day, he begged God to allow him to die if he did not possess the talent to become a great musician. That day a rafter fell on him and almost killed him. The first remark made by the child after recovering from his shock was: "I did not die, then God decided to make me a great musician after all!"

In his boyhood Grétry heard performances of Italian *opere buffe* presented by a visiting Italian company. The works of Pergolesi, Galuppi, and Jommelli moved him profoundly, and became a stimulus to his eventual choice of a career as composer for the stage. His first compositions, however, were instrumental and choral; they included six symphonies and a Mass, completed between 1758 and 1759. These works impressed Canon du Harlez, who in 1759 provided Grétry with funds to go to Rome. Grétry made this trip in the company of a

ANDRÉ MODESTE GRÉTRY

smuggler, traveling part of the way by foot. In Rome he enrolled at the Collège de Liège, which had been founded for natives of Liège. For a while he studied counterpoint with Casali, but the instructor found him so inept a student that he soon dismissed him from his class. Nevertheless, Grétry kept working at his compositions, completing several church works (including a number of motets and a De Profundis), six string quartets, a flute concerto, and his first work for the stage, an intermezzo produced in Rome during the carnival of 1765. About this time, Grétry discovered *Rose et Colas,* a successful *opéra-comique* by Monsigny. The work spurred him to cultivate the field of comic opera in particular.

In 1766 Grétry went to Geneva, where for a while he earned his living as a voice instructor. He sought out Voltaire in the hope that the celebrated writer would provide him with a libretto for an *opéra-comique.* "You are a musician and you have intelligence," Voltaire told him, "and that is a combination too rare for me not to take the liveliest interest in you." Although Voltaire declined to write a libretto for him on the grounds that he was then too busy, he did propose an idea which the playwright Favart developed into a one-act text. The result was *Isabelle et Gertrude,* produced in Geneva in December 1766.

On Voltaire's advice Grétry moved to Paris in the fall of 1767. He completed a new *opéra-comique* which reached the re-

hearsal stage but was not performed at the time. The score, however, brought him the patronage of the Count de Creutz, the Swedish ambassador to France, through whose influence Grétry acquired the libretto of *Le Huron* by Marmontel. *Le Huron* was a huge success when given at the Comédie Italienne on August 20, 1768. With *Lucile* and, in 1769, *Le Tableau parlant* (the latter described by Grimm as a masterwork), Grétry's career as one of the leading figures in French comic opera was launched.

During the next twenty years Grétry wrote about fifty serious and comic operas. Among the best are *Zémire et Azor* in 1771; *La Fausse magie* in 1775; *Les Fausses apparences* (better known as *L'Amant jaloux)* in 1778; *Théodore et Paulin* (better known as *L'Épreuve villageoise)* in 1784; and what many regard as his greatest opera, *Richard Cœur de Lion,* also in 1784. *Richard Cœur de Lion* received one of its rare revivals in the United States on August 10, 1953, when it was presented at Tanglewood, in Lenox, Massachusetts by the Berkshire Music Center. "While there is a certain innocence about Grétry's music today," wrote Cyrus Durgin in reviewing the Tanglewood presentation of *Richard Cœur de Lion,* "it is far from quaint or thin. In its own day it must have seemed bold indeed, and in the several times repeated love song of Richard, well ahead of its time. The score has substance, a good measure of melodic invention. If the range of harmonic expression is not wide, the play of rhythm is constant, varied, and unceasingly vigorous. Indeed, there is a certain clever tension, suspense almost, about story and music."

In 1771 Grétry married Mlle. Grandon, a young painter. They had three daughters, one of whom, Lucile, became a gifted composer. Tragically, all three daughters were fatally stricken by tuberculosis.

Although the French Revolution stripped Grétry of his wealth and property, he allied himself wholeheartedly with the new regime, to become one of its most prominent musical spokesmen. He received many honors. In 1785 the city of Paris named a street after him. A decade later he was appointed an Inspector of the newly founded Conservatory and a member of the newly organized Institut. A statue of Grétry was placed outside the Opéra-Comique and a bust in the foyer of the Opéra.

When the monarchy was restored, Grétry reversed his political affiliations in order to retain prestige and influence with the governing powers. In 1802 Napoleon made him a Chevalier of the Legion of Honor, when that order was first instituted, and endowed him with a handsome annual pension.

During the last ten years of his life Grétry lived in semiretirement at L'Ermitage, near Montmorency, one-time residence of Rousseau, devoting himself more assiduously to philosophy and musical theory than to composition. He died at L'Ermitage on September 24, 1813. At an impressive funeral ceremony three days later, Bouilly and Méhul delivered eulogies to the composer.

Throughout his life Grétry was a deeply religious man, but he was superstitious as well. He was also opportunistic—a trait which enabled him to ride smoothly with shifting political winds; his character was marked also by a lack of scruples and a disconcerting tactlessness. Fétis informs us that Grétry was a formidable egotist who studded his conversations with comments on his works, plans, and achievements. Throughout his life, Grétry's delicate health compelled him to pursue a strict diet, often consisting of little more than dry figs and water.

Grétry had pronounced faults as a composer, especially in the techniques of harmony, counterpoint, and orchestration. He was aware of these shortcomings and often quoted Gluck's opinion of his operas: "You received from nature the gift of appropriate melody, but in giving you this talent she withheld that of strict and complicated harmony." And, for all his vanity, he did not hesitate to agree with Gluck. But he would point out in self-defense that lyricism was the greatest gift a composer could possess. "The melody which lingers in one's mind like beautiful poetry," he once wrote, "bears the mark of genius."

There can be no argument about Grétry's lyric power, both in freshness and spontaneity of expression and poetic beauty of thought. Even the great Carl Maria von Weber was enthusiastic about Grétry's melodies. "Grétry is perhaps the only one among French composers whose spirit is essentially lyric, at times even romantic. It would be impossible to equal the really exquisite purity of his melodies which are always inspired to suit the exigencies of the moment and not according to stereotyped forms."

Characteristic of Grétry's pronounced melodic gifts are the noble air of Blondel in *Richard Cœur de Lion*, "O Richard, o mon roi," and the second-act duet of Richard and Blondel, "Une fièvre brûlante," which Beethoven used for a set of piano variations (op. 184). Frans Rühlmann arranged six dances from five of Grétry's operas for a delightful orchestral suite entitled *Danses villageoises*. Ballet suites for orchestra based on various operas by Grétry were also arranged by Felix Mottl and Selmar Meyrowitz.

Grétry published the first volume of his memoirs in 1789, and two others in 1791. He was also the author of several theoretical treatises.

Principal Works

Chamber Music—6 string quartets; trios.

Choral Music—Antiphon, Confiteor, De Profundis, Requiem, motets.

Operas—Over 60 comic and serious operas including: Les Deux avares; Zémire et Azor; Céphale et Procris; La Fausse magie; L'Amant jaloux (or Les Fausses apparences); Colinette à la cour; L'Embarras du richesses; La Caravane du Caire; L'Épreuve villageois (or Théodore et Paulin); Richard Cœur de Lion; Amphitrion; Guillaume Tell; Denys le tyran.

Orchestral Music—6 symphonies; various divertissements.

Piano Music—6 sonatas.

About

Bruyr, J., Grétry; Clercx, S., Grétry; Closson, E. André Modeste Grétry; Curzon, H. de, Grétry; Froidcourt, G. de, La Correspondance de Grétry; Grétry, A. J., Grétry en famille; Grétry, A. M., Réflexions d'un solitaire; Hulst, F., Grétry; Rolland, R., Some Musicians of Former Days; Sauvenier, J., André Grétry.

Edvard Grieg *1843-1907*

EDVARD HAGERUP GRIEG, the founder of a national school of Norwegian music, and Norway's greatest composer, was born in Bergen on June 15, 1843. He was of Scottish ancestry, his great-grandfather having emigrated to Norway in the middle of the eighteenth century. Grieg's mother, an amateur pianist, began to teach him piano when he was six. Late in life Grieg described the fascination the piano had had for him at first acquaintance. "My arms

EDVARD GRIEG

stretched out to the piano to discover—not a melody, that was yet far off—no, it must have been a harmony, first a third, then a chord of three notes, then a full chord of four, ending at last with both hands. Oh joy! A combination of five, the chord of the ninth! When I found that out, my happiness knew no bounds. That was indeed a success! No later successes ever stirred me like that."

At the Bergen school, however, Edvard was a lazy and indifferent pupil, often the object of ridicule by his teachers. "I could not understand in what respect all the torments connected with it were to a child's advantage. Even today I have not the least doubt that the school developed only what was bad in me and left the good untouched." One day, when he was twelve, he brought to school one of his compositions, *Variations on a German Theme*. The reaction of his teacher was typical: "Next time leave that stupid stuff home and come with your German homework, instead!"

At home, however, he received encouragement, for both his parents were decidedly musical, and well cognizant of his pronounced talent. Moreover, the celebrated Norwegian concert violinist Ole Bull, a frequent visitor to the Grieg household, recognized Grieg's gifts. "You must go to the Leipzig Conservatory," Bull told him firmly. It was due largely to the violinist's insistence that Grieg, at the age of fifteen, enrolled at the conservatory. During the next few years

he received a comprehensive education from Reinecke, Moscheles, Hauptmann, and Plaidy, among others.

The years at Leipzig, however, were strenuous: in 1860 Grieg, under the pressure of work, suffered a physical collapse which, in turn, brought on pleurisy. Grieg emerged from this severe illness with one lung permanently impaired. He went home to recuperate, then returned to Leipzig, to graduate from the Conservatory with highest honors in 1862.

In the spring that year Grieg returned to Bergen, where he presented a concert of his works. Soon afterwards, he established his home in Copenhagen. There he came under the influence of two remarkable musicians, Niels Gade and Rikard Nordraak. Gade, who was Denmark's foremost composer, encouraged Grieg and directed him to the writing of ambitious compositions, including a symphony. Nordraak, the distinguished young Norwegian who had written his country's national anthem, was a cousin of the celebrated dramatist Björnson and a dedicated scholar of Norwegian folk music. It was through Nordraak that Grieg first learned "what the Norwegian folk song was, and learned to know my own nature," as he later explained. From that time on, Grieg was a passionate musical nationalist.

Grieg joined Nordraak in helping to organize Euterpe, a society dedicated to performing music by Norwegians and promoting a national Norwegian music. Grieg also started to compose music in this idiom, rather than in the tradition of German Romanticism, which had heretofore influenced him. His first such composition was the *Humoresque* for piano, op. 6—written in 1865, and dedicated to Nordraak.

While visiting Copenhagen in 1864, Grieg was secretly betrothed to his cousin, Nina Hagerup, a singer. Nina's parents seriously opposed their marriage, since Grieg at the time was still an obscure musician, incapable of supporting a family. The couple was forced to wait. Grieg expressed his feelings in his most celebrated song, "Ich liebe dich," which he wrote for Nina in 1864, to a verse by Hans Christian Andersen.

Grieg spent the winter of 1865 in Italy, where he wrote his first work for orchestra, the concert overture *In Autumn*. It received first prize from the Stockholm Academy of Music. While still in Italy Grieg received the tragic news that his friend and inspirer, Nordraak, had died in Paris at the age of twenty-three. The news broke Grieg's health and spirit. After his recovery, Grieg was newly fired with the desire to carry on Nordraak's work in promoting and fostering a national musical art in Scandinavia. In Christiania (now Oslo), Grieg arranged the first concert ever devoted entirely to Norwegian music; the program given on October 15, 1866, included two of his own compositions, his Violin Sonata in F major and a piano sonata. Its success established Grieg's reputation in Norway. In 1867 he founded a Norwegian Academy of Music, began to direct the Philharmonic Society in outstanding choral and orchestral concerts which invited the work of unknown Norwegian composers, and received supplemental income as a concert pianist and teacher of music. Now financially secure, Grieg was able to marry Nina Hagerup. Their wedding took place in Denmark on June 11, 1867. The Griegs' only child, a daughter, died in 1869 when only thirteen months old.

Grieg won his first important recognition as a composer in 1869, when Liszt wrote to him from Rome, praising his F major Violin Sonata. "It evidences a powerful, logically creative, ingenious and excellent constructive talent for composition," wrote Liszt, "which needs only to follow its natural development to attain high rank." Liszt's letter was followed shortly by a Norwegian government grant of 1,600 crowns which enabled Grieg to travel to Rome to visit Liszt. On this occasion Grieg played for him a new work, the now celebrated Piano Concerto in A minor, which Liszt found had "real talent."

The Concerto was performed for the first time in Copenhagen on April 3, 1869, with Eduard Neupart as soloist. "The triumph I achieved was tremendous," Neupart reported to Grieg. "Even as early as the cadenza in the first movement the public broke into a real storm." To this day it remains one of Grieg's most famous works, a cornerstone of his fame. Frederick Niecks found in it "life itself, in its press and stress." Henry T. Finck wrote: "The first movement is replete with beautiful, haunting melody, and nothing could be lovelier than the orchestral introduction to the slow movement —one of the saddest preludes ever written— a prelude illustrating Grieg's gift of creating an emotional atmosphere upon the simplest means."

Another of Grieg's universally acclaimed compositions was written several years after the Piano Concerto—the incidental music for Henrik Ibsen's *Peer Gynt*. Ibsen had asked Grieg to write music for his play in 1874, but the composer was reluctant at first to take on the project. "For several days," recorded Grieg's wife, "he went about in a nervous, restless state, in great doubts and anxiety as to the heavy task. The more he saturated his mind with the powerful poem, the more clearly he saw that he was the right man for a work of such wild witchery, and so permeated with the Norwegian spirit. In the suburb of Sandviken, outside Bergen, he found a pavilion, with windows on every side, high up on a hill . . . with a magnificent view of the sea on one side and the mountains on the other. 'Solveig's Song' was the first number to see the light. Then 'Åse's Death.' I shall never forget the bright summer evening on the mountains, as he sang and played 'Solveig's Song.' For the first time, Grieg himself smiled, well pleased with the song. . . . Grieg himself considered 'Åse's Death' and 'Solveig's Song' to be his best work."

Grieg completed twenty-two pieces for *Peer Gynt*. The play, with Grieg's incidental music, was first performed in Christiania, on February 24, 1876. From the score the composer extracted eight pieces for two orchestral suites, which have become two of his most popular works.

In 1874 Grieg's eminence in Norwegian music was acknowledged with an annual government pension of 1,600 crowns. Until then, Grieg had earned his living by conducting, teaching, and giving piano performances. Now he could concentrate his energies on composition. During the next decade he produced several masterpieces that enhanced his already impressive reputation: the G minor String Quartet, in 1878; the twelve songs to texts by Vinje, between 1873 and 1880; the *Norwegian Dances*, in 1881; the A minor Cello Sonata in 1883; the third book of the *Lyric Pieces* in 1884; the *Holberg Suite* in 1885.

His fame assumed wider dimensions. On May 3, 1888, he was acclaimed in London at a concert of his compositions; in 1890 he was elected to the French Academy of Arts; and in 1894 he received an honorary doctorate from Cambridge. As the years passed he won other honors, including a second honorary doctorate, from Oxford, in 1906. In 1903 his sixtieth birthday was an occasion for international celebration. Concerts of Grieg's works were given throughout the world; a bust of the composer was placed in the Gewandhaus in Leipzig.

In 1885 Grieg had realized a life's dream by acquiring Troldhaugen, a beautiful villa six miles out of Bergen. In this secluded woodland setting, overlooking the Hardanjer Fjord, he spent the rest of his life, devoting himself to composition, contemplation, and enjoyment of the Norwegian countryside. Music lovers from all parts of the world visited Troldhaugen to pay him tribute.

Grieg's last public appearance took place in May 1906 in London, where he conducted two concerts of his major works. En route to his native land he suffered a heart attack, and was rushed to a hospital in Bergen. He died in his sleep on September 4, 1907. His body lay in state in the Great Hall of the Museum of Art and Industry as thousands upon thousands of his compatriots, as well as representatives from foreign countries and the world's leading musical organizations, filed by to bid him farewell. His remains were buried in a grotto on the grounds of Troldhaugen overlooking the fjord, as he himself had requested.

Gerhard Schjelderup, who knew Grieg well, described the composer as follows: "Grieg was of small stature, delicate but impressive. The fine serene forehead he had in common with many a creative artist. His light blue eyes under the bushy eyebrows sparkled like those of a child when listening to a fairy tale. They mostly had a joyful though gentle and dreamy expression, but when roused to sudden anger or indignation, they could flash like lightning. For with his short, stumpy nose, the fine flowing hair, the firm expressive mouth under the strong moustache, the resolute chin, he had dynamic energy and an impatient and passionate temperament. As in Wagner's features there was in his a marked contrast between the upper and lower parts of the face. The forehead reveals the dreamer, the mouth and chin a strong determination to live a life of untiring activity. Grieg's astounding energy gave to his frail body an elastic and impressive gait and more than once in his life he performed true feats of endurance."

Grieg was essentially a simple and reticent man who shunned public adulation, and who was happiest living in seclusion. He had a peasant streak which sometimes conflicted with his middle-class values. He enjoyed mixing with peasants; but, as his friend Percy Grainger noted, when "the communal beer bowl is passed around the table and every feaster is expected to drink from it.... Grieg's middle-class squeamishness (his sense of personal cleanliness) found him out. 'When I saw the great bowl approach me, its rim dark with tobacco juice, my heart sank within me,' he told me. This urge 'to feel at one with peasants' is a more vital necessity for a Norwegian artist than a non-Norwegian person might be able to guess."

Fishing was a favorite diversion, playing piano in solitude a beloved pastime. Grieg drank incessantly—strong tea in the morning, weak tea at night.

When he worked, he demanded monastic seclusion; he detested having anyone near him. In addition to his home he built a studio, a one-room cabin, surrounded by the natural beauty of the Norwegian countryside near the Hardanjer Fjord, where intrusion was never permitted. Grieg passionately loved the wild country landscapes near his cabin. "His great love of nature and his admiration of its wonders," said Schjelderup, "gave his conceptions a strongly pantheistic character."

In politics Grieg was a "true democrat, even a republican," deeply concerned with the social and political problems of his day. During the Dreyfus scandal in France, he fearlessly spoke out in defense of the persecuted officer, and in 1899 refused to make a concert appearance with the Colonne Orchestra in protest against this violation of justice in France. In religion, he once explained, he admired "the teachings of the Unitarians who believe in one God alone, to the exclusion of the Holy Trinity in which God the Son is equal to God the Father." On another occasion he said: "I firmly believe in the existence of God, but I find it hard to accept the idea of a personal prayer to the Deity."

Daniel Gregory Mason has pointed out the "persistently lyrical character" of Grieg's best work. "It is intimate, suggestive, intangible. It voices the gentlest feelings of the heart, or summons up the airiest visions of the imagination. It is whimsical, too, changes its hues like the chameleon, and often surprises us with a sudden flight to some unexpected shade of expression. Again,

its finesse is striking. The phrases are polished like gems, the melodies charm us with
their perfect proportions, the cadences are
as consummate as they are novel. Then,
again, the rhythm is most delightfully frank
and straightforward; there is no meandering
or uncertainty, but always a vigorous dancing progress, as candid as childhood."

Analyzing Grieg's principal works, Lawrence Gilman wrote: "He is sometimes truly
imaginative, as in passages in the *Peer Gynt*
music, in the last two sonatas for violin and
piano (opp. 13 and 45), in certain of the
songs and piano pieces. He has, too, achieved
ideas; ideas of exquisite distinction, of noble
breadth. But they lack the stamp of supreme
excellence. . . . But in a surprising degree,
Grieg has individuality—individuality that
is seizing and indubitable. That, one feels,
is his distinguishing possession. His speech
may sway one, or it may not; but always the
voice is the voice of Grieg. . . . Grieg is
thrice admirable in this: he wears no one's
mantle; he borrows no man's speech."

One of Grieg's most remarkable creations
is the *Lyric Pieces*, ten volumes of piano
pieces, comprising sixty-six compositions in
all, that appeared between 1867 and 1901.
A wide range of moods and emotions is
here explored, from the gay and the whimsical to the elegiac and the introspective.
Some of the compositions are pictures of
nature; some are tonal re-creations of Norwegian tales and legends; some reflect various facets of Norwegian life. "One of the
best groups of this ensemble," says Yvonne
Rosketh, "is that which is inspired directly
by Norwegian folklore. . . . At the side of
this series one can place those pieces in
which the artist gave his impressions of the
Norwegian people or of Norwegian Nature,
his gratitude for so much beauty, his happiness in seeing it again after a prolonged
absence, his nostalgia for it during his absence. . . . All in all, the *Lyric Pieces* reflect
the two facets of Grieg's personality, the
elegiac and the joyous. . . . The best of these
pieces is usually the briefest." Among the
most popular are the following: *To the
Spring; Erotik; Lonely Wanderer; Butterfly;
March of the Dwarfs; Wedding Day at
Troldhaugen.* Grieg himself orchestrated
four of these pieces, *Shepherd's Lad, Norwegian Rustic Dance, Nocturne,* and *March
of the Dwarfs,* and gave the new work the
title *Lyric Suite.*

PRINCIPAL WORKS

Chamber Music—3 violin sonatas; String Quartet in G minor; Cello Sonata in A minor.

Choral Music—Album; Landsighting; Scenes
from Olav Trygvason; Ave Maris Stella; Four
Psalms.

Orchestral Music—Piano Concerto in A minor;
In Autumn; Two Elegiac Melodies; Holberg
Suite; Norwegian Dances; Peer Gynt, two suites;
Sigurd Jorsalfar Suite; Symphonic Dances; Lyric
Suite.

Piano Music—Sonata in F minor; Lyric Pieces,
ten volumes; Moods; Norwegian Mountain
Tunes; Norwegian Peasant Dances; Albumblätter, ballades, humoresques.

Vocal Music—German Songs; Danish Songs;
Children's Songs; many individual songs for
voice and piano, including And I Will Take a
Sweetheart, A Dream, Eros, The First Meeting,
I Love You, I Wandered One Lovely Summer's
Eve, Old Mother, Return to Rundarne, Spring,
A Swan, Thanks for Thy Counsel, While I Wait,
With a Primrose, With a Water Lily, and The
Wounded Heart.

ABOUT

Abraham, G. (editor), Grieg: A Symposium;
Cherbuliez, A. E., Edvard Grieg: Leben und
Werk; Finck, H. T., Grieg; Finck, H. T., Grieg
and His Music; Gilman, L., Nature in Music;
Horton, J., Grieg; Lange, K., and Östvedt, A.,
Norwegian Music; Monrad, J. D., Edvard Grieg;
Rosketh, Y., Grieg.

Jacques Halévy *1799-1862*

JACQUES FRANÇOIS FROMENTAL
ELIAS HALÉVY, the composer of *La
Juive,* was born in Paris on May 27, 1799.
His father was Élie Halévy, a distinguished
Hebrew poet, who served for some time as
a cantor in a Paris synagogue. Jacques early
displayed remarkable musical gifts. In his
tenth year he entered the Paris Conservatory, where he studied piano with Lambert
and harmony with Berton. In 1810 he received first prize in solfeggio, and a year
later second prize in harmony. For five
years after that he was a pupil of Cherubini
in counterpoint, fugue, and composition.

After two unsuccessful attempts to win
the Prix de Rome (on each occasion he won
second prize) Halévy achieved the coveted
award in 1819 with *Herminie.* On March
24, 1820, just before he left for Italy, two
of his compositions were introduced in
Paris, a funeral march and *De Profundis.*

During his three-year stay in Italy, required by the Prix de Rome, Halévy continued to study music while working on
sacred compositions and operas. In 1822 he

JACQUES HALÉVY

returned to France, after paying a visit to Vienna, where he was received warmly by Beethoven. He submitted two serious operas, *Pygmalion* and *Les Bohémiennes,* to the Opéra, and a lighter effort, *Les Deux pavillons,* to the Opéra-Comique. Both houses rejected his creations. It was not until 1827 that one of his stage works was granted a performance; this was the one-act opera *L'Artisan,* produced by the Théâtre Feydeau. It was not well received. A year later, however, *Clari,* presented at the Théâtre-Italien on December 9, 1828, with Mme. Malibran scored successfully.

In 1827 Halévy was engaged as cembalist by the Paris Opéra; in 1830 he became *chef du chant* at the Opéra, a post he held for sixteen years. In 1827 Halévy also began a highly successful teaching career at the Paris Conservatory, with his appointment as professor of harmony and accompaniment. In 1833 he became the professor of counterpoint and fugue, and in 1840 of advanced composition. His many students included Gounod and Bizet; Bizet married Halévy's daughter in 1869.

In 1833 Halévy was called upon by the Opéra-Comique to complete *Ludovic,* an opera that Hérold had left unfinished at his death. Its huge success added considerably to Halévy's prestige. It was not long, however, before Halévy enjoyed triumph in his own right. In 1835 he completed major works in each of two branches of opera: *La*

Juive for the serious lyric theater, *L'Éclair* for the *opéra-comique.* They represent his supreme, unsurpassed efforts in these genres.

La Juive, a grand opera with libretto by Scribe, was introduced at the Opéra on February 23, 1835, proving a sensation from the beginning. Halévy's score was rich in dramatic interest and expressive in its lyricism. Its musical and dramatic climax, occurring at the close of the fourth act, was Éléazar's unforgettable aria "Rachel, quand du Seigneur." Sensitive and refined in musical style, yet compelling in its emotion, *La Juive* was certain to be successful with opera audiences everywhere. It soon circled the globe. The American première took place in New Orleans in 1844.

L'Éclair, introduced at the Opéra-Comique on December 16, 1835, was an entirely different creation. Strangely enough for a French *opéra-comique,* the work has an American setting and American characters. Light, amusing, and ebullient in text and music, *L'Éclair* was so popular from the time of its première that in less than half a century it had been performed more than three hundred times by the Opéra-Comique. The first American presentation took place in New Orleans on February 16, 1837.

His operas duly acclaimed, Halévy was greatly honored by his compatriots. He was made Chevalier of the Legion of Honor in 1836, a member of the Institut de France soon after that, and a permanent secretary of the Académie des Beaux-Arts in 1854.

Although Halévy wrote many operas after 1836, none of them attained the level of quality or the popularity of *La Juive* and *L'Éclair.* Some of the pages of his later operas suggest impressive creative powers, but none of these works are integrated *chefs-d'œuvre.* For one thing, Halévy was too ready to accept whatever text was offered to him, and many of his librettos were inherently unpromising. Moreover, he became involved in a competitive struggle with Meyerbeer after the enormous success of Meyerbeer's *Les Huguenots* in 1836. Bent on creating the kind of spectacles that Meyerbeer had made his specialty, Halévy failed to develop his own gift, which lay rather with refined and sensitive lyric dramas.

In 1861 Halévy, suffering from consumption, went to Nice for a rest cure. There he showed alarming symptoms of mental as well as physical deterioration. He died in

Nice on March 17, 1862. Five days later he was given a state funeral and buried in Montmartre, in Paris.

"Certainly," wrote Richard Wagner, "the talent of Halévy lacks neither freshness nor grace. His vigorous constitution, his concentrated energy assured him from the very first a leading position in our lyric theater. He knew how to succeed in the *opéra-comique* in attaining a gait of gracious elegance. But Wagner also lamented Halévy's artistic decline after *La Juive* and *L'Éclair.* "From my final visit to him, I came away grieved at the enervation, moral and aesthetic, of one of the last of the significant French musicians."

Ludovic Halévy, the distinguished opera librettist who worked with Offenbach, Delibes, and Bizet, among others, was the nephew of Jacques Halévy.

PRINCIPAL WORKS

Ballets—Manon Lescaut, Yella.

Choral Music—5 cantatas; Psalm CXXX; part songs for men's voices.

Operas—La Juive; L'Éclair; La Reine de Chypre; Les Mousquetaires de la reine; Le Val d'Andorre; La Fée aux roses; La Dame de pique; Le Juif errant; L'Inconsolable; La Magicienne.

Piano Music—Sonata, for four hands; nocturnes, romances.

ABOUT

Halévy, L., Jacques Halévy, sa vie et ses œuvres; Monnais, F., Jacques Halévy: Souvenirs d'un ami pour joindre à ceux d'un frère.

Guide Musicale, December 6, 1903; Musical Courier, June 16, 1921; Musical Quarterly, April 1953.

Andreas Hammerschmidt *1612-1675*

A NDREAS HAMMERSCHMIDT, one of the most important composers of Lutheran church music before Johann Sebastian Bach, was born in Brüx, Bohemia, in 1612. His father, a saddler, left Brüx during the Thirty Years' War, moving to Freiberg, in Saxony. It was in that city that Andreas studied music with Stephan Otto. In 1633 Hammerschmidt became organist for Count von Bünau, at Weesenstein Castle. During this period he published his first work, an eight-part chorus commemorating the victory of the Saxon army at Liegnitz in 1634.

In 1635 Hammerschmidt became organist of the St. Pierre Church in Freiberg. Three years later he was appointed to the post he held for the rest of his life—organist of the St. Johann Church in Zittau. Hammerschmidt died in Zittau on November 8, 1675. Shortly after his death the city of Zittau erected a monument in his honor; it bore an epitaph describing him as "that noble swan who has ceased to sing here below, but now increases the choir of angels round God's throne; the Amphion of Germany, Zittau's Orpheus."

Between 1638 and 1653 Hammerschmidt published five series of *Musikalische Andachten,* 187 settings of German sacred words for one to seven voices. It is a monument in seventeenth-century church music. The first volume (1638), subtitled *Geistliche Concerten,* was composed in an Italian concerted style; the second (1641), *Geistliche Madrigalien,* was in a choral-madrigal style; the third (1642), *Geistliche Symphonien,* was modeled after Heinrich Schütz; the fourth (1646), *Geistliche Motetten und Concerten,* made extended use of instruments *ad libitum;* and the fifth (1655-56), *Chor-Musik,* was again in a madrigal style.

In 1639 Hammerschmidt published *Erster Fleiss,* two sets of dance pieces for viols, a pioneer work in instrumental music. Of equal historical significance is the *Dialogi oder Gespräche zwischen Gott und einer gläubigen Seele,* issued in 1645, in which some of the new concepts of "Ars Nuova" were successfully introduced into polyphonic writing. In 1658 Hammerschmidt published *Fest'-, Buss- und Dank Lieder,* a set of thirty-two hymns for five voices and five instrumental parts *ad libitum;* here we find numerous chorale tunes that are still sung in Lutheran churches, such as "Meine Seele Gott erhebet" and "Meinen Jesum lass' ich nicht."

Fétis has written that Hammerschmidt possessed "an original genius, an exalted style and a manner of writing that was simpler and purer than most of the compositions of his time." C. Hubert Parry also finds modernity in many of Hammerschmidt's compositions: "One of the most important features of modern musical art is the clear definition of the musical idea; but it took composers a long time to arrive at the conception, and they often tried to express what touched them in a rather indefinite way. But Hammerschmidt often shows a lively instinct for the path along which art was destined to travel. . . . His efforts in the direction of expression extend even to occasional harmonic subtleties."

PRINCIPAL WORKS

Chamber Music—Erster Fleiss, for viols.

Choral Music—Chorales, madrigals, Masses, motets, odes.

ABOUT

Parry, C. H., Oxford History of Music, vol. 3; Steinhard, E., Zum 300. Geburtstage Andreas Hammerschmidts.

George Frideric Handel *1685-1759*

GEORGE FRIDERIC HANDEL was born Georg Friedrich Händel in Halle, Germany, on February 23, 1685. His father, originally a barber, became a surgeon later in life, then a valet to the Prince of Saxe-Magdeburg. The elder Handel's second marriage, to Dorothea Taust, the daughter of a pastor, took place when he was sixty-three. Georg Friedrich was the second son of this union.

His father wanted him to become a lawyer and when he began to reveal his unusual aptitude for music did everything possible to stifle his talent by discouraging further musical activity. He was forced to practice secretly, usually late at night, while his father was asleep, on an old spinet stored in the garret.

When Handel was seven his father took him to the court of Saxe-Weissenfels to visit the boy's stepbrother, who was working there as a valet. The young Handel played upon the organ for the Duke, who filled the boy's pockets with gold pieces and prevailed upon his father to permit him to study music. His first lessons took place in Halle with Friedrich Wilhelm Zachau, the organist of the Halle Cathedral, who for three years gave him instruction in organ, harpsichord, and oboe, as well as counterpoint and fugue. By 1696 Zachau confessed that there was nothing more he could teach Handel, that the boy (then only eleven) was ready to embark upon a professional career as an instrumentalist and composer.

In his eleventh year Handel paid a visit to Berlin (why he went there has never been explained). The Elector of Brandenburg, astonished by Handel's harpsichord and organ performances, offered to provide him with funds for a period of study in Italy. But Handel's father insisted that the boy return home and begin to think seriously of a career in law.

The next year his father died. For a while Handel worked as assistant organist in the Halle Cathedral. He also began to compose: motets for performance at church on Sunday, and several sonatas. But in 1702, stricken with guilt at having failed to fulfill his father's ambitions for him, he enrolled at the University of Halle for preliminary studies in law. After a year, however, Handel was sure that his future lay in music alone.

In 1703 Handel went to Hamburg, which was then a center of operatic performance under the leadership of Reinhard Keiser, director of the Hamburg Opera. Handel found employment as a violinist in the opera orchestra. While holding this post he visited Lübeck, hoping to obtain the position as organist from which Buxtehude was retiring. But upon discovering that custom required him to marry the daughter of his predecessor, he decided to return to Hamburg.

Handel's companion on the trip to Lübeck was Johann Mattheson, a member of the Hamburg Opera. After their return to Hamburg a bitter rivalry developed between the two musicians with almost fatal consequences. During a performance of Mattheson's opera *Cleopatra,* the composer was to appear in the role of Antony; for this reason Handel was asked to take over Mattheson's customary place at the harpsichord. After performing this role (Antony dies early in the opera) Mattheson descended to the pit to replace Handel at the harpsichord. Handel refused to yield his place, and a bitter quarrel ensued, culminating in a duel outside the theater. Handel's life was saved only by accident: Mattheson's sword split in two, almost piercing a button on Handel's coat.

Rivalries notwithstanding, Handel's reputation as a composer was being established. His first opera, *Almira,* was introduced in Hamburg on January 8, 1705, with such great success that his second opera, *Nero,* received a performance less than two months later, on February 25. A major choral work, the *Passion According to St. John* (one of the few compositions by Handel set to a German text) also added to his growing fame.

But by 1706 Handel had wearied of Hamburg, of the petty cabals and rivalries cluttering its musical activities. There is even good reason to believe that Reinhard Keiser, envious of Handel's growing stature in Hamburg, had begun to make Handel's life in Hamburg intolerable. In any event, Handel in 1706 embarked on an extended and productive trip to Italy. His first Italian opera, *Rodrigo*, was produced successfully in Florence in 1707. Early in 1708 he went to Rome, where he turned to the composition of religious music, soon completing his first oratorio, *La Resurrezione.* Its première took place on April 8, 1708 at the Palazzo Bonelli. Handel's greatest success in Italy was the opera *Agrippina*, produced in Venice on December 26, 1709. By the end of his prolonged stay abroad, Handel had become one of the most eminent musicians in Italy, where he was called, affectionately, *il Sassone*, "the Saxon."

The frequently described tale of his encounter in Venice with Domenico Scarlatti is probably apocryphal. The story is told that Scarlatti, attending a masked ball, was attracted by the harpsichord performance of one of the masked guests. His reaction, frequently quoted, is said to have been, "This must either be the Saxon or the Devil himself."

In 1710 Handel became *Kapellmeister* to the Elector of Hanover (later King George I of England). One of the conditions he had set for acceptance of this post was that he be permitted periodic leaves of absence. Soon after he had been installed in Hanover, he applied for leave, and made his first visit to London. On February 24, 1711, his opera *Rinaldo* was introduced there. This work sold out the Queen's Theatre for fifteen performances, brought the publisher of the score a huge profit, and established Handel's reputation solidly in England.

By mid-June 1711, Handel was back in Hanover to attend to his duties as *Kapellmeister.* But he was restless to return to the scene of his recent triumph. In the fall of 1712 he applied for a second leave, which was granted on condition that he return home within a reasonable period of time. As it turned out Handel never went back to Hanover. He remained in England permanently, and in 1727 became a British subject.

Handel produced several operas in 1712 and 1713, none with particular success. Several other compositions, however, written to commemorate special events, brought him royal favor and a generous annuity of two hundred pounds.

GEORGE FRIDERIC HANDEL

Upon the death of Queen Anne in 1714, the Elector of Hanover mounted the British throne as George I. A legend has gained credence that the new King was so angered by Handel's defection from Hanover that he would have nothing to do with his former *Kapellmeister.* According to the story, Handel reestablished himself with George I by means of his *Water Music*, whose beauty moved the King to become more kindly disposed toward the composer. There seems little substance to the tale, for the *Water Music* was not written until 1717, by which time the King had showered many favors on Handel—including an increase in his annual pension, an appointment as music master to the royal family, and an invitation to the composer to accompany the royal entourage on a trip to Hanover.

Another reason to doubt that the *Water Music* was the means by which the composer and his royal patron were reconciled is incontrovertible evidence that this work was actually commissioned by the King. A royal water pageant was planned on the Thames River for the summer of 1717, an event for which Handel was engaged to write a suite of airs, fanfares, and dances, to be performed by an orchestra floating down the river on one of the barges. According to a report in the London *Daily Courant* of July 19, 1717, "His Majesty liked [the music] so well that he caused it to be played over three times in going and returning." In its original version the *Water Music* consisted of twenty sections; as most often heard today, however, in an arrangement by Sir Hamilton Harty, it consists of only six movements.

In 1718 Handel became chapel master for the Duke of Chandos at his estate at Canons, near London. With a remarkable musical organization at his command, Handel became a prolific composer of choral and stage music, including his first English oratorio; *Esther*, the delightful secular cantata *Acis and Galatea*; and various anthems and masques. Handel also served as music master to the daughters of the Prince of Wales, in which capacity he completed a number of harpsichord pieces, including one of the most celebrated he ever wrote for the keyboard, *The Harmonious Blacksmith*. This piece of music is really a theme-and-variations movement from the harpsichord Suite No. 5 in E major; the title *Harmonious Blacksmith* appeared for the first time when this section of the suite was published separately in Bath in 1822.

When the Royal Academy of Music was founded in London in 1719 for the production of Italian opera, Handel was made its director. His opera *Radamisto* was presented there on April 27, 1720, with outstanding success. But Handel won no easy popularity. He had many enemies in London. Some resented him because he was a foreigner, some because he was uncouth, others because he was a tyrant, still others because they opposed the operatic tradition which he represented. Uniting under the leadership of the powerful Earl of Burlington, these opposing groups determined to destroy Handel. Hoping to revive the simpler and purer principles of Italian opera upheld by the Italian composers, Handel's enemies invited one of Italy's most notable and successful opera composers, Giovanni Battista Bononcini, to London. A spirited rivalry soon developed between Handel and Bononcini as each tried to woo London's audiences with new works. For a time Bononcini seemed to have won favor, but Handel's *Ottone*, produced on January 12, 1723, was so successful that it destroyed Bononcini's ascendancy. This feud was immortalized by John Byrom in a verse which is still remembered as the origin of the popular phrase "tweedledum and tweedledee":

Some say, compared to Bononcini,
That Mynheer Handel's but a ninny.
Others aver that he to Handel
Is scarcely fit to hold a candle.
Strange all this difference should be
'Twixt Tweedledum and Tweedledee.

Even now, Handel's triumph was only temporary. The English public, growing weary of Handelian opera, turned its support and enthusiasm to John Gay's *The Beggar's Opera*, whose popular tunes, realistic, satirical, and topical text, and travesty on the clichés and rituals of grand opera signaled a new era in taste. In 1728 the triumph of *The Beggar's Opera*, combined with Handel's extravagance in producing his works, brought the Academy to bankruptcy. Undaunted, Handel went into partnership with Heidegger in 1729, presenting opera at the King's Theatre. He wrote several operas for the new venture, including *Partenope* in 1730, *Poro* in 1731, *Ezio* in 1732, and *Orlando* in 1733. But his attempts were futile. His operas had lost their audience, and the King's Theatre closed in 1733. After several more disastrous efforts to present opera in London, Handel became a man broken in health, spirit, and financial resources, certain that he had come to the end of his career as a composer. Many agreed.

Handel's last opera, *Deidamia*, was produced in London on January 10, 1741. He had written over forty operas, all adhering to the traditional conventions of the period. As a composer of opera Handel was no innovator. As C. F. Abdy Williams has written: "He took the opera as he found it and simply embellished it by means of his great genius. . . . Handel, in his operas, was essentially a man of his time. . . . He simply took the forms he found ready-made and adorned them with all the beauty and solidity he was capable of producing, which far surpassed the operatic efforts of his contemporaries. . . . The orchestration of Handel's operas would probably seem monotonous to an audience accustomed to the brilliancy of modern instrumentation. . . . The subject matter of the operas is perhaps another bar to their acceptance. . . . A third obstacle is that the vocal parts were written to suit the powers of special singers and were invariably altered when it was necessary that they should be sung by others. It is scarcely possible that singers could be found to execute the more difficult songs nowadays, to say nothing of the fact that artificial male sopranos are an extinct species."

On their infrequent revivals, Handel's operas seem as dated as museum pieces. Nevertheless, he did fill these works with some of the most sublime passages of vocal music to be found in eighteenth-century opera: "Ombra mai fu" (better known as Handel's "Largo" in instrumental adaptations) from *Serse;* "Lascia ch'io pianga" and "Cara sposa" from *Rinaldo;* "Care selve" from *Atalanta;* "Caro amore" from *Floridante.*

After 1741 Handel centered his tremendous energies and creative gifts on the oratorio, the medium through which he was to achieve his greatest artistic triumphs. He had already written oratorios with notable success: his first in 1708; *Esther* (his first English oratorio) in 1720; *Deborah* and *Athalia* in 1733; *Saul,* and the remarkable *Israel in Egypt,* in 1739. With oratorio finding an increasingly prominent place in English music after 1732, Handel shrewdly recognized that this was the form through which he could recapture both his fortune and his audience.

In 1741 Handel was invited to Dublin to direct a charity performance of one of his works. For this event he planned to write a new oratorio. He chose a text from the Scriptures adapted by Charles Jennens—the *Messiah*—and he plunged himself into the project with new energy and almost frenzied inspiration. The entire score, comprising fifty pieces, took him less than twenty-five days to complete. While working he often neglected to eat or sleep, carried by an irresistible momentum which would not permit relaxation. He frequently labored as if under a spell. When he had completed the work he remarked simply: "I think God has visited me."

The *Messiah* was introduced in Dublin on April 13, 1742, with complete triumph. "Words are wanting to express the exquisite delight it afforded the admiring, crowded audience," said the *Faulkner Journal.* Less than a year later, on March 23, 1743, the *Messiah* was performed in London. It is on this occasion that a tradition was established that persists to the present time: the audience's rising during the singing of the "Hallelujah" chorus. During the first Lon-

don performance King George II was so moved by this section that he involuntarily rose from his seat; out of respect to their King, the audience rose too.

The *Messiah* is Handel's masterwork. Unquestionably it is one of the greatest and most often performed oratorios ever written. "The work," says César Saerchinger, "is too well known to require extended comment. Let us only remind the reader of the exquisite beauty of such lyric passages as 'I Know that My Redeemer Liveth,' 'How Beautiful Are Thy Feet,' and 'Behold and See,' which are among the rarest gems of aria form in our possession. Powerful and passionate expressions such as occur in 'The People That Walked in Darkness' are as rare in the literature of dramatic music, while the highly dramatic recitatives like 'Thy Rebuke Hath Broken' are, without question, one of the completest realizations of the ideal of Peri and Monteverdi. The glorious choral effects in the 'Hallelujah Chorus,' the stirring polyphony, now simultaneous, now imitative, reflect a potency and spiritual elevation that will perhaps never be surpassed. Lastly, let us not forget the beautiful 'Pastoral Symphony' in which the exquisite Calabrian melody, the song of the *pifferari* that Handel heard in the early days in Rome, is introduced."

Having renewed his creative energies with the *Messiah,* Handel was now ready to undertake some of his most superb achievements. In rapid succession, one great oratorio after another was produced, making the age of Handel, in the opinion of Arnold Schering, the greatest epoch in oratorio history with such works as *Samson, Joseph and His Brethren, Judas Maccabaeus, Joshua, Solomon, Theodora, Jephtha.*

Jephtha, first heard in London on February 26, 1752, brought this monumental cycle to an end. Handel was working on this oratorio when his sight failed him, and he became totally blind. Three times he underwent surgery, once with the surgeon who had tried to save Bach's eyes. These efforts were ineffectual. Blind, Handel continued to perform as an organist and to direct performances of his oratorios.

On April 6, 1759, while conducting a charity performance of the *Messiah* in London, Handel collapsed. He was taken home and put to bed; he never lived to leave it. "I should like to die on Good Friday," he said. His simple wish was almost realized. Handel died early on the morning of Good Saturday, on April 14, 1759, and was buried in the poet's corner of Westminster Abbey. His burial place is marked with a statue by Roubiliac representing Handel at his table, on which reposes the score of the *Messiah,* open at the portion that reads, "I know that my Redeemer liveth."

Romain Rolland described Handel thus: "They used to call him 'The Great Bear.' He was gigantic, broad, corpulent, with big hands and enormous feet. . . . He walked bow-legged, with a heavy, rolling gait, very erect, with his head thrown back under its huge white wig, whose curls rippled heavily over his shoulders. He had a long horse-like face, which with age became bovine and swamped with fat; with pendant cheeks and triple chin, the nose large, thick and straight; the ears red and long. His gaze was very direct; there was a quizzical gleam in his bold eye, a mocking twist at the corner of his large, finely cut mouth. His air was impressive and jovial. . . . He was full of humor. He had a 'sly pseudo-simplicity' which made the most solemn individuals laugh though he himself showed an unsmiling face. No·one ever told a story better. . . . This huge mass of flesh was shaken by fits of fury. He swore almost with every phrase. . . . Spiteful he was not. 'He was rough and peremptory,' says Burney, 'but entirely without malevolence.' There was, in his most violent fits of anger, a touch of originality which, together with his bad English, made them absolutely comical. Like Lully and Gluck, he had the gift of command; and like them, he combined an irascible violence that overcame all opposition with a witty good nature which, though wounding to vanity, had the power of healing the wounds it had caused. . . . This masterful character, with its violence and its transports of anger and genius, was governed by a supreme self-control. In Handel . . . tranquillity prevailed. . . . No one had any suspicion of the nervous tension or the superhuman determination which he must have needed in order to sustain this tranquillity."

In *Music in the Baroque Era,* Manfred F. Bukofzer has pointed out that Handel's oratorios fall into three categories: the choral opera, the choral cantata, and the choral drama. In the first belong works like *Semele, Hercules, Susanna,* and *Theodora,* "in which the proximity to the opera is most conspicuous. . . . In style they are comparable with the Italian operas of the Viennese court." In the second group fall works like *Alexander's Feast* and *Ode for St. Cecilia's Day* (both settings of Dryden poems) and *L'Allegro* (after Milton). Here Bukofzer finds a similarity with the English odes dealing with "allegorical subjects without dramatic action." Handel's greatest and best-loved oratorios belong to the third category, the choral drama. "The Old Testament was the ideal source for the choral drama because it provided Handel with exactly what he needed: monumental characters in a monumental setting. Handel's grand manner, his broadly sweeping style, are peculiarly fitting for these massive choral dramas so that subject matter and musical style are in perfect harmony."

In addition to opera and oratorio Handel cultivated one other field profitably: instrumental music. His main compositions in this medium include the Concerti Grossi and Suites for orchestra, various concertos for solo instruments and accompaniment, trio sonatas, and numerous suites and smaller pieces for the harpsichord. Here, as Romain Rolland remarked, Handel "had . . . an exquisite sense of form. No German surpassed him in the art of writing beautiful melodic lines. Mozart and Hasse alone were his equals in this. . . . He did not work so much through brilliancy, variety and novelty of his tone colors as by the beauty of his designs, and his effects of light and shade. With a voluntarily restrained palette, and by satisfying himself with the sober colors of the strings, he yet was able to produce surprising and thrilling effects. Volbach has shown that he had less recourse to the contrast and mixing of instruments than to the division of the same family of instruments into different groups. On the other hand, Handel, when he considered it advisable, reduced his instrumental forces by suppressing the violin and the second violin, whose places were taken by the harpsichord. All his orchestral art is in the true instinct of balance and economy which, with the most restricted means in managing a few colors, yet knows how to obtain as powerful impressions as our musicians today, with their crowded palette."

Since Johann Sebastian Bach and Handel were contemporaries and represent the greatest pillars of Baroque art, they have often been compared. "Where Handel aimed at beauty of melodic form," wrote C. Hubert Parry, "Bach strove for characteristic expression. Where Handel used orderly progressions of simple harmony, Bach aimed at contriving elaborate interweavings of subtly disposed parts to give the effect of the subtlest shade of human feeling. Where Handel used the most realistic means to convey the hopping of frogs, or the rattling of hailstones . . . Bach attempted to express the inner feelings of human creatures under the impress of any exciting causes. . . . Nowhere is the difference of their attitude better illustrated than in their use of the recitative. Handel, accepting the conventions of the Italian art without hesitation, ruined an enormous amount of his works by the emptiest, baldest, and most mechanical formulas; while Bach, dissatisfied with anything which had not significance, endeavored by the contours and intervals of his solo part, by the progressions and harmonies of his accompaniment, and by every means that was available to intensify from moment to moment the expression of the words.

"Bach's feeling for melody was not so happy as Handel's. . . . In instrumentation both of these giants among composers were equally backward, though their aims and methods, and the rest they achieved were very different. . . . Handel did as little as it is possible for a great master to do in adding to the resources of the instrumental side of music. . . . Bach, on the other hand, looking always forward, gives proof of much more purpose in his use of instrumental resources. . . . The oratorios of Handel were nearly all dramatic or epic, and the subjects were treated, as nearly as possible, histrionically. . . . But [with Bach] they are the direct outcome of personal devotion, and in them the mystic emotionalism of the Teutonic nature found its purest expression."

PRINCIPAL WORKS

Chamber Music—Trio sonatas; various sonatas for solo instruments and accompaniment.

Choral Music—Esther; Alexander's Feast; Saul; Ode for St. Cecilia's Day; Israel in Egypt; L'Allegro; Messiah; Samson; Dettingen Te Deum; Semele; Hercules; Belshazzar; Judas Maccabaeus; Joshua; Susanna; Solomon; Theodora; Jephtha; anthems.

Harpsichord Music—Capriccios, fantasias, fugues, suites, and various pieces.

Operas—Over 40, including: Almira; Agrippina; Rinaldo; Radamisto; Acis and Galatea; Floridante; Giulio Cesare; Tamerlano; Rodelinda; Scipione; Admeto; Siroe; Partenope; Poro; Ezio; Arianna; Ariodante; Alcina; Atalanta; Berenice; Faramondo; Serse.

Orchestral Music—18 concerti grossi; various concertos for solo instruments and orchestra; overtures.

Vocal Music—72 Italian cantatas for voice and continuo; various other cantatas for solo voices and instruments; 22 Italian Duets with continuo; English Songs; French Songs; German Songs.

ABOUT

Abraham, G. (editor), Handel: A Symposium; Burney, C., A General History of Music; Davison, A. T., Bach and Handel: The Consummation of the Baroque in Music; Dent, E. J., Handel; Deutsch, O. E., Handel: A Documentary Biography; Flower, N., George Frideric Handel; Hadow, W. H., Handel; Larsen, J. P., Handel's Messiah: Origins, Composition, Sources; Leichtentritt, H., Handel; Myers, R. M., Handel's Messiah; Rolland, R., A Musical Tour Through the Land of the Past; Tobin, J., Handel at Work; Weinstock, H., Handel; Young, P. M., Handel.

Johann Adolph Hasse *1699-1783*

JOHANN ADOLPH HASSE, a German was a leader in the Neapolitan school of opera. He was born in the town of Bergedorf, near Hamburg, on March 25, 1699. His father, the town organist and schoolmaster, gave him his first music instruction. In 1717 Hasse went to Hamburg, where he became acquainted with Ulrich König, the famous poet attached to the Polish court. Impressed by Hasse's beautiful singing voice, König recommended him to Reinhard Keiser, the director of the Hamburg Opera. Keiser engaged Hasse as principal tenor for his company, a post he filled for four seasons. At the end of that period, and once again on König's recommendation, Hasse joined the company of the Brunswick Theater. There he made his bow as an opera composer with *Antioco*, introduced on August 11, 1721.

Though *Antioco* was well received, Hasse recognized his own technical shortcomings and set off for Naples for additional study. His first teacher was Porpora, but Hasse was soon dissatisfied with him and became a pupil of Alessandro Scarlatti, the leading figure in Neapolitan opera. Under Scarlatti,

JOHANN ADOLPH HASSE

Hasse absorbed the traditions and techniques of the Neapolitan school and put them into practice in his opera *Tigrane,* given on November 4, 1723. This work was a huge success. But even more successful was Hasse's *Serenade* for two voices, introduced by Farinelli and Vittoria Tesi. On the strength of the *Serenade* Hasse was commissioned to write a new opera, *Sesostrate,* which on May 13, 1726 brought Hasse the greatest triumph he had yet enjoyed and made him famous throughout Italy.

In 1727 Hasse went to Venice. He became professor at the Scuola degl' Incurabili, for which he wrote a remarkable *Miserere.* He also produced five operas in Naples between 1726 and 1730; one of these, *Ezio,* was the first of the many operas that he would set to texts by Metastasio. Hasse's pronounced gifts as a singer, composer, and harpsichord-ist, combined with his striking physical presence, his gracious manner, and ready wit, won him great popularity in the fashionable salons and with the general public. Italians everywhere referred to him affectionately as *il caro Sassone,* "the beloved Saxon," though Hasse was not from Saxony.

In 1730 Hasse married the celebrated singer Faustina Bordoni. He subsequently wrote two operas for her—*Artaserse* and *Dalisa,* in both of which she won major successes in Venice that year.

In 1731 Hasse was appointed director of opera at the court of Augustus II in Dresden,

a position that held opportunity both for him and for his wife, who became *prima donna* of many performances. Hasse's first production in Dresden, on September 13, 1731 was *Cleofide;* it starred his wife in the leading female role. *Cleofide* was a triumph, as were several other operas by Hasse produced at the Dresden court. But his life there was troubled by petty competition. Various musicians, with influential backing of their own, did their best to make his work difficult, for they envied his talent and popularity. Although he kept his post until 1740, Hasse took every opportunity he could find to leave Dresden. With his wife he toured the principal cities of Germany, introducing several new operas that starred his wife. In 1734 he visited England for the first time, making a profound impression with his opera *Artaserse.* Hasse was offered the direction of an opera company competing with the one led by Handel. Since Hasse was reluctant to engage in rivalry with Handel, and not eager to settle in England, he declined the offer.

In 1739 Hasse was back in Dresden. He continued to prosper, despite the fact that rivalries and intrigues continued to plague him—and that a new singer, Regina Mingotti, had risen to eclipse the fame of his wife. After the victory of Frederick the Great at Kesselsdorf, Hasse presented a special performance of his opera *Arminio* for the royal entourage; it was performed each night for the King during his nine-day stay in Dresden. In further acknowledgment of his high esteem for the opera and its composer, Frederick presented Hasse with a diamond ring and instructed him to distribute a thousand thalers to his company of musicians.

During the siege of Dresden in 1760, Hasse lost most of his property and possessions, including many manuscripts he had been preparing for publication. He continued to write operas for the court and to direct performances until the end of the war. But when the court subsequently was forced to curtail its program of operatic activity as part of its economic retrenchment, Hasse lost his post. He visited Vienna with his wife, and was engaged by the court to write operas to Metastasio's texts in opposition to Gluck. In 1771 he returned to Italy to supervise the première of his last opera, *Ruggiero,* in Milan on October 16. The program also featured a brief intermezzo, *Ascanio in Alba,* by a thirteen-year-old composer, Wolfgang Amadeus Mozart. It has been said that when Hasse heard Mozart's little opera he exclaimed prophetically, "This child will cause all of us to be forgotten."

Hasse spent the remainder of his life in Venice, where he died on December 16, 1783.

Charles Burney, a contemporary, described Hasse as "tall and strongly built. His face must have been handsome and finely chiseled. . . . He was very . . . kindly in manner. He was very talkative and full of commonsense; equally devoid of pride and prejudice; he spoke ill of no one. On the contrary, he did justice to the talents of several of his rivals. He had an infinite respect for Carl Philipp Emanuel Bach and spoke of Handel only with reverence."

Hasse wrote about eighty operas. He set all of Metastasio's texts to music, some of them twice and even three or four times. In his operas, which followed the manner and style that had been perfected by the Neapolitan school, Hasse was an aristocrat of melody. His lyricism was as elegant as it was abundant, and he wrote for the voice with extraordinary flexibility and consummate skill. Fétis wrote: "In expression of tender sentiments, his music had an irresistible charm. . . . His harmonies were less strong, less rich in modulation than the works of other German composers of his time; they appeared feeble later when Mozart and Haydn threw into their music all the splendor of their art."

In *A Short History of Opera,* however, Donald Jay Grout emphasizes the appeal and high quality of Hasse's lyricism. "His arias are models of that musical feeling which dissolves and transmutes everything into beautiful, elegant and sensitive melody . . . with a surface of such perfection that it seems almost captious to demand more."

Hasse also created a vast library of distinguished church music. His instrumental compositions were significant in the early eighteenth century in crystalizing a classical structure and style.

Principal Works
Chamber Music—String trios, sonatas.
Choral Music—22 motets; 10 Masses; 10 psalms; 9 oratorios; 5 Litanies; 3 Requiems; Te Deum; Salve Regina.

Operas—About 80 operas, including: Antioco; Tigrane; Astarto; Ezio; Artaserse; Dalisa; Arminio; Catone in Utica; Demetrio (later renamed Cleonice); Atalanta; Asteria; Didone abbandonata; Antigono; Semiramide riconosciuta; Demofoonte; Adriano in Siria; Achille in Sciro; Partenope; Ruggiero.

Orchestral Music—Concertos; overtures.

About
Gerber, R., Der Operntypus Hasses und seine textlichen Grundlagen; Mennicke, C., Hasse und die Gebrüder Graun als Sinfoniker; Müller, W., J. A. Hasse als Kirchenkomponist.

Hans Leo Hassler *1564-1612*

HANS LEO HASSLER, one of the earliest creators of a German style of musical composition, was born on October 25, 1564, in Nuremberg, where his father, Isaac, was church organist. Hans' father was his only music teacher in Nuremberg; under his expert guidance the boy soon became a proficient organist. In 1584, financed, probably, by members of the Nuremberg community, Hassler became the first German musician to seek advanced instruction across the Alps. He arrived in Venice, where he became a pupil of Andrea Gabrieli. Gabrieli's teaching, and the music of Palestrina, had a pronounced influence on the young man.

In 1585 Hassler returned to Germany, and became a chamber musician to Octavian Fugger in Augsburg. He held this post for fifteen years, continuing his study of music, and engaging seriously in composition. In 1588 his first published pieces, two motets, appeared in a collection edited by Frederick Lindner. Two years later Hassler issued a volume of twenty-four Italian *canzonette.* In the ensuing years he published several volumes of motets, Masses, and other contrapuntal compositions which introduced the methods and style of the Venetian polyphonic masters (especially those of the Gabrielis) in Germany.

Upon the death of Octavian Fugger in 1600, Hassler returned to Nuremberg. There he was appointed organist of the Frauenkirche and town bandmaster. In 1602 he became court organist to Rudolf II in Prague, but this was mainly an honorary appointment which enabled Hassler to pursue other activities—one of which was the manufacture of musical clocks. As a token of his high regard for Hassler's abilities as

HANS LEO HASSLER

an organist and composer, Rudolph II knighted him.

In 1604 Hassler became an organist in Ulm. There he married and settled down for a number of years. In 1609 he assumed an organ post with the Elector of Saxony, and three years later traveled with the Elector to Frankfurt am Main. Long a victim of tuberculosis, Hassler broke down completely in Frankfurt and died there on June 8, 1612.

Although Hassler was responsible for carrying into Germany the traditions of the Venetian polyphonic school, he was also uniquely successful in realizing a Germanic style of musical composition, as opposed to the then popular Italian style, through his arrangements and wide use of German melodies. His main works in this area include the *Lustgarten neuer teutscher Gesäng* in 1601; the *Psalmen und christliche Gesäng mit vier Stimmen auf die Melodien fugweis componirt*, in 1607; and the *Kirchengesänge, Psalmen und geistliche Lieder auf die gemeinen Melodien mit vier Stimmen simpliciter gesetzt*, in 1608.

Karl Nef regards Hassler's many religious choral works as the "pearls of Protestant church music." He goes on to say: "How splendidly the polyphonic arrangement of *Ein' feste Burg* depicts the proud defiance of the opening words, how well it delineates the 'cruel enemy,' and in what a beautifully flowing line it calmly draws to its conclusion. Not less beautiful . . . are the simple

four-voice arrangements of the church melodies which Hassler published in 1608. This is golden treasure which the church choirs should ever cherish. Even he who stands far removed from a genuine musical appreciation can surmise what depth of spirit lay in this master who wrote the melody of "O Haupt voll Blut und Wunden". . . . His Masses are highly esteemed for their melodic wealth, and he achieved delightful results as a composer of madrigals and secular songs."

Hans Leo Hassler had two brothers, both of whom distinguished themselves as professional musicians. Kaspar Hassler (1562-1618) was an organist at the Lorenzkirche in Nuremberg and edited some important collections of sacred Italian motets. Jacob Hassler (1565-c.1618) was also a prominent organist and editor of collections of church music; in addition, he composed some distinguished works for the organ.

PRINCIPAL WORKS

Chamber Music—Canzoni, ricercari.
Choral Music—Chorales, hymns, madrigals, Magnificats, Masses, motets, psalms.

ABOUT

Leichtentritt, H., Meisterwerke deutscher Tonkunst; Moser, H. J., Geschichte der deutschen Musik, vol. 1; Denkmäler der Tonkunst in Bayern, vol. 5.

Joseph Haydn *1732-1809*

FRANZ JOSEPH HAYDN was born on March 31, 1732, in Rohrau, a town in lower Austria, near the border of Hungary. His parents were simple folk; his father was a wheelwright who served as sexton in the local church, his mother a cook in the household of a count. Both were musical. On Sundays and holidays the Haydns, sometimes accompanied by several neighbors, would give impromptu concerts at their home. The child Joseph responded sensitively to them, and his interest in music attracted Johann Matthias Frankh, a relative of the elder Haydn, who suggested that the boy go to live with him in nearby Hainburg. Joseph was only five at the time. For about three years the boy received comprehensive instruction in music from Frankh. Frankh was a severe martinet who often subjected the boy to "more blows than victuals," as Haydn later recalled, but his lessons proved

Haydn: hīd'n

an invaluable preparation, enabling Joseph, at the age of eight, to become a chorister at St. Stephen's Cathedral in Vienna. For the next nine years Joseph sang in the choir, and received additional music instruction, and lessons in Latin and psalm reading, as well. The regime at St. Stephen's was strict, the food poor, the rooms cold. Joseph was constantly hungry, and just as constantly, he was subjected to abuse by his teacher, the *Kapellmeister* Karl Georg Reutter. Moreover, being of a mischievous bent, Joseph was always in trouble.

Joseph's voice broke when he was seventeen, and he was dismissed from St. Stephen's. Without money, friends, or a home, he was forced to shift for himself in Vienna. A fellow chorister provided him with food and lodging until he could support himself through violin playing, teaching, and sundry musical tasks. Then Haydn rented a garret room for himself in the Michaelerhaus in the Kohlmarkt. He devoted himself passionately to the study of music whenever he found the spare time; most often his study consisted in memorizing the piano sonatas of Carl Philipp Emanuel Bach. He also composed music of his own. In 1752 a Viennese farce, *Der krumme Teufel*, for which he had written the music, was produced at the Burgtheater and would have enjoyed a profitable run had not a prominent Viennese nobleman regarded it as a satire on himself. The work was taken off the boards after two performances; but it was subsequently produced in several other European cities.

Also living in the Michaelerhaus at the time was Pietro Metastasio, the court poet and the most celebrated opera librettist of his day. Through Metastasio Haydn met Nicola Porpora, the eminent singing teacher and composer. Porpora was willing to give Haydn singing instruction if, in return, Haydn would serve as his house servant and accompanist, an arrangement which Haydn found agreeable. Through this influential musician, Haydn met some of Vienna's most prominent composers, including Gluck and Dittersdorf, and several of its most distinguished noblemen. Baron Karl Joseph von Fürnberg engaged Haydn to direct musical performances at his palace in Weinzierl. For these concerts Haydn wrote serenades, cassations, nocturnes—and, in 1755, his first string quartet.

JOSEPH HAYDN

Haydn next went to work for Count Ferdinand Maximilian von Morzin at his palace in Pilsen. There, in 1759, Haydn created his first symphony. Haydn's first symphonies, like his first quartets, were modeled after the Baroque suites and serenades of his predecessors—"charming, trivial pieces . . . a *galant* simplification of the Baroque style," as Wilfrid Mellers described them. "It cannot be said that he approaches Stamitz in fire or precision of effect; nor that he adds anything substantial to his other models."

The comparative financial security provided him by his post as *Kapellmeister* for Count Morzin enabled Haydn to marry. On November 26, 1760, he wed Maria Anna Keller, the daughter of a wigmaker, after her younger sister, with whom Haydn had been in love, suddenly decided to enter a convent. It was an unhappy choice. Maria Anna was a shrew—surly, extravagant, selfish, and completely incapable of understanding her husband's music or of sympathizing with his ambitions. They quarreled continuously until, after several years, they decided to separate. Haydn provided for her for the rest of her life.

In 1761 Haydn became second *Kapellmeister* at the Eisenstadt estate of Prince Paul Anton Esterházy. When the Esterházys built a new palace in Esterház in 1766, Haydn assumed the post of first *Kapellmeister*, which he retained for twenty-five years. Directing performances of opera and orchestral music, as well as concerts for special festive occasions, he wore a uniform consisting of a bright blue coat decorated with silver braids and buttons, white collar and cuffs, white stockings, and shining pumps.

Haydn now created a vast library of compositions in virtually every medium: operas, Masses, symphonies, quartets, concertos, sonatas, and other forms. "My Prince was always satisfied with my works," he confided to a friend. "Not only did I have the encouragement of constant approval, but as conductor of an orchestra I could make experiments, observe what produced an effect and what weakened it, and was thus in a position to improve, to alter, to make additions, or omissions, and be as bold as I pleased. I was cut off from the world. There was no one to confuse or torment me, and I was forced to be original." Original, indeed! The symphonies, quartets, concertos and sonatas which Haydn created while working for Esterházy not only established the classic sonata form definitely, but also rose beyond the Baroque concept of beauty of sound and from the conventions of the "gallant style" to create a musical art dramatically enriched with passion and intensity, fresh and adventurous in technique and vocabulary.

To W. W. Cobbett, the six string quartets of opus 20, completed in 1772, are "of historic and aesthetic importance. . . . There is perhaps no single or sextuple opus in the history of instrumental music which has achieved so much or achieved it so quietly." These compositions are known as the *Sun Quartets* because they represent "a sunrise over the domain of the sonata style as well as of quartets in particular." The *Farewell* and *Maria Theresa Symphony*, also completed in 1772, similarly represent for orchestral music a new character. "The tempestuous features in these works," said Mellers, "strike one's attention immediately. . . . Haydn exploits the dramatic potentialities inherent in the rococo style."

The new enrichment of Haydn's style, deepening of emotion. and intensification of the dramatic element in his writing were produced by a number of important influences: the Enlightenment; the *Sturm und Drang* epoch through which Haydn lived; his love affair with Luigia Polzelli; and, per-

haps most important, his friendship with Mozart.

Haydn and Mozart met in 1781, when Mozart was twenty-five and Haydn forty-nine. Mozart, of course, regarded Haydn with the admiration and respect due one of Europe's most celebrated composers, and willingly followed the influence of the master. But before long Haydn began to recognize in Mozart an incomparable gift, instinct and originality from which Haydn himself profited immeasurably. Familiarity with Mozart's music brought to Haydn a new technique and a new concept. When in 1785 Haydn heard the quartets which Mozart had written for and dedicated to him, he told the composer's father: "I must tell you before God, and as an honest man, that I think your son the greatest composer I ever heard." And in 1787 he wrote to a friend: "Oh, if only I could explain to every musical friend, and to the leading men in particular, the inimitable art of Mozart, its depth, the greatness of its emotion, and its unique musical conception, as I myself feel and understand it, nations would then vie with each other to possess so great a jewel within their frontiers."

When Prince Nicolaus Esterházy died in 1790, and his successor, Prince Anton, reduced the musical staff and activities at Esterház, Haydn at last left the post which he had held so long with such great distinction, and went to live in Vienna. Shortly after returning to the Austrian capital, the English impresario Johann Peter Salomon invited Haydn to London to conduct a series of orchestral concerts and to compose a new series of symphonies. On December 15, 1790, Haydn set forth for England. En route he stopped off at Bonn, where he heard and admired a Mass by young Beethoven. After a stormy Channel crossing, he arrived in London on the first day of the new year. From March to May he directed brilliant and outstandingly successful orchestral concerts featuring his new symphonies. Throughout this period of concert giving he was extensively fêted; he appeared as guest of honor at numerous banquets and other social functions; and he received an honorary degree from Oxford University.

Haydn's fabulous success in London encouraged him to return to that city in 1794, again to direct concerts featuring his new symphonies, and to enjoy the *élan* of dinners, social events, and public ceremonies honoring him.

The twelve *London Symphonies* which Haydn wrote for his two visits to England are the crown of his vast symphonic output. With Mozart's best works they represent the highest summit attained in the symphonic form in the age preceding Beethoven's. "No others of Haydn's scores," said Karl Geiringer, "show such virtuosity of instrumentation or such delightful, unorthodox treatment of musical forms and contrapuntal devices. . . . The whole nineteenth century, beginning with Beethoven and ending with Brahms, was able to draw rich inspiration from Haydn's last . . . symphonies."

After returning from his second spectacular and highly profitable visit to London, Haydn settled down to a quiet existence in the Gumpendorf district of Vienna. Though now at the dusk of his life, he was still destined to produce masterworks. The greatest of these are two oratorios, his first attempts at writing in this form: *The Creation (Die Schöpfung)* in 1798 and *The Seasons (Die Jahreszeiten)* in 1801. In addition, he completed several Masses, including the *Nelson-Missa* in 1798, the *Theresien-Messe* in 1799, and the *Harmoniemesse* in 1802. What he had said about writing *The Creation* holds true for all these religious choral works: "I felt myself so penetrated with religious feeling that before I sat down to the pianoforte I prayed to God with earnestness that He would enable me to praise him worthily." Rarely before had Haydn given voice to such spiritual exaltation as in this music.

In 1797 the Minister of Interior commissioned Haydn to write a patriotic hymn to stimulate the national feeling of the Austrian people. Haydn complied with "Gott, erhalte Franz, den Kaiser," which was performed in all the theaters of the Empire on the Emperor's birthday that year. "You have expressed what is in every loyal Austrian heart," the Emperor told him, "and through your melody Austria will always be served." Since then this song has become the Austrian national anthem. Haydn used the melody as the basis for a series of variations in the second movement of his String Quartet in C major, op. 76, no. 3, appropriately known as the *Emperor Quartet.*

Haydn conducted his last concert on December 26, 1803, in Vienna, directing a performance of his *The Seven Last Words of Christ.* He had written this work twenty-five years earlier, at the request of the canon of the Cadiz Cathedral. After 1803 Haydn's health deteriorated rapidly. His speech and memory began to falter. He became scarcely more than an invalid. His last public appearance took place on the occasion of his seventy-sixth birthday, celebrated (a few days in advance) on March 27, 1808, with a performance of *The Creation.* Haydn had to be carried into the concert auditorium in a chair to receive a tumultuous ovation.

By the end of May 1809, Haydn knew he was close to death. He drew up his will, "commending my soul to my all-merciful Creator," then called in his household to bid them farewell and to play his national anthem for them for the last time. His death came only a few days later, on May 31, 1809. Funeral services were held in all the major churches of Vienna. The city was occupied at the time by the French, and Napoleon ordered that a special guard of honor be placed at Haydn's home. Haydn was buried in the churchyard of Hundsthurm, after funeral ceremonies that included the performance of Mozart's Requiem. In 1820 his body was disinterred to be reburied in Eisenstadt.

Haydn considered himself an ugly man and was always amazed that women found him attractive. He was of medium height, with very short legs which made him seem misshapen. His face was deeply marked by smallpox, as was his hawk-like nose, which was enlarged by nasal polyps. Yet he made a favorable first impression. His kindliness, generosity, and warmth were instantly reflected in his gentle eyes and mobile facial expressions. He was generous to a fault with people in need, though otherwise he was extremely thrifty. He was always sympathetic and open-hearted. "Anybody can see by the looks of me," he once said of himself, genially, "that I am a good-natured sort of fellow." He was also fervently religious; habitually he began and ended his manuscripts with the phrases "In nomine Domini" or "Laus Deo."

The carefully planned program Haydn set for himself each day, and to which he adhered rigidly, pointed to his partiality for discipline and order—just as his personal appearance emphasized his extreme tidiness. He was a conscientious workman, industrious and systematic. He was fully conscious of his gifts and powers. "I know," he once said, "that God has bestowed a talent upon me, and I thank him for it. I think I have done my duty and have been of use in my generation and by my works." And again: "I look back with heartfelt cheerful satisfaction on the works to which I devoted such a long succession of years and such persevering efforts and exertions." This was no self-aggrandizement, for Haydn's genius can hardly be overestimated.

"His vision of the world," explained Daniel Gregory Mason, "was more that of an accountant or statistician than that of a poet. He saw simply and clearly; for him objects stood in the hard light of reason, not surrounded by any haze of revery or atmosphere of emotion. . . . Haydn was distinctly an uneducated man. . . . He knew Italian and a little French, but never had any English until he went to London at nearly sixty. He read little, and did not care to discuss politics, science, or any art but music. He spoke always in the strong dialect of his native place. . . . On the other hand, the impressive peculiarity of his emotional nature is its normality. Emotionally he was typical rather than personal, centered in the common interests and instincts rather than eccentric to them, conservative and conventional rather than radical and individual."

Haydn was not (as he has often been loosely described) the "father" of the symphony, quartet, and sonata. Many others preceded him, helping to evolve these forms, and to establish their structure and style. But with Haydn the symphony, quartet, and sonata acquired new structural dimensions, a new dramatic intensity, and a more varied range of emotion than had yet been achieved. He was an innovator who introduced a new concept of thematic development and variation form, who enriched the harmonic vocabulary, who introduced new colors and timbres into orchestration, and who, in his quartets, brought a new individuality to the four instruments. In these ways he was the great, and requisite, predecessor of Mozart and Beethoven. As Paul Henry Lang wrote, Haydn was a musician "who opened the classical era," and who was permitted "to accompany a new world of art from its inception to its supreme flowering. . . . With him music shed its courtly etiquette and playfulness to become a most personal expression, the expression of an Austrian peasant, of love of life, of the colorfulness of nature, moving about in a kaleidoscope of wit, humor, joy and sorrow."

J. Cuthbert Hadden described Haydn's style in this manner: "To say that a composition is 'Haydnish' is to express in one word what is well understood by all intelligent amateurs. Haydn's music is like his character—clear, straightforward, fresh and winning, without the slightest trace of affectation or morbidity. Its perfect transparency, its firmness of design, its fluency of instrumental language, the beauty and inexhaustible wealth of its melody, its studied moderation, its childlike cheerfulness—these are some of the qualities which mark the style of this most genial of all composers."

Several of Haydn's long-forgotten operas were presented in revivals in the 1950's and 1960's. His last opera, Orfeo ed Euridice, never performed during his own lifetime, was revived in 1950 for a complete recording made in Vienna for the Haydn Society. Il Mondo della luna was heard for the first time in almost two centuries at the Holland Music Festival in 1959. Die Feuerbrunst, whose manuscript was discovered in the Yale University library, was given its first modern performance in Sweden in 1961. And in 1962 the Stockholm Festival revived the long-neglected L'Infedeltà delusa.

PRINCIPAL WORKS

Chamber Music—125 trios for various combinations; 82 string quartets; 35 piano trios; 18 string trios; cassations, divertimenti, duos, nocturnes, quintets, sextets, sonatas.

Choral Music—14 Masses; Die Schöpfung (The Creation); Die Jahreszeiten (The Seasons); offertoriums, Te Deums, Salve Regina.

Operas—Lo Speziale; L'Infedeltà delusa; Il mondo della luna; La Vera costanza; L'Isola Disabitata; Die Feuerbrunst; Armida; Orfeo ed Euridice.

Orchestral Music—104 symphonies; 15 piano concertos; 3 violin concertos; 2 cello concertos; 2 horn concertos; other concertos for solo instruments and orchestra; Die sieben Worte des Erlösers am Kreuz (The Seven Last Words of Christ); divertimenti, German dances, marches, minuets, nocturnes, overtures, scherzandi.

Piano Music—52 sonatas; Fantasia in C major; Capriccio in G major; Arietta con variazioni; Variations in F minor; 10 German Dances.

Vocal Music—Various songs for voice and piano, including Das Leben ist ein Traum, My Mother Bids Me Bind My Hair, Piercing Eyes, The Sailor's Song, She Never Told Her Love, The Spirit Song; 4 cantatas; vocal duets, vocal trios, vocal quartets; canons, rounds.

ABOUT

Brenet, M., Haydn; Geiringer, K., Haydn: A Creative Life in Music; Gotwals, V. (editor), Joseph Haydn: Eighteenth Century Gentleman and Genius; Hadden, J. C., Haydn; Hughes, R., Haydn; Jacob, H. E., Haydn: His Art, Times and Glory; Nohl, L., Haydn; Pohl, C. F., Joseph Haydn; Reich, W., Joseph Haydn: Leben, Briefe, Schaffen; Singer, H. (editor), The Haydn Yearbook.

Ferdinand Herold *1791-1833*

LOUIS JOSEPH FERDINAND HEROLD, distinguished composer of *opéras-comiques*, was born in Paris, January 28, 1791. He was the only son of François Joseph Herold, a piano teacher and composer who had studied with Carl Philipp Emanuel Bach in Hamburg. Though Ferdinand started to play piano and compose at the age of six, his father discouraged him from musical activity. At ten Ferdinand entered the Hix school in Paris. One of its teachers was Fétis, who was struck by the boy's musical gifts. "His progress," Fétis later recorded, "was more rapid than that of other pupils. Nature had made him a musician."

After his father died in 1802, the boy began to consider studying music seriously. Despite her severe financial difficulties, Ferdinand's mother was willing to submit to his wishes if an acknowledged authority could be found ready to vouch for his talent. She thereupon took some of his work to the *opéra-comique* composer Grétry. "Rest assured, madam," Grétry told her. "Your son will be a distinguished musician."

In 1806, having completed his course at the Hix school, Herold entered the Paris Conservatory. He studied harmony with Catel and composition with Méhul. In 1812 the youth won the Prix de Rome.

After he had written two symphonies and several string quartets, Herold decided that he preferred to write music for the stage. In Naples, where he served as court pianist for Queen Caroline, he completed his first opera, *La Jeunesse de Henri V*. It was introduced in that city on January 5, 1815.

Upon his return to Paris, Herold became a friend of Boieldieu, who asked Hérold to write the second half of an opera he had been unable to complete. *Charles de France,* the result of this joint effort, was produced at the Opéra-Comique on June 18, 1816 and

FERDINAND HEROLD

was so well received that Herold was commissioned to write an opera. His first opera, *Les Rosières*, was introduced at the Opéra-Comique on January 27, 1817.

Herold continued to write in this genre with remarkable productivity. *La Clochette* was completed in 1817; *Le Premier venu* in 1818; *Le Troqueurs* in 1819; and *L'Auteur mort et vivant* in 1820. Some were well received, but the last work was a dismal failure. In an effort to win back his public, Herold began to imitate the style of successful French composers; the results had neither merit nor appeal. He regained success, however, with *Le Muletier* in 1823, and *Marie* in 1826, retaining from that time a dominant position in French opera.

Between 1820 and 1827 Herold was an accompanist at the Théâtre-Italien. In 1824 he was made choirmaster of the Académie. During these years he turned to writing music in areas other than theater and produced a large amount of piano music.

In 1827 Herold married Adèle Élise Rollet. They established their home at Les Ternes in Paris, where Herold lived with his wife and three children for the remainder of his life.

In 1831 Herold completed the first of the two operas for which he is best remembered today. It was *Zampa*, produced at the Opéra-Comique on May 3, 1831. The libretto, by Mélesville (A. H. J. Duveyrier),

Herold: ā-rôld'

was a variation of the Don Giovanni legend in which a marble statue comes to life to destroy the central character. Though the dramatic element was pronounced in *Zampa*, lyricism was not sacrificed. As B. Jouvain wrote: "The melody of the composer, overflowing in abundance, is at turns passionate and buoyant. The harmony, endowed with force and with elegance, adopts, under a skilled hand, all the undulations of sonority. . . . But all has not been said when one has praised the melody, and the harmony. There is 'Song,' beautifully attired; the musician takes it by the hand and places it in a setting of instrumentation which has languor, grace, buoyancy, and color."

R. A. Streatfeild noted that while *Zampa* is often called a French *Don Giovanni*, "the music owes far more to Weber than to Mozart, while the fantastic and absurd incidents of the plot have little of the supernatural terror of Mozart's opera. . . . It would be vain to look in Herold's score for an echo of the passion and variety of Mozart, but much of the music of *Zampa* is picturesque and effective."

Zampa was well received in Paris at its première, establishing itself immediately as a classic in *opéra-comique*. But the work enjoyed even greater triumphs in Germany, where it has continued to be a favorite of opera audiences. The first American presentation took place at the Park Theatre in New York on August 12, 1833. The overture is a staple of the light music repertory throughout the Western world.

Herold's second major *opéra-comique* was *Le Pré aux clercs*, which opened in Paris on December 15, 1832, at the Opéra-Comique. The French have been even more faithful to this work than to *Zampa*. *Le Pré aux clercs* was performed over fifteen hundred times during the nineteenth century. The libretto, by Planard, was based on a historical tale of Mérimèe. Herold's score has been characterized in Grove's *Dictionary of Music and Musicians* as possessing "unity of style, variety of accent, and sustained inspiration always kept within the limits of truth." The first American performance of the work took place in New York on July 3, 1843.

Le Pré aux clercs was Herold's last work. On January 19, 1833, only a month after its première, the composer died of consumption at his home in Les Ternes. On his deathbed, Herold remarked sadly: "I go too soon! I have only just begun to learn how to write for the theater." He left an unfinished opera, *Ludovic,* which was completed by Jacques Halévy and produced on May 16, 1833.

"Herold," wrote Arthur Pougin, "was the most important musician in the first half of the nineteenth century, and his name marks an important epoch in the history of national art. . . . With him, dramatic music freed itself from the fetters which had formerly bound it; it soared fully and freely into the air, definitely and permanently repudiating former formulas."

PRINCIPAL WORKS

Ballets—Astolphe et Joconde; La Somnambule; Lydie; La Fille mal gardée; La Belle au bois dormant; La Noce de village.

Chamber Music—3 string quartets; 2 violin sonatas; Trio concertant, for two bassoons and horn.

Operas—Les Rosières; La Clochette; Le Premier venu; Le Troqueurs; L'Amour platonique; Le Muletier; Marie; Zampa; La Médicine sans médecin; Le Pré aux clercs; Ludovic (completed by Halévy).

Orchestral Music—4 piano concertos; 2 symphonies.

Piano Music—23 rondos; 10 sonatas; 9 caprices; 7 sets of variations.

ABOUT

Berlioz, H., Les Musiciens et la musique; Herold, F., Souvenirs inédits; Jouvin, B., Herold: Sa vie et ses œuvres; Pougin, A., Herold.

Johann Adam Hiller *1728-1804*

JOHANN ADAM HILLER was one of the originators of the *Singspiel,* which predated and developed into German comic opera. He was born Johann Adam Hüller in Wendisch-Ossig, near Görlitz, Silesia, on December 25, 1728. His father, a schoolmaster and parish clerk, died when Johann was just six. The boy attended the Görlitz high school, where he received some instruction in violin and harpsichord; during this period he also sang in a choir. In 1746 he enrolled at the Kreuzschule in Dresden; there he studied harpsichord and thoroughbass with Homilius. At the Kreuzschule, Hiller had the opportunity to hear the operas of Hasse and Graun, which impressed him so deeply that he copied out some of the scores by hand. During these years he earned his living by singing, and by playing flute in various orchestras.

For all his absorption in music, Hiller at first had no intention of becoming a professional musician. In 1751 he went to Leipzig and entered the University to study law. He did, however, continue to study with local music teachers, and began to compose as well, completing several symphonies, cantatas, and German songs. Hiller also participated in performances of the Grosses Concert.

Upon leaving the University in 1754, Hiller entered the employ of Count Brühl as tutor to the Count's nephew. In 1758, when the Count and his family went to live in Leipzig, Hiller accompanied them. A few years later, however, he resigned from this post to devote himself completely to music. Hiller now became an enthusiastic promoter of concert activities in Leipzig, whose musical life had declined during the Seven Years' War. In 1763 he became director of the Liebhaber Concerte, which gave impressive performances of choral music. Eight years later he founded a school of singing, which soon enriched Leipzig with outstanding performances of the oratorios of Handel, Graun, Hasse, and others. In 1776 he established the Concert Spirituel for orchestral performances; renamed the Gewandhaus Orchestra, in 1781, this distinguished group achieved world renown. For several years Hiller conducted the Gewandhaus orchestra and was responsible not only for establishing it as a permanent institution but for creating high standards of performance.

Coincident with these varied activities, Hiller began to write the *Singspiel*, a kind of German musical comedy utilizing lively texts of mass appeal, with spoken dialogue in place of recitatives and popular German folk tunes and songs in place of opera arias. Hiller's first *Singspiel* was *Die verwandelten Weiber,* or *Der Teufel ist los,* produced in Leipzig on May 28, 1766; the score included an overture and twenty-five vocal pieces. So successful was this stage work that Hiller was prevailed upon to write many more *Singspiele* in a similar style and spirit. Thus Hiller became the founder of a branch of the German musical theater that enjoyed immense popularity for many years and a contributor of very great importance. His most successful musicals included the following: *Lottchen am Hofe* in 1767; *Die Liebe auf dem Lande* in 1768; and *Die Jagd,* in 1770, which was performed extensively throughout Germany in the nineteenth century and has been revived occasionally in the twentieth century. Hiller's music for these various pro-

ductions, said Burney, "was so natural and so agreeable that the favorite airs . . . were sung by all classes of people, and some of them in the streets."

In 1785 Hiller became court conductor at the palace of the Duke of Courland in Mitau. He held this post for only a single year; then, on June 30, 1789, he was appointed cantor and music director of the Thomasschule in Leipzig, remaining until 1801, when he was forced to resign because of poor health. He died in Leipzig on June 16, 1804. Several of his pupils raised funds to erect a monument to his memory in 1832; it was situated on a promenade near his home in Leipzig.

Hiller's great contribution to music was as a creator of the German musical theater—and it has been conceded that Mozart's German comic operas had their roots in these *Singspiele.* As Donald Jay Grout has pointed out, Hiller's *Singspiele* were filled with "all those ideas which made . . . the comic opera . . . a genuine popular manifestation."

Hiller was also a major figure in the early development of the German song, creating a species of the *Lied.*

As an editor, Hiller was responsible for new editions of works by Pergolesi, Graun, and Handel, among others, and for collections in which important compositions by contemporaries were saved from obscurity. As an author, Hiller produced several notable educational treatises.

PRINCIPAL WORKS

Chamber Music—3 string quartets.

Choral Music—Allgemeines Choral-Melodienbuch für Kirchen und Schulen; Psalm C; cantatas, Mass, oratorio, Stabat Mater, and numerous shorter works.

Operas (Singspiele)—Die verwandelten Weiber; Der lustige Schuster; Lisuart und Dariolette; Lottchen am Hofe; Die Liebe auf dem Lande; Die Jagd; Der Dorfbarbier; Der Ärndtekranz; Der Krieg; Die Jubelhochzeit Das Grab des Mufti.

Orchestral Music—Symphony.

Piano Music—2 sonatas.

Vocal Music—Lieder für Kinder; Lieder mit Melodien an meinem Canarienvogel; Letztes Opfer in einigen Lieder-Melodien; Sacred Songs.

ABOUT

Calmus, G., Die ersten deutschen Singspiele; Einstein, A. (editor), Lebensläufe deutscher Musiker, vol. 1; Peiser, K., Johann Adam Hiller; Schering, A., Das Zeitalter J. S. Bachs und Johann Adam Hillers.

Johann Hummel *1778-1837*

JOHANN NEPOMUK HUMMEL was born in Pressburg, Hungary, on November 14, 1778. His father, who was director of the Imperial School of Military Music, tried to teach Johann violin when he was just three, but the child showed such indifference to this instrument that his father wisely directed him to piano. From the first Hummel loved the keyboard and practiced incessantly.

When the Imperial School closed in 1785, the Hummel family moved to Vienna, where Johann's father became a conductor at Schikaneder's theater. Through Schikaneder the child Hummel, aged seven, was introduced to Mozart. Delighted with Hummel's performance of several Bach compositions, Mozart offered to become his teacher, and invited the boy to live with him in his apartment on the Grosse-Schulerstrasse so that he might better supervise Hummel's education. Hummel remained with Mozart for two years.

In 1787 Johann made his piano debut in Dresden, at a concert at which Mozart was principal performer. This performance was highly successful, and in 1788 he was engaged to make an extensive concert tour. He toured most of Europe during the next few years, acclaimed everywhere as an outstanding prodigy. At a concert in Oxford, in October 1788, he introduced his first string quartet. Early in 1791 Johann arrived in London. There he met Haydn, who referred to him as the "wonder child" and dedicated a piano sonata to him. Hummel's stay in London was a profitable one. In 1792 he gave a remarkable concert, performing a Mozart concerto and one of his own sonatas. His first publications appeared: three *Airs variés* and several sonatas. And before leaving England he was able to receive piano instruction from Clementi.

By the time he returned to Vienna in 1793, the fifteen-year-old boy was regarded as one of Europe's foremost piano virtuosos. His father, however, insisted that he needed further instruction in music, so Johann continued to study with Albrechtsberger, Salieri, and Haydn. During these years his performances were confined mainly to private salons. He devoted himself, rather, to teaching piano and to composition, completing among other works a set of three fugues, several series of variations, and a few sonatas, all for piano.

In 1804, after several concert appearances in Russia, Hummel, on Haydn's recommendation, became *Kapellmeister* to Prince Esterházy at Eisenstadt. The position enabled him to engage in several creative efforts. He completed his first sacred work, the Mass in B-flat major, in 1805. His first opera, *Mathilde von Guise,* was performed in Vienna in 1810. He also completed several scores for ballets and pantomimes, works of chamber music, and compositions for piano.

In 1810 a rift occurred between Hummel and Beethoven, often detailed in biographies of Beethoven. Hummel and Beethoven had crossed paths frequently since about 1787, and Beethoven had often expressed his admiration for the younger musician. But in 1810, after a performance of Beethoven's Mass in C major in Eisenstadt, Beethoven misinterpreted Hummel's laughter as criticism of his music. Without asking for an explanation, Beethoven refused to have anything to do with Hummel and dismissed rudely every effort on Hummel's part to clarify the misunderstanding. By 1814, however, his wrath had apparently subsided, for he invited Hummel to conduct the battery of "drums and cannonades" in a projected performance of Beethoven's *Battle Symphony.* Hummel and his wife visited Beethoven years later, at his deathbed in 1827, and Hummel was a pallbearer at Beethoven's funeral.

In 1811 Hummel was dismissed from Eisenstadt, accused by Esterházy of neglect of duty. For a while he earned his living teaching piano in Vienna. On May 16, 1813, he married Elisabeth Roeckl, an opera singer. Three years later Hummel became *Kapellmeister* in Stuttgart, and in 1819 he accepted a similar post in Weimar. While holding these offices, he made numerous concert tours, maintaining a leading position among Europe's great piano virtuosos with his unsurpassed gifts of improvisation. Some of his advanced ideas of piano technique, particularly of fingering, were incorporated into a theoretical treatise, *Piano School,* one of the finest works on piano method that had yet appeared.

After leaving Weimar, Hummel visited Paris and London several times. In 1825 he was made Chevalier of the Legion of Honor in Paris. In the early 1830's Hummel gave up concert work to devote himself to conducting. In 1833 he became conductor of German Opera at the King's theatre in London, but remained only a single season.

The last years of Hummel's life were marred by poor health and physical pain. He died in Weimar on October 17, 1837.

Hummel did not give a favorable impression at first sight. Karl Czerny described him as "a very striking young man, with an unpleasant, common-looking face that constantly twitched." He was large, ungainly and coarse; was extremely careless of his dress and manners; wore expensive diamond rings on almost all his fingers. Harold C. Schonberg adds: "His face was pitted by small-pox. . . . In later life he grew monstrously stout, and a place had to be cut into his dining room table, both at home and at court. When he played he puffed, blew and perspired." But his personal charm, ingratiating sense of humor, and warmth compensated for his appearance and endeared him to all who knew him.

Hummel's contemporaries and immediate successors tended to magnify his gifts as composer. Schumann, for example, maintained that Hummel's Piano Sonata in F-sharp minor would have been enough to ensure his immortality. Fétis insisted that had Beethoven been born twenty-five years later, Hummel would have been recognized as the "greatest instrumental composer of his era." A later generation has gone to an opposite extreme, underestimating Hummel. Today his work is virtually unknown in the concert hall. Yet on occasions when his chamber music is revived or made available on recordings, music lovers become strongly aware of his considerable gifts and contemporary appeal. Though Hummel lacked profundity of emotion, he possessed an aristocratic style and grace and a commanding technique. These virtues invariably make for pleasant listening.

PRINCIPAL WORKS

Ballets—Helene und Paris; Das belebte Gemälde; Harlekin und Kolumbine; Sapho de Mitylène.

Chamber Music—6 piano trios; 3 string quartets; 3 violin sonatas; 2 quintets; 2 septets; various sonatas for solo instruments and piano.

Choral Music—3 Masses; Polymelos russischer Nationallieder.

Operas—Mathilde von Guise; Die gute Nachricht; Die Rückfahrt des Kaisers; Jeannette und Colin.

JOHANN HUMMEL

Orchestral Music—4 piano concertos; Piano Concertino in G major; Les Adieux, for piano and orchestra; Oberons Zauberhorn, for piano and orchestra; Potpourri, for viola and orchestra; Potpourri, for cello and orchestra; Variations for oboe (or clarinet) and orchestra; dances, nocturnes, waltzes.

Piano Music—Dances, fantasies, fugues, marches, minuets, preludes, rondos, sonatas, variations; 2 sonatas for piano duet; Rondo, for two pianos.

ABOUT

Bacharach, A. L. (editor), The Music Masters, vol. 1; Batka, J., and Wodianer, E., Johann Nepomuk Hummel; Benyovszky, K., Johann Hummel: Der Mensch und Künstler; Schonberg, H. C., The Great Pianists.

Engelbert Humperdinck *1854-1921*

ENGELBERT HUMPERDINCK, composer of *Hänsel und Gretel,* was born in Siegburg, near Bonn, Germany, on September 1, 1854. He attended the Paderborn School, preparing himself to study architecture in Cologne. It was in music, however, that he distinguished himself, showing such pronounced gifts that he was asked to write the music for a school production of a Goethe drama. In Cologne, the renowned musician Ferdinand Hiller persuaded Humperdinck to give up architecture for music; and in 1872 he entered the Cologne Conservatory. Under such teachers as Hiller, Jensen, and Gernsheim he made marked progress. In 1876 he won the Mozart Prize,

ENGELBERT HUMPERDINCK

which enabled him to go to Munich. After a period of study with Lachner, Humperdinck attended the Royal School of Music from 1877 to 1879, studying with Rheinberger.

In 1879 Humperdinck won the much-coveted Mendelssohn Foundation Award, which gave him an opportunity to travel in Italy. At the Villa d'Angri, near Naples, Humperdinck met Richard Wagner, who took an interest in him and playfully nicknamed him "*Humpchen.*" Wagner invited Humperdinck to Bayreuth to assist in the production of the world première of *Parsifal.* Humperdinck arrived at the Wagnerian shrine in 1880, and worked eagerly at any task he was given to perform, whether it was as stage manager, rehearser, or copyist. There is reason to believe that several bars in one of the opera's transitional passages were written by Humperdinck and allowed to remain in the score with Wagner's consent.

In 1881 Humperdinck received a third prize, the Meyerbeer Award, from Berlin, amounting to about two thousand dollars. With these funds he was able to go on an extended trip to France, Italy, and Spain. In Venice, where Wagner was vacationing, the older composer asked Humperdinck, as a birthday gift to his wife, Cosima, to direct a private performance of Wagner's early Symphony in C. Soon afterwards Wagner tried without success to obtain for Humperdinck the post of director of the Benedetto Marcello Conservatory in Venice. Humper-

dinck went on to France. He was in Paris when he received the news of Wagner's sudden death in February 1883. Humperdinck remained a close friend of the Wagner family; he was the only teacher entrusted with the musical education of Wagner's son, Siegfried.

After moving to Spain in 1885, Humperdinck was appointed professor of musical theory at the Barcelona Conservatory. He remained for two years, then returned to Germany, to work for a while in the publishing establishment of Schott in Mayence. In 1890 he transferred his home to Frankfurt am Main, assuming a professional post at the Hoch Conservatory. During his six-year tenure, he also gave voice instruction at Stockhausen's school and wrote music criticism for the *Frankfurter Zeitung.*

Thus far Humperdinck had accomplished little creatively. In 1880 he had written a *Humoreske* for orchestra, which was performed by several German orchestras; between 1884 and 1887 he completed two ballads for chorus and orchestras; and in 1889 he prepared a new adaptation of Auber's *opéra-comique, Le Cheval de bronze.* None of these works, however, hinted at the sudden and widespread fame that would soon attend his opera, *Hänsel und Gretel.*

The work was, originally, a modest undertaking. Humperdinck's sister, Adelheid Wetter, had adapted the fairy tale into a play with which she planned to entertain the children of the Humperdinck family. She asked her brother to write some music for this performance. In preparing several songs for this amateur production, Humperdinck grew so enthusiastic about the project that he decided to set the entire play to music. By the time he had completed it he was convinced that the work was worthy of operatic production. He revised and expanded the score, and dispatched the manuscript to Richard Strauss. Strauss not only described the opera as "a masterwork of the first order," but agreed to conduct its world première on December 23, 1893, in Weimar.

The opera took its audience by storm. Nor was Weimar alone to succumb to its fairy-tale charm and enchantment. Within a year there was hardly a stage in Germany that had not presented *Hänsel und Gretel to* delighted audiences. The opera rapidly circled the globe. Its first American presentation took place on December 8, 1895, at Daly's Theatre in New York in an English translation. On November 25, 1905, it was performed for the first time by the Metropolitan Opera, this time in the original German. Since then *Hänsel und Gretel* has become a children's classic, particularly favored during the Christmas season, though it has no topical connection with the Yuletide.

In his first work for the operatic stage, Humperdinck leaned heavily on Wagner. As H. E. Krehbiel wrote, "Humperdinck built up his musical structure in *Hansel and Gretel* in the Wagnerian manner, and he has done so with such fluency and deftness that a musical layman might listen to it from beginning to end without suspecting the fact save from the occasional employment of what may be called Wagnerian idioms. The little work is replete with melodies nearly all of which derive their physiognomy from two little songs which the children sing at the beginning of the first and second acts, and which are frankly borrowed from the folksong literature of Germany. These ditties, however . . . contribute characteristic themes out of which the orchestral part is constructed; and these themes are developed in accordance with an interrelated scheme every bit as logical and consistent as the scheme at the bottom of *Tristan and Isolde.*"

Paradoxically enough, in view of its Wagnerian derivations, *Hänsel und Gretel* attained its overwhelming success in Germany partly because some of its admirers regarded it as a reaction against Wagner. Many of those who were most enchanted with *Hänsel und Gretel* had no sympathy for the Wagnerian music drama. What delighted them was the beauty of the folk-like songs and dances, the spontaneity and charm of the style, and an opera libretto that was devoid of any kind of symbolism or heavy philosophical implication. For the great strength of Humperdinck's opera lay in the fact that, as R. A. Streatfeild said, it "reproduced with infinite art, the tender and childlike charm of the delightful old fairy tale." Indeed, *Hänsel und Gretel* brought into being a new genre of opera popular in Germany in the early 1900's, which drew its texts from fairy tales.

The world-wide success of *Hänsel und Gretel* made it possible for Humperdinck to resign his duties as teacher and critic in order to concentrate on composition. In 1895 he wrote a fairy play with music, *Die sieben Geislein,* following it with two operas, *Dornröschen* in 1902 and *Die Heirat wider Wil-*

len in 1905. His next work was *Die Königskinder,* the only other opera by Humperdinck besides *Hänsel und Gretel* to be heard in European opera houses today. Its world première took place in America, during Humperdinck's only visit to the United States, at New York's Metropolitan Opera, on December 28, 1910. This opera was still deeply rooted in Wagnerism, though its libretto was again derived from a fairy tale. Humperdinck's score, however, was revolutionary, often replacing formal lyricism with a kind of song speech in which dialogue is declaimed rather than sung, and set off against orchestral accompaniment.

In 1900, four years after the Kaiser had bestowed on him the honorary title of Professor, Humperdinck returned to pedagogy, becoming director of the Akademische Meisterschule in Berlin. At this time he was also a member of the Senate of the Royal Academy of Arts.

In 1910 Humperdinck wrote the incidental music for Max Reinhardt's production of *The Miracle.* The following winter he suffered an apoplectic stroke that paralyzed his left arm. He went into complete retirement, attended only by a faithful servant. During World War I, Humperdinck drew up a manifesto, signed by ninety-five German professors, denying that atrocities were being perpetrated by German soldiers, and insisting that Germany was the victim, not the aggressor, in the war.

Humperdinck's last opera, *Gaudeamus,* was produced in Darmstadt on March 18, 1919. He died of an apoplectic stroke in Neustrelitz on September 27, 1921.

Humperdinck's music was influential in arousing the interest of German composers in their folk music. As Paul Bekker said, "The example set by Humperdinck's treatment of the orchestra—combination of simple melody with an appearance of artistic polyphony and harmonic logic—proved handy for German composers of household music, and was exploited in a rich, practical literature of genre pieces, idylls, comic or light operas in small forms."

PRINCIPAL WORKS

Chamber Music—String Quartet.
Choral Music—Das Glück von Edenhall; Die Wallfahrt nach Kevlaar; various choruses for mixed or male voices.
Operas—Hänsel und Gretel; Die sieben Geislein; Dornröschen; Die Heirat wider Willen; Königskinder; Die Marktenderin; Gaudeamus.

Orchestral Music—Humoreske; Maurische Rhapsodie; Five Songs, for voice and orchestra.

Vocal Music—Kinderlieder; various songs for voice and piano, including Am Rhein, Weihnachten, Wiegenlied.

ABOUT

Besch, O., Humperdinck; Kuhlmann, H., Stil und Form in der Musik von Humperdincks Oper Hänsel und Gretel; Newman, E., Stories of the Great Operas, vol. 3.

Musical America, October 8, 1921; Musical Quarterly, April 1915.

Clément Jannequin *1485-1560*

CLÉMENT JANNEQUIN (JANNEQUIN), an important Renaissance composer, was born in Châtellerault, France, in or about 1485. Almost all available biographical information is conjecture. It is believed that he received his musical education from Josquin des Prés, of whom he became a disciple. He then, presumably, entered the service of Louis Ronsard (father of Pierre Ronsard, the poet) and in all probability accompanied his employer during the Italian campaigns between 1507 and 1515. In or about 1520 he probably visited Paris and Spain. After a period in Bordeaux he served with the Cardinal of Lorraine, whose victories he celebrated in several significant *chansons*. From 1545 to 1558 he was the curate of Unverre. His old age was spent in poverty and bitterness, which he lamented in a poetic dedication written in 1559. He died in or about 1560; the place of his death is not known.

Jannequin was a leading exponent of the sixteenth century polyphonic *chanson*. His numerous four-voice *chansons*, which appeared from 1529 on, are remarkable for their descriptive, and at times realistic, tone painting. "By resorting to this device," says Karl Nef, "Clément Jannequin introduced a species of portraiture *chanson* which gives precious illustrations of the life of the day. Well known is his *Bataille de Marignan,* which paints with realism the entire course of events. Indeed, the realism goes so far that at the close, the voices of the defeated Swiss suddenly resound in a Swiss German dialect, as the French understand it. . . . In *La Chasse* we are present at a court hunt. At the end, the king despatches the deer with his own hand. In *Le Chant des oiseaux* we hear a piquant bird concert, of starlings and nightingales; also something similar, inter-

mixed with references to the gallant life, in *L'Alouette. . . . Les Cris de Paris* is a theme which modern orchestral composers have again taken up. The title *Le Caquet des femmes* scarcely savors of gallantry; its execution demands, above all, great lingual facility. In their vivacity and joviality, with their characteristic tonal effects, these creations are thoroughly original. Through them, Jannequin, as a true national composer, has given expression to a vein of French national genius."

In addition to his realistic *chansons,* Jannequin wrote others that are amorous, humorous, or satirical.

PRINCIPAL WORKS

Choral Music—2 Masses; Proverbs de Salomon; Octante deux psaumes de David; Motet; chansons.

ABOUT

Levron, J., Clément Jannequin, musicien de la Renaissance; Reese, G., Music in the Renaissance.

Le Ménestrel, January 21, 1927; Revue de musicologie, February 1923; Revue musical belge, March 1934.

Niccolò Jommelli *1714-1774*

NICCOLÒ JOMMELLI, an outstanding representative of the Neapolitan school of opera, was born in Aversa, near Naples, on September 10, 1714. He received some preliminary music instruction from the canon Mazillo, and it is probable that he attended one or two of the music schools in Naples. His first opera, *L'Errore amoroso,* was produced in Naples in 1737 and was well received. The legend that Jommelli was so unsure of its worth that he presented it under an assumed name is clearly false, for the original libretto carries his name. Jommelli's second opera, *Odoardo,* in 1738, was also successful.

In 1740 Jommelli went to Rome where, under the patronage of the Cardinal Duke of York, he wrote and produced two new operas, *Ricimero* (1740) and *Astianatte.* These led to a commission from Bologna for a new work. While working on this project—*Ezio,* produced in 1741—Jommelli met Padre Martini and asked to be his pupil. Martini provided Jommelli with a theme to be developed fugally. When Jommelli completed the assignment, Martini asked him: "Do you come to mock me? It is *I* who should study with

Jannequin: zhăn-ē-kăn′   **Jommelli:** yōm-mĕl′lē

you." Jommelli did not become Martini's pupil, but he profited greatly from the master's advice and criticism.

By 1743 Jommelli's reputation had spread throughout Italy. That year he was appointed director of the Conservatorio degli Incurabili, in which capacity he expanded his creative efforts, writing a great deal of sacred music as well as opera. Indicative of his eminence in Naples is the fact that he was asked to select the candidate for an important *maestro di cappella* post which had become vacant.

In 1749 Jommelli visited Vienna, and became friendly with Metastasio, the distinguished poet and librettist. Jommelli's opera *Didone abbandonata,* which had been introduced two years earlier in Rome, proved a triumph in Vienna. As its librettist, Cesareo, reported to the Princess of Belmont, "Its music fairly astonished the court. It is so full of elegance of ideas, novelty of harmony, and above all deep expression." The Empress Maria Theresa showered Jommelli with gifts. The composer wrote two operas that year, *Catone in Utica* and *Achille in Sciro,* before leaving Vienna.

After his return to Rome, Jommelli was assistant *maestro di cappella* at St. Peter's Cathedral from 1751 to 1753. In 1753 he went to Stuttgart, where for sixteen years he was *Kapellmeister* for the Duke of Württemberg, at the extraordinary salary of four thousand florins a year. He continued to write operas with extraordinary productivity. Hardly a year passed without the production of at least one of his works in Stuttgart, or in various Italian opera houses. He also completed several significant choral works, including a Requiem and an oratorio.

In 1769 Jommelli returned to his native land because of his health. After 1770 he lived in Aversa, supported by a handsome pension that had recently been presented to him by the King of Portugal. Jommelli wrote three operas for the king; they were produced in Lisbon between 1772 and 1775. In these last years the failure of two of his operas in Naples broke his spirit, and he sought refuge in writing church music. One of these pieces, a Miserere in G minor, is regarded by some critics as his masterpiece.

Niccolò Jommelli died in Naples on August 25, 1774, the victim of an apoplectic stroke. "Yesterday," reported his friend Saverio Mattei, "all the musicians of the

NICCOLÒ JOMMELLI

city united in attending the funeral of the great Jommelli. The church was very finely ornamented; and a great number of wax tapers placed about the pompous bier. Two orchestras of three rows . . . executed the music that was expressly composed for this occasion by the worthy Sabatini. . . . At the desire of Signor Manna, not only every musician attended the funeral and performed gratis, but contributed likewise towards the expenses of this solemnity."

Although he was strikingly handsome in his earlier years, Jommelli's excessive corpulence in middle age destroyed all traces of his former physical beauty. He retained, nevertheless, the gracious, worldly manners and cultivation which charmed all who knew him.

Jommelli was one of the most prolific opera composers of his time, completing about eighty works for the stage. His earlier operas followed rigidly the aesthetics and methods crystallized by the Neapolitans. But after his stay in Germany, Germanic influences began to be evident in his writing. His later operas were so rich in harmonic structure, dramatic in lyricism, and attentive to orchestration, that many came to call him "the Italian Gluck."

Donald Jay Grout pointed out, however, that while Jommelli's later operas may anticipate Gluck in certain respects, they did not break with Neapolitan traditions altogether: "In spite of all changes in details.

the works remain singers' operas, with the old virtuoso display, improvised embellishments and cadenzas. Furthermore . . . the style of the music itself is still essentially rococo; it is, for the most part, primarily elegant and polished rather than simple and passionate."

PRINCIPAL WORKS

Choral Music—Laudate; Dixit; In convertendo; Magnificat; Hymn to St. Peter; Miserere in G; Oratorio of the Passion; Requiem.

Operas—About 80, including: Merope; Ezio; Achille in Sciro; Catone in Utica; Eumene; Alessandro nell' Indie; Didone abbandonata; Artaserse; Demetrio; La Clemenza di Tito; Armida; Ifigenia in Tauride.

ABOUT

Abert, H., Niccolò Jommelli als Opernkomponist.

Musical Standard, June 2, 1917.

Josquin des Prés 1450-1521

JOSQUIN DES PRÉS, master of the Netherlands or Flemish school of contrapuntists, and one of the leading composers of his age, was born in Hainaut (possibly in Condé-sur-l'Escaut) in or about 1450. As a boy he sang in the choir of the Collegiate Church at St. Quentin; he subsequently became canon and choirmaster of the Collegiate Church. Josquin is believed to have studied with Okeghem, whom he admired profoundly, and whose influence upon him was far-reaching. In 1475 Josquin went to Milan, and served five years in the court of Duke Galeazzo Sforza. After that, for a brief period, he resided in Florence, attached to the brilliant court of Lorenzo the Magnificent. From 1486 to 1494 he was a member of the papal choir under Popes Innocent VIII and Alexander VI. In 1494 he left Italy to join the chapel of Louis XII in France, and from 1495 to 1499 was choirmaster of the Cambrai Cathedral.

Josquin's first book of Masses, and some of his earliest motets, appeared in 1502. The second and third volumes of Masses followed in 1512 and 1516, respectively. In or about 1516 Josquin became canon of the Collegiate Church of Condé. His last years were spent in Condé-sur-l'Escaut, where he died on August 27, 1521.

Josquin des Prés was an extremely self-critical composer who refused to publish any of his works that did not meet his most

JOSQUIN DES PRÉS

exacting standards. He wrote music only when he was moved to do so; even the most handsome commission could not persuade him to compose when he did not feel the inclination.

Josquin exerted a powerful influence as a teacher. Adrian Petit Coclius, one of his pupils, recalled: "My teacher never gave a lecture on music or wrote a theoretical work, and yet he was able in a short time to form complete musicians. He did not keep his pupils busy with long and useless instructions, but he taught them the rules in a few words during singing."

Josquin was the greatest composer to appear in Europe before the age of Orlando de Lasso and Palestrina. His impact on his contemporaries and immediate successors was enormous. He developed canonic writing and imitation from a comparatively primitive technique into a highly subtle and complex art. He brought to polyphonic writing a mastery that was inconceivable before him, and introduced to it a poetic expressiveness and a lyrical beauty which it had never known. He was also perhaps the first important composer to emphasize melody and harmony.

The historian Ambros considered Josquin "the first musician [in history] who impresses us with genius. There speaks in the music of Josquin a warm sensitiveness, a capacity for urgent emotion, a mystic awe of worship. His Masses are noble with the no-

Josquin des Prés: zhôs-kăɴ' dä prā'

bility of the heart's depth. .... In his other works, the abstract, elevated style of the earlier composers is broken up by the prism into a glowing play of many colors. Here are sadness, pain, and bitter revolt; and here are intimate love, tender sympathy, and playful jest. It is an unprecedented stride forward which occurs with Josquin; in him there is 'lived through' an art development such as is found in no artist previously."

In *Music in History,* Howard D. McKinney and W. R. Anderson wrote: "Like Beethoven, Josquin lived and wrote in two epochs: in him was united the Gothic ideal of art, the ability of creating a universal expression out of a multiplicity of individual elements, with that of the Renaissance, the idea of creating art for its own sake. He may be said to have been the first composer to express in music the ideals of the Renaissance. His imagination was able to seize on the spirit of a text, whether solemn or majestic, passionate or serious, secular or sacred, and to express it with something like definite exactness."

Josquin was Martin Luther's favorite composer. Luther said of him: "He is the master of his notes. They have to do as he bids them. Other composers have to do as the notes will."

Of Josquin's seventeen Masses, one of the most significant is *L'Homme armé,* found in the first volume of his Masses, issued in 1502. *L'Homme armé* is, of course, the famous French *chanson* that for two centuries was used by almost every outstanding contrapuntist as basic material for a Mass. Josquin used the song in a novel way by transposing it, in each section of the Mass, one step higher in the hexachord—in C for the Kyrie, D for the Gloria, and so on.

One of the most beautiful of Josquin's motets is an Ave Maria for four voices, in which contrapuntal technique is made subordinate to a compelling motif. The thematic material is here derived from the Gregorian chant and embellished by Josquin.

PRINCIPAL WORKS

Choral Music—Chansons, Masses, motets.

ABOUT

Blume, F., Josquin des Prés; Delpvech, L. C., Josquin des Prés, l'homme, le musicien; Osthoff, H., Josquin Desprez; Reese, G., Music in the Renaissance; Sollitt, E. R., From Dufay to Sweelinck; Wooldridge, H. E., Oxford History of Music, vol. 2.

Vassili Kalinnikov *1866-1901*

VASSILI SERGEIVICH KALINNIKOV was born in Voin, near Mtsensk, Russia, on January 13, 1866. He was the son of a police official. As a boy, Kalinnikov attended the Orel Seminary, where he sang in the choir. Attempting to obtain more advanced music instruction, he went to Moscow in 1884 and attended the Conservatory for about a year, but was forced to leave because he could not obtain the money for tuition. He next enrolled in the free music school of the Moscow Philharmonic, where he was taught bassoon. He supported himself by playing bassoon in theater orchestras. One of his efforts as a student at the music school was a tone poem, *The Nymphs,* introduced in Moscow on December 28, 1889.

Kalinnikov graduated from the music school in 1892, and the next year was appointed second conductor of the Italian Opera in Moscow. He held this post only one year, for in 1894 he discovered that he was suffering from tuberculosis. Seeking a cure in a more favorable climate, he settled in the Ukraine and devoted himself to composition. It is there that he completed the work which spread his name throughout the world of music, the Symphony No. 1 in G minor, introduced in Kiev on February 20, 1897. This richly melodic work of strong national identity was highly acclaimed and was soon introduced in Berlin, Vienna, Paris, and London. "This work," wrote Charles O'Connell, "is not designed along the lines of the massive Tchaikovsky symphonies, yet in its more modest way it can be considered of value equal to any of them. Like them, it is influenced by Russian folk music, though it does not appear that there is any literal use of a folk tune." Kalinnikov's Second Symphony, heard in Kiev on March 12, 1898, was far less successful.

As a result of his irregular habits and undisciplined behavior, Kalinnikov's health soon broke down completely. He went to Yalta for treatment, and there he died on January 11, 1901, at the age of thirty-five. The handful of orchestral works he wrote in his short life are of such distinction, so fresh and spontaneous in content, that it is apparent his premature death robbed the music world of a highly gifted composer.

In 1951, on the fiftieth anniversary of Kalinnikov's death, the Soviet government, in an attempt to popularize his music, pub-lished some of his manuscripts.

PRINCIPAL WORKS
Chamber Music—String Quartet.
Choral Music—John of Damascus; Russalka.
Orchestral Music—2 symphonies; The Nymphs, The Cedar and the Palm; Overture and entr'actes to Czar Boris; Prelude to In the Year of 1812; Suite; Bylina; Serenade, for strings; 2 symphonic sketches; 2 intermezzi.
Piano Music—4 Pieces.
Vocal Music—9 songs, including On the old Burial Ground.

ABOUT
Paskhalov, V. S., Kalinnikov, Life and Works.

Reinhard Keiser *1674-1739*

REINHARD KEISER, one of Germany's earliest composers of opera, was born in Teuchern, near Weissenfels, on January 9, 1674. His father, an eminent composer of church music and an organist, gave him his first music lessons. After that Keiser entered the Thomasschule in Leipzig, where he studied with Johann Schelle. Then, in 1692, he went to Brunswick and studied for a while with the court conductor, Kusser. When Kusser left Brunswick in 1694, Keiser succeeded him at court, serving both as con-ductor and as chamber musician. During that year three operas by Keiser were intro-duced; *Basilius*, his first, was presented in Hamburg, the other two in Salzthal and Brunswick.

In 1696 Keiser followed Kusser to Ham-burg, where he was engaged as principal conductor of the Opera, then one of the lead-ing musical institutions in Europe. His first work for the Hamburg Opera was *Mahumeth II*, produced in 1696. During the next forty years, Keiser composed a vast number of operas, most of them for performance in Hamburg. In some years as many as four or five operas were performed in a single season. In all, Keiser wrote about 125 works for the stage.

Keiser's operas were highly important for the development of that form in Germany. They were among the first to use German-language librettos, which were often based on popular rather than historical or mytho-logical themes. In his works Keiser combined his exceptional facility for melodic creation with a mastery of orchestration unusual for the operas of that period; he was also one of the few composers of his time to pay strict attention to the demands of his texts. The renowned Mattheson, a rival opera com-poser, echoed the general consensus in de-scribing Keiser as the most significant dra-matic composer in the world. Still another eminent opera composer of the time, Hasse, placed Keiser at the head of his generation in writing for the theater. Scheibe and Reichardt were also unsparing in their praise.

In 1700 Keiser inaugurated in Hamburg a series of winter concerts in which outstand-ing singers and instrumentalists joined with an orchestra. Three years later he became codirector, with Drüsicke, of the Hamburg Opera. The extravagance of the two men in mounting productions almost brought the theater to financial ruin, and Drüsicke was forced to flee Hamburg. Keiser was also compelled to go into hiding temporarily in order to escape creditors, but he later took over the direction of the opera house and preserved its status as the first musical thea-ter of Europe. In 1709 he married the daughter of a wealthy Hamburg merchant, Oldenberg, acquiring financial security and social status. Keiser was now able to indulge his lifelong weakness for soft living, luxury, and dissipation. His dissolute ways were notorious. In 1931 they were made the sub-ject of an opera entitled *Der tolle Kapell-meister*, whose score was derived and adapted from Keiser's own music by Benno Bardi.

In 1717 Keiser went to Copenhagen, en-joying immense popularity during his stay. Between 1719 and 1721 he was court com-poser in Stuttgart, and from 1722 to 1724 lived in Copenhagen, where he produced several operas and filled an honorary post as conductor to the king. He had returned to Hamburg by 1724; four years later he be-came canon and cantor of the Katharien-kirche in that city.

In the last years of his life Keiser produced a library of sacred music, although he con-tinued to write opera as well. His last work for the stage was *Circe*, produced in Ham-burg in 1734. Keiser died in Hamburg on September 12, 1739. Just before his death, the Hamburg Opera closed, after sixty years of historic achievement.

In both his operas and his choral music, Keiser had a remarkable gift of song. He was, as Karl Nef said of him, "one of those fortunate creatures who always have an inspiration, with whom everything turns into song. He might be compared with Mozart or Schubert, if his nature had been somewhat more profound. Depth is a quality which is always lacking in Keiser. He delights, flatters, pleases, but scarcely ever is one really moved by his music. He understood his trade and his forms are artistic."

Mattheson noted that Keiser's lyricism falls on the ear "like charmed accents after the dull pedantries of the contrapuntists of the day. . . . I believe assuredly that in the time he flourished there was no composer who . . . had set words to music so richly, naturally, flowingly, attractively or (above all) so distinctly, understandably and eloquently."

PRINCIPAL WORKS
Choral Music—Cantatas, motets, oratorios, Passions, psalms.

Operas—About 125, including: Mahumeth II; Der geliebte Adonis; Orpheus; Die wunderschöne Psyche; Almira; Aurora; Der hochmüthige . . . Croesus; L'Inganno fedele; Ulysses; Der Hamburger Jahrmarckt; Der lächerliche Printz Jodelet; Circe.

ABOUT
Grout, D. J., A Short History of Opera; Leichtentritt, H., Reinhard Keiser in seinen Opern; Lindner, E. O., Die erste stehende deutsche Oper.

Friedrich Kuhlau *1786-1832*

DANIEL FRIEDRICH RUDOLPH KUHLAU, distinguished Danish composer, was born in Ülzen, Hanover, Germany, on September 11, 1786. One day in early boyhood, on his way to draw water from a well, Friedrich lost his balance, hit his head, and permanently injured his right eye. During his long period of convalescence he was given piano lessons by his father, a member of a military band. A number of years later he studied flute and voice in Brunswick. At that time he also sang in the streets to earn a living. Later, in Hamburg, studying theory and composition with E. F. G. Schwencke, he taught piano to support himself. In 1808 he made his debut as a concert pianist, and published his first work, a piano sonata.

When Napoleon occupied Hamburg in 1810, Kuhlau escaped conscription by fleeing to Copenhagen, where he lived under an assumed name. When he emerged from his anonymity, he gave a concert of his works at the Theatre Royal whose success won for

FRIEDRICH KUHLAU

him a prompt invitation to give a command performance for the Queen. In 1813 he was appointed first flutist in the court orchestra. In 1814, his first score for the stage was heard, incidental music for *The Robber's Castle*. His incidental music for *The Magic Harp* in 1817, *Elisa* in 1820, and *Lulu* in 1824 added greatly to his fame. (*Lulu* is the play by Wieland which Alban Berg in the twentieth century used for his provocative expressionist opera.)

While on a brief visit to Vienna in 1825, Kuhlau met Beethoven. Though the master was not impressed with Kuhlau's improvisations, a warm friendship developed between the two composers. Beethoven composed a canon on a verse which punned on Kuhlau's name ("Kühl, nicht lau").

Returning to the town of Lyngby near Copenhagen, where he had settled permanently some years before, Kuhlau now devoted himself assiduously to composition. He wrote many works for the piano. On November 6, 1828—on the occasion of the marriage of Prince Frederick to the daughter of Frederick VI—Kuhlau's national opera, *The Fairies' Mound*, was produced; it was his most successful, as well as finest, work. In recognition of his contributions to Danish music, the honorary title of professor was conferred upon Kuhlau in 1828.

In 1830 Kuhlau's property and many of his valuable manuscripts, including an about-to-be published treatise on counter-

Kuhlau: kōō'lou

point, were destroyed in a fire. The tragedy undermined his always sensitive health. He became an invalid, and died in Copenhagen on March 12, 1832.

Piano students the world over are familiar with Kuhlau's sonatas and sonatinas which, though they have disappeared from the concert hall, retain their pedagogical value. More significant, however, are Kuhlau's many compositions for the flute, which, as Philip Hale once remarked, "afford estimable models of construction and originality."

A writer for *Etude* magazine noted the influence of the flute on works by Kuhlau which were not written for that instrument. This influence is evident in many of his piano compositions, which "abound in charming passages in the higher octaves of the piano," and "in the flowing style of his music—a style peculiar to composers who are accustomed to play on an instrument capable of sustaining long voice-like tones and at the same time capable of great flexibility."

PRINCIPAL WORKS

Chamber Music—8 violin sonatas; 3 flute quintets; 3 flute quartets; 3 piano quartets; trio concertantes for flute; duets for flute and violin; String Quartet; Divertimento, for flute and piano.

Choral Music—Part songs for male voices.

Operas and Incidental Music—The Robber's Castle; The Magic Harp; Elisa; Lulu; William Shakespeare; The Fairies' Mound.

Orchestral Music—2 piano concertos.

Piano Music—Sonatas, sonatinas.

Vocal Music—Songs for voice and piano; male quartets.

ABOUT

Thrane, K., *Friedrich Kuhlau.*

Etude, October 1914; Flutist, October-November 1927; Musician, June 1909.

Johann Kuhnau *1660-1722*

JOHANN KUHNAU was the first German composer to write sonatas for a keyboard instrument and the most important composer for the clavier before the time of Bach and Handel. He was born in Geising, Saxony, on April 6, 1660. At the age of nine he entered the Kreuzschule in Dresden, studying music with Hering and Bental. His talent soon attracted the strong interest of *Kapellmeister* Vincenzo Albrici, who would frequently keep the child as a household guest when he gave him music lessons.

In 1680 an epidemic broke out in Dresden, and Kuhnau left the city for Zittau, continuing his music studies with Edelmann. On the occasion of a municipal election he wrote a motet for two choirs. Its excellent reception brought him a cantorial post in one of the city's churches.

In 1682 Kuhnau enrolled at the University of Leipzig for the study of law. For years thereafter, he divided his interests between law and music. In 1684, while still a student, he became organist of the renowned St. Thomas Church in Leipzig. In 1688, the year in which he received his law degree, he helped found the Collegium Musicum, which gave regular series of public concerts in Leipzig. And for the next thirteen years Kuhnau pursued both law and music.

Even these two areas, however, were confining to his quick and restless intelligence. Kuhnau also studied Greek, Hebrew, and mathematics; translated books from French and Italian; wrote several treatises and a novel satirizing Italians. He was also learned, one of his contemporaries noted, in theology, rhetoric, and poetry.

In 1700 Kuhnau became music director of the University of Leipzig and of two local churches. On May 6, 1701 he became cantor of the Thomasschule. In accepting that office, he gave up his law practice to devote himself to music. For the next two decades he directed the famous choir of the school, and devoted himself to composing.

Kuhnau's last years were unhappy, marred by the tragic death of two sons and a daughter. He died in Leipzig on June 5, 1722. His post at the Thomasschule was taken over by Johann Sebastian Bach.

Kuhnau composed a large body of admirable church music, including motets, chorales, and cantatas. In these works, Camille Bellaigue remarked, "one finds . . . young and truly fresh . . . those grandiose Scholastic forms which Bach was soon to bring to maturity."

Nevertheless, Kuhnau is best known for his music for clavichord, which brought new character and articulateness to instrumental writing. "He did, indeed, possess a depth of feeling, and at the same time a beauty of form, a grace compounded of strength and lucidity which even today would make his name a household word," wrote Romain Rolland. "Kuhnau was one of the creators of the modern sonata; he wrote 'suites' for

Kuhnau: kōō′nou

the clavichord which are the models of spirited grace, occasionally tinged with reverie. He composed some descriptive poems —program music—under the title of *Biblical Sonatas;* cantatas, sacred and profane, and a Passion which make him, if we are to tell the truth, not only the immediate predecessor of Bach at the Thomasschule in Leipzig but also, in a great many respects, his indisputable model."

Kuhnau's greatest single achievement was perhaps to bring the Italian *sonata da chiesa* into German piano music for the first time in a publication entitled *Neue Clavierübung* which appeared in 1692. "I have added a Sonata in B-flat," he explained in his preface. "Why should not such things be attempted on the clavier as well as on other instruments?" The Sonata in B-flat is in three movements: Allegro, Adagio, Allegro.

In 1696 Kuhnau published *Frische Clavier Früchte* in which seven more sonatas appeared. In the preface to this volume, he explained in great detail how he had written these works: "It did not take me long to produce these; it was with me just as it is in certain countries where, thanks to the unusual heat, everything grows with such rapidity that the harvest may be reaped a month after sowing. While writing these sonatas, I experienced such eagerness that without neglecting my other occupations I wrote one every day, so that this work, which I began on a Monday, was completed by the Monday of the next week. I mention this merely so that no one shall expect in them anything rare or exceptional."

These sonatas are in four or five movements. In some of the fast movements a binary form of two contrasting themes is often suggested; in others Kuhnau remains faithful to the old polyphonic traditions with his fugal writing; and in some of the slow movements he belongs to the new age of homophony, presenting a clearly defined melody against a harmonic background.

The most famous group of sonatas by Kuhnau appeared in 1700: the *Biblische Historien nebst Auslegung in sechs Sonaten (Musical Representations of Some Stories of the Bible in Six Sonatas).* It is of particular importance as an early example of program music, though on frequent occasions the tonal representations of nonmusical episodes are too naïvely literal. The six sonatas are entitled *The Combat Between David and Goliath, David Healing Saul, The Marriage*

JOHANN KUHNAU

of *Jacob, Hezekiah's Illness, Gideon,* and *The Tomb of Jacob.*

The Combat Between David and Goliath (Der Streit zwischen David und Goliath) is the most celebrated sonata in this group; it is still performed today occasionally at concerts. Its six movements recreate the biblical story of David and Goliath realistically, with the titles that hint at the episodes they describe in the movements: "The Bravado of Goliath," "The Terror of the Israelites and Their Prayer to God," "David's Courage Before the Terrible Enemy," "The Dispute and the Slinging of the Stone by David," "The Plight of the Philistines," and "Paeans of Victory by the Israelites." Here, as Wanda Landowska said, we have "a marvelous example of early tone painting. . . . Kuhnau was more than a pioneer composer. He had a lucid sense of form, and in his clavier music used an outline that is graceful and elegant. He had a fine fluidity of musical expression and a wonderful resourcefulness in enriching his melodic materials."

PRINCIPAL WORKS

Choral Music—Cantatas, chorales, motets, Passion.

Keyboard Music (clavichord)—Neue Clavierübung; Frische Clavier Früchte; Biblische Historien.

ABOUT

Rolland, R., A Musical Tour Through the Land of the Past; Shedlock, J., The Pianoforte Sonata.

Le Guide musicale, January 17, 1904; Zeitschrift für Musikwissenschaft, August-September 1923.

Édouard Lalo *1823-1892*

VICTOR ANTOINE ÉDOUARD LALO was born in Lille, France, on January 27, 1823. He was of Spanish ancestry. His father, who held a provincial government job in Lille, had been an officer in the Grande Armée, and had been decorated on the field by Napoleon for his heroic exploits in the battle of Lützen. The elder Lalo dreamed that his son would follow in his footsteps by becoming a soldier in the French army; but he did not prevent the boy from expressing his innate musical nature, not realizing, doubtless, what the consequences would be. Édouard studied violin with Müller and cello with Baumann at the Lille branch of the Paris Conservatory, soon becoming convinced that he wanted no part of the army. His decision brought about a break with his father that was not healed until his father lay on his deathbed.

When he was sixteen, Lalo left home to make his way in Paris. He attended the Conservatory, a pupil of Habeneck, Schulhoff, and Crèvecœur. These were trying times for the young man. He was unhappy with the strict discipline and inflexible curriculum of the Conservatory. In addition, he suffered intense poverty. His poverty and personal deprivation were to continue for some time, but he soon left the Conservatory to undertake the independent study of theoretical texts and scores of masterworks. He also began to compose, and completed several songs and a piece for violin and piano. In 1847 Lalo competed for the Prix de Rome with a cantata, but won only second prize. A year later his first publication, a group of songs, appeared.

In 1848 Lalo left composition and for a number of years devoted himself more conscientiously to violin and viola performance. In 1855 he became violist of the eminent Armingaud-Jacquard Quartet, which had been founded to promote German chamber music in France. The ensemble was renamed the Société Classique when a wind section was added to it.

In 1865, Lalo married Mlle. Bernier de Maligny, one of his harmony pupils. (This was his second marriage. An earlier marriage to a woman twenty-five years his senior, Mme. Moine, had been unhappy and brief.) Lalo's wife encouraged him to return to creative work, and urged him to try writing for

the stage. Stimulated by a competition for new operas, Lalo completed *Fiesque,* based on a Schiller drama, in 1866. Although it won only third prize, its score made a deep impression on the director of the Paris Opéra, who promised to produce it. Unfortunately, *Fiesque* was never performed during Lalo's lifetime. Its presentation was delayed first by the outbreak of the Franco-Prussian War, then by the fire that destroyed the Opéra. The Brussels Opera accepted the work, but before it was mounted, the opera company had gone into bankruptcy.

Other works by Lalo, however, were performed in Paris. At a concert of the Société Nationale in 1871 Lalo's wife sang some of his songs. On December 8, 1872, the Concert Populaire, directed by Pasdeloup, gave the première of his *Divertissement* for orchestra (it was actually the ballet music from *Fiesque*).

It was the world-renowned violinist Pablo de Sarasate who was responsible for bringing Lalo his first major successes, with two important works. The first was his Violin Concerto in F major, which Sarasate performed in London with the London Philharmonic on January 18, 1874. The romantic ardor of Lalo's lyricism and the brilliant virtuosity of his instrumentation aroused great admiration. Spurred on by this acclaim, Lalo wrote for Sarasate an even more impressive composition, the *Symphonie espagnole* for violin and orchestra, generally conceded to be his finest work for the concert stage. Using Spanish rhythms and melodies, as a tribute to the violinist for whom the work was intended, Lalo created one of the most effective pieces of music by a Frenchman to picture colorful Spain through its folk melodies and dances. Despite its title, the *Symphonie espagnole* is not a symphony, but a cross between a suite and a concerto. Lalo doubtless used the term "symphony" (though he made no attempt to use the symphonic structure) to emphasize the importance of the orchestra and to point up the work's symphonic breadth. Sarasate introduced the *Symphonie espagnole* in Paris, at a Colonne concert, on February 7, 1875. It was popular from the start. Tchaikovsky, hearing it for the first time, remarked that it gave him the "greatest pleasure," that it was "delightfully fresh and light, with piquant rhythms and beautifully harmonized melodies." It has never lost its great appeal for concert audiences and violin virtuosos.

Lalo: là-lō′

The *Symphonie espagnole* was followed by an important Concerto for cello and orchestra in D minor (still a great concert favorite), which Adolphe Fischer played with the Pasdeloup Orchestra on December 9, 1877; and by the *Rapsodie norvégienne* for orchestra (adapted from an earlier work for violin and orchestra), first presented by the Colonne Orchestra on October 26, 1879.

For over a decade Lalo labored on what he, and many of France's foremost critics, considered his masterwork—the opera *Le Roi d'Ys*. He had begun writing it in 1875, then in 1886 destroyed most of the score. He later returned to the work with renewed zest, and brought it to completion in 1888. The world première took place at the Opéra-Comique on May 7, 1888. "When two years ago I destroyed the first score of *Le Roi d'Ys*," wrote Lalo in 1888, "I had the desire of making it a lyrical drama in the modern acceptance of the term; but after some months of reflection, I drew back, frightened at this task which seemed too heavy for my strength. Until now the colossus Wagner, the inventor of the real lyrical drama, has alone been strong enough to carry such a weight; all those who have had the ambition to walk in his footsteps have failed, some piteously, some honorably. . . . It will be necessary to surpass Wagner in order to fight on his own ground with advantage, and the fighter capable of doing so has not yet revealed himself. As for myself, I have realized in time my impotence, and I have written a simple opera."

This "simple opera" had a libretto by Édouard Blau based on the same Breton legend that had inspired Debussy's piano prelude *La Cathédrale engloutie*. The opera impressed both audiences and critics. One music critic found it "noble, strong, puissant, not free from faults, but evidently the work of an artist of the first rank and endowed in a superior degree."

R. A. Streatfeild summed up the strength and weakness of *Le Roi d'Ys:* "[It] is an excellent specimen of the kind of opera which French composers of the second rank used to write before the sun of Wagner dawned upon their horizon. It is redolent of Meyerbeer and Gounod, and though some of the scenes are not without vigor, it is impossible to avoid feeling that in *Le Roi d'Ys* Lalo was forcing a graceful and delicate talent into an uncongenial groove. He is at his best in the

ÉDOUARD LALO

lighter parts of the work, such as the pretty scene of Rozenn's wedding, which is perfectly charming."

Le Roi d'Ys was first seen in the United States on January 23, 1890, in New Orleans; the first production by the Metropolitan Opera in New York took place on January 5, 1922. The work has never been very popular in America, but its overture has acquired a permanent place in the orchestral repertory.

The last years of Lalo's life were somber. He had suffered an attack of paralysis in the early 1880's, and the effects grew worse with the years, finally crippling him completely. His failure to be elected to the Institut de France also darkened his spirit. He received other honors, however: election as Officier of the Legion of Honor, and the Prix Monbinne, given by the Académie des Beaux-Arts.

Lalo died of a heart attack in Paris on April 22, 1892, and was buried in the cemetery of Père Lachaise. "Lalo," said Jules Massenet in a eulogy, "will be counted among the French composers of whom we must be proud because his music, sometimes exquisite or sparkling, sometimes dramatic or elegiac, is always the pure music of Lalo."

Philip Hale described Lalo's appearance as follows: "Slight in stature, he limped a little as a result of paralysis, which attacked him during the rehearsals of *Namouna*. He was otherwise of distinguished appearance, fastidious in dress, with a good deal of color in his cheeks, bright-eyed, with snow-white hair, a white beard and moustache 'which gave him the appearance of an Austrian diplomat.' "

In a discussion of Lalo's music, Julien Tiersot wrote that it is "essentially an aristocratic art. It is a sculpture created with extreme delicacy, outlined without any visible effort, and brought to being—so it seems—with the utmost naturalness. It possesses no romanticism, discloses little restlessness, and its intimate feeling is not very profound. But his forms are of a rare ingenuity. Its tonality is clear and endowed with a color not too excessive but always bathed in light; it is founded upon a diatonism that is almost constant and hardly ever depends upon the resources of chromaticism. His melodies, generally short, are elegant and fresh. His rhythms are well formed, so neat that they often give the feeling of energy."

PRINCIPAL WORKS

Ballets—Namouna; Néron.

Chamber Music—3 piano trios; 2 quintets; 2 string quartets; Violin Sonata; Cello Sonata; Soirées parisiennes, for violin and piano; Guitare for violin and piano.

Choral Music—O Salutaris; Veni Creator; Litanies de la Sainte-Vierge.

Operas—Fiesque; Le Roi d'Ys; La Jacquerie (completed by Arthur Coquard).

Orchestral Music—3 symphonies; 2 violin concertos; Divertissement; Deux aubades; Symphonie espagnole, for violin and orchestra; Allegro symphonique, for violin and orchestra (also for cello and orchestra); Cello Concerto in D minor; Rapsodie norvégienne; Scherzo; Piano Concerto in C minor.

Piano Music—La Mère et l'enfant, for piano duet.

Vocal Music—Six Romances populaires; 12 Mélodies; Cinq Lieder; various songs for voice and piano, including L'Esclave, Marine, Souvenir.

ABOUT

Cooper, M., French Music; Dufour, M., Édouard Lalo; Servières, G., Lalo.

Musical Quarterly, January 1925; La Revue musicale, March 1923 (Lalo issue).

Orlando di Lasso *1532-1594*

ORLANDO DI LASSO (Roland de Lassus, Orlandus Lassus), the last and greatest exponent of the Flemish or Netherlands polyphonic school, and one of the musical giants of the Renaissance, was born in Mons, Hainaut, in 1532. When he was seven he joined the chorus of the St. Nicolas Church in Mons. His voice was so beautiful that on three occasions agents of powerful noblemen attempted to kidnap him. In 1544 his parents permitted him to join the service of Ferdinando Gonzaga, the Viceroy of Sicily, with whom he traveled throughout Italy and Sicily.

When his voice broke in 1548, di Lasso left Gonzaga and proceeded to Naples, finding employment with the Marchese della Terza, an art patron. In 1552 di Lasso went to Rome, where in all probability he met Palestrina. From April 1553 to December 1554 he served as choirmaster at St. John Lateran Church in Rome. Then he was engaged by Cesare Brancaccio, a Neapolitan nobleman, with whom he may have visited England and France.

In 1555 di Lasso settled in Antwerp, becoming, within a short time, one of its most prominent cultural figures. He published his first two volumes in 1555, both devoted to Italian madrigals; a year later he issued his first volume of motets. His individual approach to polyphony was apparent even in these early compositions, in his emphasis on particular words in the text by means of unusual melodic and harmonic processes and unorthodox chromatic modulations.

In 1556 di Lasso was invited to Munich by Albert V, Duke of Bavaria, to become a member of the ducal chapel; in or about 1563 he rose to the position of *Kapellmeister*. Di Lasso traveled widely in Italy and throughout Germany to engage singers and musicians for his court. One of these court guests was the renowned Venetian composer and organist Giovanni Gabrieli, whom di Lasso brought to Munich in 1575. In 1558 di Lasso married Regina Wechinger (or Weckinger), a member of an aristocratic family.

Di Lasso's first great work, the *Sacrae cantiones* for five voices, was issued in Nuremberg in 1562. "This work," says J. R. Milne, "shows the master in full possession of all the resources of his art for the devout expression of the various phases of religious feeling, from penitential sorrow and prayerful meditation to joyous praise and thanksgiving." Even more deeply emotional and expressive was the *Seven Penitential Psalms of David*, published in 1563, which many historians regard as di Lasso's greatest work. "These powerful, magnificent, serious pieces," wrote Hugo Leichtentritt, "are eminent classical masterpieces of the first rank, and find their equal only in certain Palestrina and Bach compositions. They show, besides the fullest mastery of contrapuntal technique, Lasso's individuality, with its dark pathos, its passionate outcries, differing considerably from Palestrina's more serene, more celestial, pure manner."

In 1567 di Lasso issued in Munich his first setting of German words, the *New German Songs* for five voices (or instruments). A year later he wrote a festival Te Deum for the marriage ceremony of the daughter of Duke William to the Duke of Lorraine; it is reported that the music held the audience so spellbound that food and conversation were forgotten.

Di Lasso visited Paris in 1571. He was received ceremoniously by King Charles IX, to whom he presented a new work, a book of five-part French *chansons*. After his return to Munich, he received a generous offer from Paris to become chamber musician to the French King. But, though di Lasso provided music for the French court during the next few years, he preferred to stay in Munich. When other flattering offers threatened to lure him away, the Duke of Bavaria had him sign a lifetime contract in return for a large increase in salary. Except for brief visits to Italy and Regensburg, di Lasso remained at the Munich court until his last days.

Di Lasso's closing years were painful. By 1587 his health had begun to deteriorate so alarmingly that he was given a leave of absence; his duties at court were assumed by his son Rudolph. Eventually his poor health brought on a siege of melancholia, then mental disorder. Despite his declining physical and intellectual powers, di Lasso completed a new volume of *Cantiones sacrae* for six voices in 1592. He knew he would never write anything else, for in his dedication he referred to the work as his "swan song."

Di Lasso died in Munich on January 14, 1594, and was buried in the Franciscan Cemetery, where a monument of the composer, with his children and grandchildren, was erected to his memory. The monument was subsequently removed and placed in the garden of the National Museum. Its epitaph reads: "Here lies Lasso, who revives a world in lassitude and resolves its discord into harmony." In 1604 di Lasso's sons,

ORLANDO DI LASSO

Ferdinand and Rudolph, issued a volume entitled *Magnum Opus Musicum Orlandi de Lasso,* containing 516 motets.

Di Lasso was greatly honored in his own day. Pope Gregory XIII made him a Knight of the Golden Order, and in 1570 the Emperor Maximilian conferred on him a hereditary rank of nobility. Some of his most important contemporaries recognized his high station in the music of that period, and referred to him persistently as "the prince of music," "the divine Orlando," or "the Belgian Orpheus."

He was, indeed, as Charles van den Borren said of him, "one of the peaks in the history of music." The number of his compositions has been estimated at from twelve hundred to two thousand. In any event, there is no question that he was remarkably prolific, just as there is little doubt that he was one of the most versatile composers of his generation. He composed a variety of forms with equal mastery of technique and loftiness of style—French *chansons,* German and Neapolitan songs, Italian madrigals and villanellas, as well as numerous Masses, motets, Magnificats, and psalms. He could be robust and earthy in his drinking songs, witty and gay in his settings of ribald verses, tender in his love songs, elevated and exalted in his religious music. On whatever he touched he left the imprint of a master.

"Profoundly human, and a profound believer—such was Orlando," wrote Charles van den Borren. "With this was combined a propensity to interest himself in everything, to leave nothing in the shade, to explore to the furthermost depths all the domains of his art. Universality and fecundity —these were the distinctive traits of his genius. . . . If one penetrates more deeply into the labyrinth of his immense production, one is struck by the multiplicity of his attention to detail, and the infinity of his means which is combined with the diversity."

Di Lasso's most distinguished contemporary was Palestrina, the great Italian composer, who was seven years his senior. Ernest Closson has pointed out some of the differences between these two Renaissance masters. "Lasso has less grace than the Italian; he is less luminous, less perfect, above all else less mystic. However, if he is inferior to him from the point of view of religious sentiment, he surpasses him in secular composition, through the originality of the harmony, his energy, his vigor, and puissant vivacity, his strong conceptions, and more especially through his vernal freshness."

PRINCIPAL WORKS
Choral Music—Chansons, German songs, madrigals, Magnificats, Masses, motets, psalms, villanellas.
ABOUT
Balmer, L., *Orlando di Lassos Motteten*; Boetticher, W., *Orlando di Lasso*; Borren, Charles van den, *Orlande de Lassus*; Closson, E., *Rolande de Lassus*; Expert, H., *Orlande de Lassus*; Huschke, J., *Orlando di Lassos Messen*.

Jean Marie Leclair *1697-1764*

JEAN MARIE LECLAIR is sometimes called the "French Corelli" because he was one of the first great French composers for violin. He was born in Lyons on May 10, 1697, the oldest of eight children. Six of them became professional musicians, and Jean Marie is designated "l'aîné," or the "elder," to distinguish him from a younger brother who had the same name.

Leclair's father was a lacemaker. Early in boyhood, Jean Marie seemed destined for a similar calling, for he served as an apprentice in his father's shop. But in 1716, after his marriage to Rose Catignie, a singer, Leclair began to study dancing and music. It was dancing that at first interested him more, and by 1722 he had progressed sufficiently in his command of the field to be

appointed ballet master in Turin. Some of the ballet music he wrote at this time impressed Somis, a distinguished teacher of the violin, who encouraged Leclair to study with him and thus deflected his interest from the dance. In 1723 Leclair published his first volume of violin sonatas, and a few years later he made his successful debut as a violinist in Paris, impressing his audience with his virtuosity.

From 1729 to 1735 Leclair was a violinist in the orchestra of the Paris Opéra. From 1728 to 1736 he appeared frequently as soloist with the Concert Spirituel. In 1734 he was engaged as concertmaster of the royal orchestra, but held the post for only a short time because of a bitter rivalry with a fellow violinist for leadership of the second violins. While he pursued a career as virtuoso, Leclair continued to study composition with Chéron.

Meanwhile, Leclair's wife had died and he was married a second time, to Louise Roussel, a widow who owned a prosperous music publishing and engraving enterprise. Although the marriage ended in separation, Louise continued as publisher and engraver of her husband's music.

After 1736 Leclair withdrew from his concert work to concentrate on teaching and composition. During the next sixteen years he wrote most of his celebrated violin sonatas (of which the D major Sonata, op. 2, no. 4, is still highly popular on concert programs) together with a great deal of other chamber music and orchestral concerti grossi. He became one of the first creators of violin music in France. Building solidly on the foundations established in Italy by Corelli and Tartini, Leclair contributed to his works a French elegance and refinement, contrast of material, and increased virtuosity not encountered in the early Italian masters.

A high point in the baroque violin concerto in France was reached in two volumes of six concertos each which Leclair published between 1737 and 1744. A. B. Hutchings has described these works as follows: "He cast his concertos in Vivaldi's three-movement form, adding an introductory slow movement to two of them. His allegros are further advanced towards the classical, post-symphony concerto, than in any of Vivaldi's printed sets. . . . Within his small field, Leclair reveals a trait which is rarely observed outside the music of much greater artists. . . . I refer to the constant extension and variation of his ideas. He does not often repeat them exactly (when he needs them in a new key), nor present them in a former context except where the repetition serves a better purpose than development."

Except for a brief visit to Holland on an invitation from the Princess of Orange, and a brief excursion to Spain (both in 1743), Leclair lived a fairly secluded, sedentary life in Paris. On October 4, 1746, his opera *Scylla et Glaucus* was given at the Opéra. Four years later he wrote the music for *Apollon et Climène,* an opera-ballet. In 1748, Leclair served as concertmaster of the orchestra of the Duke of Gramont in Puteaux.

Leclair was murdered at his home in Paris on October 22, 1764. He was stabbed three times, in the left shoulder, stomach, and chest. Near his blood-covered body were found a book (*L'Élite des bon mots),* some manuscript paper, and a hunting knife without traces of blood. These items seemed to have been placed carefully near the dead body. The reason for this is as mysterious as the identity of the murderer, for it soon became apparent that robbery had not been a motive. Three people were suspected, the gardener (who had a prison record), the gardener's mistress, and Leclair's nephew, who had been furious at the composer's refusal to recommend him for a post with the Duke of Gramont's orchestra. The following report was entered by the police inspector after the inquest: "The nephew merits attention; his extraordinary state of agitation and trembling at Leclair's interment noted by my men, whom I had sent to the funeral, and also by others, adds to the circumstantial evidence against him, and makes him highly suspect. I also know that he enjoys the favor of Leclair's widow, which justified my interest in her part as well. At the same time I do not abandon my suspicions against the gardener as some information seems to point against him."

All three suspects, however, were cleared, and the mystery of Leclair's murder was never solved. In *A Thing or Two About Music,* Nicolas Slonimsky constructs a case to illustrate that the murderer was Leclair's estranged wife, Louise. Louise, in Slonimsky's opinion, had gone to Leclair to persuade him to place his nephew in the Duke's orchestra. Leclair stubbornly refused to assist, partly because he was jealous of his

JEAN MARIE LECLAIR

own position at court and did not wish to endanger it, partly because he resented his nephew's *liaison* with his estranged wife. In rage, Louise killed him.

PRINCIPAL WORKS

Chamber Music—48 violin sonatas; 6 trios; 2 easy trios; Récitations de musique, for two flutes (or two violins).

Operas—Scylla et Glaucus; Apollon et Climène.

Orchestral Music—Concerti grossi.

ABOUT

Hutchings, A. B., The Baroque Concerto; Pincherle, M., Jean-Marie Leclair l'aîné; Slonimsky, N., A Thing or Two About Music.

La Revue musicale, April 1923; The Score, June 1930; Strad, April 1930.

Giovanni Legrenzi *1626-1690*

GIOVANNI LEGRENZI was an important Italian composer of chamber music in the generation preceding Corelli and a distinguished creator of operas and church music. He was born in Clusone, near Bergamo in August 1626. His father, a local musician, gave him his first instruction in music, after which the boy studied with Pallavicino. For a while Legrenzi served as organist of the Santa Maria Maggiore Church in Bergamo. Then he went to Ferrara, where he was appointed *maestro di cappella* at the Spirito Santo Church. His first opera, *Achille in Sciro,* was produced in Ferrara in 1663.

GIOVANNI LEGRENZI

A year later Legrenzi settled permanently in Venice. He wrote seventeen more operas; most were performed in that city, some achieving great popularity and influence. In 1672 Legrenzi became director of the Conservatorio de' Mendicanti. In 1681 he was appointed second *maestro di cappella* at San Marco, and from 1685 until his death was its first *maestro di cappella*. One of his accomplishments at San Marco was the expansion of its orchestra to thirty-four members.

Legrenzi's last opera, *Pertinace,* was produced in Venice in 1684. He died in that city on May 26, 1690. Through the years, his influence as a teacher was absorbed by a generation of younger composers, including Gasparini, Lotti, and Caldara.

Legrenzi was a gifted composer in several genres, writing with equal felicity for the church, stage, and chamber music ensembles. As one of the earliest distinguished creators of sonatas and trio sonatas, he prepared the ground for Corelli, who continued where he had left off. In his expansive writing of arias and recitatives and his interest in increasing the prominence of the orchestra, he pointed to new directions for Italian opera. And in his church music he greatly advanced the skill of polyphonic writing. His reputation spanned Europe. It is indicative of his high place in the regard of his contemporaries and successors that Johann Sebastian Bach and Handel used his material in their own compositions, Bach in his organ Fugue

in C minor, Handel, for one of his choruses in *Samson.*

PRINCIPAL WORKS

Chamber Music—Sonatas, trio-sonatas.
Choral Music—6 oratorios; cantatas, Masses, motets, psalms.
Operas—Achille in Sciro; Zenobia e Radamisto; La Divisione del mondo; Eteocle e Polinice; Germanico sul Reno; Totila; I due Cesari; Mercure galant; Giustino; Pertinace.

ABOUT

Fogaccia, P., Giovanni Legrenzi.
Musica d'oggi, April 1937.

Guillaume Lekeu *1870-1894*

GUILLAUME LEKEU was born in Heusy, near Verviers, Belgium, on January 20, 1870. As a boy he studied organ with a local musician. When he was nine his family moved to Poitiers, where Guillaume attended the Lycée, showing unusual aptitude in sciences, literature, and the plastic arts. He also studied music with a physics instructor at the school.

In 1885 Lekeu heard some music by Beethoven, and was inspired to become a composer. He began earnestly to study piano and solfeggio, and to memorize the scores of the masters. In 1888, after graduating from the Poitiers Lycée he went to Paris, where, without having taken a single lesson in composition, he completed his first work for orchestra, *Chant de triomphale délivrance.* It was introduced in Verviers in 1889.

Realizing his need to develop a technique in composition, he began to study harmony with Gaston Vallin. Vallin was so impressed with Lekeu's talent that in two months he introduced the young man to César Franck. Between 1889 and 1890 Lekeu studied composition with Franck. Franck's aim, as Oscar Sonneck explained, "was to stimulate the productive imagination of his pupil, first by guiding him into every nook of the workshop of a Bach or a Beethoven, and secondly by urging him on to unconventional musical utterance of his own.

" 'That marches on wheels,' he would exclaim, and would encourage Lekeu to write from lesson to lesson as much as he possibly could, with the result that the fascinated pupil would submit ten or twelve pages of music for examination by a master, than whom there was no greater teacher in Europe." César Franck's influence on Lekeu was decisive, and Franck's death in 1890 was a personal disaster to Lekeu. "I was completely bewildered," he confided to a friend. "I passed four or five days a week smoking and watching the implacable rain pour down, and telling myself how wise it would be to jump out of the window. But, since verily there are other things to do than to watch the downpour, I forced myself, best as I knew how, to do regular work. I plunged back into counterpoint, double chorus and fugue, and that sort of thing now marches *cahin-caha*." He also found a new teacher in Vincent d'Indy, one of Franck's most noted pupils and disciples.

Vincent d'Indy urged Lekeu to enter the competition for the Belgian Prix de Rome. He did so in 1891 with a cantata, *Andromède*, but won only second prize. Portions of this composition were introduced at the Verviers Conservatory on March 27, 1892. Eugène Ysaÿe, the distinguished Belgian violinist, recognized Guillaume Lekeu's creative potential and commissioned the young man to write a composition for him. The result, in 1891, was Lekeu's Sonata in G major, one of his most remarkable works. Ysaÿe introduced it the following year. The Sonata is a masterwork, bubbling, in Oscar Sonneck's words, "with the freshness and joyousness of youth, though of youth meditative, not flippant. . . . The themes of the Sonata . . . possess breadth. . . Instead of dissecting, doubling, telescoping, breaking up his themes, and juggling with their component parts, . . . Lekeu prefers to leave his themes more or less intact and seeks to make the thematic narrative more convincing by repetition of important phrases at different pitches."

Another of Lekeu's distinguished compositions, still heard frequently, is the beautiful *Adagio for Strings,* also completed in 1891. This elegiac music was inspired by a motto from Georges Vanor's "Des Fleurs pâles du souvenir" ("the pale flowers of memory"). Scored for divided strings, except for double basses, the work develops an elegiac subject that appears at the opening.

In 1893 Lekeu himself directed the première of his *Fantaisie sur deux airs angevins* for orchestra in Paris. He was now planning several ambitious compositions, and was hard at work on a cello sonata and a quartet for piano and strings. But on January 21, 1894, at the age of twenty-four, Lekeu died in Angers, stricken by typhoid fever. His

GUILLAUME LEKEU

last words were, "So many works unfinished —my quartet!" The quartet, and Lekeu's cello sonata, were completed by Vincent d'Indy.

Four months after Lekeu's death, a concert of his works was arranged in Paris. Eugène Ysaÿe performed the Violin Sonata, and Vincent d'Indy directed the *Fantaisie sur deux airs angevins* and *Andromède.*

Though Lekeu produced only a handful of works in his short life, the quality of his slim output places him, as Romauld Vandelle wrote, "at the head of all composers of his generation. None of his rivals . . . manifested a genius more original, or an inspiration more exalted. From his music there comes a breath of grandeur, and an intensity of life which are not deceiving.... When faith took possession of him, when for a moment he attained the peaks towards which he threw his gaze, his song became unique and large, powerfully harmonized with an intuitive feeling for timbres which astonishes and ravishes. . . . These moments mark the peak of his inspiration."

Debussy considered Lekeu next to Franck himself as "one of the most remarkable representatives of the Belgian school." Philip Hale said: "Lekeu's voice is his own. His music is not like that of any other men; he thought in his own way and his emotional eloquence . . . is genuine and convincing.... Such music does not suffer when played after a noble work by Beethoven."

PRINCIPAL WORKS

Chamber Music—2 piano trios; String Quartet in D minor; Violin Sonata in G major; Cello Sonata (completed by Vincent d'Indy); Piano Quartet (completed by Vincent d'Indy).

Choral Music—Andromède; Chanson de mai; Chant lyrique.

Orchestral Music—Prelude to Act III of Phèdre; Chant de triomphale délivrance; Fantaisie sur un cramignon liégeois; Hamlet; Adagio for Strings (also for string quartet); Epithalame; Fantaisie sur deux airs angevins; Introduction and Allegro, for brass; Suite, for cello and orchestra.

Piano Music—Sonata; Fugue, in four parts; Trois pièces.

Vocal Music—Trois poèmes.

ABOUT

Lorrain, M. G., Lekeu: sa correspondance, sa vie, son œuvre; Prist, P., Guillaume Lekeu; Sonneck, O. G., Miscellaneous Studies in the History of Music; Stengel, R., Lekeu.

Guide musicale, April 12, 1895; Musical Quarterly, January 1919; La Revue musicale, January 1921.

Leonardo Leo *1694-1744*

LEONARDO LEO (Lionardo Oronzo Salvatore de Leo), a founder of the Neapolitan school of opera, was born in San Vito degli Schiavi (now San Vito dei Normanni), near Brindisi, on August 5, 1694. He went to Naples when he was fifteen, and there attended the Conservatorio della Pietà de' Turchini about four years, studying with Fago and Basso. While a student he completed a sacred drama, *L'Infedeltà abbattuta,* which was presented first at the Conservatory during the Carnival in 1712, then, at royal command, at the Viceroy's palace. A second sacred drama, *Il Trionfo della castità di S. Alessio,* was produced at the Conservatory early in 1713.

In April 1713 Leo became a supernumerary organist at the royal chapel. At first he received no compensation, but in 1715 he was given a nominal salary for his services. On June 14, 1713, he married Anna Losi; they had five children.

In 1714 Leo's first secular opera, *Pisistrato* was produced at the Teatro di San Bartolomeo. It was in 1718, however, that Leo began to enjoy his immense popularity as an opera composer, with the production of *Sofonisba.* In the ensuing years Leo wrote opera with remarkable productivity. In 1723 he tapped a new, rich vein of operatic writing with his first comic opera, *La mpeca scoperta (L'imbroglio scoperto).*

Through the years Leo held several important positions in the Neapolitan musical world. In 1716 he was appointed *maestro di cappella* at the Santa Maria della Solitaria Church, and second *maestro* at the Conservatory. He became third *maestro di cappella* of the royal chapel in 1731, second *maestro* in 1738, and first *maestro* in 1741.

Leo also enjoyed an immense following as a teacher. In 1725 he succeeded Alessandro Scarlatti as instructor at the Conservatorio di Sant' Onofrio and kept this post until his death. There is hardly a significant Neapolitan opera composer of that day who did not study under him or come under his influence. Among his pupils were such outstanding representatives of Neapolitan opera as Jommelli, Piccini, Sacchini, and Pergolesi.

Leo's greatest success as an opera composer was *Demofoonte,* given in 1735; an aria from this work, "Misero pargoletto" was regarded by Piccini as a model of Neapolitan writing. The last of Leo's operas were *La Fedeltà odiata* and *La Contesa dell' amore colla virtù,* produced in 1744. He wrote more than sixty operas during his lifetime.

Leonardo Leo died in Naples on October 31, 1744.

Edward J. Dent described Leo as follows: "In person Leo was of middle height and handsome features; in manner he was dignified and urbane. He was a man of serious character, working hard at night when his other occupations left him little opportunity for composition in the daytime, and so careful in the preparation of music for performance that he would begin on Ash Wednesday rehearsing the Miserere to be sung in Holy Week. As a teacher he was severe, but greatly beloved of his pupils."

Leo's music is distinguished in areas outside the theater. In 1732 he completed his first two celebrated oratorios, *La Morte di Abele* and *Sant' Elena al Calvario,* and in 1739 he wrote a noteworthy **Miserere.** He also produced a great deal of instrumental music, including concertos, organ fugues, and toccatas for harpsichord.

PRINCIPAL WORKS

Chamber Music—6 cello concertos with string quartet; Concerto in D, for four violins and bass.

Choral Music—Credos, Dixit, hymns, Magnificats, Masses, Misereres, motets, oratorios, psalms, and responses.

Harpsichord Music—Toccatas.

Operas—Over 60 serious and comic operas, including: Sofonisba; La mpeca scoperta; Timocrate; L'Amore fedele; Trionfo di Camilla; Catone in Utica; Il Castello d' Atlante; La Clemenza di Tito; Demofoonte; Siface; Demetrio; L'Andromaca; La Fedeltà odiata; La Contesa dell' amore colla virtù.

Organ Music—Fugues.

ABOUT

Leo, G., Leonardo Leo.
Musical Review, November 1948.

Ruggiero Leoncavallo *1858-1919*

RUGGIERO LEONCAVALLO, composer of *Pagliacci*, was born in Naples on March 8, 1858. His father was a magistrate. As a child Ruggiero studied piano with Siri and Simonetti; then he entered the Naples Conservatory. At sixteen he wrote a cantata of real merit and gave several piano recitals.

After receiving his diploma from the Naples Conservatory he went to Bologna, enrolling in literature courses at the University. In 1878 he completed his first opera, *Tommaso Chatterton,* and arranged with a local impresario to have the work produced in Bologna. When the impresario absconded with his funds, the youth, overwhelmed and disillusioned, took on menial musical chores for his subsistence. Seeking to escape his disappointment, he traveled aimlessly about Europe, earning his living by playing piano and singing in cafés. It was a squalid existence, marked continually by frustration, disappointment, and personal deprivation. His road eventually led to Egypt, where he was engaged to play the piano for the Viceroy's brother. But soon after his arrival, an insurrection erupted in Egypt against the English, endangering the lives of all Europeans. Leoncavallo fled from Cairo in the dead of night, riding for twenty-four hours on horseback disguised as an Arab until he was safe outside the borders of Egypt. He arrived at Port Said. There he gave a piano recital, using the income to buy his passage to France.

In Paris Leoncavallo led a bohemian life, working as a pianist in various cafés, writing *chansonnettes* and popular ditties for café performers. But he had also undertaken serious composition, including an opera, *A Midsummer Night's Dream,* which was given a private performance in a salon. Leoncavallo's main influence at the time was

RUGGIERO LEONCAVALLO

the Wagnerian music-drama, which he studied assiduously from the published scores. They inspired in him a single-minded ambition to compose a Wagnerian trilogy set in the Renaissance.

His meeting with Victor Maurel, one of the most celebrated French opera singers, proved to be a turning point in Leoncavallo's career. The two soon became friends, and Maurel asked Leoncavallo to accompany him on a trip to Milan. In Milan the young composer was introduced to the influential publisher Ricordi, and confided to him his plan for writing an opera trilogy about the Renaissance. The publisher, impressed with the project, commissioned Leoncavallo to work on the first of these three operas. It took Leoncavallo a year to complete *I Medici.* But Ricordi found that the work would be too expensive to produce and procrastinated in arranging the performance. Having waited in vain for about three years for *I Medici* to reach the stage, Leoncavallo came to an important decision. He would abandon his Renaissance project temporarily and attempt to win producers and the public with a realistic, passionate, dramatic opera in the *verismo* style that had recently been popularized by Mascagni with *Cavalleria rusticana.* Recalling an episode he had witnessed in Calabria in his youth, in which a jealous actor killed his unfaithful wife during an actual performance, Leoncavallo fashioned the libretto for *Pagliacci.* He wrote a gripping text, using an effective play-within-a-play technique. Once the text was written, Leoncavallo spent a year composing the score.

Through the efforts of Lison Frandin, a prima donna, Leoncavallo was able to gain an audience with a rival publisher, Sonzogno. Leoncavallo started to play his score, but had not gone far before the publisher rushed over to him, embraced him, and announced his eagerness to publish the work on the strength of what he had just heard. The world première of *Pagliacci* took place at the Teatro dal Verme in Milan on May 21, 1892, Arturo Toscanini conducting and Victor Maurel appearing as Tonio. "The crowded Dal Verme theater," reported Claude Trevor, "was literally in a frenzy. A scene of such wild enthusiasm took place as is only to be seen rarely."

Pagliacci alone established Leoncavallo's wealth and fame. It was an immediate success everywhere. The American première, which took place at the Grand Opera House in New York on June 15, 1893, was a complete triumph. F. Bonavia gave some reasons for the universal and immediate popularity of the work: "The text has the rare merit of a poignant story and rapid action, and the music has all the typical flow of the Italian school; but the texture is infinitely more substantial than is the case with Mascagni. . . . The orchestration is also carefully balanced and is free from vulgarities."

Now a composer in great demand, Leoncavallo had no difficulty winning performances of his earlier operas. *I Medici* was given in Milan on November 9, 1893; *Tommaso Chatterton* was seen in Rome on March 10, 1896. Both were failures. In 1896 it seemed briefly that Leoncavallo had recovered his stride with *La Bohème*, an opera that was acclaimed when given in Venice on May 6, 1897. But Giacomo Puccini's opera on the same subject, which had been introduced a year earlier, received such admiration in all parts of the world that Leoncavallo's opera was soon obscured.

The only opera with which Leoncavallo was able afterwards to win popular favor was *Zaza*, introduced at the Teatro Lirico in Milan on November 10, 1900. It was soon performed in Germany, Holland, France, and the United States, the American première taking place at the Tivoli Opera House in San Francisco on November 27, 1903.

Shortly after the successful première of *Zaza,* Leoncavallo was commissioned by Emperor Wilhelm II of Germany to write an opera glorifying the house of Hohenzollern. *Der Roland von Berlin* was produced at the Berlin Royal Opera on December 13, 1904. Despite a lavish presentation, royal patronage, and the splendor of its première, *Der Roland* failed to make a strong impression.

In 1906 Leoncavallo toured the United States and Canada, conducting *Pagliacci*. He completed a new opera for this tour, *La Jeunesse de Figaro,* but it failed so disastrously that he never attempted to mount it in Europe. Leoncavallo visited the United States again in 1913, as guest conductor of the San Francisco Opera.

Though he continued to write opera until the end of his life, Leoncavallo was never able to recapture the spark that had illuminated *Pagliacci*. The première of one of his last operas, *Edipo re,* was heard in Chicago on December 13, 1920. It was a posthumous performance, Leoncavallo having died in his villa in Montecatini, Italy, on August 9, 1919.

PRINCIPAL WORKS

Ballet—La Vita d'una marionetta.

Operas—I Medici; Pagliacci; La Bohème; Zaza; Der Roland von Berlin; Maia; Malbruk; La Reginetta delle rose; I Zingari; La Candidata; Goffredo Mameli; Prestami tua moglie; Edipo Re; Il Primo bacio.

Orchestral Music—Serafita.

Vocal Music—Songs for voice and piano, including Lasciati amar, Mattinata, Sérénade française, Sérénade napolitaine.

ABOUT

Biancolli, L. (editor), The Opera Reader; Newman, E., More Stories of Famous Operas.

Monthly Musical Record, September 1919; Musical America, September 6, 1919; Musical Times, September 1919.

Jean François Lesueur 1760-1837

JEAN FRANÇOIS LESUEUR was born in Drucat-Plessiel, near Abbeville, France, on February 15, 1760, the son of humble peasants. He reacted sensitively to musical experiences as a child: to the hymns in church; to a military band that passed through his town, which he followed for miles until he fell by the wayside in exhaustion. At seven he became a chorister in Abbeville. For two years, beginning in

Lesueur: lē-sü-ûr'

1774, he took academic courses in Amiens, but broke them off to concentrate on music. He became *maître de musique* at the Séez Cathedral in 1779, then assumed the post of *sous-maître* at the Church of the Innocents in Paris, where he studied harmony with the Abbé Roze. In 1781 he was appointed *maître de musique* of the Dijon Cathedral. After serving as *maître de musique* in Le Mans and Tours, he returned to Paris in 1784 to take over the Abbé's chores as choirmaster at the Church of the Innocents. The year 1784 also marked his official debut as composer with the introduction of several of his motets at a Concert Spirituel in Paris. Two years later, the Concert Spirituel also presented the première of his cantata *L'Ombre de Sacchini,* which Lesueur had written upon that composer's death.

In 1786 Lesueur competed successfully for the splendid office of *maître de musique* of the Notre Dame Cathedral in Paris. He introduced a full-sized orchestra into the services, so that he could give performances of world-famous choral compositions. This move was part of a major reform he was attempting to institute in French church music which included not only the presentation of ambitious, large-scale compositions but the introduction of religious music dramas into the church to excite the enthusiasm of worshipers. Lesueur's performances attracted huge audiences, including many poor people from all parts of Paris who had never before attended a religious service at Notre Dame.

The more conservative branch of the clergy looked askance upon Lesueur's reforms, feeling that religious services were being cheapened through the presentation of huge musical spectacles which it derisively dubbed "beggars' operas." In addition, this segment of the clergy objected vehemently to the enormous expenses involved in the execution of Lesueur's musical activities.

In an effort to justify his reforms, Lesueur published in 1787 the *Essai de musique sacrée* in which he clarified his ideas. He explained that his aim was to apply to church music the principles previously established by Gluck in opera; that church music, like the music of Gluck's operas, should reflect with sensitivity the mood and message of the text, and thus should not hesitate to be descriptive, programmatic, expressive, or dramatic. He felt too that the

JEAN FRANÇOIS LESUEUR

character of church music should vary with the different holidays and festivals of the year. It is interesting to note that Lesueur in this essay was one of the earliest theorists to suggest the use of a *Leitmotiv* technique, as well as to promote the cause of program music. To answer Lesueur's arguments, a violent anonymous attack was published in 1787. Lesueur replied with still another monograph, *Exposé d'une musique,* in which he reaffirmed his ideas.

The opposition of some of his superiors compelled Lesueur to resign his post at Notre Dame in 1788 and to go into temporary seclusion in a country home. When he returned to Paris in 1792 he was no longer a propagandist for church music, but a composer of opera. On February 16, 1793, *La Caverne* (based on the celebrated novel of Lesage, *Gil Blas*) was produced at the Théâtre Feydeau with extraordinary success. *Paul et Virginie,* derived from the novel of Bernardin de Saint Pierre, followed on January 13, 1794, and *Télémaque* on May 11, 1796, both at the Théâtre Feydeau. Now one of France's most highly esteemed opera composers, Lesueur received many official honors. Soon after the triumph of *La Caverne* he became professor at the École de la Garde Nationale; upon the founding of the Paris Conservatory in 1795 he was made one of its Inspectors.

In 1802 Lesueur became again embroiled in bitter controversy when two of his operas, scheduled for performance at the Opéra, were displaced to make room for the work of another composer. He launched a fierce tirade against the Opéra, and against the Conservatory, which had sponsored his rival. In addition, a pamphlet he had written the preceding year—*Projet d'un plan général de l'instruction musicale en France*—severely criticizing the curriculum of the Conservatory, was not taken lightly by the head of that institution. Consequently, in the fall of 1802, Lesueur lost his post at the Conservatory. For two years he knew poverty and the disdain of his fellow musicians. But in 1804 he was restored to favor with his appointment as *maître de chapelle* to the First Consul, on the recommendation of Paisiello. His high status as a composer was also regained with the production of *Ossian* on July 10, 1804, and with the performance later that year of a Te Deum and a Mass at Notre Dame for Napoleon's coronation.

Honors came his way again. He was made a member of the Legion of Honor, and performances of his work won wide attention. When Lesueur married Adeline Jamart de Courchamp in 1806, Napoleon and Josephine signed the marriage contract. In 1813 Lesueur succeeded Grétry as a member of the Institut de France.

The downfall of Napoleon did not appreciably change Lesueur's fortunes. After the Restoration, he was made principal composer and music master at the chapel of Louis XVIII. In 1818 he became professor of composition at the Conservatory, retaining this post until his death.

Lesueur died in Paris on October 6, 1837. Fifteen years after his death a monument to him was erected in Abbeville; for this occasion Ambroise Thomas composed the *Song of Triumph.*

A contemporary thus described Lesueur: "His features were hard, noble, lit with superior intelligence which, so to speak, embellished his face. His brow was high and polished like a marble-top table, destined to receive and efface the thousand impressions which confronted it. His mouth was finely shaped, his lips were sensitive. . . . His cheeks were pale, made thin by constant study and by the many battles of his life." With his shock of gray hair, the piercing intensity of the eyes beneath heavy brows, and his ascetic face he had "the air of a patriarch," as Gounod said of him. He was

unworldly and impractical in matters pertaining to social position, money, or career, but he was endowed with inordinate pride and vanity. It was said of him that he had three guiding stars: Homer, the Bible, and Napoleon. A devotee of Greek music, he often insisted in his classroom, with utter seriousness, that one Greek mode represented morality, another license.

Lesueur is today remembered primarily as a teacher, theoretician, and musical personality. "His music," says Mary Hargreave, "is a mixture of simplicity and complexity. He was a poet, philosopher and a writer, as well as a musician, and was full of ideals which were too difficult of execution, especially with his primitive notion of harmony."

PRINCIPAL WORKS

Choral Music—Cantatas, Masses, motets, oratorios, Passions, psalms, Stabat Mater, Te Deums.

Operas—La Caverne; Paul et Virginie; Télémaque; Ossian; Tyrtée; Artaxerse; Alexandre à Babylone.

ABOUT

Boschot, A., La Jeunesse d'un romantique; Fouqué, O., Les Révolutionnaires de la musique; Hargreave, M., The Early French Musicians; Lamy, F., Jean François Lesueur; Servières, G., Épisodes d'histoire musicale.

Franz Liszt *1811-1886*

FRANZ LISZT was born in Raiding, Hungary, on October 22, 1811. His father was a humble employee on the Esterházy estate, and a dedicated musical amateur. He recognized his son's musical talent and had him begin piano lessons at the age of six. Only three years later Franz was giving impressive concerts in Hungarian cities—concerts that prompted several Hungarian aristocrats to finance the boy's further musical education in Vienna. Provided with a handsome annual subsidy for six years, Franz and his family settled in Vienna in 1821. There he studied the piano with Karl Czerny and composition with Salieri, making a highly successful Vienna début as a pianist on December 1, 1822. In 1823 Franz gave a second concert in Vienna which was attended by Beethoven; the master took the boy into his arms, kissed him, and prophesied for him a magnificent future. The boy also made his official bow as a composer in Vienna by contributing a piece to the *Vaterländische Künstlerverein*, a series of variations by several composers on a melody by Diabelli, published in 1823.

Toward the end of 1823, Franz left Vienna for Paris, intending to enter the Conservatory. En route he played in Munich and Stuttgart. In Paris, he passed his entrance examinations brilliantly, but Cherubini, the director of the Conservatory, denied him admission because the child was a foreigner and because of his own violent prejudice against prodigies. The twelve-year-old Liszt was then placed with private instructors in Paris, notably Paër and Reicha in composition; but he took no further lessons in piano, preferring to work out his technical and artistic problems by himself. He made swift strides. On March 8, 1824, he played a concerto by Hummel at the Opéra and made a decisive conquest of musical Paris.

Now a pet of Parisian high society, Liszt performed in the most important salons of the city. He was also lionized in London, where he appeared later in 1824. His concerts in England were so sensational that he was invited to give a command performance for George IV. One London critic went so far as to say that Liszt, in his virtuosity, yielded the palm "to Hummel alone."

After his return to Paris Liszt's one-act opera *Don Sanche* was produced at the Opéra on October 17, 1825. It was presented only five times and was never performed again; nor did Liszt attempt again to write for the stage. (The score, long believed to have been destroyed in a fire, was discovered intact in 1903 and two excerpts were published in *Die Musik,* issue of May 1904.)

For two years Liszt gave concerts throughout Europe with phenomenal success. Then, in 1827, the death of his father brought about his pious resolution to change his way of life. He was weary of the pomp and brilliance of a virtuoso's career, "a musician in the pay of the great folk," as he himself described it at the time, "paid for by them like a conjurer or a clever dog." Turning his modest funds over to his mother, Liszt found simple lodgings in Paris and decided to lead a more ascetic and dedicated life. Supporting himself by teaching piano, he was consumed at first by religious ardor. But he soon grew weary of religion, and turned with equal fervor to literature and philosophy, devouring works by Montaigne, Voltaire, Chateaubriand, Rousseau, Sainte-Beuve, and other French masters. The in-

FRANZ LISZT

fluence of French Romanticism was later apparent in his compositions.

Then (though the route was circuitous) Liszt went back to music. Three eminent musicians were responsible for reviving his passion for music. The first was Paganini, whose violin performances stirred in Liszt the ambition to become a "Paganini of the piano," a virtuoso of virtuosos. He hurled his formidable energies into further developing his piano technique: "Here is a whole fortnight that my mind and fingers have been working like two lost spirits. . . . Beethoven, Bach, Hummel, Mozart, Weber are all around me. I study them, meditate on them, devour them with fury; besides this, I practise four to five hours of exercises (thirds, sixths, eighths, tremolos, repetitions of the notes, cadenzas, and so forth). Ah! provided I don't go mad, you will find an artist in me!"

Out of this concentrated two-year period of study and exercise Liszt emerged in 1833, as he had hoped he would, the foremost piano virtuoso of his generation. At this time two other important musicians, Chopin and Berlioz, turned him in still another musical direction. Those composers, whom he admired profoundly, inspired Liszt to create Romantic music, rich in poetic thought, vitalized by dramatic feeling, vibrant with realistic approaches. The incomparable virtuoso was also growing into an outstanding creative figure, a giant of the German Romantic movement.

In 1833 his personal life began to encroach upon his career. Always susceptible to women and highly attractive to them, Liszt embarked on a passionate relationship that kept him from the concert stage for two years. His beloved was the Countess d'Agoult. In her *Memoirs,* which appeared under the pseudonym Daniel Stern (as did her other literary efforts), she recalled; "Strong affinities of race and temperament brought them together, but the extreme differences in their education and station in life of necessity raised up innumerable difficulties around them. A thousand obstacles arose between them and endowed the passion that drove them towards each other with a dolorous intensity which, in more balanced days than these, love will never know again."

The Countess, who was estranged from her husband (by whom she had three children), went with Liszt to Geneva in 1833. They lived together for four years, during which time three children were born to them. One of the children, Cosima, duplicated her mother's convention-shattering adventure years later by deserting her own husband, Hans von Bülow, to live with Richard Wagner.

By 1839 their love idyll had run its course. The clash of two strong artistic personalities produced a perhaps inevitable rupture. Liszt was now engaged in the triumphal series of tours that carried him throughout Europe and made him the idol of concert audiences everywhere from England to Russia and Turkey.

It is with Liszt that the modern piano virtuoso can be said to have emerged: Liszt was the first pianist with sufficient audience appeal to succeed in giving an entire concert without the aid of other soloists or an orchestra, bringing about the first piano recital in concert history. This development took place in Rome in 1839 with a solo performance which Liszt described as a "musical soliloquy"; his concert in London on May 1, 1840 was the first to be designated as a "recital." He was one of the first to establish the concert stage tradition of having the pianist perform with his profile facing the audience, for he was particularly vain about his profile. And Liszt was also one of the first to introduce head tossing, facial contortions, and sweeping hand motions to dramatize his performances.

Certainly never before, and perhaps never since, has a concert artist known the kind of adulation that Liszt enjoyed everywhere. At his concerts, women threw jewels on the stage, even fainted. His public fought savagely at the end of his concert to gain possession of his gloves, which he sometimes left on the piano, or the stub of his cigar, which was always to be found backstage. Heine described a concert at which two Hungarian countesses tore each other's hair for possession of Liszt's snuff-box. Simply to look at him, or touch him, was a privilege that threw his admirers into raptures.

He had no rivals, and when some contender threatened his supremacy in the concert hall, he went out of his way to put him in his place. Hearing that Sigmund Thalberg had scored triumphs in Paris with several piano recitals, Liszt set out for the French capital to prove that he was still king. In 1837 each pianist performed, and since each was a remarkable virtuoso, the issue was subject to considerable argument. To decide the matter conclusively, Princess Cristina Gelgojoso invited both pianists to her salon for a "musical duel." Thalberg played his highly technical fantasy on Rossini's *Moïse;* Liszt followed with his dazzling arrangement of melodies from a now forgotten opera. The final consensus gave the victory to Liszt.

In 1847 a second *grand passion* began for Liszt. While performing in Kiev, he attracted the interest of Princess Carolyne von Sayn-Wittgenstein, who invited him to her estate. Liszt went and remained. He and the Princess felt a strong physical and intellectual attraction for each other. Both were devotees of literature, both had a natural bent for religion and mysticism.

In 1848 Liszt was appointed court *Kapellmeister* in Weimar, where his duties included the direction of symphonic concerts and operas. Princess Carolyne joined him, and for a decade they lived together in Weimar, making their home a center of artistic activity. But such open flouting of convention caused much resentment and Liszt's musical activities were almost as controversial. For, determined to maintain the highest artistic standards, he was indefatigable in his efforts to support the cause of New Music, and too many of his offerings proved unpalatable to bourgeois tastes. Yet Liszt transformed Weimar into one of the great music centers of Europe.

In his passionate dedication to New Music, Liszt became one of the first to enter the battle in behalf of Wagner. He produced *Tannhäuser* and *Der fliegende Holländer* in magnificent performances. After Wagner had been discredited in Germany because of his involvement in revolutionary activities, it was to Liszt's door that he came in 1849, an exile seeking refuge. When the rest of Germany regarded him as an outcast, Liszt welcomed him with open arms. And Liszt was courageous enough to give the world première of Wagner's *Lohengrin,* on August 28, 1850.

During his decade in Weimar, Liszt also emerged as a composer of first significance. Largely through the influence of Princess Carolyne, Liszt extended the scope of his creative activities. Formerly a writer of music primarily for piano, in which area he had opened new vistas for piano style and technique, Liszt was now encouraged to work in larger orchestral forms, to embark on new techniques and approaches, and to experiment with dramatic and poetic expressions, bringing the Romantic era in music to a new, rich phase.

With *Ce qu'on entend sur la montagne,* inspired by Victor Hugo, Liszt completed the first of thirteen orchestral works which brought a significant musical structure into existence: the tone poem or symphonic poem. Liszt's aim was to bring to orchestral music some of the dramatic expressiveness and aesthetic principles of the Wagnerian music-drama. In his hands the tone poem became a flexible structure for translating into musical terms some poem, story, painting, or idea. Through the tone poem Liszt introduced a new dramatic vividness to programmatic writing and an increased articulateness to orchestral music. His most famous tone poem is *Les Préludes,* based on Lamartine; it was introduced in Weimar on February 28, 1854. Also popular are *Tasso, Lamento e trionfo,* after Byron, and *Mazeppa,* after Victor Hugo, both introduced in 1854.

In addition to creating the tone poem Liszt helped popularize the form of the rhapsody. This was another elastic, freely developed form, for piano, in which popular melodies were used in a rhapsodic manner. Liszt wrote nineteen *Hungarian Rhapsodies,*

the first in 1846. They were among the earliest successful attempts to use the rhapsody form, and at the same time proved a pioneer effort in musical nationalism. The second of these rhapsodies is one of the most frequently played compositions in this form.

In two so-called symphonies—*Dante,* introduced in Weimar on July 8, 1856, and *Faust,* heard in Weimar on September 5, 1857—Liszt extended the boundaries of the tone poem to epic dimensions. At the same time he embarked on new approaches to harmony, tonality, orchestration, sonority, thematic presentation and development; some of these techniques foreshadowed methods employed by the avant-garde composers of the twentieth century.

Though Liszt remained in Weimar until 1861, he resigned from his musical post in 1859. The antagonism of Weimar to his passionate and untiring efforts on behalf of New Music—specifically, the hostility toward the world première of Cornelius' comic opera *The Barber of Bagdad*—had convinced him that his immediate environment was not congenial to music making of the highest order. "I had dreamed of a new art period for Weimar like that of Karl August, in which Wagner and I should have been leaders as formerly Goethe and Schiller were," he lamented, "but unfavorable circumstances brought these dreams to naught." Rather than lower his standards he decided to withdraw.

After his attempt to marry Princess Carolyne failed in 1861, Liszt embraced religion, and lived mainly in Rome for several years. His aim now was to become a priest, but his past made this ideal impossible. He did, however, take minor orders and received the tonsure in 1865. Pope Pius IX having conferred upon him the dignity of Abbé in the Third Order of St. Francis of Assisi, he was henceforth known as the Abbé Liszt.

Despite this preoccupation with religion, Liszt continued to dedicate himself to music. He taught piano to students who flocked to him from all parts of the world, bringing to this task both high-minded purpose and generosity. An entire generation of great piano virtuosos received some of their training from him, including Hans von Bülow, Tausig, Sgambati, Moritz Rosenthal, and Emil Sauer. In 1875 Liszt extended his teaching activities, becoming president of the New Hungarian Academy of Budapest.

Liszt never accepted payment from his students. Harold C. Schonberg has described his classes: "The students would gather and restlessly wait, talking in whispers. At around 4 P.M. everyone would begin to murmur: 'Der Meister kommt.' The Meister walks into the room. All stand and move respectfully toward him. The ladies kiss his hand. Liszt grandly tells all to be seated. He is never spoken to unless he speaks first. He looks over the pile of music on one of the pianos. A piece interests him. The pianist who has prepared it comes to the piano at the royal summons. Liszt listens. He comments. Sometimes he impatiently sweeps the miserable wretch from the piano and plays the piece as it should be played. All of the young girls in the class immediately start swooning. The Meister smiles deprecatingly, but he is pleased."

Though Liszt never wavered in his admiration and stout support of Wagner's music-dramas and theories, he became estranged from Wagner in 1866 when the latter (less than two years younger than Liszt) began to live with Liszt's daughter Cosima, the wife of Hans von Bülow. Wagner and Liszt remained unfriendly until 1872 when Liszt went to Bayreuth to attend the groundbreaking ceremonies of the Wagner festival theater. Though Liszt was a frequent visitor at the Bayreuth festival after that, and maintained a more sympathetic relationship with Wagner, Cosima herself never forgave her father, and would not allow him to visit her at the Wagner villa, Wahnfried. She refused even to permit Liszt to attend Wagner's funeral in 1883.

While attending the Bayreuth Festival in 1886, Liszt fell seriously ill during the performance of Tristan and Isolde and was forced to leave the theater. Pneumonia set in and proved fatal. Liszt died in Bayreuth on July 31, 1886. The last word he uttered was "Tristan."

Amy Fay, an American who studied with Liszt, described him as "tall and slight, with deep-set eyes, shaggy eyebrows, and long iron-gray hair which he wears parted in the middle. His mouth turns up in the corners which gives him a most crafty and Mephistophelean expression when he smiles, and his whole appearance and manner have a sort of Jesuitical elegance and ease. His hands are very narrow, with long and slender fingers that look as if they had twice as many joints as other people's! They are so flexible and supple that it makes you nervous to look at them. Anything like the polish of his manner I never saw. When he got up to leave the box, for instance, after his adieu to the ladies, he laid his hand on his heart and made his final bow—not with affectation, or in mere gallantry, but with quiet courtliness which made you feel that no other way of bowing to a lady was right or proper. It was most characteristic. But the most extraordinary thing about Liszt is his wonderful variety of expression and play of feature. One moment his face will look dreamy, shadowy, tragic. The next he will be insinuating, amiable, ironic, sardonic; but always the same captivating grace of manner."

Saint-Saëns said that "the influence of Liszt on the destiny of the piano was immense. . . . We owe to him the invention of picturesque musical notation, thanks to which, by an ingenious disposition of the notes, and an extraordinary variety in presenting them to the eye, the author contrived to indicate the character of the passage and the exact way in which it should be executed. Today, these refined methods are in general use. But, above all, we owe to Liszt the introduction of the piano of orchestral effects and sonority."

Daniel Gregory Mason has explained that Liszt's method in composing symphonic music lay in "combining the musical organization of the classics with the dramatic organization of Berlioz. . . . By the use of program and leading motives, he secured the advantages of the realistic school: freedom from the shackles of the strict traditional sonata form and a 'poetic' principle of coherence. By retaining thematic development, he reinforced this poetic coherence by musical logic, and avoided to some extent the fragmentary effects into which unmodified realism generally falls. To the thirteen orchestral pieces in which he most strikingly embodied this plan of interlinked dramatic and musical structure he gave the name of poèmes symphoniques, generally translated as "symphonic poems" [or tone poems]. He owes his chief historical importance to his creation of this form, which he exemplified also on a larger scale in his Faust and Dante symphonies."

Because Liszt is most famous for his lesser and more sentimental compositions—the Hungarian Rhapsodies, the two piano concertos, the *Liebesträume* for piano solo, *Les Préludes, La Campanella*, and so forth—his true creative importance, as manifested in his more ambitious productions, has often been sadly underestimated and misunderstood. "The real, fundamental Liszt," wrote Cecil Gray, "is not the brilliant and facile rhetorician that he is invariably made out to be, delighting principally in grandiose sonorities and triumphant apotheoses; the essence of his art, on the contrary, consists in a sadness, a melancholy, a disillusion, a despair, of depth and intensity unequaled, perhaps in all music. . . . This is the essential Liszt. It is here that his true greatness lies, here that he is original, unique, unsurpassed." The "essential Liszt" can be found in the best pages of his remarkable sets of piano pieces collectively entitled *Années de pèlerinage,* and in *Harmonies poétiques et religieuses,* also for the piano; in the monumental Piano Sonata in B minor; in the *Dante* and *Faust* Symphonies.

PRINCIPAL WORKS

Choral Music—Hungarian Coronation Mass; Mass in C minor; Missa Choralis in A minor; Requiem; Die Legende von der heiligen Elisabeth; Christus; Hungaria; Die heilige Cäcilia; 9 choruses with organ; various other choruses; psalms.

Orchestral Music—13 tone poems; 2 piano concertos; A Faust Symphony; A Symphony to Dante's Divine Comedy; Two Episodes from Lenau's Faust; Second Mephisto Waltz; Hungarian Fantasy, for piano and orchestra; Totentanz, for piano and orchestra.

Piano Music—19 Hungarian Rhapsodies; 2 concert études; Deux Légendes; Études d'exécution transcendante; Album d'un voyageur; Années de pèlerinage; Harmonies poétiques et religieuses; Sonata in B minor Weihnachtsbaum; Albumblätter, ballades, caprices, Consolations, Czardas, Ländler, Liebesträume, mazurkas, rhapsodies, and numerous transcriptions.

Vocal Music—Songs for voice and piano, including: Du bist wie eine Blume, Es muss ein Wunderbares sein, Kling leise, mein Lied, O Lieb', so lang du lieben kannst (original song version of the celebrated Liebestraum for piano), Oh quand je dors.

ABOUT

Agoult, M. de, Mémoires; Beckett, W., Liszt; Chantavoine, J., Franz Liszt; Corder, F., Franz Liszt; Friedheim, A., Life and Liszt; Haldane, C., The Galley Slaves of Love: The Story of Marie d'Agoult and Franz Liszt; Harsányi, Z. von, Hungarian Melody; Hill, R., Liszt; Huneker, J. G., Franz Liszt; Newman, E., The Man Liszt; Pourtalès, G. de, Franz Liszt: The Man of Love; Searle, H., The Music of Liszt; Westerby, H., Liszt, Composer, and His Piano Works.

Pietro Locatelli *1695-1764*

PIETRO LOCATELLI, early eighteenth century composer for the violin, was born in Bergamo, Italy, on September 3, 1695. Little is known of his early life beyond the fact that he studied in Rome with Corelli. After completing these studies he wrote and published twelve concerti grossi in 1721. Four years later he entered the service of the Landgrave of Hesse-Darmstadt, then residing in Mantua. Next he toured Europe as a concert violinist, achieving renown for his dynamic technique. His occasional exploitation of unique pyrotechnical effects is reflected in some of his violin studies and caprices.

Locatelli established permanent residence in Amsterdam, where he inaugurated a series of highly popular violin concerts. His activity as a composer continued unabated. He published a volume of flute sonatas in 1732; a volume of concertos and caprices, under the title of *L'Arte del violono*, in 1733; a series of concertos in 1735; and a series of trio-sonatas and a second group of violin sonatas in 1737. Six *concerti a quattro* and a group of trios appeared in 1741.

Locatelli's influence as a performer and composer was far-reaching. He brought violin virtuosity to a new stage of development, largely through his effective use of double stops and the high positions. As a composer for violin, remarked Edmund van der Straeten, Locatelli's "share in the de-

PIETRO LOCATELLI

velopment of the sonata form is by no means inconsiderable. Paganini owes a great deal of his art to a close study of Locatelli's twenty-four caprices, which are really transcendental technique." Locatelli was also important in developing the structure and enriching the musical content of the concerto grosso, a form which he had mastered under the tutelage of Corelli.

Pietro Locatelli died in Amsterdam, Holland, on March 30, 1764.

PRINCIPAL WORKS

Chamber Music—Quartet-concertos; trio-sonatas; violin sonatas; flute sonatas.
Orchestral Music—Concerti grossi; violin concertos.
Violin Music—Caprices, études.

ABOUT

Koole, A., Leven en Werken van Pietro Locatelli; Phipson, T. L., Biographical Sketches of Celebrated Violinists; Pincherle, M., Les Violonistes; Straeten, E. van der, The History of the Violin.
Bolletino della Biblioteca Civica di Bergamo, May 1920.

Matthew Locke *1630-1677*

MATTHEW LOCKE, England's most eminent composer for the stage before Henry Purcell, was born in Exeter in or about 1630. At the age of eight he became a chorister at the Exeter Cathedral, where

MATTHEW LOCKE

for three years he was trained by its organist, Edward Gibbons, brother of the celebrated Orlando Gibbons. It is believed that he studied music further with William Wake.

In 1648 Locke visited the Low Countries, where he was first introduced to, and influenced by, Italian contrapuntal music, particularly the motet. He had returned to England by 1651, the year in which he completed his first work, the *Little Consort of Three Parts* for viols or violins, published in 1656. In 1652 he completed a set of duos for two bass viols.

Locke's first attempt to write for the stage was the score for Shirley's *Cupid and Death,* which he wrote in 1653 in collaboration with Christopher Gibbons. Three years later he wrote part of the score for Davenant's *The Siege of Rhodes,* a play in which he also appeared as vocal soloist. His most important music for the stage was written for Shakespeare's *Macbeth* in 1663, Shadwell's *Psyche* in 1673, and Shakespeare's *The Tempest* in 1674. These and similar efforts have won Locke his reputation, with many musicologists, as the first great English composer of music for the theater.

Locke also achieved prominence in English music with creations in areas outside the theater. In 1661 he wrote a remarkable work for brass (one of the earliest of its kind in England), which was performed during the coronation ceremonies of Charles II, for the King's procession through London from the Tower to Whitehall on April 22. That year, Charles II appointed Locke "composer in the private musick" and "composer in Ordinary." Locke was later engaged as personal organist for Queen Catherine.

Locke died in London in August 1677. and is believed to have been buried in the chapel of the Savoy Palace. Henry Purcell wrote an elegy for Locke's funeral.

Locke's music, according to Frederick Bridge, was "exceedingly dramatic and melodious." His harmony, said W. H. Cummings, "evinces a freshness and variety far in advance of the period in which it was composed."

Summing up Locke's place in English music, Jeffrey Pulver remarked that all of Locke's music is "marked by an obvious desire to do his best—often in a style that did not suit him. Thus his sacred music, though good, lacks that spontaneity which his dramatic work exhibits."

Chamber Music—Courtly Masquing Ayres; Little Consort of Three Parts; Consort of Four Parts.
Choral Music—Anthems, hymns.
Stage Music—Cupid and Death (with Christopher Gibbons); The Siege of Rhodes (with others); Psyche; Macbeth; The Empress of Morocco; The Tempest.
Vocal Music—Various songs for voice and accompaniment.

ABOUT
Bridge, F., Twelve Good Musicians; Pulver, J. A., A Biographical Dictionary of Old English Music; Walker, E., A Short History of English Music.
International Music Society Congress, May-June 1911.

Jean-Baptiste Loeillet *1680-1730*

JEAN-BAPTISTE LOEILLET, early eighteenth-century composer of music for the flute, was born in Ghent, Belgium, on November 18, 1680. His music study began in Ghent and was completed in Paris, where he also wrote his first compositions. Some of these works were published in Amsterdam and dedicated to various French patrons.

In 1705 Loeillet moved to London and remained for the rest of his life; his Anglicized name was John Loeillet. For five years he played flute and oboe in the orchestra of the Queen's Theatre in Haymarket, then resigned in 1710 to teach and play the harpsichord. At his home in Hart Street, he inaugurated a series of weekly concerts which were responsible for introducing Corelli's concertos to English audiences. It is also through Loeillet's performances on the German transverse flute that this instrument became favored by English flautists.

Loeillet died in London, on July 19, 1730. He bequeathed a modest legacy and a valuable collection of musical instruments to various relatives. (He had never married.) His brother Jacques was a well-known oboist; his half-brother Pierre and his uncle Pierre Emmanuel also were distinguished professional musicians.

Loeillet wrote many works for flute and keyboard. From Grove's *Dictionary* we learn that he "was not a genius," but that nevertheless he had a "noticeable gift for melody. . . . His writing for harpsichord shows distinct traces of Italian influence and his not infrequent use of ornamentation points

to a knowledge of the French school. His slow movements in particular have much charm and grace. His flute and oboe music is well adapted to its purpose."

Chamber Music—Numerous sonatas for various solo instrument, or instruments, and accompaniment.
Keyboard Music—Lessons for harpsichord (or spinet); Suites of Lessons, for harpsichord (or spinet).

ABOUT
Music Review, May 1955.

Karl Loewe *1796-1869*

JOHANN KARL GOTTFRIED LOEWE, outstanding composer of German ballads, was born in Löbejün, near Halle, on November 30, 1796. He was the youngest child of the village schoolmaster and choirleader. Karl's father gave him his first music lessons. In 1807 the boy became a chorister in the court chapel in Cöthen, where, as he later wrote in his autobiography, "the people admired and made much of me." After two years he proceeded to Halle to enter the Franke Institut, directed by Türk. Türk took the boy under his wing and gave him private instruction in singing and theory. Loewe's vocal talent made a strong impression wherever he appeared at public or private functions. On one occasion Mme. de Staël, the celebrated patroness of the arts, gave him a valuable gift; on another, King Jerome of Westphalia, brother of Napoleon, endowed him with an annual grant of three hundred thalers which enabled him to complete his music studies. It was during this period that Loewe completed his first two songs, "Klothar" and "Das Gebet des Herrn und die Einsetzungsworte des Abendmahls."

After the war of 1812-1813 and the downfall of the Bonapartes, Loewe's annuity was terminated. He enrolled at the University of Halle as a student of theology, while continuing his music studies at the Singakademie. He also joined a vocal quartet which gave public concerts and which, in time, expanded in size and influence until it was capable of performing oratorios and operas. There he met and fell in love with the soprano Julie von Jacob.

Loewe now became interested in the ballad. This was a setting for voice and piano of an extended poem that utilized dialogue

KARL LOEWE

as well as narrative. English in origin, the form is generally thought to have been introduced in Germany by Johann Zumsteeg (1760-1802). Loewe (like Franz Schubert) was stimulated by Zumsteeg's example to write ballads and to make that vocal form a vibrant and compelling musical art.

Loewe's first two ballads, written in 1818, are considered to be among his finest; both were published through the generosity of Loewe's friend Adolf B. Marx. One of these is "Edward," written to a poem by Herder. The other, "Der Erlkönig," is based on the same poem by Goethe which Schubert had set to music three years earlier. It speaks profoundly for the high quality of Loewe's "Der Erlkönig" that his ballad does not suffer in comparison with the Schubert masterpiece.

In 1819 Loewe visited Dresden, where he met and became a friend of Carl Maria von Weber. Then he proceeded to Jena to present a copy of "Der Erlkönig" to Goethe. "Goethe was exceedingly kind," Loewe later recalled, "and while walking up and down with me, conversed pleasingly about the nature of the ballad. . . . I told him that I liked the ballad above all other forms of poetry and how the popular legend of the Erlking in the grand romantic garb of his poem had quite captivated me; so much so, indeed, that I could not help setting it to music."

In 1820 Loewe passed the examinations for a professorship at the Gymnasium and Seminary in Stettin. A year later he also became director of the municipality of the town and organist of the St. Jacobus Church. Loewe was now able to marry his fiancée, Julie von Jacob, on September 7, 1821. But their marriage ended suddenly and tragically, less than two years later, with Julie's death. For a year Loewe isolated himself from the society of friends. It was at this time that he composed his celebrated ballad "Der Wirtin Töchterlein." A year later, in 1824, Loewe was married a second time, to Augusta Lange, one of his pupils.

His fame as a composer grew rapidly. He was a particular favorite of King Frederick William III of Prussia and his son Frederick William IV. In 1830 he completed the oratorio *Die Zerstörung Jerusalems,* winning high acclaim. He scored an even greater success with the opera *Die drei Wünsche,* introduced in Berlin in 1834, for which the Crown Prince decorated him with a gold medal. In 1837 he was made a member of the Academy of Berlin; he subsequently received an honorary doctorate from the University of Greifswald.

Between 1837 and 1857 Loewe traveled a great deal, often in concert performances of his songs. In 1837 he appeared throughout Germany, in 1844 visited Vienna, in 1847 was heard in London (where he performed at court), and in 1857 toured Sweden, Norway, and France.

In 1864 Loewe's active career as singer, teacher, organist, and composer came to an abrupt halt, when he was stricken with what was then described as a "trance" but apparently was a form of mental derangement. By 1866 his health had deteriorated so drastically that the authorities in Stettin were obliged to request his resignation as organist and professor. As if in compensation, Loewe received royal honors soon after his resignation when Kaiser Wilhelm I elevated him to a higher grade in the Order of the Red Eagle, of which he was already a member.

Loewe left Stettin and went to live in Kiel. He died there on April 20, 1869, and was buried near the organ at St. Jacobus in Stettin.

Although Loewe wrote oratorios, five operas, and a number of orchestral, chamber music, and piano works—many of which were highly regarded by such eminent contemporaries as Schumann, Mendelssohn, and Wagner—it is through his songs and ballads that he achieved immortality. Indeed, some regard him as the foremost composer of German songs between the periods of Schubert and Brahms. Francis Toye and Dyneley Hussey have written: "Loewe is the most important of all minor song writers, owing to the fact that he may be said definitely to have created the German dramatic ballad. Even now his setting of the '*Erlkönig*' has not been entirely swamped by Schubert's, and in the opinion of some competent judges his interpretation of the text is more conscientious if not more effective."

"The musical form of the ballad was first created through Loewe," wrote Hugo Riemann, "so far as he understood it by clinging to the development of a plastic principal motive of epical breadth without losing any of his sharp characteristic details."

Principal Works

Chamber Music—4 string quartets; Piano Trio.
Choral Music—17 oratorios.
Operas—5 operas, including Die drei Wünsche.
Orchestral Music—Concertos, overtures, symphonies.
Piano Music—Sonatas.
Vocal Music—368 ballads and songs for voice and piano, including Archibald Douglas, Edward, Das Erkennen, Der Erlkönig, Fridericus Rex, Heinrich der Vogler, Der Nöck, Odins Meeresritt, Prinz Eugen, der edle Ritter, Süsses Begräbnis, Tom der Reimer, Die Uhr, Der Wirtin Töchterlein.

About

Bach, A. B., The Art Ballad: Loewe and Schubert; Buhlthaupt, H., Karl Loewe: Deutschlands Balladenkomponist; Engel, H., Karl Loewe; König, K., Karl Loewe; Loewe, K., Autobiography; Sietz, R., Karl Loewe; Ein Gedenkbuch zum 150. Geburtstag; Wellmer, A., Karl Loewe.

Albert Lortzing *1801-1851*

GUSTAV ALBERT LORTZING was born in Berlin on October 23, 1801. Many members of his father's family were actors, and his father followed suit, giving up a leather business to enter the theater in 1811. Since the nomadic life of stage performers kept young Albert traveling with his family from one town to another during his boyhood and youth, he had no systematic education. But he did learn some French and Latin, and studied piano, violin, cello, and theory. He also made several appearances as an actor.

ALBERT LORTZING

In 1819 Lortzing turned to composition, completing several songs and choral works within the next few years. These impressed Karl Herlssohn, a novelist, who encouraged Lortzing to undertake comic opera. Lortzing's first score for the stage, *Ali Pascha von Janina,* was written in 1824 and produced four years later, on February 1, 1828, in Münster.

In his twenty-first year, Lortzing married a young actress, Rosina Regina Ahles. She bore him eleven children, five of whom died in infancy. The young couple made a number of stage appearances in several German cities, including the Cologne Theater and the court theater in Mannheim. In 1832 Lortzing wrote music for two successful stage productions. A year later he was engaged as principal tenor of the Leipzig Municipal Theater. He remained four years.

Lortzing's first successful opera was *Die beiden Schützen (The Two Marksmen)* which the Municipal Theater in Leipzig presented on February 20, 1837. It was subsequently produced in Dresden, Prague, Berlin, Munich, and Vienna. Lortzing's first masterwork was written soon after: *Zar und Zimmermann (The Czar and the Carpenter),* one of the crowning achievements of nineteenth-century German light opera. The première of this work took place at the Municipal Theater in Leipzig on December 22, 1837. Writing his own libretto, Lortzing drew his plot from an actual historical episode: the time when Peter the Great of Russia worked as a carpenter in Holland. While the central character in Lortzing's opera is Czar Peter, the role of the Burgomaster Van Bett provides most of the charm and comic interest. His opening song, "O Sancta justia," became a classic of the German comic-basso repertory, and his third-act air with chorus, "Heil sei dem Tag," is equally delightful. On the other hand Peter's romantic songs, of which "Sonst spielt' ich mit Zepter" is the most celebrated, provide the variety of emotional interest that led Lortzing to describe his work as "a sentimental comedy of contrasts."

Zar und Zimmermann won immediate success throughout Germany and Austria. Liszt thought so highly of it that he conducted it in Weimar in 1851. The first American production took place in New York on January 13, 1857.

After several dismal failures, Lortzing regained success with one of his greatest operas, *Der Wildschütz (The Poacher)*, whose première took place in Leipzig on December 31, 1842. This was Lortzing's first comic opera which fused the popular and gay elements of the old *Singspiel* with the pronounced Romantic tendencies of Weber's operas. Humorous characterizations, light and tuneful melodies, delightful parodies and travesties are here combined with spacious writing for chorus and orchestra which elevate the work to the status of folk opera. Lortzing's richness of expression and skill in writing choruses and ensemble numbers are found in the children's chorus that comes towards the end of the opera and in the vocal quartet "Kann es im Erdenleben." His felicitous touch in comedy and satire is in evidence in an episode in which Mendelssohn's *Antigone* is parodied and in Baculus's second-act air, "Fünftausend Thaler," a comic classic in German song literature. The American première of *Der Wildschütz* took place in New York on March 25, 1859.

In 1844 Lortzing was appointed conductor of the Leipzig Opera. He lost this post after several months because of intrigues within the opera company which deeply involved the director. Without a salaried post and deprived of royalties because his music was being published in pirated editions, Lortzing knew real poverty for over a year, earning a meager living through hack work. He completed a major project, however, a "light fairy opera," *Undine*, based on the famous legend of the water sprite who mar-

ries a mortal. Introduced in Magdeburg on April 21, 1845, it effectively brought German Romanticism to the light musical theater. But Lortzing's lovely melodies are more strongly influenced here by Mendelssohn than by Weber. The best of these were Undine's first-act song, "Ich scheide nun" and the second-act romance, "Es wohnt am Seegestade."

In 1846 Lortzing was invited to Vienna to direct the world première of his new opera, *Der Waffenschmied (The Armorer)*, at the Theater-an-der-Wien on May 31. Here, as in *Der Wildschütz*, we find a successful union of *Singspiel* and German Romantic opera. The marriage of *Singspiel* and Weber's nationalism is fully consummated here. The lilting tunes for Marie represent *Singspiel* at its best and most popular, as does the first-act "Armorer's Song." On the other hand, the opening chorus of the journeymen and the chorus to Spring in the second act are worthy offspring of Weber's *Der Freischütz*. The first American performance of *Der Waffenschmied* was given in New York on February 4, 1867.

After serving as principal conductor of the Theater-an-der-Wien for a short time, Lortzing returned to Leipzig, where his opera *Zum Grossadmiral* was produced in 1847. The revolution of 1848 had a disastrous effect upon his personal fortunes. With no position available, he was forced to return to acting in order to support himself and his large family. A new opera, *Rolands Knappen*, produced in Leipzig in 1849, did nothing to alleviate his distressing situation. The several songs he wrote on commission brought him small financial rewards. In 1850 he was hired as musical director of the Friedrich-Wilhelmstadt, a small theater in Berlin, which promised at least a steady, if small, income. But the position lasted for only a few months, and the loss of even this menial work brought on severe depression and physical deterioration. Lortzing died of a stroke in Berlin on January 21, 1851.

One day before his death, his last opera, *Die Opernprobe*, was introduced in Frankfurt am Main.

Lortzing was throughout life a deeply religious man. His letters are filled with expressions of profound faith in God, and this faith never left him even in the face of extreme poverty and sorrow. When he could obtain them, he enjoyed life's smaller pleasures, clothes and good wine particularly. He had a happy disposition and a ready wit. "Unlike many professional humorists," explained Ralph W. Wood, "his jocoseness flowed straight out of his own temperament. Although as prone as the next man to be quickly downcast by misfortune and disappointment, he had to reinforce the acquired consolation of religion, with a natural sanguineness and elasticity."

Lortzing's sunny nature was reflected in his music. "He never ruffled his placid audiences by any too cruel thrusts of satire," wrote Eric Blom. "It has, in fact, a great deal of the sentimentality of the old German *Singspiel*, a quality which often characterizes and frequently disfigures his music. The comic portions of his operas always have a lively aptness, enhanced by a happy knack of neat orchestration; but where it is a question of displaying tender or melancholy feelings, he lapses sadly into an almost unendurable triviality."

PRINCIPAL WORKS

Choral Music—Die himmelfahrt Christi.
Operas—Die beiden Schützen; Zar und Zimmermann; Hans Sachs; Casanova; Der Wildschütz; Undine; Der Waffenschmied; Zum Grossadmiral; Regina; Rolands Knappen; Das ersehnte Glück; Die Opernprobe.
Vocal Music—Songs for voice and piano.

ABOUT

Blom, E., Stepchildren in Music; Düringer, P. J., Albert Lortzing: sein Leben und Wirken; Kruse, G. R., Albert Lortzing; Kruse, G. R. (editor), Lortzings Briefe; Schumann, O., Albert Lortzing, sein Leben in Bildern.

Musical America, October 9, 1926; Musical Opinion, January 1923.

Jean-Baptiste Lully *1632-1687*

JEAN-BAPTISTE LULLY (Giovanni Battista Lulli), the Italian-born founder of French opera, was born in Florence on November 28, 1632, the son of a humble miller. As a child he learned to play guitar and received lessons in music theory from a Franciscan monk. In 1646 the Chevalier de Guise, en route from Malta to Paris, hired Giovanni as a page for the establishment of Mademoiselle de Montpensier, cousin to Louis XIV. Thus the boy was brought to Paris. His post with Mademoiselle de Montpensier was a humble one, his duties including teaching her Italian. He devoted his

JEAN-BAPTISTE LULLY

leisure to music, playing violin and composing tunes, and liked to entertain the domestics in the kitchen with his violin playing. The Count de Nogent, impressed by his performances, persuaded Mademoiselle de Montpensier to employ him in the house orchestra. Lully did not remain long: his musical setting of a malicious verse satirizing Mademoiselle de Montpensier resulted in his dismissal.

Lully's next post was in the orchestra of the court of Louis XIV. He soon gained considerable favor and was permitted to organize and direct an orchestra of his own, "les petits violons," for which he wrote numerous instrumental compositions. It was the stage, however, that fascinated him most. He wrote the score for a ballet, *La Nuit*, whose successful première at court on February 23, 1653, determined his career. From that time Lully was charged with writing music for court ballets, including several comic ballets based on plays by Molière (*Le Bourgeois gentilhomme, Le Mariage forcé*, and *L'Amour médecin*). In 1660, on the occasion of the King's marriage, Lully wrote a motet for the religious service.

In 1661, as a mark of royal favor, Louis XIV appointed him "composer to the King," and the next year raised him to the rank of *Maître de musique* to the royal family, also granting him a patent of nobility. Lully's fame had so overwhelmed France by this time that many French poets and essayists extolled him and his music in their writings.

Lully: lü-lē′

During the earlier years of his activity at court, Lully continued to study music assiduously, concentrating on harpsichord and composition with Nicolas Metru and François Roberday.

On July 24, 1662, Lully married Madeleine Lambert, the daughter of Michel Lambert, a court musician. It was largely a marriage of convenience, and Lully, who had frequently been involved in amorous scandals, did not change his libertine ways after he took a wife. The marriage nevertheless endured, and three sons and three daughters were born of the union.

In 1672, largely through intrigue and conniving, Lully obtained the patent for the Académie Royale de Musique, which had been founded in 1668 by the Abbé Perrin and Cambert for public performance of ballets and operas. As head of a great opera company (which eventually became the renowned Paris Opéra), Lully turned his remarkable gifts and energies to the theater. The first production with which he became involved as composer was *Les Fêtes de l'Amour et de Bacchus,* for which the French dramatist and poet Quinault pieced together pastoral scenes from various ballets. On April 27, 1673, there followed *Cadmus et Hermione,* a "tragédie en musique" with text by Quinault and music by Lully. This was Lully's first opera, and it made a deep impression. After that Lully wrote the scores for eleven more tragedies by Quinault, and three to librettos by Corneille and Campistron. It was with these works that French opera was solidly established for the first time, with traditions to which French composers were to adhere for many years.

Lully's prime contribution was to adapt Italian opera to French tastes and temperament. By associating himself with the gifted Quinault he was able to satisfy the French preference for classic drama and poetic flights. He made a study of French poetic diction by listening to recitations of Racine by Champmeslé, the celebrated actress of the Comédie Française; thus he was able to write recitatives which for the first time lent themselves gracefully to French poetry. He knew that the French were partial to ballets, spectacles, and pastoral scenes, so he introduced these elements into each of his operas. He recognized that the French preferred grace and refinement to Italian passion and emotion, and his musical style was adapted accordingly. Most important, he pleased

French audiences by making music the servant of the play rather than the reverse, as was the case with Italian opera. His recitatives were expressive and dramatic, carrying on the action, providing insight into character, or underscoring moods and emotions. His choruses had power and majesty. His orchestral writing was vivid and pictorial, creating tonal images of tempests, battles, pastoral episodes, infernal scenes, processions, and metamorphoses, with telling effect.

Lully's operas usually followed a pattern which Henri Prunières elucidated as follows: "The overture is followed by a patriotic prologue in the pastoral style with allusions to recent victories, the blessings of peace and the greatness of Louis XIV. *Chansons* and danced choruses are combined with recitations exalting 'Le Roi Soleil.' The usual theme of the five-act tragedies is love thwarted by the jealousy of a god or sorceress who raises supernatural powers against the lovers, thereby providing the stage-setter with an opportunity of raising a tempest, of changing a radiant grove into a hideous desert inhabited by monsters, or of showing his audience scenes from the Underworld. The action of the drama finds its musical expression in the recitative." Recitatives are the spine of Lully's operas, but in each opera can be found three or four arias in which Lully's lyricism is permitted to soar.

One of Lully's innovations was the so-called "French overture," as distinguished from the "Italian" employed by the Neapolitan composers. With Lully, the overture was composed in two sections, the first slow and majestic, the second lively and often in fugal style.

Lecerf de La Viéville revealed that Lully "produced one opera a year and he took three months to write it. He applied the whole of his energies to it, and worked with extreme assiduity. The rest of the year he did little to it, except for an occasional hour or so at night when he could not sleep, and on mornings, which he could not spend in pleasure. He kept his mind always fixed, however, on the opera that he was evolving, or had just evolved, and if anyone happened to learn what he was singing at any time it always proved to be an extract from an opera on hand."

Discussing Lully's operas, C. Hubert Parry wrote: "Lully developed a scheme of opera which was more mature and complete than any other of the time. The texture of his work as a whole is crude and bald, but the definition of the various items which go to make up his operatic scheme is complete as far as it goes. . . . In the first place, the plan of his overture is thoroughly distinct, and very happily conceived as an introduction to what follows. . . . Lully shows excellent sense of relief and proportion, and in regulating the relation of the respective acts and scenes to one another; and he is conspicuously successful for his time in shaking himself free from the ecclesiastical associations of the modes, and adopting a thoroughly secular manner. . . . His instinct for orderliness and system in laying out the musical material was in advance of the age. . . . He was among the first to make a notable use of what is called the aria form. . . . Lully's type of opera was an immense advance over the first experiments in plan, in definiteness of expression and rhythm, and in variety of subdivision into component ballet movements, choruses, instrumental interludes, arias, recitatives, and so forth."

Lully's creative strength grew steadily through the years. Some of his finest operas were written at the dusk of his career: *Persée* in 1682; *Phaéton* in 1683; *Amadis de Gaule* in 1684; *Roland* in 1685; and *Armide et Renaud* in 1686.

"As Lully became more master of his work," wrote Romain Rolland, "he tried not only to harmonize its different elements but to unite them, and establish a certain relationship between them. For example, in the fourth act of *Roland* he gets a dramatic feeling out of a pastoral interlude. The scene is a village wedding, with hautboys, choruses, shepherds and shepherdesses, concerted duets, and rustic dances; and quite naturally, the shepherds talk among themselves in Roland's presence and tell the story of Angélique, who has just gone off with Médor. The contrast between the quiet songs and Roland's fury has a great dramatic effect, and it has often been used since."

Armide et Renaud was described by Lecerf de La Viéville as "a supremely beautiful piece of work, with a beauty that increases in every act. . . . I do not know how the human mind could imagine anything finer than the fifth act."

In 1681 Lully was appointed "Secrétaire du roi," a position that brought with it an exalted social status.

Early in 1687 Lully directed a performance of his Te Deum, written to celebrate the recovery of the King from a serious illness. It was his last public appearance. He died in Paris, on March 22, 1687, of gangrene, a condition brought about by the incessant pounding of a heavy walking stick on his foot as he tried to beat time while conducting. Amputation of the leg, necessary to save his life, had been vigorously rejected by the composer, who preferred to place himself in the hands of a charlatan.

According to a widely circulated story, the confessor summoned to Lully's deathbed demanded of him that he burn the manuscript of his last opera in order to obtain absolution. Lully did so, but with an easy heart: he had saved a second copy in his desk.

"In person," wrote George Hogarth, "Lully was rather thick and short. His complexion was dark, and his features very far from handsome; but his face had the expression of spirit and talent. He had not the politeness which might have been expected from so long a residence at the French court; but he was gay, good humored, and his deportment was not without dignity. He was too much addicted to the pleasures of the table. . . . He was fond of money and left behind him a sum equal to a hundred thousand dollars. He was called a miser by the extravagant courtiers. He had much vivacity and wit, and told a story with admirable humor." Hogarth might have added that the composer was arrogant, unscrupulous, and even ruthless when driven by his overpowering ambitions. He was as contemptuous of his inferiors as he was obsequious to his superiors.

"He led a merry life," revealed Romain Rolland. "Lecerf says that 'he inclined to wine and the table like a rather dissolute Frenchman, but he inclined to avarice like an Italian.' His debauchery in company with the Chevalier de Lorraine was known to all; this open profligacy, in which even some of his admirers find the explanation if not the excuse for a certain carelessness in his work, contributed perhaps to his premature death. All these things did not prevent him from being a family man at times. He divided his life into two parts, but up to the end he knew how to remain on good terms with his wife. . . . He had so much confidence in his wife's wisdom that he gave his money into her care, and in his will it was to her, not to his sons or followers, that he left absolute control and management of his work—the Opéra."

Lully's immediate family erected a handsome monument to his memory which can still be seen at the church near the Place des Victoires in Paris. His epitaph reads: "God, who had given him a greater gift of music than any other man of his century, gave him also, in return for the inimitable chants he composed in His praise, a truly Christian patience in the sharp pain of the illness of which he died . . . after having received the sacraments with resignation and edifying piety."

PRINCIPAL WORKS

Ballets—Alcidiane; La Raillerie; Les Arts; Les Amours déguisés; Le Triomphe de Bacchus; Flore; La Jeunesse; Le Triomphe de l'amour; Le Temple de la paix.

Choral Music—Miserere; Mass; Te Deum; motets.

Operas—Cadmus et Hermione; Alceste; Thesée; Atys; Isis; Psyché; Bellérophon; Proserpine; Persée; Phaéton; Amadis de Gaule; Roland; Armide et Renaud; Achille et Polyxène.

Vocal Music—Au clair de la lune.

ABOUT

Borrel, E., Jean-Baptiste Lully; La Laurencie, L. de, Lully; Prunières, H., Lully; Valensi, T., Louis XIV et Lully.

Guide de concert, February 1, 1952; Musical Quarterly, October 1925.

Edward MacDowell *1861-1908*

EDWARD ALEXANDER MacDOWELL, America's foremost nineteenth-century composer, was born on Clinton Street, New York City, on December 18, 1861. His father, of Scottish descent, was a prosperous businessman. His mother was of Irish stock.

Edward received his first piano lessons from Juan Buitrago, a friend of the family. Buitrago was so impressed with the extraordinary talent of his pupil that he brought him to the attention of Teresa Carreño, the renowned concert virtuoso. Between tours, Carreño taught and coached the boy, who made such remarkable progress that Carreño prophesied a brilliant career for him as a concert pianist. When he was fifteen, Edward left with his mother for Paris. After

a year of piano study with Marmontel, MacDowell took and passed the entrance examinations for the Paris Conservatory, where he became a fellow-pupil of Debussy in Savard's class in theory.

MacDowell was never a Francophile, much less so in his earlier years. He was intolerant of French manners, behavior, music, music instruction, and general way of life. Upon hearing a recital in Paris by Nicholas Rubinstein in 1878, MacDowell exclaimed to his mother: "I can never learn to play the piano like that if I stay here." Consequently, he moved on to Germany that summer. First he attended the Stuttgart Conservatory for a brief period; then he studied theory and composition with Louis Ehlert in Wiesbaden; finally he enrolled at the Frankfurt Conservatory, where his teachers included Joachim Raff (the Conservatory director) and Karl Heymann.

The composer's widow has recorded how MacDowell came to write his first ambitious composition, the *First Modern Suite,* for piano: "MacDowell had not been long with Raff before this fine and interesting composer one day came to his pupil. 'I should like to see what you can do—not in writing exercises, but in producing a piano composition that would be your own.' MacDowell did not take the idea seriously, but promised to work on it. He spent two weeks writing his first piano suite. After this was completed he took it to Raff. When the latter had examined it, he said, 'I would like to have you show this to Franz Liszt.' "

With a letter of introduction from Raff in one hand and the manuscript of his suite in the other, MacDowell called on Liszt in Weimar, in 1882. After the master had gone through the music, he remarked, "This young American is going to be someone." He arranged for MacDowell to appear at a forthcoming music festival and persuaded his own publishers, Breitkopf and Härtel, to issue MacDowell's first compositions, including the Piano Suite, and later MacDowell's First Piano Concerto.

When Karl Heymann resigned as professor at the Frankfurt Conservatory, he recommended MacDowell for his job. This suggestion was not adopted and MacDowell left Frankfurt in 1881 to accept a post as piano teacher at the Darmstadt Conservatory. The hours were long; the demands on his time and energy exacting; the pay modest. But it ensured a certain degree of financial security, enabling MacDowell to devote his leisure to classic literature and poetry, which he devoured, and to concentrate his energies on composition.

The hard work and long hours proved so injurious to MacDowell's health that a change of occupation and scene was prescribed. He returned to Frankfurt, dividing his activity between giving private piano lessons and composition. He completed his First Piano Concerto, which was introduced in Zurich on July 11, 1882, the composer appearing as soloist. He also wrote an orchestral tone poem, *Hamlet and Ophelia,* whose immediate success brought it performances in Darmstadt, Wiesbaden, Frankfurt, and Baden-Baden.

One of MacDowell's piano students was a young American, Marian Griswold Nevins. In June 1884 MacDowell and Miss Nevins returned to the United States to marry, then returned to Europe for the honeymoon. They settled in Frankfurt, intending to remain in Germany permanently. A few years later they acquired a secluded cottage in Grubweg, a suburb of Wiesbaden, surrounded by woods.

In 1888 MacDowell finally returned to the United States, establishing himself in Boston. "Gradually," recalled T. P. Currier, "the figure of MacDowell the composer became a familiar one on the Common's walks and the nearby streets. For some time he had clung . . . to the high, full-crowned felt hat, the rather fiercely curled mustache, and the goatee. . . . Then suddenly he appeared in a derby hat, which became him extremely well; and shortly afterward the goatee vanished."

By 1889 MacDowell already was recognized as a composer of some importance. Teresa Carreño had played some of his solo piano music, including the *Second Modern Suite.* The First Piano Concerto was successfully introduced in Boston in 1888. On that occasion W. F. Apthorp wrote, "We can hardly recall a composition so full of astonishing and unprecedented effects. The work was evidently written at white heat; its brilliance and vigor are astounding." Another major work by MacDowell scored even greater success in America—the Second Piano Concerto in D minor, still one of the works most often representing him today on concert programs. It was first heard in New York on March 5, 1889, with the composer

EDWARD MacDOWELL

as soloist and Theodore Thomas conducting. Soon afterwards it was heard in Paris and Boston. James Gibbons Huneker, in reviewing the première performance, said that this concerto "easily ranks with any modern work in this form." John F. Porte subsequently described the concerto as a work "full of feeling, brilliantly cohesive and logical, with good material that is handled with confident skill. . . . Its character . . . is strong and virile, containing many passages of pure tonal beauty and eloquent expressiveness."

MacDowell lived in Boston for eight years, supporting himself by teaching piano, but devoting his main energies to composition. This period saw the creation of some of his finest works: the *Tragica* and *Eroica* sonatas for piano; the *Indian Suite,* for orchestra; various vocal pieces, including the *Six Love Songs,* op. 40; and the *Woodland Sketches* for piano, in which are found two of his most popular keyboard pieces, "To a Wild Rose" and "To a Water Lily."

When a department of music was established at Columbia University, the college president, Seth Low, and the University trustees invited MacDowell to become its head, describing him at that time as "the greatest musical genius America has produced." In 1896 MacDowell was appointed to the Robert Center Chair of Music. He hurled all his energies and dedication into teaching music "scientifically and technically," as he explained in a carefully prepared program of instruction, "with a view to training musicians who shall be competent to teach and to compose." He also aspired to "treat music historically and aesthetically as an element of liberal culture." He developed a progressive, far-sighted and independent curriculum of music study; in his own classes (for MacDowell taught all the music courses for the first two years) he was an inspiration to his pupils.

But, as Henry T. Finck later remarked sadly, it was a mistake to "harness Pegasus." The routine and clerical work involved in administering a department and conducting classes were oppressing chores, and working with many mediocre students an endless trial. To make matters worse, the new president of Columbia, Nicholas Murray Butler, objected to some of the reforms which MacDowell regarded as essential. MacDowell expressed his opposition to the new president openly and fearlessly. Then, in January 1904, seeing no other solution, he resigned from Columbia.

The conflict of interests and aims between Columbia and MacDowell was discussed at great length in the press. The "MacDowell affair," as it came to be known, aroused much bitterness in both camps. MacDowell's final words on the subject were these: "For seven years I have put all my energy and enthusiasm in the cause of art at Columbia, and now at last, recognizing the futility of my efforts, I have resigned the chair of music in order to resume my own belated vocation." Today, however, a professorship of music at Columbia University is called the Edward MacDowell Chair.

Having acquired a small, secluded farm near Peterboro, New Hampshire, in 1896, MacDowell hoped to withdraw and devote himself entirely to creativity. But his health, severely taxed, probably, by his recent conflict with Columbia, began to show startling signs of deterioration, and in 1905 all creative work ended when he suffered a mental collapse. His mind now destroyed, he would sit near a window completely oblivious of his surroundings or his company, unaware of his own identity, thumbing the pages of a fairy-tale book that seemed to bring him inexplicable pleasure. As Mary Craig put it, "He retreated into an inner solitude, a silence and a darkness of soul impenetrable to the affection of friends and the self-denying love of his brave wife. The great traditional melancholy of the star-crossed Celt covered his mind with the black heaviness of a shroud."

A fund raised in 1906 by some of America's leading musicians relieved financial pressure on the MacDowell household. But the composer did not have long to live. Tended patiently and devotedly by his wife, MacDowell died in a hotel room in New York on January 23, 1908. His body was transferred to his Peterboro farm, to be buried on an open hilltop commanding a view he loved dearly. After his death, in memory of her husband, his widow established at the farm a colony for artists, writers, and poets, where they could work in congenial surroundings at a negligible weekly rate. The colony remained Mrs. MacDowell's prime interest up to the time of her death in 1956.

This is how T. P. Currier described MacDowell's appearance: "His finely shaped head, carried a little to one side, was well set on slightly drooping shoulders. His very dark hair was close-cut. . . . There was about him no trace of the 'professional artist.'. . . His skin was light and clear, showing a slight color in his rather delicately rounded cheeks. Light blue eyes, with light bordering of eyebrows and lashes, a well-cut aquiline nose, and an agreeable mouth and firm chin, completed what anyone would call a handsome face. It was equally expressive. Even casual acquaintances could read in it a kindly disposition, strong sense of humor, energy and determination. In conversation, he regarded one frankly and intently; and his mouth mirrored with extreme quickness his instinctive response. Anything pleasant or humorous would bring a lively twinkle into the eyes, rapid winking of eyelids, and a contagious smile or deep hearty laugh, as the case may be. Profuse compliments would be received with a mingled look of boyish bashfulness and sly suspicion."

He was a man of expansive intellectual interests that included literature, philosophy, and politics. His conversation was lively, piqued with an engaging wit and irony. Whether he was at home with friends, or in class. his sense of humor and wisdom captured and enchanted his audience. He combined his compelling intellectual force and dynamic personality with a kindness and generosity that permanently endeared him to all who knew him.

As Lawrence Gilman has described the salient qualities of MacDowell's best music, "Hearing certain melodic turns, certain harmonic formations, you recognize them at once as belonging to MacDowell and to no other. . . . He suggested, at his best, no one save himself. He was one of the most individual writers who made music. . . . His manner of speech was utterly untrammeled, and wholly his own. Vitality—an abounding freshness, a perpetual youthfulness— was one of his traits; nobility of style, another." Also characteristic of his work were a "great buoyancy," "constant juxtaposed tenderness and strength," and a "pervading nobility of tone and feeling." MacDowell's music "is charged with emotion. Yet it is not brooding or hectic, and it is seldom intricate or recondite in psychology. It is music curiously free from the fevers of sex."

In 1960 Edward MacDowell was elected to the Hall of Fame at New York University in New York City. He became the fourth New Yorker and the second musician to be thus honored. (His musical predecessor was Stephen Foster.) A bust of MacDowell by Paul Jennewein was unveiled in October 1964 during ceremonies featuring performances of several MacDowell compositions, including his Second Piano Concerto.

PRINCIPAL WORKS

Choral Music—Love and Time; The Rose and the Gardener; The Witch; War Song; Two Northern Songs; Two Songs from the Thirteenth Century; College Songs; Summer Wind; various choruses for men's voices.

Orchestral Music—5 tone poems including: Hamlet and Ophelia, Lancelot and Elaine, and Lamia; 2 piano concertos; 2 suites, including Indian Suite; Romance, for cello and orchestra.

Piano Music—4 sonatas (Eroica, Norse, Tragica, and Keltic); 2 Modern Suites; Six Idyls after Goethe; Six Poems after Heine; Woodland Sketches; Sea Pieces; Fireside Tales; New England Idyls; Virtuoso Studies; Moon Pictures.

Vocal Music—Two Old Songs; From an Old Garden; Six Love Songs; various individual songs for voice and piano including The Blue Bell, The Robin Sings, The Sea, Thy Beaming Eyes.

ABOUT

Gilman, L., Edward MacDowell: A Study; Humiston, W. H., MacDowell; MacDowell, M., Random Notes on Edward MacDowell and His Music; Matthews, J. B., Commemorative Tributes to MacDowell; Page, E. F., Edward MacDowell: His Works and Ideals; Porte, J. F.,

A Great American Tone Poet: Edward MacDowell; Sonneck, O. G., Suum cuique: Essays in Music.

Musical Quarterly, January 1915, October 1942.

Guillaume de Machaut *1300-1377*

GUILLAUME DE MACHAUT (or Machault or Machaud) was the leading French musical figure of his time, a major representative of *Ars Nova,* and a hardly less distinguished poet. He was born in the diocese of Rheims, in or about 1300. One of his narrative poems, *Confort d'amil,* provides us with some biographical information. He was of humble birth, took holy orders at an early age, studied theology (probably in Paris), and from 1323 to 1340 was employed by the King of Bohemia, John of Luxembourg. In this post he traveled with the King to Poland, Lithuania, and Italy. In 1330 he rose to the position of almoner, in 1332 to notary, and in 1335 to secretary.

In or about 1340 Machaut left the service of King John to work for the king's daughter, Bonne, wife of the Duke of Normandy. For the coronation of Charles V at Rheims, in 1364, Machaut wrote the work often described as his masterpiece—the *Notre Dame Mass* for four voices. This is the first polyphonic setting of a Mass by a single composer. Its music is characterized by the continuous repetition of a rhythmic pattern ("isorhythmic technique") used, as Gustave Reese explains, "to tie together at the most ten short consecutive sections." Reese singles out another technique used here by Machaut with extraordinary effect, "a brief melodic generating cell which appears at various points, sometimes in its original form, sometimes modified, but never beyond recognition."

After leaving the employ of Bonne, Machaut was employed in the court of Charles V. He also held various ecclesiastical posts in Houdain, Arras, and Verdun. From 1337 on he served as canon of Rheims. In that city he indulged his passion for hunting and poetry, as well as music. He died there in 1377.

Machaut was the foremost exponent in France of *Ars Nova,* the polyphonic style prevalent during the fourteenth century.

Machaut: mà-shō′

Besides the Mass, he wrote several motets, and with them a variety of secular songs, including ballades, rondeaux, and virelais. Here, said Paul Henry Lang, Machaut produced a "deeply felt expressive music, which breathes a romantic spirit full of fantasy, raising the polyphonic ballad at the end of the Gothic period to a position equal to that of the motet."

To Edward Dannreuther, Machaut's ballades represented a particularly significant achievement. "The poetry of the ballades reveals Machaut as the true exponent of the medieval chivalrous ideas with their religious, moral, and social code—a belated *trouvère*. He praises love with all the effects of the *seconde rhétorique;* mythology, the Old Testament, and allegory. Their music is not constructive as is that of his motets, but expressive and capable of rendering various and varying moods."

Two volumes of Machaut's poetry, *Poésies lyriques de Guillaume de Machaut,* were published in Paris in 1909.

Principal Works

Choral Music—Notre Dame Mass; Sacre de Charles V Mass; ballades, chansons, motets, rondeaux, virelais.

About

Chailley, J., La Messe Notre-Dame de Guillaume de Machaut; Douce, A., Poésies lyriques de Guillaume de Machaut; Douce, A., Guillaume de Machaut: musicien et poète rémois; Levarie, S., Guillaume de Machaut; Machabey, A., Guillaume de Machaut: la vie et l'œuvre musicale; Reese, G., Music in the Middle Ages.

Musical Quarterly, April 1948, April 1950; La Revue musicale, May 1930, April-May 1931.

Gustav Mahler *1860-1911*

GUSTAV MAHLER was born in the Bohemian town of Kalischt on July 7, 1860, the son of a shopkeeper. He grew up in an unhappy household in which his mismated parents quarreled frequently and loudly, and where tragedy was a perpetual visitor. Five of his brothers and sisters died in childhood of diphtheria; a sixth child, a boy to whom Gustav was particularly devoted, died of hydrocardia when he was twelve; another sister suffered a brain tumor soon after her marriage; an eighth child committed suicide; two others were simpleminded and given to hallucinations.

Gustav soon found in music an escape from his grim surroundings. When he was six he discovered a piano in the attic of his grandmother's house, and from that time on was absorbed in music. His father hoped that he would be a shopkeeper, but noting his passion for music and recognizing his talent, decided to seek out expert advice on whether or not the boy should be allowed to dedicate himself to music. He took Gustav to Vienna to play for Professor Julius Epstein of the Vienna Conservatory. Professor Epstein's verdict was brief and unequivocal: "This boy is a born musician."

Mahler entered the Vienna Conservatory at fifteen. For the next three years he studied the piano with Professor Epstein, harmony with Robert Fuchs, and composition with Krenn. Between 1877 and 1879 he also took courses in history and philosophy at the University of Vienna.

After leaving the Conservatory, where he received prizes in piano and composition, Mahler began his career as a professional musician rather modestly, as a conductor. His first post was with a disreputable music hall in Vienna where he was paid about twelve dollars and fifty cents a month to direct operetta performances. In 1881 he became a conductor in Laibach, in 1882 in Olmütz; from 1883 to 1885 he was a conductor in Cassel. All these positions were with third-rate opera companies, whose execrable performances were an ordeal. Nevertheless Mahler gained an all-important apprenticeship which served him well in his later illustrious career.

In 1885 Mahler was invited to Leipzig to direct a special performance of Mendelssohn's *St. Paul.* With this first opportunity to lead thoroughly competent musical forces, Mahler gave a performance of such compelling power and insight that he attracted the interest of several important musicians, including the opera impresario Angelo Neumann. Neumann offered Mahler the prominent position of principal conductor of German opera in Prague, as successor to Anton Seidl.

In Prague Mahler achieved his first distinction as an interpreter of Wagner's music-dramas. Then Artur Nikisch, one of Germany's leading conductors, invited him to Leipzig in 1886 as his assistant. Two years later Mahler became music director of the Budapest Opera, where, during the next three seasons, he completely reorganized the company, revitalized the repertory, and set a new standard of performance. "Such a *Don Giovanni* performance as has been heard in Budapest," said Brahms, "is not to be heard even in Vienna." From Budapest Mahler went on to the Hamburg Opera for another three-year stay.

Mahler's great achievement as a conductor was his work as director of the Royal Opera in Vienna, to which post he was appointed in 1897 on the recommendation of Brahms and other musicians. The Opera had fallen upon sorry days when Mahler arrived. He applied Herculean energies and a tyrannical will to reshaping the repertory, strengthening the company, reconstructing scenery, redesigning costumes, and making painstaking preparations for each performance. He insisted on playing the Wagner music-dramas without cuts, and each season introduced one innovation after another. In his determination to establish the loftiest artistic standards, he banished the claque and refused to permit latecomers to be seated while the performance was in progress. He was severe with all who worked with him, and severest with himself. He was hated by many—because he had been born a Jew, (though converted early in life to Catholicism), because he was a despot, because he was ruthless in his perfectionism. Yet none could question the fact that he had inaugurated a new era of operatic performance in Vienna. And the same integrity, idealism, and driving passion for flawless performance characterized his presentation of the symphonic repertory with the Vienna Philharmonic, which became, under him, one of Europe's greatest symphonic ensembles.

"When he conducted," wrote Guido Adler, "both his own personality and that of the composition found expression. He plunged into the work of art, it drew him to itself, he surrendered himself utterly. Subject and object became one. When he was recreating a work of art, he exerted an irresistible power of suggestion on those who labored with him, those he led, his companions; he magnetized them to his conception. . . . At rehearsals, you could watch how the terrain was taken step by step, how he kept his eye on the cohesion of the whole, even during the punctilious polishing of the most minute detail. . . . When the little man with the lively movements approached the podium, silence fell. . . . The instant he raised his baton they [the musicians] yielded

GUSTAV MAHLER

to the fascination of his glance, surrendered themselves to his will. His face spoke earnestness and holy zeal; the flashing eyes cast forth brilliant light; at mystic passages they gave dreamily before them. . . . Mahler's conducting grew more and more spiritual, and his will communicated itself like an electrical discharge, remaining invisible to the observer's eye."

Although he became one of the world's foremost conductors, Mahler attributed far greater significance to his creative work. His first major compositions were *Das klagende Lied* (1880), for soprano, contralto, tenor, chorus, and orchestra—to which he had written a text based on the Grimm brothers' tale; the song cycle *Lieder und Gesänge aus der Jugendzeit* (1882); and a second song cycle, *Lieder eines fahrenden Gesellen*, completed in 1883. Although he later wrote other compositions for voice and piano or orchestra, some of them masterworks, it is essentially as a symphonist that Mahler achieved renown. In his nine symphonies (a tenth remained unfinished), Mahler proved himself a descendant of Beethoven and Bruckner rather than Brahms. He went beyond those masters, however, in expansiveness of structure, in the prodigious size of his orchestra, in his immense sonorities, and in his continuous aspiration to have his music express the problems of life and death. "All my works," he said, "are anticipations of a future life."

Mahler long suffered abuse and personal invective on the part of critics who saw in his ambitious aims only pretension and megalomania. His First Symphony, which he entitled *The Titan* and described as "the sound of Nature," was a complete failure when Mahler introduced it in Budapest on November 22, 1889. Even the members of the orchestra were so hostile to the composer-conductor that they deliberately sabotaged the performance. Audience and critics were no less antagonistic. The critics remained at their battle stations, equipped with potent verbal artillery, for the Second Symphony, the *Resurrection,* a brooding, philosophical work which probed the reasons for human existence. This work was introduced in 1895, first with three of its movements, conducted by Richard Strauss in Berlin, then in its entirety with Mahler as conductor, in Vienna. One critic saw in the music the "cynical impudence of this brutal . . . music maker." In 1897 the première of three movements of the Third Symphony, which took place in Berlin, with **Felix Weingart-ner** conducting, was again largely a disaster. "I engaged in two battles yesterday [the general rehearsal and concert]," Mahler reported in a letter, "and am sorry to be compelled to report that the enemy was victorious. There was much approval, but also just as much opposition. Hissing and applause! Finally Weingartner called me and I took a bow. That was the signal for the audience to become really noisy. The papers will tear me to pieces."

But Mahler had little doubt about his ultimate victory as a composer. He concluded his letter with the following sentence: "In ten years those 'gentlemen' and I may meet again," and in another communication he said firmly, "My time will come." In the meanwhile he continued to build his mighty symphonic edifices, the Fourth Symphony in 1900, the Fifth in 1902, the Sixth in 1904, the Seventh in 1905.

The apathy of audiences and the hostility of critics were not his only crosses; he suffered severe personal misfortune as well. On March 9, 1902, Mahler married Anna Maria Schindler, the daughter of a Viennese painter. A daughter born to them in 1903 died of scarlet fever in 1906. The loss to Mahler was almost insupportable, and his immense grief was compounded by an overwhelming sense of guilt. Three years earlier he had completed a setting of elegies for dead children, *Kindertotenlieder,* and now he could not dissuade himself from the conviction that he had thus tempted fate into taking his child away from him.

Soon after his daughter's death, Mahler began to show symptoms of a serious heart ailment. He was warned by his physicians that he would have to exercise extreme caution in his habits. But Mahler refused to spare himself, either in his creative efforts or as a conductor; indeed, the knowledge that he probably did not have long to live spurred him to greater efforts to fulfill his self-imposed mission.

Mahler's situation at the Vienna Opera held added frustrations. He met with obstruction everywhere—from those who envied his genius; those whom he abused mercilessly in his slavish perfectionism; those who held anti-Semitic sentiments in spite of his early conversion. So charged did the atmosphere become at the Opera House, so often were his most zealous efforts subjected to internal sabotage, that Mahler felt he could no longer work fruitfully and decided, rather than make compromises, to withdraw from the conflict. On October 15, 1907 he gave his last performance at the Opera—Beethoven's *Fidelio.* In his resignation he said: "Instead of the complete accomplishment of my dreams, I can only leave behind me fragments, as man is ever fated to do. . . . I have always put my whole soul in my work, subordinated my person to the cause, my inclination to duty. I have not spared myself and could, therefore, require of others their utmost exertions. In the press of the struggle, in the heat of the moment, neither you nor I have escaped wounds and misunderstandings." But to his closest friends he said, "I must keep on the heights. I cannot let anything irritate me or drag me down."

Mahler's next appointments as a conductor were in the United States, first at the Metropolitan Opera, where, as director of German operas, he made a brilliant debut with *Tristan und Isolde* on January 1, 1908. "Mr. Mahler did honor to himself, Wagner's music, and the New York public," reported Henry Krehbiel in the New York *Tribune.* "It was a strikingly vital reading which he gave to Wagner's familiar score." In the autumn of 1908 Mahler combined his work at the Metropolitan Opera with the exacting position of principal conductor of the New

York Philharmonic Orchestra. Despite his poor health and the warnings of physicians not to overtax himself, he drove himself mercilessly, at the Opera and in the symphony hall, in order to give his best to his work, and to arrive at a consistently exalted level of performance.

On September 12, 1910, Mahler directed the première of a new symphony, his Eighth, the so-called "symphony of a thousand voices." "It is the biggest thing I have done so far," he had informed the conductor Willem Mengelberg, "and so individual in content and form that I cannot describe it in words. Imagine that the whole universe begins to vibrate and resound. These are no longer human voices, but planets and suns revolving." To another friend he said, "All my earlier symphonies are but preludes to this one. My other works are all tragic and subjective; this one is the great dispenser of joy."

The Eighth Symphony was a giant work calling for a mighty orchestra, eight solo voices, a double chorus, a boys' choir, and an organ. Its text was derived from Maurus' hymn, "Veni, Creator Spiritus," and portions of the final scene from the second part of Goethe's *Faust.* The Eighth Symphony, said Neville Cardus, "embraces, in intention at any rate, earth and heaven; the music speaks not of the individual but of the universal soul. . . . [In it he places] his art, now that he is technically a master, at the service of all people. . . . He would bequeath his inheritance to the world."

The première of this work was the first unqualified triumph Mahler had yet enjoyed as a composer, receiving enthusiastic response from both audience and critics. "In the overwhelming demonstration of joy that followed the last note, the whole world of music, eminently represented upon that significant occasion, joined," wrote Gabriel Engel. "Mahler, his pale, pain-lined, ascetic features transfigured with happiness by so unparalleled a tribute to his accomplishment, stood motionless on the huge stage while the great storm of enthusiastic applause kept raging."

But the victory won at last for his vast symphonic concepts had come, as is so often the case, late in the day. Mahler completed only one more symphony, his Ninth. It was introduced posthumously in Vienna on June 26, 1912; Bruno Walter conducted.

Mahler worked upon a tenth symphony, which he did not live to complete. These fragments were not heard for half a century. At last, in the summer of 1963, Mahler's widow finally gave permission for their performance. On October 21, 1963, Leopold Stokowski and the American Symphony Orchestra presented two movements of Mahler's Tenth Symphony—an opening adagio lasting twenty-one minutes, and a four-minute scherzo entitled "Purgatorio," intended as a third movement. Writing in the New York *Times,* Ross Parmenter described this music as "striking." He added: "Of the two, Purgatorio is the more original, for it is curiously elfin in its tone and very distinctive in its instrumentation. Yet the Adagio, though it does not seem so strongly individual, makes a deep impression because it is the work of a great composer who was near the death he dreaded so deeply."

In his lifetime, however, Mahler did complete another masterwork of the first order, *Das Lied von der Erde,* a song cycle, with orchestra, based on old Chinese poems. This work was also presented posthumously, in Munich on November 20, 1911, again with Bruno Walter as the conductor.

Mahler's health broke down completely on February 21, 1911, his strength drained by the effort of directing the Philharmonic, his spirit sorely tried by the demands of directors that he popularize his concerts. He was taken back to Paris for serum treatments, and from there to Vienna, where he died on May 18, 1911. On his deathbed he moved a finger as if it were a baton with which he was directing some great performance; the last word he uttered was the name of Mozart.

Although he was often described as "the ugly Mahler," the composer had a striking appearance which made a forceful impression. "He was a little below average height," noted Gabriel Engel, "but a wiry, slender figure of perfect proportions obviated any impression of shortness. He had flowing black hair and dark brown eyes which under stress of great emotion would take on an almost fanatical gleam." His scorching eyes, the tense muscles of the face, his square jaw, all suggested his inner strength and iron will.

"Mahler," said Guido Adler, "was a nature founded on goodness and energy. His strength of will was fanatic, alike in the divine mania of the artist and in the inexorable drive toward truth in all the manifestations of life. Like a child, he let the moment carry him away; at such times he seemed a creature utterly free and unfettered. Yet his actions were in fact ultimately governed by a clear intelligence. His will showed itself inflexible, yet his temper was mild, his heart soft. He was generous; like a child he felt with his fellow men, with great and small, with grownups and with the young. He was touching in his friendship, in his attachment; he was open, reserved to the point of self-abnegation. He could enjoy everything—and he could lose his temper over the merest trifle that did not match his mood of the moment. Extremely sensitive and irritable, he could yet bear the most acute pain without complaint—and the next moment show annoyance at the slightest discomfort. He was communicative and confiding toward friends whom he won and recognized as such, mistrustful and reserved with disagreeable people in whom he found no understanding—and he was capable of striking out with the harshest home truths, so that now and then he hurt. This explains the enmities that not infrequently arose from wounded vanity."

Since his death, Mahler's nine symphonies have achieved ever wider recognition among discriminating musicians and music lovers, thanks largely to the efforts of such noted conductors as Bruno Walter, Willem Mengelberg, Richard Strauss, Otto Klemperer, Dimitri Mitropoulos, and Leonard Bernstein. To Bruno Walter, Mahler unfolded in his first four symphonies an "important part of the history of . . . [his] soul. . . . While in the First the subjective experience with its tempest of emotions is exerting its influence upon the music, metaphysical questions strive to find an answer and deliverance in music in the Second (the *Resurrection*) and in subsequent symphonies." Walter found that in the Fifth Symphony Mahler is at "the summit of his life, of his power, and of his ability." In the Sixth and Seventh Symphonies "the composer aims at a further intensification of the symphonic idea." Of the epic Eighth Symphony, Walter said, "No other work of Mahler is so saturated with the spirit of fervent affirmation." In conception, technique, and polyphony, the Ninth Symphony continues the line of the Fifth, Sixth, and Seventh. "While it,

too, is pure orchestral music, it differs from the central group and comes nearer again to the earlier symphonies by the strong influences of a decidedly spiritual and fundamental mood."

There are many who regard Mahler's symphonies as bombastic, prolix, and pretentious. Philip Hale remarked: "One has found through his symphonies restlessness that at times becomes hysterical; reminders of Wagner, Berlioz, Strauss; melodies in folk song vein, often naïve, at times beautiful but introduced as at random and quickly thrown aside; an overemployment of the woodwind, used too often as solo instruments; passages for the bass which recall the fact that as a child Mahler delighted in military bands. Sudden changes from screaming outbursts to thin and inconsequential instrumentation; trivial moments when the hearer anticipates the movement of a country dance; diffuseness, prolixity that becomes boresome; an unwillingness to bring speech to an end; seldom genuine power or eloquence; yet here and there measures that linger in the memory."

Many others, however, are as firmly convinced that Mahler achieved a plane of sublimity which few symphonists before him had realized; that in his best pages he plumbed emotional depths and soared to spiritual heights; that he was a poet, a dreamer, a seer who brought new dimension to the symphonic structure and a new articulateness and eloquence to the musical language.

PRINCIPAL WORKS

Orchestral Music—9 symphonies (a tenth, unfinished); Das klagende Lied, for soprano, contralto, tenor, chorus, and orchestra; Lieder eines fahrenden Gesellen, for voice and orchestra; Lieder aus des Knaben Wunderhorn, for voice and orchestra; Kindertotenlieder, for voice and orchestra; Das Lied von der Erde, for contralto, tenor, and orchestra.

Vocal Music—Lieder und Gesänge aus der Jugendzeit; Five Songs to Poems by Rückert; individual songs for voice and piano, including Ich atmet' einen linden Duft, Ich bin Der Welt abhanden gekommen, Revelge, Der Tambourg'sell and Wer hat dies' Liedlein erdacht.

ABOUT

Adler, G., Gustav Mahler; Cardus, N., A Composer's Eleven; Engel, G., Gustav Mahler; Mahler, A., Gustav Mahler: Memories and Letters; Mitchell, D., Gustav Mahler: The Early Years; Newlin, D., Bruckner, Mahler, Schoenberg; Redlich, H., Bruckner and Mahler; Stefan, P., Gustav Mahler; Walter, B., Gustav Mahler.

Benedetto Marcello *1686-1739*

BENEDETTO MARCELLO was born in Venice on July 24, 1686, the descendant of an illustrious Venetian family that had included senators, ambassadors, prelates, and a doge. His father was a professional violinist whose home (which still stands on the Grand Canal) was a gathering-place for some of the city's most distinguished musicians. Benedetto started to study violin early, but since his musical interests leaned strongly to composition and singing, he made better progress in theory with such masters as Gasparini and Lotti. Later he memorized theoretical writings of Zarlino, and spent hours poring over the published works of Palestrina and Monteverdi.

His father sent him to Rome to study law. After obtaining his degree in jurisprudence, Benedetto Marcello returned to Venice, combining the practice of law and politics with composition. For a number of years he held various political posts, first in the Great Council, then in 1711 as a member of the Council of Forty, and from 1730 to 1738 as the *provveditore* of Pola. Active also as a musician, he was elected a member of the Accademia Filarmonici of Bologna in 1712, and later joined the Pastori Arcadi of Rome.

Marcello's biographer Leonida Busi, relates an incident in 1728 that had a powerful and decisive influence on the composer. Until then, Marcello had led an irresponsible and dissipated life. One day, while he was participating in services at church, a slight mishap occurred: a sepulchral slab gave way under his foot as he stepped up to the altar, and he slipped into a grave. Marcello was not hurt, but he did see in the accident the warning of imminent death and he decided immediately to abandon his wild ways. Living in almost monastic seclusion, he gave himself up to religious pursuits and dedicated application to composition. A year later, on March 28, 1729, he married Rosana Scalfi, one of his singing pupils.

After his eight years of service at Pola, Marcello's health gave way, and his physicians advised him to return to a more favorable climate. He spent his last years in Brescia, holding the post of town treasurer. He died in that city on July 24, 1739, and was buried in the church of San Giuseppe,

BENEDETTO MARCELLO

where a monument was erected to his memory. The epitaph referred to him as a "nobleman, magistrate, philologist, poet, and musician."

Marcello produced a library of choral music that included numerous cantatas and what many musicologists regard as his masterwork, fifty psalms for one, two, three and four voices and instrumental accompaniment, to texts by Girolamo Giustiniani. These psalms appeared in eight volumes published between 1724 and 1726. "In your sublime and imperishable psalms," Telemann wrote to Marcello, "there reigns a majesty which all masters before you have failed to enthrone." The French musicologist Fétis found in these compositions "a rare merit of poetic expression, much originality, a boldness of ideas, and lastly a singular variety of means."

Marcello also wrote concertos and sonatas which have been revived in the past quarter of a century in concerts and on recordings.

"The music of Marcello was essentially lyric," explained Camille Bellaigue. "But to me Marcello's power is more to be admired than his sweetness—now, in the assurance of his faith and the impetuosity of his prayer, now in the tragic emotion of his repentance. [His] musical individuality was noble, proud, and vigorous; in every particular, it stemmed from the force and beauty which the Renaissance created throughout all art."

In 1720 Marcello published a brilliant satire on the affectations and clichés of Neapolitan opera, the pamphlet *Il Teatro alla moda*. He himself wrote several works for the stage, including an opera, *La Fede riconosciuta*, which was performed in Vicenza in 1707, as well as various pastorales and intermezzi.

Benedetto Marcello's brother, Alessandro (1684-1750), was a distinguished philosopher and mathematician, as well as a composer. Under the assumed name of Eterico Stinfalico he wrote numerous concertos, sonatas, and cantatas.

PRINCIPAL WORKS

Chamber Music—Various sonatas for solo instruments and accompaniment.

Choral Music—Giuditta; Canzoni madrigaleschi ed arie per camera; cantatas, oratorio, psalms.

Harpsichord Music—Sonatas.

Operas—Calisto in Orsa; La Fede riconosciuta; Arianna.

Orchestral Music—Concerti grossi.

ABOUT

Angeli, A. d', Benedetto Marcello; Bellaigue, C., Portraits and Silhouettes; Busi, L., Benedetto Marcello.

Monthly Musical Record, March 1890; Musical Quarterly, April 1948.

Luca Marenzio *1553-1599*

LUCA MARENZIO, one of the masters of the Italian madrigal, was born in Coccaglio, near Brescia, Italy, in 1553. As a chorister at the Brescia Cathedral he received music instruction from Giovanni Contino. It is believed he went to Rome in 1572, serving for six years as *maestro di cappella* for Cardinal Madruzzo; it is also believed that he studied with various Roman music teachers during these years.

On August 1, 1579, Marenzio was appointed to the musical court of Cardinal Luigi d'Este, where he remained for seven years. His salary was meager, but as compensation he was afforded the opportunity to indulge in the luxurious life encouraged at the Cardinal's palace. During this period he traveled with the Cardinal's entourage to several important Italian courts, and on one occasion he visited Paris.

In 1580 Marenzio published the first of nine books of five-voice madrigals. It was a success of the first order, so highly regarded

LUCA MARENZIO

by musical authorities as well as the general public that by 1602 it had gone through six editions. The first of Marenzio's six volumes of six-voice madrigals, and a volume of five-part *Madrigali spirituali*, appeared in 1584. In 1584 Marenzio also issued a volume of three-voice *Villanelle ed arie alla napoletana*, and the next year the first of two volumes of four-voice motets.

From 1588 to 1599 Marenzio lived in Florence, where he was employed by the Medicis. When Ferdinando de' Medici and Christine of Lorraine were married in 1589, Marenzio wrote his *Intermedi e concerti* for the ceremony. From 1591 to 1595 he lived in Rome, employed by Cardinal Aldobrandini, and from 1596 to 1598 in Cracow, serving in the court of Sigismund III of Poland. After returning to Rome he worked in the establishments of several notable Romans. He died in Rome, in the garden of the Villa Medici on Monte Pincio, on August 22, 1599, and was buried in the church of San Lorenzo in Lucina.

As one of the foremost creators of the Italian madrigal, Marenzio was greatly honored by his contemporaries and successors. They frequently referred to him as "the divine composer" or "the sweetest swan." In 1622 Henry Peacham wrote that "for delicious aires and sweet invention in madrigals, Luca Marenzio excelleth all others."

Later historians have emphasized Marenzio's historic importance in bringing the

Italian madrigal to its most advanced stage of technical development as well as artistic fulfillment. With Marenzio, more than with any of his predecessors, a recognizable homophonic style began to assert itself, as well as a modern tonality as distinguished from the older modality. But Marenzio's greatest contribution lay, perhaps, in his attention to the text. In attempting to discover the musical equivalent of the emotion or mood of the poem he was setting, Marenzio used a vivid imagery and pictorialism that were new to madrigal writing. Virtuoso sounds, color effects, striking contrasts of tempo and rhythm were made to emphasize the message of the poem. "For the expression of the word in its liveliest, most vivid form," said Carl von Winterfeld, "is the goal towards which his endeavors are particularly directed. . . . His domain was secular music, where the individual takes precedence over the universal; this stands out as sharply as possible in his every creation. Seldom is the mode he chooses grasped into its essential relationships; as a rule, through the correspondence of beginning and end, it serves him only as a general frame for his multifarious, many-colored images, particularly when he openly reveals his desire for the new and unheard of in strange and unusual modulations and in this way endeavors to disclose the sense and spirit of his texts."

Characteristic of the way in which he turned to graphic word setting are such madrigals as "Strider faceva" and "Solo e pensoso." In the first he imitates the singing of birds and the drone of a bagpipe; in the latter he finds the appropriate musical translation for the poignant opening line, "alone, thought-sick, I pace where none has been."

Marenzio set to music numerous pastoral and love poems of Dante and Petrarch, among other Italian poets. At times he touched profound emotional depths, as in "Dura legge d'amor," which speaks of the poet's unhappy love. In general, what Karl Nef said of "Parto ò non parto" applies to most of Marenzio's madrigals, whatever their atmosphere or mood: "The composer utilizes his vocal resources with complete freedom, allowing to each voice its full development, its individual life; one does not know which to admire more, the intimate, spiritual expression, or the dramatic force, the effect upon the sensibilities."

PRINCIPAL WORKS

Choral Music—Madrigals, Mass, motets, villanellas.

ABOUT

Einstein, A., The Italian Madrigal; Engel, H., Luca Marenzio; Engel, H., Marenzios Madrigale und ihre dichterischen Grundlagen; Reese, G., Music in the Renaissance

Padre Martini *1706-1784*

GIOVANNI BATTISTA (GIAMBATTISTA) MARTINI, better known as Padre Martini, was born in Bologna on April 24, 1706. His father, a violinist and a member of one of Bologna's most prominent music societies, taught Giovanni the fundamentals of music. Then the boy received training in harpsichord and voice from Padre Predieri, and in counterpoint from Riccieri.

The church, however, drew the boy more strongly than did music. He pursued the study of theology and philosophy with the monks of San Filippo Neri, and after passing his novitiate at the Franciscan monastery at Lago, was ordained a priest on September 11, 1722.

In 1725 Padre Martini returned to his native city, where he became *maestro di cappella* of the San Francesco church. During this period he went through a period of intensive study of church music with Giacomo Perti. Music, however, was not his only absorption, for he also studied mathematics with Zanotti, undertook a course in medicine, and learned philosophy through extensive reading. The scope of Martini's intellectual interests was a source of no little admiration to his contemporaries. He possessed one of the finest private libraries in Europe (about seventeen thousand volumes) which was divided, after his death, between the Liceo Filarmonico in Bologna and the court library of Vienna.

Despite the variety of his interests and pursuits, Martini composed music in all forms. In the years 1738-1739 he completed two outstanding oratorios with St. Peter as the theme. He also wrote many instrumental works, the most important being the twelve sonatas published in 1742, and six sonatas for organ and cembalo, which appeared in 1747.

Martini then founded a music school in Bologna, where he distinguished himself as a teacher. His reputation as a musical

PADRE MARTINI

scholar and theoretician was so widespread that pupils came to him from all parts of Europe; among those who profited from his advice and instruction were Gluck, Mozart, Grétry, and Jommelli. He was sought out by scholars everywhere for the solution of musical problems and difficult questions of musical science. Fétis regarded him as "the most erudite musician of the eighteenth century." His high position in Italian music was acknowledged with his appointment as a member of the Accademia Filarmonica of Bologna, and of the Accademia degli Arcadi in Rome.

Martini's last years were darkened by illness. He suffered severely from asthma, a disease of the bladder, and a leg wound. Yet his spirit remained gentle and resigned, and his outlook optimistic. He died in Bologna on October 4, 1784. A Mass, the composite work of thirteen distinguished Italian composers, was performed in his memory at the Accademia Filarmonica in Bologna on December 2.

Charles Burney, who met Martini when the composer was already old, described him as follows: "He is advanced in age, and in bad health. He has a distressing cough; his legs are swollen; and his whole appearance is that of a sick man. . . . His character is such that it inspires not only respect but affection. With the purity of his life and the simplicity of his manners he combines gaiety, kindness, and philanthropy. I have never liked anyone so well after so slight

an acquaintance. I was no more reserved with him at the end of a few hours than I should have been with an old friend or a beloved brother."

Martini's most significant works were for the church, and included numerous oratorios, Masses, and litanies, as well as other forms. But his rich output of instrumental music—comprising, largely, concertos and sonatas—was hardly less distinguished. Romain Rolland wrote that Martini's works "exhibited a certain rococo grace." Martini was not an experimenter or innovator, but he was a master of form and style, and the charm of his best works provides rewarding experiences for the music lover.

Two short compositions often ascribed to Martini are the work of other men. One is the celebrated song "Plaisir d'amour," which was written by another Martini— Jean Paul Egide Martini (1741-1816), who is often designated *il Tedesco,* or "the German," to distinguish him from the Padre. The other piece is an Andantino "transcribed" for violin and piano by Fritz Kreisler. Kreisler, however, confessed that this piece, like many of his other alleged transcriptions, was his own composition.

Martini completed three volumes of a history of ancient music, and was working on a fourth at the time of his death. He also wrote a two-volume treatise on counterpoint.

PRINCIPAL WORKS

Chamber Music—Various sonatas for solo instruments and accompaniment.

Choral Music—Antiphonies, cantatas, litanies, Masses, oratorios, psalms, Requiems, and various other church compositions.

Operas—3 Intermezzi.

Vocal Music—Duets for two voices and bass.

ABOUT

Busi, L., Il Padre Giovanni Battista Martini; Pauchard, P. A., Ein italienischer Musiktheoretiker: Pater Giambattista Martini.

Jules Massenet *1842-1912*

JULES ÉMILE FRÉDÉRIC MASSENET, the composer of *Manon* and *Thaïs,* was born in Montaud, in the Loire region of France, on May 12, 1842. He was the youngest of twenty-one children. "My father was a superior officer under the First Empire," Massenet wrote in his autobiography, "but when the Bourbons were restored,

Massenet: màs-nā′

my father resigned. He was a graduate of the Polytechnic School, and later devoted himself to manufacturing and to starting the famous iron works near Saint-Étienne. My mother gave me my first piano lesson. How well I remember the day! The lesson was strangely interrupted by the noise of street firing. The revolution [of 1848] had begun."

The revolution shut down the elder Massenet's iron works, and the family moved to Paris in 1851. They lived in abject poverty, their only support derived from the meager income earned by Mme. Massenet, who gave piano lessons. Soon after his arrival in Paris, Jules enrolled at the Paris Conservatory, where he remained for about ten years. His teachers included Reber in harmony, Laurent in piano, and Ambroise Thomas in composition. During some of his student years, Massenet supported himself by playing the triangle and drums in theater orchestras, working on his Conservatory lessons during the stage intervals. In spite of his difficulties, Massenet won first prizes in piano and fugue in 1859, and four years later was awarded the Prix de Rome for a cantata, *David Rizzio.*

Massenet's three-year residence in Rome was extremely pleasant, for it afforded him the opportunity to move among sculptors, painters, and musicians. One of the last was Franz Liszt, who took an interest in him and referred a young lady to him for piano lessons—Mlle. de Sainte-Marie. Massenet married her on October 8, 1866.

Soon after returning to France Massenet wrote his first opera, *La Grand' tante,* in one act, introduced at the Opéra-Comique on April 3, 1867. It had a run of only fourteen performances, but it found favor among critics and musicians because of its dramatic interest and inventive orchestration. Massenet scored a greater success in 1867 with his *First Suite* for orchestra, performed by the Pasdeloup Orchestra.

During the Franco-Prussian War Massenet served with the National Guard. After the war's end, his second opera, *Don César de Bazan,* was given on November 30, 1872. It met with only moderate success. But Massenet was to earn acclaim at last less than two months later with his incidental music for Leconte de Lisle's drama *Les Érinnyes,* presented at the Odéon on January 6, 1873. One of its numbers, "Invocation,"

JULES MASSENET

was later transcribed by the composer for cello and piano and retitled "Élégie." In this version (and in another for voice, with lyrics by E. Gallet), it has become one of Massenet's most popular pieces.

Two major works now brought Massenet high esteem in French musical life. One was the oratorio *Marie-Magdeleine,* completed in 1873; the other, the opera *Le Roi de Lahore,* was given at the Opéra on April 27, 1877. In 1878 Massenet became the youngest member ever honored by election to the Académie des Beaux-Arts. In the same year he was appointed professor of advanced composition at the Conservatory, beginning a distinguished career as a teacher whose influence was to be absorbed by such noted French musicians as Rabaud, Pierné, Charpentier, Bruneau, and Isidor Philipp, among many others.

"In class," recalled Isidor Philipp, "Massenet sat himself at the piano and carefully examined the fugues which had been prepared. There was no pedantry in his criticisms, which were severe, but always encouraging. He noted the defects in these compositions with speed and clarity but gently emphasized their virtues. How much life, how much vigor in everything that he said, never speaking for a moment of himself or his own works! All of music he knew, played admirably on the piano and sang with the utmost charm. One could not help loving such an exceptional being."

Massenet achieved his greatest operatic successes between 1880 and 1900. *Hérodiade* was introduced in Brussels on December 19, 1881. His masterwork, *Manon,* was first seen at the Opéra-Comique on January 19, 1884, to be followed on November 30, 1885 by *Le Cid,* at the Opéra. *Werther* received its première performance in Vienna on February 16, 1892. *Thaïs,* based on Anatole France's novel, was produced by the Opéra on March 16, 1894. (In this work is found another of Massenet's well-loved instrumental compositions, the "Méditation," an orchestral entr'acte with violin obbligato.) *Sapho* followed in 1897, and *Cendrillon* in 1899, both opening at the Opéra-Comique.

Georges Jean-Aubry, discussing Massenet as a composer for the stage, praised his "theatrical sense, developed to a degree the more rare insomuch as he makes no use of blatant means. He is always ready to retain a degree of distinction that is indisputable even when it is only relative. He has yielded no more to noisy realism than he has attempted to attain to lofty grandeur."

Massenet's operas, wrote Édouard Schure, are distinguished for "the elegant . . . thrust with which he drove to the very source of a melody of which he availed himself with so much grace. . . . Massenet had two personal and original notes: on the one hand an intriguing tenderness which rises at times to passion; on the other hand, a penetrating melancholy, singularly incisive."

Manon is Massenet's most famous opera. The text, by Henri Meilhac and Philippe Gille, was derived from the celebrated story by the Abbé Prévost. "The whole of Prévost's story," said Martin Cooper, "is set in an atmosphere of coquetry and amorous intrigue which cries aloud for the accompaniment of music such as Massenet's, . . . 'melodies which are delicate and caressing rather than deeply felt, and orchestration rich in pretty and clever filigree work but without any depth.' From the opening scene . . . the story is a succession of ambiguous erotic situations. . . . One may find this ceaseless harping on the erotic interest tedious and cloying, but it is admirably suited to Massenet's talent, and [it] called out the very best of which he was capable."

Manon was first produced in the United States at the New York Academy of Music on December 23, 1885.

Though Massenet remained prolific after 1900, completing eleven operas, as well as ballets and compositions for orchestra, he never rose again to the dramatic and musical heights of *Manon, Thaïs,* and *Hérodiade.* M. D. Calvocoressi commented: "For the plain reason that he never attempted to renovate his style he sank into sheer mannerism. Indeed, one can but marvel that so gifted a musician, who lacked neither individuality nor skill, should have so utterly succeeded in throwing away his gifts." His determination to remain successful, to win the favor of audiences, to arouse the adulation of female admirers, led him to repeat outworn formulas that had once proved popular. But a few of his operas, though decidedly mediocre, met with some degree of favor. These include *Le Jongleur de Notre Dame* and *Don Quichotte,* both introduced in Monte Carlo, the first on February 18, 1902, the latter on February 19, 1910.

George Servières described Massenet as follows: "His eyes are very quick in their movements; the expression is very gentle. His profile is finely cut. His shoulders are slightly stooping and he seems short, although . . . of medium height. His movements are full of ever-present nervous vivacity."

Massenet, wrote M. D. Calvocoressi, suffered as a man and an artist from his "overwhelming desire to court success. His object was to seduce; and from the time when he found that his music proved effective and became popular, he carefully avoided changing his manner." In his personal behavior, as in his music, Massenet went to extravagant lengths to be liked and praised. Isidor Philipp described an incident illustrating Massenet's indefatigable efforts to create a favorable impression. When Philipp was still an unknown composer, he had performed his own *Barcarolle* at the office of Heugel, the publisher; Massenet had been present. Thirty years later Philipp called on Massenet to discuss several transcriptions which he planned to prepare of Massenet's music. On that occasion the master, to Philipp's astonishment, asked him about the little *Barcarolle,* went to the piano, and played the entire piece from memory! Only later did Philipp discover from Heugel that a week earlier Massenet, expecting Philipp's visit, had gone out of his way to procure a copy of that *Barcarolle.*

Massenet died suddenly in Paris on August 13, 1912, having gone to the capital

from his home in Egreville to consult with physicians about his declining health. When *Don Quichotte* was successfully revived at the Opéra-Comique in 1934, a bust of Massenet was unveiled in the foyer, where it still stands.

PRINCIPAL WORKS

Ballets—Le Carillon; La Cigale; Espada.

Choral Music—Marie-Magdeleine (also an opera); Ève; La Terre promise; Narcisse; La Vierge.

Operas—Le Roi de Lahore; Hérodiade; Manon; Le Cid; Esclarmonde; Werther; Thaïs; La Navarraise; Sapho; Cendrillon; Grisélidis; Le Jongleur de Notre Dame; Chérubin; Ariane; Thérèse; Don Quichotte.

Orchestral Music—7 suites, including: Scènes pittoresques; Scènes napolitaines; Scènes alsaciennes; 3 overtures, including Phèdre; Visions; Marche solennelle; Fantaisie, for cello and orchestra; Piano Concerto; incidental music to 13 plays, including Les Érinnyes and Phèdre.

Vocal Music—About 200 songs, including Élégie, Noël paien, O si les fleurs avaient des yeux, Ouvre tes yeux bleus, Pensée d'automne, Sérénade du passant.

ABOUT

Brancour, R., Massenet; Bruneau, A., Massenet; Cooper, M., French Music; Finck, H. T., Massenet and His Operas; Massenet, J., My Recollections; Morin, A., Massenet et ses opéras; Pougin, A., Massenet; Schneider, L., Massenet, l'homme et le musicien.

Étienne Nicolas Méhul *1763-1817*

ÉTIENNE NICOLAS MÉHUL was born in Givet, Ardennes, France, on June 22, 1763. His father, a cook at the time of Étienne's birth, later became a wine merchant and a restaurant proprietor. Étienne studied organ with a local musician, mastering the instrument so well that at the age of ten he was called upon to serve as organist of the monastery of the Récollets in Givet. Two years later the boy was admitted as a novice to the Val Dieu monastery in order that he might continue his organ studies with Wilhelm Hauser. Upon completion of this training, he became Hauser's assistant.

One day in 1777 a wealthy music amateur heard Méhul perform upon the organ, and immediately provided the boy with funds to continue his study of music in Paris. There Méhul earned his living by giving piano lessons while he studied piano with Edelmann. In 1779 Méhul heard Gluck's

ÉTIENNE NICOLAS MÉHUL

Iphigénie en Tauride and was moved so profoundly that he determined to seek out the master, who was then in Paris. He arrived at Gluck's home one day to find him seated at his harpsichord, half undressed. "All the magnificence of the toilette of Louis XIV," commented Méhul, "could not have fascinated me as much as Gluck's negligée!"

Gluck encouraged Méhul to write for the stage. Although he took this advice seriously, Méhul first completed several harpsichord sonatas, published in 1782, and a cantata which was performed that year at a Concert Spirituel. The theater remained uppermost in his mind, however, and as an experiment he completed no fewer than three operas during the next few years. He destroyed all these works. A fourth opera, composed at this time and accepted for performance, was not given until 1791. It was not until September 4, 1790, that Méhul made his official bow as an opera composer, with the presentation of *Euphrosine et Coradin* at the Comédie-Italienne. Its extreme popularity brought it thirty performances within a five-month period.

His work now in great demand, Méhul became an indefatigable composer of opera, completing within the next seventeen years thirty-three operas and three ballets, most of which were produced at the Opéra-Comique. The most successful included *Stratonice* in 1792, *Horatius Coclès* in 1794, and *Doria* in 1795.

Méhul: mā-ül′

During the French Revolution Méhul allied himself and his music with the new regime. His opera librettos reflected the temper of the times; he composed many patriotic songs and choruses that enjoyed considerable favor, such as "Le Chant du départ," which almost rivaled the "Marseillaise" in popularity, and others which were sung in public squares and at official events. His *Fête de l'Être suprême* was performed by a chorus of over two thousand voices in June 1794 to celebrate Robespierre's decree proclaiming a three-day festival. (Later he was to compose a choral work for the dedication of a statue to Napoleon, and a Mass for his coronation.)

Méhul's politically oriented compositions won him high official honor. "In the front rank of republican composers the nation places and proclaims Citizen Méhul," read one official proclamation. In 1795 Méhul was appointed to the music section of the newly formed Institut de France, and made an Inspecteur of the newly founded Conservatory where he also served as professor of composition. In 1802 he became a Chevalier of the Legion of Honor.

In addition to his numerous works for official events, Méhul's creative output continued to include opera. *Le Jeune Henri*, given in 1797, has survived largely because of its delightful overture, which is now named *La Chasse du jeune Henri*. Méhul's masterwork for the operatic stage, composed a decade later, was *Joseph*, introduced at the Opéra-Comique on February 17, 1807. There is reason to believe that Méhul wrote this work as a result of a challenge made at a fashionable dinner party. The subject of the play *Joseph*, then being seen at the Comédie Française, had been attacked by some of the guests; Méhul came to the defense of the play, pointing out the strong theatrical interest of the biblical story and asserting that an excellent opera libretto could be derived from it. Thereupon one of the guests, the poet Alexandre Duval, challenged Méhul to write the opera and offered to provide him with the libretto.

Joseph was a complete triumph, moving Guizot to write a poem about it and the Emperor Napoleon to present Méhul with a prize of five thousand francs. The opera's fame spread eventually to Austria, Hungary, Russia, Holland, Switzerland, Belgium, England, Italy, and the United States.

The music of *Joseph,* in Berlioz' estimate, "is nearly always simple, touching, rich in successful if not very bold modulations, in broad, full harmonies, in graceful accompaniments. The expression is always truthful."

Except for several symphonies modeled after Haydn, which he completed between 1808 and 1810, Méhul wrote little for many years. He was consumptive, and his personal life was also marred by his unhappy marriage to Mlle Gestaldy, the daughter of a physician.

When Méhul returned at last to his operatic endeavors, he found that he could no longer recapture the freshness, vitality, and charm of *Joseph*. The five operas he completed during this period were all failures. To add to the numerous difficulties that darkened his last years—his bad health, depressed spirits, broken marriage, and failures as a composer—the downfall of Napoleon caused a severe blow to his personal fortunes. Other composers—Spontini most notably—usurped the limelight he had once held, and the ailing man now was convinced that he was the victim of the jealousies and intrigues of rival composers.

Mortally ill with consumption in 1817, Méhul went to the Mediterranean island of Hyères for a rest cure. He was restless and unhappy there. "I have broken up all my habits," he wrote at the time. "I am deprived of all my old friends. I am alone at the end of the world, surrounded by people whose language I scarcely understand. And all this sacrifice to obtain a little more sun!" He recovered sufficiently to attend a demonstration in his honor at Marseilles, but once back in Paris his health broke down completely. He died there on October 18, 1817 and was buried in Père Lachaise cemetery.

Carl Maria von Weber pointed out that the salient qualities of Méhul's operas were "dramatic truth, animated advance free from injudicious repetitions, great effects frequently by the simplest of means, and economy in instrumentation giving, in fact, only that which is absolutely essential."

PRINCIPAL WORKS

Ballets—Le Jugement de Paris; La Dansomanie; Daphnis et Pandrose, ou La Vengeance de l'amour; Persée et Andromède.

Chamber Music—Overture burlesque, for violin, woodwind and piano; violin sonatas.

Choral Music—Chant du départ; Chant national; Fête de l'Être suprême; Chant de victoire; Chant de retour; various other patriotic hymns; cantatas, Masses.

Operas—Euphrosine et Coradin; Stratonice; Horatius Coclès; Doria; La Caverne; Le Jeune Henri; Adrien; Ariodant; Bion; Une folie; Le Trésor supposé; Joanna; Héléna; Les Deux aveugles de Tolède; Uthal; Joseph.

Orchestral Music—Symphonies.

Piano Music—Sonatas.

ABOUT

Brancour, R., Méhul; Hargreave, M., Earlier French Composers; Pougin, A., Méhul: Sa vie, son génie, son caractère; Viellard, P., Méhul: Sa vie et ses œuvres.

Musical Quarterly, October 1951.

Felix Mendelssohn *1809-1847*

J AKOB LUDWIG FELIX MENDELS-SOHN-BARTHOLDY was born in Hamburg, Germany, on February 3, 1809. His grandfather, Moses Mendelssohn, was the distinguished philosopher sometimes described as "the modern Plato"; he had been the prototype for Lessing's drama *Nathan der Weise*. Mendelssohn's father, Abraham, was a successful banker; his mother, Leah, a woman of rare cultural attainments, of whom Henry F. Chorley said, "There have lived few women more honorably distinguished than she by acquirement."

When in 1811 French troops occupied Hamburg, the Mendelssohn family established residence in Berlin, in the fashionable Neue Promenade. There little Felix began to study the piano with his mother. He studied music more intensively in Berlin with Ludwig Berger (piano) and Karl Friedrich Zelter (theory), then went to Paris to study with Mme Bigot. At nine he made his first public appearance as a pianist.

In 1819 Mendelssohn became a member of the Singakademie in Berlin, directed by Zelter. Through this group the boy was initiated into the world of great choral music. Its influence on him was reflected in a choral psalm which he completed in 1819, and which the Singakademie introduced that year. The boy then wrote prolifically in various forms; by 1821 he had written several symphonies, two operas, some fugues for string quartets, and a variety of shorter compositions.

To insure the future safety of her children, Frau Mendelssohn had long urged her

FELIX MENDELSSOHN

husband to consider conversion from Judaism to Christianity. For a while Abraham resisted "out of respect for my father's memory." One day, however, the child Felix came home from the Singakademie weeping because some children had mocked him for his religion. The episode settled the matter for Abraham Mendelssohn, and the entire family—Abraham, Leah, Felix, and Felix's sister, Fanny—were converted to Lutheranism. To distinguish his own family from the other Mendelssohns who had remained Jewish, Abraham added to his own name that of Bartholdy, the name that had been assumed by one of Felix's uncles when he had converted.

Sir Julius Benedict, who met the boy Mendelssohn in 1821, provides a picture of the young genius: "[As I was] walking in the streets of Berlin with my master and friend, Carl Maria von Weber, he directed my attention to a boy, apparently about eleven or twelve years old, who, on perceiving the author of *Der Freischütz* ran towards him, giving him a most hearty and friendly greeting. 'This is Felix Mendelssohn,' said Weber, introducing me at once to the prodigious child, of whose marvelous talent and execution I had heard so much at Dresden. I shall never forget the impression that day on beholding that beautiful youth, with his auburn hair clustering in ringlets around his shoulders, the ingenuous smile of innocence and candor on his lips. He would have it that we should go with him at once to his father's house; but as Weber had to attend a rehearsal, he took me by the hand and made me run a race till we reached his home. Up he went briskly to the drawing room where, finding his mother, he exclaimed: 'Here is a pupil of Weber's, who knows a great deal of his music and of the new opera. Pray, mama, ask him to play it for us.' And so, with irresistible impetuosity, he pushed me to the piano, and made me remain there until I had exhausted the store of my recollections. When I then begged of him to let me hear some of his own compositions, he refused, but played from memory such of Bach's fugues or Cramer's exercises as I could name."

In 1821 Mendelssohn also met Goethe for the first time, through the efforts of his instructor, Zelter, who took the boy to Weimar for this purpose. Young Mendelssohn performed Bach and Beethoven, and spent hours improvising. "You will be a great composer," Goethe told him. Mendelssohn later visited Goethe on several occasions. "I am Saul and you are David," Goethe once wrote to Mendelssohn. "Come to me when I am sad and discouraged and quiet my soul with your sweet harmonies."

Mendelssohn astounded others with his remarkable gifts. After he had improvised on several themes by Bach for the venerable Johann Schelble, director of the Cäcilien-Verein in Frankfurt, Schelble said, "This boy is one of God's own." When Mendelssohn's comic opera *The Two Nephews* was heard during one of the Sunday musicales held in the Mendelssohn home, his teacher Zelter told him: "You are no longer an apprentice but an independent member of the brotherhood of musicians." Ignaz Moscheles, one of the most eminent pianists and piano instructors of his day, exclaimed, "Mendelssohn stands in no need of lessons. . . . He is a mature artist."

In 1825 the Mendelssohns moved to a new, spacious home on the Leipzigerstrasse in Berlin. A little theater was built in the garden for the presentation of weekly concerts. It was here that Mendelssohn's first masterwork was introduced—the Overture to *A Midsummer Night's Dream,* which was completed on August 6, 1826 and introduced soon afterwards in a two-piano version with his sister. Six months later he conducted the première of the orchestrated version in Stettin. "All is exquisitely designed, thought out with flawless logic, and reverently adapted to the spirit of Shakespeare's play," Wallace Brockway and Herbert Weinstock have commented on this exquisite work. The same elfin delicacy and diaphanous texture of the Overture, evoking a fairy kingdom with so sensitive a touch, is found in another important work which Mendelssohn wrote that year, the Octet, op. 20. "Not even Mozart or Schubert," wrote John Horton, "accomplished at the age of sixteen anything quite as astonishing as this major work of chamber music."

In 1829 Mendelssohn realized a great ambition and at the same time brought about a decisive event in music history. From childhood on he had performed and admired the music of Johann Sebastian Bach. As a member of the Singakademie he had sung parts of the *Passion According to St. Matthew.* One of his most prized possessions was a copy of the score of this work, presented to him by his grandmother. In 1829, however, Bach's music was little known and rarely performed, and it was Mendelssohn's first ambition to bring to that forgotten and neglected master some of the deserved recognition which had so long been denied him. Mendelssohn dreamed of performing the complete score of the *St. Matthew Passion,* which had not been given since Bach's own day. With the cooperation of Eduard Devrient, a well-known actor and singer, Mendelssohn arranged to conduct the Singakademie in this masterwork. The concert took place in Berlin on March 11, 1829, with monumental success. "Everyone was filled with the most solemn devotion," wrote Mendelssohn's sister, Fanny. "One heard only an occasional involuntary exclamation that sprang from deep emotion." Indeed, so enthusiastic was the response that the concert was repeated ten days later. There is little question that these performances of the complete *St. Matthew Passion* helped precipitate the Bach revival that swept the world of music during the next few decades, finally elevating the master to his present position of supremacy among composers. "To think," Mendelssohn remarked in one of his rare references to his religious origins, "that it should be an actor [Devrient] and a Jew who gave back to the people this greatest of Christian works!"

In the spring of 1829 Mendelssohn made his first visit to England, where he returned often throughout his life to receive higher honor than any foreign-born composer since Handel. He made his debut in England directing the première of his Symphony in C minor. A few months later the Philharmonic Society elected him an honorary member. After an active season in England he traveled to Scotland, where he sketched his *Fingal's Cave* or *Hebrides Overture* and planned his *Scotch Symphony.* He then proceeded to Italy, and was inspired to begin his *Italian Symphony.* After stopping in Paris to meet Chopin, Liszt, and Meyerbeer, among others, Mendelssohn returned to London to direct the world première of his *Fingal's Cave* or *Hebrides Overture* on May 14, 1832, and perform his G minor Piano Concerto on May 22. During this period he also completed the *Capriccio brillant* for piano and orchestra, and published the first volume of his *Songs Without Words.*

In 1833 Mendelssohn applied for, but was denied, the post of conductor of the Singakademie in Berlin. Later that year, however, he was made general music director of the city of Düsseldorf, in charge of its Opera, church music, and two choral groups. He was not happy in this post, largely because his artistic aims were higher than the means at his disposal. After leaving Düsseldorf, Mendelssohn received, in the spring of 1834, his first official honor—election to membership of the Berlin Academy of Fine Arts.

In 1835, Mendelssohn became the principal conductor of the Gewandhaus Orchestra in Leipzig, a position which provided him with resources to match his aims. The five years of his tenure in Leipzig are a period of prime importance in music history. Through his painstaking performances and his dedication to new works and unknown composers, Mendelssohn brought the orchestra to a position of world prominence. He developed the art of conducting. He was responsible for making Leipzig the greatest music center in Germany.

On May 22, 1836, Mendelssohn directed the successful première of his oratorio *St. Paul* at the Lower Rhine Festival. Less than a year later, on March 28, 1837, he married Cécile Jeanrenaud, the daughter of a minister. Their marriage was idyllic, and five children were born to them.

In 1840 Mendelssohn was asked by the King of Prussia, Frederick William IV, to head a music department planned in conjunction with a proposed Academy of Arts, in Berlin. He assumed the post in 1841, and almost at once found himself embroiled in numerous court intrigues, rivalries, and other difficulties. Promptly requesting a temporary leave of absence, Mendelssohn revisited Leipzig to direct the world première of his *Scotch Symphony* on March 3, 1842, then continued to London for two command performances for Queen Victoria. Upon his return to Berlin that fall, Mendelssohn resigned from the music department. The King then prevailed on him to accept an honorary appointment as General Music Director, which carried with it no obligations other than to write music for special events and help organize music performances at the Cathedral. Perhaps the only significant creative result of Mendelssohn's Berlin adventure was the writing of the incidental music to *A Midsummer Night's Dream,* which the King commissioned him to compose for a presentation of the Shakespearean play in Potsdam. To the early Overture, written in his youth, Mendelssohn now added thirteen new sections; the best of these, including the "Nocturne," the "Scherzo," and the extremely popular "Wedding March," retain magically the high standards, and at times the delicate style, of the incomparable Overture.

Again Mendelssohn made his home in Leipzig, reappearing occasionally as a conductor of the Gewandhaus Orchestra. He was now able to realize an all-consuming ambition to create a Conservatory of the first rank. He received the requisite permission from the King in 1843, and on April 3 that year the Leipzig Conservatory opened, with a faculty that included Ferdinand David, Robert Schumann, Hauptmann, Becker, and Mendelssohn himself.

For the next few years several noteworthy activities absorbed Mendelssohn's energies. In addition to teaching and conducting in Leipzig, he made important guest appearances in England in the summer of 1844. He also occupied himself with the creation of some of his greatest works, including the Violin Concerto in E minor, and the oratorio *Elijah.* He directed the world première of his oratorio on August 26, 1846, at the Birmingham Festival, where it received a thundering ovation. Since then *Elijah* has been a favorite of English music audiences, who regard it second in significance only to the *Messiah.*

Hard work now seriously taxed Mendelssohn's health, which had always been extremely delicate. He began to suffer excessive fatigue, and severe headaches which forced him to give up his duties with the Gewandhaus Orchestra and the piano department of the Conservatory. Despite his weariness and physical ailments, he made a tenth, and last, visit to England in April 1847. Upon his return to Leipzig he received the crushing news that his beloved sister, Fanny, had died on May 14. The shock sent him into a severe depression and further damaged his nervous system. He aged suddenly, his strength dissipated rapidly, and he died in Leipzig on November 4, 1847. "In the afternoon," wrote Eduard Devrient, "the immense throng of the funeral procession began to gather in front of the house. Streets and open places were filled with people; all the windows were crowded on the long and circuitous route that the procession was to pass, through the town and by the Gewandhaus, the scene of Mendelssohn's labors. The musicians led the way, playing a hastily instrumented *Song Without Words* (the one in E minor, Book 5). Six clergymen in full robes followed the bier." Memorial services were also held in the principal cities of England, Germany, France, and the United States. After the funeral service in Leipzig, Mendelssohn's body was transferred to Berlin for burial in the family vault.

As Eduard Devrient described Mendelssohn's physical appearance, "he was of middle height and slender frame. His features, of the Oriental type, were handsome; a high, thoughtful forehead, much depressed at the temples; large, expressive dark eyes, with drooping lids, and a peculiar veiled glance through the lashes; this, however, sometimes flashed distrust, or anger, sometimes happy dreaming and expectancy. His nose was arched and of delicate form, still more so the mouth, with its short upper and full underlip, which was slightly protruded and hid his teeth when, with a slight lisp, he pronounced the hissing consonants. An extreme mobility about the mouth betrayed every emotion that passed within him."

"Excitement," continued Devrient, "stimulated him to the verge of frenzy, from which he was restored only by his sound, deathlike sleep. . . . The habit of constant occupation . . . made rest intolerable to him. To spend any time in mere talk caused him to look frequently at his watch, by which he often gave offense; his impatience was pacified only when something was being done, such as music, reading, chess. He was fond of having a leaf of paper at hand when he was conversing, to sketch down whatever occurred to him. . . . His bearing retained from boyhood the slight rocking of the head and upper part of the body, and shifting from foot to foot; his head was much thrown back, especially when playing the piano."

Mendelssohn was not a composer of emotional or conceptual profundity. Daniel Gregory Mason points out these and other shortcomings, which have kept Mendelssohn from first rank as a composer. "We cannot escape the impression of a certain thinness of blood, straitness of sympathy, and inelasticity of mind. His personality is tenuous, overrarefied; he seems more like a faun than a man. And hence it comes about that when, leaving his world of fairies, elves, visionary landscapes, and ethereal joys and sorrows, he tries to sound a fuller note of human pain and passion, he is felt to be out of his element. His style is too fluent, too suave, too insinuating and inoffensive, to embody tragic emotion. It lacks the rugged force, the virile energy, the occasional harshness and discordance even of the natural human voice; its reading of life, in which there is ugliness, crudity, and violence as well as beauty, is too fastidiously expurgated."

These faults notwithstanding, Mendelssohn was ever an aristocrat in form and style, and achieved whatever he attempted with utmost skill and artistry. His forte, as Hugo Leichtentritt wrote, was "light, aerial, fairy music," and in this he has never been surpassed. "Many of his scherzos have a delightfully fantastic play of the most delicate tones, suggestive of a dance of spirits that float in the air like clouds, soaring lightly in most graceful undulations, hardly touching the ground with their nimble feet, wrapped in veils, like clouds or smoke mounting towards the sky." He was also a master at painting landscapes in music. In this connection H. H. Statham wrote, "The *Scotch* and *Italian* Symphonies are entirely occupied in giving through music the local color of the landscapes and life of the two countries indicated, or, more properly, the impression which they produced in the composer's imagination. The same is true of the *Fingal's Cave Overture* and the *Meeresstille Overture*."

Analyzing Mendelssohn's style, Frederic H. Cowen found it characterized by "extreme grace and refinement and musical scholarship, at times full of sparkling vivacity, at other times tinged with melancholy. If he had comparatively few really great moments, so are there few traces of absolute weakness. . . . He was an inspired melodist, though his themes, beautiful as they are, were not infrequently molded after the same pattern. He also possessed a strongly marked . . . individuality . . . [and] in addition a gaiety and animation, a *joie de vivre* which was the outcome of his happy and light-hearted nature. . . . If Mendelssohn did not rise to the greatest heights, he came within measurable distance of them. His music bears the stamp of his cultured mind, and his high level of excellence is undeniable."

Principal Works

Chamber Music—6 string quartets; 3 piano quartets; 2 string quintets; 2 piano trios; 2 cello sonatas; String Octet in E-flat major; Piano Sextet in D major; Violin Sonata in F minor.

Choral Music—St. Paul; Lobgesang; Die erste Walpurgisnacht; Elijah; anthems, English church pieces, hymns, motets, psalms, sacred pieces, Te Deum, unaccompanied part songs.

Operas—Die Hochzeit des Camacho; Die Heimkehr aus der Fremde; Loreley (unfinished).

Orchestral Music—5 symphonies (not including his early symphonies); 2 piano concertos; Violin Concerto in E minor; A Midsummer Night's Dream, suite; Fingal's Cave (or Hebrides) Overture; Calm Sea and Prosperous Voyage (Meeresstille und glückliche Fahrt); Ruy Blas; Capriccio brillant, for piano and orchestra; Rondo brillant, for piano and orchestra.

Organ Music—6 sonatas; preludes and fugues.

Piano Music—3 sonatas; Seven Characteristic Pieces; Rondo capriccioso; Songs Without Words (Lieder ohne Worte); Variations sérieuses; Kinderstücke; caprices, études, fugues, preludes, scherzos.

Vocal Music—Songs for voice and piano, including Abschiedslied der Zugvögel, Auf Flügeln des Gesanges (On Wings of Song), Gruss, Ich wollt, meine Liebe ergösse sich, Morgengruss, Sonntagsmorgen, Wasserfahrt; vocal duets.

About

Devrient, E., My Memories of Felix Mendelssohn; Hiller, F., Mendelssohn: Letters and Recollections; Jacob, H., Felix Mendelssohn and His Times; Petitpierre, J., The Romance of the Mendelssohns; Radcliffe, P., Mendelssohn; Stratton, S., Mendelssohn; Werner, E., Mendelssohn: A New Image of the Composer and His Age; Young, P. M., Introduction to the Music of Mendelssohn.

Giacomo Meyerbeer *1791-1864*

GIACOMO MEYERBEER, who helped establish the traditions and ritual of French grand opera, was born Jakob Liebmann Beer in Berlin on September 5, 1791. His father, a banker, had a rich cultural background, and made his home a rendezvous for foremost intellectual figures. The boy thus grew up in a milieu well suited to fostering his musical talent. Indeed, his maternal grandfather bestowed on him a huge legacy that was to give him financial independence throughout his life, thus enabling him to pursue a career in music, with the sole stipulation that he add the name of "Meyer" (his grandfather's name) to his own. It is for this reason that the boy became known as Meyerbeer; the Italianization of his first name was made after he had won distinction as a composer of Italian opera.

The young Meyerbeer was remarkably precocious as a pianist and composer. He started to play piano at the age of four, made his first public appearance as a virtuoso at seven, giving a phenomenal performance of Mozart's D minor Piano Concerto, and was only eleven when he completed the writing of a cantata.

In 1802 Muzio Clementi, the renowned pianist and teacher, visited Berlin and heard young Meyerbeer play, and was so impressed that he decided to emerge from retirement to teach the boy piano. The boy soon afterwards studied theory with Karl Friedrich Zelter, and then with Anselm Weber.

While a student of Anselm Weber, young Meyerbeer sent one of his exercises, a fugue, to the Abbé Vogler, the distinguished theorist in Darmstadt. Vogler's reply consisted of a lengthy dissertation on the technique of writing fugues, together with a devastating criticism of the composition Meyerbeer had submitted. Undismayed, Meyerbeer proceeded to write a new eight-part fugue along the lines that Vogler had set down. This time Vogler's answer was: "Art opens to you a glorious future. Come to me, and I will receive you as a son."

In 1810 Meyerbeer went to live with Vogler in Darmstadt, studying with him for two years. As Vogler's pupil, Meyerbeer engaged more industriously in composition. He wrote a set of songs to religious poems by Klopstock; an oratorio, *Gott und die*

GIACOMO MEYERBEER

Natur, performed in Berlin on May 8, 1811; and two operas: *Jephthas Gelübde,* introduced in Munich on December 23, 1812, and *Wirt und Gast* (or *Alimelek*), first given in Stuttgart on January 6, 1813. Both operas failed.

In 1813 a Viennese production of *Wirt und Gast* brought Meyerbeer to the Austrian capital. There he was so taken with the piano performances of Hummel that he decided to retire temporarily in order to work on his piano technique and become a virtuoso of the first order. After an intensive ten-month period of study, he did become an outstanding performer, and might have, had he so desired, become one of the greatest pianists of his time. But he still aspired to be a composer, particularly a composer for the stage. So, on the advice of Antonio Salieri, he decided in 1815 to go to Italy to study music and absorb its operatic traditions. He arrived in Venice at a time when that city was smitten with a passion for Rossini, and he was soon victimized as well. He began to write opera in the Rossini manner. "I was caught," he later confessed, "like the rest . . . in this fine web of sound. I was bewitched in a magic garden which I had no wish to enter but which I could not avoid. All my thoughts, all my faculties became Italian; when I had lived there a year, I thought of myself as a native. . . . That so complete a transformation of my inner life must have a radical effect upon the style of my music will be readily

understood. I did not want, as is commonly supposed, to imitate Rossini or to write in the Italian manner, but I had to compose in the style which I adopted under the compulsion of my state of mind."

His first Italian opera, *Romilda e Costanza,* was produced in Padua on July 19, 1817. *Semiramide riconosciuta* and *Emma di Resburgo* followed in 1819, *Margherita d'Anjou* in 1820, and *L'Esule di Granata* in 1822. The last work was introduced at La Scala in Milan, then performed in Munich, France, England, and Belgium.

In 1823 Meyerbeer returned to Berlin. Carl Maria von Weber, his former fellow-student under Vogler, directed performances of Meyerbeer's *Alimelek* and *Emma di Resburgo* (the latter renamed for Germany, *Emma von Leicester*) at the Dresden Opera. But Weber was highly critical of Meyerbeer's defection to the traditions of Italian opera. Although Weber's influence could not bring Meyerbeer into the German camp, it prompted him to revaluate his aims and purposes, and soon to become dissatisfied with the Italian style. The effects of his considerations are apparent in *Il Crociato in Egitto,* an Italian opera which he composed in Berlin, and which was introduced in Venice on March 7, 1824, with great success. This opera is of particular interest in Meyerbeer's creative growth, pointing up a change in style, which now attempted to combine Italian lyricism with the sounder harmonic and orchestral values of German opera, blending these with spectacle and pageantry. *Il Crociato* is a transitional work, connecting Meyerbeer's Italian period with the later French operas of his full maturity. "*Il Crociato,*" says Dyneley Hussey, "is a synthesis of various styles, manipulated with Meyerbeer's astonishing capacity for absorbing and coordinating other men's ideas which did in the end produce a style that may be called his own."

For several years Meyerbeer wrote no opera. In 1826 he went to Paris. There he moved among the foremost musicians and devoted himself to research in French history, culture, and art, as well as opera. He married his cousin, Mina Mosson, in Berlin; then in the next years suffered personal anguish through the deaths, in rapid succession, of his father and his own two children.

When he went back at last to writing opera, Meyerbeer produced what was not only his first masterpiece but also the first opera ever written in a distinctly French style—combining Italian lyricism with strong declamation, French dramatic force, and emphasis on ballets and large scenes. The opera was *Robert le Diable,* produced by the Paris Opéra on November 21, 1831. It was a sensation, bringing a fortune to the Opéra, and establishing a new genre of opera that was to flourish in France for the next half century. To William F. Apthorp, *Robert* is Meyerbeer's "freshest and most original work." Apthorp adds that Meyerbeer may have had greater maturity and deeper emotional content in his later operas, but in *Robert* there is "a superior freshness of melodic invention, more genuine dash and brilliancy." The American première of *Robert le Diable* took place at the Park Theatre in New York on April 7, 1834.

Meyerbeer's next work, *Les Huguenots* (first presented by the Paris Opéra on February 29, 1836, and introduced in the United States in New Orleans on April 29, 1839), did not have the immense success of its immediate predecessor; but it revealed the expanding creative powers in its composer, and a greater range of dramatic writing. "Had he written nothing else but the fourth act," said Arthur Hervey, "he would be entitled to rank as one of the greatest dramatic composers of all time," an estimate which Richard Wagner also had made at one time. Berlioz was another major composer who was most enthusiastic about *Les Huguenots.* "The effervescence of the emotions excited by this masterpiece," he wrote, "makes one desire to be a great man in order to place one's glory and one's genius at the feet of Meyerbeer."

With *Robert le Diable* and *Les Huguenots,* Meyerbeer became the most celebrated composer in France, and one of the most highly honored in all Europe. He received many honors: the Order of the Oak Crown from the Netherlands; an appointment to the Royal Academy of London; an offer from Frederick William IV to become general music director in Berlin. He assumed the last post in 1843, and devoted himself for several years to directing opera performances and writing special works and functional pieces for court. He also completed a new opera, *Ein Feldlager in Schlesien,* which was introduced in Berlin on December 7, 1844.

During a leave of absence from Berlin, Meyerbeer revisited Paris, where his librettist, Eugène Scribe, provided him with the text of a new opera. It was *Le Prophète,* an elaborate historical spectacle based on the career of John of Leyden. The work was triumphantly introduced at the Opéra on April 16, 1849. Critical esteem, however, has not matched the popularity of the work. "Meyerbeer's besetting sin," commented R. A. Streatfeild, "his constant search for the merely effective, is even more pronounced in *Le Prophète* than in *Les Huguenots.* The Coronation Scene (with its famous march) has nothing of the large simplicity necessary for the proper manipulation of mass of sound. The canvas is crowded with insignificant and confusing detail, and the general effect is finicking and invertebrate rather than solid and dignified."

After *Le Prophète,* Meyerbeer wrote two works in a lighter style and a new genre for the Opéra-Comique. His first comic opera, *L'Étoile du nord,* was seen on February 16, 1854; the second, *Le Pardon de Ploërmel,* now better known as *Dinorah,* was first performed on April 4, 1859. "These French operas, although containing much that is charming, were like his Italian 'wild oats' the results of an effort of will—the will to be whomsoever he chose," wrote Mrs. Julian Marshall. Both operas are among Meyerbeer's less significant achievements and are rarely given. When *Dinorah* is occasionally revived, it is mainly because of the appeal of one of its big arias, the "Shadow Song," a favorite with coloraturas.

Meyerbeer next concentrated his energies on *L'Africaine,* an opera that occupied him for about twenty-five years. He regarded it as his masterwork, and expended on it infinite care and devotion. Even after it had been scheduled for performance and was in rehearsal, he continued to revise details; and he was still working upon this opera when he died suddenly in Paris on May 2, 1864.

This last work was produced posthumously at the Opéra on April 28, 1865, and introduced in the United States at the Academy of Music in New York on December 1, 1865. There are many who consider it to be Meyerbeer's greatest opera. "When Meyerbeer succeeds in *L'Africaine,*" wrote Wallace Brockway and Herbert Weinstock, "it is, perhaps, on the highest musical level he ever attained. . . . There are enough fine things in *L'Africaine* to make it tragic that Meyerbeer never managed to produce an opera in which he was consistently at his best from beginning to end. Such an opera would unquestionably have been among the finest ever composed." To Cecil Gray, Verdi's *Aïda* is "musically little more than a grandiose pendant or sequel to *L'Africaine.*"

In a discussion of Meyerbeer's operatic work, C. Hubert Parry wrote: "Musically it is a huge pile of commonplaces, infinitely ingenious and barren. There is but little cohesion between the scenes, and no attempt at consistency to the situations in style and expression. No doubt Meyerbeer had a great sense of general effect. The music glitters and roars and warbles in well-disposed contrasts, but the inner life is wanting. It is the same with his treatment of characters. They metaphorically strut and pose and gesticulate but express next to nothing; they get into frenzies but are for the most part incapable of human passion. The element of wholesome musical sincerity is wanting in him, but the power of astonishing and bewildering is almost unlimited. His cleverness is equal to any emergency."

Notwithstanding his faults, Meyerbeer was an important composer. He was, as Arthur Hervey explained "an innovator. His operas contain great beauties; he showed extraordinary dramatic perception and marked originality; he devised new instrumental effects; he helped to prepare the way for the modern music drama. . . . With more strength of character, Meyerbeer would have done yet greater things. He had at his command the genius and the opportunities."

Above everything else, Meyerbeer was "one of the greatest masters in writing for the human voice," as Robert Lawrence remarked in *Musical America,* adding that "his influence in the development of casting and of vocal types as we know them today is not to be underestimated. . . . Every kind of operatic singer found new outlets through his skill. The bass role in *Robert le Diable* became the first of the great Mephisto parts; the mezzo in *Le Prophète* created the grand tradition from which were later to spring Eboli, Amneris and Ortrud; the music for Meyerbeer's tenors brought fresh scope to the virtuoso performer."

And Hugo Riemann, summing up Meyerbeer's place in music, wrote: "History will point to Meyerbeer's music as one of the most important steps to Wagner's art."

Meyerbeer's greatest weakness, both personal and artistic, was his insatiable love of glory. He sought public adulation as others hunger for wealth. He exerted himself to gain affection for himself and admiration towards his work, was profoundly concerned with, and sensitive to, public opinion. Heine once criticized Meyerbeer's weakness with a devastating quip: "When Meyerbeer is dead," Heine asked, "who will look after his glory?"

A wealthy man all his life, Meyerbeer lived simply and unostentatiously. He was extraordinarily generous in helping musicians, contributing to charitable causes, creating trust funds for families of musicians. Music, particularly his own, was the most important element in his life—dearer, Heine believed, than even life itself. "When the cholera broke out in Paris," Heine revealed, "I implored him to leave as soon as possible, but he had a few days' urgent business—he had to arrange for an Italian version of the libretto of *Robert le Diable.*"

PRINCIPAL WORKS

Operas—Il Crociato in Egitto; Robert le Diable; Les Huguenots; Ein Feldlager in Schlesien; Le Prophète; L'Étoile du nord; Le Pardon de Ploërmel (Dinorah); L'Africaine.

ABOUT

Blaze de Bury, H., Meyerbeer; Curzon, H. de, Meyerbeer; Dauriac, L., Meyerbeer; Dieren, B. van, Down Among the Dead Men; Hervey, A., Giacomo Meyerbeer; Kapp, J., Giacomo Meyerbeer: eine Biographie; Pougin, A., Meyerbeer.

Stanislaus Moniuszko *1819-1872*

STANISLAUS MONIUSZKO, composer of Poland's most important national opera, *Halka,* was born in Ubiel, in the province of Minsk, on May 5, 1819. His father was a former army captain who became adjutant to the King of Naples and acquired a small estate in Ubiel; his mother was a fine amateur musician. When Stanislaus revealed an unmistakable gift for music, the family moved to Warsaw in 1827 so that he might benefit from competent instruction. From 1827 to 1830 he studied with August Freyer. In 1830 the family settled in Minsk where the boy continued his music studies with local instructors. From 1837 to 1839 he attended the Berlin Singakademie, where he was a pupil of Rungenhagen. Moniuszko's first published works, three songs, appeared in Berlin in 1838, and

Moniuszko: mô-nyōōsh′kô

were described by a critic of the *Allgemeine Musikalische Zeitung* as "national in word and tune . . . distinguished by surety and decisiveness."

In 1840 Moniuszko settled in Vilna as a teacher of music and as an organist of the St. John Cathedral. Soon after he was married to Alexandra Müller. In 1842 he published a volume of songs that attracted much attention and praise, and began to write music for operettas and other light stage diversions. In 1846 one of his operettas, *The Lottery*, was successfully produced in Minsk and Warsaw.

The work that gave Moniuszko his eminence as the first great Polish operatic composer was *Halka*, introduced on January 1, 1848, in an amateur production. In his original version Moniuszko wrote two acts. Then, convinced of its artistic potential, and spurred by the ambition to have his work mounted by the Warsaw Opera, he revised it extensively and expanded it into four acts. For many years the Warsaw Opera failed to show interest in *Halka*, largely because its own repertory emphasized Italian opera. After many years, however, on January 1, 1858, it did produce *Halka*, with success that was matched by few, if any, of its other productions. The opera was soon translated into twelve foreign languages and given throughout Europe (including Russia) and in New York City (at the People's Theatre in June 1903). When Hans von Bülow saw the score in 1858, he wrote in the *Neue Zeitschrift für Musik*: "In *Halka* a highly gifted composer energetically expresses the strength of the national spirit. . . . His opera contains a striking beauty for us Germans."

Analyzing the specific merits of *Halka*, Zdislaw Jachimecki wrote, "The listener is carried upon the stream of the music, and always feels the personality of the composer and the sincerity of his inspiration. The songs of the opera are very melodious, characteristic, and dramatic. There are, however, also other remarkable factors which raise it to the rank of masterpiece. No Polish dramatic composer had previously expressed by dance scenes the Polish national temperament so perfectly as did Moniuszko."

Halka has retained its popularity in Poland, and is occasionally revived in other European countries. The work was also made into a Polish-language motion picture that was released in Europe and the United States.

STANISLAUS MONIUSZKO

Although Moniuszko never wrote an opera to equal *Halka*, several of his other dramatic works enjoyed great favor in Poland. The best were *The Bargemen* in 1858, *The Countess* in 1860, and *The Haunted Castle* in 1865. Moniuszko also composed many songs that were widely performed and that placed him with Europe's most important song composers of the day. "Not for a moment," wrote the eminent Russian composer Serov in 1869, "do I hesitate to put the songs of Moniuszko in the highest class of lyric composition, as represented by the great names of Schubert and Schumann in Western Europe and in our own country by Glinka and Dargomizhsky."

After the triumph of *Halka*, Moniuszko was appointed professor of theory at the Warsaw Conservatory in 1858. The failure of his last two operas, *The Pariah* in 1869 and *Beata* in 1872 broke his spirit, and probably his health too. He died in Warsaw on June 4, 1872.

Moniuszko was the author of an important text on harmony.

PRINCIPAL WORKS
Chamber Music—2 string quartets.

Choral Music—Cantatas, hymns, Litanies, Masses, motets, Requiems.

Operas—The Lottery; The New Don Quixote; Jawnuta; Halka; The Bargemen; The Countess; The Haunted Castle; The Pariah; Beata.

Orchestral Music—Bajka; incidental music to various plays.

Vocal Music—About 250 songs, including At the Spinning Wheel, Evening Song, Knowest Thou the Land?, The Spinster, Spring, War Song.

ABOUT

Arct, A. S., Moniuszko: Life and Works; Jachimecki, Z., Stanislaus Moniuszko; Rudzinski, W., Stanislaus Moniuszko; Stromenger, K., Moniuszko.

Musical Quarterly, January 1928.

Pierre-Alexandre Monsigny
1729-1817

PIERRE-ALEXANDRE MONSIGNY, a founder of *opéra-comique*, was born in Fauquembergues, near Saint-Omer, France, on October 17, 1729. At the Jesuit College of Saint-Omer, which he attended as a boy, he was given violin instruction. When his father died, Monsigny, aged eighteen, sought several means to support his family. In 1749 he moved to Paris, finding employment as a clerk in the Bureaux des Comptes du Clergé. Later he became the *maître d'hôtel* for the Duke d'Orléans, a post that enabled him to live in luxury and provide amply for his family.

In 1754 Monsigny heard a performance of Pergolesi's *La Serva padrona*, performed in Paris by a visiting Italian company. This pioneer work, with which *opera buffa* had come into existence as an art form, impressed Monsigny so deeply that the young man determined to become a composer of comic opera. He began to take lessons in harmony from Gianotti, a double-bass player in the Opéra orchestra who followed Rameau's harmonic system. Then, a bare five months later, he composed his first *opéra-comique*, *Les Aveux indiscrets*. It was introduced at the Théâtre de la Foire Saint Germain, on February 7, 1759, and enjoyed huge success. Equally popular were his three succeeding operas, presented at that theater: *Le Maître en droit* in 1760; *Le Cadi dupé* and *On ne s'avise jamais de tout*, in 1761.

The competitive Comédie-Italienne regarded the rising popularity of the Théâtre de la Foire and its composer Monsigny with considerable envy. The directors, consequently, effected a merger with their competitor. Thus Monsigny now began to compose opera for the Comédie-Italienne, beginning with *Le Roi et le fermier* on November 22, 1762. His triumphs continued as he created a series of brilliant operas,

PIERRE-ALEXANDRE MONSIGNY

including *Rose et Colas* in 1764, *Le Déserteur* in 1769 (rapturously praised by Berlioz), *Le Faucon* in 1772, and *Félix* in 1777.

Although *Félix* was an overwhelming success, bringing Monsigny to the peak of his popularity and creative ability, he suddenly decided to abandon composition for the theater. Years later he confided to Fétis that he had refused to write opera after *Félix* because no more ideas came to his head. "*Félix*," he said "was like death for me."

The French Revolution destroyed Monsigny's position in France as well as his fortune. Years of suffering and poverty followed, partially alleviated in 1798 when the Opéra-Comique presented him with an annuity of 2400 francs. When Napoleon heard of this grant he immediately tripled it, and expressed amazement at discovering that Monsigny, whom he had so long admired, was still alive.

In 1800 Monsigny was appointed Inspector of the Conservatory. He soon realized that he was not suited for the post and resigned in 1802. In 1813 he succeeded Grétry as a member of the Institut de France, and in 1816 was made a member of the Legion of Honor.

Pierre-Alexandre Monsigny died in Paris on January 14, 1817.

A writer thus described Monsigny's appearance and manner: "He was of medium height; his appearance was noble and benevolent, and his manners at the same time both simple and elegant. He preserved until his extreme old age all that distinguished a man who has lived in the best society. His character, full of sweetness and kindness, without a trace of pettiness or envy, brought him the affection and high esteem of all those who knew him. The most salient trait of his make-up was a most exquisite sensibility."

Although none of Monsigny's *opéras-comiques* has survived, his importance in French music is unquestionable. He was one of those who helped crystallize the form, style, and traditions of *opéra-comique*. He had an inadequate technique, and his musical construction left much to be desired, but he more than made up for what he lacked in musical science with the beauty of his melodies and the charm of his style. Adolphe Adam, who profited greatly from Monsigny's works, spoke of his "exquisite sensibility," "comic verve," and "dramatic movement and expressive force." Berlioz said that in his own field of light musical endeavor, Monsigny had proved as significant as Gluck had been in music-drama.

PRINCIPAL WORKS

Operas—Les Aveux indiscrets; Le Maître en droit; Le Cadi dupé; On ne s'avise jamais de tout; Le Roi et le fermier; Rose et Colas; Aline, Reine de Golconde; Le Déserteur; Le Faucon; La Belle Arsène; Félix.

ABOUT

Druilhe, P., Monsigny, sa vie et son œuvre; de Ménil, F., Les Grand musiciens du Nord: Monsigny; Pougin, A., Monsigny et son temps.

Philippe de Monte *1521-1603*

PHILIPPE DE MONTE (Filippo di Monte, Philippe de Mons), one of the last important representatives of the Flemish school of counterpoint, was born in Malines in 1521. Little is known of his boyhood beyond the fact that he was a chorister at the Saint-Rombaud Cathedral, then patronized by Queen Margaret of Austria. From 1541 to 1554 he was a music instructor at the Pinelli household in Naples. During this period he came to know Orlando di Lasso.

In 1554 de Monte went to Rome, became acquainted with Palestrina, and published his first volume, a set of five-voice madrigals. From Rome he proceeded to Antwerp, then to England, where for a while he served

PHILIPPE DE MONTE

in the choir of Philip II, husband of Queen Mary Tudor.

After returning home, Philippe de Monte spent several years traveling, making appearances as a singer. In 1568 he was appointed *Kapellmeister* at the court of Maximilian II in Vienna. He held this post until his death. In 1572 he received the honorary, and nonresidential, post of treasurer of the Cathedral of Cambrai, and three years later was made canon.

Toward the end of his life, de Monte went to Prague in the entourage of Rudolph II of Austria. De Monte died in Prague on July 4, 1603. Three months before his death his ninth and last volume of madrigals, written for six voices, was issued. De Monte, at his own request, was buried in the courtyard of the St. James Church in Prague.

Philippe de Monte was a prolific creator of madrigals, Masses, motets and other church and secular choral compositions. His style, according to G. van Doorslaer, was "simple and pure," and at the same time "profound in its technique of harmony and counterpoint."

"With de Monte," wrote Charles van den Borren, "the edifice is slowly and patiently put together by means of little pieces fitted one upon another with the most marvelous suppleness and most impeccable sureness. He has, like Lasso, a vigorous *sens-plastique* of which the delicate materiality is in opposition with the more ethereal substance of Palestrina's work."

PRINCIPAL WORKS

Choral Music—French chansons, madrigals, Masses, motets, villanellas.

ABOUT

Doorslaer, G. van, Philippe de Monte: la vie et les œuvres; Reese, G., Music in the Renaissance.
Chesterian, December 1929; Musical Times, November 1931.

Claudio Monteverdi *1567-1643*

CLAUDIO GIOVANNI ANTONIO MONTEVERDI, opera's first genius, was born in Cremona, Italy, in 1567, the son of a physician. He was baptized on May 15. As a boy chorister at the Cremona Cathedral, he studied music with distinguished choirmaster Marc'Antonio Ingegneri. When he was only fifteen he published his first opus, a volume of three-part motets. This was followed by a book of canzonettes in 1587, and the first three volumes of madrigals between 1587 and 1592. In all these compositions he demonstrated a consummate mastery of polyphonic technique and sound adherence to traditional procedures.

After failing to obtain an appointment in Milan through the sponsorship of Senator Ricardi (to whom Monteverdi had dedicated his second volume of madrigals), the young composer was engaged as viol player and madrigal singer at the Mantuan court of Vincenzo Gonzaga. It was a well-paying position, in which Monteverdi performed with a competence that won the high regard and friendship of his employer. On several occasions when the Duke embarked on his travels he took Monteverdi with him —to Hungary in 1595 and Flanders in 1599. In 1595 Monteverdi married a singer in the ducal court, Claudia Cattaneo. She bore him two sons before her untimely death in 1607.

In 1602 Monteverdi was elevated to the post of *maestro di cappella*, which brought with it more prestige and renown than financial reward. It is known that on more than one occasion the composer experienced great difficulty in obtaining his compensation. The work was exacting, for a great deal of composition was demanded of him; and Monteverdi was an artist who worked slowly and meticulously. Frequently the necessity of completing assignments within the period of a few days made him ill. "I do most heartily pray your Most Serene Highness," he was compelled to write to the Duke on one occasion, "for the love of God, no longer to put so much work on me; and to give me more time, for my great desire to serve you, and the excess of my fatigue will not fail to shorten my life."

Between 1603 and 1605, Monteverdi published two more volumes of madrigals, in which his command of polyphonic technique was combined with bold innovation. He was a pioneer in introducing unresolved discords for dramatic effect by means of passing notes, syncopations, and appoggiaturas. His harmonic writing grew more daring in the fifth volume, where we find for the first time "chords of the dominant seventh and ninth . . . used without preparation to determine the tonal cadences," as Henri Prunières pointed out. In this volume he also revolutionized the structure of the madrigal through the introduction of a continuo, or thorough-bass, in some of the madrigals (*madrigale concertato*). "The fact is," concluded Henri Prunières, "he was constructing a new harmonic language and threatened the foundations of polyphony by the introduction of a dramatic and personal sentiment."

Monteverdi wrote his first opera, *La Favola d'Orfeo*, only ten years after the musico-dramatic form and the style of monody had been devised by the Florentine *Camerata* (see sketches on Emilio del Cavaliere and Jacopo Peri). Ever seeking new musical worlds, Monteverdi seized upon the new medium to compose *Orfeo* at the behest of his employers at the ducal court in Mantua. The text, by Alessandro Striggio, was based on the ancient mythological story of Orpheus and Eurydice which Peri and Caccini had used for *Euridice,* and which numerous composers would later use. The new opera was introduced at the Accademia degli Invaghiti in February 1607 (probably on the 22nd), as part of the ceremonies celebrating the marriage of a member of the Gonzaga family to the Infanta of Savoy.

With *Orfeo,* the form of *dramma per musica* was raised for the first time to an elevated artistic status. "The dramatic genius of Monteverdi," as Manfred F. Bukofzer wrote, "that had expressed itself hitherto in the medium of madrigals, finally found its most congenial form in this opera, unquestionably the first masterpiece of operatic history. Its stylistic complexity sets it sharply apart from all earlier operas. Accepting the radical *stile rappresentativo* of the Florentines and infusing it with his intense pathos, Monteverdi realized at the same time the dramatic possibilities of the closed musical forms, the strophic aria, the dance song, the chamber duet, the madrigal, and the instrumental interlude, which the Camerata had discarded. In spite of their adherence to strictly musical laws, these forms were made subservient to the drama."

The new dimension and eloquence that the declamation of the Camerata achieved with Monteverdi are apparent in such affecting passages as "Ecco purch'a voi ritorno" and "Tu se' morta," which are not far from *bel canto* and the aria. Vocal solos were generously supplemented with vocal duets and trios, dances, and instrumental passages, all of which helped to extend the composer's artistic canvas. He used rhythm, harmony, and tempo to intensify dramatic action and suggest moods. Through his music the character of Orfeo becomes real, whereas with Caccini and Peri he had remained an abstraction.

Perhaps most revolutionary of all was Monteverdi's use of the orchestra. Whereas only a few primitive instruments had accompanied voices in the operas by Peri and Caccini, Monteverdi called upon an orchestra of forty instruments—the family of strings, flutes, cornets, trumpets, trombones, a harpsichord. This surely was the first modern symphony orchestra ever to be assembled. For this ensemble Monteverdi wrote not only an overture and accompaniments, but also independent pieces—sinfonie and ritornelli. Thus Monteverdi was one of the earliest creators of orchestral music to realize a purely instrumental style. "He produced," said Adam Carse, "that which is only possible on instruments; music, in which the interest is that of harmony, texture, and tone color, and is completely independent of imitative movement of parts."

Monteverdi's innovations produced a play throbbing with musical force, convincingly human, deeply emotional, and varied in dramatic appeal. As the first musical drama

CLAUDIO MONTEVERDI

ever written, *Orfeo* is understandably the earliest extant opera that can still be appreciated by modern audiences.

What is generally regarded as the American stage première of *Orfeo* took place in Northampton, Massachusetts, on May 12, 1929; prior to that time, however, the opera had been heard several times in concert versions.

Monteverdi's second opera was *L'Arianna,* produced in Mantua on May 28, 1608. From this score only a single fragment remains— "Lasciatemi morire," the lament of Arianna. It has been reported that the audience hearing it for the first time burst into tears; and to this day it does not fail to touch the heart. It is undoubtedly the most famous and remarkable piece of music created in the *stile rappresentativo,* and ranks high among Monteverdi's masterpieces. The composer himself apparently regarded the melody highly; he adapted it into a five-part madrigal and published it in his sixth volume in 1614, then used the melody again as a setting for a sacred text in 1641.

In 1613 Monteverdi became *maestro di cappella* at St. Mark's Cathedral in Venice. He held the post until the end of his life. He lived in seclusion and comparative simplicity in the house provided him, devoting himself with uninterrupted industry to the composition of religious and secular music. He issued the sixth volume of his madrigals in 1614, the seventh in 1619. In

1624 he completed one of his major operas, *Il Combattimento di Tancredi e Clorinda,* introduced at the palace of Senator Mocenigo. This is a work of outstanding historic importance since it is here that Monteverdi invented a new style, *stile concitato,* for the expression of agitated and passionate moods. "In the works of the composers of the past," Monteverdi explained, "I have found examples of the 'soft' and 'moderate' types but never of the 'agitated' style described by Plato in the third book of *Rhetoric* in these words, 'Take that harmony that would fittingly imitate the brave man going to war.' Aware that contrasts move our soul, and that such is the purpose of all good music as Boethius asserts by saying 'music is a part of us, and either ennobles or corrupts our behavior'—for this reason I have applied myself diligently to the rediscovery of this style. . . . I resorted to the divine Tasso, . . . and I chose his description of the combat between Tancredi and Clorinda, as the theme for my music expressing contrary passions aroused by war, prayer, and death." To project such agitated moods, Monteverdi invented several new devices which henceforth became basic to instrumental performance; among these are pizzicato and tremolo.

In 1632 Monteverdi took holy orders. Such a decision was not uncommon with *maestri di cappella* at St. Marks's, but Monteverdi appears to have had a special motivation to enter the church: gratitude at having been spared during the terrible plague of 1631.

In 1637 the first public opera house ever to be established opened in Venice—the Teatro San Cassiano. Its first attraction, *Adone,* was long believed to be an opera by Monteverdi, but this has been disproved. Monteverdi did write two outstanding operas for Venice's public opera houses: *Il Ritorno d'Ulisse,* produced at San Cassiano in 1641, and *L'Incoronazione di Poppea* at the Teatro SS. Giovanni e Paolo in 1642. The latter, one of the first operas to be based on a historical subject, was Monteverdi's last work for the stage, and his greatest. Written when he was seventy-four, it found him at the peak of his creative powers, and realized almost fully the devices of Italian opera which the Neapolitan school would soon integrate within the operatic framework—the *da capo* aria, *secco recitativo, bel canto.* Indeed, Dyneley Hussey found in *Poppea* "every element of grand opera, including even scenes of comedy skillfully placed to give light relief to the more somber passages. The whole work has a more considered and artistic form as compared with the casual and tentative *Orfeo.*" Henri Prunières described *Poppea* as "one of the most precious ornaments of the musical drama, along with *Don Giovanni, Tristan und Isolde,* and *Pelléas et Mélisande.*"

In 1643 Monteverdi decided to leave Venice to revisit his native city. He never reached his destination. He fell seriously ill en route and was taken back to Venice, where he died on November 29, 1643.

Monteverdi had "a noble forehead, melancholy eyes, and a wry twist of the lower part of his bearded face, half sad, half humorous," wrote Dyneley Hussey, describing a posthumous portrait. "This portrait certainly accords well with the strength and seriousness of Monteverdi's character. As a man he was honest and forthright in his dealings; as a musician he pondered deeply upon the technique and aesthetics of his art without allowing theory to interfere with his imagination when it came to the actual work of creation."

In summing up Monteverdi's achievements, Prunières wrote: "This immense work is inexhaustible. It astonishes us by its richness as by its incredible variety. Yet the personality of Monteverdi gives to this work, written in styles not only different but incongruous, a surprising unity. Everything bears the mark of his genius; the contrapuntal motets, the madrigals with their barbaric dissonances, the graceful canzonette, the dramatic narrations. The slightest arietta by Monteverdi has so peculiar a quality that the composer can be recognized in the very first bars. . . . The music of Monteverdi, like that of Bach, is never empty of thought and feeling; it does not find its end in itself but in the emotion it expresses. His vehement soul is revealed entire, with its passionate sadness, its powerful sensuality, its love of life; for this great Latin artist, who suffered so greatly, preserved to the end that love and feeling for life."

PRINCIPAL WORKS

Choral Music—8 books of madrigals; canzonettes, Magnificats, Masses, motets.

Operas—La Favola d'Orfeo; Tirsi e Clori; La Maddalena; Andromeda; Le Nozze di Peleo e di Tetide; Il Combattimento di Tancredi e Clorinda; Il Ritorno d'Ulisse in Patria; L'Incoronazione di Poppea.

ABOUT

Arnold, D., Monteverdi; Le Roux, M., Claudio Monteverdi; Malipiero, G. F. Claudio Monteverdi; Paoli, D. de, Claudio Monteverdi; Prunières, H., Claudio Monteverdi; Roche, M., Monteverdi; Schrade, L., Monteverdi: Creator of Modern Music.

Opera News, March 10, 1962.

Cristóbal de Morales *1500-1553*

CRISTÓBAL DE MORALES, the most distinguished Spanish composer of contrapuntal music in the sixteenth century, was born in Seville in or about 1500. For approximately six years he was a chorister at the Seville Cathedral, whose chapel master, Fernández de Castilleja, trained him in music. From 1526 to 1530, he was choirmaster of the Ávila Cathedral, then in 1535, went to Rome, where he became a member of the papal choir. His first important work, a six-part cantata entitled *Jubilemus omnis terra,* written to celebrate the peace jubilee at Nice, was heard in June 1538. A year later his first publication, two four-part motets, appeared and in 1540 three Masses were issued.

In 1540 Morales received an extended leave of absence from the papal choir. After a period of travel, he returned to Rome for a second five-year tenure as papal chorister. During this interval he produced a number of important publications; one of the most significant was a volume of sixteen Masses that appeared in 1544. From 1545 to 1547 Morales was a choirmaster at the Toledo cathedral, and from 1551 until his death he held a similar position in Málaga.

Cristóbal de Morales died in Málaga in 1553, sometime between September 4 and October 7.

Morales was one of the earliest important Spanish contrapuntists whose music impressed the rest of Europe. His technique was admired by some of the leading theoreticians in Europe. In 1711 Adami listed Morales as the most important composer to have been attached to the papal choir in the time of Josquin des Prés and Palestrina. Padre Martini often praised the mastery of structure in Morales' works. J. B. Trend noted that "Morales is saved from dullness by his imagination; he had such a complete command of the methods of his time that he could afford to break the strictest rules . . . when the occasion demanded it."

CRISTÓBAL DE MORALES

Cecil Gray wrote, "The art of Morales is perhaps less directly moving than that of most of his compatriots, and it has in it something of the ceremonious stiffness and solemn courtly demeanor of a Spanish grandee; nevertheless, this somewhat forbidding aspect conceals a vein of somber and passionate intensity which is often exceedingly compelling and impressive."

PRINCIPAL WORKS

Choral Music—Cantatas, Lamentations, Magnificats, Masses, motets.

ABOUT

Anglés, H., Morales: Opera omnia; Chase, G., The Music of Spain; Trend, J. B., The Music of Spanish History; Van Vechten, C., The Music of Spain.

American Musicological Society, Spring 1953; Music and Letters, January 1925.

Thomas Morley *1557-1602*

THOMAS MORLEY, one of England's foremost madrigalists, was born in 1557 in England; the precise place of birth is unknown. He was a boy chorister at St. Paul's Cathedral until his voice broke in 1573, then studied music and mathematics with William Byrd. In 1588 he received a baccalaureate in music from Oxford. While serving as organist at St. Giles's Church in Cripplegate, Morley was married. (All that is known of his wife is that she was in the

Morales: mō-rä′läs

service of Lady Periam.) Four children were born to the marriage; three died in infancy or childhood.

In 1589 Morley was appointed organist of St. Paul's Cathedral, remaining for several years. During this period he was implicated as an anti-Catholic political agent in Flanders through the interception of some of his letters by one of his enemies. Imprisonment seemed inevitable, but after his ardent pleas for mercy he was allowed to leave. It is strongly believed that in spite of his seeming repentance he continued his activities.

In 1592 Morley became a Gentleman of the Chapel Royal. During the next decade he produced all of his major works. His first volume was a set of canzonets for three voices, issued in 1593, in which a madrigal style was suggested. A year later he turned directly to the writing of madrigals, producing the *First Book of Madrigals to Four Voices*, a work in which the English madrigal emerged at last as a mature form—as in such gems as "April Is in my Mistress's Face," "Now in the Gentle Season," and "Since My Tears and Lamenting." In 1595 Morley published a second set of canzonets for two voices, and a volume of ballets for five voices. The latter is of particular importance, for it introduced the "ballet" into English music and established Morley as its surpassing master. The "ballet" is really a madrigal, but more homophonic in style, with a repeated refrain of "fa-la-la." (For this reason "ballets" are sometimes known as "fa-las.") In the collection can be found some of Morley's most famous compositions, including "Now Is the Month of Maying" and "Sing We and Chant It."

In 1603 an epochal event took place in the history of the English madrigal for which Morley was directly responsible. It was the appearance of *The Triumphs of Oriana*, a collection of madrigals by twenty-three English composers, edited by Morley. "Oriana" was the name used in pastoral poetry to identify Queen Elizabeth, and the volume was intended as a tribute to the Queen— each madrigal ending with the line "Long Live Fair Oriana." Containing two madrigals by Morley himself, and others by such masters as Wilbye, Weelkes, and Gibbons, *The Triumphs of Oriana* completed a job initiated by Morley in his own compositions—to establish the personality, style, and character of the English madrigal.

"So far as greatness in handling of material [is concerned] there can be no doubt that the concerted vocal music of the chief men of the time represents the supreme flower of English art," wrote Ernest Walker. "Limited by necessary historical conditions as their technical resources are, they can between them cover a wide range of emotional expression, and portray it from end to end, with a subtle directness that places their work very high among the things worthy of permanent remembrance by musicians of all nationalities. . . . They can look in the face of any composer who has ever lived; if they are not among the supreme divinities they are at any rate Titans among the earth-born."

Commenting on Morley's madrigals, E. F. Fellowes wrote: "[They] reflect the lighthearted spirit of the composer, who excelled all the English madrigalists in this particular vein. . . . They are written with consummate skill and with extraordinarily full harmonic effect, while their phrasing and melodic beauty go near perfection."

On September 28, 1598 Morley received a grant for the patent of song books and music paper. A competitor, John Day, claimed priority to this patent, but after considerable litigation Morley was decreed the exclusive lessee.

By 1597 Morley had been complaining severely about his poor health. He wrote at the time, "My health since you saw me, has been so bad, as if it had been the pleasure of Him who made all things, to have taken me out of the world, I should have been very well contented; and have wished it more than once." His poor health compelled him to give up his duties at the Chapel Royal in or about 1602 and to lead a solitary existence. He died in late 1602 or early 1603, probably the former.

In addition to his madrigals, canzonettes, and ballets Morley wrote several fine songs (or "ayres"). One or two of these—including "It Was a Lover and His Lass"—are the only ones written in the sixteenth century for Shakespeare's plays that have survived.

Although Morley was at his best in moods that were light, gay, and graceful, he was also capable of more sober and serious attitudes, notably in some of his highly significant choral music for the church. As A. E. F. Dickinson remarked, "He . . . touched deeper springs . . . in the simple *Burial Service* in G minor, in 'Hark, allelulia,' the elegy for Henry Noel, and the stately 'Out of the Deep.' "

Morley was the author of a remarkable theoretical treatise in Platonic dialogue, *A Plaine and Easie Introduction to Practicall Musicke* (1597). It throws considerable light on English modal music, the performance of unaccompanied choral works, the madrigal and ballet, other facets of English music making in Morley's day, and even on Morley's own personality and way of life. A modern edition, prepared by John Harman, was issued in London in 1952.

PRINCIPAL WORKS

Chamber Music—Fantasias, for strings.
Choral Music—Anthems, ballets, canzonettes, madrigals, motets, and Services.
Vocal Music—Several songs (ayres), including It Was a Lover and His Lass.

ABOUT

Anderton, H. O., Early English Music; Fellowes, E. H., The English Madrigal; Fellowes, E. H., English Madrigal Composers.

Moritz Moszkowski *1854-1925*

M ORITZ MOSZKOWSKI was born in Breslau, Germany, on August 23, 1854. He studied music in Dresden, and at the Stern and Kullak Conservatories in Berlin, where he specialized in piano. In 1873 he made an impressive concert début in Berlin, then embarked on a tour throughout Europe. In the meantime he had been appointed to the piano faculty of Kullak Conservatory.

Although German born and trained, Moszkowski wrote his finest works in an essentially Spanish style. The first composition of this nature was a set of *Spanish Dances* for piano solo (also for piano duo), op. 12. The volume includes the highly popular dances in C major, G minor, and D major. A second volume of *Spanish Dances* for piano, op. 65, was as successful as the first.

Moszkowski also worked within the larger forms. His opera *Boabdil*, introduced in Berlin on April 21, 1892, was highly acclaimed, and as a result performed soon afterwards in Prague and New York. The "Malagueña" from this opera has become one of its composer's most popular composi-

Moszkowski: môsh-kôf'skē

MORITZ MOSZKOWSKI

tions. In 1896 his ballet, *Laurin*, was also a huge success in Berlin.

In 1897 Moszkowski established permanent residence in Paris, where he was active as a teacher, concert pianist, and composer. In 1899 he was elected a member of the Berlin Academy.

The last years of Moszkowski's life were in grim contrast to his former triumph. Having disposed of all of his copyrights for a handsome sum which might have ensured life-long financial security, Moszkowski proceeded to invest his entire fortune in European securities. When World War I broke out, he lost everything. Unable to attract audiences or pupils, he could not earn a living, and lived in the most appalling poverty and in broken health. A fund was started by several European musicians to help support him, but by the time their project materialized Moszkowski could no longer benefit from it. He died in Paris on March 4, 1925.

One of Moszkowski's pupils, Fannie Edgar Thomas, described him as follows: "Moszkowski is one of those 'ever-will-be-youthful' types of men, tall, slender, of a certain easy grace in carriage, a gentle air. . . . Hair and moustache are somewhat auburn and not over-plentiful, face rather long, with high brow, kindly eyes, the hands long and slender, with a few freckles on them, the speaking tones clear, gentle, good-humored and haunting."

Moszkowski's most famous compositions are for the piano. Paderewski once maintained that they cover the whole gamut of piano technique. Most famous are his pieces in a Spanish national style—not only the *Spanish Dances* but the *Bolero* (op. 12, no. 5) and the *Guitarre* (op. 45, no. 2). Beyond these Spanish compositions, Moszkowski produced a rich and varied piano literature which, in the words of George Lowe, "follows in legitimate line that of Schumann and Chopin. It is romantically conceived and built up out of well-sustained melodies and bold harmonies not too remotely related. The wealth of melody and the generally attractive quality of the rhythms are marked features in the work of this composer. There is no hesitancy in the sequence of his musical themes. They flow from a source that is clear and undisturbed. . . . It is by his delightful dance music that Moszkowski will probably always be best known. . . . Moszkowski, like Chopin, has shown how dance music may be both scholarly and artistic, and if he fails to stimulate our intellect or stir any depths of emotions, he sets our pulses tingling, and makes us feel the glamour of the world, wayward doings of youth beneath sunny Spanish skies, and the various characteristics that dominate the people of his country. It may be the life of action only that he has the power to picture vividly, but he does it with a subtle and compelling fascination. That is the essence of his genius." In the opinion of Harold C. Schonberg, "No better salon music has ever been composed, or any so gratefully conceived for the piano."

PRINCIPAL WORKS

Ballet—Laurin.
Chamber Music—2 Concertstücke, for violin and piano; Scherzo, for violin and piano; Three Pieces, for cello and piano.
Opera—Boabdil.
Orchestral Music—2 suites; Piano Concerto; Violin Concerto; Jeanne d'Arc; Phantastischer Zug; Aus aller Herren Länder (also for piano four hands); Prelude and Fugue, for strings.
Piano Music—Spanish Dances; Bolero; Guitarre; Serenata; Skizzen; barcarolles, caprices, concert études, gavottes, Humoresques, mazurkas, tarantellas, waltzes.
Vocal Music—Various songs for voice and piano.

ABOUT

Collins, W. F., Laurel Winners.
Gramophone Magazine, July 1925; Monthly Musical Record, May 1915; Musical Opinion, August 1927.

Modest Moussorgsky

see Modest Mussorgsky

Wolfgang Amadeus Mozart *1756-1791*

WOLFGANG AMADEUS MOZART (christened Johannes Chrysostomus Wolfgangus Theophilus Mozart) was born in Salzburg, Austria, on January 27, 1756. His father, Leopold, was a professional musician, long employed in the court orchestra of the Archbishop of Salzburg; he married Anna Maria Pertl in 1747. Of their seven children only two survived, Wolfgang and his sister Marianne (nicknamed Nannerl), who was born in 1751. A year after Wolfgang's birth, his father was elevated to the post of court composer. In this capacity he wrote many operas, symphonies, oratorios, concertos, and other compositions; his most significant achievement was probably the *Versuch einer gründlichen Violinschule,* published in 1756, one of the earliest known texts on violin playing. It was translated into many languages, and in 1948 was issued in London in a new English translation.

The phenomenal musical exploits of the child Mozart read like fables, but they are facts and not embellishments of romantic biographers. At three Wolfgang would seek out pleasing harmonic combinations on the harpsichord, and when he succeeded he would shout with joy. His father began to teach him composition and harpsichord when he was only four. The child required little guidance; with just a few basic lessons he was soon able to play not only harpsichord but also violin with facility. His musical memory was developed to an extraordinary degree; he could play a composition after hearing it once. His ear was so sensitive that he could identify tones and chords sounded on the piano while he was blindfolded, his musical invention so rich that he could improvise on a given subject for a half hour. At five he wrote several delightful minuets, still familiar to beginners of piano; at seven he completed a sonata; at eight, a symphony.

Mozart's father, aware of the treasure that had been entrusted to him, decided to exhibit his wonder child to the world. When Mozart was six, his father took him and sister Marianne to the court of the Elector of Bavaria in Munich, then to the palace of Emperor Francis I and Empress Maria Theresa in Schönbrunn in Austria. Mozart's performance elicited rapturous praise in both places. At Schönbrunn the Emperor described him as a "sorcerer," and the distinguished composer Georg Christoph Wagenseil (whose concerto Mozart performed) burst into tears.

In 1763 Leopold Mozart took Wolfgang to Frankfurt, Paris, and London for further demonstrations of his incredible powers. In Frankfurt, as an announcement revealed, Mozart performed a violin concerto, accompanied symphonies on a harpsichord or organ whose manual or keyboard was covered by a cloth; named all notes played for him from a distance whether "singly or in chords"; and improvised "in any key" on the harpsichord or organ. Goethe, aged fourteen, heard him play, and many years later remembered that performance, saying: "A phenomenon like that of Mozart remains an inexplicable thing."

In addition to his performance at Versailles, Mozart's first appearance in Paris was signalized by the publication of four violin sonatas. In London, at the court of George III, the child captured the hearts not only of royalty and nobility but of the venerable *Kapellmeister* John Christian Bach, son of Johann Sebastian Bach. Mozart's earliest symphonies were introduced at Vauxhall Gardens.

Vienna was revisited in 1768. There Mozart was commissioned by the Emperor to write his first opera, *La Finta semplice.* Intrigues generated by musicians envious of his genius and resentful that a mere child should be asked to write an opera kept Mozart's first stage work from being produced. But another of his little works was performed, albeit privately. It was a delightful little *opera buffa* entitled *Bastien et Bastienne,* a parody of Rousseau's *Le Devin du village,* performed at the home of Dr. Franz Anton Mesmer (whose name was later used to coin the word "mesmerize"). In addition Mozart appeared at a public concert on December 7, directing one of his Masses, an offertorium, and a trumpet concerto.

Next an extensive tour of Italy was begun in December 1769. In Mantua, the Società Filarmonica gave a concert of Mozart's music in honor of his visit. In Milan, Mozart received a commission to write an *opera*

WOLFGANG AMADEUS MOZART

seria in the Italian style. In Bologna, Mozart was elected an honorary member of the Accademia Filarmonica after passing examinations, although the rules specifically forbade the admission of anyone under twenty. In Rome, Mozart provided still further evidence of his incomparable genius. During Holy Week each year there took place performances of Allegri's *Miserere* which, by papal decree, was denied presentation anywhere else in the world. The only manuscript copy was kept under lock and key. Mozart heard the *Miserere* twice, then went on to write the whole complicated polyphonic score from memory. A few months after this incredible exhibition, the Cross of the Order of the Golden Spur was conferred upon Mozart by the Pope.

The *opera seria* Mozart wrote on commission for Milan was *Mitridate, re di Ponto,* introduced on December 26, 1770. "Before the first rehearsal," Leopold Mozart reported to his wife, "there was no lack of people to run down the music and pronounce it beforehand in satirical language to be something poor and childish, alleging that so young a boy, and a German to the bargain, could not possibly write an Italian opera, and that, although they acknowledged him to be a great executant, he could not understand or feel the *chiaroscuro* required in the theater. All these people have been reduced to silence since the evening of the first rehearsal . . . and say not a word." The opera was an outstanding success. The newspapers praised Mozart's "rarest musical grace" and "studied beauty." The opera had twenty performances, all directed by the composer.

In March 1771 Mozart returned to Salzburg, where he remained for the next few years, except for several brief visits to Italy or Germany for specific performances. This was one of the most unhappy periods in his life. A new Archbishop was installed in Salzburg in 1772—Hieronymus, Count of Colloredo, who was completely indifferent to music and was thoroughly incapable of evaluating Mozart's genius. As a musician in the Archbishop's chapel Mozart was miserably paid, treated as a menial servant, and often subjected to personal abuse and insults. The remarkable music he now wrote with unprecedented productivity received no recognition whatever: his serenades (including the famous *Haffner Serenade;* symphonies (such as No. 25 in G minor and No. 29 in A major); five violin concertos (among them the remarkable concertos in D major and A major); piano concertos; string quartets; operas; and many other works. To the Archbishop these works could have been produced by a complete incompetent.

Mozart was impatient to leave Salzburg; to recapture the moments of triumph he had formerly enjoyed; to find again receptive audiences and an admiring nobility; above all to gain some profitable post in an influential court. In 1777 he was finally able to set forth on an extended trip, this time in the company of his mother since the Archbishop had denied his father permission to leave his post. They passed through Munich, where Mozart applied for a court appointment and was rejected. They stopped in Mannheim, where he fell in love with Aloysia Weber, and for a while thought of eloping with her to Italy. At last, on March 23, 1778, they arrived in Paris. Disappointments followed in swift succession. Although a symphony of his was played at a Concert Spirituel, Mozart did not succeed in leaving a strong impression. Powerful patrons who had once showered him with gifts and praises now ignored him—for he was no longer a fabulous child prodigy. And tragedy came in the wake of disappointments: Mozart's mother died in Paris on July 3, 1778.

Alone and unemployed, Mozart had no choice but to return to Salzburg, to his hum-

ble post. Two years followed, their drabness and misery relieved temporarily when his *opera seria, Idomeneo,* met with notable success in Munich on January 29, 1781. Ramm, the oboist, and Lange, the horn player, "were half crazy with delight," as Mozart wrote. Lange exclaimed, "I must own that I have never yet heard any music which made such a deep impression upon me!"

Mozart now knew he would have to make a permanent break with Salzburg, and with his employer, the Archbishop. In 1781 the Archbishop went to Vienna to attend the funeral services of Maria Theresa, and while there he summoned Mozart to join his entourage. When the Archbishop highhandedly refused Mozart permission to appear at several benefit concerts in Vienna, the composer lost his temper, and the Archbishop responded with abuse. The final explosion came when the Archbishop, without warning, ordered Mozart back to Salzburg at once. Mozart refused, heatedly announced his resignation and left.

Mozart had good reason to be optimistic about his future. Soon after establishing permanent residence in Vienna, he was invited to court to compete with the renowned pianist Clementi, and to allow the Emperor to decide who was the greater performer of the two. The Emperor called the contest a "draw," and thus established Mozart among the foremost piano virtuosos in Europe. Besides gaining a distinguished reputation as a concert performer, Mozart had an opportunity to prove himself as a composer with the Emperor's commission for a new opera. It was *The Abduction from the Seraglio* (*Die Entführung aus dem Serail*). Although some of Vienna's most powerful musicians, including Salieri, attempted to prevent its performance, the opera was given at the Burgtheater on July 16, 1782. At the première, Mozart's enemies tried to create disturbances, but the opera was still a triumph. "The populace is quite crazy over this opera," Mozart wrote. "It does one good to hear such applause. . . . The people will hear nothing else, and the theater is constantly filled to the doors." Prince Kaunitz said that a genius like Mozart "appeared only once in a century." Gluck, the foremost composer in Vienna, and the Emperor were both effusive in their praise.

The Abduction from the Seraglio is a masterpiece for its enchanting lyricism, the verve of its humor, the subtlety of its characterization, and the inexhaustible invention of its orchestral and harmonic writing. It is also the first important opera to be written in the German language, and as such it marks the real beginning of German-language opera in general, German comic opera in particular. To this day it remains the earliest German comic opera to be given in regular performances. Carl Maria von Weber felt that while Mozart may have written great operas after *The Abduction,* he never again captured the same kind of vivacity, effervescence, and youthful vitality. The American première took place in New York on October 10, 1862.

Convinced that his future was secure, and that a well-paying post at court would not be slow in coming, Mozart married Constance Weber on August 4, 1782. She was a younger sister of Aloysia, with whom Mozart had formerly fallen in love. The only ones present at their simple wedding ceremony were the bride's mother and youngest sister, two witnesses, and a friend of the Weber family. "The moment we were made one," Mozart wrote his father, "my wife and I began to weep, which touched everyone, even the priest. . . . We are married now; we are man and wife! And we love each other enormously. We feel that we are made for one another."

But the post Mozart expected did not materialize. He was forced to earn his living by giving private music lessons, and the little he earned was hardly enough to support him and his wife. He was continually upset by the obstacles placed in his way by Salieri, who envied his gifts and feared a powerful competitor. Other rivals were equally influential in keeping him from important engagements. But he also had admirers, among these Joseph Haydn, who spoke of him in the highest terms. His admirers, however, could not obtain for him either permanent employment or lucrative commissions.

These disappointments and frustrations might have distressed Mozart but could not arrest his productivity. Between 1782 and 1785 he completed the set of six remarkable string quartets which he dedicated to Haydn and had performed for that master at his home at the Schulerstrasse. "I tell you before God and as an honest man," Haydn told Mozart's father after the performance,

"your son is the greatest composer I know, either personally or by name."

In 1785 Mozart collaborated with Abbé Lorenzo da Ponte, who had recently been appointed poet to the Viennese imperial theaters, on an opera based on Beaumarchais's *Le Mariage de Figaro.* Despite the Emperor's interest in the new work, Mozart's enemies and rivals did their best to prevent its performance. Fortunately, their efforts were in vain. The musicians and singers were beside themselves with sheer joy at Mozart's opera during rehearsals. "I can still see Mozart," wrote Michael Kelly, one of the singers, "dressed in his red fur hat trimmed with gold, standing on the stage with the orchestra at the first rehearsal, beating time for the music. . . . The players on the stage and in the orchestra were electrified. Intoxicated with pleasure, they cried again and again, and each time louder than the preceding one: 'Bravo, Maestro! Long live the great Mozart!'. . . . It seemed as if the storm of applause would never cease. . . . Had Mozart written nothing but this piece of music it alone would, in my humble opinion, have stamped him as the greatest master of his art. Never before was there a greater triumph than Mozart and his *Figaro!*"

The Marriage of Figaro (*Le Nozze di Figaro*) was introduced at the Burgtheater on May 1, 1786. "The theater was packed," continued Michael Kelly, "and so many arias were repeated that the length of the opera was nearly doubled. The Emperor himself expressed his delight." But this success was short-lived, thanks to the apparently limitless ingenuity of Mozart's enemies. Salieri saw to it that a slight and catchy little opera was produced at the Burgtheater in competition to Mozart—*Una cosa rara,* by Vicente Martín y Solar. Its great popularity caused the public to lose interest in Mozart, and *The Marriage of Figaro* closed after nine performances. (It is believed that the first American performance of *Figaro* took place in New York in 1799.)

What Mozart earned from *Figaro* was hardly enough to pay his debts. He was penniless. But for repeated loans from friends he would not have been able to purchase the food or fuel to sustain him and his wife. (Their child, Raimund, had died three months after birth.) Mozart wrote pathetic letters to people in high station and to publishers, trying to gain their interest in his works, but in vain. He sank deeper and deeper into depression. Nevertheless the masterworks kept coming: the G minor and E-flat major Piano Quartets; the C major, D minor, A major and C minor Piano Concertos; the Sonata and Fantasia in C minor, for piano; the E-flat major Violin Sonata; and possibly the greatest of all, the opera *Don Giovanni*, written again to a text by Lorenzo da Ponte. Introduced in Prague on October 29, 1787, *Don Giovanni* was perhaps the greatest triumph of Mozart's mature years. "Connoisseurs and artists say that nothing like this has been given in Prague," reported a contemporary journal. "Mozart himself conducted, and when he appeared in the orchestra, he was hailed by a triple acclamation." (The American première of *Don Giovanni* was given at the Park Theatre in New York on May 23, 1826.)

Soon after his return from Prague and the première of *Don Giovanni*, Mozart was at last offered a court position, succeeding the recently deceased Gluck as chamber musician and court composer. Mozart's salary, however, was greatly reduced, and his eight hundred gulden a year hardly enabled him to subsist. He was compelled to beg friends for loans "at a suitable interest." As if life were not sufficiently discouraging, Mozart soon began to suffer an alarming deterioration in health. His work and creative powers, however, were unflagging. In 1788 he produced his last three, and his greatest, symphonies—the E-flat major, the G minor, and the C major known as the *Jupiter*. In the same year he also completed the *Coronation Concerto* for piano. A year later he wrote three extraordinary string quartets (the D major, B-flat major, and F major), the *Clarinet Quintet*, and the incomparable opera *Così fan tutte*, to da Ponte's libretto. And in 1791—beset though he was by illness and despair—he wrote the opera *The Magic Flute* (*Die Zauberflöte*), the Requiem, the *Ave Verum*, the B-flat major Piano Concerto, the E-flat major String Quintet, and the opera *La Clemenza di Tito*.

The Magic Flute had been commissioned by a Viennese impresario, Emanuel Schikaneder, who wanted a German comic opera in the style of the old *Singspiel* for the Theater-auf-der-Wieden. It was performed there on September 30, 1791 with such suc-cess that it was presented one hundred times; the American première was given at the Park Theatre in New York on April 17, 1833.

The story surrounding the writing of Mozart's last work, the Requiem, has often been narrated. It reads like the invention of some imaginative biographer, but it is grounded in fact. One day, in July 1791, a masked stranger appeared at Mozart's house to commission him to write a requiem for a generous price. The only condition imposed upon Mozart was that he make no effort to uncover the identity of the man ordering the work from him. Actually, the stranger was a messenger from Count von Walsegg, who made it a practice thus to commission pieces of music from eminent composers and then to pass them off as his own. But to Mozart, oppressed by sickness, poverty, frustration, the stranger seemed to be a messenger from the other world urging him to write his own requiem. As he worked feverishly on this assignment, Mozart knew he did not have much longer to live. He continued to work, sometimes even while wracked with pain. Then, when he felt he no longer had the strength to continue, he instructed one of his pupils, Süssmayr, as to the manner in which he wished the Requiem to be completed. As it turned out, Mozart finished twelve of the fifteen sections, while Süssmayr completed the other three from materials provided him by Mozart and according to the master's specific instructions.

On December 4, 1791, Mozart summoned a few friends to his bedside and joined them in the singing of the "Lacrymosa" from his Requiem; midway he burst into tears. That same night he received extreme unction and bade his family farewell. He died the next morning. His funeral was pitiable, with only a handful of friends attending the services at St. Stephen's Cathedral. Then he was consigned to a pauper's grave with no marking or tombstone to designate the place.

Mozart "was a remarkably small man," said Michael Kelly, "very thin and pale, with a profusion of fine hair of which he was rather vain. . . . He was remarkably fond of punch, of which beverage I have seen him take copious draughts. He was also fond of billiards, and had an excellent billiard table in his home. Many and many a game have I played with him, but always came off second best. He gave Sunday con-

certs which I always attended. He was kind-
hearted, and always ready to oblige, but so
very particular when he played that, if the
slightest noise were made, he instantly left
off."

In many respects he was like a child. "He
never knew how properly to conduct himself," wrote Adolph Heinrich von Schlichtegroll. "The management of domestic affairs,
the proper use of money, the judicious selection of his pleasures, and temperance in
the enjoyment of them, were never virtues
to his taste. The gratification of the moment
was always uppermost with him."

Von Schlichtegroll revealed too that "of
his operas, Mozart esteemed most highly *Idomeneo* and *Don Giovanni.* . . . The time
which he most willingly employed in composition was the morning, from six to seven
o'clock when he got up. After that he did
no more for the rest of the day, unless he
had to finish a piece that was wanted. He
always worked very irregularly. When an
idea struck him, he was not to be drawn
from it. If he was taken from the piano, he
continued to compose in the midst of his
friends, and passed whole nights with his
pen in his hand. At other times he had such
a disinclination to work that he could not
complete a piece till the moment of its
performance."

In Romain Rolland's opinion, "His true
happiness was creation. In restless and unhealthy geniuses creation may be a torture
—the bitter seeking after an elusive ideal.
But with healthy geniuses like Mozart creation was a perfect joy and so natural that
it seemed almost a physical pleasure. . . .
He was able to do what he wished, and he
never wished to do what was beyond him.
. . . So easy was creation to him that at
times it poured from him in a double or
triple stream, and he performed incredible
feats of mental activity. He would compose
a prelude while writing a fugue; and once
when he played a sonata for violin and
piano at a concert, he had composed it the
day before, between eleven o'clock and midnight, hurriedly writing down the piano part
to rehearse it with his partner. The next
day he played from memory what he had
composed in his head. This is only one of
many examples. Such genius was likely to
be spread over the whole domain of his art
and in equal perfection."

There is no field of music that was not
touched by Mozart's genius. Opera, symphony, the sonata, the string quartet, the
concerto, the Mass, and the requiem were
all enriched by his inexhaustible imagination, invention, and technical innovation.

With *The Marriage of Figaro, Don Giovanni, The Magic Flute,* and *Così fan tutte*
Mozart created a new epoch for opera. Eric
Blom has discussed these masterworks. He
found *The Marriage of Figaro* to be "the
perfect *opera buffa*," with music that is
"sunnily civilized" and filled with "a profound humanity, a sympathetic penetration
into the hearts of men and women—especially women. . . . *Figaro* is Italian comic
opera in its final stages of perfection." For
Blom, *Don Giovanni* was "the greatest of
all. . . . Everything is in character, everything colored by the particular mood into
which this great tragi-comic subject cast
him." After *Don Giovanni* we enter into
a different world altogether, that of *Così fan
tutte.* Blom described this world as "only
a show of marionettes. . . . Once again
Mozart achieved a miraculous feat of writing
a score which, consistent in style from start
to finish, could not by any conceivable
chance lend a single one of its numbers to
any other work of his. The whole perfume
and flavor of the music are new and unique.
Artifice is the keynote of it." In *The Magic
Flute,* Blom found "not declamation but
spontaneous emotional expression, not grandly ordered drama but the variety of life. . . .
Here was a good deal of nonsense, but it
was good theater, it was alive, and there was
a multiformity of setting, of situation, of
character such as he had never before had
the occasion to handle. . . . All this and
more is by some marvel of genius fashioned
into a single gem of many facets—and of
inestimable value."

The symphony was another branch of
music brought to new fruition by Mozart's
genius. The crown of his symphonic output
are the three last works, the E-flat major,
the G minor, and the *Jupiter.* In a little-
known essay, Edvard Grieg commented upon
these works: "We note at once the great
step from Haydn's to Mozart's treatment of
this, the highest of instrumental forms, and
our thoughts are involuntarily transferred
to the young Beethoven who, without any
specially noteworthy break, rises from where
Mozart left off to these proud summits which
none but he was destined to reach. In the

introduction of the E-flat major Symphony, just before the first Allegro, we come upon harmonic combinations of unprecedented boldness. They are introduced in so surprising a way that they will always preserve the impression of novelty. . . . In the G minor Symphony, Mozart shows himself to us in all his grace and sincerity of feeling. It is worth noting what astonishing effect he gets here by the use of chromatic progressions. In the *Jupiter Symphony* we are astounded, above all, by the playful ease with which the greatest problems of art are treated. No one who is not initiated suspects in the Finale, amid the humorous tone gambols, what an amazing contrapuntal knowledge and superiority Mozart manifests. And then this ocean of euphony! Mozart's sense of euphony was, indeed, so absolute that it is impossible in all his works to find a single bar wherein it is sacrificed for other considerations."

"The same animation that dominates Mozart's operas, the same lively change of ideas and personalities, and the same virtuoso polyphonic summary of characters live in his chamber music," wrote Paul Henry Lang. In the six quartets of 1785, which Mozart dedicated to Haydn, he arrived at such freedom of thought, such iconoclasm of technique, such daring structural innovations that Haydn could only shake his head with incredulity and say: "If Mozart wrote it he must have had good reason to do so."

There remain Mozart's remarkable concertos, for piano and for violin. "The concerto, particularly the piano concerto," remarked Donald Jay Grout, "was more important in Mozart's work than in that of any other composer of the second half of the eighteenth century. Mozart's concertos are incomparable. Not even the symphonies reveal such a wealth of invention, such breadth and vigor of conception, such insight and resource in the working out of musical ideas."

In Mozart, summed up Eric Blom, "Classicism and Romanticism meet and . . . once and for all we see a perfect equilibrium between them."

Principal Works

Chamber Music—42 violin sonatas; 26 string quartets; 7 string quintets; 7 piano trios; 2 piano quartets; quintets for wind and piano; Clarinet Quintet in A major; Quintet in E-flat for horn, violin, violas and cello; flute quartets; Oboe Quartet in F major.

Choral Music—Ave Verum Corpus, Cantatas, Litanies, Kyries, Masses, motets, psalms, Requiem.

Operas—Idomeneo; Die Entführung aus dem Serail; Le Nozze di Figaro; Don Giovanni; Così fan tutte; Die Zauberflöte; La Clemenza di Tito.

Orchestral Music—49 symphonies; 31 divertimentos, cassations, and serenades; 25 minuets, German dances, and country dances; numerous concertos for solo instrument or instruments and orchestra; Sinfonia concertante, for viola and orchestra; solo arias with orchestra.

Piano Music—23 sonatas; fantasies, fugues, minuets, rondos, variations.

Vocal Music—Songs for voice and piano, including Abendempfindung, Als Luise die Briefe ihres ungetreuen Liebhabers verbrannte, An Chloe, Das Veilchen, Der Zauberer; arias, canons.

About

Anderson, E. (editor), The Letters of Mozart and his Family; Biancolli, L. (editor), The Mozart Handbook; Burk, J. N., Mozart and His Music; Dent, E. J., Mozart's Operas; Einstein, A., Mozart: His Character, His Work; Holmes, E., The Life of Mozart; Hutchings, A., A Companion to Mozart's Piano Concertos; Jahn, O., Wolfgang Amadeus Mozart; Landon, H. C. R., and Mitchell, D. (editors), The Mozart Companion; Prod'homme, J. G., Mozart raconté par ceux qui l'ont vu; Schenk, E., Mozart and His Times; Tenschert, R., Wolfgang Amadeus Mozart; Turner, W. J., Mozart: The Man and His Works.

Modest Mussorgsky *1839-1881*

MODEST MUSSORGSKY was born in Karevo, district of Pskov, Russia, on March 21, 1839, the son of a prosperous landowner. From an autobiographical sketch (which he wrote in the third person) we learn that as a child "he became familiar with old Russian tales. . . . It was mainly his familiarity with the very spirit of the life of the people that impelled him to extemporize music before knowing even the elementary rules of piano playing. His mother gave him his first piano lessons. When at the piano he hated having to do as he was told. Nevertheless, he made such progress that at the age of seven he was able to play small pieces by Liszt; and at a party in his parents' home at the age of eleven he performed in front of a large audience a concerto by Field. His father, who worshipped music, decided to develop his ability, and his musical education was carried on under Anton Herke in St. Petersburg." In 1852 his first published work, a piano piece entitled *Porte-enseigne Polka,* appeared.

It was to a military career, however, that Modest was directed. After completing his preliminary studies in St. Petersburg, he entered the cadet school of the Imperial Guards in 1852. Following his graduation in 1856 he became an officer in the regiment of the Guards. "He was a true little dandy," recorded a fellow officer, "a very handsome young officer in a tightly fitting uniform. His feet were small and finely turned. His hair was smoothly groomed, combed down and pomaded; his dainty hands were chiseled. His manners were elegant and aristocratic. He spoke a little through his teeth, and interspersed his conversation with French expressions in a rather affected way. There was a certain air of foppishness about him, but well in moderation. His politeness and civility were out of the ordinary. The ladies liked him. He would sit down at the piano and coquettishly throw his hands and then play very sweetly and gracefully some melodies from *Il Trovatore* and *La Traviata*. The ladies, buzzing around him, exclaimed: '*Charmant! Délicieux!*' "

As an officer he sketched an opera which remained unfinished because, as he remarked, "the composer was seventeen years old and knew nothing." Then, in 1857, a fellow officer, impressed with Mussorgsky's musical interests, introduced him to Alexander Dargomizhsky, creator of *Rusalka,* an early experiment in national Russian opera. Dargomizhsky in turn brought Mussorgsky into contact with Balakirev, the passionate musical nationalist, who undertook to teach Mussorgsky theory and composition. Balakirev was responsible not only for feeding Mussorgsky's musical ambitions but also for directing him to musical nationalism. In 1858 Mussorgsky decided to leave military life and make a deliberate attempt to become a professional musician. On January 23, 1860 he made his official début as a composer when his Scherzo in B-flat, for orchestra, was introduced in St. Petersburg by the Russian Musical Society, Anton Rubinstein conducting.

By 1861, Mussorgsky had become a dedicated partner of Balakirev, Cui, Borodin, and Rimsky-Korsakov in creating the national school of composition known as "the Russian Five" or "the Mighty Five." Like his partners, Mussorgsky was inspired in his compositions by Russian history, backgrounds, and culture. Like theirs, his own writing

MODEST MUSSORGSKY

was to be rooted deeply in the soil of Russian folk songs and dances, and church music. Mussorgsky's first significant work in this folk idiom was the orchestral tone poem *A Night on Bald Mountain,* begun in 1860, completed six years later, and still extremely popular.

The loss of his financial resources after the liberation of the serfs in 1861 compelled Mussorgsky to find a way to earn his living. In 1863 he became a clerk in the Ministry of Communications, holding the position for four years. During this period he sought and received intellectual stimulation from a group of dilettantes with whom he set up a communal kind of existence and from whom he acquired an insight into fields outside music—philosophy, politics, art, and literature. It was mainly through this association that Mussorgsky became the most cultivated and best-informed member of the Russian Five in areas outside music. For musical stimulation and advice he went to Rimsky-Korsakov among others, and in this area—the techniques and science of music— he was unquestionably inferior not only to his instructor but to the other members of the "Five."

The death of his mother in 1865 had a profound impact on Mussorgsky. From this time on, he grew increasingly morbid and neurotic, a helpless victim of alcoholism, subject to attacks of delirium tremens. Yet, despite the steady and continued deterioration of his physical resources and the rapid breakdown of his spirit, he continued to write music in a highly personal style and with original material—such songs as "Hopak," "Darling Savishna," and "The Magpie"; a major work for chorus and orchestra entitled *The Destruction of Sennacherib;* and a piano suite dedicated to the memory of his mother: *From Memories of Childhood.*

His thinking as well as his style grew more audacious, iconoclastic, and individual with the opera which he began in 1868, based on Gogol's *The Marriage.* It was with this work that he made his first experiments in "melodic recitative"—expressive melodies patterned after the inflections of human speech. He called this new kind of lyricism "the melody of life," explaining, "What I want to do is to make my characters speak on the stage as they would in real life and yet write music which will be thoroughly artistic. . . . If you forget all operatic conventions and admit the principles of musical discourse carried out in all simplicity, then *The Marriage* is an opera. If I have succeeded in rendering the straightforward expression of thoughts and feelings as it takes place in ordinary speech, and if my rendering is artistic and musicianly, then the deed is done."

Mussorgsky completed only a single act of *The Marriage.* That act was performed in St. Petersburg on October 26, 1917. Subsequently, Alexander Tcherepnine wrote the other acts and orchestrated the entire opera; this version was given in Essen, Germany, on September 14, 1937.

In his next opera, the one which was to become his crowning work, Mussorgsky proceeded even more boldly in his experiments in realistic musical writing. In order that he might better project his "melodic recitative," he now used a prose instead of a poetic text. The opera was *Boris Godunov,* for which the composer prepared his own libretto based on the Pushkin drama. Mussorgsky completed the first version of the opera in 1869, having spent three years working on it. The Imperial Opera of St. Petersburg rejected it, considering the work too unorthodox and unusual for popular consumption. What was objected to was not simply the uniqueness of Mussorgsky's lyricism, but also the fact that the opera had no formal arias or ensemble pieces, no

major love episodes, no grand scenes. To meet these objections, Mussorgsky made extensive revisions (1871-1872), introducing several lyrical vocal pieces and a love scene. But even this version was unpalatable to the St. Petersburg Opera, and was turned down again. However, the influence of some of Mussorgsky's friends was soon brought to bear on the Opera, and a decision was reached to produce a few scenes of *Boris* on February 17, 1873. These extracts were impressive enough to persuade the Opera directors to mount the entire work, on February 8, 1874. The critics, and many leading musicians in St. Petersburg, were violently antagonistic. They considered the opera to be the work of an illiterate musician and a boor—mistaking its inherent strength and originality for ineptitude. Not until Rimsky-Korsakov had revised, edited, and reorchestrated the opera did it finally win public and critical favor. The Rimsky-Korsakov version was given for the first time in St. Petersburg on December 10, 1896, and went on to circle the globe. The American première took place at the Metropolitan Opera on March 19, 1913, Toscanini conducting. "The musical subject matter," reported W. J. Henderson in the New York *Sun,* "is thoroughly Russian. The principal themes are either actual Russian melodies or melodies fashioned by the composer in the national idiom. All of them are aptly chosen or made. They embody the moods and pictures of the drama with eloquence. They are woven together in a score of marvelous richness and power. The voices utter for the most part arioso which is original and characteristic. . . . Its fitness for the drama is perfect, and the higher flights of the arioso reach melodic beauty of unusual nobility. The orchestra has a place in the denotement of the work quite equal to that of the voices. One follows the opera with unceasing admiration for the use of musical resource."

Kurt Schindler has provided the following informative analysis of *Boris Godunov:* "With *Boris Godunov* a new type of historical opera has been founded. . . . This is the work of the simple and compelling logic of a master playwright, in which the great emotional forces, the revolutionary sentiments of a period, are depicted through the medium of music. Mussorgsky was not only a wonderful composer individually, but behind him lay the unexplored musical wealth of the great Slav nation—a mine of rhythmically and melodically unusual folk songs; of Byzantine church chants flavoring of the mysterious early Christian periods; of old bard tunes, rhapsodic and full of grandeur; of new and violent vocal inflections rooted in the dialects of a rich and varied language. . . . In *Boris Godunov* the people are actually in the foreground of the happenings, the great masses are really the principal actor; at first dumb, oppressed, easily guided, then stirred up, threatening, finally in open revolt and jubilant war spirit. The strong veracity of these folk scenes can be likened to such eternal masterpieces as Shakespeare's *Coriolanus* and *Julius Caesar*. And in all dramatic music there is nothing so near to *Macbeth* as the specter scene of *Boris.* Since Wagner's death there is no work that has so stirred the musical world through its freedom from convention, its direct truth, and its compelling sincerity."

Paul Bekker thus described Mussorgsky's highly individualized lyricism: "Mussorgsky proceeds from the sentence structure and not, like Wagner, from the individual word. From the sentence structure he builds a sort of recitative-like arioso. For this construction, to be sure, the simple and natural singable quality of the Russian language was a prerequisite. There is, in fact, no language except Italian that lends itself so readily to singing as Russian, and none that disposes of such rich material as Russian, particularly among men's voices. Mussorgsky found formal support for his style in Russian folk song, and for his treatment of speech-melody and of harmony in Russian church music."

Several versions of *Boris Godunov* are extant today. There is, first and foremost, the edition by Rimsky-Korsakov—the one with which most operagoers are familiar. Here Mussorgsky's often crude and primitive writing is refined through extensive modifications and changes of harmony and orchestration. This version is really a variation of an older one which Rimsky-Korsakov had prepared four years earlier, and in which he attempted to conform somewhat more faithfully to Mussorgsky's original intentions. *Boris Godunov* also exists as Mussorgsky originally wrote it, without modifications and so-called improvements; this version was reintroduced to the music world at the Bolshoi Theater on February 26, 1928, when it proved that it could stand quite solidly on its own merits. Karol Rathaus and Dimitri Shostakovich are others who attempted to revise *Boris* and whose versions have been produced.

Between 1870 and 1880, Mussorgsky wrote two other folk operas, *Khovanchina* and *The Fair at Sorochinsk;* both remained unfinished. He did, however, complete two noteworthy song cycles, *Sunless* in 1874 and *Songs and Dances of Death* in 1875. In 1874 he also composed the memorable suite for piano solo, *Pictures at an Exhibition,* inspired by his visit to a posthumous showing in St. Petersburg of canvases of the painter Victor Hartmann, Mussorgsky's friend. Since Mussorgsky's time, this suite has become famous in an orchestral transcription by Maurice Ravel.

While he was engaged in the creation of these significant compositions, Mussorgsky's moral and physical disintegration grew alarming. He became a hopeless alcoholic, often associating with disreputable company. Reduced to the condition of a beggar, he wore ragged, filthy clothes, and was often locked out of his rooms for failing to pay rent. Time and again friends came to his assistance with financial support to pay for his food and lodging.

He even changed physically and in his everyday deportment. As Mikhail Zetlin wrote: "He grew stouter and more ungainly; his voice thickened and his nose was now the color of a ripe plum. His elocution became more elaborate and confused. . . . As soon as he lapsed into one of his 'spells' he became cantankerous and arrogant, got into brawls in public places, quarreled with servants and waiters for preferential treatment and was obnoxious to a high degree. . . . At first, as is the case with so many inveterate drunkards, Modest carefully concealed his weakness and when dining with friends, would stubbornly refuse their offers of wine, only to disappear suddenly with some innocuous alibi which everybody recognized as meaning that he was off again on one of his binges. . . . Although, by some miracle of subconscious will power, he was always able to sober up and turn up at his office at the Ministry when required to do so, he was nevertheless becoming increasingly incapable of systematic work. For a long time this was tolerated. He even received his promotions when these were due, but the last one was already merely by way of a consolation prize; his early retirement was a foregone conclusion and he knew it."

Mussorgsky was able in 1879 to tour the Ukraine in joint recitals with the singer Daria Leonova.

In February 1881, at a party one evening in St. Petersburg, Mussorgsky suffered an attack which led to his death. "A doctor in the company had gone to attend him," recalled Mme. Leonova. "By the time the gathering broke up, Mussorgsky was all right again. We took a cab together. When we got to the neighborhood of my house, he implored me to let him stay with me; he said his nervous condition was getting worse, he felt a fit of anxiety coming on. . . . I took him with me. . . . He slept through the night in a sitting position. While I was taking tea the next morning he came in looking very cheerful. I asked him how he was; he thanked me and said he was fine. But even while he was saying this I saw him stagger, and suddenly he fell flat on the floor. . . . We rushed to his aid and I sent for the doctor. In the course of the day he had two more attacks. . . . The next day he was taken to the hospital in a carriage."

He died in the hospital on March 28, 1881. A few weeks before his death, in the hospital room, Repin drew the now celebrated portrait of the composer which shows him unkempt and disheveled, with stark, staring eyes and hollow cheeks. Mussorgsky was buried in the Alexander Nevsky Cemetery in St. Petersburg.

Of the "Five," wrote M. Montagu-Nathan, "Mussorgsky alone appears to have possessed the true seer's vision. His art is to be described as an expression of socialism in simultaneous relation to people and to music. In opera, as in song, he was a follower of his master [Dargomizhsky]. His dramatic, as well as his vocal works, are informed by that steadfast desire for naturalness which Dargomizhsky seems to have been the first to awaken in him. For, more than either Balakirev, Cui, or Borodin, Mussorgsky reflects the spirit of the sixties in Russia; his works are in much closer touch with the literature and painting of that period. They show us that, although he was regarded with some alarm by his friends as a revolutionary, his ideals were of a kind that could not fail, when realized, to promote the evolution of the musical art."

PRINCIPAL WORKS

Choral Music—Shamil's March; The Destruction of Sennacherib; Joshua; Three Vocalises, for female voices; Five Russian Folk Songs, for male voices.

Operas—The Marriage (only one act); Boris Godunov; Khovanchina (unfinished); The Fair at Sorochinsk (unfinished).

Orchestral Music—Scherzo in B-flat; Alla marcia notturna; Night on Bald Mountain; Intermezzo symphonique in modo classico; Triumphal March.

Piano Music—Impromptu passionné; Ein Kinderscherz; Intermezzo in modo classico; From Memories of Childhood; Duma; Scherzino; The Seamstress; Pictures at an Exhibition; On the Southern Shores of the Crimea; Meditation; Une Larme; Au Village.

Vocal Music—Nursery; Sunless; Songs and Dances of Death; individual songs for voice and piano, including Hebrew Song, Hopak, The Little Star, Night, Song of the Flea, and Yeremoushka's Cradle Song.

ABOUT

Barzel, C., Moussorgsky; Brook, D., Six Great Russian Composers; Calvocoressi, M. D. Moussorgsky: His Life and Works; Calvocoressi, M. D., and Abraham, G., Masters of Russian Music; Leonard, R. A., A History of Russian Music; Leyda, J., and Bertensson, S. The Musorgsky Reader; Montagu-Nathan, M., History of Russian Music; Riesemann, O. von, Mussorgsky; Seroff, V. I., The Mighty Five; Zetlin, M., The Five.

Pietro Nardini *1722-1793*

PIETRO NARDINI, distinguished eighteenth-century composer for the violin, was born in Leghorn, Italy, on April 12, 1722. He received his first violin lessons in his native city, then became a pupil of the renowned Tartini in Padua. After returning to Leghorn, Nardini participated in church concerts. In 1753 he became solo violinist at the court of the Duke of Württemberg at Stuttgart. Here he achieved a reputation as a violinist that soon spanned all of Europe. Leopold Mozart, father of Wolfgang Amadeus, described the "beauty, purity, and equality of his tone, and the tastefulness of his *cantabile* playing . . . which cannot be surpassed." When Emperor Joseph II heard Nardini play he was so delighted that he presented the musician with a golden snuffbox.

In 1767 Nardini left the Duke's court at Stuttgart to return to Leghorn. It was there that he wrote many of his violin compositions. In 1769 he settled in Tartini's house in Padua, tending solicitously to that master

PIETRO NARDINI

until the time of his death in 1770. After Tartini died, Nardini proceeded to Florence, where he was engaged as *maestro di cappella* at court. Then he entered the musical service of the Grand Duke of Tuscany. His last years were spent in Florence, where he died on May 7, 1793.

Among Nardini's compositions which are still part of the concert repertory are a melodious Concerto in E minor, for violin and orchestra, and the violin sonatas in A major and B-flat major.

Thomas Lambe Phipson has written that Nardini's music, like his character, "was of serious cast. . . . His style is large, his ideas and expression natural." Paul David further explained that the main characteristics of Nardini's style are "vivacity, grace, a sweet sentimentality. . . . Nardini's style is altogether more modern in form and feeling than Tartini's. His Allegros are often largely developed, and already display the full sonata form, while his slow movements are not unlike Viotti's."

PRINCIPAL WORKS

Chamber Music—6 string quartets; 6 flute trios; 6 sonatas for two violins; 6 violin sonatas.
Orchestral Music—6 violin concertos.
Violin Music—6 solo sonatas.

ABOUT

Pfäfflin, C., Pietro Nardini: seine Werke und sein Leben; Phipson, T. L., Biographical Sketches of Celebrated Violinists.

Otto Nicolai *1810-1849*

KARL OTTO EHRENFRIED NICOLAI, the composer of *The Merry Wives of Windsor,* was born in Königsberg, Germany, on June 9, 1810. His parents separated when he was a child. Otto's father, a teacher of music and elocution, was a ruthless autocrat, determined to rear his son as a musical prodigy. Piano lessons were accompanied by severe blows and violent outbursts of temper. On one occasion, the boy's father shut him in a dark and cold loft where he almost froze to death. By the time he was sixteen, Otto could no longer bear this treatment and ran away from home. He eventually reached Stargard, where he found a patron in *Justizrat* Adler. Adler made it possible for Nicolai to go on to Berlin to continue his music studies with Zelter, Berger, and Bernhard Klein. The young student developed quickly as a musician. In 1830 he wrote several choral compositions and published a vocal duet, a vocal quartet, and a book of *Lieder,* the latter dedicated to Mendelssohn. In 1831 Nicolai became a member of the renowned Singakademie conducted by Zelter. In 1832 he completed a Te Deum and a *Christmas Overture* for orchestra, both of which were given in public performances the next year.

In December 1833 Nicolai went to Rome. There he gained the friendship and patronage of Karl von Bunsen, Prussian Ambassador to the Papal Court. Through Bunsen, Nicolai obtained a position as organist at the embassy chapel. During his stay in Rome, Nicolai made an intensive study of old Italian sacred music with Giuseppe Baini; he also heard operas by Bellini and Donizetti which deeply impressed him. Eventually he was able to gain acquaintance with Donizetti.

Strikingly handsome, with unusual gifts as pianist and singer, Nicolai established himself as a favorite in the foremost salons of Rome. He became one of the city's most sought-after music teachers. He also wrote a symphony, and a funeral march for the recently deceased Bellini, which was performed as a memorial to the master between acts of *La Sonnambula.*

In the summer of 1836 Nicolai left Rome. After much traveling in Italy he went to Vienna in June 1837, was appointed conductor of the Kärnthnerthor Theater, and re-

OTTO NICOLAI

mained for a year. Then he resumed his travels, eventually settling again in Rome. It was there that he completed his first opera, *Rosmonda d'Inghilterra,* performed in Turin in 1838 and in Trieste in 1839. The work was strongly influenced by Donizetti, as was the work that succeeded it, *Il Templario,* based on Sir Walter Scott's *Ivanhoe,* which was introduced in Turin on February 11, 1840, with great success. *Il Templario* was soon staged in Genoa and Naples, and at La Scala in Milan. The two operas that followed this work, however, *Odoardo e Gildippe* in 1840 and *Il Proscritto* in 1841, were failures.

An invitation to help stage *Il Templario* in Vienna brought Nicolai back to the Austrian capital in 1841. There, too, the opera was highly successful, and brought Nicolai an appointment as principal conductor of the Vienna Royal Opera. The six years of tenure there constituted one of the great artistic periods in the history of Viennese opera. In 1842 Nicolai further added to his fame as a conductor by founding the Vienna Philharmonic Orchestra, which he directed in distinguished performances of the symphonic repertory for several years.

In 1847 Nicolai left Vienna for Berlin, assuming positions as *Kapellmeister* at the Berlin Royal Opera and director of the newly founded Domchor. In the meanwhile he had completed *The Merry Wives of Windsor (Die Lustigen Weiber von Wind-*

sor), the comic opera that brought him true greatness. The Shakespearean comedy, adapted for him by Salomon Hermann Mosenthal, was introduced at the Royal Opera of Berlin on March 9, 1849, the composer conducting. *The Merry Wives of Windsor* was an immediate success in Germany, and it repeated its initial triumph at its premières in Vienna, in 1852, Philadelphia, in 1863, and London, in 1864. Nicolai's effervescent lyricism, combined with uncommon skill in writing for ensembles, his deft recitatives, and his remarkable synthesis of the styles of German and Italian opera, all helped to make *The Merry Wives of Windsor* one of the greatest comic operas ever written. The work is still a favorite in German-speaking countries, and it occasionally receives successful revivals elsewhere. Its overture is, of course, a classic in the repertory of salon music.

The première of *The Merry Wives of Windsor* took place so tragically close to Nicolai's death that the composer may be considered fortunate in having witnessed the introduction of his greatest work. After directing only four performances of this opera, Nicolai succumbed to a fatal apoplectic stroke on May 11, 1849. On the day of his death, his election to the Berlin Academy of Arts was announced. Nicolai was buried in the churchyard of the Dorotheenstadt in Berlin, where a monument to his memory was erected in 1851.

"His music," said John S. Weissmann in summarizing Nicolai's style, "is characterized by two influences: on the one hand his works manifest a highly accomplished technique, the roots of which lay in church music—that is, the strict style of the great polyphonists (especially the Italians); on the other, a fresh, flexible, soaring melodic invention comparable only to Mozart's. His brilliant orchestration, full of surprising and novel ideas, is remarkable."

PRINCIPAL WORKS

Chamber Music—String Quartet; Cello Sonata.
Choral Music—Requiem; Te Deum; motets.
Operas—Rosmonda d'Inghilterra; Il Templario; Odoardo e Gildippe; Il Proscritto; Die Lustigen Weiber von Windsor.
Orchestral Music—2 symphonies; Piano Concerto; Christmas Overture; Festival Overture.
Vocal Music—Songs for voice and piano; part songs.

ABOUT
Altmann, W. (editor), Otto Nicolais Tage-bücher; Bacharach, A. L. (editor), The Music Masters, vol. 2; Kruse, G. R., Otto Nicolai: Ein Künstlerleben; Mendel, H., Otto Nicolai: Eine Biographie.

Jacob Obrecht *1452-1505*

JACOB OBRECHT, a distinguished member of the Flemish contrapuntal school, was born in Berg-op-Zoom on November 22, 1452. He was the son of the city trumpeter. Jacob received music instruction at an early age, then left his native town to attend the University of Louvain. Upon returning to Berg-op-Zoom he took holy orders, celebrating his first mass in 1480. Four years later he was appointed *maître des enfants* at the Cambrai Cathedral. He held the post for only fifteen months, then was dismissed on the grounds of having neglected the boys under his tutelage. Between 1485 and 1487 Obrecht resided in Bruges, where, on October 13, 1485, he was made succentor at the Saint-Donatien church. In 1487, at the request of the Duke of Ferrara, he took a short leave of absence to work at the ducal court, then returned to Bruges to continue his musical activities from 1488 to 1491.

In 1491 Obrecht was engaged as the choirmaster of the Notre Dame Cathedral in Antwerp. At this time his health began to decline, and in 1496 he was forced to resign as choirmaster and return to his native city. Although his health continued to deteriorate he held various musical posts as choirmaster in Antwerp and in Berg-op-Zoom. In 1501 two of his secular compositions appeared in the first volume of music ever printed. In 1503 a volume of his Masses appeared in Italy. During the next few years other works by Obrecht were included in publications and collections edited by Petrucci.

In 1504 Obrecht went to Italy, hoping that its milder climate would benefit his health. There he re-entered the service of the ducal court in Ferrara. His death in Ferrara in 1505 was due, ironically, not to his chronic ailments but to the plague.

Obrecht was the creator of many Masses, motets, hymns, and other choral works. Among Obrecht's compositions is a four-part setting of the *Passion According to St. Matthew;* it is probably the first musical treatment ever given that text. Although the Passion (in the old Catholic Church service) included a narrative recited in the style of the Gregorian chant, with the Commentary of the People given over to the chorus, Obrecht was first to provide a polyphonic setting of the entire Gospel text.

Particularly distinguished were Obrecht's Masses, of which the *Sine nomine, Maria zart,* and *Malheur me bat* are most outstanding.

Paul Henry Lang has pointed out that Obrecht was strongly influenced by the folk music of his native Flanders. Because of the impact of this folk art on him, there exists a cleavage between his music and the purer polyphony of another Flemish master, Ockeghem. Obrecht retained, said Lang, "the profound religious mysticism" of the Flemish contrapuntal school, "but his Masses and motets emit a new sonority and show clear and balanced periodic construction based on well-founded harmonies." Because Obrecht's music was so deeply rooted in folk influences, his writing was endowed with "an earthly, human touch," even in his most "mystical religious compositions."

PRINCIPAL WORKS
Choral Music—Chansons, hymns, Masses, motets.
ABOUT
Gombosi, O. J., Jakob Obrecht; Piscaer, A., Jakob Obrecht; Reese, G., Music in the Renaissance.
Musical Quarterly, October 1957.

Johannes Ockeghem *1430-1495*

JOHANNES OCKEGHEM (Jan Okeghem), one of the founders of the second Flemish contrapuntal school, was born in 1430, probably in the village of Ockeghem, near Dendre, in Flanders. He was a boy chorister at the Notre Dame Cathedral from 1443 to 1444, and in the chapel of Duke Charles of Bourbon at Moulins from 1446 to 1448. He is believed to have studied with Binchois during these early years, though confirmation of this fact is lacking.

In 1449 Ockeghem went to Cambrai, where he became a pupil of Dufay, the leading creative figure in Flemish music of that period. From 1452 to 1453 he was a

Ockeghem: ō′kĕ-gĕm

chorister in the royal chapel in Cambrai; then, in 1454, he was appointed composer and first chaplain to Charles VII at the royal court in Paris. He served in similar capacities under two later French monarchs, Louis XI and Charles VIII. In addition, he was made *maître de la chapelle du chant du roi* in the court of Louis XI in 1465. He also held the important post of treasurer at the Abbey of St. Martin at Tours in 1459. He was granted royal permission to visit Spain in 1469 and Flanders in 1484.

Ockeghem died in or about 1495, probably in Tours. His teacher and distinguished predecessor, Dufay, composed a musical epitaph in his honor.

Though many of Ockeghem's works were destroyed or lost during the half-century following his death, enough has survived to place him with the foremost exponents of Flemish contrapuntal music. Just as Dufay was the preëminent figure in what is now regarded as the first Flemish, or Netherland, school of contrapuntal composers, Ockeghem was the dominant creative figure of the later Flemish school, and one of its surpassing masters of form. "The purely technical aspects of his compositions," wrote Theodore M. Finney, "such as the possibilities of thematic augmentation and diminution, inversion and cancrizans in canonic and fugal compositions, were brought close enough to perfection by him, so that his successors could use them with perfect freedom."

Ockeghem's works are marked not only by their remarkable polyphonic structure and style, but by their mysticism and profound religious content. One of the most notable of his compositions in this respect is the Mass *Fors seulement* (the name is derived from the melody used as the *cantus firmus* for the three sections of the Mass that have survived).

Kiesewetter distinguishes between the second Flemish school, of which Ockeghem was the most distinguished representative, and the first, headed by Dufay, in this manner: Ockeghem and his contemporaries possessed "a great facility in counterpoint and fertility in invention. Their compositions, moreover, are no longer mere premeditated submissions to the contrapuntal operation, but for the most part are indicative of thought and are sketched out with manifest design, being also full of ingenious contrivances of an obbligato counterpoint, at that time just discovered."

PRINCIPAL WORKS
Choral Music—Canons, chansons, Masses, motets.

ABOUT
Brenet, M., Jean de Ockeghem; Burbure, L. de, Jean de Ockeghem; Krenek, E., J. Ockeghem; Reese, G., Music in the Renaissance.
Musical Quarterly, October 1937; La Revue musicale, February 1928.

Jacques Offenbach *1819-1880*

JACQUES OFFENBACH, genius of the *opéra-bouffe*, was born in Cologne, Germany, on June 20, 1819. He was the seventh child and second son of Isaac Judah Eberst, a voice instructor and synagogue cantor. His father had come to Cologne from the town of Offenbach-am-Main, and some time before his marriage had changed his name, taking the name of the town of Offenbach as his own. He was a competent violinist as well as a singer, and often supplemented his income by performing in local taverns. He gave his son Jacques violin lessons, but Jacques preferred the cello. Since cello instruction was denied to him because of his delicate health, Jacques studied the instrument secretly, soon acquiring enough proficiency to participate in performances of chamber music. He became a member of his own family instrumental trio that performed in cafés and other public places.

In 1833 Jacques went to Paris to enter the Conservatory. The rules forbade admission to foreign-born students, but when Cherubini, the director of the Conservatory, heard him perform on the cello he waived the restriction and permitted the boy to enter the cello class taught by Vaslin. Offenbach remained at the Conservatory for only a year. After that he worked as a cellist in the Opéra-Comique orchestra, where he became notorious for his pranks. He studied music privately with various teachers, notably Norbin for cello and Jacques Halévy for composition. Halévy had high regard for the young man's talent; Offenbach, he said at the time, "appears destined for real success."

From the beginning Offenbach seems to have preferred to direct his creative activity to the lighter forms of music. Among his first compositions were several popular dances, songs, and fantasies. Some of these pieces were included in a vaudeville show produced at the Palais Royal on March 2, 1839.

After withdrawing from the orchestra of the Opéra-Comique, Offenbach became a successful performer on the cello in concert auditoriums and in fashionable salons. At one Parisian salon he met and fell in love with Herminie d'Alcain. Herminie consented to marry Offenbach if he fulfilled two conditions. He would have to achieve success in England as a cello virtuoso, and convert to Catholicism. When both conditions were met, Offenbach and Herminie were married on August 14, 1844.

In 1848 Offenbach went to Germany to visit his family. Upon his return to Paris he was appointed conductor of the Théâtre Français, where he remained for five years and instituted several major musical reforms. His ambitions, however, had turned to composition rather than performance, particularly composition for the stage. In 1850, at the request of Alfred de Musset, he wrote an outstandingly successful song, "Chanson de Fortunio," for a production of Le Chandelier. Three years later his first operetta, Pépito, was given at the Théatre des Variétés.

Offenbach's dream was now to have a theater of his own, where he could produce his operettas. "I said to myself," he wrote subsequently, "that the Opéra-Comique was no longer the home of comic opera, and that the idea of really gay, cheerful, witty music —in short, the idea of music with life in it—was gradually being forgotten. The composers who wrote for the Opéra-Comique wrote little 'grand operas.' I felt that there was something that could be done by the young musicians who, like myself, were being kept waiting in idleness outside the portals of the lyric theater."

His dream was realized in 1855, when he took a lease on the Théâtre Comte in the Passage Choiseul and renamed it the Bouffes Parisiens. There, on July 5, he presented a program of light musical entertainment that included his operetta Les Deux aveugles. This comic opera was received so enthusiastically that it had a run of some four hundred performances.

During the five-year existence of the Bouffes Parisiens, Offenbach wrote over

JACQUES OFFENBACH

thirty operettas. In Le Violoneux, introduced on August 31, 1855, the glamorous Parisian stage star Hortense Schneider made her début as an interpreter of Offenbach's music. Later, some of Offenbach's greatest triumphs were achieved with Hortense Schneider appearing in the leading female role. On November 19, 1859, the Bouffes Parisiens offered Offenbach's Geneviève de Brabant. Today this operetta is remembered only because one of its melodies was taken for the celebrated American Marine hymn, "From the Halls of Montezuma."

It was also for the Bouffes Parisiens that Offenbach wrote his first opéra-bouffe masterwork, one of the crowning achievements in French light opera: Orpheus in the Underworld (Orphée aux enfers), introduced on October 21, 1858. The text, by Hector Crémieux and Ludovic Halévy, was a burlesque on mythology and the Olympian gods, centering on the marital bickerings of Orpheus and Eurydice, and placing the gods Pluto and Jupiter in an infamous intrigue to win Eurydice for themselves. Offenbach's music was hardly less irreverent than the play. A staid minuet was followed by a riotous can-can by the gods and goddesses; the lament of Orpheus in Gluck's opera Orfeo ed Euridice, "Che faro senza Euridice," was parodied; the sound of snoring was made the accompaniment to airs by Cupid and Venus. Elsewhere in the score an engaging, infectious lyricism replaced irony, malice, and burlesque.

Gabriel Grovelz commented: "Offenbach never produced a more complete score. . . . It is impossible to analyze adequately a piece wherein the sublimest idiocy and the most astonishing fancy clash at every turn. The overture is gay and lively, the recitative of the shepherd Aristeus is almost on the level with one of Iopasin in *Les Troyens* of Berlioz. The songs . . . of John Styx are masterpieces of fatuity and naïveté."

Orpheus in the Underworld was not at first a success. Many critics and theatergoers objected violently to this desecration of antiquity and the Olympian gods; others were shocked by some of the more provocative scenes in the play. But when the critic Jules Janin leveled a devastating attack on the opera in the *Journal des débats,* Parisians began to flock to the Bouffes Parisiens to see for themselves what had provoked the eminent journalist to such extreme pronouncements. Before long, *Orpheus in the Underworld* became a major topic of discussion and the theater was filled. *Orpheus* had an initial run of 227 performances. Its melodies were heard everywhere in Paris. The can-can became a rage. In later revivals *Orpheus* proved even more successful. By the time of World War I it had been seen in Paris over a thousand times. In the United States it was first seen in New York in March 1861.

Now that *Orpheus in the Underworld* had made him one of the most famous composers in Paris, Offenbach found theaters clamoring for his scores. In 1860 he decided to give up his own theater to write operetta for other producers. Some of his greatest operettas were given at the Théâtre des Variétés—*La Belle Hélène* on December 17, 1864; *Barbe-bleu,* on February 5, 1866; *La Grande Duchesse de Gérolstein,* on April 12, 1867; and *La Périchole,* on October 6, 1868.

The success of the last-named work is attested by the fact that its American première took place in New York on January 4, 1869, barely three months after its introduction in Paris.

La Périchole enjoyed a triumphant revival in New York on December 21, 1956 at the Metropolitan Opera. It was presented in a new English translation, with the British actor Cyril Ritchard as stage director and star in the role of the Viceroy. One of Offenbach's most beloved melodies is found in *La Périchole*—the heroine's farewell letter, "O mon chèr amant, je te jure."

After *La Périchole,* Offenbach's great creative powers declined. Most of his operettas after 1868 were mediocre, and failed to hold much interest for audiences. In 1873 Offenbach again became his own director, taking over the management of the Gaîté theater, and he presented new versions of *Orpheus in the Underworld* and *Geneviève de Brabant,* along with several new, and undistinguished, works. Audiences, however, neglected these works; and poor attendance, combined with his extravagance in mounting productions, brought him into bankruptcy in 1875.

In order to raise funds to repay his creditors, Offenbach in 1876 undertook a tour of the United States, conducting concerts of his music in New York and Philadelphia. He recorded his impressions of the country in two volumes, *Notes d'un musicien en voyage* (1877) and *Offenbach en Amérique* (1877). The latter appeared in a new English translation in 1957 under the title *Orpheus in America.*

After returning to Paris, Offenbach wrote and produced ten more operettas, none successful. Embittered by failure and ravaged by illness, Offenbach nevertheless burned with the ambition to attempt his first serious opera. He became a virtual recluse, expending whatever physical and creative resources remained to him on a work that he was convinced would be his crowning achievement. Thus it was that he completed *The Tales of Hoffmann* (*Les Contes d'Hoffmann*), a "fantastic opera" with a text by Jules Barbier and Michel Carré based on tales by E. T. A. Hoffmann. He did not live to see this work performed. On October 5, 1880, in Paris, he died of rheumatic heart disease.

On February 10, 1881, four months after his death, *The Tales of Hoffmann* was introduced by the Opéra-Comique. Ernest Guiraud provided the recitatives which Offenbach had not lived to complete, as well as some of the unfinished orchestration.

The Tales of Hoffmann was an immediate success; it has since become one of the staples of the French lyric theater. "The music Offenbach wrote for the kaleidoscopic succession of fantastic incidents," wrote Herbert F. Peyser, "is as amazing, as diverse, and as colorful as the episodes it enlivens. Some of it might have come straight out of the operettas which made their creator a world figure. Some of it is sensuously charming, some astoundingly dramatic, some sweetly nostalgic, some out-and-out macabre." The most popular single excerpt from this beloved opera is, of course, the second-act "Barcarolle." Interestingly, Offenbach had not written this famous melody for *Tales of Hoffmann,* but borrowed it from one of his earlier operetta-ballets: it is the ghost song from *Die Rheinnixen.*

The Tales of Hoffmann was first heard in the United States at the Fifth Avenue Theatre in New York on October 16, 1882, but it did not achieve popularity in America until its production at the Manhattan Opera House on November 14, 1907.

PRINCIPAL WORKS
Ballets—Pierrot Clown; Polichinelle dans le monde; Les Bergers de Watteau; Le Papillon.
Operas—About 100 opéra-bouffes, including Les Deux aveugles; Orphée aux enfers; Geneviève de Brabant; La Belle Hélène; La Vie parisienne; La Grande Duchess de Gérolstein; La Périchole; Les Brigands; Les Contes d'Hoffmann.

ABOUT
Brindejont-Offenbach, J., Jacques Offenbach, mon grand-père; Kracauer, S., Orpheus in Paris; Offenbach, J., Orpheus in America: Offenbach's Diary of His Journey to the New World; Schneider, L., Offenbach; Sitwell, S., La Vie Parisienne: A Tribute to Offenbach.

Jan Okeghem

See Johannes Ockeghem

Johann Pachelbel *1653-1706*

JOHANN PACHELBEL, an important predecessor of Johann Sebastian Bach in the art of organ performance and composition, was born in Nuremberg, Germany, in August 1653 (his baptismal date being September 1). His first music lessons were with Heinrich Schwemmer. He then attended the University of Altdorf, and received additional organ instruction from J. Kaspar Kerl, organist of the imperial chapel; on several occasions Pachelbel served as Kerl's stand-in at the chapel.

Pachelbel: päк'ĕl-bĕl

In 1677 Pachelbel received his first important appointment with his engagement as organist for the court at Eisenach. He then served as organist at the Predigerkirche in Erfurt in 1678, at the court of Stuttgart from 1690 to 1692, at Gotha from 1692 to 1695, and, after 1695, at the St. Sebaldus Church in Nuremberg. Esteemed as one of the leading organists of his day, Pachelbel succeeded in introducing to German organ performance some of the subtleties and refinements of the Viennese school.

Pachelbel's numerous compositions for organ are so important as landmarks in Baroque organ music that Pachelbel is often described as the spiritual ancestor of Johann Sebastian Bach. He helped crystallize the forms of the chorale prelude, chaconne, fugue, toccata, fantasia, and instrumental Magnificat, and developed the techniques of organ performances. Such chorale preludes as *Von Himmel hoch* and *Durch Adams Fall* anticipate Bach in variety and skill of polyphonic improvisation. Pachelbel's keyboard Magnificats, as Wanda Landowska wrote, are "fervent and mystical, . . . touching in [their] simplicity. The Magnificats have all the poetic intensity of the hour of vespers. They evoke the atmosphere of a quiet village, with its small wooden church resounding and vibrating to the sounds of bells and organ, while its fields are illuminated by the rays of the setting sun." Miss Landowska also explained why Pachelbel's work exerted so powerful a fascination on Bach: "In spite of its contrapuntal skill, it is essentially simple and naïve. For a mind as complex as Bach's, the very transparence of this art must have added to its charm."

Pachelbel preceded Bach in still another significant aspect, that of "well-tempered tuning." In one of his organ suites, he wrote compositions in seventeen of the twenty-four keys then available to him. "This collection of preludes and fugues," said Manfred F. Bukofzer "represents the most important document in the evolution of the temperament before Bach. It served as the direct model for the *Well-Tempered Clavier,* not only with regard to the order of the keys, but sometimes even with regard to the fugue themes."

One of Pachelbel's sons played a major role in the early history of concert performance in the United States. He was Carl

Theodorus (1690-1750), who emigrated to Boston in the early eighteenth century. In Boston he helped found the Trinity Church, of which he became the organist. He later was the organist of St. Philip's Church in Charleston, South Carolina, and on January 21, 1736 he gave the first known organ recital in New York.

Another of Pachelbel's sons, Wilhelm Hieronymus (1685-1764), was organist of the Jacobkirche and of St. Sebaldus in Nuremberg and a composer of various organ compositions.

PRINCIPAL WORKS
Harpsichord Music—Chaconnes, fugues (with organ), Magnificats.
Organ Music—Arias with variations, chaconnes, chorale preludes, fantasias, fugues, Magnificats, preludes, ricercari, suites, toccatas.
Violin Music—6 suites for two violins.

ABOUT
Beckmann, G., Pachelbel als Kammerkomponist; Born, E., Die Variation als Grundlage handwerklicher Gestaltung im musikalischen Schaffen Johann Pachelbels; Bukofzer, M. F., Music in the Baroque Era; Eggebrecht, H. H., Johann Pachelbel als Vokalkomponist.

Niccolò Paganini *1782-1840*

NICCOLÒ PAGANINI, one of the greatest violin virtuosos of all time and an outstanding composer of brilliant violin music, was born in Genoa, Italy, on October 27, 1872. It is said that when he was born his mother insisted that a Holy Messenger had come to her side to prophesy that the child would become the world's greatest violinist. Niccolò, however, barely survived his childhood. At the age of four, stricken with a grave illness, he was thought dead, wrapped in a shroud, and almost buried alive. Only accidentally was the startling discovery made that the child was still breathing. Although Niccolò survived that illness, he remained sickly for the rest of his life.

Niccolò's father, who worked at the port of Genoa for a shipping company, aspired to make his son a musical prodigy. He gave Niccolò lessons on the mandolin, then turned him over to Giovanni Servetto and Giacomo Costa for instruction in composition and violin. Niccolò's progress fulfilled his father's wildest hopes. At the age of eight he wrote an extraordinary piano so-

nata; a half year later he gave a remarkable demonstration of his virtuosity with his performance of Pleyel's Violin Concerto at a church concert; and in 1793, giving a violin recital in a public auditorium, he overwhelmed the audience with a dazzling performance of one of his own variations on *La Carmagnole*. His fellow townspeople, eager to foster his astonishing gifts, raised funds to finance his musical education. Niccolò's studies thus continued in Leghorn, with Ferdinand Paer, and in Parma, with Alessandro Rolla. By the time Paganini was fourteen, Rolla insisted that there was nothing more he could teach him; the distinguished violinist Kreutzer would not believe his ears when Paganini played for him.

In 1797 Paganini toured many of the principal cities of northern Italy, where he enjoyed immense personal triumph, and reaped lavish financial reward. His early success gave him the courage to shake loose from his father's influence, and to set off on his own without further parental guidance or interference. But this newly won freedom, combined with his mounting fame, turned his head. At sixteen, he had begun to pursue women, gamble recklessly, and lead a dissipated life. His gambling losses were often so large that he would occasionally pawn his violin in order to pay his debts.

In or about 1800, Paganini disappeared from public view. A wealthy Tuscan lady whose identity has always remained a mystery became his patroness and supported him in her château for several years. Since she was an amateur guitarist, Paganini now wrote several works for that instrument. He continued, however, to work assiduously at perfecting his technique.

The second woman to sponsor Paganini's career was Elisa Bacciochi, Princess of Lucca, sister of Napoleon. Through her influence, Paganini in 1805 was appointed conductor of the Lucca Opera and music director at her court. He held both positions until 1813. In the meanwhile, he had also returned to the concert stage with violin performances that electrified his audiences. By 1813 there was little doubt in all of Italy that Paganini was the greatest violinist, and one of the most adulated concert artists, of his age. His cadaverous appearance and his fabulous violin exploits inspired rumor and legend. Some maintained he was the son of the Devil and crossed themselves when they passed him; others insisted that he was Cagliostro, or that he was the original "wandering Jew." Meyerbeer, enraptured by his performance, followed him from concert to concert, from city to city. "Where our powers of thought end, there Paganini begins," Meyerbeer exclaimed. "Paganini knows how to surpass all your imaginings with his realities." Women worshipped him. "When they hear my music, my melting tones," Paganini remarked, with his customary lack of modesty, "they begin weeping and then I become their idol. They lie at my feet."

In 1824 Paganini fell in love with Antonia Bianchi, a singer. They lived together for about three years, in which time a son was born to them, Achilles Cyrus Alexander. Paganini lavished extraordinary affection on the child. When he and Antonia separated in 1828, he agreed to provide for her handsomely on the condition that he retain sole custody of the boy.

Until 1828 Paganini's consistently poor health forced him to confine his career to performing in Italy. In that year, however, he yielded to pressure to tour other parts of Europe. On March 29, 1828, he gave his first concert in Vienna. The reception accorded him has few parallels in the history of Viennese concert music. The poet Grillparzer wrote a poem in his praise. Operas and plays were written about him. The Emperor appointed him "imperial and royal virtuoso." Food, sweets, clothing were named after him. Crowds swarmed outside his hotel, hoping to catch a glimpse of him. Women vied with each other for the joy of meeting him personally. And the press reached almost the same peak of hysterical praise as did his admirers.

Paganini next toured Germany, then in 1831 went to Paris and London. The triumphs of Vienna were repeated everywhere. Famous musicians expressed superlatives: Schumann said, "Paganini is the turning point in the history of virtuosity." The young Liszt gasped, "What a man! What a violinist! What an artist!" (It was after hearing Paganini that Liszt was inspired to become the greatest piano virtuoso of his age.) Rossini confessed that he had cried only three times in his life, "the third time when I first heard Paganini play." In London, Henry Chorley, the eminent critic, said, "Paganini is a solitary man in his art."

NICCOLÒ PAGANINI

Paganini returned to Italy broken in health but greatly enriched in material resources. He purchased an estate near Parma, where he hoped he would be able to recuperate. He also made a foolhardy speculation, setting up a gambling casino in Paris which lost him a fortune.

Worry and entanglements with creditors and the law further sapped his strength. In the winter of 1839 he fled to Nice, where he died on May 27, 1840, of a disease of the larynx. Since he had failed to receive the final sacraments from the church, and because wild rumors still circulated about him, the composer was denied burial in holy ground. Five years after his death his devoted son, Achille (now a baron), effected the removal of this ban. In May 1845 Paganini's remains found their permanent resting place in a village church near Parma.

Paganini's appearance was Mephistophelian. His cheeks were pale and sunken, his eyes like burning charcoal in their intensity; his thin lips usually curved in a sardonic smile. Heinrich Heine described him: "A black-clad figure which seemed to have ascended from Hades appeared on the stage. That was he, Paganini, in his black gala: black tails and vest, as it might be enforced at Proserpina's Court by the Devil's etiquette, the black trousers anxiously fluttering around his thin legs. . . . His face, pale as a corpse, in the blinding stage lights."

One of Paganini's early biographers, Weiss, wrote: "He was under five feet ten inches in height. He was . . . exceedingly thin, and his arms and hands unnaturally long. His bony fingers seemed to stretch from one end of the violin fingerboard to the other without an effort; and it has been asserted that without such a length of finger he never could have played the passages he is known to have executed. He wore his hair (of which he was very proud) in long ringlets over his shoulders. Its color was a rich brown (not black, as some have stated); and although he looked many years older than his age (forty-seven) he was proud that he had not a gray hair on his head."

Most of Paganini's compositions remained unpublished during his lifetime. Whenever publishers approached him, he demanded exorbitant fees that precluded further negotiation. It is more than probable that he did not wish most of his music published, feeling that if other violinists did not perform his works audiences would believe that no one else could play them. The only pieces whose publication he permitted were the twenty-four caprices for violin (which, because of their extraordinary technical problems, Paganini was sure would not often be performed), twelve sonatas for violin and guitar, and six string quartets with guitar. The two violin concertos—No. 1 in D major and No. 2 in B minor—did not appear until eleven years after Paganini's death.

There is a great deal in Paganini's compositions that is meretricious, exploiting amazing virtuosity and pyrotechnical feats for their own sake rather than for musical values. Despite these faults, Paganini is pre-eminent among composers for the violin. None before him did so much to extend the technical resources of violin performance. Through the most brilliant and varied use of harmonics, arpeggios, pizzicati, tremolos, staccato and octave passages, double and triple stops, and other devices, Paganini gave new dimensions to violin music; it has been said, with complete justification, that the modern technique of violin performance emerged with Paganini and his music.

The foremost composers of his day were among those who recognized the significance of his works. Robert Schumann said, "His compositions contain many pure and precious qualities." Berlioz wrote, "A volume might be written in telling all that Paga-

nini has created . . . of novel effect, of ingenious contrivances, noble and grandiose forms, and orchestral combinations unknown before his time. His melodies are broad Italian melodies, but full of passionate ardor seldom found in the best pages of dramatic composers of his country. His harmonies are always clear, simple, and of extraordinary sonority."

Paganini's masterwork is the group of twenty-four Caprices for unaccompanied violin, written in 1820. This is sometimes described as a lexicon of violin technique in general and of Paganini's technique in particular. These pieces are not merely technical exercises for the violin but music rich in poetic and expressive content. Some of them were transcribed for piano by Schumann and Liszt; Georges Enesco and Fritz Kreisler, among others, gave them a piano accompaniment. The most celebrated of these pieces, the Twenty-Fourth Caprice, was the inspiration for major works by Brahms, Rachmaninoff, and Boris Blacher.

Paganini wrote three violin concertos. The most frequently performed is the First, in D major, op. 6, which Paganini wrote for his first appearance in Paris in 1831. This work is frequently heard in edited and greatly shortened versions by Fritz Kreisler or August Wilhelmj. From Paganini's Second Concerto in B minor, op. 7, Liszt derived the now popular *La Campanella*. In the concerto it forms the second movement called "Ronde à la clochette"; Liszt named it *La Campanella* in his transcription for piano.

Principal Works

Chamber Music—12 sonatas for violin and guitar (or piano); 6 quartets for violin, viola, cello and guitar; various other quartets, trios, duets and sonatas.

Orchestral Music—3 violin concertos; Moto perpetuo, for violin and orchestra; various variations for violin and orchestra including Le Streghe, God Save the King, and Di tanti palpiti.

Violin Music—24 caprices for unaccompanied violin; sonatas for unaccompanied violin; various shorter pieces for violin and piano, including fantasias, minuets, polonaises, sonatinas, and variations.

About

Bonaventura, A., Niccolò Paganini; Chiesa, M. T., Paganini; Codignola, A. (editor), Paganini intimo; Courcy, G. I. C. de, Paganini: The Genoese; Day, L., Niccolo Paganini of Genoa; Komroff, M., The Magic Bow: A Romance of Paganini; Pulver, J., Paganini, the Romantic Virtuoso; Saussine, R. de, Paganini, the Magician; Spivacke, H., Paganiniana; Valensi, T., Paganini.

Giovanni Paisiello *1740-1816*

GIOVANNI PAISIELLO, prolific and successful composer of Italian opera in the eighteenth century, was born in Taranto on May 8, 1740. His father, a veterinary surgeon employed by the king of Naples, enrolled Giovanni in the Jesuit school when he was five. The boy remained for eight years, studying voice with Don Carlo Resta, a priest. Resta was so impressed by Giovanni's beautiful voice that he urged his father to permit him to develop his musical talents. Another musician profoundly impressed by the boy's gift was Maestro Guaducci of the Capuchin Church. It was through Guaducci's urging that Giovanni's father in 1754 finally permitted him to enter the Conservatorio di Sant' Onofrio in Naples. Until 1759 Paisiello received a comprehensive musical training under such masters as Durante and Contumacci. For the next four years he taught composition at the Conservatory.

First as a Conservatory student, then as an instructor, Paisiello took a deep interest in church music. He wrote numerous choral works, including Masses, oratorios, motets, and psalms. However, one of the compositions he wrote at this time was for the stage: a slight one-act interlude given at the Conservatory in 1763. This work brought him a commission from the Marsigli Theater in Bologna for the comic opera *La Pupilla*, a major success when introduced in 1764. Many other commissions now came to Paisiello from some of Italy's leading opera companies. Extraordinarily prolific, he wrote approximately fifty operas during the next twelve years. The most important were *Le Finte contesse*, given in Rome in 1766; *L'Idolo cinese*, introduced in Naples in 1767; *La Frascatana*, seen in Venice in 1774; and a remarkable parody on classical opera, *Socrate immaginario*, also given in Venice a year later. By 1775 Paisiello had become one of Italy's most highly esteemed opera composers, a formidable rival to such established masters as Piccini and Cimarosa. In the meantime he entered upon a marriage arrangement, in 1769, after being imprisoned for breach of promise.

In 1776 Paisiello went to Russia to serve as *Kapellmeister* for Catherine II at a handsome salary. Paisiello remained in Russia for nine years, during which period he wrote

GIOVANNI PAISIELLO

several operas. One of these, composed in 1781, was a new setting of *La Serva padrona,* a work which, a half-century earlier, had served Pergolesi as the text for the first *opera buffa* ever written. Much more significant was Paisiello's *The Barber of Seville (Il Barbiere di Siviglia)*, his masterwork in the *buffa* style. This opera preceded by more than twenty-five years the more famous *opera buffa* by Rossini on the same subject and with the same title. After the première at the Hermitage in St. Petersburg, on September 26, 1782, the *opera buffa* was given throughout Italy, becoming one of the most popular stage works of its time. Fresh in its musical material, alternately witty and lyrical, graceful in style, filled with subtle characterizations and expert writing, Paisiello's *The Barber of Seville* was an *opera buffa* classic delighting the audiences of the music world until Rossini's opera eclipsed it. The first American performance of Paisiello's work took place in Philadelphia in 1794, in an English translation.

Recent revivals of Paisiello's opera (including an outstanding one at the Komische Oper in East Berlin in 1959-1960), and a complete recording made in 1960, provide convincing testimony to contemporary audiences that Paisiello's opera can still afford a good deal of listening pleasure; a work of the first order, Paisiello's *opera buffa* might very well have retained its popularity up to the present time. As Howard Taubman wrote in his review of the Berlin revival: "It is easy to see how it won the hearts of eighteenth- and early nineteenth-century patrons. It is also easy to see how Rossini's immense gusto overwhelmed a public accustomed to a politer form of expression." Conrad L. Osborne remarked with wisdom, "If the listener will accept Paisiello's music on its own terms he will find the score full of charm and wit. The melodies fall very easily on the ear, and as in Mozart, the working of them contains countless unexpected little turns that keep the theatrical pot bubbling. Everything is done with the simplest of materials, but done with precision and dramatic shrewdness."

Early in 1784 Paisiello gave up his post in Russia. En route back to Naples he stopped off at Vienna, where he wrote twelve symphonies on a commission from Emperor Joseph II. He also completed a new opera, *Il Re Teodoro,* produced in Vienna on August 23, 1784. It contains some of his finest writing within the *opera seria* format.

Later that year, in Naples, Paisiello was appointed *maestro di cappella* at the court of Ferdinand IV. During the fifteen years he held this office he produced numerous new operas. *Pirro,* in 1787, was one of the earliest operas to introduce the concerted finale. *La Molinara,* in 1788, is of particular interest to us today because the young Beethoven took one of its airs, "Nel cor più," for a set of six piano variations in 1795. *Nina* (1789) has historic importance as an early example of "opera of sentiment." As Francis Toye explained, "Previously sentiment had been almost unknown on the opera stage, *opera seria* dealing only with incredible nobility and rage, *opera buffa* with farce and satire. Doubtless this innovation owed its primary impetus to the ideas of Rousseau and other pre-Revolutionary purveyors of democratic emotion."

When a republican government was established in Naples in 1799, Paisiello became director of national music. With the restoration of the monarchy, his former royal patrons refused to reinstate him as *maestro di cappella.* For two years Paisiello remained unemployed, then in 1802 was invited to Paris by Napoleon to direct music at his chapel. This was the period in which Paisiello completed his only opera on a French text, *Proserpine,* produced at the Opéra in 1803.

Partly because of his wife's poor health, partly in disappointment at the indifferent reception of *Proserpine,* Paisiello decided to leave France and return to Naples. Napoleon gave him permission to do so, but on condition that he name his own successor. Paisiello's choice, surprisingly, was Lesueur, who by 1803 had fallen on evil days and was completely neglected and impoverished.

In Naples, further honors awaited Paisiello. Joseph Buonaparte bestowed on him a handsome pension and reinstated him as *maestro di cappella.* But with the return to power of the Bourbons, Paisiello's good fortune was again reversed, coming to a sudden and permanent end. His pension was terminated, though he was permitted to continue working at the royal chapel. The loss of financial security and prestige, and the death of his wife, combined to shatter his health. He died in Naples on June 5, 1816.

The critics and musicians of Paisiello's day regarded him highly. The *Quarterly Musical Review* of 1818, for example, described his "fertility of invention, an extraordinary and happy facility of finding subjects full both of nature and originality, a talent unique in developing them by the resources of melody, and embellishing them by interesting details, an arrangement always full of fancy and learning, a taste, grace, and freshness of melody. . . . His composition is always very simple, and divested of all affectation of learning . . . exceedingly elegant; his accompaniments are always very clear and at the same time full of brilliant effect. . . . He knows perfectly how to introduce variety . . . to pass from the comic, from the simple and unaffected, to the pathetic, to the majestic, and even to the terrible, without losing . . . grace and elegance."

Paisiello was, indeed, a far greater composer than the present-day obscurity of his operas suggests. In addition to his ingratiating style and lyricism, richness of orchestral texture, and uncommon skill in writing for ensembles, Paisiello boasted a dignity and dramatic truth not often encountered in the Italian operas of his day. Donald Jay Grout has written, "Paisiello was . . . a many-sided genius, a master of musical characterization, perhaps the greatest figure in eighteenth-century *opera buffa* next to Mozart himself, and one who exercised a strong influence on the musical style of the latter."

PRINCIPAL WORKS

Chamber Music—12 quartets with continuo; 6 string quartets; Harp Sonata; Sonata for Violin and Cello.

Choral Music—Cantatas, oratorios, various sacred compositions.

Operas—Over 100 comic and serious operas, including: Le Finte contesse; L'Idolo cinese; La Frascatana; Socrate immaginario; Il Barbiere di Siviglia; Il Re Teodoro; L'Olimpiade; La Molinara; Nina; I Zingari Proserpine.

Orchestral Music—12 symphonies; 6 harpsichord concertos; Harp Concerto.

ABOUT

Della Corte, A., Settecento italiano: Paisiello; Faustini-Fasini, E., Opere teatrali, oratori e cantate di G. Paisiello; Prota-Giurleo, U., Paisiello ed i suoi primi trionfi a Napoli.

Music and Letters, April 1939; Opera News, April 14, 1962.

GIOVANNI PIERLUIGI DA PALESTRINA

Giovanni Pierluigi da Palestrina
1525-1594

GIOVANNI PIERLUIGI DA PALESTRINA, the dominant figure of the Roman polyphonic school, was the most important composer before the age of Bach and Handel. His name at birth was Giovanni Pierluigi, but he is known as Palestrina from the place of his birth, a hill town of that name twenty miles from Rome. He was born in or about 1525, the son of a property owner in comfortable circumstances. As a boy, Palestrina sang in the choir of the local cathedral. When the Bishop of Palestrina was summoned to Rome to become Archbishop of S. Maria Maggiore in 1534, he took young Palestrina with him. There for about five years the boy studied in the choir school and sang in the choir. It is believed that he studied later in Rome with the choirmaster of Maria Maggiore. In 1544 Palestrina returned to his native city, there to become choirmaster and organist of the Cathedral of Saint Agapitus. While holding this post he married Lucrezia Gori, the daughter of a prosperous landowner.

In 1551 the Bishop of Palestrina was elevated to the Holy See as Pope Julius III. Soon afterwards, the new Pope called Palestrina to Rome to become director of the Julian Choir, which performed regularly at St. Peter's. In 1554 Palestrina issued his first publication, a volume of Masses dedicated in the most flattering terms to the Pope. Probably in grateful acknowledgment of this dedication, the Pope made Palestrina a member of the pontifical choir, an appointment that forthwith aroused considerable antagonism among the other singers since Palestrina had been elevated to this post without taking the prescribed examination. When Pope Julius died, about a year later, Palestrina was removed from the choir on the grounds that he was a married man.

For a brief period, mainly because of ill health, Palestrina held no office of any kind. But in October 1555 he became musical director of St. John Lateran, where he remained four years, and completed a volume of Magnificats and Lamentations. Between 1561 and 1568 he filled a similar post at S. Maria Maggiore, publishing his first volume of motets in 1563.

In 1567 Palestrina published a second volume of Masses which contained one of his most celebrated works, the *Missa Papae Marcelli*. For a long time a legend was circulated that Palestrina had written this remarkable work to convince the Church authorities that no reform of liturgical music, as requested by the Council of Trent, was required. The Council had objected severely to the use of secular tunes in religious worship and had suggested the substitution of the old plainsong for the complex polyphonic style then in use. The story goes that Palestrina created the *Missa Papae Marcelli* to prove that music of great dignity, beauty, and spiritual exaltation could be written in a contrapuntal idiom, and proved it so decisively—the legend went on—that reform was considered unnecessary. There is no evidence to show that the *Papae Marcelli* had such an origin. But it is known that the Church authorities listened to some of Palestrina's Masses while studying the existing repertory, and it is possible that some of Palestrina's works were influential in the final decision to avoid any change. (The legend of Palestrina's writing the *Missa Papae Marcelli* to maintain the existing style, and the supposed influence of the work on the Church authorities, is the subject of a compelling twentieth-century opera, *Palestrina*, by the German composer Hans Pfitzner.)

Palestrina left S. Maria Maggiore in 1567 to join the establishment of Cardinal Ippolito d'Este, a prominent Renaissance figure who encouraged Palestrina to write some of his greatest choral compositions. In 1571 Palestrina returned to his former post as director of the Julian Choir. He was now one of Italy's most celebrated composers, a man to whom considerable homage was accorded. In 1575 fifteen hundred singers walked from the town of Palestrina to Rome to pay him tribute, singing his music as they marched.

Personal tragedy—the death of his wife and two of his sons—led Palestrina to consider entering the Church. He abandoned this plan, however, and was remarried in 1581. His second wife was Victoria Dormuli, a woman engaged in the fur business, and for the remainder of his life Palestrina managed to combine his musical activities as a composer and director of the Julian Choir with the pursuit of business. Early in 1594 he issued his last publication, a volume of spiritual madrigals. While working on these pieces, Palestrina was stricken with pleurisy, which proved fatal. He died in Rome on February 2, 1594. His body was encased in lead on which his name was inscribed in Latin with the designation "Princeps Musicae."

"To Palestrina," wrote Zoë Kendrick Pyne, "the practical and material side of his profession was of utmost importance. . . . It has been made a subject of implied reproach that he was never indifferent to the financial aspect of a question, nor ever neglected an opportunity of attaching himself to a wealthy patron; but he should rather be praised for precisely those qualities which prove him to have been a good husband, careful father, and prudent man. . . . His monthly salary at S. Maria Maggiore amounted at first to thirteen, later, sixteen scudi on the addition of another chorister to the three already in charge, in all about one hundred and ninety-two scudi [approximately seven hundred and fifty dollars a year]. For this sum Palestrina was expected to feed the boys and give them musical instruction. . . . Presents were customary after the great festivals of the Church. . . . To these sources of income must be added Palestrina's pension as ex-member of the Pontifical Choir, amounting to a yearly sum of about two hundred and fifty dollars. Then comes an uncertain sum for dedications to rich patrons—habitual at the time—and the organization of music for occasions festive or mournful. The present was an epoch in which men of wealth and position desired to pose as excellent musicians, so that there were always compositions to be corrected and put into shape, or lessons to give. . . . Palestrina also had property and turned it to practical account. . . . He was certainly not rich, but . . . his income compares not unfavorably with many a church musician of high repute today."

Except for some secular madrigals, Palestrina was exclusively a composer for the Church—Masses, motets, hymns—the richest musical contribution made by the Counter Reformation. Cecil Gray divided this repertory into three periods. "In his first book of Masses, and in several other compositions published later, but probably written at the same time, he appears rather in the light of a disciple and follower of the Netherland school. . . . They are highly complex and artificial, and as full of ingenious contrapuntal contrivances as the most elaborate productions of the Flemish (or Netherland) school. His second period is characterized by a constantly increasing tendency in the direction of melodic suavity and harmonic clarity, culminating in the *Missa Papae Marcelli*—the most famous as it is likewise one of the best of all his Masses—in which the utmost sensuous beauty is united to a great wealth and subtlety of technical resource, without, however, detracting from the profoundly devotional character of the music. Finally, in the work of his third period, the formal structure becomes more concentrated and precise, the polyphonic texture still more refined and simplified, and the harmonic and melodic idiom undergo a further process of clarification, resulting in the formation of a style from which every vestige of the old Flemish style has been eliminated."

Palestrina marks the end of an old era in music rather than the beginning of a new one. His art is essentially an extension of medieval music, with its dependence on the Gregorian chant and its often archaic vocabulary and language. As Richard R. Terry has pointed out, Palestrina was "content to work in the modes as his forefathers had done, and we see no signs of his attempting to break away from this medieval system of tonality. . . . Unlike his English contemporaries, he tried no bold experiments in the direction of a newer tonality, and this contented habit of mind gives his music very frequently an uneventful character. But the note of mysticism was always present. Serene, aloof, and detached from mundane affairs, there is no note of materialism to be found in it. When he rises to his highest flights, they are flights of spiritual ecstasy, not those of declamation or pictorialism."

Zoë Kendrick Pyne has made an apt comparison between Palestrina's music and Renaissance tapestries, likening Palestrina's music to the art of "some marvelous piece of needlework, of weblike pattern, gleaming with gold, silver and soft colors, obeying the hidden laws of design, but presenting an indefinite yet gorgeous whole. The ear, like the eye, endeavors to distinguish the course of one thread, only to be deflected by another. It receives no exact impression, but the vague perception it conveys to the brain is of an agreeable, harmonious whole, rising to sensations of acute pleasure. This simile, however, fails in one important aspect: no general perception of color could affect the mind so powerfully as sound or produce the same moral effect. Palestrina's music penetrates the depths of the soul, and its selflessness widens the conception of things appertaining to the spirit. More, far more than a new formula of art, it was founded on antiquity and built up on international inspiration."

Principal Works

Choral Music—256 motets; 93 Masses; 4 books of madrigals; 3 books of Litanies; 3 books of Lamentations; 2 books of Madrigali Spirituali; Stabat Mater; hymns, offertories, psalms.

About

Coates, H., Palestrina; Einstein, A., The Italian Madrigal; Pyne, Z. K., Palestrina; Reese, G., Music in the Renaissance.

Felipe Pedrell *1841-1922*

AS A COMPOSER, theoretician, and scholar, Felipe Pedrell was the father of the Spanish nationalist school of music that began with Isaac Albéniz, continuing through Manuel de Falla. Pedrell was born in Tortosa, Spain, on February 19, 1841. As a boy chorister at the Tortosa Cathedral he was familiar with, and powerfully affected by, Spanish church music; in later life he often described the terror aroused in him by one of the old Spanish chants he was required to sing during a Good Friday procession. Most of Pedrell's musical education was self-acquired, but for a period he did receive formal instruction from Juan Antonio Nin y Serra, who encouraged Pedrell to use the folk tunes he had learned from his mother as thematic material for his exercises; thus Pedrell's life-long fascination with Spanish folk songs was first stimulated. His earliest compositions, written when he was about fifteen, show signs of dependence on Spanish folk sources.

Pedrell's first published music appeared in 1871. His first opera was completed three years later; it was *El último Abencerraje,* based on a Catalan libretto which he himself had prepared. The opera was produced at the Barcelona Liceo on April 14, 1874. In 1867 Pedrell had begun to write articles on music for Spanish journals, and between 1873 and 1874 he earned his living conducting operettas in Barcelona.

For a time Pedrell traveled in Italy and visited Paris. By 1882 he had returned to Barcelona, where he founded a weekly journal and a firm devoted to the publication of religious music. In 1888 he organized, and from then until 1896 edited, the *Ilustración musical Hispano-Americana.* He also absorbed himself in extensive researches in both Spanish folk music and the church and secular compositions of the early Spanish polyphonic masters.

Pedrell's major creative activity at that time was an opera trilogy entitled *Los Pirineos,* based on a Catalan libretto by Victor Belaguer, in which he hoped to embody his theories and concepts of Spanish musical nationalism. He explained his ideas in a monograph, *Por nuestra música,* published in Barcelona in 1891 as an explanatory preface for his opera. Here he maintained that "the character of a truly national music is to be found not only in the popular song and in the instinct of primitive ages, but also in the genius and in the masterpieces of the great centuries of art."

Los Pirineos was performed for the first time in Barcelona on January 4, 1902, in an Italian translation. Its first presentation in Spanish took place in Buenos Aires on September 10, 1910. César Cui, one of the members of the renowned Russian national school "The Five," admired this opera. He wrote, "[Its] nobility of style, the strength of its conviction, the avoidance of any and every concession to the prevailing taste, together with its originality and maturity, render this work a gratifying phenomenon amid the commercialized products of modern opera music. It is the creation of a great and high-minded artist."

In 1894 Pedrell settled in Madrid, where he became one of the city's most prominent and active musicians. He became a member of the Royal Academy of Fine Arts, and was chosen by the government to carry out a reform of Spanish church music. Between 1895 and 1903 he was a professor at the Madrid Conservatory, where his influence was absorbed by pupils who were destined to carry on his ideals—Granados, Falla, and others. Pedrell also lectured on music history at the Ateneo.

Pedrell's activities in music research were ambitious. In 1894 he started to edit the monumental *Hispaniae scholae musica sacra,* an eight-volume anthology of great Spanish church music. From 1896 to 1899 he edited the journal *Música religiosa.* His subsequent achievements in scholarship included his editions of the complete works of the sixteenth-century polyphonic master Tomás Luis de Victoria, and of the entire keyboard literature of Antonio de Cabezón, as well as the compilation of two anthologies: the first, of classical organ music by Spanish masters; the second, of Andalusian, Moorish, Catalonian, and Basque folk music.

Despite his varied activities, Pedrell continued his composition. He wrote several operas after *Los Pirineos,* including *La Celestina,* based on a sixteenth-century Spanish literary classic, *Comedia de Calisto y Melibea,* which Camille Bellaigue once described as the Spanish *Tristan und Isolde.* Pedrell also wrote various orchestral works and several large-scale compositions for chorus. But his music never proved popular even in Spain, and none of it has survived in the living repertory. Gilbert Chase explained: "Pedrell's chief aesthetic failing was probably that he interpreted his own doctrine too literally. In attempting to give a national color to his operas he often borrowed entire passages from the works of the old Spanish masters; and the popular themes that he uses in his operas, while exquisitely harmonized, are not always sufficiently integrated into the texture of the work."

Anthony Clyne further analyzed the weaknesses of Pedrell's music: "He was himself incapable of entirely discarding the meretricious sentimentality, acquired through the influence of foreigners, especially the Germans, of an age when true romance was in all the arts so often counterfeited. So anxious to make his music expressive, he did not see that it was not sufficient to use the material of folk music with the technique of European music, but that its own technique must be involved. Its rhythmic and modal characteristics were the essence of its beauty and value. Intensely patriotic, he nevertheless overlaid the racial and traditional qualities with a structure un-Spanish, producing a mixture of irreconcilable styles."

Nevertheless, for J. B. Trend, Pedrell's best works were characterized by "serenity as well as strength in his emotions, and an unusual sense of mystery, or of poetry." And for Manuel de Falla (as quoted by Gilbert Chase), Pedrell's music possessed "individuality in the means of expressions, serene emotional strength, and extraordinary evocative power."

In 1904 Pedrell returned to Barcelona, where he devoted himself to writing, editing, research, and composition. Though he was greatly honored, particularly on the occasion of his seventieth birthday in 1911, he was bitter that his own works were never properly appreciated. "They have never done me justice," he told Manuel de Falla, "either in Catalonia or in the rest of Spain. They have constantly tried to belittle me, saying that I was a great critic, or a great historian, but not a good composer. It is not true. I *am* a good composer! I do not want respect for my years, but for my work. Let them hear it and study it; they will then be able to judge!"

Illness and poverty further darkened Pedrell's last years. He died in Barcelona on August 19, 1922.

Pedrell's influence in Spanish music can hardly be exaggerated. He brought to the attention of the entire world of music the riches to be found in Spanish music of the past; pointed up the importance of Spanish folk songs and dances; directed the creative talent of many of his most significant contemporaries to musical nationalism. "For my part," said Manuel de Falla, "I affirm that it is to the lessons of Pedrell and to the powerful stimulation exercised on me by his works that I owe my artistic life." André Cœuroy said, "He made of Spanish music a living and vibrant art. The Joaquín Turinas and the Manuel de Fallas of our day would not have become what they are if this predecessor—he of the white beard—had not guided them. Thus Pedrell has known the purest joy that can be experienced by pioneers—that of having assisted, while living, to the triumph and culmination of his life's ideal."

Principal Works
Chamber Music—String Quartet.
Choral Music—Canço llatina; Misa da gloria; Requiem; Hymne à Ste. Thérèse; Te Deum; antiphons, cantatas, motets.
Operas—El último Abencerraje; Quasimodo; Mazeppa; Tasse à Ferrare; Cléopâtre; Los Pirineos; La Celestina (Comedia de Calisto y Melibea).
Orchestral Music—Excelsior; Arnau (with chorus); Glosa (with chorus); Cant de la montanya; I Trionfi; Marcha de la coronación a Mistral.
Piano Music—Escenas de niños (for piano duet).
Vocal Music—Les Orientales; Canciones arabescas; Consolations.

About
Blom, E., Stepchildren of Music; Chase, G., The Music of Spain; Trend, J. B., Manuel de Falla and Spanish Music.
Music and Letters, July 1926; Musical Quarterly, April 1924; La Nouvelle Revue, January 1912; La Revue musicale, February 1923.

Giovanni Battista Pergolesi *1710-1736*

GIOVANNI BATTISTA PERGOLESI, composer of *La Serva padrona*, with which *opera buffa* originated, was born in Jesi, near Ancona, Italy, on January 4, 1710.

Pergolesi: pār-gō-lā′sē

GIOVANNI BATTISTA PERGOLESI

His ancestors, named Draghi, had come from the town of Pergola, from which they took their name. Pergolesi's father was a surveyor and a sergeant in the Jesi militia. Three of his children died in infancy. The fourth, Giovanni Battista, was so sickly from birth that he was not expected to live either.

A musical child, he received his earliest instruction from the Marchese Gabriele Ripanti, who gave him violin lessons. The boy then became a pupil of Francesco Santi, director of the cathedral choir, and of Francesco Mondini. A local nobleman, the Marchese Cardolo Maria Pianetti, provided the funds for young Pergolesi to go to Naples in or about 1726 and enroll at the Conservatorio dei Poveri di Gesù Cristo. Pergolesi remained in Naples five years, a pupil of Greco and Durante in counterpoint and of Domenico de Matteis in violin. Pergolesi's talent on the violin made a particularly strong impression. On several occasions he drew fees for performing during the carnival season in Naples. He also made notable progress as a composer. His first major work was a large-scale choral composition in dramatic style, *La Conversione di S. Guglielmo d'Aquitania*, performed at the Sant' Agnello Maggiore Monastery during the summer of 1731. His first opera, *Sallustia*, was performed the following winter at the Teatro San Bartolomeo in Naples. At that time it was customary to give short comic scenes (intermezzi) between the acts of a serious opera in order to provide a change of mood and pace. During the performance of *Sallustia,* Pergolesi introduced such an intermezzo, his first attempt at writing comic opera. The production of still another comic stage work, *Lo frate 'nnammorato,* enjoyed immense success at the Teatro dei Fiorentini. Pergolesi was commissioned by the city of Naples to compose a Mass after a series of earthquakes.

In 1733 Pergolesi completed his masterwork, *La Serva padrona.* Its première took place at the Teatro San Bartolomeo in Naples on August 28, 1733, between the acts of Pergolesi's serious opera *Il Prigionier superbo.* The "intermezzo in two parts," as it was then described, took Naples by storm, and the rest of Europe was hardly less appreciative. In its use of everyday characters and simple situations; in its avoidance of a large cast and elaborate sets and costumes; in its humor derived from a scheming servant and the wily machinations of a valet; in its unpretentious, unornamented melodies —in all this *La Serva padrona* helped to establish some of the methods, approaches, and materials adopted by later composers of *opera buffa.*

Music historians now regard *La Serva padrona* as the first *opera buffa,* even though it is not the first comic opera ever written; certainly it is the first of this genre still able to afford pleasure to a sophisticated musical audience. "The little opera," remarked Karl Nef, "is so lively in its music, so telling in its characterization, so full of jests and humor that it has continued as a masterpiece of the first rank until the present day."

Only three characters are employed, and one of them, a valet, is a mute. There is no chorus. In each of the two sections of what is essentially a one-act opus, there are arias for the two principals and a duet. The plot concerns the efforts of Uberto to find himself a wife in order to extricate himself from the wiles and whims of his servant, Serpina: but Serpina, with the help of the valet, so manages to arouse his jealousy that he finally marries her.

For Paul Bekker *La Serva padrona* was among "the most astonishing things the theater has to show in any age. Two speaking characters, no decorations—nothing could be more primitive. . . . The astonishing thing is the variety exhibited within that narrow circle. Nothing more can be said about the interplay of man and woman than bass and soprano tell each other and enact in their raving, dancing and singing. It may be this element of eternal validity that gives Pergolesi's work its incomparable effect. . . . It remains . . . alive and inimitable. While it contained, as the first work, the essence of the entire species, it left to later times the possibilities of formal expansion and productive elaboration. But everything essential it had itself established beyond excelling."

The impact of *La Serva padrona* on composers of opera throughout Europe was immediate and profound. In Italy, it became the model which such composers as Cimarosa, Galuppi, Paisiello, and Rossini followed in writing their own comic opera. In France, where the opera was performed for the first time in 1752 by a visiting Italian company, it created a schism among French musicians. Some regarded it as the ideal opera, as opposed to the more cerebral and dramatic creations of Rameau. Among those who extolled Italian opera in general, and Pergolesi in particular, were Diderot and Rousseau; the latter wrote a little comic opera of his own in frank imitation of Pergolesi, *Le Devin du village,* introduced at Fontainebleau in 1752, and at the Paris Opera in 1753. Opposing Diderot and Rousseau were those convinced that Rameau was the true apostle of opera. The struggle between the two factions is now identified as *"le guerre des bouffons."* Rousseau was not the only Frenchman to write operas in the style of Pergolesi. Monsigny and Grétry were others who wrote little light operas, helping to create a French school of comic opera.

Early in 1734 Pergolesi became a deputy to the *maestro di cappella* of Naples. Later that year, the Duke of Maddaloni invited him to Rome to direct a performance of his Mass in F major at the San Lorenzo Church. It proved so successful that Pergolesi was given a commission to write an opera for the Teatro Tordinona in Rome: *L'Olimpiade,* produced early in January of 1735. This (the first of Pergolesi's stage works to get a hearing outside Naples) did not do well. The audience, in fact, proved so hostile that, at one point, someone in the theater threw an orange at the composer, who was directing the performance from the harpsichord.

Pergolesi appears to have been employed briefly by the Duke of Maddaloni. After returning to Naples, Pergolesi was engaged as organist at the court chapel. He now completed several important choral works including four Salve Reginas and a cantata, *Orfeo*. His last work for the stage was an *opera buffa*, *Flaminio*, successfully performed at the Teatro Nuovo in the fall of 1735.

By 1736 Pergolesi's health had gravely deteriorated. A victim of consumption, he was ordered by his physician to take a rest cure, and he went to Pozzuoli where he found shelter in a Capuchin monastery. There he completed his last work, the Stabat Mater, much of it written while he was feverish. This work, commissioned by the Confraternity of S. Luigi di Palazzo of Naples, had brought him a paltry advance of ten ducats.

Pergolesi died in Pozzuoli on March 16, 1736, at the age of twenty-six. He was buried in a pauper's grave on the grounds of the cathedral. His meager possessions were sold in order to raise the sum of eleven ducats needed to defray the expenses of the shabby funeral.

Though Pergolesi wrote a good deal of instrumental music, many of the works in this category long attributed to him have recently been found to be the work of other composers. Some of the material used by the twentieth-century composer Igor Stravinsky for two suites presumably based on Pergolesi's melodies—the *Suite italienne* and *Pulcinella*—is now believed to lack authenticity.

Nevertheless, there remains a considerable amount of instrumental music—together with operas and numerous choral works—which are unquestionably by Pergolesi and which place him with the foremost Italian masters of his day. Paul Marie Masson went so far as to compare Pergolesi favorably with Mozart. "There exists between Pergolesi and the author of *Don Giovanni* a close parental tie," said Masson. "One finds with each of them the same quality of soul, the same nimble gaiety or, in the sadness, the same elegiac sweetness. And it is not only in sentiment that they resemble each other but in style as well, by the general form of their art. There are entire pages of Pergolesi which one would say had been written by Mozart; there are the same melodic out-lines, the same method of harmonization and accompaniment."

PRINCIPAL WORKS

Chamber Music—Various sonatas for solo instruments and continuo.
Choral Music—Cantatas, Masses, oratorios, Salve Reginas, Stabat Mater.
Harpsichord Music—Sonatas; 16 Lessons.
Operas—Salustia; Lo frate 'nnammorato; Il Prigioner superbo; La Serva padrona; Adriano in Siria; La Contadina astuta; L'Olimpiade; Flaminio.
Orchestral Music—Concertos for solo instrument or instruments and orchestra; 2 sinfonie.

ABOUT

Luciani, S. A., Giovanni Battista Pergolesi: Note e documenti; Schlitzer, G., Giovanni Battista Pergolesi.
Monthly Musical Record, October 1950; Music and Letters, October 1949; Rassegna musicale, Special Issue, 1936.

Jacopo Peri *1561-1633*

JACOPO PERI, composer of the first opera in musical history, was born in Florence on August 20, 1561; he was descended from Florentine nobility. He was nicknamed "Il Zazzerino" by his contemporaries, because of his thick shock of hair. After studying music with Cristofano Malvezzi in Lucca, Peri became a member of the musical establishment at the palace of the Medicis in Florence, first with Ferdinando I, and later with Cosimo II. He soon achieved considerable note in Florence as a singer and composer, his earliest compositions having been published by his former teacher, Malvezzi. In 1601 he was appointed court musician in Ferrara.

In or about 1580, Peri became a member of the *Camerata* in Florence, a group of the city's leading noblemen and dilettantes who aspired to revive the dramatic forms, and who created a new style of music—the *stile rappresentativo* consisting of declamation or monody. (For a more detailed discussion of the Camerata and the "Nuove musiche" or "New music," see the sketch on Emilio del Cavalieri.) After other members of the Camerata, notably Cavalieri and Vincenzo Galilei, had made important experiments and progress with this new style, Jacopo Peri became the composer to set a stage work entirely to musical recitative. In doing so he was the first composer to write an opera.

That opera—or, as Peri officially designated it, *"dramma per musica"*—was *Dafne,* written to a text by Rinuccini, and completed in 1597. In his preface to his second opera, *Euridice,* Peri explained in detail his aim and purpose in evolving this new genre in music:

"It pleased Signor Corsi and Rinuccini to have me set to music the play of *Dafne* . . . treating it in a new manner. I was to show by a simple experiment of what the song of our age is capable. I decided that I must accordingly seek in my music to imitate one who speaks. . . . For it seemed to me that ancient Greeks and Romans . . . must have made use of a sort of music which, while surpassing the sounds of ordinary speech, fell far short of the melody of singing, and assumed the shape of something intermediate between the two. . . . Therefore, abandoning every style of vocal writing hitherto known, I gave myself up wholly to contriving the sort of imitation demanded by this poem. And, considering that the sort of vocal delivery applied by the ancients to singing . . . could be somewhat accelerated, so as to hold a mean course between the slow and deliberate pace of singing and the nimble, rapid pace of speaking (thus making it serve my purpose); considering this, I also recognized that we pass through other sounds in speech which are not so intoned until we return to the one which is capable of forming a new consonance. And, having regard for the accents and modes of expression we use (in grief, rejoicing, and so on), I made the bass move at a rate appropriate to them, now faster, now slower, according to the emotions that were expressed. And I sustained the bass through both dissonances and consonances, until the speaker's voice, after passing through various degrees of pitch, comes to those sounds which, being intoned in ordinary speech, facilitate the formation of a new consonance."

Words such as these sounded an emancipation proclamation for music, establishing a permanent break with the old polyphonic style which had dominated music for several centuries; they announced the new homophonic idiom which emphasized a single melody based on a harmonic foundation.

Dafne was based, of course, on the classical myth in which the nymph is changed into a laurel tree by her mother to protect her from the pursuing god Apollo, to whom the laurel then becomes sacred. Peri's opera told the story in a series of recitatives, punctuated occasionally by short dances and choral episodes; a harpsichord, lute, or lyre was used to accompany the voice. *Dafne* was heard for the first time during the carnival of 1597 in Florence, at the Palazzo Corsi, with Peri himself enacting the part of Apollo. This performance was so successful that the opera was revived several times in the next two years, with various changes and additions.

The score of *Dafne* has been lost, but Peri's second opera, *Euridice,* published in 1601, has survived. Consequently, this is the first opera in music history to come down to us intact. *Euridice,* also composed to a text by Rinuccini, was the first operatic treatment of the legend of Orpheus and Eurydice, which was to become a favorite subject with opera composers. Written on commission for the wedding ceremonies of Henry IV of France and Maria de' Medici, *Euridice* was introduced at the Palazzo Pitti in Florence on October 6, 1600, with Peri appearing in the part of Orpheus. There was neither overture nor any independent instrumental interludes. The vocal accompaniment was provided by four instruments behind the scenes: a harpsichord, two lutes, and a lyre. The story was told in a succession of recitatives by the principal characters, some in free rhythm, others in regular meter. Several dances and choruses injected a note of variety.

Alan Rich, expressing a twentieth century reaction to Peri's *Euridice* in a review of the first complete recording of the opera ever made (1963), wrote in the New York *Times:* "Truth to tell, the interest in this Peri album lies far more in its mere existence as a historical document than as a genuinely exciting musical experience. One can admire the simple plasticity of Peri's melodies and his graceful subservience to the demands of the prosody of Ottavio Rinuccini's libretto. But the music remains an experiment, not a realization. . . . Peri, as an ardent proselytizer, constantly overstates the need for the new simplicity and ends with a piece that is dramatically so flaccid as to have no musical life at all."

Nevertheless, the success of *Euridice* in 1600 proved beyond doubt that the new monodic style and the new musico-dramatic form evolved by the Camerata, had public acceptance. Three days after Peri's *Euridice* was introduced, a second operatic setting of the Orpheus and Eurydice legend was staged by another member of the Camerata, Caccini. (A few sections from the Caccini opera had been interpolated in Peri's *Euridice* at its première.) Comparing the two versions of *Euridice* which came so close to each other, Donald Jay Grout wrote, "Peri is perhaps somewhat more forceful in tragic expression, whereas Caccini is more tuneful, excels in elegiac moods, and gives more occasion for virtuoso singing."

After *Euridice*, Peri wrote music for two plays which were never produced (*Tetide* in 1608, and *Adone* in 1620). In 1608 he also wrote the recitatives for *Ariadne*, an opera to which Monteverdi contributed the arias; and in 1628 he collaborated with Marco da Gagliano on the opera *Flora*. In addition, he wrote a large body of music for court spectacles and entertainments; much of it has been lost.

In 1608 Peri was Marco da Gagliano's deputy as music director at the San Lorenzo Church, and between 1622 and 1623 he wrote music for the choir at San Nicola in Pisa. Peri died in Florence on August 12, 1633.

PRINCIPAL WORKS

Choral Music—Madrigals.
Operas—Dafne; Euridice.

ABOUT

Grout, D. J., A Short History of Opera.
Rassegna musicale, April 1933; Sammelbände der Internationalen Musik-Gesellschaft, 1913.

François André Philidor *1726-1795*

FRANÇOIS ANDRÉ DANICAN PHILIDOR, a highly successful and prolific composer of *opéra-comique,* was born in Dreux, France, on September 7, 1726. His family was one which had enriched French music for generations. His father, André Philidor *l'aîné*, who died in 1730, was a member of the music staff of Louis XIV and had composed a large body of music for royal entertainments.

As a boy, François André Philidor showed as much talent for chess as for music; throughout his life he pursued both activities with rewarding results. He received lessons in harmony from André Campra

FRANÇOIS ANDRÉ PHILIDOR

while serving as a page at the royal chapel. Later he moved to Paris, where he earned his living giving lessons and copying music. Probably in despair at ever succeeding as a musician, he decided to forsake art for chess. By the time he was eighteen he had become one of Europe's foremost chess players. For a number of years he toured Europe, challenging the foremost chess masters of the time. In London, in or about 1749, he made chess history by winning three games simultaneously against three formidable opponents without once looking down at the boards. He also published a highly popular treatise on chess.

In 1754 he was back in Paris. Soon thereafter he returned to music, completing motets with which he hoped to secure a post as Surintendant de la Musique to the King. To Philidor's acute disappointment, the job went to his competitor. But this fact did not dissuade him from composition. He arranged several popular airs for *Le Diable à quatre*, his first stage work, which was produced at the Théâtre de la Foire Saint-Laurent in 1756. Success came with *Blaise le savetier*, performed at the Théâtre de la Foire Saint-Germain on March 9, 1759. Convinced by now that writing opera was his forte, Philidor combined his career as a chess player with that of composer for the theater. Between 1759 and 1795 he completed over thirty operas. The most successful were *Le Maréchal ferrant* in 1761; *Sancho*

Pança dans son île in 1762; *Le Sorcier in* 1764; *Tom Jones* (based on Fielding's novel) in 1765; the grand opera *Ernelinde, princesse de Norvège* in 1767; *La Nouvelle école des femmes* in 1770; *Le Puits d'amour* in 1779; and *La Belle esclave* in 1787. His last opera, *Bélisaire*, was produced posthumously at the Théâtre Favart more than a year after his death.

Philidor was one of the most popular composers of his generation. Although few of his works have survived, he was also one of the most significant. In his use of harmony, orchestra and chorus, in his deployment of voices singly and in ensemble, in the dramatic force of his lyricism, and in the originality of his structure he was superior even to such distinguished contemporaries as Monsigny and Grétry.

Philidor spent a part of each year in London, where he received a regular pension from the Chess Club, and where his fame as a composer was almost equal to his success in Paris. He died in London on August 24, 1795.

PRINCIPAL WORKS

Chamber Music—L'Art de modulation.
Choral Music—Motets.
Operas—About 50 comic and serious operas, including: Blaise le Savetier; Le Maréchal ferrant; Sancho Pança; Le Sorcier; Tom Jones; Ernelinde, princesse de Norvège (later renamed Sandomir, Prince de Danemark); Le Jardinier de Sidon; L'Amant déguisé; La Nouvelle école des femmes; Le Bon fils; Les Femmes vengées; Le Puits d'amour; Persée; L'Amitié au village; La Belle esclave; Le Mari comme il les faudrait tous; Bélisaire.
Vocal Music—Ariettes périodiques.

ABOUT

Allen, G., The Life of Philidor; Blom, E., Stepchildren of Music; Bonnet, G. E., Philidor et l'évolution de la musique française au XVIIIe siècle; Lardin, A., Philidor peint par lui-même.

Niccolò Piccini *1728-1800*

NICCOLÒ PICCINI (or Piccinni), a dominant figure in eighteenth-century Italian opera, serious and comic, was born in Bari, near Naples, on January 16, 1728. His father though a professional musician—a violinist in the orchestra of the Basilica di San Nicola—preferred to prepare his son for the Church rather than for a career in music. It was the Archbishop of Bari himself who, impressed with young Niccolò's talent

for improvisation on the harpsichord, prevailed on the elder Piccini to permit his son to develop his gifts. In 1742 Piccini entered the Conservatorio di Sant' Onofrio. At first he was dissatisfied with the school because one of his instructors was a ruthless martinet; but when the Conservatory director, Leo, took the boy under his wing, Piccini responded more favorably and began to make excellent progress. Later Piccini became one of Durante's favorite pupils; that master once remarked, "The others are my students, but this one is my son."

Piccini remained at the Conservatory for about twelve years. Then, through the help and influence of the Prince of Ventimiglia, he saw the production of his first opera, the *opera buffa Le Donne dispettose*, which was introduced with outstanding success at the Teatro dei Fiorentini in the fall of 1754. Demands for more operas led Piccini to write several successful works. Two of these were operas in a dramatic vein that revealed his rapidly expanding creative powers: *Zenobia*, seen at the Teatro San Carlo in Naples on December 18, 1756, and *Alessandro nell'Indie*, presented at the Teatro Argentina in Rome on January 21, 1758.

In 1756 Piccini married Vincenzia Sibilla, a gifted singer who had been one of his pupils. When Piccini married Vincenzia, she had already made her mark in opera, and Piccini felt certain that no one could sing his music better than she; yet he insisted that his wife abandon a professional career and devote herself entirely to domesticity. She willingly acceded.

The work generally regarded as Piccini's masterwork in the *buffa* style, and one of the most popular works of *opera buffa* written in the latter half of the eighteenth century, was produced at the Teatro delle Dame in Rome on February 6, 1760. It was *La Buona figliuola*, or *La Cecchina*, written text by Goldoni, freely based on Samuel Richardson's novel *Pamela*. *La Buona figliuola* took the world by storm. It was performed by every kind of troupe, including a marionette theater, and entered the repertory of virtually every important opera company in Europe. Clothes, wines, villas, toys were named *alla cecchina*. Its tunes were heard everywhere. Performance took place even in such remote countries as China, where the Emperor demanded a private performance at his palace.

Piccini: pēt-chē′nē

Eric Blom has written that this opera "is replete with a fluency and vivacity that are quite in the best vein of the comic opera of this period. . . . It is mellifluous, pretty music, written without any great care to fit it to the stage situation, yet with more of that care than the public of the time, who simply wanted to hear agreeable music, ever suspected. There are some delightful harmonies and surprising modulations in this little opera, besides occasional attempts to create dramatic effect by means of tremolos and other conventional tricks." Verdi remarked to Boito that he considered *La Buona figliuola* to be the first genuine comic opera, and that its quintets and sextets were models which composers of choral music should be required to study.

Piccini now marched from success to success, in both comic and serious opera. He was amazingly prolific: in 1761 he had ten operas produced; in 1762, seven. For several years there was no composer in all of Italy to rival him in popularity or artistic importance. This fortunate state of affairs, however, was eventually to change. In 1773 the young composer Anfossi, one of Piccini's former pupils, gained extreme popularity, robbing Piccini's fame of much of its luster. Indeed, at a performance of one of Piccini's operas, the followers of Anfossi created a mild scandal. This incident affected Piccini so deeply that he decided to leave Rome and return to Naples, the scene of his first triumphs. There his popularity was still unblemished. He prepared a second version of *Alessandro nell'Indie* in 1774, and a new *opera buffa, I Viaggiatori,* which was so highly acclaimed it remained on the boards for four seasons.

In December 1776 Piccini was invited by the Paris Opéra to go to the French capital and write works for the Opéra at a yearly income of six thousand francs. Piccini enjoyed great favor at the French court, where twice a week he gave singing lessons to the Queen. He was also appointed director of an Italian opera troupe that performed at the Opéra on alternate nights. Musicians and the general public adulated him.

Piccini's first French opera, *Roland,* produced on January 27, 1778, was an immense success. After that he helped to produce at the Opéra some of his more celebrated Italian works, including *La Buona figliuola.* His numerous admirers now banded together to

NICCOLÒ PICCINI

use him in an attack on Gluck, who then also enjoyed great successes in Paris. Thus a bitter feud began between those who favored the Italian opera traditions carried out by Piccini and those who sided with Gluck in his revolution against the Italian school. It should be emphasized that in this schism Piccini himself played no active part, for he himself admired Gluck greatly and had no sympathy with any attempts to discredit him.

The climax of the war between the two camps occurred when both composers were commissioned by the Paris Opéra to write works on the same subject, *Iphigénie en Tauride.* Gluck's was produced first, on May 18, 1779, with such triumph that Piccini's adherents were effectively silenced. Piccini did not complete his own opera within the prescribed time; and when it was finally produced, on January 23, 1781, it proved far less successful than Gluck's, largely because of a series of unfortunate accidents that marred the performance—including the fact that Mlle Laguerre, who sang Iphigénie, was obviously inebriated.

After Gluck left Paris, Piccini continued for some time to occupy an exalted position in the operatic life of the city. *Didon,* probably his greatest French opera, was performed on October 16, 1783 at Fontainebleau at the request of the King; soon afterwards it was produced at the Opéra, where it retained its popularity for almost half a century. But before long, Piccini's fame went into sharp decline as a new Italian composer arose to win Parisian favor—Sacchini.

The French Revolution deprived Piccini of his pension and of his position as *maître de chant* at the École Royale de Chant et de Declaration, which he had held since 1784. He now returned to Naples, where he was given a modest pension by the King. But he soon became embroiled in political difficulties. When his daughter married a Frenchman with pronounced revolutionary leanings, he was suspected of being a Jacobin. Discredited at the Neapolitan court, he found that his operas were also being booed and hissed.

For about four years Piccini suffered extreme poverty and personal abuse; for a while he was even subjected to house arrest. Finally, through the intervention of some powerful friends he was granted permission to leave Naples. After a short stay in Rome he returned to Paris, where in 1798 he was given a warm welcome. The French government presented him with a purse of five thousand francs to provide for his immediate needs, and promised him a pension; the latter, however, was paid only at irregular intervals. Napoleon commissioned him to write a military march and the Conservatory appointed him Inspecteur.

But the reverses he had suffered undermined his health. Paralysis set in, and his waning strength was further sapped by the continual bleedings to which surgeons subjected him. He went to Passy for a rest cure, and there he died on May 7, 1800.

One of Piccini's contemporaries described him as being "under middle size, but well-made, his carriage bespeaking dignity. His figure had been very agreeable, his forehead was large and open, his eyes blue and . . . with an expression both sweet and spirited and sometimes animated and sparkling. . . . The form of his nose, and the union of this feature with the forehead, reminded one of the Greeks. .·. . His mind was quick, extended, and cultivated. . . . His principles in art were severe."

"As a man," said Francis Toye, "Piccini must rank as one of the most charming musicians who ever lived. He was simple, modest, quite devoid of jealousy and incapable of intrigue. When Gluck died, Piccini tried to raise money to establish an annual memorial concert. The project failed for lack of support, but the benevolence of the gesture remains. Less known but equally remarkable is the fact that he insisted on pronouncing the funeral oration on Sacchini—his new rival, who had been imported when Gluck left Paris."

Cecil Gray lamented the fact that a composer of Piccini's endowments should have been used as a weapon in the attack against Gluck in Paris, insisting that "Gluck is incontestably a great musical dramatist, but as a musician pure and simple, he is incontestably the inferior of his rival." Gray also deplored the fact that "such a noble and highly gifted artist . . . should have been held up in musical histories to derision and contempt, and regarded as a typical representative of all the most pernicious tendencies in operatic art."

"He [Piccini] was a strong personality and a considerable intellect and technically well equipped," commented Bernard van Dieren. "His music has an elegant stateliness, an easy flexibility, and a balanced clarity such as are rarely found combined with so much strength and purpose. He has dramatic muscle, together with exquisite nervous sensibility. His melody emotionally pulsated with a subtlety that has been rarely equaled before the advent of Verdi."

Niccolò Piccini left two sons. Ludovico (1766-1827) was a *Kapellmeister* in Sweden and died in Paris; he was the composer of many operas. Little is known about Piccini's other son, Giuseppe; but Giuseppe's son, Louis Alexandre (1779-1850), wrote over two hundred works for the French stage, including twenty-five comic operas.

PRINCIPAL WORKS

Choral Music—3 oratorios; Mass; psalms.

Operas—Over 115 comic and serious operas, including: Le Donne dispettose; Zenobia; Alessandro nell'Indie (two settings); La Buona figliuola (or, La Cecchina); Demofoonte; Artaserse; L'Olimpiade (two settings); Demetrio; Catone in Utica; La Contessina; I Viaggiatori; Roland; Atys; Iphigénie en Tauride; Didon; Le Faux lord; Pénélope; Le Mensonge officieux; Griselda.

ABOUT

Blom, E., Stepchildren of Music; Curzon, H. de, Les Dernières années de Piccini; Della Corte, A., Piccini; Dieren, B. van, Down Among the Dead Men; Pascazio, N., L'Uomo Piccini, e la "querelle célèbre."

Opera News, April 14, 1962.

Amilcare Ponchielli *1834-1886*

A MILCARE PONCHIELLI, composer of *La Gioconda,* was born in Paderno Fasolaro, near Cremona, Italy, on August 31, 1834. His father, a humble shopkeeper, was the local church organist. A musical child, Amilcare received instruction from his father before entering the Milan Conservatory at the age of nine. While a student, he collaborated with three other Conservatory pupils in writing an operetta that was produced in Milan on March 3, 1851. He was graduated from the Conservatory in 1853.

In 1854 Ponchielli became organist of the Church of S. Ilario in Cremona. For some years he devoted himself to the composition of an ambitious serious opera, *I Promessi sposi,* based on Manzoni's famous novel. The work received moderate recognition when it was introduced in Cremona on August 30, 1856.

For a number of years following the première of *I Promessi sposi,* Ponchielli served as bandmaster of the National Guard at Piacenza, also undertaking other uninspired musical activities and orchestrations in order to earn a living. At the same time he completed a number of operas which were produced in Cremona or Piacenza without particular success.

In an attempt to improve his financial situation and escape his drab occupations, Ponchielli applied for a position as professor of counterpoint at the Milan Conservatory. Although his references were excellent, the post went to Franco Faccio, who the Conservatory authorities felt needed the job more than Ponchielli. It is indicative of Ponchielli's lack of bitterness and envy that when a newspaperman in Milan attempted to create a controversy out of the issue Ponchielli quickly silenced him.

At this point Ponchielli, past his thirtieth birthday, obscure as a composer, and unsuccessful as a musician, had reconciled himself to a humble existence. "I accepted," he later admitted, "whatever fate had in store for me."

Then he submitted a revised version of his opera, *I Promessi sposi,* to the director of the Teatro dal Verme, a new opera house about to open in Milan. The director liked it so well that he decided to mount it as the opening presentation of his theater. Teresina Brambilla, who later became Pon-

AMILCARE PONCHIELLI

chielli's wife, performed the leading role of Lucia at the première of the opera on December 5, 1872. The work was a complete triumph: the overture and several arias were repeated, at the audience's insistence, and there were forty curtain calls. On the following morning, the powerful publishing house of Ricordi promptly contracted with Ponchielli for a new opera. La Scala commissioned a ballet score. When Verdi learned of Ponchielli's success he commented sadly, "Of all the operatic composers I know, Ponchielli is the best. But, alas! he is no longer young; I think he must be about forty, and he has seen and heard too much. You know my opinions on hearing too much!"

Ponchielli wrote the scores for two ballets presented by La Scala: *Le Due gemelle,* presented in February 1873, and *Clarina,* which followed it at the Teatro dal Verme in September the same year. Both were well received. In the meanwhile, he was completing the opera he had agreed to write for Ricordi. *I Lituani* was presented at La Scala on March 7, 1874, with such success that it was performed soon afterwards in St. Petersburg by command of the Czar.

Ponchielli now went to work on the opera that brought him world fame and that has assured the survival of his name. It was *La Gioconda,* written to a libretto by Arrigo Boito (under the pseudonym of Tobia Gorrio) which was based on Victor Hugo's his-

Ponchielli: pōng-kyĕl'lē

torical drama *Angelo, tyran de Padoue*. The world première took place at La Scala on April 8, 1876. An Italian critic, evaluating *La Gioconda* after the première, wrote: "Ponchielli's score shows that he has fully grasped the poet's intentions. True to the school of which Boito made himself the champion, and after many years of hard struggle, Ponchielli had endeavored to write dramatic music which being descriptive of the action abounds in color and instrumental effects. . . . *La Gioconda* is an energetic and laudable effort to infuse fresh vigor into Italian opera."

La Gioconda placed Ponchielli with the foremost Italian opera composers of his time. Its première in England, at Covent Garden in 1883, was also a huge success. The first American performance was given during the first season of the Metropolitan Opera—on December 20, 1883—as the only new work presented that year. Its popularity in the United States is indicated by the fact that Oscar Hammerstein used it to open his second season of the Manhattan Opera in 1907, and that in 1909 Henry Russell chose it as the first presentation of his newly founded Boston Opera Company.

The contemporary critic Robert Lawrence has appraised *La Gioconda* as follows: "It makes no pretense at education or ennoblement; it is simply a good show. . . . What other opera can offer *three* leading women, a trio of male stars, a big chorus, an ensemble of children, a mammoth ballet divertissement, a regatta and—by way of scenic representation—the ducal palace of Venice. With all these ingredients, *Gioconda* can't miss and—provided there is a sympathetic audience—it usually doesn't." Yet, as Lawrence remarked, this opera, a "work of blood and guts, . . . has a way of courting the obvious, of trumpeting a thrice-told tale. . . . Its vulgarity is sumptuous, its emotional appeal direct and unashamed."

Without minimizing the musical or emotional effect of several leading arias—notably Enzo's romance, "Cielo e mar" and La Gioconda's dramatic narrative, "Suicidio!"—one may state that the most celebrated single excerpt from the opera is undoubtedly the "Dance of the Hours," a piece of orchestral music for ballet, symbolizing the victory of Right over Wrong, in which the dancers come out in groups of six to impersonate the hours of dawn, day, evening and night. "The ballet music," said R. A. Streatfeild, "shows many favorable examples of Ponchielli's fondness for fanciful melodic designs, a mannerism which has been freely imitated by his pupils and followers."

Ponchielli wrote three operas after *La Gioconda,* of which *Il Figliuol prodigo,* performed in 1880, was the most successful. From 1881 until his death Ponchielli was *maestro .di cappella* at the Bergamo Cathedral, writing church music for performance at the Cathedral. In 1883 he became professor of composition at the Milan Conservatory; one of his pupils was Giacomo Puccini. Ponchielli died of bronchial pneumonia in Milan on January 16, 1886.

PRINCIPAL WORKS

Ballets—Le Due gemelle; Clarina.
Choral Music—Cantata; Hymn; various church compositions.
Operas—I Promessi sposi; La Savoiarda (revised under the title Lina); Roderico; Bertrand de Born; I Lituani (revised under the title Aldona); La Gioconda; I Mori di Valenza; Il Figliuol prodigo; Marion Delorme.

ABOUT

Cesare, G., Amilcare Ponchielli nell'arte del suo tempo; Damerini, A., Amilcare Ponchielli; Napoli, G. de, Amilcare·Ponchielli.

Opera News, March 31, 1962.

Henry Purcell *1659-1695*

Henry PURCELL, the great English composer often described as "the father of English music," was born in the Westminster section of London in or about 1659. His father was Thomas Purcell, a distinguished musician and Gentleman of the Chapel Royal, not, as was long believed, Henry Purcell (who died in 1664) who was also a Gentleman of the Chapel Royal and master of the choristers at Westminster Abbey.

It is probable that in his childhood Henry Purcell received music instruction from his father. In 1669 the boy was admitted as a chorister to the Chapel Royal, where he studied music with Cooke, Humfrey, and John Blow. He wrote several compositions during this period, including several anthems, and in 1670 a birthday ode to King Charles II.

Purcell: pûr's'l

When Purcell's voice broke in 1673, he left the Chapel Royal and was appointed "keeper, maker, mender, repairer, and tuner of the King's instruments" at a salary of thirty pounds a year together with an allowance for his wardrobe. In 1676, through the influence of John Blow, Purcell was made copyist at Westminster Abbey, and in 1677 became "composer to the King's band." The year 1675 marked the appearance of his first publication, a song in the first volume of Playford's *Choice Ayres;* four years later Playford included several pieces by Purcell, including an elegy on the death of Matthew Locke, in the second volume of his anthology. A more important publication appeared in 1680—a group of twelve fantasias for viols in three and four parts. In this work the fantasia, a form of instrumental composition in contrapuntal style that had been favored by English composers since Byrd and Morley, came to its last phase of structural and artistic development. Even during Purcell's time it was regarded as outmoded, but Purcell succeeded in infusing it with new life through his immense technical skill and creative imagination. The most famous of his fantasias did not appear in this group of twelve pieces, but was released independently. It is the *Fantasia on One Note,* in F major, in five parts, with one viol holding throughout the piece a sustained "C" while the other viols weave fanciful melodies around it.

When John Blow resigned as organist of Westminster Abbey in 1679, Purcell succeeded him. Provided with adequate financial security, Purcell married Frances Peters the following year. Four sons and a daughter were born to the marriage. In 1682 (the year in which his first son, John Baptista, was born) Purcell was made organist of the Chapel Royal. A year later he published a noteworthy set of twelve sonatas for two violins and bass in the style of Corelli and Vitali. As he confessed in his preface, he imitated the work of the Italian masters. One of the works in this group is the *Golden Sonata* (Sonata in F major), among Purcell's most famous works in the sonata form. (Precisely who called this work "golden," and why, has never been explained.) Even more significant artistically is the Sonata No. 6 in G minor, an extraordinary chaconne which traverses a wide gamut of emotion and mood.

HENRY PURCELL

In 1685 Purcell received a new court appointment, assigned again to be keeper, repairer, and tuner of the King's instruments, this time including the winds.

Purcell's first association with the theater, for which he would write much of his most outstanding music, occurred in 1680, when he produced several airs and dances for *Theodosius.* He wrote incidental music for many plays after that, but only one of his stage works can be regarded as an opera, being the only one set to music throughout. This is his crowning masterwork, *Dido and Aeneas,* written to a libretto by Nahum Tate based on the fourth book of Virgil's *Aeneid.* Purcell wrote this opera in 1689 on a commission from Josias Priest, a ballet master who was the proprietor of a girls' boarding school in Chelsea; it was in this school that the opera was first performed.

Dido and Aeneas is one of the most important operas created in the seventeenth century, and the only English opera composed, in fact, before World War II that has held the stage. In writing his opera, Purcell profited greatly from Lully in his expressive recitatives, powerful dramatic writing, grand choruses, and effective ballets. But where Lully, even at his best, is dated today, Purcell's *Dido and Aeneas* remains a vibrant aesthetic experience throughout for a twentieth century audience. And where Lully had crystallized a French style, Purcell succeeded in creating an English style in many of his airs, dances, and choruses. *Dido and Aeneas,* said Gustav Holst, is "one of the most original expressions of genius in all opera."

Relating the style of the opera to the libretto, Eric Blom writes: "Tate had a knack of contriving rapid action, emotional climaxes, and a variety of *dramatis personae,* all of which was at any rate good enough to give a great dramatic composer his chance of, so to speak, throwing into relief what the libretto merely outlined in two dimensions. And what a great dramatic composer Purcell certainly was. His way of writing from beginning to end of this very condensed but superb masterpiece music that is perfectly satisfying by its own form and invention, yet fits every situation, intensifies every emotion, and outlines every character with unfailing aptness is not equaled by any other composer of his time. Lully is pallid and monotonous, Scarlatti formal by comparison. We have to look back to Monteverdi for anything to equal *Dido and Aeneas* in all respects and forward to Mozart for anything to surpass it in range and organization."

Certainly there is nothing in seventeenth-century opera—and few episodes in *all* opera —to equal the eloquence and affecting emotion of the closing scene of *Dido and Aeneas.* Its highlight is Dido's lament, "When I am laid in Earth," one of the highest points of inspiration in the entire score.

Purcell wrote admirable incidental music for many plays by England's foremost playwrights, including Dryden, Congreve, Shadwell, John Fletcher, and Shakespeare. In 1690 he contributed two songs to Dryden's *Amphitryon;* they made so deep an impression on the poet that Dryden sought Purcell out to initiate a collaboration and friendship. Purcell contributed music to more than half a dozen Dryden plays, the most important being *King Arthur,* produced in London in 1690. For Ernest Walker, *King Arthur* was one of Purcell's most significant achievements: "Purcell never wrote anything more finely organized than the spacious passacaglia in the fourth act, the structure of which is remarkable." A. K. Holland has said, "It is perhaps Purcell's most notable achievement on the purely musical plane. The sheer tunes are of unsurpassed beauty. 'How Blest are Shepherds,'

'Come if You Dare,' 'Two Daughters of This Aged Stream,' and 'Fairest Isle' are enshrined among the immortalities of music. . . . The pastoral tunes, the sturdy choruses, the three-four measures with their varying accents, the dramatic declamation, the racy word-setting, the consummate use of descriptive devices as in the celebrated 'Frost Scene' are all here."

Outstanding in Purcell's theater music was his uncommon gift for adapting his writing to the inflections of the English tongue. "It can truthfully be said," J. A. Westrup has written, "that no other composer, before or since, has succeeded so well in translating into music the accents of the English language. This mastery is not confined to pieces in the recitative style, effective though these are. It extends also to purely lyrical works. Purcell's particular excellence as a song writer lies in his extraordinary flair for writing melodies which seem to float on the words and to gather new energy as they proceed; they often defy formal analysis because they do not depend for their effect on artificial symmetry or simple repetition."

It is generally believed that Purcell's health was undermined by hard work and late hours. He died, probably of tuberculosis, on November 21, 1695 in Dean's Yard in Westminster, London. He was buried in the north aisle of Westminster Abbey. On a tablet near his grave, the following inscription appears: "Here lyes Henry Purcell, Esq., who left this life and is gone to that Blessed Place where only his harmony can be exceeded." John Dryden's ode in memory of Purcell contains the following couplet:

Sometimes a hero in an age appears,
But scarce a Purcell in a thousand years.

This is Alec Robertson's description of Purcell: "The drawing attributed to Jonathan Richardson depicts the face of a visionary. It is Purcell as Blake would have seen him. The Kneller portrait in the National Gallery emphasizes the rather sensuous curve of the mouth and the weakness of chin observable in the Richardson drawing, but shows us the broad forehead of the intellectual and the lustrous eyes of the romantic. . . . Wig and cravat replace the open tunic and flowing hair of the Kneller portrait, the chin has become double, as it threatened, the mouth set and the eyes hard. It is hard to believe that this is Purcell at twenty-four. One gathers that Purcell had distinct personal beauty and grace; and surely the man who wrote on one of his own scores 'God bless Mr. Henry Purcell' must have been very lovable."

The eminent historian John Hawkins gives us further insight into Purcell's personality: "Mirth and good humor seemed to have been habitual to him; and this is perhaps the best excuse that can be made for those connections and intimacies with Brown and others which show him not to have been very nice in the choice of his company. Brown spent his life in taverns and alehouses; the Hole in the Wall in Baldwin's Gardens was the citadel in which he baffled the assaults of creditors and bailiffs, at the same time that he attracted thither such as thought his wit atoned for his profligacy. Purcell seems to have been of that number, and to merit censure for having prostituted his invention, by adapting music to some of the most wretched ribaldry that was ever obtruded on the world of humor."

Gustav Holst has singled out some salient qualities of Purcell's music: "It is surely unnecessary nowadays to dwell on Purcell's gift of melody. According to some it is excelled only by Mozart's. Others hold that Purcell's best melodies—and how numerous they are!—are inferior to none. In addition to his gift of melody there are his sense of harmony, his feeling for orchestral color, his humor, his intensity, his lyrical power. . . . Yet all these details of compositions were subordinate to his amazing power of dramatic characterization. . . . His music is full of movement—of dance. His is the easiest music in all the world to act. . . . At the end of his life, Purcell was the master of every branch of musical technique."

"To call him the greatest English composer of the second half of the seventeenth century," wrote Eric Blom, "would be ridiculously obvious, so . immeasurably did he out-top even the best of his compatriots. To speak of him, on the other hand, as almost the only great composer of that age is scarcely an exaggeration, surprising though the statement may seem. We have only to survey musical Europe from 1650 to 1700 to find that at any rate he stands isolated among the great as a master of all-round versatility. There are some seventeenth-century figures —astonishingly few— who must be regarded as his peers in one domain of music or another, and indeed as to some extent his mod-

els, as Lully was in opera and Corelli in the chamber sonata; but look where we may, there is no composer anywhere within his lifetime and some years beyond on either side who is his match in every field of creation then cultivated by composers. Indeed no other great man attempted to till anything like so many fields. . . . Purcell was supreme in all sorts of ways except in the handling of the largest formal schemes: a daring harmonist, a contrapuntist of unlimited skill, a superb inventor of great tunes and an enterprising innovator in rhythm."

Like Bach's reputation, Purcell's fame was eclipsed after his death. For seventy years his music was neglected, and there were few anywhere to guess the extent of his genius and the immensity of his contributions. Then in 1876 the Purcell Society was founded to publish his complete works, a monumental project that resulted in the issue of some forty volumes during the next half century. Revivals of Purcell's music in 1895, on the bicentenary of his death, further helped to point up his versatility and greatness.

The present-day symphonic repertory has been enriched by suites arranged by eminent twentieth-century musicians from Purcell's works. Two suites for strings were adapted by John Barbirolli. For the score to the ballet *Comus*, Constant Lambert adapted Purcell's incidental music for several plays— including *The Fairy Queen, Dioclesian, The Indian Queen, The Tempest,* and *The Virtuous Wife.* Sir Henry J. Wood's *Suite in Five Movements* is based on music from two Purcell sonatas as well as from *Dioclesian, Timon of Athens* and *Dido and Aeneas.* And Benjamin Britten's *Young Person's Guide to the Orchestra* is a series of variations on a theme from Purcell's *Abdelazer.*

PRINCIPAL WORKS

Chamber Music—22 sonatas in three or four parts for two violins and figured bass; various sonatas for violin and figured bass.

Choral Music—Anthems, canons, cantatas, catches, hymns, odes, psalms, sacred songs, Services.

Harpsichord Music—Airs, chaconnes, gavottes, grounds, minuets, preludes, suites, toccatas, voluntaries.

Opera—Dido and Aeneas.

Orchestral Music—Fantasias in three, four or five parts for viols; chaconnes, overtures, pavane.

Theater Music—Incidental music to about 50 plays, including: Amphitryon (Dryden); King Arthur (Dryden); The Gordian Knot Untied; The Fairy Queen (Settle, based on Shakespeare's

Midsummer Night's Dream); The Old Bachelor (Congreve); Love Triumphant (Dryden); Timon of Athens (Shadwell, based on Shakespeare); The Indian Queen (Dryden and Howard); The Tempest (Dryden and Davenant, based on Shakespeare); Abdelazer.

Vocal Music—Songs for voice and accompaniment, including Ah, How Pleasant 'Tis to Love; If Music Be the Food of Love; I Love and I Must; On the Brow of Richmond Hill; Silvia, Now Your Scorn Give Over; and Sweet, Be No Longer Sad; vocal duets, three-part songs.

ABOUT

Arundell, D., Henry Purcell; Cummings, W. H., Henry Purcell; Dupré, H., Henry Purcell; Holland, A. K., Henry Purcell: The English Musical Tradition; Moore, R. E., Henry Purcell and the Restoration Theater; Runciman, J. F., Purcell; Westrup, J. A., Purcell.

Musical Quarterly, July 1916; Musical Times, October 1934.

Joachim Raff *1822-1882*

ALTHOUGH the music of Joseph Joachim Raff has lapsed into comparative obscurity in the twentieth century, he was in his time one of the most highly esteemed and popular of the German Romantic composers. The son of an organist, Raff was born in Lachen, on the lake of Zurich, on May 27, 1822. His penchant during his boyhood was toward languages rather than music. After completing his early studies in Wiesenstetten and at the Württemberg Institute, he attended the Jesuit Lyceum of Schwyz, where he won first prizes in German, Latin, and mathematics.

The necessity of earning a living forced Raff to terminate his formal education. At this time he began to devote himself assiduously to music, which had heretofore been merely a passing hobby. Too poor to afford lessons, he taught himself composition, violin, and piano.

In 1843 Raff sent several of his compositions to Mendelssohn. "The composition is elegant and faultless throughout," Mendelssohn replied, "and in the most modern style. If my hearty recommendation will have any weight, I most willingly add it to the request of my young friend." On the weight of Mendelssohn's recommendation the young composer was able to approach the important publishing house of Breitkopf und Härtel, which issued some of his early piano pieces.

Encouraged by Mendelssohn's praise and by his own first publications, Raff gave up schoolteaching to devote himself to music. During the years that followed he was often in dire financial straits, but this circumstance did not hinder his creativity.

In the middle 1840's Franz Liszt, impressed with Raff's talent, urged the young man to accompany him on a concert tour. Raff accompanied Liszt as far as Cologne, where in 1846 he met Mendelssohn at last. He remained, accepting Mendelssohn's invitation to become his student, but the death of the master soon afterward forestalled his plans. Raff then sought music instruction from Hans von Bülow who, on January 1, 1848, introduced Raff's first major work, the *Konzertstück*, for piano and orchestra. During this period Raff also wrote music criticism for *Cäcilia*, a Cologne music journal.

The friendship and mutual admiration of Liszt and Raff deepened and Liszt did much to promote the interests and career of the younger man. He recommended Raff to the Viennese publisher Mecchetti, but the latter died just before Raff could visit him. Raff, by then an ardent advocate of the "music of the future," settled in Weimar to be closer to Liszt. For several years he worked as Liszt's secretary while studying under the master. In 1854 he published a valuable treatise on Wagner and Wagnerism, *Die Wagnerfrage*. Liszt's patronage of Raff resulted in the première in Weimar of Raff's opera *König Alfred,* on March 9, 1851. The opera had three more performances in Weimar, then was produced in Wiesbaden in 1856.

William Mason, an eminent American pianist and teacher who lived in Weimar during these years, has left the following impressions of the young musician: "He was hard to become acquainted with, and not disposed to meet one half way. He was fond of argument, and if one side was taken, he was apt to take the other. . . . Upon better acquaintance . . . one found a kind heart and a faithful friend. . . . He was very poor and there were times when he seemed hardly able to keep body and soul together. Once he was arrested for debt. . . . He was a hard worker and composed incessantly."

In Weimar Raff met and fell in love with Doris Genast, the daughter of an actor. When she moved to Wiesbaden in 1856,

Raff followed her and settled there, soon acquiring a substantial reputation as a piano teacher. Raff married Doris in Wiesbaden in 1859.

His eminence as a composer was also increasing. The overture to *Bernhard von Weimar*, which he had written in 1858, was being performed throughout Germany. In 1863 he received first prize from the Gesellschaft der Musikfreunde for his first symphony, *An das Vaterland*. In 1870 *Dame Kobold*, a comic opera, and *Im Walde*, one of his finest symphonies, were successfully introduced in Weimar. Two years later another symphony, *Lenore*, was acclaimed at its première in Sonderhausen on December 13, 1872.

By 1877 Raff was regarded in Germany as one of the country's leading composers. He was appointed director of Hoch's Conservatory in Frankfurt am Main, a post he held until his death. Raff died in Frankfort of an apoplectic stroke on June 25, 1882.

As a composer Raff was both prolific and versatile. He filled his writing with euphonious melodies and harmonies, and was particularly successful in projecting subtle moods and atmosphere. Arthur Hervey wrote, "The wonderful ease with which he was able to employ scholastic devices revealed itself in all his larger compositions. . . . If he was occasionally prolix in his utterances and not invariably inspired, he was always comprehensible and rarely dull. . . . His Romanticism was grafted on a classical stem, and the broadness of his outlook resulted in his endeavoring to conciliate opposing tendencies."

Raff was at his best in his orchestral music, most notably in his symphonies. "The best point that strikes the student of these symphonies," said Ebenezer Prout, "is their individuality. They possess, it is true, that family likeness which shows them to be productions of the same brain. . . . His ideas are by no means of equal merit, but at all events the well never runs dry, and inexhaustible fluency seems to be one of the composer's striking characteristics. . . . I have no hesitation in saying that since Beethoven nobody has equaled Raff in the absolute mastery of thematic treatment. By his skill in this respect, he frequently succeeds in constructing an interesting movement out of the most unpromising material; and when, in addition, he has been happy

JOACHIM RAFF

in the choice of themes, he produces music worthy to rank with the masterpieces of our art. No less remarkable . . . is his complete command of counterpoint."

Though Prout's estimate may seem excessively enthusiastic to a present-day audience, there is no question about some of the sound aesthetic and musical values of at least two of Raff's symphonies which are occasionally revived: the third, *Im Walde*, and the fifth, *Lenore*.

Paradoxically, in view of his vast output of hundreds of works in the larger forms, the composition by Raff most often performed today is a slight piece for violin and piano, the Cavatina in A-flat major, op. 85, no. 3, also familiar in orchestral adaptations.

Principal Works

Chamber Music—8 string quartets; 5 violin sonatas; 4 piano trios; Octet in C major, for strings; String Sextet; Piano Quintet in A minor; Cello Sonata.

Choral Music—Wachet auf; Deutschlands Auferstehung; Psalm CXXX; Two Songs for Chorus and Orchestra; Morgenlied; Einer Entschlafenen; Die Tageszeiten; Weltende, Gericht, Neue Welt; various part songs.

Operas—König Alfred; Dame Kobold.

Orchestral Music—11 symphonies; 5 overtures; 3 suites; 2 violin concertos; Piano Concerto in C minor; Cello Concerto in D minor; Suite for Violin and Orchestra; Suite for Piano and Orchestra; Two Scenes, for voice and orchestra.

Piano Music—4 suites; 4 fantasies; Sonata; numerous smaller pieces, including capriccios, rhapsodies, scherzos, waltzes; pieces for piano duet and for two pianos.

Vocal Music—Songs for voice and piano; vocal duets.

ABOUT

Raff, H., Joachim Raff: Ein Lebensbild.

Monthly Musical Record, August 1, 1882; Neue Musik Zeitung, March 1922.

Jean Philippe Rameau *1683-1764*

JEAN PHILIPPE RAMEAU is distinguished not only as one of the earliest masters of French opera, but as one of the first significant music theorists. Son of the organist of the Dijon Cathedral, Rameau was born in Dijon on September 25, 1683. He began the study of music early, learning organ, harpsichord, and violin. Between 1693 and 1697 he received an academic education at the Jesuit College in Dijon.

When he was eighteen Rameau paid a visit to Italy. For several months he performed on the organ at church services, and on the violin in small orchestras. He also made a study of Italian opera, gaining little respect for that form.

Returning to France later in 1702, Rameau became violinist in the orchestra of a traveling opera company. He was soon afterwards appointed organist at Clermont-Ferrand, and during this period became active as a composer, writing delightful harpsichord pieces and several cantatas. In 1705 he moved to Paris and found residence on the Rue du Temple, not far from the church where France's foremost organist, Louis Marchand, performed regularly. For a brief period Rameau studied with Marchand; but his main efforts were directed toward playing the organ, the intense study of musical theory, and the publication of his first book of harpsichord pieces, *Pièces de clavecin,* in 1706.

This volume, together with a second issued in 1724, was a monumental pioneer work in French keyboard music. In these works new techniques of performance were developed, and with them daring innovations in tone color and pictorial writing. It is important to recall that Rameau's first set predated Couperin's historic first volume of *Pièces de clavecin* by some eight years, for in many respects Rameau anticipates Couperin. Some of his pieces in these two volumes are classic dances (allemandes, sarabandes, gavottes, minuets, gigues, and so forth); some have descriptive or witty programmatic titles whose style reminds one of Couperin: "La Poule," "Les Soupirs," "La Joyeuse," "Le Rappel des oiseaux," and so forth. Louis Laloy wrote: "He knows how to say a great deal with only a few notes. Throughout his tonality is firm, with as much force as delicacy. One can hardly imagine a language more pert or choicer than that found here."

In 1709 Rameau left Paris to succeed his father as organist at the Dijon Cathedral. He next performed on the organ in Lyons, and after that in Clermont-Ferrand. In the latter city he published, in 1722, *Le Traité de l'harmonie,* his first volume on musical theory, and the one which was to form the basis of the science of modern harmony. A second volume, *Le Nouveau système de musique théorique,* appeared in Paris in 1726. In these studies Rameau established definitively the harmonic system of building chords by thirds and classifying them with all their inversions.

In 1723 Rameau returned to Paris, to remain for the rest of his life. His first attempt to write for the stage took place in the year he finally settled permanently in the French capital; it consisted of music for dances and various divertissements. After that he completed the scores for two light operas. In February 1726 he married Marie-Louise Mangot, a singer.

It was his eminence as a theorist rather than as a composer that brought him an important post in 1727 as music master to the household of Le Riche de la Pouplinière, a powerful patron of the arts. For La Pouplinière, Rameau served as organist, teacher, and conductor of a private orchestra. La Pouplinière encouraged Rameau to write operas, and introduced him to Voltaire in the hope that the distinguished writer might provide a suitable libretto. When Rameau failed to respond to several ideas suggested by Voltaire, La Pouplinière used his influence to persuade the Abbé Pellégrin to prepare for Rameau an opera text based on Racine's *Phèdre—Hippolyte et Aricie.* The Abbé had so little faith in Rameau that he bound the composer to a contract guaranteeing the librettist against any financial loss. However, when the Abbé heard a rehearsal of Rameau's score at La Pouplinière's palace, he destroyed the agreement. *Hippolyte et Aricie* was produced at the Opéra on October 1, 1733. (More than two hundred years were to pass before the first American presentation, which took place in New York on April 11, 1954.)

With his first opera—or as he designated it, *tragédie*—Rameau reached full maturity; Campra, a venerable French opera composer preceding Rameau and Lully, maintained that there was more good music in this one masterwork than in any ten operas in the then current repertory. Yet *Hippolyte et Aricie* was a failure, largely because of the efforts of the followers of Lully, who felt that Rameau represented a negation of Lully's ideals and principles and who feared that Rameau might displace their own favorite composer in public esteem.

Rameau was not discouraged by his initial failure with *Hippolyte*. He completed the score for a ballet-opera, *Les Indes galantes,* which was produced at the Opéra on August 23, 1735, to a most enthusiastic reception. The work was an elaborate spectacle set in four parts of the world, detailing four different love stories. In it French ballet music boasted a versatility of color and rhythm and a richness of material rarely before encountered in French opera. Program music arrived at a new articulateness, achieving new dramatic power through Rameau's gift for describing orchestrally various natural phenomena, such as an earthquake. Choral writing, too, found a new dimension in such stirring pages as "Brillant soleil!" Beauty and freshness of lyricism are encountered in such exalted pages as Love's air in the prologue, "Ranimez vos flambeaux," and the two songs of Huscar, "Clair flambeau du monde" and "Permettez, astre du jour."

Rameau's masterwork, *Castor et Pollux,* followed *Les Indes galantes* on October 24, 1737. French music drama achieved unparalleled artistic heights, as Rameau enlisted the fullest resources of harmony and orchestration and enriched powers of lyricism and recitative, to tell his mythological story, a variation of the old Orpheus and Eurydice theme. In Rameau's opera, Pollux descends to the lower regions to replace his dead brother, Castor. For this act of nobility, the gods deify both men and place them in the heavens as a constellation.

Rameau's vivid descriptive powers unfold compellingly in the scenes describing the lower regions and Elysium. The chorus of the demons, the dance of the infernal spirits, and Castor's unforgettable air to the

JEAN PHILIPPE RAMEAU

blessed spirits in Elysium are pages that must have exerted an inescapable influence on Gluck in his own *Orfeo ed Euridice.* In addition, Rameau revealed new depths in his choral writing, as in the funeral music of the first act and in his music for ballet, such as the mighty chaconne of the closing scene.

By this time, Rameau's innovations in harmony, orchestration, and lyricism were creating a stir in Paris. There was so much interest in his new opera, *Dardanus,* that all the boxes were sold out eight days before the première. Introduced on November 19, 1739, *Dardanus* was an immense success despite the efforts of the Lullists. Dardanus, according to Greek legend, was the founder of the royal house of Troy. Rameau's text was inspired by the lines about Dardanus in the third book of Virgil's *Aeneid.* In the score, Rameau gave some of his finest invention to the ballet music and created some of his passionate moods in the choruses. Of the score as a whole, Cuthbert Girdlestone found "martial vigor and strength" as "predominating qualities." He added: "From the extreme dreaminess of the original Act IV, the tragic lament of Iphise and . . . of Dardanus on the one hand, to the martial or demoniac power of the duet of Act I, the magician's chorus, the fury chorus, 'Dardanus gémit' and . . . 'Le désespoir et la rage,' in Act III . . . there runs a tremendous range of feeling and all points along the scale are marked by first-rate music."

Rameau was now recognized as one of the most eminent composers in France, and unquestionably its foremost musical dramatist and exponent of classical French opera. In recognition of his place in French music King Louis XV bestowed on him the honorary title of *compositeur de la musique de chambre,* and with it an annual pension of two thousand francs.

After the presentation of *Dardanus,* the efforts of the Lullists to discredit Rameau and his operas collapsed. What the Lullists objected to in this composer was his complexity of style, his emphasis on harmony and orchestration above pure lyricism. Jean Jacques Rousseau maintained that "French airs are not airs at all, and the French recitative is not recitative." A widely circulated verse also took Rameau to task for his supposed cerebralism:

> If the difficult is pretty
> What a great man is Rameau!
> But if, by chance, whate'er is witty
> Must be simple, then I know
> He is but a little man.

But in truth Rameau's operas were not a rejection of Lully but an extension and development of his innovations—as Rameau took pains to explain in a lengthy introduction to the published score of *Les Indes galantes.* It is true that in some ways he deviated from the dramatic ideals of Lully. Too often he was willing to set to music pedestrian texts, even doggerel verse. He did not have Lully's gift of sharp delineation of his character; Rameau's characters are mere stereotypes and he was more ready than Lully to clutter his operas with ceremonials, processions, massive scenes, and ballets at the expense of dramatic action and continuity.

But in many other respects Rameau represented a major advance over Lully as a musical dramatist. More than Lully, he succeeded in making the orchestra a partner in the projection of the dramatic action: his orchestral portraits of storms, earthquakes, sunrises mark a new day for French program music. He endowed the aria and the recitative with increasing expressiveness, reaching at times a grandeur never before heard in opera. And, far more than Lully, he made the chorus an integral part of the drama, often endowing it with a distinct identity, making it the voice of some of his most majestic utterances.

Karl Nef has proclaimed Rameau one of "the most original discoverers of all time. . . . [He] created a well-rounded work of art which combines in unified manner, poetry, action, solo, chorus, and orchestra, an accomplishment that is to be reckoned among the greatest achievements in the field of musico-dramatic art."

G. Jean-Aubry wrote, "Rameau embodies the most astonishing balance of science, will-power and inspiration. Nothing extravagant characterizes him. It may be said that he is crabbed and savage, because the obsession of problems on which he aspires to throw light compels him to solitude; but how much more thoroughly does the most vivid feeling pierce through in a thousand places! . . . Plasticity of rhythm, a sense of orderly life, delicacy and care to maintain the balance of expression, these are the features of Rameau."

In spite of his interest in and great contributions to the science of music, Rameau was not an academician. "It is often by seeing and hearing musical works," he wrote, "rather than by rules, that taste is formed." And again, "While composing music it is not the time to recall the rules which might hold our genius in bondage. We must have recourse to the rules only when our genius and our ear seem to deny what we are seeking."

In 1752, at a time when the opposition and cabals of the Lullists had long been forgotten, a new storm centered around Rameau. A visiting Italian opera company presented in Paris Pergolesi's *opera buffa La Serva padrona,* whose success immediately created a new schism in French music. Rousseau, Diderot, and other Encyclopedists saw Pergolesi's simple and forthright style as an example of true operatic art, and used Pergolesi as a spearhead to attack Rameau and the French classical opera. Others sided with Rameau. "Rameau," said Voltaire, "has made of music a new art."

Rameau himself provided an amusing and significant footnote to this operatic war now known as *le guerre des bouffons.* In his old age he remarked to the Abbé Arnaud: "If I were twenty years younger, I would go to Italy, and take Pergolesi for my model, abandon something of my harmony and devote myself to attaining truth of declamation, which should be the sole guide of musicians.

But after sixty one cannot change; experience points plainly enough the best course, but the mind refuses to obey."

In the *guerre des bouffons,* as in the earlier struggle against the Lullists, Rameau emerged triumphant; the principles of French opera which he had espoused were embraced and acclaimed by French opera audiences. A revival of *Dardanus* at the Opera in the early 1760's was a triumph of the first order. The municipal authorities of Dijon and the French Academy honored Rameau as France's leading composer.

Rameau spent the last years of his life in virtual seclusion, producing theoretical treatises, opera, ballet, and instrumental compositions. His last operas were *Les Paladins,* a comedy-ballet produced at the Opéra on February 12, 1760, and *Abaris,* a tragedy written in 1764 for the Opéra but not performed.

Stricken by typhoid fever, Rameau died at his home in the Rue des Bons Enfants in Paris on September 12, 1764.

Tall, thin, and spare, Rameau was sometimes described by his contemporaries as resembling a pipe organ. His voice was loud and harsh, his manners rude, his behavior boorish. For the most part he was an unsociable and disagreeable person, always ready to drive a hard bargain, avaricious in gathering money and honors, and living with the parsimony of a miser. "He was a stranger to all humane sentiments," Grimm said of him. "His ruling passion was avarice. . . . He wanted money and he died rich." Charles Collé, an eighteenth century playwright, wrote of Rameau: "He was a hard man, very difficult to get along with, as narrow and mulish as he was unjust. . . . Rameau was even . . . cruel to his family."

PRINCIPAL WORKS

Ballets—Les Fêtes d'Hébé; Les Fêtes de Polimnie; Les Sibarites.
Chamber Music—Pièces de clavecin en concert.
Choral Music—Cantatas; motets.
Harpsichord Music—Pièces de clavecin; Nouvelle suite de pièces de clavecin.
Operas—Hippolyte et Aricie; Les Indes galantes; Castor et Pollux; Dardanus; La Princesse de Navarre; Platée; Zoroastre; Abaris.

ABOUT

Gardien, J., Jean Philippe Rameau; Girdlestone, C., Jean Philippe Rameau; La Laurencie, L. de, Rameau; Laloy, L., Rameau; Masson, P. M., L'Opéra de Rameau; Migot, G., Rameau et le génie de la musique française.

Ernest Reyer *1823-1909*

ERNEST REYER was born Louis Étienne-Ernest Rey in Marseilles on December 1, 1823. From his sixth to his sixteenth year he attended the Free School of Music in Marseilles. During these years his enthusiasm for music was far greater than his apparent talent, and his parents tried to discourage him from attempting to become a musician. In 1839 they sent him to Algiers, where he lived with his uncle, a governmental official, and found work in the government financial office. He continued his study of music and wrote several songs that gained a certain degree of popularity. In 1847 he completed a Mass which was performed in the Algiers Cathedral in honor of the new French governor, just arrived in Algiers. This work was well received.

In 1848 Reyer returned to Paris. His parents, convinced by the success of the Mass that their son was gifted, did not place further obstacles in the way of his musical development. He went through an intensive period of study with his aunt, Louise Farrenc, who was herself a composer. At the same time, he became acquainted with several distinguished French writers, including Gautier and Flaubert, who shared his enthusiasm for the Oriental and for exotic subjects and styles. Gautier provided him with a text for a symphonic ode, *Le Sélam,* which was staged and performed on April 5, 1850. It did not make a strong impression, largely because it was regarded as an imitation of Félicien David's *Le Désert,* which had achieved considerable vogue in Paris five years before.

Reyer's one-act opera, *Maître Wolfram,* performed at the Théâtre Lyrique on May 20, 1854, fared much better. When Berlioz heard it he exclaimed, "God be praised! We have gone out of the kitchen into the garden. Let us breathe deeply." And Reyer's ballet-pantomime, *Sacountala,* again written to a text by Gautier, was an even greater success, upon its introduction at the Opéra on July 14, 1858.

On April 11, 1861, the Théâtre Lyrique produced Reyer's first significant opera, *La Statue,* based on an episode from *The Arabian Nights.* Bizet considered this one of the most remarkable French operas in twenty years. A composer of established

Reyer: rā-yâr'

reputation, Reyer was honored with the decoration of the Legion of Honor a year later.

Reyer's next opera, *Érostrate*, received its world première in Baden-Baden on August 21, 1862. Because the première took place in Germany, Reyer dedicated his opera to the Queen of Prussia, a gesture that had unpleasant repercussions a decade later with its first performance in Paris. The Franco-Prussian war had started in 1870, and much antagonism was stirred up by the opera because it bore a dedication to the queen of an enemy country.

In 1866 Reyer was appointed librarian of the Paris Opéra, a post he retained until his death. Between 1865 and 1875 he also devoted much time and energy to music criticism, particularly for the *Journal des débats*. In his capacity as journalist, Reyer attended the world première of Verdi's *Aida* in Cairo in 1871. As a critic he fought vigorously to bring recognition to composers who were neglected or misunderstood by the general public—Franck, Lalo, Berlioz, Wagner. Some of his most significant writings were assembled in two volumes: *Notes de musique* (1875) and *Quarante ans de musique* (1909).

In 1876 Reyer was elected to the Institut de France. At about this time he completed his most ambitious and significant opera, *Sigurd*, based on virtually the same textual material used by Wagner for his *Nibelungen Ring*. Despite this theme and Reyer's pronounced admiration for Wagner, the opera is thoroughly Gallic in style, grounded in the traditions of French grand opera. Donald Jay Grout wrote: "In the music there is no sign whatever of Wagner; we find the old separate numbers of grand opera, a distinctly periodic melody, and very little chromaticism. There is some recurrence of motifs, but this is not a distinctly Wagnerian trait. The musical style is serious and even has a certain nobility; its model, clearly enough, is *Les Troyens*."

The world première of *Sigurd* took place at the Théâtre de la Monnaie in Brussels on January 7, 1884. The following July, *Sigurd* was produced at Covent Garden; in January of 1885 in Lyons; and on June 12, 1885 at the Paris Opéra. Though the initial performance of *Sigurd* at the Opéra was so poor that the composer fled from the theater, the opera achieved considerable popularity in

Paris; by 1925 it had been presented more than three hundred times in that city. The American première took place in New Orleans on December 24, 1891.

Julien Tiersot described *Sigurd* as full of "color, of movement, and—in certain spots—of poetry. The melodic vein here is abundant. . . . It is 'full of ideas.' . . . His songs have a spontaneous force, a grace which is neither effeminate nor affected. And if his orchestra does not have that transparency which one admired in the past, it is colorful, striking and expressive."

Reyer's last opera also proved a notable contribution to the French lyric theater. It was *Salammbô*, based on the Flaubert novel; it was first heard at the Théâtre de la Monnaie in Brussels on February 10, 1890, then given at the Paris Opéra in May 1892.

During the last years of his life Reyer lived quietly and in semiretirement on the fifth floor of the Opéra, quarters assigned to him by virtue of his position as librarian. In 1906 he was given the Grande Croix of the Legion of Honor. Reyer died in Le Lavandou, Hyères, France on January 15, 1909.

"His style," said Arthur Hervey, "has been described as proceeding from Gluck and Weber, while his admiration for Berlioz and Wagner reveals itself in the richness and variety of his instrumentation. . . . It may be said with truth that Reyer's individuality is not of the most marked, that his melodies sometimes lack distinction, and that his inventive faculty is scarcely equal to his skill in making the most of his materials; but none will contest the true artistic feeling that presides over all his compositions, nor deny him the possession of strongly pronounced convictions."

Alfred Bruneau said of Reyer that he had "genius without talent." Following this line of thought Donald Jay Grout explained further that Reyer possessed "lofty and ideal conceptions without the technique for realizing them fully in an attractive musical form."

PRINCIPAL WORKS

Ballet—Sacountala.

Choral Music—Victoire; L'Union des arts; L'Hymne du Rhin; Le Chant des paysans; Chœur de buveurs; Chœur des assiégés; Salve Regina; Ave Maria; O Salutaris.

Operas—Maître Wolfram; La Statue; Érostrate; Sigurd; Salammbô.

Orchestral Music—Le Sélam, symphonic ode for voices, chorus and orchestra; La Madeleine au désert, for voice and orchestra.

ABOUT

Curzon, H. de, Ernest Reyer, sa vie et ses œuvres; Jullien, A., Ernest Reyer; Roujon, H., Notice sur la vie et les travaux de Ernest Reyer.

Josef Rheinberger *1839-1901*

JOSEF GABRIEL RHEINBERGER, distinguished nineteenth-century composer of organ music, was born in Vaduz, Liechtenstein, on March 17, 1839. His father was a treasurer at the Prince's palace. Josef's talent for music became obvious while he was still a child. When he was only five he was given instruction on the piano; soon afterwards he began to study theory and organ. When he was seven he began playing the organ in the local church.

At the age of eight Josef completed his first Mass; its performance made so strong an impression on the Bishop of Chur that he summoned the boy to demonstrate his gifts further. The Bishop placed the music of a Salve Regina before the boy and asked him to play it at sight while he sang the vocal part. Josef played the organ accompaniment faultlessly, and in one case corrected the Bishop for singing several wrong notes.

Another incident pointed up the boy's sensitive ear. When he was ten he was called upon to turn the pages for a violinist who was performing in a string quartet. As the violinist finished tuning his instrument, the boy told him, "Your A string is a semitone higher than the A on your piano." This observation proved accurate and prompted the violinist to persuade Rheinberger's father to permit him to study music intensively. Rheinberger was sent to Feldkirch each week (traveling ten miles on foot) to study theory with Philipp Schmutzer. In 1851 he entered the Munich Conservatory, where for three years he studied piano with Émile Leonhard, organ with J. G. Herzog, and counterpoint with J. J. Maier.

Rheinberger graduated from the Conservatory in 1854 with highest honors. For a while he continued to study music privately with Franz Lachner, earning his living by giving private lessons and serving as accompanist for the Munich Choral Society.

JOSEF RHEINBERGER

When in 1859 Leonhard resigned from the faculty of the Munich Conservatory, Rheinberger took his place; a year later he was given a full professorship in composition.

From 1860 to 1866 Rheinberger was organist of the St. Michael Church in Munich. While holding this post he held various other assignments as well. In 1864 he became conductor of the Munich Choral Society. A year later he was engaged as a coach of the Munich Court Theater, where he distinguished himself by transposing at sight the score of Wagner's *The Flying Dutchman.*

In 1867 Rheinberger married Franziska Jaegerhuber, a gifted writer. In that year the Munich Conservatory was reorganized and placed under the direction of Hans von Bülow. Rheinberger now became professor of organ as well as composition, and also an inspector of the classes in theory and instrumental performance. He held all these posts until the end of his life, and was honored with the title of Royal Professor. He achieved such renown as a teacher that pupils from all parts of Europe were drawn to Munich to study with him.

In 1877, when Hoch's Conservatory was founded in Frankfurt am Main, Rheinberger was offered the post of director. He turned it down, preferring to remain in Munich; this sacrifice led Ludwig II to confer on him the knighthood of St. Michael. It was only one of many honors he received through the years. In 1894 he was elevated to the nobility, and in 1899 he received an honorary doctorate from the University of Munich.

The year 1877 also marked Rheinberger's appointment as director of church music at court. This office inspired him to write ambitious works of choral music in the larger forms: a Stabat Mater, an oratorio, and several Masses. One of the latter was dedicated to Pope Leo XIII who, in gratitude, conferred on him the knighthood of Gregory the Great.

During the last years of his life, Rheinberger was in poor health. He died in Munich on November 25, 1901.

Josef Rheinberger was a gregarious person. He enjoyed large and convivial dinners, to which he would invite many friends. He was not only a gourmet but a skilled cook, having been trained in the culinary art by one of Napoleon III's chefs, and he usually took some part in preparing the meals served to his guests. His other interests included hunting (which he gave up after his marriage because his wife objected to the killing of animals), reciting poetry to his own piano accompaniment, and appearing as an actor in bit parts. A strict adherent to the Roman Catholic faith, he was as charitable as he was religious; it was his practice every Christmas to distribute gifts to the poor.

Rheinberger was an extraordinarily prolific composer. There is no area of musical composition which he did not cultivate, and in most fields he produced several hundreds of works. Frederick Niecks, surveying this immense output, found that "thoroughness of workmanship" distinguished his most important creations. "This thoroughness is combined with another, not less characteristic, trait of the artist and his work—namely, unpretentiousness. . . . Rheinberger is a master of his craft and yet never makes a bravado of his skill. The matter, the intellectual and emotional substance of his compositions, is of the nature of his workmanship—unpretentious. We may describe it as simple, and even as homely. . . . For him, the Classic temperament predominates over the Romantic. . . . Moreover, his Romanticism differs . . . in its being neither violent, extravagant, voluptuous, fantastic, nor transcendentally sentimental. . . . His art is deeply rooted in folk music; even in his grandest and most scholastic compositions

the soil from which it sprang is easily discernible. Health, simplicity and clearness pervade everything he has written."

Rheinberger's most important work was for the organ: his twenty-one organ sonatas are among the most significant contributions made to organ literature in the nineteenth century. "The whole series," wrote J. A. Fuller-Maitland, "covering as they do a period of over twenty years, has a richness of coloring, a mastery of effect, and a constant flow of beautiful ideas that are by no means found in his other works."

PRINCIPAL WORKS

Chamber Music—4 piano trios; 3 string quartets; 3 violin sonatas; 2 string quartets; Nonet, for strings and wind; Piano Quintet; Horn Sonata; Suite, for violin and organ; Six Pieces, for violin and piano.

Choral Music—Cantatas, hymns, Masses, motets, oratorios, Requiems, Stabat Maters; male choruses; part songs.

Operas—Die sieben Raben; Der arme Heinrich; Des Türners Töchterlein; Das Zauberwort (for children).

Orchestral Music—3 overtures; 2 symphonies; 2 organ concertos; Piano Concerto in A-flat major; Suite, for organ, violin, cello and orchestra.

Organ Music—24 fughettas; 22 trios; 20 sonatas; Twelve Characteristic Pieces; Twelve Meditations; Twelve Monologues; Twelve Pieces.

Piano Music—Humoreskes, Pieces, sonatas, Studies, toccatas, Theme and Variations; duets.

Vocal Music—Hymns; elegiac, sacred and secular songs for voice and piano (or voice and organ); vocal quartets; vocal duets.

ABOUT

Grace, H., The Organ Works of Rheinberger; Kroyer, T., Rheinberger; Molitor, P. J., Rheinberger und seine Kompositionen für die Orgel.

Musical Times, September 1926.

Nikolai Rimsky-Korsakov *1844-1908*

NIKOLAI ANDREIVICH RIMSKY-KORSAKOV was born to an aristocratic family in Tikhvin, near Novgorod, Russia, on March 18, 1844. In his autobiography he describes how even in infancy he responded to musical sounds: "I was not fully two years old when I clearly distinguished all the tunes that my mother sang to me. Later, when three or four years of age, I beat a toy drum in perfect time, while my father played the piano. Often my father would suddenly change the tempo and rhythm on purpose, and I at once followed suit. Soon afterwards, I began to sing quite correctly whatever my father played and often I sang along with him. Later on, I myself began to pick out on the piano the pieces and accompaniments I had heard him perform and having learned the names of the notes, I could from an adjoining room recognize and name any note on the piano."

Other important early experiences included the performances given for the household by a small group of Jewish musicians employed on the family estate and the church music which the child heard regularly from a nearby monastery. When he was eight Nikolai came upon some excerpts from Glinka's folk opera *A Life for the Czar* and was immediately captivated by this music. Glinka became one of his favorite composers. Later, he eagerly attended performances of *A Life for the Czar* and *Ruslan and Ludmila,* describing the latter ecstatically as "the best opera in the world." He also transcribed parts of Glinka's operas for orchestra. This passion for "the father of Russian music" is undoubtedly the main force that nurtured his enthusiasm for and interest in Russian musical nationalism.

At six Rimsky-Korsakov began to study piano with a local teacher; at nine he made his first attempts at composition. As the son of an aristocratic family, however, he was not permitted to consider music as a career; he was directed instead to the Navy. At twelve he went to St. Petersburg to enroll at the Naval School, from which he graduated in 1862. In the meanwhile he kept alive his musical interests, and for a period of time continued piano studies with Feodor Kanillé. Through him Rimsky-Korsakov met Balakirev in 1861; and through Balakirev he came to know Mussorgsky, Cui and Borodin. Thus it was that Rimsky-Korsakov began to associate with those with whom he would soon form a strong artistic bond, espousing the cause of Russian musical nationalism as a member of the "Russian Five" or "Mighty Five," as the group came to be known.

But first Rimsky-Korsakov had to pursue his chosen profession: he would be a midshipman. In the fall of 1862 the youth set sail on the *Almaz,* which, for the next two and a half years, took him around the world (it stopped in the United States in 1864). Rimsky-Korsakov returned to his native land

NIKOLAI RIMSKY-KORSAKOV

in the summer of 1865. During that trip he had completed a symphony. It was not only his first symphony, but also one of the earliest works in that form ever written by a Russian. It was introduced by the Free Music Society in St. Petersburg on December 31, 1865, Balakirev conducting; and it scored a decisive success. Cui wrote: "All who believe in a great future for our music . . . got up as one man and hailed the young beginner composer with thunderous applause."

Stimulated by this success and his close associations with his fellow nationalists, Rimsky-Korsakov completed several ambitious works for orchestra during the next three years. In 1866 he wrote the *Overture on Russian Themes;* in 1867 the *Fantasia on Serbian Themes* and the tone poem *Sadko;* in 1868 the first of his major works to survive in the repertory: the *Antar Symphony,* inspired by an old Oriental legend. The symphony was introduced in St. Petersburg in January 1876 after the composer had subjected it to much revision. He revised it again in 1897.

In 1871 Rimsky-Korsakov entered upon a career which brought him achievements hardly less fruitful than those of his creative effort: he became professor of instrumentation and composition at the St. Petersburg Conservatory. He had been poorly equipped for this job, for his own knowledge of the technical phases of music (as he himself fully realized) was spotty: "At the time I could not harmonize a chorale properly, had never written a single contrapuntal exercise in my life, and had only the haziest understanding of the strict fugue. I didn't even know the names of the augmented and diminished intervals of the chords." Nevertheless, he assumed the teaching post and undertook so comprehensive a study of theory that in time he became one of the most knowledgeable and most brilliantly trained musicians in all Russia. He also became one of Russia's most distinguished teachers. An entire generation of composers came under his influence: Liadov, Arensky, Ippolitov-Ivanov, Glazunov, Gretchaninov, and Stravinsky, among many others.

The genre in which Rimsky-Korsakov proved most productive was opera. His first was *The Maid of Pskov,* written between 1868 and 1872 and introduced with outstanding success in St. Petersburg on January 13, 1873. In this drama, dealing with episodes during the reign of Ivan the Terrible, Rimsky-Korsakov's "harmonic coloring, his fine choruses, and his brilliant orchestration unite in rendering the work a very notable first venture in the theater," according to M. Montagu-Nathan.

Rimsky-Korsakov's first significant opera, the third he had written, was heard in St. Petersburg on February 10, 1882. It was *Snegourochka (The Snow Maiden),* in which the composer penetrates the worlds of folklore and fantasy. Based on a fairy tale by Ostrovsky, which in turn was based on an old Russian legend, *The Snow Maiden,* it created, as Richard Anthony Leonard pointed out, "something essentially new in the field of lyric drama. It is not strictly the magic opera of German Romanticism. . . . In spite of its mortal characters, *The Snow Maiden* is pure fairy tale. The Maiden herself is the embodiment of a fanciful pantheistic goddess, and so are the Fairy Spring, King Winter, and the Faun; while the birds, trees, bushes, clouds, snowflakes, the wind and the sky are all a living part of the enchanting tale." In his music, the composer used old Russian folk tunes, and melodies of his own modeled after folk songs, and such programmatic devices as bird calls. His harmony was characterized by a "copious use of ancient modes" and "unusual chords based on whole tones."

In 1873, two events changed the course of Rimsky-Korsakov's personal life and artistic career. He married Nadezhda Purgold,

an outstanding pianist, who influenced him profoundly in every phase of his career. In addition he received government sanction to leave his normal duties as a naval officer and concentrate on music. The special position of Inspector of Military Orchestras of the Navy was created expressly for him; he filled this post until it was abolished in 1884.

On March 2, 1874, Rimsky-Korsakov made his début as a conductor, in a program which introduced his Third Symphony. He continued to conduct until the end of his life. From 1874 to 1881 he was director of the Free Music Society; from 1883 to 1894 he conducted choral and orchestral concerts at the Court Chapel; from 1886 to 1900 he directed the Russian Symphony; and from 1889 to 1907 he led outstanding concerts of Russian music in Paris and Brussels.

Despite the exacting demands which teaching and conducting made upon his time and energy, Rimsky-Korsakov was active also as an editor. Between 1875 and 1877 he issued *One Hundred Russian Songs*—the first important attempt to complete and present in modern adaptation the best pieces of Russian folk music. In addition, he worked painstakingly through the years on a definitive edition of Glinka's operas.

Rimsky-Korsakov continued also to create important music. His most notable works for orchestra were composed in the late 1880's. In 1887 he completed the *Capriccio espagnol,* one of his rare excursions into the folk styles òf another culture; and in 1888 the *Russian Easter Overture (Grande pâque russe)* and the suite *Scheherazade.*

Today *Scheherazade* is unquestionably Rimsky-Korsakov's most frequently played composition; it was first heard in St. Petersburg on November 3, 1888. The composer himself provided a description of his music. "The program . . . consists of separate, unconnected episodes and pictures from *The Arabian Nights,* scattered through all four movements of my suite; the sea and Sinbad's ship, the fantastic narrative of the Prince Kalendar, the Prince and the Princess, the Baghdad festival, and the ship dashing against the rock with the bronze rider on it. . . . Given motives thread and spread over all the movements of the suite, alternating and intertwining with each other. Appearing as they do each time under different illumination, depicting each time different traits and expressing different moods, the self-same given motives and themes correspond each time to different images, actions, and pictures."

It is not difficult to see why concert audiences everywhere have found *Scheherazade* attractive. "First," explained Richard Anthony Leonard, ". . . Rimsky-Korsakov had succeeded in a form for which there was practically no precedent. The repertory of Romantic music was full of short pieces in the picturesque fairy tale genre, but no one had produced a long work of this type which was symphonic in plan and elaboration. Besides, its exotic Eastern coloring, which originally gave a new titillation to Western ears, *Scheherazade* has two advantages as picture music—its delightful melodic material and an orchestration of surpassing brilliance."

A new phase of creative energy began for Rimsky-Korsakov in the 1890's and early 1900's, this time in opera. During the next fourteen years he produced some of his greatest works for the stage, including *Sadko* in 1896 (not to be confused with the earlier tone poem of the same name), *The Czar's Bride* in 1898, *The Tale of the Czar Saltan* in 1900, *The Invisible City of Kitezh* in 1905, and his last and undoubtedly greatest opera, *Le Coq d'or* (*The Golden Cockerel*) in 1907, shortly before his death.

Le Coq d'or, with a libretto by Vladimir Bielsky based on a fanciful, satirical tale by Pushkin, was first performed in Moscow on October 7, 1909, a year and a half after the composer's death. The American première took place at the Metropolitan Opera on March 6, 1918, in a French translation. W. J. Henderson wrote at the time: "The singular charm of the play lies in its curious union of picture, action, and music. Rimsky-Korsakov has treated the story with mock gravity, which sometimes becomes realistic. Thematic suggestions are proffered, and in them are food for fancy. But more frequently the composer finds his expression by those larger and older means in which rhythm, melody and harmony unite in the creation of mood pictures. Perhaps the greatest tribute that can be paid to the music is the fact that its influence on the listener is sure, while almost unnoticed. It proves a most transparent medium for the illumination of the action." The most celebrated single excerpt from this opera is the

second-act aria of the Queen of Shemakha, "Hymn to the Sun."

H. C. Colles has described the qualities distinguishing Rimsky-Korsakov's best operas. He turned away, said Colles, "from the naturalism of the historic drama (Mussorgsky's *Boris Godunov*) to the symbolism of the pictorial stage, of which the ballet is the ideal representation. Vocal melody was not Rimsky-Korsakov's strong point as it was Tchaikovsky's. Rather the keen-edged instrumental phrase in appropriate coloring of violin, trumpet, or oboe, the counterpart of gesture, the incisive rhythm, and the languorous arabesque were the groundwork of his inspiration. . . . In the main . . . if we say that it was Rimsky-Korsakov who gave form and consistency to the Russian opera, we must also say that it was the Russian preoccupation with the ballet which imbued Rimsky-Korsakov with a distinctive sense of those qualities."

In the opinion of Gerald Abraham, Rimsky-Korsakov was at his best in his operas rather than his orchestral music: "Though he never wrote anything quite as fine as *Boris Godunov* or *Prince Igor*, Rimsky-Korsakov must be granted the quite peculiar power of evoking a fantastic world entirely his own, half-real, half-supernatural, a world as limited, as distinctive, and as wonderful as the world of the Grimms' fairy tales or as *Alice in Wonderland*. It is a world in which the commonplace and matter-of-fact are inextricably confused with the fantastic, naïveté with sophistication, the romantic with the humorous, and beauty with absurdity."

In 1905 police pressure was brought down upon the students of the Conservatory for their revolutionary sympathies. Rimsky-Korsakov published a letter in *Russ* violently attacking the government for its ruthless and despotic measures against the young people. Because of his stand he was dismissed from the Conservatory, and performances of his works were forbidden for a two-month period. A wave of protest against the move swept over St. Petersburg, emanating from the indignation of cultural organizations and celebrated Russian musicians. Glazunov and Liadov resigned their posts at the Conservatory in sympathy with Rimsky-Korsakov. In the face of mounting criticism, the government hastily retreated. It ordered the reorganization of the Conservatory, appointed Glazunov as its new director, and reappointed Rimsky-Korsakov to his old teaching post, which he held until his death.

Rimsky-Korsakov's last public appearance took place in Paris in 1907, when he directed some of his own works at a festival of Russian music. He suffered a heart attack in St. Petersburg on April 23, 1908 and died in that city less than two months later on June 21.

Rosa Newmarch provided the following description of Rimsky-Korsakov: "His long, brown beard, his spectacles, and the natural gravity of his demeanor, gave him a slightly severe and pedagogic air. . . . He was one of the delightful exceptions to those cosmopolitan, expansive, emotional, and sometimes frothy Russians who give such false impressions of the national character. . . . Each time I saw Rimsky-Korsakov I was more and more struck by his simplicity and dignified reserve."

In *The Five*, Mikhail Zetlin gives us the following insight into the man: "Rimsky-Korsakov was one of those professionals who had learned to separate art from life. He had decided early to forgo the unusual, to forgo perhaps even dreaming about the unusual. Instead he had chosen to live the habitual routine life of an ordinary human being, with its every-day routine joys and sorrows, . . . a life based on method, system, hard work. . . . Children were born to him, the first four—children of his youth—healthy, strong, capable; the last three—children of his old age—more frail (two of them died). His work at the Conservatory continued apace. Only his friends and acquaintances changed, and occasionally also his home. At one time the Rimsky-Korsakovs and the Borodins lived as neighbors, so that it was even agreed that every time Rimsky-Korsakov signaled out of his window, Borodin would give up his chemical experiments and turn to music! In the summer the whole family would leave town, occasionally traveling abroad. Toward the end of his life, Rimsky-Korsakov took a special liking to his estate Vechasha, where he found it particularly easy to work. Shortly before his death he bought another estate, Lubensk, situated nearby, which had a magnificent fruit garden. It was there that he died."

Platon Brounoff singled out four qualities characterizing Rimsky-Korsakov's music: "His melodies are of the old Russian style, entirely original in rhythm and character; his harmony is brilliant and daring, in which he uses the old Greek scales; he has an extraordinary talent for instrumentation —dazzling combinations of colors, strong, radiant and brilliant, and at the same time, transparent and clear; finally, qualities which you meet so seldom in the works of other Russian composers—namely, sunshine and warmth."

Commenting on Rimsky-Korsakov's contribution to Russian nationalism, M. Montagu-Nathan wrote: "By his resolve to make a thorough study of the theoretical aspect of music, with which his comrades' acquaintance was far from exhaustive, he was eventually able to supplement and even to eclipse the efforts of César Cui in upholding the banner of nationalism. . . . He proved that nationalism was not, as alleged, a mere cloak for technical ignorance, and in the course of time he gave the world a treasury of nationalistic musical art, and an army of pupils, each of whom was able to reflect no little glory on the master."

PRINCIPAL WORKS

Chamber Music—String Sextet in A major; Quintet in B-flat major for winds; String Quartet in G major; Piano Trio in C minor.
Choral Music—Four Variations and Fughetta on a Russian Folk Song; Fifteen Russian Folk Songs; various choruses, settings from the Liturgy, chants, and so forth.
Operas—The Maid of Pskov; Snegourochka; Christmas Eve; Sadko; Mozart and Salieri; The Czar's Bride; The Tale of the Czar Saltan; Kaschei the Immortal; The Legend of the City of Kitezh; Le Coq d'or.
Orchestral Music—3 symphonies; Overture on Russian Themes; Sinfonietta on Russian Themes; Capriccio espagnol; Scheherazade; Russian Easter Overture; Piano Concerto in C-sharp minor; Fantasy on Russian Themes, for violin and orchestra.
Piano Music—Six Variations on the Theme B.A.C.H.; fugues, pieces, variations.
Vocal Music—In Spring; To the Poet; By the Sea; individual songs for voice and piano, including In the Silence of the Night, It Is Not the Wind, The Messenger, Oh, If You Could for a Moment, The Rose and the Nightingale; vocal duets.

ABOUT

Abraham, G., Rimsky-Korsakov; Calvocoressi, M. D., and Abraham, G., Masters of Russian Music; Leonard, R. A., History of Russian Music; Montagu-Nathan, M., History of Russian Music; Rimsky-Korsakov, N., My Musical Life; Seroff, V., The Mighty Five; Zetlin, M., The Five.

Pierre Rode *1774-1830*

JACQUES PIERRE JOSEPH RODE, eminent nineteenth-century composer of violin music, was born in Bordeaux, France, on February 26, 1774. At the age of four he began to study violin with local teachers, and from 1782 to 1786 was a pupil of Fauvel. In 1786 he went to Paris. There he was heard by Punto, a famous horn player, who brought him to the attention of Viotti. From 1787 to 1789 Rode received violin instruction from Viotti, then, in 1790, made an impressive début in Paris in a program that included a Viotti concerto.

Shortly after his début, Rode was appointed leader of the second violins at the Théâtre Feydeau. He retained this post for four years; then, in 1794, he began a career as violin virtuoso, touring Holland and Germany, where he was well received. When his ship, bound from Hamburg to Bordeaux, was driven by a raging storm to the English shore, he visited London for a single concert.

Upon his return to Paris, Rode became professor of violin in the newly founded Conservatory. He was also made the solo violinist at the Opéra. His restless nature, however, impelled him to give up these secure positions to embark on a new concert tour. This time he visited Spain and met Boccherini, who wrote several compositions for him.

Rode returned to Paris, where in 1800 he received the important appointment of solo violinist to Napoleon. He was at the height of his fame, one of the foremost contemporary French violinists. Louis Spohr wrote, "The more I heard him, the more I admired his playing. Indeed, I do not hesitate for a moment to place his style . . . above that of my own master, Eck, and I did my utmost to master his style by a most careful study of same."

In 1803 Rode toured North Germany and Russia in the company of Boieldieu. He decided to settle in St. Petersburg, where he was solo violinist to Alexander I for five years. The pressure of work, however, destroyed not only his health but his powers as a violin executant. When he left Russia to perform throughout Europe, he found that many former admirers had now become highly critical of his performances. Spohr expressed his disappointment in no uncertain terms; and Beethoven—who had

PIERRE RODE

written his G major Sonata, op. 96, for him —maintained that there was a good deal lacking in Rode's introduction of this sonata at a private concert.

In 1814 Rode visited Berlin, where he married. In Berlin he also met the boy prodigy Mendelssohn. Realizing that his career as a virtuoso was now over, he decided to retire to his native city of Bordeaux, where he purchased a country home.

In 1828 several well-meaning but ill-advised friends persuaded Rode to return to the concert stage. He gave a single recital in Paris. It was a fiasco, and the hostile reaction of audience and critics shattered his spirit. His health declined after the experience, and he frequently succumbed to severe depression. He died in Château de Bourbon, near Damazan, on November 25, 1830.

Rode made a significant contribution to violin literature. His twenty-four caprices (or études) have been indispensable to violin students for over a century, and rank with those of Kreutzer and Paganini as basic studies. "They are," said Arthur Pougin, "truly model works in this form, and remain one of the best exercises for our young violinists. . . . [They] are true pieces of style, with an inspiration that is sometimes melancholy and elegiac, sometimes ardent and fiery, sometimes warm and passionate."

Rode wrote thirteen violin concertos, the most significant of which is the one in A minor. "It is remarkable in many ways," commented Brent Smith on this work. "Written in an age which we, at this distance, regard as dominated by Mozart, the concerto, despite its many styles, shows no traces of Mozart's influence. . . . That the concerto is ill-knit, that it is a conglomeration of styles, that it has no intellectual development, is obvious criticism. But that it has endured and that it has very real beauties and freshness entitle it to our occasional release from the strings of students."

Principal Works

Chamber Music—5 groups of quartets.

Orchestral Music—13 violin concertos.

Violin Music—24 caprices (or études); 12 other études; 7 sets of variations; 3 volumes of violin duos.

About

Ahlgrimm, H., Pierre Rode; Pougin, A., Notice sur Rode.

Strad, September 1927.

Gioacchino Rossini *1792-1868*

G IOACCHINO ROSSINI, the foremost composer of Italian opera in the first half of the nineteenth century, was born in Pesaro on February 29, 1792. His father was the town trumpeter; during Gioacchino's childhood he lost his post and was imprisoned for his pro-French republican sympathies during the conflict attendant upon Napoleon's invasion of Pesaro. Later he traveled about, playing horn and trumpet in provincial theater orchestras. The child, meanwhile, was raised by his grandmother and aunt. In 1804, when the Rossinis settled in Bologna, Gioacchino returned to live with his parents, who could now devote themselves to his musical training. In 1807 Rossini entered the Bologna Conservatory. He studied theory with Padre Mattei and cello with Cavedagni. Having already demonstrated creative talent through the composition of chamber and vocal music, Rossini soon began an ambitious cantata, *Il Pianto d'armonia sulla morte d'Orfeo*, which the Conservatory had commissioned him to write and which it presented on August 8, 1808.

In 1810 Gioacchino's family found itself in serious financial difficulty, and the young man had to give up his music studies to earn a living as a chorusmaster and performer on the cembalo. A chance opportunity now brought him a commission to write an opera. A Venetian company had been planning a program comprising five one-act operas by local composers. When one young musician failed to complete his opera in time, the company manager was persuaded by one of Rossini's friends to ask Rossini for a substitute work. In three days' time Rossini completed *La Cambiale di matrimonio*. It was introduced in Venice on November 3, 1810.

Rossini wrote several more operas, and had them produced in various Italian cities, before he first experienced success with *La Pietra del paragone*, first presented at La Scala in Milan on September 26, 1812. This work was so well received that it ran for fifty performances that season alone, and won for its composer an exemption from army duty. *Tancredi*, an *opera seria* given at the Teatro la Fenice in Venice on February 6, 1813, scored an even greater success. One of its arias, "Di tanti palpiti," gained such wide circulation outside the opera house that the law courts in Venice forbade citizens from singing, humming, or whistling it in the streets—so much of a nuisance had the hearing of this melody become! No less successful was the *opera buffa L'Italiana in Algeri*, first given at the Teatro San Benedetto, in Venice, on May 22, 1813. With these works, performed in the same city within a brief period of time, Rossini became the idol of Venice, and one of its most critically esteemed opera composers.

In 1815 Rossini contracted with Domenico Barbaja, an opera impresario who produced works in Naples, Milan, and Vienna, to write two operas a year for his various theaters. Rossini fulfilled this assignment for eight years. In that time he completed twenty operas beginning with *Elisabetta, regina d'Inghilterra*, introduced in Naples on October 4, 1815. In *Elisabetta*, Rossini established new traditions for Italian opera by replacing the cembalo (until then used as accompaniment for the recitatives) with the orchestra, and by writing down embellishments for the singers which until then performers had improvised.

Rossini also wrote operas for other theaters. One of those was his crowning masterwork, *The Barber of Seville (Il Barbiere di Siviglia)*, one of the greatest and most beloved works in the *opera buffa* repertory, and the standard by which all later Italian comic operas were measured. One of Rossini's most inspired scores, an apparently inexhaustible source of melodic riches, the work was completed in about thirteen days. Rossini did not even trouble to write a special overture for it, taking one he had previously used for *Elisabetta*.

It is surprising, in view of its success in all areas of the world for more than a century and a half, to learn that the première of *The Barber* was a fiasco. One reason for its failure was the widespread resentment in Rome that Rossini had dared to write an opera on the same text used by one of its particular favorites, Paisiello. Paisiello's *Barber of Seville* had been a prime favorite of Italian audiences from its première in 1782. The fact that it was common practice for many different composers to write music to the same text; that Rossini had asked Paisiello if he had any objections and had received that composer's blessing; and that Rossini's opera appeared at its première under the title of *Almaviva,* in order to distinguish it from Paisiello's masterwork—all these circumstances were irrelevant to Paisiello's admirers. At the première they created severe disturbances, so that by the second act, it was virtually impossible to hear the singers. Nor did a poor performance, and several ludicrous accidents, help matters. Don Basilio fell through a trap door; a string from Almaviva's guitar snapped; a cat walked calmly across the stage. At the end of the opera there were laughter, shouts of disapproval, and hissing. Rossini, who had officiated as conductor, rushed out of the theater in dismay and hid himself in the privacy of his apartment.

The second performance was more fortunate. For some reason Paisiello's followers were no longer present, and a few important additions to the score (including the beautiful serenade "Ecco ridente") improved the opera itself. After the final curtain, there was a sustained ovation. The third performance of the work was a complete triumph.

Five years after its première, *The Barber* was taken on tour throughout Italy with great success. Outside Italy, too, the opera found articulate admirers. Beethoven told Rossini in 1822, "It will be played as long as Italian operas exist." Later, Berlioz, Brahms, and Wagner praised it highly.

GIOACCHINO ROSSINI

Today there is hardly a critic or operagoer who does not consider it one of the finest Italian comic operas ever written, if not, indeed, the finest. As Francis Toye wrote, "Every situation, almost every idea, seems to have suggested to him one musical train of thought after another, nearly all equally felicitous. Indeed, the spontaneity of the score is such that one has an impression of music sprouting from his pen, as it were, under high pressure."

The role of Rosina was originally written for a mezzo-soprano. But because sopranos have been so attracted to the part—since Henriette Sontag sang the role in 1826—it has become habitual to perform it in that higher range. On several occasions, however, Rossini's original intention has been adhered to and the part assigned to a mezzo-soprano. In several other ways, contemporary performances do not follow Rossini's original intent. The music he wrote for the "Lesson Scene" has been lost, and it is now the general practice for sopranos to interpolate into this episode any one of several songs or arias by other composers of their own preference—usually Payne's "Home, Sweet Home," Alabiev's "The Nightingale," or Arditi's "Il Bacio." And Rossini's second-act aria for Bartolo, "A un dottor della mia sorte," is frequently replaced by Romani's "Manca un foglio," since Rossini's own air is not regarded as flattering to the voice.

The first American performance of *The Barber of Seville* took place, in an English translation, at the Park Theatre in New York on May 3, 1819. Four years later, *The Barber* became the first opera to be sung in Italian in New York, where it was presented at the Park Theatre with a cast including Mme Malibran, Manuel del Popolo Vicente Garcia, and the younger Manuel Garcia. The opera was heard at the Metropolitan Opera during its first season, on November 23, 1883.

During the next six years, Rossini wrote sixteen operas, comic and serious. They included *La Cenerentola* (1817), based on the Cinderella fairy tale; *La Gazza ladra* (1817), and *Mosè in Egitto* (1818). Now the most celebrated Italian opera composer of his day, Rossini sought new worlds to conquer. After marrying a Spanish singer, Isabella Colbran, on March 16, 1822, he left Italy for the first time to spend a season in Vienna. Three of his operas were performed there, and the city was delirious in his praise. Everyone sang his genius; the great Beethoven, welcomed him warmly. His airs were hummed everywhere. A benefit performance, arranged in his honor at the Kärnthnerthor Theater just before his departure for Italy, was attended by thousands, and thousands more, unable to gain admission to the theater, stood outside. For their benefit, Rossini arranged an impromptu concert from a balcony.

On February 3, 1823, Rossini attended the première of his opera *Semiramide* in Venice. His wife appeared in the leading female role. But the opera was received so apathetically that Rossini's stay in Italy was brief. Seeking favor elsewhere, he went to London in 1823. There he was received by King George IV and earned over seven thousand pounds in various concerts for the nobility within a single year.

In 1824 he settled in Paris. For two years he was the manager of the Théâtre Italien, and offered several of his serious works at the Paris Opéra. In 1826 he was appointed by King Charles X as *premier compositeur du roi*. His contract specified that he would write five new operas during the next decade, for an extraordinary sum, and he was promised a handsome yearly pension for life upon termination of the agreement.

In addition to presenting several of his older operas in French versions, Rossini completed a new work, *William Tell* (*Guillaume Tell*), a serious opera many critics regard as his greatest. It was introduced at the Paris Opéra on August 3, 1829. Critics and leading musicians were delighted. Fétis proclaimed that Rossini had achieved the impossible, having progressed beyond the elevated standards of his earlier masterworks. Later, such composers as Bellini, Berlioz, Mendelssohn, Verdi, and even Wagner were unqualified in their praise. Yet it did not at first appeal to the general public. It was performed only fifty-six times in its original version. Audiences enjoyed the libretto but found much of the music dull, and the opera as a whole much too long to sustain interest. Because of its extreme length, Rossini himself later authorized a shortened version. Still the Paris Opéra frequently presented only one act of *William Tell* at a time, completing the program with the performance of another opera. According to an oft repeated anecdote, Rossini, informed on one occasion that the second act of *William Tell* had been scheduled by the Opéra, inquired with mock surprise: "What —*all* of it?"

Today *William Tell* is acknowledged as one of Rossini's two greatest operas. Its overture is one of the most popular in the symphonic and semiclassical repertory. Donald Jay Grout conceded that the opera as a whole is "uneven in quality" and that too much of it is distended and dull, but noted where its greatness lies: "The first act is well planned to furnish contrast between the pastoral music at the beginning, in which Rossini employed many authentic Alpine horn motifs (*Ranze des vaches*) and the magnificent finale. . . . Act II is the most nearly perfect both in general arrangement and in detail. . . . The third and fourth acts contain . . . numbers of great beauty, such as the introduction to Act IV, and Arnold's aria, 'Asile héréditaire,' the canonic trio for women's voices, 'Je vends à votre amour,' and the final hymn to freedom."

The American première of *William Tell* took place at the Park Theatre in New York on September 19, 1831. It entered the repertory of the Metropolitan Opera during its second season, on November 28, 1884.

When he completed the writing of *William Tell*, at the age of thirty-seven, Rossini was at his peak of creativity and fame. He lived thirty-nine years longer but never again was he to write an opera. This "great renunciation," as his remarkable creative abstinence is often described, is without parallel in music, if not in all art. Francis Toye inquired, "Is there any other artist who thus deliberately, in the very prime of life, renounced that form of artistic production which has made him famous throughout the civilized world?"

Many theories have been offered to explain this mystery. Rossini himself stubbornly refused to provide a clue, even to his closest friends. Some believe that he resented the fact that audiences did not recognize the greatness of *William Tell* and was so embittered that he vowed never again to write an opera. Some maintain that he was envious of Meyerbeer's growing popularity in French opera and refused to compete with him. Others point to his reputed indolence and insist that Rossini, now wealthy, preferred to avoid work. Still others cite the deterioration of Rossini's mental and physical health after the 1830's—his acute neurasthenia, and the disease of the bladder and urinary tract (possibly of venereal origin) that afflicted him.

Certain explanations are more plausible than others. It seems highly doubtful that Rossini was overwhelmed by the public rejection of *William Tell;* he had encountered too many failures to be troubled by excessive sensitivity. Nor can one describe as lazy a composer who wrote thirty-nine operas in nineteen years. Envy of his colleagues had never been one of his failings, and it is improbable that he was overly oppressed by Meyerbeer's ascent to fame.

His waning health seems to provide the most logical explanation. After 1835 Rossini was indefatigable in his efforts to improve his health. His nerves were in such a turbulent state that at times he thought he was going mad. His first experience riding in a railway train in 1836 sent him into a dead faint. The death of a friend made him violently ill. For several years Rossini, then living in Florence, was virtually bedridden, tortured by insomnia and indigestion.

Rossini did not remain completely silent as a composer during these years. Though he avoided opera, he wrote church music, including the Stabat Mater in 1842, and the *Petite Messe solennelle* in 1863. He also created many minor vocal and piano pieces.

One hundred and eighty of his piano compositions were gathered into the volume entitled *Péchés de vieillesse.*

Rossini's cures in watering resorts seem to have revitalized him. In August 1846, ten months after the death of his wife, Rossini married Olympie Pélissier, who had been his mistress since 1832. After 1855 they lived mainly in Paris, where Rossini became a prominent figure in Parisian social and cultural life. He entertained in the grand manner at his apartment on the Rue de la Chaussée d'Antin, and at his summer villa in Passy, outside Paris. The greatest European musicians coming to Paris would visit him Saturday evenings to enjoy his wit. Once, asked to hear two compositions by a visiting composer, Rossini remarked hurriedly after the first had been performed: "I like the second one better." On another occasion, encountering Meyerbeer, he poured out a detailed list of his distressing physical symptoms. When Meyerbeer left him, Rossini remarked to a friend, "I feel perfectly well, but dear Meyerbeer would be *so* delighted to hear of my death tomorrow that I didn't have the heart to deny him a little pleasure today."

The last time Rossini played host to his guests was on September 26, 1868. Two weeks later he suffered a heart attack, which led to other complications. A special papal nuncio administered extreme unction. Rossini died in Passy on Friday, November 13, 1868, and was buried at Père Lachaise in Paris. Some years later, at the request of the Italian government, his remains were transferred to the Santa Croce church in Florence.

As a composer Rossini was a curious combination of genius and hack. He wrote too much, too quickly, with too little concern for editing or revision or selection. He permitted too much inferior music to remain in his operas because better material would have required expenditure of energy and effort. He continually borrowed from himself, lifting passages from his earlier music; and there were several occasions when he even plagiarized from other composers. He did not hesitate to interpolate the work of other men—even in his masterwork *The Barber of Seville.* He was always willing to write functional music to specifications. And he was sublimely indifferent to the quality of the texts provided by his librettists. When he once said lightly, "Give me a laundry list and I will set it to music," he spoke almost literally; many of his librettos were as contrived, prosaic, and functional as a laundry list. Of the great composers in music history, he probably had the lowest artistic standards.

He knew his weaknesses, as he knew his strength. He asserted that of his works only *The Barber of Seville, William Tell,* and parts of *Othello* would survive; and he would have been correct had he included some of his sparkling, effervescent overtures to other operas. He knew he was incapable of profundity or deep emotion. "The German critics wish that I compose like Haydn or Mozart," he said after his visit to Vienna. "But if I took all the pains in the world I should still be a wretched Haydn or Mozart. So I prefer to remain a Rossini. Whatever that may be, it is something, and at least I am not a bad Rossini."

He was not "a bad Rossini." For all his shortcomings, he was a genius, remarkably spontaneous, facile, and inventive. His best music had the gifts of both laughter and inspired melody; deathless vitality; consummate skill in construction; and exceptional knowledge of the human voice. It was continuously alive with experiment and innovation. Ernest Newman wrote: "Rossini altered the form and spirit of Italian opera in a way and to an extent that must have been rather disturbing to the conservative minds of his own day. . . . He broke away, bit by bit, from a good deal of the older formalism of structure." Newman elaborated, explaining that Rossini shortened "the long and dreary recitatives . . . common in older operas" by replacing them with a "more animated and natural dialogue"; by developing the expressive power of choral ensembles and using them not at the end of the act as had been customary but whenever the text demanded. Important, too, was the way in which he refused to allow his singers to ornament melodies at will but insisted they follow the notes he had written out for them; his effective use of alternating slow and fast passages, and crescendos for climaxes; his deployment of strings, instead of merely the cembalo, to accompany recitatives; the enrichment of his orchestration through the interpolation of instruments rarely if ever used at that time.

Richard Wagner had this to say about Rossini: "His station is no lowly one, for with the same title as Palestrina, Bach and Mozart belonged to their ages, Rossini belongs to his."

The twentieth-century British composer Benjamin Britten prepared two orchestral suites based on Rossini's melodies: *Soirées musicales* and *Matinées musicales,* both of which borrow themes from *William Tell* and *Péchés de vieillesse.* The twentieth-century Italian composer Ottorino Respighi also created two works based on Rossini: the ballet score for *La Boutique fantasque,* introduced by Diaghilev's Ballet Russe on June 5, 1919, and the orchestral suite *Rossiniana.*

PRINCIPAL WORKS

Choral Music—Stabat Mater; Saul; Pietà signore; Petite messe solennelle; cantatas, hymns.

Operas—La Scala di Seta; Il Signor Bruschino; Tancredi; L'Italiana in Algeri; Elisabetta; Il Barbiere di Siviglia; Otello; La Cenerentola; La Gazza ladra; Armida; Mosè in Egitto; Semiramide; Le Comte Ory; Guillaume Tell.

Piano Music—Péchés de vieillesse.

Vocal Music—Arias, ariettas, cavatinas, and various songs.

ABOUT

Bonavia, F., Rossini; Curzon, H. de, Une heure avec Rossini; Rognoni, L., Rossini; Stendhal, The Life of Rossini; Toye, F., Rossini: A Study in Tragi-Comedy.

Anton Rubinstein *1829-1894*

ANTON GRIGOREVICH RUBINSTEIN was born in Vykhvatinetz, Volhynia, on November 28, 1829. His father, a merchant of Jewish descent, was converted to Christianity when Anton was two. Later the family moved to Moscow, where the elder Rubinstein opened a small pencil factory. Anton started to study piano with his mother and made such rapid progress that he was soon sent to one of Moscow's foremost piano teachers, Alexander Villoing, for instruction.

On July 11, 1839, Rubinstein made his piano début in a concert in Moscow which featured a Hummel concerto. "He certainly has the soul of an artist and the feeling for the beautiful," commented the Moscow *Galatea,* "and there lies with him so much musical talent that in time, after the complete perfecting and developing of it, the young artist will undoubtedly be able to procure for himself an honorable rank among European celebrities."

The success of this performance encouraged Villoing to take his prodigy to Paris and London. "In Paris, I remained a whole year," Rubinstein later recalled in his autobiography, "but had no lessons except with Villoing, who jealously guarded me from all approach; not a being could gain access to me. At one of my concerts, Liszt, Chopin and other musical celebrities were present. In London, I was graciously received by the young and then handsome Queen Victoria, and subsequently in all the aristocratic circles. Although but a boy of twelve, I felt no shyness nor timidity in the presence of these formal lords and ladies."

Rubinstein remained in Paris two years. After that he toured many parts of Europe. In 1844 he settled for a while in Berlin, studying composition with Dehn. Then he proceeded to Vienna where he became a friend of Liszt. Returning to Berlin, he spent two years teaching piano and appearing in concerts.

In 1848 he returned to his native land, settling in St. Petersburg for eight years. He gained the patronage of the Grand Duchess Helen, who appointed him chamber virtuoso. At her summer residence in Kamenoi-Ostrow, Rubinstein completed a piano suite of twenty-four portraits which, in tribute to his patroness, he named after the town of Kamenoi-Ostrow. One of its movements (originally called "Rêve angélique," but now known as "Kamenoi-Ostrow") has become one of Rubinstein's most popular melodies. Another of his now celebrated piano pieces had been written several years earlier. It was the Melody in F, the first of two pieces in opus 3. He also wrote works in more ambitious forms, including three operas in the years 1852-1853.

In 1854 Rubinstein undertook a grand concert tour of Europe. He was acclaimed as one of the very greatest piano virtuosos of his time. In his command of keyboard technique he was compared to Liszt, while in majesty of musical conception and in profundity of insight he was declared to have no rival. "This Russian boy," the distinguished pianist Ignaz Moscheles said, "has fingers as light as feathers and with them the strength of a man."

In 1858, after the tour ended, Rubinstein was appointed court pianist and conductor of the court concerts in St. Petersburg. In 1859 he became director of the Russian Musical

ANTON RUBINSTEIN

Society. He played a significant role in the musical life of St. Petersburg through his adventurous program-planning and high standards of performances. He also influenced musical pedagogy in Russia by founding the St. Petersburg Conservatory in 1862 and serving as its director for five years.

At about this time, Rubinstein completed several of his finest works. These include the twelve *Persian Songs*, op. 34; the *Ocean Symphony*, which during his lifetime was heard in concerts throughout the world; the piano suite *Soirées de St. Petersburg*, op. 44, one of whose movements is the popular Romance in E-flat; the excellent Third Piano Concerto in G major, which is still a favorite in the concert hall; and, perhaps most significant of all, the opera *The Demon*. The world première of *The Demon* took place in St. Petersburg on January 25, 1875 (Rubinstein conducting). The work was so well liked that it enjoyed over a hundred presentations in less than a decade. It was also produced throughout Europe (Italy excepted), and was a triumph when heard at Covent Garden in London in 1881. It was acclaimed when staged in the United States—in New York City on May 13, 1922. It has frequently been revived in the Soviet Union, and a performance by the Bolshoi Opera was recorded in its entirety and released in 1964.

The libretto by Lermontov tells the story of a demon who pursues Tamara, a princess, with the hope of finding redemption through her love; in the end he is responsible for her death. "Rubinstein's wildly uneven, overchromatic, intermittently banal, and occasionally very forceful pre-Wagnerian Romantic music, rises at its best to a dramatic strength worthy of *Boris Godunov*," said Herbert Weinstock in the *Saturday Review*. He added: "The first two scenes of Act II are magnificent music drama. As they unfold, one forgets that this is a superannuated opera by an extraordinarily uncertain composer. One is completely taken over by the subtly, vigorously presented struggle of the Demon to alter his inner nature and offer the wavering Tamara a purely human love. For Tamara's struggle to repress both the Demon and herself and the hair-raising moments when she finally kisses him and dies are transformed into completely convincing music."

Between 1870 and 1872 Rubinstein was in Vienna directing performances of the Vienna Philharmonic and choral concerts as well. He made several concert tours as a pianist between 1867 and 1873, one tour taking him to the United States. At his American début in New York, on September 23, 1872, Rubinstein performed his own Concerto in D minor among other works. Later he gave over two hundred concerts (often in joint appearances with the violinist Wilhelmj), for which he received forty thousand dollars, then an unprecedented fee. Before returning home, he added to his already crowded schedule a monumental historical series of seven recitals in New York, which took place from May 12 to May 20, 1873. The last program was made up entirely of his own compositions, and included a series of variations on "Yankee Doodle" which he had created for the occasion. His American tour was a triumph of incomparable magnitude and reaffirmed his imperial position among the concert performers of his generation.

Between 1885 and 1887 Rubinstein gave farewell recitals all over Europe. From 1887 to 1891, he resumed his post as director of the St. Petersburg Conservatory, and from 1891 to 1894 lived in semiretirement in Dresden, where he completed his autobiography. In 1890, he established the Rubinstein Prize, an international competition for young pianists and composers.

Rubinstein died at Peterhof, near St. Petersburg, on November 20, 1894. In spite of the numerous tributes he had gathered, Rubinstein became in his last years a bitter man. He felt he had never received the recognition he deserved for his compositions. He wrote to his publishers in 1889, "I confess to you frankly and honestly, that complete disappointment is the sum total of all my artistic activity! That to which I have attached especial importance all my life, and to which I have devoted all my knowledge and built all my hopes upon—my work as a composer—has met with failure."

As Arthur Pougin described Rubinstein, "He had the body of a Hercules, with a solid frame, huge developed chest, and broad, powerful shoulders. His head was square, without either beard or moustache. The forehead was high and prominent, the hair was thick and black. The nose was strong, the mouth sensual, and the eyes, which were sunk in their orbits, had a look which, though piercing, seemed a little vague and undecided."

One of Rubinstein's favorite diversions was billiards, though he was not especially competent at the game. "I play billiards only for exercise," he would remark apologetically after making a poor shot. He smoked cigarettes profusely, was partial to Italian cooking, and was particularly fond of cucumbers, which he liked to have at every meal.

Leonid Sabaneyev evaluated Rubinstein's vast and varied output as a composer in this manner: "In most cases, Rubinstein shows himself to be a successor of Beethoven and Mendelssohn, but his defective sense of style leads him to blend these influences with those of Glinka, the Italian school, Meyerbeer, and even Liszt. In his symphonic and chamber works, he is Mendelssohn without the stereotyped form and feeling for style of the original, but on the other hand, he often approaches Beethoven in the intensity and dramatic quality of his emotions (the Fourth Piano Concerto in D minor). In opera and music for the stage, he is more like Meyerbeer and Glinka. His work is inundated with an abundance of what are called commonplaces. Nevertheless, it cannot be denied that we find in it oases of inspiration which compel us to bear in mind his rank as musician. . . . The oases of great thoughts and even of grandiose conceptions are evidence that if he had not written at journalistic speed, there is no reason why he should not have been the proclaimer of a great musical idea."

Arthur Pougin noted that Rubinstein wrote too hastily and paid too little attention to pruning and polishing. "Every now and again he lapses into writing which is clumsy and is not characterized by purity of style; and he sometimes is rather too ready to be content with the first idea that came into his head." But Pougin emphasized that there is also a good deal in Rubinstein's best works to compensate for these serious faults. "He had ample inspiration and wide, expansive temperament which made it possible for him to take up all branches of composition, if not exactly with success, at least with uncommon vigor. His music is undoubtedly alive, picturesque, and full of warmth and movement, and in moments of inspiration it carries the listener along in its train and rouses him to a high pitch of enthusiasm."

His greatest fault lay, perhaps, in the fact that his style, too eclectic, never achieved a strong personal identity. Rubinstein recognized this shortcoming, saying, with greater bitterness than wit: "For the Christians I am a Jew. For the Jews I am a Christian. For the Russians I am a German. For the Germans I am a Russian."

Anton Rubinstein's brother, Nicolas (1835-1881), was a celebrated musician. He was an outstanding pianist and conductor and the founder and director of the Moscow Conservatory.

PRINCIPAL WORKS

Ballet—The Vine.

Chamber Music—10 string quartets; 5 piano trios; 3 violin sonatas; 2 cello sonatas; Quintet in F major, for piano and wind; String Quintet in F major, Piano Quintet in G minor.

Choral Music—3 oratorios; 2 cantatas; part songs.

Operas—Dmitri Donskoi; The Siberian Hunters; Thomas the Fool; Die Kinder der Heide; Feramors; The Demon; Die Makkabäer; Nero; The Merchant Kalashnikov; Sulamith; Unter Räubern; Der Papagei; Goriusha.

Orchestral Music—6 symphonies; 5 piano concertos; 2 cello concertos; Violin Concerto in G major; Concertstück, for piano and orchestra; overtures, suites, tone poems.

Piano Music—4 sonatas; Kamenoi-Ostrow; Two Melodies; Soirées de St. Petersburg; The Months; barcarolles, caprices, études, funeral marches, mazurkas, nocturnes, pieces, polonaises, preludes, serenades.

Vocal Music—Twelve Persian Songs; Five Fables by Krilov; various individual songs for voice and piano, including Der Asra, A Bard, Du bist wie eine Blume, Es blinkt der Tau, Wanderers Nachtlied; various Russian songs.

ABOUT

Bowen, C. S. D., Free Artist: The Story of Anton and Nicolas Rubinstein; Glebov, I., Anton Rubinstein: His Musical Activities and Opinions of His Contemporaries; Hervey, A., Anton Rubinstein.

Musical Quarterly, October 1939; Musical Times, December 1945.

Camille Saint-Saëns *1835-1921*

CHARLES CAMILLE SAINT-SAËNS was born in Paris on October 9, 1835. His father, a government official in the Ministry of the Interior, died when Camille was three months old. The child was entrusted to a baby farm until his second year, when he was taken over and raised by a great-aunt, Charlotte Masson.

His precociousness in music has been compared with that of Mozart. Saint-Saëns was attracted to pleasant musical sounds, repelled by unpleasant ones when he was only two. When he was just two and a half, his aunt playfully started to teach him piano, and to her astonishment found him completing the first book of exercises in about a month. For fear of overtaxing him she stopped these lessons, but the child protested so that they had to be resumed. At three Camille was taught notation; at four and a half he played the piano part of a Beethoven violin sonata at a salon concert; and at five he began to compose songs and piano pieces. His greatest delight was to read through an opera score such as Mozart's *Don Giovanni*.

Camille's study began in earnest when at seven he became a piano pupil of Camille-Marie Stamaty, and studied theory with Pierre Maleden. His progress was so swift that on May 6, 1846, at the age of ten and a half, he made his public début in Paris in an exacting program that included a Mozart concerto and a movement from Beethoven's C minor Piano Concerto.

From 1848 to 1853 he attended the Paris Conservatory; there, as a pupil of Benoist, he won first prize for organ playing. On December 26, 1852, his *Ode à Sainte-Cécile* was performed, after winning first prize in a competition. When his first symphony was introduced in Paris on December 11, 1853, Charles Gounod prophesied that if he used his native gifts properly, Saint-Saëns would surely develop into "a great master."

Saint-Saëns: săn säns′

CAMILLE SAINT-SAËNS

Despite his exceptional gifts, Saint-Saëns never won the Prix de Rome. He competed for it twice, first in 1852, and again twelve years later, when he was already a composer of some consequence.

Having left the Conservatory in 1853, Saint-Saëns became organist at the Church Saint-Merry in Paris for four years. In 1858 he was appointed to one of the most esteemed organ posts in Paris, at the Madeleine Church. He remained until 1877, winning recognition as one of the foremost French organ virtuosos of that period. He was lauded by such eminent musicians as Anton Rubinstein, Pablo de Sarasate, Clara Schumann, and Robert Franz.

Saint-Saëns was also industriously pursuing a career as composer. He won first prize for his Second Symphony in 1857, in a contest sponsored by the Société Sainte-Cécile. In 1858 he completed his First Piano Concerto, introduced in Leipzig on October 26 of that year. In 1863 he wrote his first major secular choral work, the Oratorio de Noël.

A man of great energy, Saint-Saëns was engaged in many musical activities. He toured extensively as a concert pianist and conductor, usually in performances of his own music. From 1861 to 1865 he taught piano at the École Niedermeyer, influencing such eminent French musicians as Fauré and Messager, among many others, as pupils. He wrote theoretical treatises and edit-

ed the music of the old French masters. In 1871 he helped found the Société Nationale de Musique to promote the music of French composers, and was one of its leaders until 1886. Hans von Bülow considered him to have the finest musical gifts of any musician of his generation, an estimate all the more remarkable in view of von Bülow's association with Wagner.

These activities were matched by Saint-Saëns' extreme versatility in fields outside music. He was, as Philip Hale once remarked, a "caricaturist, dabbler in science, enamored of mathematics and astronomy, amateur comedian, feuilletonist, critic, traveler, archaeologist." He wrote poetry, plays, and books on philosophy, literature, painting, and the theater. He was a linguist, familiar with the classical languages, and a student of natural history and physics.

Between 1868 and 1877, Saint-Saëns completed several works that established his greatness in French music: the Second Piano Concerto in G minor (still the most popular of his five piano concertos), which he introduced in Paris on May 6, 1868, with Anton Rubinstein conducting; his first tone poem, Le Rouet d'Omphale, an illustration, the composer explained, of "feminine seduction, the triumphant struggle of weakness over strength," introduced at a Concert Pasdeloup on April 14, 1872; his first cello concerto, in A minor, the more popular of the two cello works, first performed at the Paris Conservatory on January 19, 1873 with August Tolbecque as soloist; the popular Danse macabre, a picture of ghostly dancers as Death plays the tune, which had its première at a Concert Colonne on January 24, 1875; and, perhaps most significant, the opera Samson et Dalila (Samson and Delilah).

Samson and Delilah, written to a libretto by Ferdinand Lemaire, was first heard in part in Paris in 1875, when a concert version of a single act was performed. The music was severely criticized at the time. "Never," said the Chronique musicale in a typical reaction, "has a more complete absence of melody made itself felt as in this drama. And when to the lack of melodic motives there is added at times a harmony extremely daring and an instrumentation which never rises above the level of the ordinary, you will have some idea of what Samson is like!" No one in France cared to produce the opera. Franz Liszt, however, became convinced of its originality and importance and used his influence to have it mounted in Weimar, on December 2, 1877. There the public and critical reaction was more favorable, though not fully appreciative of its true artistic merits. *Samson and Delilah* was performed in Brussels in 1878, in Hamburg in 1882, in Rouen in 1890. Only then was it staged in Paris, at the Opéra, on November 23, 1892. The American première took place in New Orleans on January 4, 1893, and its New York premiére at the Metropolitan Opera on February 8, 1895.

Samson and Delilah is not only the most celebrated of its composer's twelve operas but a peak in the French lyric theater. "Altogether," say Wallace Brockway and Herbert Weinstock in *The Opera,* "the score is vastly entertaining, even at times thrilling. Throughout *Samson* is the work of an admirable musician—colorful, but not to excess, cleverly orchestrated, dramatic. The choral writing is solid and telling, and even the seeming lack of balance caused by Saint-Saëns' passion for his enchantress is evened up by the tenseness of the struggling Samson who does not, appropriately, gain heroic stature until, at the very end, he pulls the temple down on the heads of the Philistines."

Two more outstanding works appeared in the 1880's, both for the concert hall. One was his admirable Third Violin Concerto in G minor, written for Pablo de Sarasate, who introduced it in Paris on January 2, 1881. The other was the remarkable Third Symphony in C minor, with organ, which he wrote for the Royal Philharmonic; Saint-Saëns conducted its first performance with that orchestra in London on May 19, 1886.

"The Saint-Saëns symphonies, notably the one in C minor with organ, are stylistic models," wrote Louis Vuillemin. "True to classical form, they extend it without doing much of the renovation until the Finale makes its appearance. His symphonic poems, on the other hand, better affirm the musician's personality. They instantly establish a genius: the 'poem' for orchestra has a legendary cast. As to the concertos for piano and orchestra, it seems to me that even more than anything already mentioned, they characterized the composer's 'manner.' Radiantly wrought, ingenious in their instrumental disposition, often rich in the picturesque, they

dominate the ensemble of the composer's work and, I believe, constitute their most original feature."

Saint-Saëns married Marie-Laure Truffot in 1875. Their relationship, unhappy at the start, ended in disaster with the death of their two children. One day, while on vacation with his wife, Saint-Saëns quietly disappeared; a few days later he sent her a note telling her he could live with her no longer.

Despite his extensive traveling throughout his life, Saint-Saëns remained unusually prolific to the end. He completed operas, concertos, large chamber music works, choral music, incidental music for the theater, songs, and numerous pieces for piano and organ.

He was a composer who preferred conservative approaches to experimentation. He possessed one of the most consummate, extraordinary techniques of any French composer of his time. What he wrote might, on occasion, be superficial, trivial, or derivative, but it never lacked distinction of structure and style. He had an uncommon gift for writing in styles far different from the French Romantic idiom of his great works. At will, he composed music that was identifiably Algerian, Persian, Breton, Russian, Arabian, Portuguese, and even Egyptian. He also had an uncanny gift for bringing into the music of the late nineteenth century the styles and manners of an older day, by imitating classic forms and recreating the style and structures of an earlier century.

In the words of M. D. Calvocoressi, the basic traits of Saint-Saëns' music are the "surpassing excellence of his technique . . . his lucidity, his versatility, his sense of proportion, and the perfection of what he achieved within the limits of his outlook— limits carefully thought out, deliberately adopted, which he never fell short of or overstepped. . . . His qualities of emotion and imagination were inferior to his capacity for building and working out, but what his works lack in glow and profundity they almost make up for in technical interest and beautiful finish, in fineness of proportion and perfection of texture."

Arthur Hervey summarized: "He may not have the rugged power of a Berlioz, the emotional feeling of a Gounod, the mystic fervor of a César Franck, the insinuating charm of a Massenet, but he possesses an extraordinary faculty for assimilation, and certain characteristics peculiarly his own. He has been taxed with dryness, with lacking that warmth of feeling which vivifies a work and establishes a communication between the composer and his audience. The fact is that, of all composers, Saint-Saëns is most difficult to describe. He eludes you at every moment—the elements constituting his musical personality are so varied in their nature, yet they seem to blend in so remarkable a fashion. . . . Saint-Saëns is a typical Frenchman. . . . He is pre-eminently witty. . . . It is this quality which has enabled him to attack the driest forms of art and render them bearable. There is nothing ponderous about him."

A restless traveler, Saint-Saëns visited the remote corners of the world, even in old age. He twice visited the United States, first in 1906 on a concert tour, and again ten years later to perform a concert of French music at the Panama Exposition, in which he introduced his own *Hail Columbia*. When he was eighty-one he toured South America, and at eighty-five gave concerts in Algiers and Greece. He gave his last piano recital and conducted his last orchestral concert in 1921. He died while on vacation in Algiers on December 16, 1921, at eighty-six. His body was brought back to Paris. His funeral was attended by France's foremost musicians, and eulogies were given by Alfred Bruneau and Charles M. Widor.

Saint-Saëns was one of the most highly honored French musicians of the late nineteenth century. He received the Legion of Honor in 1868, was elected to the French Institut in 1881, and was given an honorary doctorate by Cambridge in 1893.

Georges Servières gave the following description of the composer: "Saint-Saëns is of short stature. His head extremely original, the features characteristic: a great brow, wide and open where, between the eyebrows, the tenacity of the man reveals itself; hair habitually cut short, and brownish beard turning gray; a nose like an eagle's beak, underlined by two deeply marked wrinkles starting from the nostrils; eyes a little prominent, very mobile, very expressive."

Though his social evenings at his Paris home were celebrated—particularly the Monday musicales, attended by the great and near-great—Saint-Saëns was essentially partial to solitude. He would often slip away from his friends for weeks at a time to take solitary holidays.

A brilliant conversationalist, he also had a well-developed gift for mimicry. He would delight his friends by performing the role of Marguerite in Gounod's *Faust*, bedecked in an outlandish costume; or by parodying early Italian operas; or by enacting a scene from Offenbach's *La Belle Hélène* with extravagant gestures. On a visit to Moscow, stopping at an empty concert hall in the company of Tchaikovsky and Anton Rubinstein, he startled his colleagues by mounting the stage without warning and performing pirouettes like a ballerina.

PRINCIPAL WORKS

Chamber Music—2 string quartets; 2 piano trios; 2 violin sonatas; 2 cello sonatas; Septet, for trumpet, strings and piano; Piano Quintet in A minor; Piano Quartet in B-flat major; Havanaise, for violin and piano; Oboe Sonata; Clarinet Sonata; Bassoon Sonata.

Choral Music—Messe solennelle; Oratorio de Noël; Le Déluge; Requiem; Psalm CL; Chants d'automne; La Gloire; Ave Maria; Tu es Petrus; Quam Dilecta; Laudate Dominum; canticles, hymns, motets, other secular and church compositions.

Operas—La Princesse jaune; Le Timbre d'argent; Samson et Dalila; Étienne Marcel; Henry VIII; Proserpine; Ascanio; Phryné; Les Barbares; Hélène; L'Ancêtre; Déjanire.

Orchestral Music—5 piano concertos; 3 symphonies; 3 violin concertos; 2 cello concertos; Introduction and Rondo Capriccioso, for violin and orchestra; Le Rouet d'Omphale; Phaëton; Danse macabre; La Jeunesse d'Hercule; Suite algérienne; Jota aragonesa; Rapsodie d'Auvergne, for piano and orchestra; Le Carnaval des animaux, for two pianos and orchestra; Ouverture de fête; incidental music to plays, including Antigone, Andromaque, and On ne badine pas avec l'amour.

Organ Music—7 improvisations; 3 Rhapsodies on Breton Themes; 3 fantasies; 3 preludes and fugues.

Piano Music—Souvenir d'Italie; Feuillet d'album; Variations on a Theme of Beethoven, for two pianos; Caprice héroïque, for two pianos; bagatelles, études, fugues, waltzes.

Vocal Music—Mélodies persanes; La Cendre rouge; individual songs for voice and piano, including Le Bonheur est chose légère, La Cloche, Danse macabre, and Les Pas d'armes du roi Jean; vocal duets.

ABOUT

Aguétant, P., Saint-Saëns par lui-même, d'après des lettres reçues; Bonnerot, J., Saint-Saëns, sa vie et son œuvre; Chantavoine, J., Camille Saint-Saëns; Cooper, M., French Music; Dandelot, A., La Vie et l'œuvre de Saint-Saëns; Hervey, A., Saint-Saëns; Lyle, W., Camille Saint-Saëns: His Life and Art; Rolland, R., Musicians of Today; Servières, G., Saint-Saëns.

Giovanni Battista Sammartini
1698-1775

IN THE WRITING of symphonic and chamber music, Sammartini was an important predecessor of Haydn. Little biographical information about him has come down to us. Identified as "Il Milanese" (to distinguish him from his brother, "Il Londinese"), Giovanni Battista Sammartini was born in Milan in 1698. It is not known who his teachers were, but we do know that in the 1720's he was an organist in several churches in Milan. From 1730 to 1770 he was *maestro di cappella* at the Convent Santa Maria Maddalena. In this office he wrote choral music, motets, and psalms. As early as 1734 he had become interested in instrumental music and had written his first symphony, one of the first works to define symphonic structure and style. "It was an outstanding success," recorded Carpani in his biography of Haydn published in 1812, "and became all the rage in that large capital where music is held to be a very agreeable pastime." Sammartini also produced several chamber works which added greatly to his reputation; these included a set of six trio-sonatas issued in London in 1744. His fame as a composer spread throughout Europe, bringing him many pupils from outside Italy, including Gluck, who studied with him between 1737 and 1741. Sammartini died in Milan on January 15, 1775.

It is believed that Sammartini produced over two thousand compositions, including operas and church music as well as symphonies and chamber music.

According to Denis W. Stevens, Sammartini's greatest contribution to music was his "sensitive handling of the melodic line. . . . The melody is never overdressed or weighed down with ornament, and it is worthy of note that the slow movements in many of Sammartini's symphonies are extremely short, thus tending to preclude the usual decorative adjuncts to a slowly moving melodic line."

Giovanni's older brother, Giuseppe (c. 1693—c. 1750), known as "Il Londinese" because of his extended stay in England, was a distinguished oboe virtuoso, a composer of excellent chamber and orchestral music, and director of chamber concerts at the palace of the Prince of Wales.

PRINCIPAL WORKS
Chamber Music—6 trio-sonatas for two violins and bass; Sonatas, for flute, two violins, and bass; Nocturnes, for two violins and bass.
Choral Music—Masses, motets, psalms.
Orchestral Music—24 symphonies.

ABOUT
Sondheimer, R., Giovanni Battista Sammartini. Journal of the American Musicological Society, Summer 1953.

Pablo de Sarasate *1844-1908*

PABLO MARTÍN MELITÓN SARASATE Y NAVASCUES, composer of violin music, was born in Pamplona, Navarre, Spain, on March 10, 1844. He began to study violin during his childhood, and gave his first public appearances in the town of Corunna when he was six. Shortly afterwards he toured Spain. At ten he performed for the Queen, who presented him with a Stradivarius. When he was twelve he went to Paris and attended the Conservatory for several years. He won first prizes as a pupil in violin of Alard, and in harmony of Reber.

At fifteen, he was pronounced ready for the concert stage. From then on he toured most of the world, acclaimed everywhere as a virtuoso of the first order. He had an extraordinarily beautiful tone, and with it an aristocratic style and impeccable taste. Until 1872 his programs consisted mainly of fantasies of opera arias, or his own transcriptions or adaptations of Spanish folk songs and dances. After 1872, however, he devoted himself also to the great classics of violin music, which he performed with consummate technical mastery and musicianship. Many composers wrote major compositions for him, including Édouard Lalo (*Symphonie espagnole* and the Concerto in G minor), Max Bruch (Scottish Fantasy), and Saint-Saëns (Concerto No. 3 in G minor).

"When one saw this little well-set man—with elegant figure, black eyes, and abundant, flowing hair," wrote Arthur Pougin, "holding in one hand both his fiddle and bow—advance to the platform, greet his public with great simplicity and without timidity, then place his instrument under his chin and prepare to launch upon his solo in his irreproachably correct position, . . . one instantly felt that one was in the presence of a veritable artist." A contempo-

Sarasate: sä-rä-sä′tä

PABLO DE SARASATE

rary critic reported: "Sarasate's distinguishing characteristics are not so much fire, force and passion, though of these he had an ample store, as purity of style, charm, flexibility, and extraordinary facility."

Sarasate produced a library of violin music familiar to violin students, concert audiences, and performers the world over. One of his most celebrated compositions is the *Zigeunerweisen (Gypsy Airs)*, op. 20, no. 1, a brilliant fantasia on gypsy melodies. Equally familiar are his four sets of *Danzas españolas (Spanish Dances)* (op. 21, 22, 23 and 26) in which can be found the extremely popular "Malagueña," "Habanera," "Caprice Basque" and "Zapateado."

Sarasate died in his villa, Navarra, in Biarritz, France, on September 20, 1908, a victim of acute bronchitis. In his will he bequeathed his violins and large sums of money to music schools in his native city. He also turned over to the city all the gifts that had been showered on him during his lifetime and which, after his death, were placed in a museum.

The following portrait of Sarasate was written by Luisa Sobrino, one of his close friends: "He was a model of courtliness and courtesy, particular to a degree as to the neatness and good taste of his dress—exactness personified. At his Biarritz home, he breakfasted in his room, then walked for a little time in his garden, attended by his favorite dog. . . . Then he would drive to his favorite café—the same café, invariably —walk to the same table, and sit down in the same chair, Sarasate's chair. . . . He lunched to the minute at the appointed hour, and then there would be a short walk to the beach. At ten minutes to nine precisely, he would take a cab and be driven to the Casino which he would always enter by the same door, sharp at the stroke of nine. . . . Then the homecoming—dominos, and a glass of beer.

"Sarasate, the man, was devoid of ostentation. . . . The possessor of a treasury of royal jewels, chiefly the gifts of admiring monarchs, he wore no jewelry but a simple chain. To money he gave no thought. . . . In his early days he was careless as to money. . . . Yet he had an eccentric fancy for carrying money about him. He liked to see it. I have often seen the special place in his violin case in which it was his habit to put his money and thus carry it about with him through an entire season."

PRINCIPAL WORKS

Violin Music—Danzas españolas; Zigeunerweisen; Introduction and Tarantelle; Navarra, for two violins; Peteneras; Jota de San Fermín; Adios montañas mias; Carmen Fantasia; Le Chant du rossignol; Introduction and Caprice-Jota; Jota aragonesa.

ABOUT

Sagardie, A., Pablo de Sarasate; Zárate, L., Sarasate.

Music and Letters, July 1955; Musical America, March 25, 1940; Scribner's Magazine, March 1896.

Alessandro Scarlatti *1660-1725*

PIETRO ALESSANDRO GASPARE SCARLATTI, the leading figure in the Neapolitan school which dominated Italian opera in the late seventeenth and early eighteenth centuries, was born in Palermo, Sicily, on May 2, 1660. It is believed that his father was a musician who had gone to Palermo from Trapani in early manhood and married a girl from that town. Little is known of Alessandro's early life, beyond the fact that his family moved to Rome in 1672; that he studied music in Rome with Carissimi as a boy, and that he started composition early, his works strongly influenced by such Italian masters as Stradella and Legrenzi.

On April 12, 1678, Alessandro Scarlatti married Antonia Anzalone. They had ten children, one of whom was the celebrated composer Domenico (*see* following sketch). A year after his marriage, Scarlatti began to establish himself as a composer. A Latin oratorio for the Lenten season, commissioned by the Arciconfraternità del SS Crocifisso, made a strong impression. In February that year his first opera, *Gli equivoci nel sembiante,* was produced at the Teatro Capranica.

His first opera brought Scarlatti an appointment as *maestro di cappella* to Queen Christina of Sweden. In making this appointment the Queen defied papal authorities who frowned upon Scarlatti because one of his sisters had been involved with an ecclesiastic. Under the Queen's patronage, Scarlatti wrote a second opera, *L'Honestà negli amori,* which was performed at her palace in Rome on February 6, 1680.

Scarlatti left Rome for Naples in 1682; he remained for the next two decades. The success of his new opera, *Psiche,* at the Palazzo Reale in Naples on December 23, 1683, and the first presentations in Naples of *Gli equivoci* and *Pompeo,* which had been previously performed in Rome, brought Scarlatti to the forefront of the Neapolitan composers. In 1684 he was appointed *maestro di cappella* at the Royal Chapel. In the succeeding years he wrote many operas for performance at the palace and at the Teatro San Bartolomeo, as well as music for various royal entertainments. Most of the operas completed by Scarlatti during this period reveal the haste with which they were written. Though his style is often vulgarized by his studied attempts to win public favor, one can discern even in these works some of the innovations which were soon to characterize the Neapolitan opera, notably the development of the *da capo* aria; the subdivision of recitative writing into two categories, *secco* (accompanied by harpsichord alone) and *stromentato* (accompanied by the orchestra); the introduction of ensemble numbers; and the development of the three-part "Italian overture," as opposed to the two-part "French overture" adopted by Lully in France.

Dissatisfied with his post at court (for both financial and artistic reasons) and with the disturbed political situation in Naples, Scarlatti requested a leave of absence in 1702. He hoped to find employment in Flor-

ALESSANDRO SCARLATTI

ence, where Prince Ferdinand de' Medici, eldest son of the Duke of Tuscany, was a noted patron of the arts. But Ferdinand took no interest in Scarlatti, and Florence offered him few opportunities to write and produce new operas. He consequently went on to Rome though there was little operatic activity in that city. There he attracted the support of Cardinal Ottoboni, through whose influence he obtained a fairly humble post as assistant director of music at the Santa Maria Maggiore Church. In 1707, by which time his post in Naples had been declared officially vacant, Scarlatti became the principal *maestro di cappella* at the Santa Maria Maggiore and obtained a similar post at Cardinal Ottoboni's palace. Scarlatti now produced a great amount of church music as well as some of his finest chamber cantatas. He did not, however, neglect the composition of opera. *Mitridate Eupatore,* one of his best and most ambitious works for the stage until then, and *Il Trionfo della libertà* were both produced in Venice at the Teatro San Giovanni Crisostomo in 1707. Two other operas were heard in Rome in 1708, and three in Naples and Rome in 1709. By 1710 Scarlatti had written his hundredth opera.

In 1709 Scarlatti returned to Naples to his old post as court *maestro di cappella.* Except for occasional brief visits to Rome, he remained in Naples permanently. He achieved distinction not only as a composer but equally as a teacher, his pupils including

Johann Adolph Hasse, Francesco Durante, and Nicola Logroscino, among many others.

Scarlatti's operas continued to be staged successfully in Naples and Rome. Between 1715 and 1721, three operas generally regarded as his masterworks were performed: *Tigrane*, given at the Teatro San Bartolomeo in Naples on February 16, 1715; *Il Trionfo dell'onore*, produced at the Teatro dei Fiorentini in Naples on November 26, 1718; and *Griselda*, introduced at the Teatro Capranica in Rome in January 1721.

Il Trionfo dell'onore is one of the earliest comic operas ever written, and the first to be written in Italian rather than in some dialect, as was customary. This is not yet *opera buffa*, though the work is sometimes designated as such; *opera buffa* proper did not emerge for another fifteen years, with Pergolesi. But its light mood and comic overtones foreshadows the *opera buffa*. *Il Trionfo* has enjoyed several successful revivals in England and Italy since 1938. It was recorded in its entirety in Italy in 1951, in an edition by Virgilio Moratri which was first introduced in Siena in 1940.

By 1721 Scarlatti was at the height of his creative power and popularity. He was honored by his country with knighthood, by the Pope with the Order of the Golden Spur. His influence was absorbed by an entire generation of opera composers in Italy. It was as a result of his genius that a new school of opera composers sprang up in Naples, dominating Europe as Monteverdi and Cavalli had dominated Venice in an earlier period.

In a discussion of Scarlatti's operas, Edward J. Dent has written: "The libretti of his day offered him hardly a guarantee of heroic sentiments which he could set to dignified recitative, as well as straightforward emotions which he could express in a neat aria at the end of the scene. . . . Writing every air (and each opera would contain some fifty or sixty) in the same form, Scarlatti attained a wonderful mastery over his material and besides displaying an infinite variety of style within the given limits, he gradually developed the form to a very high degree of emotional and structural organization."

Beyond his great contributions to Italian opera, Scarlatti composed highly accomplished chamber cantatas; he was, in fact, an outstanding exponent of that form in his generation, pouring into it some of his finest and freshest inspiration. He was also an important pioneer in instrumental music. In lifting the sinfonia from the context of the opera and using it as an independent composition he became one of the earliest masters of orchestral music in general, and of the symphony in particular. And he was one of the first composers of the string quartet; in his two string quartets the figured bass of the harpsichord was for the first time completely dispensed with, and the four stringed instruments (violins, viola, and cello) given full independence.

Despite his impressive achievements and development of new techniques and methods, Scarlatti was not essentially a reformer or iconoclast. "He made no attempt to alter the conventions of the cantata," said Philip Radcliffe, "and he left opera the same odd mixture of tragic and comic elements that he found. What he did realize more than any of his predecessors was the significance of classical tonality, and his power of combining, when at his best, beauty of melody and expressive harmony may well have exercised some inspiring influence even upon Bach and Mozart."

Professor Dent has summarized Scarlatti's place as follows: "He has gathered up all that was best of the tangled materials produced by that age of transition and experiment, the seventeenth century, to form out of them a musical language, vigorous and flexible as Italian itself, which has been the foundation of all music of the classical period."

PRINCIPAL WORKS

Chamber Music—2 string quartets; sonatas and suites for various solo instruments, or combination of instruments, and figured bass.

Choral Music—Chamber cantatas, madrigals, Masses, motets, oratorios, serenades.

Operas—About 115 operas including: Olimpia vendicata; Statira; Pirro e Demetrio; Mitridate Eupatore; Il Trionfo della libertà; Tigrane; Telemaco; Il Trionfo dell'onore; Marco Attilio Regolo; Cambise; Griselda; La Virtù negli amori.

Harpsichord Music—Variations on Follia; sundry other pieces.

ABOUT

Borren, C. van den, Alessandro Scarlatti et l'esthétique de l'opéra napolitain; Dent, E. J., Alessandro Scarlatti: His Life and Works; Foss, H. J. (editor), The Heritage of Music, vol. 2.

Musical Times, November 1926; La Revue musicale, January 1929.

Domenico Scarlatti *1685-1757*

GIUSEPPE DOMENICO SCARLATTI was the composer of over five hundred sonatas which rank among the crowning works in literature for the harpsichord. In them, too, a modern technique of keyboard performance is perfected. The sixth son of the ten children of Alessandro Scarlatti, the celebrated Neapolitan opera composer (*see* preceding sketch), Domenico was born in Naples on October 26, 1685. He received his musical training from his father.

In 1701 Domenico was appointed organist and composer at the Royal Chapel in Naples. A year later he left with his father for Rome. There his first operas were produced: *Ottavia restituita al trono,* during the carnival of 1703; *Giustino,* at the royal palace in December 1703; and *Irene,* in 1704, a revision of an opera by Pollarolo for which Scarlatti wrote thirty-three new arias.

Convinced of his son's remarkable talent, Alessandro urged Domenico to go to Venice where his gifts might find greater scope. As Alessandro wrote to Ferdinando de' Medici in 1705: "This son of mine is an eagle whose wings are grown. He ought not to stay idle in the nest, and I ought not to hinder his flight. Since the virtuoso Nicolino of Naples is passing through Rome on his way to Venice, I have thought fit to send Domenico with him; and under the able escort of his own artistic ability (which has made great progress since he was able to be with me and enjoy the honor of obeying Your Royal Highness' command in person, three years ago) he sets forth to meet whatever opportunities may present themselves for making himself known—opportunities which it is hopeless to wait for in Rome nowadays."

In Venice Scarlatti studied with Gasparini, then went on to achieve renown as a virtuoso of the harpsichord. When he returned to Rome in 1709, Cardinal Ottoboni arranged to have him compete with Handel (then visiting Italy) in harpsichord and organ performance. The consensus was that Scarlatti was superior at the harpsichord, while Handel excelled at the organ.

In 1709 Scarlatti joined the musical staff of Queen Maria Casimira of Poland, then residing in Rome. For her theater Scarlatti wrote seven operas. When the Queen left Rome in 1714, Scarlatti became assistant, then *maestro di cappella,* at the Vatican. He

DOMENICO SCARLATTI

wrote numerous church compositions in this capacity, but did not abandon the stage. *Narciso,* a new adaptation of an earlier opera, was produced at the Haymarket Theatre in London on May 30, 1720, with outstanding success.

In about 1719 Scarlatti became the *maestro di cappella* at the Royal Chapel in Lisbon, serving also as a teacher of the harpsichord for Princess Maria Barbara. When the Princess went to Madrid to marry the Prince of Asturias in 1729, Scarlatti went with her, settling in Madrid. Upon the ascent of Maria Barbara to the Spanish throne he became *maestro di cappella* at the royal palace, and remained in Madrid for the rest of his life, though he made several visits to Lisbon and Italy. In 1728, on a visit to Rome, he married Maria Caterina Gentile; five children were born to the marriage. Soon after the death of his wife in 1739, Scarlatti was married again, to Anastasia Ximenes, a native of Cádiz. She bore him four children.

It was for his royal pupil, Maria Barbara, that Scarlatti wrote the first of the great harpsichord pieces on which his historic importance rests: the *Esercizi per gravicembalo,* better known to us today as "sonatas." The first volume of these compositions was published under the composer's personal supervision in 1738. In its introduction Scarlatti spoke of these pieces almost apologetically: "Reader, do not expect, whether you are a dilettante or a professor, to find any profundity of intention in these compositions, but rather an ingenious bantering with the medium which will give you practice in playing the harpsichord boldly. I have published them with no selfish or ambitious end in view, but out of duty; perhaps you will find them agreeable and then I shall, more freely, obey all other orders to amuse you by using a more easy and more varied style. Therefore, show yourself more human than critical and you will increase your own pleasure. . . . *Viva felice!"*

Scarlatti wrote approximately five hundred of these "sonatas." They are not "sonatas" in the present-day definition, but rather brief little tone pictures in a two-part form built usually from a single theme. More accurately, they are "exercises" as the composer designated them, and as such they revolutionized and extended keyboard writing and performance of the late Baroque era by originating or perfecting a variety of techniques —runs in thirds and sixths, crossing of hands, broken chords in contrary motion, leaps across the keyboard in intervals greater than the octave, shakes, arpeggios, trills, and so on. But since he carried to them an extraordinary creative imagination and variety of style and mood, these exercises, like the études of Chopin, are elevated to the status of art. His compositions are, in turn, lyrical, witty, moody, graceful, dramatic, or delicate. Some are grounded in Neapolitan folk music, as for example the C major Sonata (L. 205). Most, however, are deeply rooted in the soil of Spain: their rhythms are those of the Spanish dance (most often the *jota*); their accompaniments and dissonances simulate the strummings of a guitar; their use of repeated notes suggest the clicking of castanets.

"His instinct for the requirements of his instrument," wrote C. Hubert Parry, "was so marvelous and his development of technique so wide and rich, that he seems to spring full-armed into the view of history. That he had models and types to work upon is certain, but his style is so unlike that of familiar old suites and fugues and fantasias and ricercare, and other harpsichord music of the early times, that it seems likely that the work of his prototypes had been lost. . . . He knows well the things that will tell, and how to awaken interest in a new mood when the effects of any particular line are exhausted. Considering how little attention

had been given to technique before his time, his feats of agility are really marvelous. The variety and incisiveness of his rhythms, the peculiarities of his harmony, his wild whirling rapid passages, his rattling shakes, his leaps from end to end of the keyboard, all indicate a preternaturally vivacious temperament; and unlike many later virtuosos, he is thoroughly alive to the meaning of music as an art and does not make his feats of dexterity his principal object."

Among the more popular of these sonatas are the following: E major, L. 23,* known as the "Cortège" because of its pictorial representation of procession; E major, L. 375 and D minor, L. 413, named respectively "Capriccio" and "Pastorale" by Karl Tausig in his famous transcriptions for the piano; D major, L. 461, which Wanda Landowska said "reads like a page from a music drama"; G minor, L. 499, sometimes identified as the "Cat's Fugue" because the leaps in the melody sound as if they came from a cat running pell-mell across the harpsichord keyboard.

Scarlatti's influence was responsible for the emergence of a new school of Spanish instrumental composers headed by Antonio Soler (1729-1783). There was hardly a composer of piano music after Scarlatti who did not benefit from his works; those perhaps most strongly affected by them were such Romantic masters as Chopin, Schubert, and Mendelssohn in their shorter pieces.

Themes from seven of Scarlatti's sonatas were taken by the twentieth century Italian composer Vincenzo Tommasini for the score to his ballet *The Good Humored Ladies.* The ballet, based on Goldoni's *Le Donne di buon umore* and choreographed by Leonide Massine, was introduced in Rome on April 12, 1917. Another twentieth century Italian composer, Alfredo Casella, used material from Scarlatti's sonatas for a divertimento for piano and orchestra, entitled *Scarlattiana,* performed for the first time in New York on January 23, 1927

Domenico Scarlatti was knighted in Madrid on April 21, 1738. He died in the same city on July 23, 1757. A chronic gambler, he had squandered all his resources on games of chance, leaving his widow and children destitute. The Queen, who had

---

* The designation after each sonata of the letter "L" followed by a number refers to the place of the sonata in the definitive Longo catalogue.

often come to his assistance when he was in financial difficulty, bestowed a generous pension on Scarlatti's survivors, equal almost to the composer's income at court.

PRINCIPAL WORKS
Chamber Music—Sonatas for violin and figured bass.

Choral Music—4 oratorios; 2 Misereres; chamber cantatas; Salve Regina, Stabat Mater.

Harpsichord Music—Over 500 esercizi (sonatas).

Operas—Giustino Silvia; Orlando; Ifigenia in Aulide; Ifigenia in Tauri; Amor d'un ombra e gelosia d'un aura; Narcisco

ABOUT
Kirkpatrick, R., Domenico Scarlatti; Luciana, S. A., Domenico Scarlatti; Valabrega, C., Il Clavicembalista D. Scarlatti: Il suo secolo, la sua opera.

Music and Letters, 1939, 1941; Musical Quarterly, July 1927.

SAMUEL SCHEIDT

Samuel Scheidt *1587-1654*

SAMUEL SCHEIDT, an early master of German baroque music, was born in 1587 in Halle, where his father was an overseer of the salt works. The most gifted of several children, Samuel was dispatched in or about 1605 to Amsterdam, where he studied the organ with Sweelinck. Three years later Scheidt became the organist of the Moritzkirche in Halle. In 1620 his first publication appeared: the *Cantiones sacrae octo vocum*, thirty-nine vocal compositions that included fifteen settings of Lutheran chorales. This was followed in 1621-1622 by the *Concerti sacri*, ambitious polyphonic works for chorus and orchestra, and *Ludi musici.*

Without relinquishing his organ post at the Moritzkirche, Scheidt became the *Kapellmeister* to the Margrave of Brandenburg, Christian Wilhelm, at the court chapel of Halle in 1620. He remained *Kapellmeister* until 1625. He kept the organ post until 1637 when the Moritzkirche was destroyed by fire.

Scheidt's life after 1637 is shrouded in mystery, though it is known that in 1642 he applied to Duke Augustus of Brunswick for patronage and a job. Scheidt's personal fortunes, however, could not have been seriously impaired. On his death, in Halle on March 30, 1654, he left a sizable amount of money to pay for an organ at the rebuilt Moritzkirche.

The history of German organ music can be said to begin with Scheidt. His masterwork in this department is *Tabulatura nova,* a monumental three-volume collection of organ chorales, toccatas, fantasias, and fugues, together with choral psalms, hymns, a Mass, and a Magnificat, issued in 1624. Brahms expressed great admiration for this work. The *Tabulatura nova,* said Paul Henry Lang, "bids farewell to the old Nordic style and definitely associates music with the new Italo-German baroque." In 1650 Scheidt published another distinguished collection of organ pieces, the *Tabulaturbuch.*

With Scheidt, said Manfred F. Bukofzer, German organ music achieved stature. Not only did Scheidt "abandon the traditional German organ tablature in favor of the Italian keyboard partitura which reserved for each voice a separate staff" (an innovation in German music whose importance cannot be overestimated), he also was among the first in Germany to cultivate and work out artistically the forms of the chorale, fantasy, and chorale variation for the organ. "Fantasy and variation," according to Bukofzer, "were the only forms of the organ chorale known in the early baroque period."

Other significant Scheidt publications are several volumes of the *Neue geistliche Conzerten,* between 1631 and 1640; the *Lieb-*

liche Krafft-Blümlein in 1625; the *Symphonien auf Conzerten-Manier* in 1644. A collected edition of Scheidt's works was issued between 1923 and 1937.

PRINCIPAL WORKS

Chamber Music—Preludes, Interludes, for two violins and accompaniment.
Choral Music—Cantiones sacrae, concerti sacri, conzerten, hymns, Mass, Magnificats, psalms.
Organ Music—Chorale fantasies, chorale variations, fugues, symphonien, toccatas.

ABOUT

Hünicken, R., Samuel Scheidt; Mahrenholz, C., Samuel Scheidt; Serauky, W., Scheidt in seinen Briefen.
Musica, March 1954.

Johann Hermann Schein *1586-1630*

L IKE SAMUEL SCHEIDT, Johann Hermann Schein was an influential figure in early German baroque music. The son of a Lutheran pastor, he was born in the Saxon town of Grünhain on January 20, 1586. When his father died in 1599, Johann moved to Dresden where he became a member of the court chapel choir. He attended the *Gymnasium* at Schulpforta from 1603 to 1607, and later studied law at the University of Leipzig. After occupying the posts of Praeceptor and house musician at the establishment of Captain von Wolffersdorf in Weissenfels, he was appointed court *Kapellmeister* in Weimar in 1613. One year later he became cantor of the Thomasschule in Leipzig, a post that Johann Sebastian Bach would fill in a later period. Schein stayed on as cantor until the end of his life. He died in Leipzig on November 19, 1630.

Schein's first publication was the *Cantional*, in 1627, a set of over three hundred German and Latin sacred songs and psalms harmonized for practical church use; eighty of these were original with Schein. "If Schein still retains the old rhythms in the melodies," wrote J. R. Milne, "in his harmonies he almost entirely lost . . . the feeling for the peculiarities of the old church modes in which these melodies are written, though otherwise his harmonies are serious and dignified."

In this, and in his subsequent publications, Schein became one of the first masters to introduce the monodic and instrumental style of the Italian baroque composers into German music. With Scheidt, he was one of the first to adapt the chorale for the organ. In his suites for strings, published in 1617 under the title of *Musical Banquet (Banchetto musicale)*, Schein was a pioneer in the writing of instrumental music. "The music is dignified, aristocratic, vigorously rhythmic, and melodically inventive," said Donald Jay Grout, "with that union of richness and decorum, of Italian charm and Teutonic gravity, so characteristic of the early baroque in Germany."

Schein's important publications include *Venus-Kräntzlein*, 1609; *Cymbalum Sionium*, 1615; *Opella nova*, 1618, 1626; *Musica Boscareccia* in three parts, 1621-28; *Fontana d'Israel* in 1623; *Diletti pastorali*, 1624; *Studenten-Schmauss*, 1626. Included here are strophic songs, motets, instrumental canzone, chorales, madrigals, and sundry other choral and instrumental compositions. A complete edition of Schein's works was issued in Germany in seven volumes between 1901 and 1923.

PRINCIPAL WORKS

Choral Music—Chorales, madrigals, motets, psalms, sacred songs, secular songs.
Instrumental Music—Suites, canzone, etc.

ABOUT

Prüfer, A., Johann Hermann Schein.
Neues Musikblatt, No. 42, 1939.

Franz Schubert *1797-1828*

F RANZ PETER SCHUBERT was born in the Lichtenthal district of Vienna on January 31, 1797. His father was a parish schoolmaster who had purchased a schoolhouse where he taught; his mother was a cook. Being an amateur musician, the elder Schubert encouraged all his children to make music. Performances of chamber music were frequent events in the Schubert household. Franz received musical training from childhood on. His father taught him the violin; his brother Ignaz, the piano; and the parish organist, Michael Holzer, singing, the organ, viola, and thorough bass. "He seems to know the lessons perfectly before I begin to explain them to him," Holzer once told Schubert's father.

When he was ten, Schubert became a chorister in the local church. A year later he passed the examinations for admission to the Konvict school in Vienna, a seminary which trained boys as court singers. He sang the required trial pieces with such facility that his acceptance was immediate. For five years Schubert boarded at the school, receiving comprehensive musical training under various teachers including Ruzicka and Salieri. It was not an easy life for the students; the rooms were cold, the food poor and inadequate. Schubert was hungry so often that he had to write appealing letters home begging for money with which to buy bread or apples. But he was not unhappy. As a member of the school orchestra he was introduced to the literature of Haydn, Mozart, and Beethoven, all of which made a powerful impact upon him. In his classes he made remarkable progress. "I can't teach him anything," Ruzicka once said. "He's learned it all from God himself." And Salieri told Schubert: "You can do everything, for you are a genius."

Provided with music paper by Joseph von Spaun, a fellow pupil who later became a lifelong friend, Schubert soon started composition. His first song, "Hagars Klage," was written in March 1811. This was an extended vocal composition in at least twelve movements with numerous changes of key. Here, as Donald Francis Tovey said, "the real development of the art forms of song was worked out by the child Schubert with the same fierce concentration as that with which the child Mozart laid the foundations of his sonata forms." After that came more songs, piano pieces, choral compositions, chamber music, and, in 1813, his first symphony.

In 1813 Schubert's voice broke and he was compelled to leave the seminary. He went to live in his father's house to prepare himself for a career as a teacher. After completing a preparatory course at St. Anna Normal School he assumed a post in his father's school in the fall of 1814.

He worked as a teacher for about two years, during which time he composed feverishly. He worked not only during the evenings and often late into the night, but even in the classroom, while the children were engaged in scribbling in their notebooks. During 1814 he wrote an opera, a Mass in F major (performed in a Lichtenthal church on October 16 of that year), two string quartets, two pieces for piano, and songs. Among the last was his first masterwork, "Gretchen am Spinnrade," after

FRANZ SCHUBERT

Goethe, written at a single sitting. That song would have been a phenomenal achievement by anybody in 1814, when the art of songwriting was still in its infancy. As the work of a boy of seventeen it is little short of a creative miracle. The climactic point of the song at the words *"Und ach! sein Kuss,"* where the spinning stops short only to be resumed with difficulty, is creative invention without parallel in the song literature of the early nineteenth century.

Schubert was even more prolific in 1815. In quick succession he completed two symphonies, two Masses, one opera and four operettas, four piano sonatas, several choral works, smaller pieces for the piano, and one hundred and fifty-six songs including the masterpiece "Der Erlkönig," once again with a text by Goethe.

With "Der Erlkönig," the art song, or lied, is fully realized. In it, as P. F. Radcliffe remarked, "the dramatic tension is wonderfully sustained, . . . and behind the drama there is a feeling of vast spaciousness that no other setting of the poem has achieved." M. J. E. Brown wrote: "From the first the Schubert song was practically without ancestry; even before 'Gretchen am Spinnrade' he was writing passages which have no precedent. . . . Many of Mozart's and Beethoven's songs, considered as music, are superior to his own earlier efforts. The miracle he achieved was to match with a reality of music poetry whose depth of human emotion would have appeared to the older masters as rendering it unsuitable for song."

From the beginning, Schubert detested teaching and resented the time it stole from his creative work. By 1816 he had decided to give it up for good. He went to live with Franz von Schober, and from then on had to depend upon the bounty of his friends for life's essentials. In addition to Schober, these friends included the poet Johann Mayrhofer, the famous Viennese singer Johann Michael Vogl, Schubert's friend from the seminary Joseph von Spaun, and Anselm Hüttenbrenner. Schubert lived now in the apartment of one friend, now at the home of another. His daily life was for the most part a happy-go-lucky existence. When one had money everybody had the price for food and drink. Schubert and his friends visited the coffeehouses to drink wine and engage in discussions. They played schoolboy pranks and indulged in innocent merriment. Many an evening was given up to informal, improvised parties which came to be known as "Schubert Evenings" (Schubertiaden) because their main attraction invariably was the performance of one or more of Schubert's latest compositions.

For Schubert there was always work, hard work. He was as indefatigable as he was prolific. "Every day at six," recalled Anselm Hüttenbrenner, "Schubert seated himself at his writing desk and composed without a break till one o'clock, smoking a few small pipes. If I came to see him in the morning, he would play to me what he had already composed and wait to hear my opinion. If I praised any song especially, he would say, 'Yes, that was a good poem; and when one has something good the music comes easily —melodies just stream from one, so that it is a real joy.' "

In 1818 Schubert spent the summer working as a music teacher for the family of Count Johann Esterházy at Zélész, Hungary, a post he held a second time during the summer of 1824. These two brief intervals as teacher, six years apart, were Schubert's only jobs after leaving the schoolroom. On various occasions he made a bid for a post as Kapellmeister at court or as a conductor in Vienna and elsewhere, but these efforts proved to no avail. For his livelihood he had to depend upon his music alone, and that provided him almost nothing. Although by 1820 he had written over five hundred

works in every branch of composition, nothing was published, and only a youthful Mass and a song had even been performed. "His situation was really oppressive," his friend Spaun recalled. "There was not a publisher who would have ventured to pay even a small sum for his wonderful creations. For years he remained the victim of money worries; the man so rich in melody could not afford a piano. But his troubles did not in the least lessen his diligence. He had to write, it was his life. And he was always cheerful. For many years he was my guest, the guest of an old friend, at sociable, gay suppers which mostly went on past midnight; he liked coming and was good company. If it was late he did not go home but made himself comfortable on a very modest couch in my room, where he always slept soundly, often with his perennial eyeglasses on. In the morning he would sit down in his shirt and trousers and write the most beautiful things, mostly songs, and once in a while he surprised us dance lovers with the loveliest German dances and écossaises, then much in fashion. Schubert himself never danced."

"Nobody," asserted Spaun, "who has once seen him at work composing in the morning, radiant, eyes glowing, even his speech different, like that of a somnambulist, can ever forget it."

The year 1820, however, brought some promise of recognition. Through the influence of his friend Vogl, Schubert's operetta Die Zwillingsbrüder, was performed on June 14 at the Kärnthnerthor Theater. A few months after that the Theater-an-der-Wien introduced a second Schubert operetta, Die Zauberharfe. Both works were failures. The Wiener Sammler condemned Die Zwillingsbrüder for its "somewhat antiquated" arias and "unmelodious" score. This operetta survived only six performances. Die Zauberharfe did hardly better at the hands of critics who described it as "much too long, ineffective, and fatiguing."

Appreciation and encouragement had to come to him from his friends, and it was through their generosity that Schubert's first publication appeared. A public performance of Schubert's youthful song "Der Erlkönig" by Vogl on March 7, 1821, aroused so much enthusiasm that Schubert's friends decided to get it published. One hundred subscribers helped to defray the expenses. In 1821

Schubert's first opus—a number of songs including "Der Erlkönig"—finally appeared.

But this publication did nothing at all to lift him out of his obscurity and neglect. Succeeding events managed only to mount failure upon failure. When Schubert showed Carl Maria von Weber the score of his new opera, *Alfonso und Estrella,* in 1822, the master told him that "first operas and first puppies should always be drowned." In 1823 Schubert's incidental music to Helmina von Chézy's *Rosamunde* was performed, only to be described as "bizarre." "At present," one critic remarked sardonically, "he [Schubert] is too much applauded."

His natural capacity for enjoying life and work, his pleasure in his friends and in the *Schubertiaden,* his intense love of nature and his delight in taking excursions into the country—all this was soon smothered by his disappointments and frustrations, and by his constant defeats at the hands of public and critics. He recognized that he was a failure, dependent for his shelter and food upon the generosity of his friends. And as if this recognition and frustration were not enough to torment him there was the deterioration of his health after 1823. "Picture to yourself someone whose health is permanently injured," he wrote to Kupelwieser on March 31, 1824, "and who, in sheer despair, does everything to make it worse instead of better; picture to yourself, I say, someone whose most brilliant hopes have come to nothing, someone to whom love and friendship are at most a source of bitterness, someone whose inspiration (whose creative inspiration at least) for all that is beautiful threatens to fail and then ask yourself if that is not a wretched and unhappy being. *'Meine Ruh ist hin, mein Herz ist schwer, ich finde sie nimmer und nimmer mehr.'* That could be my daily song now, for every night when I go to sleep I hope never to wake again, and each morning I am only recalled to the griefs of yesterday. So I pass my days, joyless and friendless." The line quoted by Schubert in this letter is the opening line of "Gretchen am Spinnrade."

He had to be satisfied with crumbs of recognition. In 1823, the Musikverein of Graz elected him an honorary member, an award that carried no remuneration and very little prestige. But Schubert was so overwhelmed with gratitude that he decided to write a symphony for that society. The

work he despatched to Anselm Hüttenbrenner, then the president of the society, was his most famous instrumental composition, the Symphony No. 8 in B minor, known as the *Unfinished* because Schubert completed only the first two movements and a hundred measures of the third. The reason why Schubert did not complete the symphony has never been uncovered, and all hypotheses posed by biographers and critics hold little conviction. But, even unfinished, it is a work so incomparably perfect, so exquisite in style and structure that, as Philip Hale once noted, we should perhaps be grateful that Schubert never finished it; not even he could have sustained such a high level of inspiration through two more movements.

It was characteristic of the frustrations dogging Schubert that this symphony never reached the society. For some reason Hüttenbrenner never delivered the work but allowed it to lie neglected on a shelf in a closet, where it was found more than thirty years after the composer's death. Its première performance took place in Vienna on December 17, 1865.

Beethoven, the composer Schubert admired above all others, died in 1827, and his death plunged Schubert into an even deeper gloom. It is doubtful if Schubert had ever met Beethoven, as some unauthoritative sources have stated; but it is known that just before he died Beethoven said about some of Schubert's songs, "Surely there is a divine spark of genius in this Schubert!" At Beethoven's funeral, Schubert was one of the torch bearers, and immediately afterwards he expressed the wish to be buried next to the master.

Schubert's despondency is apparent in some of his important works of 1827: in the funereal song cycle *Die Winterreise,* with its foreboding of death; in the C major String Quintet, whose slow movement is one of the most tragic utterances in all chamber music; in the E-flat major Mass; in parts of the song cycle *Schwanengesang.*

Recognition seemed finally to be at hand in 1828. On March 26 there took place at the Musikverein in Vienna a program devoted entirely to Schubert's music. It inspired such enthusiasm that Schubert's friends were convinced that here and now was the beginning of Schubert's success. Confident of his future, Schubert considered taking lessons in counterpoint with Sechter to strengthen his technique, and he was planning many new major compositions.

But he did not have long to live. At his brother's home in the Kettenbrückengasse, in the Neue Wieden suburb of Vienna, his life was slowly ebbing away. On November 12, 1828, he wrote to his friend Schober: "For eleven days I have neither eaten nor drunk anything. I am tottering from chair to bed and vice versa. . . . Whenever I eat anything, I promptly throw it up." On the night of November 16 delirium set in. He kept raving that he was not lying next to Beethoven. When reassured by his brother Ferdinand that he was near Beethoven, Schubert remarked softly, "Then I am happy."

Schubert died on November 19, 1828. The funeral services were held at the St. Joseph Church, where Schubert's friend Schober recited a eulogy and Schubert's "Pax Vobiscum" was sung. Then the composer was buried, not next to Beethoven—since this could not be arranged at the time—but not far away from him. A few months later a monument was erected over his grave with an epitaph by Franz von Grillparzer, Vienna's renowned poet: "Music has here entombed a rich treasure, but still fairer hopes."

Grillparzer could refer to "still fairer hopes" because in 1828 very few, indeed, were aware of the vast quantity of masterworks produced by Schubert. Since only a scattered few of Schubert's many compositions were known either through publication or performance, it was many years before the world of music became aware of Schubert's greatness. A decade after Schubert's death, Robert Schumann, on a visit to Vienna, discovered the manuscript of the great C major Symphony (No. 7), lying in a disordered state in a closet at Ferdinand Schubert's home. Schumann was instrumental in having this symphonic masterwork published and introduced in Leipzig on March 21, 1839, under the direction of Mendelssohn. The *Unfinished Symphony,* as we have noted, was introduced in 1865. Soon after this, Arthur Sullivan and George Grove made an expedition to Vienna to try to find other Schubert manuscripts. They found a treasure trove in the apartment of a Dr. Schneider, including Symphonies Nos. 1, 2, 3, 4, and 6, the music of *Rosamunde,* a trio, songs, and a Stabat Mater. They came upon some sixty lieder in the publishing house of Spina. Only the rediscovery of the works of Bach surpassed in historic importance the finding of these Schubert manuscripts.

Once the extent of Schubert's genius was revealed, it became apparent that here was a giant in Austrian instrumental and vocal music, the first of the great Austrian Romanticists in music. Schubert was one of the earliest Germanic composers to arrive at a new concept of form, and to create such small structures for piano literature as the *Moments musicaux.* He was the first to evolve the art song or lied, which was to be a favored form of the Romantic composer. He was one of the first to derive strength and stimulus from the German folk song and to fill his writing with subjective feelings.

Liszt characterized Schubert as the most poetic of all composers, and the essence of his poetic expression was melody. Schubert poured his wonderful lyricism into every medium he employed, but most of all into the song form of which he was probably the greatest exponent.

Discussing Schubert's songs, Daniel Gregory Mason wrote: "Simple in style and design, wonderfully direct and sincere, conceived as idealizations of the beautiful old German *Volkslieder,* and carried out with all the artistic perfection and appropriateness of detail that good craftsmanship could give, they are among the few things in music that are absolutely achieved. Especially remarkable is the art-concealing art by which Schubert, through some perfectly simple and unobtrusive feature of rhythm, melody or harmony knows how to suggest exactly the spirit and atmosphere of his text. . . . In short, Schubert strikes at once . . . the exact tone and style needed to transfigure the particular feeling with all the magic of music, and throughout the song maintains the mood perfectly, with no mixture or clouding. And this, too, with the greatest actual diversity of mood in the different songs, to which his art flexibly responds. . . . Schubert is often sublimely simple . . . ; but sometimes he is merely flat and obvious. Indeed, writing as he did over six hundred songs in a score of years, not the most inspired of men could have always avoided platitude. Thus we must set aside many melodramatic and many trite compositions before we can get an unimpeded view of his real masterpieces. But after that has been done, we have left about twenty or thirty songs of such incomparable loveliness as to give him a secure place among the great masters of the musical lyric."

In Schubert's greatest symphonies, quartets, piano trios, piano sonatas, and other instrumental works we find, as Philip Hale said, the same "striking characteristics of Schubert's songs, spontaneity, haunting melody, a birthright mastery over modulation, a singular good fortune in finding the one inevitable phrase for the prevailing sentiment of the poem and in finding the fitting descriptive figure for salient detail. . . . Then there is the ineffable melancholy that is the dominating note. There is a gaiety such as was piped naïvely by William Blake in his *Songs of Innocence;* there is the innocence that even Mozart hardly reached in his frank gaiety; yet in the gaiety and innocence is a melancholy—despairing, as in certain songs of the *Winterreise,* when Schubert smelled the mold and knew the earth was impatiently looking for him—a melancholy that is not the Titanic despair of Beethoven, not the whining or shrieking pessimism of certain German and Russian composers; it is the melancholy of an autumnal sunset, of the ironical depression due to a burgeoning moon in the spring, the melancholy that comes between the lips of lovers."

Much has been written about Schubert's technical shortcomings, his inadequate contrapuntal technique and feeling for structure, his lack of subtlety in development, and his harmonic weakness. We know now, however, that these weaknesses were his strength, that as a supreme melodist—the greatest music had known up to then and probably since—he could call upon his seemingly inexhaustible lyricism to serve every artistic demand. We know now that Schubert was always able to make technique and form the servant to his poetic thought and emotion; indeed, as Alfred Einstein has indicated, Schubert's modulations, criticized by some for their awkwardness, enabled him to plumb depths never before reached in music. He did not have a poor sense of form, but a *new* sense of form. Einstein also pointed out that not even Beethoven "achieved anything more striking or more terse than the volcanic climax" of the first movement of the *Unfinished Symphony,* while the great C major Symphony, "with its tremendous trombone calls in the first movement . . . declares Schubert to be Beethoven's peer." Einstein continued: "Schubert's apparent failings are only the reverse side of his immortal greatness. His thoughts seem to spring from the primal fount of sound and melody. . . . The great Schubert strikes his lyre as the greatest of all nature-musicians and pantheists."

Anselm Hüttenbrenner described Schubert's appearance as follows: "Schubert was not of a very striking appearance. He was very short, somewhat corpulent, with a full round face. His brow had a very agreeable curve. Because of his near-sightedness he always wore eyeglasses which he never removed, not even while sleeping. He never concerned himself with his dress, and he detested going into higher society because it necessitated careful dressing. In general, he found it impossible to discard his soiled frockcoat for a black suit."

Hüttenbrenner then went on to say: "His opinions on musical matters were acute, succinct, penetrating and to the point. When, at social gatherings, there was serious conversation about music, Schubert enjoyed listening and rarely joined in. But if a presumptuous amateur would show complete ignorance, Schubert's patience would snap and he would bark: 'Better say nothing about things you do not understand at all, and never will!' Schubert rarely spoke about his works or himself, and when he did it was usually in a few well chosen words. His favorite subjects were Handel, Haydn, Mozart, and Beethoven. He had the highest esteem of all for Beethoven. Schubert was enchanted by the operas of Mozart. His favorite works were the *Messiah* of Handel, *Don Giovanni* and the Requiem of Mozart, and the Fifth Symphony and the Mass in C major of Beethoven."

PRINCIPAL WORKS

Chamber Music—15 string quartets; 3 violin sonatinas; 2 piano trios; Octet in F major; String Quintet in C major; Piano Quintet in A major, Die Forelle (The Trout); String Trio in B-flat major; Violin Sonata in A major; Fantasy in C major, for violin and piano; Sonata in A minor, for arpeggione (a cellolike instrument) and piano.

Choral Music—Cantatas, offertories, Stabat Mater, Masses, Salve Reginas; compositions for chorus and piano; compositions for unaccompanied chorus.

Operas—Die Zwillingsbrüder; Die Zauberharfe; Alfonso und Estrella; Fierrabras; Der häusliche Krieg.

Orchestral Music—8 symphonies; 7 overtures; Konzertstück, for violin and orchestra; German dances; Minuets; incidental music to Rosamunde.

Piano Music—22 sonatas; Wanderer Fantasy; écossaises, German dances, impromptus, Ländler, Minuets, Moments musicaux, waltzes.

Vocal Music—Die schöne Müllerin; Die Winterreise; Schwanengesang; over 600 individual songs for voice and piano including Die Allmacht, Am Meer, An die Leier, An die Musik, Auf dem Wasser zu singen, Du bist die Ruh', Der Erlkönig, Die Forelle, Gretchen am Spinnrade, Hark, hark, the Lark, Heidenröslein, Im Abendroth, Die junge Nonne, Der Tod und das Mädchen, Der Wanderer, Who Is Sylvia? Wiegenlied; vocal duets, vocal trios, vocal quartets.

ABOUT

Abraham, G. (editor), Schubert: A Symposium; Bie, O., Franz Schubert: Sein Leben und sein Werk; Brown, M. J. E., Schubert; Capell, R., Schubert's Songs; Deutsch, O. E., Schubert: A Documentary Biography; Deutsch, O. E., Schubert: Memoirs by His Friends; Einstein, A., Schubert; Flower, N., Franz Schubert: The Man and His Circle; Hutchings, A., Schubert; Kobald, K., Franz Schubert and His Time; Kreissle, H. H. von, Franz Schubert; Prod'homme, J. G., Schubert raconté par ceux qui l'ont vu; Schauffler, R. H., Franz Schubert: The Ariel of Music.

Heinrich Schuetz

see Heinrich Schütz

Robert Schumann *1810-1856*

ROBERT ALEXANDER SCHUMANN was born in Zwickau, Saxony, on June 8, 1810. His father was a publisher and bookseller who encouraged his son's early disposition toward music. Robert began to study piano when he was six, started composition at seven, and at eleven completed several choral and orchestral works. He formed a little orchestra among eight of his friends, directing them in concerts. With a neighbor, he played four-hand arrangements of the symphonies of Haydn, Mozart, and Beethoven. The boy demonstrated no less a passion for literature, reading the Greek classics and the Romantic poets when he was fourteen. One year after this he formed a society for the discussion of great books, and at seventeen he was convinced that he wanted to become a poet. "Whether I am a poet—for I cannot become one," he said at the time, "posterity must decide. . . . The strange thing is that where my feelings make themselves most strongly felt I am forced to cease being a poet; at such times I can never arrive at adequate ideas."

Between 1820 and 1828 Schumann attended the high school in Zwickau. During his last years there his father died, and with him went whatever sympathy and understanding the boy could expect at home for his musical and literary interests. Schumann's mother was a strong-willed, practical woman who could not appreciate or understand her son's artistic temperament and aspirations. She insisted he forget all nonsense about music and poetry and devote himself to preparing for a career in law. For this purpose, Robert entered the University of Leipzig in 1828. His utter detestation of his law courses at the University, combined with his frustrations in being unable to devote himself to music and literature, induced an attack of melancholia. A change of scene now seemed in order. In 1829 he went to Heidelberg to continue his law studies there. By the end of that year he knew with finality he would become a musician, and not a lawyer. By this time he had completed a significant work for the piano, *Theme and Variations on the Name Abegg*, his first published composition. Abegg was an attractive young lady whom he had met at a ball, and in her honor he wrote this composition in which his first theme was derived from the letters of her name, "A," "B" (German for B-flat), "E," "G," and "G." This work was still more unusual for the time in that the variations were based on an original melody rather than on some familiar tune, aria, or excerpt by some other composer, as was then the general practice in the writing of a theme-and-variations.

On November 11, 1829, Schumann wrote to his mother: "If ever I were to have achieved anything in the world, it would have been in music. From the first I have had within me a powerful drive toward music, and without overrating myself, the creative spirit as well." This letter finally brought him his mother's consent to give up law for music. Returning to Leipzig, Schumann took up lodgings with Friedrich Wieck, with whom he studied the piano. He also took lessons in harmony from Dorn. "I have . . . arrived at the conviction," he wrote to his mother from Leipzig, "that with work, patience and a good master, I shall within six years be able to challenge any pianist. . . . Besides this, I also possess imagination, and perhaps aptitude, for individual creative work." Wieck agreed with him. "I pledge myself to turn him into one of the greatest pianists," Wieck wrote Schumann's mother in August 1830.

His ambition to become a supreme piano virtuoso led Schumann to devise a new method whereby the fourth finger could become as flexible as the others: He kept it rigid and extended while using the others. After a prolonged period of holding his fingers in this artificial position, Schumann developed a paralysis of the hand which proved incurable. His dream of becoming a virtuoso shattered, he hurled his industry and passion into creative channels. If he could not become one of the world's great pianists, he would aspire to be one of its leading composers. In 1832 he wrote three movements of a symphony which he never finished; the first movement was introduced at Zwickau on November 18, 1832. In the same year he completed the *Papillons* (op. 2), *Paganini Études* (op. 3), the *Six Intermezzi* (op. 4), and the Toccata (op. 7), all of them for the piano. In 1833 came a second set of *Paganini Études* (op. 10), and work was begun on his first piano sonata, in F-sharp minor (op. 11).

Besides his intensive preoccupation with composition, he became active in other areas of music. In 1833 he helped form the *Davidsbündler,* a society of idealistic, iconoclastic young music lovers. Just as the Biblical King David had destroyed Philistinism, so these new young Davids of music hoped to defeat false musical standards, shams, and corrupt artistic practices, while marching under the banner of the highest artistic ideals.

The voice of the *Davidsbündler* was the *Neue Zeitschrift für Musik,* edited by Schumann, the first issue appearing on April 3, 1834. While the life of the *Davidsbündler* was brief, the magazine continued to flourish for a decade under the vigorous, progressive, and astute editorship of Schumann. It was here, in pieces written by Schumann himself, that the unknown and unrecognized Chopin and Brahms were first brought to the attention of musicians in prophetic examinations of their creative futures. The *Neue Zeitschrift* continued to be one of the world's foremost music journals even after Schumann's retirement as editor.

H. Truhn, who knew Schumann during the composer's first years in Leipzig, described him as follows: "He had a big, roomy head, true Germanic, richly adorned with soft, dark blond hair, a full, beardless face, with

ROBERT SCHUMANN

lips so shaped and held that he always looked as if he were about to begin whistling very softly; his eyes were a beautiful blue but neither large nor expressive of energy or power; they always looked as if he had something he must fathom and listen to intently deep in his own soul. His posture was rigidly erect, but he walked with a soft, yielding step, as if the strong, broad-shouldered body had no bones at all. He was shortsighted and made much use of the lorgnette but without a trace of coquetry—an observation hardly necessary since his nature was diametrically opposed to everything studied or affected."

When his day's work was over, Schumann liked to go to the *Kaffeebaum* late in the evening for conversations with friends and drinks of wine. Karl Franz Brendel said: "He used to sit sideways at the table so that he could lean his head on his hand; he would sit and from time to time stroke back his hair, which often fell over his forehead, with his eyes half-closed, withdrawn into himself, sunk in dreams. But then when something evoked an interesting exchange of ideas among his companions, he would liven up, even become talkative and animated; it may be said that you could actually see him awakening from his abstraction, emerging to the outer world—and you could see too how his eyes, usually turned backward, looking into himself, now turned toward the external world, displaying at one and the same time an acute intelligence and a fantastic splendor." Every once in a while Schumann rushed out of the *Kaffeebaum* precipitately without even bothering to say good night to his friends. At such times his head was swarming with musical thoughts which he had to put down on paper.

He was already beginning to show signs of those emotional disturbances which would eventually destroy him. In 1833 he suffered an attack of fainting spells and violent rushing of blood to the head. This was followed by an attack of severe melancholia which, on October 17, 1833, made him attempt suicide by jumping out of his window. At certain times he was sure he was going mad.

But hard work, both as composer and as editor, helped to lift him out of his depressions. By 1835 he had completed three masterworks for the piano which could leave no doubt about his creative powers: the *Carnaval* (op. 9), the first piano sonata (op. 11), and the *Études symphoniques* (op. 13).

If his fulfillment as critic and composer helped to bring about a certain degree of emotional stability and equilibrium, these were soon destroyed by a tempestuous love affair which caused him indescribable anguish for a number of years.

The object of his love was Clara, the young daughter of his teacher, Friedrich Wieck, herself a piano prodigy. She was nine years younger than Schumann. From her twelfth year on she had adored him from a distance. Though Schumann was deeply impressed by her pronounced musical gifts and found her to be a lovable playmate, he did not realize how much she really meant to him for a long time. Then one day in 1835, when she was departing for a concert tour, he kissed her good-bye. "When you kissed me for the first time I thought I should faint," Clara confessed to Schumann in a letter dated November 25, 1835. "Everything went black before my eyes." Robert also realized that he was in love with a girl who was only sixteen.

Wieck refused to consider the possibility of a marriage between his daughter and Schumann, mainly because he wanted nothing to interfere with her career as a virtuoso. He did everything in his power to keep the lovers apart. He refused to permit them to communicate with one another; for a long time the only contact between the young lovers was through clandestine letters secretly exchanged, or through hurriedly arranged surreptitious meetings. Whenever Wieck discovered that one of these meetings had taken place, or that letters had been exchanged, he would fly into a rage and threaten to kill Schumann if he persisted in his efforts to woo Clara. Wieck even tried poisoning Clara's mind against Schumann through deceit and fabrications. But the more fiercely Wieck labored to keep Schumann and Clara apart, the more devoted they became to each other, and the more determined to seek each other out. "I say to you again that my love knows no bounds," Clara wrote to Schumann. "If you wanted my life today I would give it up." Schumann was no less ardent. "Some day my turn will come. Then you will see how much I love you."

The love affair dragged on for four years. Then Schumann decided to resolve the issue in the law courts. He brought suit against Wieck to compel him to consent to Clara's marriage, and won. On September 12, 1840, Clara and Schumann were married. "Now," wrote Clara in her diary, "begins a new existence, a beautiful life, a life wrapped up in him whom I love more than myself and everything else."

The four years of enforced separation from his beloved Clara had been a period of turmoil and agony. Now that Clara was his wife, a blessed peace entered Schumann's life. Out of his great love for her, he seemed to find new creative resources which demanded new directions. Until now he had concentrated mainly on the piano. In 1840, the first year of his marital happiness, he turned to the art-song (lied), producing what he himself considered "something quite new in that line." In a wonderful outpouring of inspired song he produced in that single year the two *Liederkreis* cycles on Heine's and Eichendorff's poems; the *Myrthen* cycle; the first volume of *Lieder und Gesänge;* the twenty-four *Gedichte,* op. 30, 31, 35, and 36; the *Fünf Lieder,* op. 40; the cycle *Frauenliebe und Leben;* the first three volumes of *Romanzen und Balladen;* and the monumental *Dichterliebe* cycle on Heine's poems. Songs like "Widmung," "Der Nussbaum," "Die Lotosblume," "Du bist wie eine Blume," "Im wunderschönen Monat Mai," and "Ich grolle nicht"—to mention only a few—established Schumann as Schubert's successor as monarch of the lied, one of the greatest creators in that form. "As illustrations of lyric poetry," wrote W. H. Hadow, "they are unsurpassed in the whole history of art. With him the terms 'words' and 'settings,' 'melody' and 'accompaniment' lose their distinctive meanings; all are fused into a single whole in which no part has preeminence. He follows every shade of the poet's thought with perfect union of sympathy, he catches its tone, he echoes its phrase, he almost anticipates its issue. It is not too much to say that no man can understand Heine who does not know Schumann's treatment of the *Buch der Lieder*."

Just as 1840 was Schumann's year of song, so 1841 became his year for orchestral music, and 1842 his year for chamber music. In 1841 he completed the First Symphony in B-flat major. He called his symphony *Spring*, not because it was essentially an evocation in tones of the vernal season, but because it gave voice to the springtime in his heart brought about by his marriage. The symphony received its world première in Leipzig under Mendelssohn's direction on March 31, 1841, at a concert which featured Clara Schumann as soloist. The principal chamber-music works of 1842 were his string quartets, his Piano Quartet in E-flat, and his magnificent Piano Quintet in E-flat major. Of the Piano Quintet Joan Chissell said: "In the first happiness of reunion with the piano, his creative imagination took on a new lease of life. Not only did the themes of the quintet glow with all his old irresistible charm and spontaneity, but there is also inspired craftsmanship behind their 'working out' and scoring—that is why the work is one of the supreme achievements of his entire output."

Schumann wrote four symphonies in all. The second, in C major, was introduced in Leipzig on November 5, 1846, Mendelssohn conducting; the third, the *Rhenish*, in E-flat major, was performed for the first time in Düsseldorf, on February 6, 1851, under the direction of the composer himself; the fourth in D minor, was heard in its final and definitive version in Düsseldorf on March 3, 1853, once again with the composer conducting.

Schumann's symphonic works have been subjected to a good deal of criticism, mainly because of their supposedly inadequate orchestration and the lack of skill in developing the thematic material. Philip Hale, in evaluating Schumann's strength and weakness as a symphonist, wrote: "It has been urged against Schumann that his symphonies were thought for piano and then orchestrated crudely, as by an amateur. This, however, is not the fatal objection. . . . A more serious objection is this: the genius of Schumann was purely lyrical, although occasionally there is the impressive expression of a wild and melancholy mood, as in the chords of unearthly beauty soon after the beginning of the overture to *Manfred*. Whether the music be symphonic, chamber, a piano piece, or a song, the beauty, the expressive force lies in the lyric passages. When Schumann endeavored to build a musical monument, to quote Vincent d'Indy's phrase, he failed; for he had not the architectonic imagination or skill. His themes in symphonies, charming as they often are, give one the impression of fragments, of music heard in sleep-chasings. Never a master of contrapuntal technique, he repeated these phrases over and over again instead of broadly developing them, and his filling in is generally amateurish and perfunctory."

In January 1844, Schumann went on a concert tour of Russia. Upon returning to Leipzig, he resigned from the Conservatory, (he had accepted a post in 1843) and as editor of the *Neue Zeitschrift*. The Schumanns then went to Dresden, where for five years he taught music privately, conducted two choral groups, but most of all concentrated on creative work. His major compositions included the opera *Genoveva*, introduced in Leipzig on June 25, 1850.

Upon the recommendation of Ferdinand Hiller, Schumann was appointed musical director of the city of Düsseldorf in 1850, his duties including the conducting of orchestral concerts. While holding this post, his nervousness and irritability mounted. In time he began to lose his powers of concentration. By 1853 his conducting had become so erratic and lackadaisical that an assistant had to take over for him. A special committee was formed to suggest to him, as discreetly as possible, that he resign his post.

His mental breakdown came quickly once he withdrew from his position. He began hearing voices and sounds that tormented him endlessly. He insisted that the great musical masters of the past were visiting him to dictate melodies to him. One day, in February 1854, he tried to commit suicide by throwing himself into the Rhine. Rescued, he was committed to an asylum in Endenich, near Bonn. He stayed there two years, haunted by fantasies and apparitions, noises and delusions. Clara Schumann visited him regularly.

"At first," wrote Brahms, "he lay a long time with closed eyes, and she [Clara] kneeled in front of him, more quietly than one would have thought possible. But he recognized her and again on the following days. Once he desired clearly to embrace her and threw his arm around her. Of course he was no longer able to speak; one could only make out single words (perhaps imagine them) but even that must have pleased her. He often refused the wine that was offered him, but took it eagerly from her finger, for so long at a time and so ravenously, that one was convinced he recognized the finger."

Clara Schumann was with him on July 29, 1856, when he died. "He died," continued Brahms, "as easily as you read these words. We should have breathed more freely once he had been released but could hardly believe it. His death was so gentle that it almost passed unnoticed. His body looked calm, as if all were for the best. They buried him Thursday afternoon. I carried the wreath before the coffin, with Joachim and Dietrich. The members of a choral society were pall bearers. There was trumpeting and singing." Schumann was buried in the cemetery of the Sternentor Church in Bonn where, in 1880, a monument was erected for his grave.

Schumann's last major work was the Concerto in D minor, for violin and orchestra, completed in October 1853. This work has had a strange history. Joseph Joachim, for whom it was written, did not regard it highly and refused to play it. After Schumann's death, Clara Schumann and Brahms agreed not to permit publication. The manuscript was consigned to a place in the Berlin State Library, where it lay untouched for three quarters of a century. Early in the 1930's, the concerto became news again when the violinist Yelly d'Aranyi insisted that the spirit of Schumann had come to her with a plea to perform the concerto. It took her four years to locate it and learn it. The German publishing house of Schott had meanwhile published it in a version edited by George Schünemann. Schott asked Yehudi Menuhin to give the première performance, but the Nazi regime refused to assign this honor to a non-Aryan. The world première of the concerto took place in Berlin on November 26, 1937; George Kuhlenkampf was the soloist, and the Berlin Philharmonic was conducted by Karl Boehm. Yehudi Menuhin performed it in New York on December 6, 1937, and Yelly d'Aranyi on February 16, 1938. Critics both in Europe and the United States found that the concerto, despite many beautiful passages, was structurally disorganized, occasionally pedestrian in thought, and often the product of a disordered mind. The work remains little more than a curiosity.

Schumann once indicated that three influences had shaped his musical development: "the simple Gluck, the more intricate Handel, and the most intricate of all—Bach. Only study the last-named thoroughly and the most complicated of my works will be clear."

He also wrote: "Everything that occurs in the world affects me—politics, literature, humanity. I ponder over everything in my own way until the thoughts then break forth and clarify themselves in music. But for this reason many of my compositions are so difficult to understand, because they are associated with remote interests. Often also they are significant because everything strange moves me, and I must then begin to express it musically. . . . There are moments when music possesses me so completely, when only sounds exist for me to such a degree that I am unable to write anything down."

Most critics are generally agreed that Schumann was at his greatest in his piano music and songs. "As a writer for the piano, he may be said to rank beside Schubert," wrote W. H. Hadow. "He has less melodic gift, less sweetness, perhaps less originality, but he appreciates far more fully the capacities of the instrument and possesses more power of rich and recondite harmonization. His polyphony was a new departure in the history of piano music, based upon that of Bach, but exhibiting a distinctive color and character of its own. The beauty of his single phrases, the vigor and variety of his accompaniments, the audacity of his 'bittersweet discords' are all so many claims on immortality. . . . His spirit, too, is essentially human. No composer is more companionable, more ready to respond to any word and sympathize with any emotion."

In summing up Schumann's creative importance, Philip Hale said: "The best of Schumann's music is an expression of states and conditions of soul. This music is never spectacular; it is never objective. . . . In his own field, Schumann is lonely, incomparable. No composer has whispered such secrets of subtle and ravishing beauty to a receptive listener. The hearer of Schumann's music must in turn be imaginative and a dreamer. He must often anticipate the composer's thought. The music is not for a garish concert hall; it shrinks from boisterous applause."

PRINCIPAL WORKS

Chamber Music—4 Fantasiestücke, for violin, cello and piano; 3 string quartets; 3 piano trios; 3 Romances, for oboe and piano; 2 violin sonatas; Piano Quintet in E-flat; Piano Quartet in E-flat.

Choral Music—Des Paradies und die Peri; Requiem für Mignon; Nachtlied; Der Rose Pilgerfahrt; Des Sängers Fluch; Mass; Requiem.

Opera—Genoveva.

Orchestral Music—4 symphonies; 4 concert overtures; Scherzo, Overture and Finale, E major; Piano Concerto in A minor; Violin Concerto in D minor; Cello Concerto in A minor; Overture and incidental music to Manfred; Fantasy in C major, for violin and orchestra; Introduction and Allegro (Konzertstück), for piano and orchestra.

Piano Music—3 sonatas; Abegg Variations; Études after Caprices of Paganini; Davidsbündlertänze; Toccata in C major; Carnaval; Fantasiestücke; Études symphoniques; Papillons; Kinderscenen; Kreisleriana; Fantasy in C major; Faschingsschwank aus Wien; Album für die Jugend; Waldscenen; Bunte-Blätter; Albumblätter, arabesques, fugues, Humoresques, intermezzi, marches, Noveletten, Romances.

Vocal Music—Myrthen; Lieder und Gesänge; Zwölf Gedichte; Sechs Gedichte; Liederkreis; Frauenliebe und Leben; Romanzen und Balladen; Dichterliebe; Liederalbum für die Jugend; Gedichte, Gesänge, vocal duets, vocal trios, vocal quartets, part songs.

ABOUT

Abraham, G. (editor), Schumann: A Symposium; Bedford, H., Schumann; Chissell, J., Schumann; Cœuroy, A., Robert Schumann; Dahms, W., Schumann; Harding, B., Concerto: The Glowing Story of Clara Schumann; Niecks, F., Schumann; Peyser, H. F., Robert Schumann: Tone Poet, Prophet, and Critic; Rehberg, P. and W., Robert Schumann: Sein Leben und sein Werk; Schauffler, R. H., Florestan: The Life and Work of Robert Schumann; Schumann, E., Memoirs; Wörner, K. H., Robert Schumann.

Heinrich Schütz *1585-1672*

THREE "S's" dominated the early baroque period in German music: Samuel Scheidt, Johann Schein, and most important, Heinrich Schütz. Schütz, the outstanding German composer of the seventeenth century, was born in Köstritz, Saxony, on October 8, 1585. His family occupied an important place in the social and economic

HEINRICH SCHÜTZ

life of Weissenfels, the town to which the Schütz family moved when Heinrich was six. There, in 1599, the Landgraf Maurice of Hesse-Cassel, impressed by the beauty of Heinrich's voice, took him into the chapel choir. At the same time Heinrich was permitted to receive an education in the sciences and in languages at the Collegium Mauricianum. In 1609 he went to the University of Marburg for the study of law. But his greatest interest lay in music, and when the Landgraf provided him with funds to go to Venice, Schütz left the University of Marburg the same year and became a pupil of Giovanni Gabrieli, the eminent Venetian contrapuntist. As a result of this period of study Schütz wrote a volume of five-voice madrigals which appeared in 1611.

When Gabrieli died in 1612, Schütz returned to Germany to continue his law studies. But sometime in 1613 he became convinced that his future lay solely with music. He then became organist at the court of the Landgraf in Cassel. In this office he traveled with the Landgraf to Dresden where he was put in charge of all the music performed during the ceremonies attending the christening of the Elector's son. Schütz's work attracted the interest of the Elector, Johann Georg of Saxony, who tried to persuade the composer to enter his employ. The Landgraf was reluctant to let his organist go, but by 1615 the Elector had persuaded the Landgraf to allow Schütz to work temporarily at the electoral chapel in Dresden. In 1617 this temporary assignment became permanent with Schütz's appointment as *Kapell-meister.* During the next few years Schütz effected a radical overhauling of the musical activity at the chapel by using Italian models and importing fine Italian singers and musicians.

Schütz arrived at maturity as a composer with the publication in Dresden in 1619 of *Psalmen Davids,* a book of psalms and motets in which he introduced into German music Italian techniques of polychoral writing, concerted music, and the monodic style. In 1623 he produced still another remarkable work in an Easter oratorio entitled *Historia der Auferstehung Jesu Christi,* and in 1625 he issued a new collection of noteworthy motets, *Cantiones sacrae.* Meanwhile, in 1619 Schütz had married Magdalene Wildeck. The marriage ended abruptly six years later with Magdalene's untimely death.

The loss of his wife in 1625 brought on a period of depression from which Schütz tried to find relief by paying a second visit to Italy. This time he went for the purpose of becoming more closely acquainted with the music of Monteverdi. His association with the Venetian master led Schütz in 1627 to write *Dafne,* generally regarded as the first German opera ever written. He wrote it for the marriage ceremonies of Princess Sophia, daughter of the Elector, and it was produced for the first time at Hartenfels Castle in Torgau, on April 23, 1627. The score of this opera has since been lost.

The upheavals brought about by the Thirty Years' War were responsible for the dissolution of the musical forces at the electoral chapel in Dresden. In 1633 Schütz left Germany to visit Copenhagen. There, for a two-year period, he served as *Kapell-meister* to King Christian IV, a post he also held in 1637 and 1638, and again from 1642 to 1644. In the intervals between these periods he paid visits to Hanover and Brunswick, and made periodic returns to Dresden with the hope of reorganizing the musical activity at the electoral chapel. Matters improved greatly in Dresden by 1655, and until his death, Schütz continued his devoted services to the Elector.

Towards the end of his life, Schütz began to suffer from a loss of hearing together with a general decline in his health. He spent most of his time in almost monastic seclusion, devoting himself to reading the Bible.

A setting of Psalm CXIX was one of his last compositions. Schütz died in Dresden on November 6, 1672, and was buried there in the churchyard of Notre Dame.

Martin Geier, who was at Schütz's deathbed, described the composer's last hours: "On the sixth of November . . . he arose . . . and dressed; and after nine o'clock, while he was searching for something in his room, he was seized by a sudden weakness and he was stricken by apoplexy. . . . The doctor, whom one had called without delay, applied all his care to succor him with excellent remedies . . . but there was nothing that could help him. At the same time, the spiritual father was called to his side. . . . He blessed him, and almost immediately he [Schütz] rested very tranquil. . . . And when the fourth hour struck, he died quietly and peacefully, without the least convulsion, while we, at his side, were praying and singing."

Schütz represents the connecting link between the Renaissance and Johann Sebastian Bach. To German religious music Schütz brought the dramatic character—with its capacity to translate into musical terms the moods and sentiments of a given text—of the Italian monodic style created by the Camerata in Florence. In his Passions, a form he helped to introduce in Germany and to carry to an advanced stage of structural and musical development, he successfully combined the religious feelings of the cantata with the careful word-setting and dramatic thrust of the early Italian opera composers.

For Cecil Gray, the most striking characteristic of Schütz's music lay "in its expressive depth. In the art of Schütz every means of securing musical interest is ruthlessly sacrificed to his expressive purpose, with the result that he attains a stark, elemental simplicity and a mystical grandeur and solemnity that are quite unlike anything else, and are among the most affecting things in music. . . . It is incidentally interesting to note that Schütz became deaf in his old age and that it is, therefore, probably no mere coincidence that we should encounter in his later work the same mysterious inner radiance, the same abstract and disembodied quality and thought, the same notes of wistful and tender resignation that we find in the later work of Beethoven."

E. W. Naylor further analyzed some of the traits distinguishing Schütz: his care "to accent his words with intelligent accuracy"; the tendency "to let the course of the musical notes take the natural shape of ordinary speech"; the extraordinary dramatic expressiveness combined with harmonies of varied colors, with special emphasis on chromaticism.

In summing up Schütz's place in the history of music, F. Erckmann wrote: "When he was born the purely polyphonic style had undergone a change. While studying under Gabrieli he became acquainted with the 'Nuove musiche'—solo songs with figured bass, development of instrumental music, and union of vocal and instrumental music. With this new style he became thoroughly acquainted during a second stay in Italy, and he was the first German who introduced Italian methods and musical manners into Germany."

PRINCIPAL WORKS

Choral Music—4 Passions; Weihnachts-Historie (Christmas Story); various oratorios including Die Sieben Worte Jesu Christi am Kreuz (The Seven Last Words of Christ on the Cross); chorales, madrigals, Masses, motets, sacred songs.

ABOUT

Hoffmann, H. W., Schütz und J. S. Bach; Moser, H. J., Heinrich Schütz: His Life and Works; Müller von Asow, E., Heinrich Schütz; Müller von Asow, E. (editor), Heinrich Schütz: Gesammelte Briefe und Schriften; Piersig, J., Das Weltbild des Heinrich Schütz; Pirro, A., Schütz.

Giovanni Sgambati *1841-1914*

GIOVANNI SGAMBATI stood in the vanguard of the late nineteenth century Italian composers who helped bring about a renaissance of instrumental music in their country. He was born in Rome on May 28, 1841. His mother was the daughter of Joseph Gott, eminent Italian sculptor; his father was a successful lawyer. Giovanni early proved his pronounced gift for music. He began piano lessons when he was five with Amerigo Barbieri. One year later Sgambati made his piano debut. He also sang in the church choir, directed a small instrumental group in concerts, and wrote some church music.

When he was eight his father died and the family moved to Trevi, in Umbria, where his mother remarried. Sgambati continued his music study there with Natalucci.

In 1860 Sgambati established his home in Rome. He now gave piano concerts which helped to make him famous. He was a top-ranking virtuoso as well as a scholarly musician, a powerful force in familiarizing Italian music audiences with important German piano music rarely performed in Italy. He enjoyed a considerable following. Bettina Walker described "his lovely, elastic touch, the weight and yet the softness of his wrist staccato, the swing and go of his rhythmic beat, the coloring rich and warm, and yet most exquisitely delicate, and over all, the atmosphere of grace and charm, and the repose which perfect masters alone can give." Franz Liszt, who became Sgambati's friend as well as his teacher, also expressed unqualified admiration for Sgambati's piano performances.

In 1866 Sgambati began to achieve considerable renown as a conductor of orchestral concerts at the Dante Gallery. Once again he proved to be a valuable propagandist for little-known German music: he was responsible for the first performance in Rome of Beethoven's *Eroica Symphony* and *Emperor Concerto*. Liszt selected him to conduct his *Dante Symphony*.

With his activities as pianist and conductor were combined his first major efforts as a composer. Unlike his compatriots who preferred writing operas, Sgambati interested himself primarily in abstract instrumental music. He completed a string quartet in 1864, and in 1866, a piano quintet and the orchestral overture *Cola di Rienzi*.

In 1869 Sgambati and Liszt traveled to Germany. In Munich he heard Wagner's music dramas for the first time, a memorable experience for him even though he himself never succumbed to the Wagnerian spell. A personal meeting with Wagner in 1876 provided an opportunity for Wagner to hear some of Sgambati's compositions. They made such an impression on the master that he recommended Sgambati to the publishing house of Schott which forthwith issued several of Sgambati's works, including two piano quintets and the *Prelude and Fugue*, op. 6, for piano.

In 1877 the Liceo Musicale was established in Rome by royal decree. This Liceo was an outgrowth of the free piano classes which Sgambati had organized in 1868 at the Accademia di Santa Cecilia. After 1877, and for the rest of his life, Sgambati taught piano at the Liceo.

While achieving recognition as one of Italy's foremost piano teachers, Sgambati continued producing major compositions. His first symphony in D minor was introduced in Rome on March 28, 1881. A second symphony in E minor followed in 1883, and an important suite for orchestra, *Epitalamio sinfonico,* in 1887. His String Quartet in D-flat major, completed in 1882, was made popular throughout Europe by such distinguished chamber-music ensembles as the Joachim Quartet and Kneisel Quartet. His Piano Concerto, completed in 1878, helped to introduce him to music audiences in London, where it was heard on May 11, 1882, in a performance by the composer himself. In 1887 Sgambati directed the French première of his Second Symphony in Paris, and in 1903 he toured Russia.

He was honored at home and abroad. In France he was appointed a corresponding member of the French Institute (in succession to Liszt). King Victor Emmanuel named him Commendatore of the Order of SS Maurice and Lazarus in 1903.

After 1903 Sgambati withdrew from most of his professional activities. During the next decade he lived in semiretirement in Rome where he died on December 14, 1914.

Alfredo Casella has pointed up Sgambati's importance in Italian music: "He marks the beginning of the renaissance in that country of instrumental music which had been in abeyance for a whole century. . . . The work of Sgambati, the first advocate and supporter of this return, is of real importance in musical history; if he said nothing that was absolutely new, it was he, at all events, who pointed the way which Italian composers are now treading in ever greater numbers with growing confidence and with increasing success."

"Much of his work in the larger forms," wrote Edward Burlingame Hill, "has neither the spontaneity and melodic invention which characterize Italian music nor the depth which his German models possess. . . . In spite of the dryness of much of his chamber music, the somewhat futile classicism of the symphony, and the pretentiousness of the piano concerto, we must recognize Sgambati as a composer for the piano of real distinction. His piano pieces are original in technical style, and also in musical conception; they are elevated in artistic standards." His most celebrated piano pieces include the *Intermezzo,* op. 16, the *Pièces lyriques,* and the *Mélodies poétiques.*

PRINCIPAL WORKS

Chamber Music—2 piano quintets; String Quartet in D-flat major; Gondoliera and Due pezzi, for violin and piano.

Choral Music—Messa da Requiem; Motet.

Orchestral Music—2 symphonies; Piano Concerto in G minor; Te Deum laudamus; Epitalamio sinfonico.

Piano Music—Prelude and Fugue; Quattro pezzi; Mélodies poétiques; Pièces lyriques; Suite; études, gavotte, nocturnes.

Vocal Music—Quattro canti italiani; 4 Melodie liriche; various individual songs for voice and piano.

ABOUT

Bonaventura, G., Sgambati; Streatfeild, R. A., Masters of Italian Music; Walker, B., My Musical Experiences.

Music and Letters, October 1925; Rivista musicale italiana, January 1912.

Bedřich Smetana *1824-1884*

BEDŘICH SMETANA was Bohemia's first significant nationalist composer. He was born in Leitomischl, Bohemia, on March 2, 1824, the seventh child and only son of a successful brewer. Bedřich was unusually gifted in music and gave early demonstrations of his talent. When he was five he played in a string quartet; at six and a half he appeared as pianist in an entertainment honoring Emperor Francis I; soon after that he made his first attempts at composition. But his father, who hoped to have his son succeed him in his business, was violently opposed to a career in music and refused to allow the boy musical training.

Between 1831 and 1839 Smetana received his preliminary academic education in schools in Neuhaus, Iglau, and Deutschbrod. Then he entered a Prague high school where his overpowering interest in music led him to slight all other studies. To separate him from the active musical life of Prague, Smetana's father sent him to Pilsen where he was placed under the care of a relative, Josef Franz Smetana, a historian and scholar. In Pilsen, Smetana gave piano recitals, which brought him local renown, and taught music. His cousin, Josef Franz, recognized his talent and did what he could to persuade the boy's father to allow him to pursue music study without additional obstruction and discouragement. The father's reply was to cut off his son financially and to compel him henceforth to fend for himself.

Smetana: smě'tȧ-nȧ

One of Smetana's childhood friends, Katharina Kolař, had studied piano in Prague with Proksch and urged him to become Proksch's pupil. At nineteen, Smetana returned to Prague and for the first time undertook systematic music study with Proksch. At the same time, Smetana earned his living by giving lessons, making hardly enough to feed himself adequately. Then he was appointed music teacher for the household of Count Leopold Thun where he was given food, lodging, and the respectable salary of three hundred florins a year.

In 1848 Smetana left the employ of Count Thun. He set forth on an extended concert tour to raise money with which to found a music school in Prague. That tour was a financial disaster, and he appealed for help to Liszt, who proved cooperative. Smetana was now in a position to open his music school, a venture which became successful. His new financial status enabled him to marry his lifelong friend and sweetheart, Katharina Kolař, on August 27, 1849. One year later Smetana was appointed court pianist to Ferdinand I, former Austrian Emperor now living in retirement in Prague.

Fired with nationalist ardor, Smetana began to compose piano pieces in a Bohemian idiom, none of which attracted interest. Failure to gain recognition as a composer depressed him greatly. Tragedy deepened his gloom—the death, in 1855, of his four-year-old daughter, to whose memory he wrote the poignant Trio in G minor. The following year he went to Gothenburg, Sweden, where he stayed five years conducting the Gothenburg Philharmonic, teaching, and appearing as a piano virtuoso.

He was on his way back to Prague for a visit, in 1859, when his wife died. On July 10, 1860, he married a second time. His new wife, Barbara Fernandi, found Gothenburg too provincial and prevailed on Smetana to return to his native land for good. He did so in 1861. For a season he went on an extended concert tour through Germany and Holland. Then settling again in Prague he assumed a place of first importance in the musical life of that city. He organized and conducted choral and orchestral concerts; he opened a new music school; he wrote music criticism; he became head of the music section of the newly founded Art Society; he wrote major works in a national style.

The wave of nationalism sweeping across Bohemia since 1860 (when Austria had

BEDŘICH SMETANA

granted it political autonomy) led in 1862 to the founding of a national theater devoted to performances of Bohemian operas. Smetana volunteered to write for this theater several folk operas. "I want to give my nation that which I owe to it and which I carry in my heart—a work of grand volume," he said at the time. His first national opera was *The Brandenburgers in Bohemia,* based on a historical episode which occurred when the Teutons overran Bohemia. *The Brandenburgers in Bohemia* was introduced on January 5, 1866 and was received with considerable public enthusiasm. But many critics felt that the libretto was too involved and static, and that the music was too ponderous and derivative from Wagner.

These criticisms upset Smetana. Piqued, he decided to write an opera which would prove he could be light, tuneful, vivacious, and completely free of any Wagnerian influence. He asked the librettist Karel Sabina to provide him with a text. The result was *The Bartered Bride (Prodaná Nevěsta).* This was Smetana's masterwork, one of the greatest folk operas ever written and a cornerstone of Bohemian nationalism in music.

In its first version, as produced by the National Theater on May 30, 1866, *The Bartered Bride* was more musical comedy than opera. It was a spoken play with songs and dances in a popular or folk style. As such it proved outstandingly successful, a powerful factor in finally establishing Smetana's reputation as the foremost nationalist composer in Bohemia. But the success of *The Bartered Bride* outside Bohemia came only after the opera had been subjected to several major revisions. For a projected Parisian performance that never materialized, Smetana added some new arias and a male chorus; he split up the first act into two and made other basic revisions. Later the same year he decided to include two folk dances, the popular Polka and Furiant. The opera returned to Prague in its changed format on January 29, 1869. Then, for presentations in St. Petersburg, Smetana substituted recitatives for spoken dialogue. This was the final and definitive version, produced for the first time in Prague on September 25, 1870.

From Prague, *The Bartered Bride* went on to win the praise of the music world outside Bohemia. It was a triumph in Vienna in 1892 in performances at the Vienna Royal Opera conducted by Gustav Mahler. In 1894 it was seen in Scandinavia, in 1895 in England, and in 1907 in Belgium. The American première took place at the Metropolitan Opera on February 19, 1909, Gustav Mahler directing. "The question whether there can be any sustained popularity for an opera of [this] character," wrote W. J. Henderson in the New York *Sun,* "seemed to be swiftly answered by the public enjoyment of its novelty of style and color."

"*The Bartered Bride,*" said Julien Tiersot, "is full of vivacity, movement, and color. The action, which takes place entirely in a public square, in an inn of a village of Bohemia, during a festival day, has for its subject a typical musical-comedy situation. . . . All the music which expresses all the states of soul (however simple) of the characters, is enframed here and there by purely picturesque episodes: choruses of peasants, drinking songs and, above all else, by popular elements which contribute greatly to giving life to this musical work and to justify its reputation as a representation of the art of a people."

But, as Pitts Sanborn wrote, *The Bartered Bride* is "by no means folk opera in a cramping sense. While distinctly of its native soil, it also possesses the universal qualities necessary to give it a world-wide currency. We of other countries delight in its Czech rhythms, its national dances, the characteristic contour of many of its melodies, but we find also in the music more than local color and

exotic charm; the flowing humanity is there that transcends limits and boundaries."

The success of *The Bartered Bride* brought Smetana an appointment as conductor of the National Theater. He now went to work on his third opera, *Dalibor,* whose hero was the leader of a Czech revolt against oppression. Introduced on May 16, 1868, it was a failure, with the critics once again accusing Smetana of aping Wagner.

In 1869 Smetana founded a dramatic school for the Bohemian Theater, and in 1873 he became its director. Meanwhile he had completed *Libuše,* an opera planned for performance in 1871 at the coronation of Franz Josef as king of Bohemia. When the coronation did not materialize, Smetana's enemies frustrated every effort to have *Libuše* produced. The opera was finally performed June 11, 1881, when it opened the new National Theater in Prague and scored a major success. Though rarely given, *Libuše* is one of Smetana's finest operas. When it was revived in Prague about thirty years after its première, Herbert F. Peyser reported in the New York *Times* that it was "one of the larger experiences of a musical lifetime. . . . For this is music . . . now lyrical in the grand manner (and revealing some singular and beautiful relationships to Chopin), now heroic or epic, and cast, as it were, in bronze music that has the tread of armies in it."

Realizing in 1874 that he was growing deaf, Smetana resigned his post as conductor at the National Theater. He plunged more deeply into creative work, producing some of the works by which he is most often represented today in concert programs. Between 1874 and 1879 he completed a cycle of six tone poems for orchestra in which, as Kurt Pahlen wrote, "he poured forth all his love of home." The cycle was entitled *My Fatherland (Má Vlast).* Each of the tone poems represented a different aspect of Bohemian geography and history. Pahlen went on to explain that the first of these tone poems, *Vyšehrad* "is a depiction of the times of Bohemia's ancient kings. The second is undoubtedly the most celebrated in the set, and Smetana's most popular work for orchestra: *The Moldau (Vltava),* an eloquent depiction in tone of the mighty stream as it courses through picturesque villages, listens to the song of water sprites and wood nymphs, witnesses a marriage feast and a revel of naiads, and then arrives at old

Prague. The third tone poem, *Šárka,* "takes us back to the legendary times of the bards," while the fourth, *From Bohemia's Fields and Groves,* "is a charming picturization of Nature." *Tábor* gives "sound to old Hussite motifs from the historical days of the religious wars," and *Blaník* "gloriously rounds off the work like a hymn of victory and of faith in the rebirth of the Czech nation." The entire cycle received its première in Prague on November 2, 1882.

Another instrumental masterwork, written after his deafness, was an autobiographical string quartet, *From My Life (Aus meinem Leben),* in 1876. Here the composer reviews his youth when he loved art and dancing, when he fell in love with the girl who became his first wife, and when he discovered the national element in music. In the coda he speaks of his deafness, simulating "the fatal whistling in my ear . . . that announced my deafness" with a high "E" in the first violin over a tremolo in the other strings.

Smetana's last years were filled with tragedy. His final opera, *The Devil's Wall,* in 1882, was a failure that broke his spirit. "I shall write nothing more," he exclaimed. He now became a victim of depressions which, in turn, brought on a nervous breakdown. By January 1884 he was incapable of sufficient concentration to continue writing music any longer. Soon after his sixtieth birthday was celebrated in Prague with a gala concert, he was confined to an asylum in Prague where he died on May 12, 1884.

"Smetana," wrote Jan Lowenbach, "was privileged not only to hear and imitate the spirit of the rich melodies and varied rhythms of his nation, but also to invent, to *feel,* and to *express* it in a new way and to adapt it to the spirit of modern times. He created the new song and the first symphony and great symphonic poems filled with new poetical and national ideas, he invented a modern national style of piano music . . . and he was the first to introduce a discreetly intimate note to chamber music. For national opera, he found, through his ingenious intuition, his own lyrical and dramatic purity of style which has its personal cadence and retains its value as something intermediate between Mozart and Wagner. All this makes him the great founder of the modern music of the nineteenth century, and one of the most important factors in the culture of his nation."

Otakar Hostinsky, who often saw Smetana in the leading cafés of Prague in the 1870's, provided the following description: "The afternoon would find him studying the papers with great application. . . . At such times he did not like to be disturbed in his reading; therefore conversations with him were usually short, even laconic, and after a few essential words he would read on peacefully and attentively. Sometimes, after he had finished his reading he would converse gladly and gaily with a circle of acquaintances, usually from the artistic and literary world, who joined him at the table. . . .

"Whilst dining he would remain unbending. Not until he had lit his cigar from which, after cutting its end, he would carefully tap out the dust, would he thaw, and then he would become most conversational. There was a reason for this. He usually came from the theater, and on the way thoughts that were not of the pleasantest occupied his mind. The gloom that so often clouded his brow only gradually gave way to a brighter mood. When he finally felt himself to be in a circle of friends, he sought to shake off all unpleasant impressions and liked to enjoy himself for an hour or two. . . . As a rule he spoke quietly and unhurriedly, and his wit was often tinged with irony or satire. He was always ready to understand a joke and yet he knew how to keep everyone at a respectful distance, not because he was unbending or cold, but on the contrary because of the impression he gave of a great mind, frank, and sure of himself, without any ostentation and therefore impressive. If he was in a specially good mood he laughed heartily and sometimes spoke very loudly. At moments, however, when he spoke most intimately of the great masters and their works and recalled great artistic experiences, he would involuntarily lower his voice, his eyebrows would go up above his shining eyes, and his whole appearance expressed pure enthusiasm and strength of conviction, whether he was speaking of Beethoven or Wagner, or Bach or of Liszt. There were, of course, days when he did not succeed in dispelling the gloom caused by the attacks and injustices resulting from the turmoil of the times. On such occasions Smetana would speak bitterly of how the most honest work and artistic efforts were rewarded."

Louis Spohr *1784-1859*

L OUIS (LUDWIG) SPOHR was born in Brunswick, Germany, on April 5, 1784, the oldest of six children. His father was a physician who played the flute competently, and his mother was an excellent singer and pianist. In such a musical environment, Louis early developed his innate gift for music. At four he sang duets with his mother. Shortly after that, as he recalled in his autobiography, "I had lessons (on the violin) from Herr Riemenschneider. I still remember that first lesson in which I had learned to play the G major chord on all four strings. In ecstasies over the harmony, I hastened to the kitchen to my mother, and arpeggioed the chord to her so incessantly that she was obliged to drive me away." It was not long before he was participating in chamber music performances at home.

Spohr continued his violin lessons with Dufour in Seesen, a town to which the Spohrs had moved when the boy was four. Dufour, though an amateur, recognized Spohr's potential. He managed to talk Spohr's parents out of their ambition to make Louis a physician. Instead, they allowed the boy to go to Brunswick for more professional training than Seesen could offer. Spohr went to Brunswick when he was twelve. There he studied the violin with Kunisch and Maucourt, and counterpoint with Hartung. Those lessons with Hartung were the only formal training he received in music besides the violin. All his subsequent knowledge of musical theory came from studying textbooks.

When Spohr was fourteen, his father dispatched him to Hamburg to begin his professional career as violinist. Unable to find a place for himself there, Spohr returned to Seesen discouraged and defeated. But a petition he had sent to the Duke of Brunswick proved fruitful. In 1799 Spohr received his first appointment as violinist in the ducal orchestra. The Duke became personally interested in him and arranged for him to study the violin with Franz Eck. The Duke also permitted Spohr to travel with Eck to Russia, where Spohr found the opportunity to meet John Field and Clementi.

Though he had been writing music since boyhood, beginning with pieces for the violin, Spohr's first ambitious compositions were not realized until the beginning of the nineteenth century. Between 1800 and 1804 he completed three violin concertos, his first two string quartets, and some additional chamber music.

In 1804 Spohr went on a concert tour of Germany. On December 10 his performance in Leipzig proved a dual triumph, since he performed two of his own concertos which were well received. "His concertos," reported Rochlitz, in a Leipzig music journal, "rank with the finest existing, and in particular we know no concertos superior to that in D minor, whether as regards conception, soul and charm, or also in respect to precision and firmness. His peculiar style inclines most to the grand and then to a soft and dreamy melancholy."

After this tour had been completed, Spohr was appointed in 1805 concertmaster of the ducal orchestra in Gotha. On February 2, 1806, he married Doretta Scheidler, a professional harpist, with whom he made a number of concert appearances. Despite the demands made upon him by the concert stage and his work at the ducal court, Spohr was able to complete several major works, including his first opera, *Die Prüfung*, which was given a concert performance in Gotha in 1806; a *Concertante* for two violins; a symphony; an oratorio; and numerous chamber music compositions.

Between 1812 and 1815 Spohr was the conductor of the Theater-an-der-Wien orchestra in Vienna, adding still a new dimension to his musical life. Between 1815 and 1817 he made a number of concert tours, appearing occasionally in joint recitals with his wife. For his appearance in Italy in 1816 he wrote his eighth violin concerto in A minor, entitled *Gesangscene,* or "vocal scene." The name comes from the fact that, in his attempt to interest Italian music lovers, Spohr wrote a concerto influenced by opera. He thus produced an operatic scene in instrumental style that was dramatic as well as lyrical and in which the violin often simulated the human voice. Another unusual feature of this work, at least in 1816, was that the three movements were played without interruption and represented a single unified conception.

In 1816 the première of Spohr's opera *Faust* was heard in Prague, Carl Maria von Weber conducting. This opera, though Spohr's fourth, was the first to be successful; it enhanced Spohr's fame as a composer throughout Europe. In 1818 Spohr himself directed performances of this opera in Frankfurt-am-Main, where one year later he conducted the world première of still another opera, *Zemire und Azor.*

In 1820 Spohr paid his first visit to England. As a guest conductor of the Royal Philharmonic Society of London he made history by becoming the first director of an orchestra to use a baton. He told the story in his autobiography: "I took my stand... in front of the orchestra, drew my baton from my coat pocket and gave the signal to begin. Quite alarmed at such a novel proceeding some of the directors protested against it, but when I besought them to grant me at least one trial they became pacified. The symphonies and overtures that were to be rehearsed were well known to me, and in Germany I had already directed their performances. I, therefore, could not only give the tempi in a very decisive manner, but indicated also to the wind instruments and horns all the entries, which ensured to them a confidence such as hitherto they had not known. . . . Surprised and inspired by this result, the orchestra immediately after the first part of the symphony expressed aloud its united assent to the new mode of conducting and thereby overruled all further opposition on the part of the directors. . . . The triumph of the baton as a time giver was decisive."

After his triumphs in London, and his return to Germany, Spohr was recommended by Weber for the post of court *Kapell-*

LOUIS SPOHR

meister to the Elector of Hesse-Cassel. Spohr began this assignment in 1822 and remained for thirty-five years. In that time he was responsible for many extraordinary performances of opera, including some of Wagner's earlier works. Spohr also found the time to complete an opera of his own, *Jessonda,* whose première he directed in Cassel on July 28, 1823. Soon after that, *Jessonda* was seen in most of Germany's leading opera houses and with such success that its over-all popularity was second only to that then enjoyed by Weber's *Der Freischütz.* Other distinguished works completed by Spohr in Cassel included his most famous symphony, the fourth, entitled *Die Weihe der Töne,* as well as other symphonies and concertos; three oratorios, including *Die letzten Dinge (The Last Judgment),* which remained a favorite in the choral repertory throughout the nineteenth century; and numerous chamber music works and songs.

In 1834 Spohr's wife died. She had borne him four children, one of whom died in infancy. In 1836, he married Marianne Pfeiffer, a pianist.

Because of his pronounced radical sympathies in politics, Spohr incurred the displeasure of the Elector and aroused a considerable amount of hostility at court. He finally decided to resign his post as *Kapellmeister* in 1857. A year after that a broken arm put an end to his career as virtuoso as well. His last appearance as a conductor took place in

Prague in 1858, in a performance of *Jessonda*. He died in Cassel on October 22, 1859.

Very little of Spohr's immense output has survived. Besides the A minor violin concerto, he is today represented in the concert hall only by a charming Nonet in F major and several other chamber music compositions. Most violinists, however, know him best for his *Violin Method,* which is utilized profitably by students the world over.

During his own lifetime, Spohr was one of the most highly esteemed composers of the day. In addition, he was a significant innovator. He was one of the first composers to write a three-movement violin concerto as a single, integrated entity, and one of the first to write a nonet. He was always experimenting with unusual combinations of instruments. He wrote a concerto for string quartet; a symphony for two orchestras; a work for double string quartet; and even a "sonatina" for voice and piano. He was also a pioneer in writing program music and in introducing a Romantic element into oratorios.

In the opinion of Arthur M. Abell, Spohr's violin concertos are his most significant contributions: "Spohr gave to the violin concerto a depth, breadth and nobility such as had been quite unknown before him. He took a big step in advance of Viotti; he made the violin concerto an organic whole, giving it greater unity of construction, and greater wealth of ideas. . . . Spohr, like his predecessors, recognized the fundamental nature of the violin and treated it first as a 'singing' instrument; thus his slow movements are among the most beautiful cantabile writing in existence for the violin. Unlike Paganini, he avoided showy writing for effect. There is no froth or foam in Spohr's works. . . . He had an abundance of ideas, and in melodic outlines his concertos are lyric, elegiac, and ofttimes of a certain melancholy sentimentality."

PRINCIPAL WORKS

Chamber Music—34 string quartets; 7 string quintets; 5 piano trios; 4 double string quartets; Nonet in F major; Octet in E major; Sextet in C major, Sonate concertante, for violin and harp; Violin Sonata in B major; fantasies for violin and piano (or harp); other chamber music works including duos concertants for two violins, trios concertants, and variations for various instruments and piano.

Choral Music—Mass; Die letzten Dinge; Des Heilands letzte Stunden; Der Fall Babylons; Vater unser; various hymns, part songs, psalms.

Operas—Faust; Zemire und Azor; Jessonda; Der Berggeist; Pietro von Abano; Der Alchymist; Der Kreuzfahrer.

Orchestral Music—15 violin concertos; 9 symphonies; 4 concert overtures; 2 clarinet concertos; 2 Concertantes, for two violins; String Quartet Concerto; Erinnerung an Marienbad; Fantasy on Die Tochter der Luft.

Piano Music—Sonata in A-flat major; Rondoletto in G major.

Vocal Music—German songs for voice and piano; songs for contralto or baritone and piano; Sonatina for voice and piano; vocal duets.

ABOUT

Pleasants, H. (editor), The Musical Journeys of Louis Spohr; Salburg, E. von, Louis Spohr; Spohr, L., Autobiography; Stierlin, L., Spohr.

Gasparo Spontini *1774-1851*

GASPARO LUIGI PACIFICO SPONTINI, eminent nineteenth century Italian opera composer, was born in Majolati, Ancona, on November 14, 1774. His father, a peasant, hoped his son would enter the church. With this in mind, he sent the boy off to Jesi to live with his uncle, a priest, and receive from him some preliminary religious training. The boy, however, had such little interest in religion that his uncle soon had to resort to harsh repressive measures to discipline him. In rebellion, Gasparo ran away and found refuge in Monte San Vito, at the home of another, more kindly, uncle. This uncle, noting the boy's strong inclination for music, found him a teacher, a man named Quintiliana.

After about a year, Gasparo's uncle in Jesi forgave him, welcomed him back home, and stood ready to allow him to indulge his musical interests freely. In 1793, after Spontini had been taken by his parents to Naples, he entered the Conservatorio della Pietà de' Turchini, where for several years he received sound training in composition and counterpoint from Sala, and in singing from Tritto. He began to attract attention with a number of cantatas and other church compositions performed in or near Naples. One of these works was heard by the director of the Teatro della Pallacorda in Rome, who commissioned Spontini to write an opera for his theater. That opera, *I Puntigli delle donne,* was introduced in Rome during the

Carnival of 1796 with outstanding success. Another opera, *Adelina Senese,* was produced in Venice in 1797; a third, *L'Eroismo ridicolo,* written with the advice and guidance of Piccini, was seen in 1798 in Naples.

When, toward the end of 1798, the French army advanced towards Naples, the Neapolitan court fled to Palermo. Spontini went with it, assuming in Palermo the post of *maestro di cappella.* In 1800, he quickly wrote and had produced four operas, each in the favored Neapolitan style of the time.

The climate of Palermo proved so detrimental to Spontini's health that before the end of 1800 he was compelled to leave Sicily. He went to Venice where he wrote an opera for one of the theaters, then set sail for France. He arrived in Paris in 1803, there he started to write stage works in the lighter style then favored by such French masters as Méhul and Boieldieu. *La Petite maison* and *Julie* were produced at the Opéra-Comique in 1804 and 1805; the reaction of the public to the first was so hostile that it was removed almost at once from the repertory.

Spontini's friendship with the distinguished French poet and librettist Étienne Jouy proved a turning point in his stage career in France. Jouy was convinced that Spontini's talent was ill suited to *opéra-comique* and urged him to consider texts of greater dramatic and emotional interest. They worked together for the first time in 1804, completing a one-act opera, *Milton,* that was richer in harmonic and orchestral material than anything Spontini had thus far written. *Milton* proved popular not only in France, but also, in 1805 and 1806, in Vienna and Berlin.

Spurred on by this success, Jouy now provided Spontini with an even more ambitious text, *La Vestale,* based on an episode from Winckelmann's *Monumenti Antichi Inediti.* The setting was Rome during the Republic, and the central figures were a Roman warrior and a vestal virgin enmeshed in a powerful love drama. It took Spontini three years to complete his score. So much of his musical writing was ahead of its time in dramatic power and force and in unusual orchestral colors that some of Paris' influential musicians joined forces to prevent its première. But Spontini had an influential patron on his side—the Empress Josephine, who had recently appointed him court composer. It was at her insistence that *La Ve-*

GASPARO SPONTINI

stale was finally produced at the Opéra on December 16, 1807. It was an unqualified success, bringing Spontini the first prize in a competition established by Napoleon and making him a favorite of French opera goers. The initial success was duplicated wherever it was played: in Vienna in 1810, in Berlin in 1811, and in New York and Philadelphia in 1828.

To Richard Wagner, Spontini, as represented by his *La Vestale,* was "the last member of a series of composers whose first member was Gluck." Many other historians consider *La Vestale* one of the most significant links in the development of musical drama during the period separating Gluck and Meyerbeer.

This is the way Ebenezer Prout described the opera: "The melodies are all of an Italian cast; the recitatives, always remarkable for the truth of their expression, are modeled on those of Gluck, though without servile imitation; the great ensemble movements were in their day a novelty. Berlioz spoke of him [Spontini] as the inventor of the 'colossal crescendo.' . . . There is little doubt but that his great finales were the patterns which, consciously or not, were imitated by many of the opera composers who followed him."

La Vestale was revived by the Metropolitan Opera in New York on November 12, 1925. On that occasion, Lawrence Gilman said in the New York *Herald Tribune:* "Spontini was not quite a genius. His musical imagination was far too limited to entitle him to be ranked with his great predecessor Gluck; yet he had an austerity of style that sometimes reminds one of Gluck, and a power of dramatic augmentation that often recalls the master of *Orfeo*. There is not much to be said for [his] melodic invention, nor for his harmonic resourcefulness. But he knew the orchestra, wrote for it with authority, and developed its potentialities of expression."

While working on his next opera, *Fernand Cortez*, Spontini married the daughter of Jean-Baptiste Erard. The new opera was given at the Opéra on November 28, 1809, with Napoleon's blessing, and proved almost as successful as *La Vestale.*

In 1810 Spontini was appointed conductor of the Italian Opera in Paris. He held this post for only two years, but in that time he was able to give some excellent performances, besides instituting a series of orchestral concerts in which masterworks by Haydn and Mozart were introduced to Parisian music lovers. Serious differences between him and the management of the Italian Opera brought about his dismissal in 1812. Two years after that, with the restoration of the Bourbons, Spontini was again offered his conducting post but he declined, preferring instead to accept one as court composer to Louis XVIII. He now completed several operas glorifying the Restoration, and some *pièces d'occasion*. And, for about four years, he was deep at work on an opera which he regarded as his masterwork—*Olympie*, with a text based on Voltaire. But when it was introduced on December 22, 1819, it met with an unfavorable reception. After that, Spontini—still convinced that this was his most important opera—revised it extensively. Not until *Olympie* was revived at the Paris Opéra in 1826, in the last of several revised versions, did it meet with approval.

In 1819 Spontini was engaged by King Frederick William III to become principal *Kapellmeister* and general music director in Berlin. Spontini scored a major success in 1821, with a carefully prepared presentation of *Olympie*, but its popularity was soon eclipsed by the triumph of Weber's *Der Freischütz*. Though the King and the court remained faithful to their *Kapellmeister*, most of Berlin's influential musicians rallied behind Weber. Nevertheless, Spontini continued to give important performances (including a memorable one cf *Der Freischütz* in 1826 for the benefit of Weber's widow and children) and wrote two new operas for presentation in Berlin. One of these was *Agnes von Hohenstaufen*, built around the frustrated love affair of a twelfth century princess. After its première in Berlin on June 12, 1829, *Agnes von Hohenstaufen* was revised and produced in 1837, and then was neglected for over a century. Its first performance since 1837, and the first ever heard in Italy, took place at the Florence May Music Festival in 1954. "Spontini composed several pieces of charm and attractiveness," wrote Michael Steinberg in his review for the New York *Times*, "most notably Agnes's opening aria in whose refrain the female chorus joins. It is in the pacing of the work that Spontini's achievement is most impressive, and the planning of some of the scenes shows the hand of a man very experienced indeed in the musical theater."

Spontini gathered numerous honors while serving as *Kapellmeister* in Berlin. In 1829 he received an honorary degree from Halle University. In 1833 he became a knight of the Prussian Ordre pour le Mérite and a member of the Berlin Academy. In 1838 he was appointed to the French Institute.

When Frederick William III died in 1840, Spontini lost his main supporter. Hated by his colleagues because of his tempers, conceit, arrogance, and lack of tact, and attacked by the press, he was destined to fall from favor. At one time public hostility to him achieved such a pitch that at one of his performances of *Don Giovanni* he was compelled to flee from the theater. He resigned his post in 1841, and left Berlin in the summer of 1842.

He traveled in France, Italy, and Germany. In 1844 the Pope made him Count of Sant' Andrea and Wagner helped prepare in Dresden a performance of *La Vestale* which Spontini himself directed. In 1847 Spontini led excerpts from *Olympie* at the Cologne Music Festival.

But by 1848 his health was deteriorating rapidly. He was suffering from deafness, failing memory, weakened physical resources, and melancholia. He went to live in Jesi, near the town of his birth, and devoted himself to charitable pursuits. In 1850 he returned to his native city, and there he died on January 24, 1851. He left all his wealth and property to the poor people of Jesi and Majolati.

Spontini's operas are rarely given today, but their significance has never been underestimated by the historian. In the era just before Meyerbeer, when the Italian opera was dominated by singer and song, Spontini wrote operas with dramatic power, truth of declamation, and rich orchestral resources; his works were landmarks in the age between Gluck and Meyerbeer. He had majesty of style, unity of purpose, an uncommon gift for building climaxes and for writing grand finales, and a skill in producing ensembles—all of which still reward twentieth century audiences on those rare occasions when his works are revived.

"Spontini's earnestness, nobility of aim and breadth of concept," wrote Frederick Niecks, "raise his operas to a high level. In their form there is an imposing largeness and a striving after unity that made him impatient with littleness produced by the stringing together of self-contained pieces. His dramatic power and skill, which never forsake him, shine brilliantly when at the climaxes of his subjects his soul is stirred. It is in these qualities that Spontini's greatness lies."

"Let us bow profoundly and reverently," Richard Wagner wrote, "before the grave of the creator of *La Vestale* and *Olympie.*"

PRINCIPAL WORKS

Operas—La finta filosofa; Milton; La Vestale; Fernand Cortez; Pélage; Olympie; Nurmahal; Agnes von Hohenstaufen.

ABOUT

Bouvet, C., Spontini; Fragapane, P., Spontini; Ghislanzoni, A., Spontini; Wagner, R., Gesammelte Schriften, vol. 5.

Musical Times, December 1910; La Revue musicale, September 1906.

Johann Stamitz *1717-1757*

JOHANN WENZEL ANTON STAMITZ was one of the most significant creators of the classical symphony before Haydn. He was born in the Bohemian town of Deutschbrod on June 19, 1717. From his father, an organist and teacher, he received his first instruction in music. Later he took courses in music at a Jesuit school. He showed marked talent for both composition and the violin. In 1741 he was acclaimed for his violin performance during festivities attending the coronation of Emperor Charles VII in Prague. The Elector Palatine, Duke Carl Theodor, hired him to join his electoral orchestra in Mannheim. Soon after receiving this appointment, Stamitz gave a remarkably successful violin recital in Frankfurt am Main.

In 1744 he married in Mannheim. (Of the four children born to Stamitz, two became successful musicians.) By 1745 Stamitz had risen in Mannheim to the post of concertmaster or leader of the court orchestra and director of the court chamber music. He was required to write for and direct orchestral performances at the ducal palace. In his post as the leader of the orchestra Stamitz made musical history by establishing what many now regard as the first modern symphony orchestra and by defining for the first time some of the functions of the orchestral conductor. His carefully prepared rehearsals, his rigid discipline, and his concern for details inaugurated a new era in orchestral performance. Those who heard the Mannheim orchestra under Stamitz (and these included Mozart and the eighteenth century British music historian Charles Burney) marveled at a virtuosity and technique said to be without parallel at that time—the way in which crescendos, diminuendos, and tremolos were produced; the manner in which the ensemble passed from pianissimo to fortissimo; the singing quality produced by the violins and the richness in tone of the winds. Charles Burney who described the orchestra as "an army of generals" went on to say: "No orchestra in the world has ever surpassed the Mannheim orchestra in execution. Its forte is thunder, its crescendo is cataract, its diminuendo is a crystal stream babbling along in the distance, its piano a breath of spring."

Because the city boasted such a remarkable orchestra, there arose in Mannheim a school of instrumental composers who helped inaugurate a new era in symphonic music. Their leading figure was Stamitz himself, and the most prominent members included Franz Xaver Richter (1709-1789), Ignaz Holzbauer (1711-1783), Christian Cannabich (1731-1798), and Johann Stamitz' son Carl (1745-1801). The nineteenth century musicologist Hugo Riemann, impressed by the works of the Mannheim school in general and of Johann Stamitz in particular, declared that the symphony and symphonic style were born with this group of composers. This, of course, is not so; but it is true that both the style of orchestral writing and the structure of the symphony experienced a truly remarkable development with Stamitz and his Mannheim colleagues.

Stamitz' first opus appeared in 1750. It was a set of orchestral trios which, as Romain Rolland said, initiated a new age of orchestral music. After that Stamitz produced a whole library of orchestral music that totaled in all over a hundred and fifty compositions. These included seventy-four symphonies and numerous concertos for various solo instruments and orchestra, including the first clarinet concerto ever written.

The symphonies of Stamitz are particularly important since they helped to formalize the classic structure and to point to a new manner of instrumental writing. Stamitz was one of the earliest composers to realize the classic sonata form by introducing a contrasting second theme in his allegro movements, and breaking those movements up into an exposition, development, and recapitulation section. He was also one of the earliest composers to add a fourth movement to the symphony, a sprightly finale after the minuet which up to that time had concluded most symphonies. In his orchestral style, he was uniquely successful in utilizing the basic personalities of the strings and the winds. He made dynamics, nuances, orchestral effects an end in themselves rather than the means to an end as had previously been the case with composers for the stage.

Burney acclaimed Stamitz as "another Shakespeare, who overcame all difficulties and carried the art of music further than any had ever done before his time; a genius, all invention, all fire, all contrast in the lively movements, with a tender, gracious, and seductive melody, simple and rich accompaniments, and everywhere the sublime effect produced by enthusiasm, but in a style not always sufficiently polished."

In a more recent critical evaluation, Romain Rolland said: "The roots of Beethoven exist already . . . in the Mannheim symphonies, in the work of the astonishing Johann Stamitz. . . . Through him, instrumental music becomes the supple garment of the living soul, always in movement, perpetually changing, with its unexpected fluctuations and contrasts. . . . I have no hesitation in saying that the symphonies of a Stamitz, though less rich, less beautiful, less exuberant, are much more spontaneous than those of a Haydn or a Mozart. It is made to its own measure; it creates its forms; it does not submit to them."

In September 1754 Stamitz journeyed to Paris, where he stayed about a year. He was already famous there when he arrived. In 1748 he had been influential in getting the famous French patron of Rameau, La Pouplinière, to include horns in his orchestra; in 1751 one of Stamitz' symphonies had been introduced in Paris with considerable success; and in 1752 his innovations and career had been responsible for a satirical pamphlet by Grimm, *Le petit prophète de Boehmischbroda*. Stamitz' fame in France grew by leaps and bounds during his one-year stay, during which time he worked for La Pouplinière. He appeared in concerts and at leading salons, he wrote a revolutionary new symphony that brought clarinets into the symphonic body, he had several works published, and his Mass was performed at the Jacobin Church.

Little is known of Stamitz' life after his return to Mannheim, where he died on March 27, 1757.

Two of Stamitz' sons made significant contributions to the Mannheim school. Carl Stamitz was one of the most distinguished performers of his time on the viola and the viola d'amour. He wrote about fifty symphonies, over twenty-five *symphonies concertantes*, seven violin concertos, two piano concertos, and numerous string quartets, trios, and other chamber music. Anton Stamitz (1754 - c. 1809), though of lesser stature than his father or brother, was also a creator of symphonies, concertos, and chamber music.

PRINCIPAL WORKS

Chamber Music—14 violin sonatas; 6 cello sonatas; 2 duos for violin solo; 9 dances for two violins and accompaniment; various trios.

Choral Music—Mass in D major; Kyrie and Gloria; 2 Litaniae Lauretanae; Motet.

Orchestral Music—74 symphonies; 10 orchestral trios: 12 violin concertos; 8 flute concertos; 6 harpsichord concertos; various other concertos for solo instruments and orchestra; Omni die, for bass and orchestra; De omni tempore, for soprano and orchestra.

ABOUT

Gradenwitz, P., Johann Stamitz; Nettl, P., Der kleine Prophet von Böhmisch-Brod; Rolland, R., A Musical Tour Through the Land of the Past.

Notes, December 1949.

Johann Strauss II *1825-1899*

AS THE WALTZ KING of Vienna and
the genius of Viennese operettas, Johann
Strauss II was essentially a composer of music in a light vein. But he brought such a
richness of musical invention and originality of thought and style to his waltzes that
they are frequently performed by the world's
greatest symphony orchestras under the direction of the foremost conductors; his best
operettas, moreover, are in the repertory of
many leading opera houses.

Strauss was born in Vienna on October
25, 1825. He was the eldest son of Johann
Strauss I (1804-1849), who for many years
was, in his own right, the idol of Vienna as
the conductor of café orchestras and as a
composer of waltzes. Johann Strauss I
organized his first café orchestra in 1826
for the Bock café. From then on, until the
end of his life, he was a major musical attraction at some of Vienna's greatest cafés,
as well as at the Redoutensaal. In 1833 he
was made bandmaster of the First Vienna
Militia Regiment, and in 1845 he was appointed conductor of the Viennese court
balls. He was almost as popular outside
Austria, having made numerous triumphant
tours throughout Europe. As a composer, he
produced over two hundred and fifty compositions, including such beloved waltzes as
the *Loreley Rheinklänge, Cäcilienwalzer,*
and *Donaulieder.* He also created galops,
polkas, quadrilles, and marches; of the last,
the *Radetzky March* has become a classic,
the voice and symbol of Hapsburg Austria.

The elder Strauss was so violently opposed
to a musical career for Johann that he put
every possible obstacle in his way. But the
boy was drawn to music instinctively, in
spite of his father's stern prohibitions. With
the help of his sympathetic mother, young
Strauss began to take violin lessons secretly
with Amon, a member of his father's orchestra. He learned not only to play that
instrument, but also to write light music; his
first effort, appropriately named *Erste Ge-
danke,* came when he was only six. While
giving free rein to his musical inclinations,
young Strauss attended the Schottengymnasi-
um from 1836 to 1840, and then the Tech-
nische Hochschule. Upon completing his
academic studies, he briefly took on a job as
bank clerk. But he never swerved from his
decision to become a musician.

JOHANN STRAUSS II

In 1840 his father abandoned the family
to live with Emilie Trampusch. For Johann
this desertion proved a blessing in disguise, for it meant he could now devote himself to music openly and wholeheartedly.
He studied the violin with Kohlmann, a
conductor at the Royal Opera, and theory
with Joseph Drechsler, a noted church choirmaster. Drechsler hoped to make his gifted
pupil a serious composer, but Strauss's decision was inflexible. His goals were the
café and the waltz.

The young man made his debut in both
departments on October 15, 1844, at Dommayer's Casino, in the Hietzing suburb of
Vienna. He led his own orchestra in a program of overtures and opera pieces, and
several of his own compositions. The event
aroused considerable interest and excitement
in Vienna, since there was general knowledge of the family rift. The Viennese saw
in the debut of the son an open challenge to
the authority and prestige of the father. The
latter did not attend the debut but one of
his friends was present and reported that
Johann Strauss the younger had scored a
triumph. When the young man had finished
playing one of his own waltzes, the *Gunst-
werber,* for the first time, the furor was such
that he had to repeat it three times. Another
of the younger Strauss's waltzes, *Sinnge-
dichte,* had nineteen encores. And when,
toward the end of the program, the son
paid a sentimental tribute to his esteemed

father by performing the *Loreley Rhein-klänge,* the audience was beside itself. "These Viennese!" commented Wiest in the *Wanderer.* "Exactly as they were ten years ago. A new waltz player—a piece of world history! . . . Good night, Lanner! Good evening, Father Strauss! Good morning, Son Strauss!"

During the next few years, the younger Strauss reigned in such fashionable cafés as Dommayer's, Zogernitz, and Zum Grünen Thore. After the death of his father in 1849, Johann Strauss II became the undisputed monarch of Viennese light music. Combining the principal members of his father's orchestra with his own group, he directed the augmented ensemble not only in Vienna's most popular cafés and at the Volksgarten, but also in tours throughout Europe, beginning in 1854, when he led concerts for several seasons in a park near St. Petersburg. In 1867 he made triumphant appearances at the World Exhibition in Paris, and soon thereafter went to London at the invitation of the Prince of Wales for six concerts at Covent Garden.

Meanwhile, on August 27, 1862, Johann Strauss and Henrietta Treffz, one-time prima donna, were married at St. Stephen's Cathedral. They set up home in a fashionable apartment on the Praterstrasse. Five years later Strauss inherited his father's former post as conductor of the court balls, a position he held for a five-year period.

All the while, Strauss was writing waltzes. The Strauss waltz was not just a simple, lilting tune in three-quarter time. It was a spacious symphonic composition opening with an extended introduction that sometimes had the character of a miniature tone poem. This was followed by a series of waltz melodies (usually five in number), varied in mood, feeling, and style, and rich in development. The waltz sequence ended with a coda that served as a kind of summation. So expansive was the structure, so inventive the harmonic, melodic, and orchestral writing, that some critics have since described these Strauss pieces as "symphonies for dancing." To Paul Bekker, a Strauss waltz has "more melodies than a symphony of Beethoven." Bekker also maintained that the "aggregate of Straussian melodies is surely greater than the aggregate of Beethoven's." Some of the greatest musicians of the nineteenth century were among Strauss's most ardent admirers. Wagner was so moved by

a performance of *Wein, Weib und Gesang* (*Wine, Woman and Song*) that he seized the baton from Strauss's hand and directed the rest of the performance. Of *An der schönen blauen Donau* (*The Blue Danube*), Brahms remarked wistfully, "alas, not by Brahms!" Gounod, Offenbach, Verdi, Hans von Bülow, and Karl Goldmark were some of the others who sang the praises of the Strauss waltz.

Strauss's greatest waltzes include *Accelerationen* (*Acceleration*), op. 234; *Morgenblätter* (*Morning Journals*), op. 279; *The Blue Danube,* op. 314; *Künstlerleben* (*Artist's Life*), op. 316; *Geschichten aus dem Wiener Wald* (*Tales from the Vienna Woods*), op. 325; *Wiener Blut* (*Vienna Blood*), op. 354; *Rosen aus dem Süden* (*Roses from the South*), op. 388; *Frühlingsstimmen* (*Voices of Spring*), op. 410; and *Kaiserwalzer* (*Emperor Waltz*), op. 437.

"His reform of the waltz as a species had reached a stage where it could not be improved upon," wrote Paul Bechert. "The originally simple form had been developed by him into a thing of subtle art; it was no longer pure three-quarter rhythm, supported by simple broken chords in the bass and endowed with native melodic equipment. He had made it an instrument for the expression of varying moods of the widest scope. Just as Schubert had created the lied out of the rudiments of simple folk songs, Strauss had made of the waltz an art form in the highest sense."

The most celebrated of all the Strauss waltzes—regarded by many as the most famous Viennese waltz ever written—is *The Blue Danube.* It was written in 1867 at the request of Johann Herbeck, conductor of a men's singing society in Vienna. In its first version, *The Blue Danube* was a composition for chorus and orchestra, text by Karl Beck adapted by Josef Weyl. In this form it was played for the first time at the Dianasaal on February 15, 1867. After that *The Blue Danube,* as an instrumental number, was heard at the Paris Exposition of 1867 and at Covent Garden in London in 1869. Thereafter it was played throughout the world. So insatiable was the demand for the sheet music that Spina, the publisher, had to print over a million copies from a hundred copper plates.

Besides hundreds of waltzes, Strauss wrote many other compositions. They included polkas (among them the popular *Tritsch-Tratsch*, op. 214); quadrilles; marches; and various other items, such as the famous *Perpetuum mobile* (*Perpetual Motion*), op. 257, described by its composer as a "musical jest."

But the one area outside the waltz most enriched by Strauss's genius was the operetta. He was reluctant to invade this field, but the encouragement of Offenbach and the insistence of Henrietta Strauss persuaded him.

Strauss's first operetta was *Indigo und die vierzig Räuber*, introduced on February 10, 1871. The text, by Maximilian Steiner, was so confused that at times it was difficult to follow the story line. Strauss poured a wealth of melody into this mold, highlighted by a stirring paean to home and country, "Ja, so singt man in der Stadt wo ich geboren." Strauss's high flights of lyricism notwithstanding, the operetta was a dismal failure. His score was used after his death for a completely new and more plausible text, *1001 Nacht* (*A Thousand and One Nights*), produced in 1906.

Strauss's second operetta, *Der Karneval in Rom*, in 1873, did not do much better. But with his third operetta, Strauss was lifted to the very top rank of composers for the popular musical stage. This was a masterwork by which all later Viennese operettas would be measured, one which to this day remains a perfect example of its species. It was *Die Fledermaus* (*The Bat*), first seen at the Theater-an-der-Wien on April 5, 1874. The text, by Karl Haffner and Richard Genée was based on a French vaudeville which in turn had been adapted from Benedix' *Das Gefängnis*.

The year 1874 was a most inappropriate one for the introduction of a light, frothy, vivacious operetta like *Die Fledermaus*. One year earlier a serious economic crisis had stricken Austria, and its impact was still felt strongly. Austrians were in too sober a mood to succumb to the charm and the levities of the new Strauss operetta, and they rejected it. Produced that same year in Berlin, however, it had a run of a hundred performances, and when *Die Fledermaus* returned to Vienna at the end of 1874 it found the city in a more receptive mood. The operetta was now a triumph in Austria, and elsewhere as well. In Germany alone it was seen in over one hundred and fifty theaters within a few years' time. The work had a

highly successful première at the Thalia Theatre in New York on November 21, 1874, in a German-language production; an American adaptation was mounted at the Casino Theatre on March 16, 1885. In 1876 it was introduced in London. In 1894 it was incorporated into the permanent repertory of the Vienna Royal Opera— testimony to the artistic significance of the operetta. The Metropolitan Opera gave it for the first time on February 16, 1905, with a cast including Sembrich, Dippel, and Reiss; in a café-chantant scene interpolated into the masquerade scene, Caruso, Scotti, Fremstad, Eames, Homer, Plançon, and Van Rooy appeared briefly in renditions of various vocal numbers. This Metropolitan Opera performance was the first in America with opera singers. At a gala revival of *Die Fledermaus* at the Metropolitan Opera during the 1950-1951 season, it was performed in a new English translation by Howard Dietz, with Garson Kanin recruited from the Broadway theater as stage director. *Die Fledermaus* has also enjoyed many revivals on Broadway; one of the most successful was in 1942-1943 when, under the new title of *Rosalinda*, it had a run of over five hundred performances.

Die Fledermaus is the work which, above all others, helped establish some of the ritual and tradition to which later Viennese operettas were to adhere. Perhaps the most significant single feature of the Viennese operetta is a seductive waltz to climax the grand finale of one of the acts, usually the second. In *Die Fledermaus*, this waltz is one of Strauss's greatest. It appears in the second-act masked ball at Prince Orlofsky's palace; it is also heard in the familiar overture preceding the first act. The many other outstanding excerpts in the operetta include a Hungarian czardas, "Klänge der Heimat," about which Ernest Newman said, "no genuine Hungarian music could sing more movingly of the pain of separation from the beloved homeland or of the fires in the Hungarian breast that drive them to the dance." Of the over-all musical content of *Die Fledermaus*, Bruno Walter once remarked that here "we have beauty without heaviness, levity without vulgarity, gaiety without frivolity, and a strange mixture of exuberant musical richness (somewhat resembling Schubert) and popular simplicity."

The most celebrated of Johann Strauss's later operettas is *Der Zigeunerbaron (The Gypsy Baron)*, first seen at the Theater-an-der-Wien on October 24, 1885. The book, by Ignaz Schnitzer, is based on a story by Maurus Jokai. The setting is eighteenth century Hungary. Three excerpts from this score are especially famous: the tuneful overture; the "Schatz" or "Treasure" Waltz in the second act; and the sensual entrance song of the gypsy Sandor, "Ja, das Alles auf Ehr'." *The Gypsy Baron* was heard in more than a thousand performances in Vienna alone before World War I: the American première took place at the Casino Theatre on February 15, 1866.

Johann Strauss paid his only visit to the United States in 1872, making his American debut in Boston on June 17 in a festival commemorating the centenary of the proposal of the colony of Massachusetts to separate itself from British rule. Strauss himself described what surely was a spectacular concert: "On the musicians' tribune there were twenty thousand singers; in front of them, the members of the orchestra—and these were the people I was to conduct. A hundred assistant conductors had been placed at my disposal to control these gigantic masses. . . . Now just conceive of my position face to face with a public of four hundred thousand Americans. . . . Suddenly a cannon shot rang out, a gentle hint for us twenty thousand to begin playing *The Blue Danube*. . . . The four hundred thousand . . . in the audience roared approbation" Strauss directed fourteen concerts in Boston, including the *New Jubilee Waltz* written for this tour—a waltz that concluded with "The Star-Spangled Banner." Strauss gave four additional concerts in New York.

In 1878 Strauss's wife, Henrietta, died. He married twice more after that. His union with Angelika Dietrich lasted five years, ending in divorce. He then married Adele Deutsch, who helped restore to his home the happiness and tranquillity he had not known for several years.

Mammoth festivities, spanning an entire week, celebrated Strauss's fiftieth anniversary in 1894 as a café orchestra conductor. Gifts, messages, wires came from all parts of the world. A torchlight parade through Vienna enlisted thousands of his admirers. Concerts and opera performances provided a cross section of his creative achievements.

"If it is true that I have talent," Johann Strauss said at the final concert, "I owe it above everything else to my beloved city, Vienna."

On May 22, 1899, Strauss conducted a performance of *Die Fledermaus*. Overheated, he caught cold on the way home, and a fatal bronchitis developed. Strauss died on June 3, 1899. The news spread quickly to the Volksgarten where a concert was taking place. The conductor stopped his performance, made the sad announcement to his audience, and then played *The Blue Danube* pianissimo.

His funeral on June 6 was like that of an emperor. A whole city mourned the passing of its beloved son. He was buried near the graves of Schubert and Brahms, the obsequies taking place to the strains of Brahms' *Farewell*. Max Heyck, a Viennese poet, summed up the feelings of all Austria when he wrote:

> What summer is without rain
> What heaven is without blue,
> This Vienna is without Johann Strauss!

One of Strauss's contemporaries described him as "tall, good-looking with a black mustache and flowing black whiskers. His black hair brushed back reveals a fine, imposing forehead. A quick expressive eye and a genial expression give his face a pleasant air. He is always elegantly dressed in the latest fashion. And he is a ladies' man."

"Strauss had few diversions," this editor wrote in his Strauss biography, *Tales from the Vienna Woods*. "Books were not among his pleasures; when he read anything it was usually a newspaper or magazine. Though he liked people immensely, he did not enjoy social functions of any sort. He was never much of a dancer, and therefore avoided balls and public dances. He much preferred an intimate tête-à-tête with one or two of his personal friends at his magnificent home on the Igelgasse. His leisure hours were usually devoted to a game of billiards or cards."

Strauss's two younger brothers both enjoyed considerable popularity as café conductors and composers of light music. Josef Strauss (1827-1870) is most famous for the *Sphärenklänge (Music of the Spheres)*, *Aquarellen*, *Dorfschwalben aus Österreich (Swallows from Austria)* and *Delirien* waltzes. Another brother, Eduard **Strauss**

(1835-1916) took over the direction of the elder Strauss's orchestra, with which he toured the United States in 1892 and 1901, and which he finally dissolved in 1902 after it had existed for three quarters of a century. Eduard's most famous waltz is the *Doctrinen (Faith)*.

On several occasions the brothers collaborated with gratifying results. Johann, Josef, and Eduard wrote the *Trifolienwalzer* and the *Schützenquadrille*. Johann and Josef joined to write the very popular *Pizzicato Polka*, as well as the *Monstrequadrille* and the *Vaterländischer* March.

PRINCIPAL WORKS

Operettas—Die Fledermaus; Cagliostro in Wien; Prinz Methusalem; Blindekuh; Das Spitzentuch der Königin; Der lustige Krieg; Eine Nacht in Venedig; Der Zigeunerbaron; Simplicius; Ritter Pázmán: Fürstin Ninetta; Jabuka; Waldemeister; Die Göttin der Vernunft.

Orchestral Music—Several hundred waltzes including Accelerationen, An der schönen blauen Donau, Cagliostro, Donauweibchen, Frühlingsstimmen, Geschichten aus dem Wiener Wald, Kaiserwalzer, Künstlerleben, Kusswalzer, Lagunenwalzer, Liebesliederwalzer, Morgenblätten, Promotionen, Rosen aus dem Süden, Schatzwalzer, Seid umschlungen, Millionen, Tausend und eine Nacht, Wein, Weib und Gesang, Wiener Blut, Wiener Bonbons, Wo die Zitronen blühn; Quadrilles; Marches, including Egyptischer, Jubel, Ninetta, and Perischer; Polkas including Annen, Champagner, Electrophor, Explosions, Leichtes Blut, Neue Pizzicato, Schnellpost, and Tik-Tak.

ABOUT

Decsey, E., Johann Strauss; Ewen, D., Tales From the Vienna Woods: The Story of Johann Strauss; Jacob, H. E., Johann Strauss: A Century of Light Music; Kobald, K., Johann Strauss; Pastene, J., Three Quarter Time: The Life and Music of the Strauss Family; Schenk, E., Johann Strauss; Specht, R., Johann Strauss; Strauss, A., Strauss schreibt Briefe: Teetgen, A. B., The Waltz Kings of Old Vienna.

Sir Arthur Sullivan *1842-1900*

SIR ARTHUR SEYMOUR SULLIVAN, genius of English comic opera, was the musical half of the partnership of Gilbert and Sullivan. He was born in the Lambeth district of London on May 13, 1842. His father, an Irishman, earned a poor living playing the clarinet in a theater orchestra, and teaching and copying music. When Arthur was three, his father became the master of band music at the Royal Military College and subsequently professor of the

Wide World

SIR ARTHUR SULLIVAN

brass band at the Royal Military School of Music.

Sullivan became a chorister of the Chapel Royal in 1854 and was placed under the tutelage of the Reverend Thomas Helmore. Exceptional both as chorister and as student, Sullivan remained with the Chapel Royal choir two years.

In 1856 Sullivan won the Mendelssohn Scholarship, which had just been established at the Royal Academy of Music. His teachers at the Academy included Sterndale Bennett and John Goss.

Sullivan entered the Leipzig Conservatory in the fall of 1858. He studied under Hauptmann (counterpoint and fugue), Ferdinand David (conducting), and Moscheles and Plaidy (piano). He attended the concerts of the Gewandhaus Orchestra, rubbed elbows with the city's foremost musicians, and did a good deal of composing. Among his creative efforts were a string quartet, an orchestral overture, and incidental music to Shakespeare's *Tempest*.

In 1861 he was back in London, where he received an appointment to a teaching post at the Crystal Palace School of Art. Subsequently, for several years, he served as the organist of St. Michael's Church, Chester Square. On April 12, 1862, his music for *The Tempest* was well received at a Crystal Palace concert under August Manns.

The next few years saw Sullivan's fame as a composer developing rapidly. His ballet *L'Île enchantée* was a huge success when produced at Covent Garden in 1864. In the same year his cantata *Kenilworth* was the highlight of the Birmingham Festival. In March 1866 the Symphony in E-flat, stimulated by a visit to Ireland in 1863 and sometimes known as the *Irish Symphony,* was introduced at the Crystal Palace. That same year also witnessed the premières of his orchestral overture *In Memoriam* (inspired by the death of his father) and a cello concerto. Among his most significant compositions soon after that were *Marmion,* an orchestral overture introduced in 1867, and his first score for a light theatrical entertainment, *Cox and Box,* which opened in London on April 27, 1867, and ran for about three hundred performances.

In 1864 Sullivan became organist at Covent Garden, and two years after that he was appointed professor of composition at the Royal Academy of Music. In 1867 Sullivan joined George Grove on an expedition to Vienna to seek out unpublished manuscripts of Schubert which they suspected were lying around neglected and forgotten. Through their efforts they brought to light an accumulation of valuable manuscripts that included a trio, the music to *Rosamunde,* a Stabat Mater, and many songs.

The first meeting of W. S. Gilbert and Sullivan took place in 1870. Their first collaborative work, created in 1871, was *Thespis,* a broad farce involving a group of actors in London and the gods on Mount Olympus who decide to change places with one another. *Thespis,* presented on December 26, 1871, was a dismal failure, but it proved significant, as Isaac Goldberg remarked, in forecasting "the characteristic methods, and now and then a character, of the later series."

It hardly seemed likely that the collaboration of Gilbert and Sullivan would be resumed after the discouraging reaction of audience and critics to *Thespis.* Sullivan returned to writing serious music. In 1872 he wrote a *Te Deum* to honor the Prince of Wales, and in 1873 he produced his most celebrated hymn, "Onward, Christian Soldiers," to words by Sabine Baring-Gould. "Onward, Christian Soldiers" is one of two serious compositions by Sullivan which have retained their immense popularity to the present day. The other is the song "The Lost Chord," written in 1876 at the deathbed of Sullivan's brother.

It was Richard D'Oyly Carte, manager of the Royalty Theatre in London, who was responsible for bringing Gilbert and Sullivan together again. The new Gilbert and Sullivan opera was *Trial by Jury,* presented on March 25, 1875. It was a broad one-act satire on British courts, and was the first opus by Gilbert and Sullivan in which they evoked the topsy-turvy world of absurdity and paradox for which all their later comic operas were famous. It differed from their later creations in that it contained no spoken dialogue, but consisted entirely of lyrics set to music. But in many respects it strongly foreshadowed their later procedures. The first Gilbert and Sullivan opera seen in the United States, it was produced on November 15, 1875, at the Eagle Theatre in New York.

Trial by Jury was followed on November 17, 1877, by *The Sorcerer,* a satire on English country-estate life. The Gilbert and Sullivan craze which seized and held both England and the United States did not really begin, however, until the introduction of *H.M.S. Pinafore* on May 25, 1878. Here the target for Gilbert's stinging and devastating satire was the British Admiralty—specifically, its First Lord, W. H. Smith, who had assumed his august office without once having gone to sea. At first *Pinafore* did not do well. Its iconoclasm and irreverence shocked English people proud of their traditions, institutions, and national ideals. But some of its music, directed by Sullivan at a Promenade concert, won over many converts, who now beat a path to D'Oyly Carte's theater to see an opera that boasted such tuneful melodies. The American première in Boston on November 25, 1878, was a triumph of the first magnitude.

Performances of *Pinafore* in the United States were pirated, without any payment made to the copyright owners. To protect their legal interests, Gilbert and Sullivan came to the United States late in 1879 to produce an "authorized" version of *Pinafore* on December 1, 1879, at the Fifth Avenue Theatre in New York. Sullivan conducted, and it was said that Gilbert played the part of one of the sailors. This presentation served further to heighten and intensify the passion of Americans for *Pinafore;* and it excited their curiosity in the new comic opera which Gilbert and Sullivan were completing in the United States and were planning to present there for the first time anywhere. That new opera was *The Pirates of Penzance,* the only Gilbert and Sullivan opera to have an exclusive première in the United States; it was introduced at the Fifth Avenue Theatre on December 31, 1879.

Patience came next, a hilarious takeoff on the Pre-Raphaelite movement with its fetish for a return to simplicity and to nature, and on the aestheticism of Oscar Wilde. It was presented in London on April 25, 1881. While the play was still running, the Savoy Theatre, which D'Oyly Carte had built expressly for performances of the comic operas of Gilbert and Sullivan, was opened and *Patience* was transferred there on October 10, 1881. Strictly speaking, therefore, *Patience* was the first of the Savoyard operas, since it was the first to be performed at the Savoy. The American première of *Patience* took place on July 28, 1881, in St. Louis.

From 1881 on, all the new Gilbert and Sullivan comic operas were seen first at the Savoy Theatre. *Iolanthe,* a spoof on the British Parliament, party politics, and the law in general, came on November 25, 1882, the same date on which it was heard in a première at the Standard Theatre in New York. *Princess Ida,* which made sport of the feminist movement, appeared on January 5, 1884 (American première in Boston and New York simultaneously, on February 11, 1884). After that came *The Mikado* (in London on March 14, 1885; in Chicago on July 6, 1885); *Ruddigore* (London, January 22, 1887; New York, February 21, 1887); *The Yeomen of the Guard* (London, October 3, 1888; New York, October 17, 1888); *The Gondoliers* (London, December 7, 1889; New York, January 7, 1890); *Utopia Limited* (London, October 7, 1893; New York, March 26, 1894); and *The Grand Duke* (London, March 7, 1896; New York, May 11, 1961).

It would not be difficult to build a case for *The Mikado* as the most popular of all the Gilbert and Sullivan operas. Certainly it was the most successful. "In *The Mikado,*" said Audrey Williamson, "the English character of Sullivan's music . . . reached its zenith. He has fought clear at last of sentimental Victorian balladry, oratorio and Teutonic influences and developed the style which began to be apparent in the 'Willow Waly' duet in *Patience.* In the so-called

'Madrigal' in *The Mikado* he goes back to a still earlier style, the Elizabethan, basing his composition fairly closely on the 'ballets' of Thomas Morley. . . . It is completely English in its purity and sweetness of melody."

In discussing the comic operas of Gilbert and Sullivan, Isaac Goldberg stressed their universality and timelessness: "They were not the rebels of an era, yet as surely they were not the apologists. Their light laughter carried a pleasant danger of its own that, without being the laughter of a Figaro, helped before the advent of a Shaw to keep the atmosphere clear. Transition figures they were, in an age of transition, caught between the personal independence of the artist and the social imperatives of their station. They did not cross over into the new day, though they served as a footbridge for others."

However harmonious the artistic partnership of Gilbert and Sullivan may have been, their personal relationship was jarred by discord. A trivial incident—a dispute over the cost of a carpet—was responsible for a serious rupture between the partners in 1890, soon after *The Gondoliers* had opened.

They stayed apart for over three years, Gilbert returning to writing plays without music, Sullivan to composing serious music. D'Oyly Carte, however, was determined to bring the writing partners together again, especially since he had suffered serious financial losses with the production of Sullivan's grand opera, *Haddon Hall,* on September 24, 1892. In 1892 D'Oyly Carte succeeded in effecting a reconciliation and a resumption of the collaboration. Gilbert and Sullivan were reunited with *Utopia Limited,* which opened on October 7, 1893.

But *Utopia Limited* was the beginning of the end of Gilbert and Sullivan. Throughout the writing they quarreled bitterly over their material. When *Utopia Limited* did poorly, both men lost heart in their partnership. They wrote only one more opera after that, *The Grand Duke,* which was a dismal failure. With it the most famous and the most successful words-and-music partnership in the history of the musical theater came to an end.

While writing his comic operas with Gilbert, Sullivan did not completely abandon his activities as a serious musician. He led the concerts at the Royal Aquarium in Westminster, then the Promenade Concerts at Covent Garden, after that performances at the Leeds Festival, and from 1885 to 1887 he was the conductor of the Royal Philharmonic in London. Between 1877 and 1881 he was the director of the newly founded National Training School (later renamed the Royal College of Music). In recognition of his service to English music, Sullivan was knighted in 1883.

After he had dissolved his partnership with Gilbert permanently, Sullivan wrote the scores for three more comic operas, two with texts by Basil Hood, one by Arthur Pinero and Comyns Carr. Sullivan did not live to complete the score to the last of these popular stage works, *The Emerald Isle*. Edward German finished the music where Sullivan had left off, and the opera was produced after Sullivan's death.

One serious work, the opera *Ivanhoe*, absorbed Sullivan's energies and dedication in the last decade of his life. Despite all his painstaking effort and his belief that he was producing a masterwork, *Ivanhoe* was a complete failure both artistically and commercially when it was produced on January 31, 1891 at the Royal English Opera House in London. *"Ivanhoe,"* Percy Fitzgerald said, "was certainly a ponderous work, more like a vast symphony protracted through several acts of an opera."

The failure of *Ivanhoe* helped to emphasize the paradox of Sullivan's career as a composer. As this writer remarked in *Lighter Classics of Music*: "It is irony fitting for a Gilbert and Sullivan comic opera that the work on which Sullivan lavished his most fastidious attention and of which he was most proud has been completely forgotten.... But the music upon which he looked with such condescension and self apology is that which has made him an immortal—in the theater if not in the concert hall. . . . Sullivan . . . had a reservoir of melodies seemingly inexhaustible—gay tunes, mocking tunes, and tunes filled with telling sentiment —and he was able to adapt the fullest resources of his remarkable gift at harmony, rhythm and orchestration to the manifold demands of the stage."

Sullivan's last years provided a sad anticlimax to his earlier triumphs. He drifted to Monte Carlo, where he indulged in gambling and extravagant living, with resulting dissipation of his energies. His health was bad. He was almost always in pain, and his face had become deeply lined and haggard through the overuse of morphine. His last days were spent in a physical agony that morphine could relieve no longer. In the fall of 1900 he caught a chill which developed into bronchitis, and he died in London on November 22, 1900. It was a lonely death. None of his former close friends and associates were at his bedside.

B. W. Findon described Sullivan's appearance and manner: "His face impressed at once, because it was the outward indication of the sweetness of his nature. . . . His voice was musical and persuading, and he had a pleasing directness of speech which never failed to reach its mark. His personal charm was infinite."

Sullivan was extravagant to a fault, a fact that infuriated the frugal Gilbert. He was also superstitious, putting faith in omens, lucky stars, and portents of all kinds. He was a heavy smoker and drinker and a discriminating gourmet.

Sullivan composed with facility. Hesketh Pearson said: "Many of his melodies came to him in the noise and bustle of a social crush, when he would pull out a notebook and commit them to paper. He scored with great rapidity, smoking cigarette after cigarette and chatting without effort to the visitor of the moment."

PRINCIPAL WORKS

Ballets—L'Île enchanté; Victoria and Merrie England.

Chamber Music—Romance, for string quartet; Duo concertante, for cello and piano.

Choral Music—Kenilworth; The Prodigal Son; On Shore and Sea; The Light of the World; The Martyr of Antioch; The Golden Legend; anthems, hymns, sacred part-songs, secular part-songs, Te Deums.

Operas—About 25 serious and comic operas including Trial by Jury, The Sorcerer, H.M.S. Pinafore, The Pirates of Penzance, Patience, Iolanthe, Princess Ida, The Mikado, Ruddigore, The Yeomen of the Guard, The Gondoliers, Ivanhoe, Haddon Hall, Utopia Limited, The Chieftain (a revision of an earlier opera, Contrabandista), The Grand Duke, The Beauty Stone, The Rose of Persia, The Emerald Isle (completed by Edward German).

Orchestral Music—Cello Concerto; Irish Symphony in E major; In Memoriam; Marmion; Overtura di Ballo; Imperial March.

Piano Music—Sonata; Thoughts for the Piano; Marche danoise.

Vocal Music—Numerous songs for voice and piano including The Long Day Closes, The Lost Chord, Onward, Christian Soldiers, Orpheus with His Lute; vocal duets, vocal trio.

ABOUT
Baily, L., The Gilbert and Sullivan Book; Cellier, F., and Bridgeman, C., Gilbert, Sullivan and D'Oyly Carte; Darlington, W. A., The World of Gilbert and Sullivan; Dunhill, T., Sullivan's Comic Operas: A Critical Appreciation; Findon, B. W., Sir Arthur Sullivan: His Life and Music; Godwin, A. H., Gilbert and Sullivan: A Critical Appreciation of the Savoy Operas; Goldberg, I., The Story of Gilbert and Sullivan; Jacobs, A., Gilbert and Sullivan; Pearson, H., Gilbert and Sullivan; Saxe Wyndham, H., Sullivan; Sullivan, H., and Flower, N., Sir Arthur Sullivan; Williamson, A., Gilbert and Sullivan Opera.

Franz von Suppé *1819-1895*

LIKE JOHANN STRAUSS II, Franz von Suppé was primarily a composer of light music; but also like Strauss, he brought such freshness and invention to the music of his operettas that some of them are still given by opera companies.

Suppé was born in Spalato, Dalmatia (then under Austrian rule), on April 18, 1819. Of Belgian descent, his name originally was Francesco Ezechiele Ermenegildo Cavaliere Suppé Demelli. He began to study the flute at eleven, and harmony at thirteen. In his thirteenth year he wrote music for a little play, *Der Apfel*, which received a private performance in Zara. One year after this one of his Masses was played in a church in Zara.

His father wanted to steer him away from music and sent him off to the University of Padua for a thorough academic education. There Suppé managed to continue music study with Cigala and Ferrari. After his father died, Suppé proceeded to Vienna to join his mother who had already settled there. For a while he taught Italian and even practiced medicine. Then, fully convinced that he wanted to become a professional musician, he completed his music study with Seyfried and Sechter at the Vienna Conservatory.

His first professional post as conductor was at the Josephstadt Theater in Vienna, where he made his official debut as stage composer by writing music for a play, *Jung lustig*, presented on March 5, 1841. Suppé subsequently directed theater orchestras in Pressburg and Baden, and for a number of years was the conductor of the renowned Theater-an-der-Wien in Vienna. From 1862 to 1865 he was the conductor of the Carl Theater, and from 1865 until the end

FRANZ VON SUPPÉ

of his life of the Leopoldstadt Theater, both in Vienna.

By the time he received his appointment at the Leopoldstadt Theater he had already become famous as a composer of comic operas. On August 24, 1846, *Dichter und Bauer (Poet and Peasant)*, whose overture is a classic in the light-music repertory, had been produced in Vienna. *Dichter und Bauer* helped spread Suppé's reputation throughout Europe. In 1847 another of his comic operas, *Das Mädchen vom Lande*, scored a phenomenal success at the Theater-an-der-Wien. During the succeeding years, more than twenty-five of Suppé's comic operas and operettas and over a hundred stage plays with his incidental music were produced. The most important were *Zehn Mädchen und kein Mann* (1862), almost as tremendous a success as *Das Mädchen vom Lande; Flotte Bursche* (1863), of special interest because its overture anticipated one by Brahms in the use of student songs; *Franz Schubert* (1864), a predecessor of such famous operettas as *Das Dreimäderlhaus* in Europe and *Blossom Time* in the United States in using the music of Schubert for a romanticized play about that composer; *Leichte Kavallerie (Light Cavalry*, 1865), whose overture is second only in popularity to that of *Poet and Peasant;* and *Die schöne Galatea*. The last of these, a delightful adaptation of a tale from Greek mythology about Pygmalion and Galatea, was revived at the Central City Opera House in Colo-

Suppé: zo͞op′ā

rado in 1951 with a new English translation by Phyllis Mead.

Three of Suppé's most celebrated operettas—*Fatinitza, Boccaccio,* and *Donna Juanita,* all with texts by F. Zell and R. Genée—have all been successfully produced by major opera companies. *Fatinitza* was introduced at the Carl Theater in Vienna on January 5, 1876, and in New York on April 14, 1879. One of its tunes (the march melody *"Himmel, Bomben, Element"*) became extremely popular throughout Europe in the late nineteenth century.

Boccaccio was performed for the first time at the Carl Theater on February 1, 1879; its American première followed on April 15, 1880, in Philadelphia. The libretto is built around the romance of Boccaccio and Fiametta as depicted in *L'Amorosa Fiametta,* his autobiographical tale. On January 3, 1931, the Metropolitan Opera revived *Boccaccio,* starring Maria Jeritza as Fiametta.

Donna Juanita, presented at the Carl Theater on February 21, 1880, was Suppé's last successful operetta. Fifteen months later the operetta was given in the United States, in New York on May 16, 1881. On January 2, 1932, it entered the repertory of the Metropolitan Opera, revived for Maria Jeritza.

Suppé established some of the traditions that would henceforth identify German-language operettas; by doing so, he set the stage for Johann Strauss II, whose best operettas emulated those of Suppé. Evaluating Suppé's operettas, Arthur Pougin wrote: "Suppé is not only a musician full of verve of youth and gaiety when he wrote for the theater. Eclectic in temperament, supported by an excellent education, he joined Italian grace with German profundity, writing . . . works which reveal a happily inspired and richly endowed artist."

PRINCIPAL WORKS

Chamber Music—String Quartets.

Choral Music—Missa dalmatica; L'Estremo giudizio.

Operas—Dichter und Bauer; Das Mädchen vom Lande; Zehn Mädchen und kein Mann; Flotte Bursche; Leichte Kavallerie; Die schöne Galatea; Fatinitza; Boccaccio; Donna Juanita.

Orchestral Music—Concert overtures including Pique Dame, and Ein Morgen, ein Mittag, ein Abend in Wien (Morning, Noon and Night in Vienna); Symphony.

ABOUT

Keller, O., Franz von Suppé, der Schöpfer der deutschen Operette; Rieger, E., Offenbach und seine Wiener Schule.

Johan Svendsen *1840-1911*

JOHAN SEVERIN SVENDSEN was born in Christiania (now Oslo), Norway, on September 30, 1840. His father, a bandmaster, gave him his first violin lessons. Svendsen's earliest compositions, all for the violin, came when the boy was only eleven. By the time he was fifteen he was adept at the violin, flute, and clarinet. In that year he enlisted in the army and soon was appointed bandmaster. While still in service, he often supplemented his income by performing at town dances. One day, when he was seventeen, he heard Beethoven's Fifth Symphony. This experience gave him a new direction and purpose in music, and led him to begin an intensive period of study of composition with Arnold, a German musician.

Svendsen left the army when he was twenty-one. For awhile he earned his living by playing the violin in theater orchestras in Christiania and at a dancing academy, where he adapted violin études by Paganini and Kreutzer as dance music. Before long he was touring Sweden and northern Germany as violinist, but with such little success that he often found himself in dire financial straits. But in Lübeck he impressed Leche, the Swedish-Norwegian consul, who arranged for him to get an annual stipend from Charles XV. This enabled Svendsen to enter the Leipzig Conservatory and study violin and theory with Hauptmann, Ferdinand David, and Reinecke. When neuritis of the wrist compelled him to give up all ideas of becoming a virtuoso, he directed his musical energies and ambitions into composition. He completed an impressive repertory of chamber music, including an octet, a quintet, and a quartet. He also wrote his first symphony, in D major, which was introduced in Christiania on October 12, 1867, in a program devoted entirely to Svendsen's works. Edvard Grieg was present at this performance and wrote about Svendsen's symphony in the *Aftenbladet*: "What is above all refreshing . . . is the complete balance between ideas and technique. Svendsen requires a public of high standard; he takes them to the fantastic fairyland of humor and romanticism, but he does not leave it to your own choice whether you shall be with him or not; he carries you away by force only on account of his great skill in the technique of music."

In 1867, having completed his studies at the Leipzig Conservatory and received a gold medal, Svendsen traveled in Denmark, Scotland, Iceland, and Norway. In 1868 he settled for a while in the Latin Quarter of Paris. There he divided his time between music and the study of literature and philosophy. He played the violin in Mussard's orchestra; made his French bow as composer with incidental music to *Le Passant,* a play by Coppée, produced at the Odéon on January 14, 1869; and completed a major work, his violin concerto in A major.

After leaving Paris, Svendsen returned to Germany. In Weimar he met Liszt and heard a remarkably successful performance of his own octet. In Leipzig, he directed his First Symphony which was received enthusiastically. Svendsen also became acquainted in Leipzig with Sarah Levett, an American girl, whom he married in New York in 1871. (This marriage ended a few years later in divorce. Svendsen later married a dancer named Juliette Vilhelmina.) Back in Europe with his bride, Sarah, Svendsen was invited by Liszt to Bayreuth to attend the inaugural Wagner festival. The Wagnerian music drama, and the personality of Richard Wagner, made a powerful impression on him.

Svendsen returned to his native land in 1872. At Grieg's recommendation he became the conductor of the Christiania Musical Society, holding this post for about five years and achieving recognition as one of Europe's leading conductors. In comparing Svendsen to Grieg, who during the same period also led some of the concerts of the Musical Society, Sandvik wrote: "He [Svendsen] was the superior master, the dictator, against whom no one dared to say a word, but at the same time he was very affable and agreeable and conflicts were therefore avoided."

It was during this five-year period that Svendsen achieved full maturity as a composer, completing some of the works that helped spread his fame throughout Europe and by which he is still represented on concert programs. In 1872 he completed *Zorahayde,* a legend for orchestra based on the Washington Irving tale *The Legend of the Rose of the Alhambra.* A year later he wrote *Carnaval à Paris (The Carnival in Paris),* probably his most frequently performed orchestral composition. Svendsen also produced a second symphony, and several

works in a national style and idiom. Most significant among these national compositions are the four *Norwegian Rhapsodies* and the *Carnaval des artistes norvégiens,* all for orchestra.

Besides receiving several decorations from the king, Svendsen received official recognition in 1874 when he was given an annual pension.

In 1877 Svendsen temporarily withdrew from his duties as conductor to spend several years traveling in Europe. Between 1880 and 1883 he returned to the conductor's stand of the Christiania Musical Society. In 1884 he was appointed the musical director of the Royal Opera of Copenhagen where he was responsible for distinguished performances of Wagner's music dramas.

After 1900 his health deteriorated rapidly when a kidney disease developed into dropsy. In 1908 he retired from his post at the Royal Opera. Svendsen died in Copenhagen on June 14, 1911, a victim of gangrene of the leg.

Svendsen's best works are characterized by remarkable workmanship, a fine gift for orchestration, and a personal lyricism. He was perhaps at his best in the national music to which he brought a deeply stirring emotion and a nobility of concept. Since he has been recognized as Grieg's most significant rival in Norwegian national music, it is interesting to record Grieg's own estimate of his compatriot: "I very much admire Svendsen's works, though there cannot be two things wider apart than his art and mine. He has taught me to believe in myself and in the power and authority of individuality. There was a time in Christiania when to be an individualist was the same thing as to be a criminal. But then Svendsen came, and he was an individualist, too, and the miracle that occurred was that from then on I was also tolerated. Therefore, there are few artists to whom I owe a greater debt of gratitude than to Svendsen."

PRINCIPAL WORKS

Chamber Music—Octet in A minor; String Quintet in C major; String Quartet in A minor.

Choral Music—Marriage Cantata.

Orchestral Music—4 Norwegian Rhapsodies; 2 symphonies; Violin Concerto in A major; Cello Concerto in D minor; Overture to Sigurd Slembe; Carnaval à Paris; Zorahayde; Polonaise; Carnaval des artistes norvégiens; Overture to Romeo and Juliet; Romance in G major, for violin and orchestra.

Vocal Music—French, German, and Norwegian songs for voice and piano.

ABOUT

Bacharach, A. L. (editor), The Music Masters, vol. 3; Grönwold, H. A., Norske musikere; Lange, K., and Östvedt, A., Norwegian Music; Schjelderup, G., Norges Musikhistorie.

Jan Sweelinck *1562-1621*

JAN PIETERSZOON SWEELINCK was one of the last major figures of the Flemish or Netherlands polyphonic school, and a master of early baroque instrumental music. He was born in Amsterdam in 1562, the son of Pieter Sweelinck, organist of the Old Church at Amsterdam. His father was his first and principal teacher at the organ; later on, it is believed, Jan received additional instruction from Jan Willemszoon Lossy in Haarlem.

Except for brief and occasional visits to nearby towns in the Netherlands, Sweelinck spent his entire life in Amsterdam. He acquired his first organ post there in 1577. The statement found in so many histories that he spent some time in Venice and studied there with Zarlino and Gabrieli is without any basis in fact.

In 1580 young Sweelinck inherited his father's organ post at Old Church. During the next decade he established an estimable reputation as an organist, attracting pilgrims from all over Europe to hear his performances. He also achieved such a considerable reputation as a teacher of the organ that he has been described as "the maker of organists." One of his pupils was Scheidt, who was responsible for importing Sweelinck's influence into early German baroque music. Another pupil was Johann Heintsch, who thus described his teacher: "Sweelinck was considered a 'wonder of music.' When the fame of his greatness went abroad, the young talent of Germany flocked to him. . . . The two Hamburg masters, Praetorius and Scheidemann, honored him as a father. They learned from him not only music, but also principles of contact, and carried away from their association with him a lifelong ideal, which they kept ever before their eyes, and which they set before their famous pupils."

As a composer of polyphonic choral music, Sweelinck followed the traditions of the Flemish school. To the writing of psalms, motets, and other choral pieces he brought

JAN SWEELINCK

at times an infectious gaiety, and at other times a nobility and grandeur. Technically, his compositions differ from those of his Flemish predecessors and contemporaries in their greater melodic freedom and rhythmic flexibility.

It is in his compositions for the organ and/or clavier (since many of his works could be played on either instrument) that he has acquired a place of first importance in the early history of baroque music. He wrote sacred and secular variations in which the variation technique, which he had acquired from the early English virginalists, was developed and perfected. Particularly outstanding were his variations on psalm and hymn tunes, of which *O Mensch bewein Dein Sünde gross* is a notable example; these can be said to have initiated the practice by later church organists in German Protestant services of performing organ variations on a hymn tune before the congregation sang the melody. He also developed the toccata form, which he used as a showpiece to display his organ virtuosity, and the fantasia form, in which he laid the foundations of the fugue. As a predecessor of Johann Sebastian Bach in writing fugues, Sweelinck's importance has long been recognized.

In 1590 Sweelinck married Claesgen Puyner. They had six children. One of these, Dirck Janszoon Sweelinck (1591-1652), was also a highly regarded organist and composer.

Sweelinck: svä'lĭngk

Jan Sweelinck died in Amsterdam on October 16, 1621, and was buried in the Old Church, where his organ post was taken over by his son Dirck.

Between 1895 and 1903, Breitkopf and Härtel in Germany issued the complete works of Sweelinck in a dozen volumes, edited by Max Seiffert.

PRINCIPAL WORKS

Choral Music—Over 250 compositions including Cantiones Sacrae, chansons, Psalms, rimes.

Instrumental Music—Over 70 compositions for organ and/or clavier including chorale variations, other kinds of variations, fantasias, and toccatas.

ABOUT

Borren, C. van den, Les Origines de la musique de clavier dans les Pays-Bas jusque vers 1630; Seiffert, M., Sweelinck und seine direkten deutschen Schüler; Sollitt, E. R., Dufay to Sweelinck; Tusler, R. L., The Organ Music of Jan Sweelinck.

THOMAS TALLIS

Thomas Tallis *1505-1585*

THOMAS TALLIS, sometimes identified as "the father of English cathedral music," was born about 1505, most probably in Leicestershire. His early years and the nature of his musical training are veiled in obscurity. Between 1532 and 1540, Tallis served as the organist of the Abbey of the Holy Cross at Waltham, Essex. When this Abbey was dissolved, Tallis spent about two years in Canterbury. Then, in 1542, during the reign of Henry VIII, he was appointed Gentleman of the Chapel Royal. He held the post for the remainder of his life, serving also under the reigns of Edward VI, Mary, and Elizabeth. At court he enjoyed high esteem as organist and was the recipient of many honors. In 1547 he received his livery for the coronation of Edward VI; in 1557 he was granted by Queen Mary a lease of the Manor of Minster on the isle of Thanet; Queen Elizabeth endowed him with an annual grant. He married in 1552.

With William Byrd, who shared his organ bench at the Chapel Royal and who became his pupil and friend, he received in 1575 an exclusive patent for printing and selling music paper, and for publishing music. The venture was a financial failure, largely because neither man boasted great business acumen; but the establishment continued to function throughout Tallis' life and after that with Byrd. Its first publication, which appeared in 1575, was a volume containing sixteen motets by Tallis. This, however, was not the first time Tallis had appeared in print: Between 1560 and 1565 five of his anthems were issued in *Certain Notes*. These two publications, however, represent the only occasions upon which Tallis saw his music issued. All his other music appeared posthumously.

Thomas Tallis died in Greenwich on November 23, 1585. He was buried in the parish Church of St. Alphege in Greenwich.

The break of the English Church with Catholicism during the Reformation compelled English composers of religious music to develop new forms and styles to replace the Masses and motets used by the Catholic faith. They proceeded to write unpretentious anthems and simple offertories suitable for the new services. Tallis was the first composer to set English texts to music for the services of the Church of England. He brought a grandeur of utterance and a nobility of style which carried English church music to a place of artistic importance. "The majestic and architectural splendor of [his] works," said Ernest Walker, "may quite fitly claim for them a place beside all but the very highest flights of contemporary Italian art. In massive music . . . we see Tallis at his grandest; there are none of the angularities of phrasing . . . that mar the effect of occasional works by Tye. . . . But Tallis also could, when he so pleased, employ with equal success a tender and more expressively graceful style."

Tallis' music, said W. H. Hadow, "has little intimacy, little involution; it is strong, simple, dignified, caring more for solidity of structure than amenity of decoration."

Donald Jay Grout felt that the *Lamentations* of Tallis "are among the most eloquent of all settings of these verses from the prophet Jeremiah." And he singled out the motet *Audivi vocem de caelo* as "an excellent specimen of mid-16th century English style. . . . One remarkable feature of the work . . . is the essential vocality of the melodies; one senses on hearing or singing them that they have been conceived not as an interplay of abstract melodic lines, but as an interplay of *voices*—so closely is the melodic curve wedded to the natural cadence of the words, so imaginatively does it project their content, and so naturally does it lie for the singer." It is, however, the opinion of many musicologists that Tallis' masterwork is the giant song in forty parts, *Spem in alium*.

The twentieth century English composer Ralph Vaughan Williams achieved his first international success in 1910 with an orchestral work entitled *Fantasia on a Theme by Thomas Tallis*. The Tallis theme utilized by Vaughan Williams for his fantasia is the third of eight tunes from the *Metrical Psalter of Matthew Parker, Archbishop of Canterbury*.

PRINCIPAL WORKS

Choral Music—52 motets; 18 English anthems; 3 sets of psalms; 2 Magnificats; 2 Masses; 2 Lamentations.

Instrumental Music (for virginal, or organ) —In nomine's; Felix namque's.

ABOUT

Terry, R. R., A Forgotten Psalter; Whittaker, W. G., Collected Essays.

Music and Letters, April 1929; Musical Quarterly, April 1951; Musical Times, July 1952.

Sergei Taneiev *1856-1915*

S ERGEI IVANOVICH TANEIEV was born in the district of Vladimir in Russia on November 25, 1856. His uncle, Alexander Sergeievich Taneiev (1850-1918) was a composer of operas, symphonies, and string quartets, a musical amateur who

earned his living in the high government position of head chancellor. Sergei's father was also a government official who loved music devotedly and pursued it assiduously. Recognizing early that his son had a pronounced gift for music, the elder Taneiev engaged a local teacher to give him piano lessons. She, in turn, brought the boy to the attention of Nicholas Rubinstein, director of the Moscow Conservatory. Rubinstein entered young Taneiev in his school in 1866 and placed him under E. L. Langer for piano instruction. During the next few years Taneiev studied piano with Rubinstein himself, theory with Hubert, and composition with Tchaikovsky. In 1875, upon being graduated, Taneiev received the first gold medal ever presented by the Conservatory. During his long stay there Taneiev completed a .symphony and a string quartet among other compositions.

In 1875, Taneiev made a distinguished debut in Moscow as concert pianist, performing Brahms' D minor Piano Concerto. "Besides purity and strength of touch," wrote Tchaikovsky of this performance, "grace and ease of execution, Taneiev astonished everyone by his maturity of intellect, his self-control, and the calm objective style of his interpretation. He has his own artistic individuality." Tchaikovsky's enthusiasm for Taneiev's pianism was expressed later the same year when he selected the young man to perform the Moscow première of his own B-flat minor Concerto.

Soon after this, Taneiev toured Russia in joint concerts with Leopold Auer, the famous violinist, and Turkey, Greece, and Italy with Nicholas Rubinstein. The winter of 1877-1878 was spent in Paris where he met the French composers Gounod, Saint-Saëns, Fauré, and Vincent d'Indy.

Following a concert tour of the Baltic region in 1878, Taneiev returned to Moscow where he succeeded Tchaikovsky as professor of harmony and orchestration at the Conservatory. Three years later, upon the death of Nicholas Rubinstein, Taneiev took over his classes in piano. From 1885 to 1889, Taneiev was director of the Conservatory, and from 1889 to 1896 its professor of composition. During these years he became one of Russia's most eminent music teachers and scholars, and an outstanding authority on counterpoint.

Taneiev: tŭ-nyā'yĕf

While thus involved in pedagogical duties he was writing major works, few of which were performed in his own lifetime. The first of his important compositions to get a hearing while he was still alive was the cantata *John of Damascus,* based on a text by Alexei Tolstoy, written in memory of Nicholas Rubinstein and performed in Moscow in 1892. Three years after that came the première of Taneiev's opera trilogy, *Oresteia*—actually not a trilogy but an opera with three extended acts—which was introduced in St. Petersburg on October 29, 1895. "If he does not achieve Wagnerian effects," said Rimsky-Korsakov, "he has written many beautiful pages filled with extraordinary beauty and expressiveness." Nevertheless *Oresteia* was rarely performed after that time and has since been totally neglected.

Today very little by Taneiev is given a hearing outside Russia. But in his native land he has always been highly regarded because of his successful blend of Romanticism of style with classical structure, and his highly effective merger of Russian melody with Germanic techniques and methods. Taneiev is often described as "the Russian Brahms." M. Montagu-Nathan found a kinship with Brahms in Taneiev's "ringing rhythmic changes," but here, he felt, the similarity ends. "He has nothing at all of the sensuous charm which constitutes the essentially appealing quality of his master's music, and his merit as composer lies in the sphere of unusual technical proficiency."

Taneiev's remarkable architectonic structures, his command of harmonic and contrapuntal devices, and his skill at thematic development are heard to best advantage in his symphonies and chamber music. "In respect to his style," said Leonid Sabaneyev, "Taneiev stands out as a master of the highest rank. It is hardly possible to mention another composer after Beethoven, save perhaps Brahms, who can stand comparison to him in respect to maturity of style in the sense of making the most of the instruments and creating a tonal web that commands interest. But at the same time there are apparent the characteristic faults of the melody, lack of inner emotional temperament, an occasional odd blindness to artistic differences of style, a blindness that permits Taneiev in one and the same composition to combine imitative traces of Mozart and Tchaikovsky."

On June 19, 1915, Taneiev died of a heart attack in Moscow. He was a man of the highest ideals who attended to both his teaching duties and his creative activity with complete dedication. A man of retiring disposition, he preferred solitude to social gatherings. He devoted himself not only to music but also to the natural and social sciences, mathematics, philosophy, and history.

As a composer he showed little interest in experimentation. As he once wrote to Tchaikovsky: "Least of all do I care to represent in my works samples of a style that was not invented before me, or to create new, unheard of music." He had an obsession for counterpoint, on which he was an undisputed authority, spending hour upon hour in writing out contrapuntal exercises on original themes in copybooks. His method of composition was to precede the writing of a work with elaborate exercises in counterpoint. "Before starting the actual writing of some composition," Rimsky-Korsakov revealed, "Taneiev used to prepare a vast number of sketches or studies; he wrote fugues, canons and different contrapuntal combinations upon a simple theme and motifs of his future composition. Only then, after sufficient practice in the principal parts, did he begin the general outline of his composition, knowing well the material at his command and what he could build from this material."

He had a pronounced bent for whimsy which sometimes asserted itself even in his compositions. Among his unpublished works are all kinds of comedy fugues, toy symphonies, humorous choruses, mock ballet music, and tongue-in-cheek contrapuntal pieces.

PRINCIPAL WORKS

Chamber Music—6 string quartets; 2 string quintets; 2 string trios; Piano Quartet; Piano Trio.

Choral Music—John of Damascus; The Rising Sun; From Border to Border; At the Reading of the Psalm; various choruses for men's or mixed voices.

Opera—Oresteia.

Orchestral Music—4 symphonies; 2 duets, for mezzo-soprano, tenor, and orchestra; Suite, for violin and orchestra; Terzetto, for soprano, contralto, tenor, and orchestra.

Piano Music—Prelude and Fugue in G-sharp minor; Prelude in F major.

Vocal Music—About 50 songs for solo voice and piano including Dreams, In the Silence of the Night, My Heart Is Throbbing, and When Autumn Leaves are Falling; vocal trios, vocal quartets.

ABOUT

Bernandt, G., Taneiev; Calvocoressi, M. D., and Abraham, G., Masters of Russian Music; Leonard, R. A., A History of Russian Music; Montagu-Nathan, M., History of Russian Music; Montagu-Nathan, M., Contemporary Russian Composers; Sabaneyev, L., Taneiev.

Musical Quarterly, October 1927, January 1958.

Giuseppe Tartini *1692-1770*

GIUSEPPE TARTINI, one of the foremost violinists and composers of violin music of his age, was born in Pirano, Istria, Italy, on April 8, 1692. He was one of five children. His father was a prosperous landowner and philanthropist. Since a career in the church was planned for him, Giuseppe was entrusted to the care of a priest of the Oratorio of St. Philip Neri for early religious training. Afterwards he was enrolled in the Padri delle Scuole Pie at Capo d'Istria, where instruction in religion was combined with music study. During this period Tartini became convinced he was not interested in theology. In 1709 his father obtained the bishop's consent to permit the boy to go to Padua to study law at the University. He stayed there three years.

After leaving the University without his law degree, Tartini worked passionately at his violin studies, supporting himself by giving music lessons. About 1713 he became the teacher of an attractive young lady, Elisabetta Premazone, fell in love with her, and married her secretly since she was under the protection of the powerful Cardinal Giorgio Cornaro. The Cardinal became so enraged on hearing that Tartini and Elisabetta had married that he ordered the young musician's arrest. Tartini was forced to flee from Padua disguised as a monk, leaving his wife behind. For a while he wandered about aimlessly, often going hungry and without a roof over his head. But a distant relative soon came to his aid and offered him asylum in a monastery in Assisi of which he was custodian.

While not much information exists about Tartini's life in Assisi, we do know that he worked long and hard on his violin technique, did a good deal of experimentation in acoustics and in the structure of violin and bow, and completed a number of works for his instrument. In 1713 he

GIUSEPPE TARTINI

wrote what today is considered his most famous and finest composition, the Sonata in G minor for violin and continuo, better known as the *Devil's Trill Sonata*. Tartini himself recorded how he came to write this work: "One night . . . I dreamed that I had made a compact with the devil, who promised to be at my service on all occasions. . . . Everything succeeded. . . . At last I thought I would offer my violin to the devil, in order to discover what kind of musician he was, when to my great astonishment I heard him play a solo so singularly beautiful and with such superior taste and precision that it surpassed all the music I had ever heard or conceived in the whole course of my life. I was so overcome with surprise and delight that I lost my power of breathing, and the violence of the sensation awoke me. Instantly, I seized my violin in the hopes of remembering some portion of what I had heard, but in vain! The work which this dream suggested, and which I wrote at the time, is doubtless the best of my compositions. I call it the *Devil's Trill Sonata [Il Trillo del diavolo]*." This sonata is in three movements. The trills which gave the work its name appear in the finale. Liszt transcribed this sonata for the piano, and Fritz Kreisler edited it for present-day concert performance.

By 1726 Tartini was allowed to return to Padua. He never left Italy again, though he continually received flattering offers to go to London and Paris. In 1740, however, he toured Italy and stayed for a while in Rome. After that he remained in Padua, playing the violin, composing, and teaching.

By 1740 he had become one of the most admired violin teachers in Italy, having established in Padua in 1728 a violin school that had become famous throughout Europe. Among his many pupils were Nardini, Manfredi, and Graun.

He died in Padua on February 26, 1770. He was buried in the graveyard of the St. Catherine Church, mourned by the entire city which had come to regard him (as Burney testified) as "its chief and most attractive ornament" and as a "philosopher, saint, and sage."

Since he had distributed most of his property while he was still alive, there was little left when he died. This generosity represents just one facet of a gentle and lovable man who was as humble as he was pious, as cultured as he was unpretentious. His love of poetry was second only to his passion for music. Often he combined the two interests by reading the poetry of Petrarch, or some other favorite writer, before sitting down to compose. On several occasions the music interpreted a poem he had just read, and he frequently identified the poem that had inspired him by a code which only he and a few intimate friends were able to unravel.

Tartini was one of Corelli's most significant successors in crystallizing a style and creating a mature literature for the violin. Though his indebtedness to Corelli cannot be mistaken, Tartini represented an important step forward in violin music, not only because of the advanced techniques and idioms he employed for the violin, but also because of the increased expressiveness of his material and the heightened subtlety of his thought.

"He built," said Arthur M. Abell, "upon the foundation laid by his great predecessor, Corelli, but . . . he greatly enlarged upon his models. He employed broader and more pregnant themes, while his passage work reveals organic development. Tartini understood the importance of light and shade; his passages stand out in bold contrast to the melodic passages, and they are not a mere collection of notes for the sake of variety; but they reveal a certain kinship to the whole structure."

PRINCIPAL WORKS

Choral Music—Miserere; Stabat Mater.

Orchestral Music—About 150 violin concertos.

Violin Music—About 100 violin sonatas including Il Trillo del diavolo, and Didone abbandonata.

ABOUT

Capri, A., Giovanni Tartini; Schökel, H. P., Giovanni Tartini; Spalding, A., A Fiddle, A Sword, and a Lady.

Strad, June 1905, October 1929.

Peter Ilich Tchaikovsky *1840-1893*

PETER ILICH TCHAIKOVSKY was born in Votkinsk, in the district of Viatka, Russia, on May 7, 1840. His father's profession of mining engineer kept the Tchaikovsky family in comfortable financial circumstances. Peter Ilich was the third of seven children.

He demonstrated an extraordinary sensitivity for things musical early in life. As a child of three he was fascinated by a little mechanical instrument (an "orchestrion") which tinkled out an air from Mozart's *Don Giovanni*. Before long he tried to reproduce this melody on the piano. At five he was given some piano instruction. He was also occasionally taken to concerts. Late one night, after a concert, the child cried out that he could not go to sleep because one of the melodies he had heard that night kept running through his head.

When Peter was ten, his family moved to St. Petersburg where the boy was enrolled in the preparatory classes for the School of Jurisprudence. While there, when he was fourteen, his mother died of cholera. Having always adored her with an almost unhealthy intensity, Peter was completely shattered by her death. It is likely that the emotional imbalance that characterized Tchaikovsky throughout his life dates from this tragedy.

Tchaikovsky remained in the School of Jurisprudence until he was nineteen. Towards the end of this period he studied piano with Kündinger; he also took lessons in theory, from Lomakin. Though he spent hours at the piano improvising, and though he had already tried his hand at composition, music had to be relegated for a long time to the role of an avocation. From 1859 to 1862 Tchaikovsky worked as a clerk in the Ministry of Justice, a job he detested but to which he devoted himself conscientiously.

Tchaikovsky: chī-kôf'skē

PETER ILICH TCHAIKOVSKY

More and more he felt himself drawn into the orbit of music. Tchaikovsky studied harmony and counterpoint with Zaremba and on the latter's advice finally left his government post in 1862 to enter the newly founded St. Petersburg Conservatory. There his teachers included Zaremba and Anton Rubinstein. "I promise you," Tchaikovsky wrote to his sister at the time, "something will come of me. Fortunately, I still have time." He fulfilled this promise. Upon graduating from the Conservatory in 1865 he received a silver medal for his cantata based on Schiller's *Ode to Joy*. Another of his compositions, *Characteristic Dances* for orchestra, was performed the same year in Pavlosk by an orchestra directed by Johann Strauss II. Besides these works, in 1865-1866 a string quartet and an orchestral overture were given at the Conservatory. Hermann Laroche, an eminent critic, could now write to Tchaikovsky: "You are the greatest musical talent of contemporary Russia, more powerful and original than Balakirev, more creative than Serov, infinitely more cultivated than Rimsky-Korsakov. In you, I see the greatest, or rather, the only hope of our musical future." Tchaikovsky, however, was more modest about his creative potential. In writing to his sister he said: "Do not for a moment think that I expect to be a great artist."

When Nicholas Rubinstein founded the Moscow Conservatory in 1866, he appointed Tchaikovsky a professor of harmony. The salary was a meager one but it provided the young man with opportunities to devote himself to composition. The most ambitious of his works at this time was his first symphony, called *Winter Dreams*. It was introduced with modest success in Moscow on February 15, 1868.

His tone poem *Fatum*, performed both in St. Petersburg and Moscow in 1869, and his first opera, *The Voyevoda*, produced in Moscow on February 11, 1869, brought him varying degrees of success. But Tchaikovsky was so dissatisfied with both these scores that he destroyed them. Almost a century after its première, the opera was restored from various drafts and scraps of manuscript which Tchaikovsky had failed to eliminate; and it was revived by the Leningrad Opera on September 28, 1949.

The original version of Tchaikovsky's first masterwork was written in 1869 and 1870. On the suggestion, and with the guidance, of Balakirev he wrote a symphonic fantasy based on Shakespeare's *Romeo and Juliet*. It was given on March 16, 1870, and was received coolly. Tchaikovsky revised his score one year later, but the composition we hear today was the product of a third revision in 1879.

Romeo and Juliet is the first of Tchaikovsky's works in which his mature style is finally crystallized. Richard Anthony Leonard wrote: "*Romeo and Juliet* contains most of the elements which were to give his music its astonishing vitality and its special coloring. Here, first of all is his gift of melody—profuse, often touching, and evocative of romantic melancholy. At the same time there is great force and directness of presentation. The ideas are marshaled swiftly and with dramatic skill; the orchestration is a model of clarity and richness. The whole work exhibits Tchaikovsky's gift for establishing a personal mood or emotion, a vivid episode or scene, and then intensifying his conception on a canvas full of romantic color and fire."

An important stimulus for the writing of this passionate, even sensual music, was a love affair, perhaps Tchaikovsky's only one, with a singer, Désirée Artôt. They even spoke of marriage. "I love her with all my heart and soul, and I feel I cannot live without her," confessed Tchaikovsky in one of his letters. But the singer jilted Tchaikovsky to marry a Spanish baritone. Never again was Tchaikovsky to be so completely, so emotionally involved with a woman.

It seems clear that Tchaikovsky had homosexual tendencies and was aware of them. A profound sense of guilt on this score doubtless contributed to his natural shyness, melancholia, and emotional disturbance. It also impelled him to embark upon a marriage that was a disaster from the very beginning.

His wife, Antonina, had been a neurotic music student who had come to him expressing rapturous adoration on bended knees. She wanted nothing more from life, she told him, than to serve him humbly. "Some mysterious power drew me to the girl," Tchaikovsky said. "One evening I went to her, told her frankly that I could not love her, but that I would be her faithful and grateful friend. I described my character in detail, my irritability, the unevenness of my temperament, my misanthropy, and my material condition. Then I asked her to marry me. The reply was, of course, in the affirmative." There can be no question but that Tchaikovsky embarked upon this loveless marriage so precipitately in order to stifle rumors that were already beginning to circulate about his homosexuality. He said as much in a letter to his brother Modest: "What a dreadful thought that people close to me may be ashamed of me! In a word, I am determined by means of marriage or public connection with a woman to shut the mouths of sundry despicable creatures whose opinions I despise but who may cause pain to people I love."

Tchaikovsky and Antonina were married on July 18, 1877. The first few weeks of marriage proved a harrowing experience for the composer. He was on the brink of a nervous breakdown when he fled from his home and went to live with his brother. After that he spent a year traveling about in Europe. He was never reunited with Antonina. She outlived him by a quarter of a century, the last twenty years of her life being spent in a mental hospital.

If this relationship with Antonina was a strange one, then the one that followed with another woman was more curious still. In 1877 he received word from Nadezhda Filaretovna von Meck, an affluent widow and dilettante who expressed her interest in his genius. Before long, she offered to provide Tchaikovsky with an annual subsidy to allow him to pursue his creative work without the necessity of earning a living. One condition was laid down for the continuance of this subsidy: They were never to meet personally. Thus, for thirteen years, Tchaikovsky and Mme. von Meck exchanged letters filled with expressions of friendship, and then of love—letters in which Tchaikovsky poured out his most secret feelings and torments as well as his artistic hopes and goals. Yet in all that time they never had a single meeting.

For Tchaikovsky this arrangement proved ideal. He had found financial security. He had also acquired the love and friendship of a woman who would make no emotional demands upon him.

Thus relieved of the necessity of earning a living, Tchaikovsky embarked upon a creative period in which he produced a succession of masterworks to place him with the foremost composers of his generation: the Fourth Symphony in F minor, which he dedicated to Mme. von Meck and which he often described to her as "our symphony," introduced in Moscow on March 4, 1878; the opera *Eugene Onegin*, produced in Moscow on March 29, 1879; the Violin Concerto, completed in 1878 and performed for the first time in Vienna on December 4, 1881; the *Capriccio italien (Italian Caprice)*, heard in Moscow on December 18, 1880; the *Ouverture solennelle*, better known as the *1812 Overture*, presented in Moscow on August 20, 1882. Recognition of his lofty place in Russian music came in 1884 when the Czar presented him with the award of the Order of St. Vladimir. Four years after that, the government bestowed on him a munificent life pension.

In 1885 Tchaikovsky went to Klin where he spent the next few years in comparative isolation. A sign on his door warned visitors to keep away except on Mondays and Thursdays, from three to five in the afternoon. He took daily walks in the country, did a good deal of reading (mainly philosophy), drank considerably, and devoted himself systematically to composition.

In 1887 Tchaikovsky directed a performance of one of his operas. Previously, he had avoided conducting, but he scored such a triumph, and he enjoyed the experience so completely, that he lost his inhibitions against conducting his compositions. As a guest conductor, he appeared in Germany,

Paris, and London in 1888, enjoying huge success everywhere. In 1891 he paid his first visit to the United States, making his American debut in New York on May 5 in conjunction with the opening of Carnegie Hall. He gave several more concerts in New York, Baltimore, and Philadelphia, before returning to Russia.

While traveling in the Caucasus in 1890, Tchaikovsky received the news that Mme. von Meck was bringing her annual subsidy to an end, and with it terminating both her correspondence and her friendship. Tchaikovsky no longer needed the subsidy; but that she should suddenly end a friendship that had come to mean so much to him was shattering. He tried in vain to persuade Mme. von Meck to reconsider her decision, but all his letters went unanswered. The cause for this precipitate break on Mme. von Meck's part after thirteen years has never been explained. Whatever the reason, the rupture broke Tchaikovsky's spirit and severely taxed his health.

After returning from the United States, Tchaikovsky sank deeper into his lifelong morbidity, seized more helplessly than ever by his fears. In such a mood he wrote his last symphony, sometimes described as the most pessimistic document in tones: the *Symphonie pathétique* (*Pathetic Symphony*) in B minor. Tchaikovsky himself had intended to call the work a "Program Symphony"; it was his brother, Modest, who suggested *Pathétique*.

It is reasonably certain that in completing this tragic music, Tchaikovsky was conscious he did not have much longer to live, that in effect he was writing his own symphonic requiem. In the first movement, he had the first trombone quote a phrase from the Russian Requiem service—a theme that has no logical place within that context, which is not developed any further, and which is half concealed within the orchestration.

"The *Pathetic*," explained Richard Anthony Leonard, "is what its name indicates—an essay in pathos. Even the barbaric clamors of the third movement are an exultation that hides but does not obliterate a substratum of morbidity; it is a wild and desperate irony in the face of terrible grief." And the plangent Adagio lamentoso with which the symphony comes to an unconventional conclusion is "an elegy which belongs with the noblest expressions of human grief."

To R. A. Streatfeild, the *Pathétique* is the most characteristic of all Tchaikovsky's symphonies, the one into which "he put most of himself. The Fourth Symphony may excel it in point of sheer picturesqueness, the Fifth in poetic feeling, but in the Sixth we feel that strongly personal note which rarely fails to appeal to sympathetic souls. Tchaikovsky affixed no program to it, but the story of a tortured soul, seeking an anodyne for its misery in the rapture of pleasure and in the ecstasy of battle, and finally sinking to hopeless pessimism and suicide, is scarcely to be misread. . . . When Tchaikovsky wrote the *Symphonie pathétique* he had attained such mastery of his material as gives him right to rank among great musicians. Whatever he chose to say he could express with absolute certainty of touch. In the *Symphonie pathétique* there are no effects that miss fire, no details that do not 'come off.' . . . It must stand as a very interesting and complete picture of a certain frame of mind, probably the completest expression in music of the *fin de siècle* pessimism that has ever been written."

In a discussion of Tchaikovsky's orchestral music, James Gibbons Huneker wrote: "His feelings for hues, as shown in his instrumentation, is wonderful. His orchestra fairly blazes at times. . . . He was not a great symphonist like Brahms; he had not the sense of formal beauty, preferring instead to work in free fashion within the easy and loosely flowing lines of the overture-fantasie. . . . He takes small, compact themes, nugget-like motives, which he subjects to the most daring and scrutinizing treatment. He polishes, expands, varies and develops his ideas in a marvelous manner, and if the form is often wavering the decoration is always gorgeous. . . . He is first and last a dramatic poet. He delineates the human soul in the convulsions of love, hate, joy and fear; he is an unique master of rhythms and of the torrential dynamics that express primal emotions in the full flood. . . . Give Tchaikovsky one or two large figures, give him a stirring situation, and then hark to the man as his dramatic impulse begins to play havoc."

The première of the *Symphonie pathétique* took place on October 28, 1893, the composer conducting. The work made only a slight impression. But when it was repeated about two weeks later, this time directed by Napravnik, it was a triumph.

Five days after he had led the première of his *Symphonie pathétique*, Tchaikovsky drank a glass of unboiled water, even though an epidemic of cholera was then spreading through St. Petersburg. His carelessness in doing this—combined with the fact that his mother had died of cholera—has led to the general belief that the composer was trying to commit suicide. However, there is no convincing evidence to substantiate such a contention. In any event, Tchaikovsky became infected with the dread disease. Delirium set in, during which he often repeated the name of Mme. von Meck and mumbled the two words, "accursed one." Suddenly, as Modest recalled, "Peter Ilich opened his eyes. There was an indescribable expression of unclouded consciousness. Passing over the others standing in the room he looked at the three nearest him, and then toward heaven. There was a certain light for a moment in his eyes which was soon extinguished, at the same time with his breath. It was about three o'clock in the morning." The date was November 6. At his funeral, the procession extended for half a mile, with tributes and expressions of grief coming from all parts of the world.

In his description of Tchaikovsky, Edward Lockspieser wrote: "At first sight he seems a benign old gentleman, with snow white hair, full features, not especially striking in appearance, not recognizably Slavic, but decidedly old for his years. In his forties he already approached old age. In the year of his death, at the age of fifty-three, he looks like a man of seventy. A photograph taken in his youth shows a triangular face with a pointed chin, an aquiline nose and a massive forehead. So at any rate he looked when a law student. A few years later he was wearing long hair in the romantic manner of the 1860's, and his large eyes, which we are told were of a 'wonderful blue,' were beginning to show signs of suffering. . . . A more convincing portrait is the one taken at the age of thirty-nine, two years after his marriage. . . . Here undoubtedly is some suggestion of the terror of the mind against which he fought for the greater part of his life. There is nothing idealized in this picture. The knit brows, the agonized stare, the heavy,

despondent expression give for the first time a glimpse of the man in mental torture."

Edwin Evans has given us further insight into the man: "Outwardly timid and nervous, he was inwardly capable of great strength, though its exertion in the strong situations of life usually left him afterwards in a state of collapse, and even of dangerous illness. His extreme discomfort whenever brought into contact with strangers, however amiable and flattering their intentions towards him, was so accentuated as to afford a fitting subject for a psychologist; but his mental attitude at the same time was not one of timidity . . . but was merely a kind of reserve, which in no way prevented him from forming lasting friendships. . . . His actions and letters reveal him as possessing a generous and amiable disposition which would shrink from causing any one a moment of pain. Like many men of this type he was long-suffering, and though his sensitiveness might cause him to wince many times, the offender had a long shrift before Tchaikovsky allowed resentment to get the better of him. When, however, this point had been reached, he could be most unforgiving, though not unjust."

He drank tea and alcohol in great quantities, liked taking solitary walks, and enjoyed an occasional game of cards (solitaire when he was alone). His working hours were usually between half past nine in the morning and one o'clock, but a good deal of creative thinking took place in the afternoons when he was out walking. He loved flowers. "When I am old and past composing," he once wrote to Mme. von Meck, "I shall spend the whole of my time growing them."

Though Tchaikovsky's music is unmistakably Russian in its personality—and though at times he quoted Russian folk songs and dances—he was not essentially a nationalist, and for this reason he was held in disdain by the members of the "Russian Five." They felt that Tchaikovsky was too strongly influenced by Western musical culture and too eclectic. Nevertheless, to many others Tchaikovsky's works represented the essence of the Russian land and its people. Igor Stravinsky said: "Tchaikovsky's music, which does not appear specifically Russian to everybody, is often more profoundly Russian than music which has long since been awarded the facile label of Muscovite picturesqueness. This music is quite as Russian as Pushkin's verse or Glinka's song. While not specially cultivating in his art the 'soul of the Russian peasant,' Tchaikovsky drew unconsciously from the true, popular sources of our race."

Outside Russia, Tchaikovsky has often been severely criticized for his excessive sentimentality and emotional extravagances. Philip Hale has written in explanation: "The heart of Tchaikovsky was that of a little child; the brain was that of a man weary of the world and all its vanities. And so we have the singular phenomenon of naïveté accompanied by superficial skill—and all this in the body and mind of a man fundamentally Oriental in his tastes and especially in his love of surprising or monotonous rhythms and gorgeous colors. . . . When faith returns again to the world, his music may be studied with interest and curiosity as an important document in sociology. But in the present we are under his mighty spell."

Principal Works

Ballets—Swan Lake; Sleeping Beauty; The Nutcracker.

Chamber Music—3 string quartets; String Sextet in D minor (Souvenir de Florence); Piano Trio in A minor; Souvenir d'un lieu cher, for violin and piano.

Choral Music—Vesper Service; Hymn to St. Cyril and St. Methodius; Six Church Songs; various cantatas and compositions for mixed chorus.

Operas—The Voyevoda; Undine; Oprichnik; Vakula the Smith; Eugene Onegin; The Maid of Orleans; Mazeppa; The Enchantress; Pique Dame (The Queen of Spades); Iolanthe.

Orchestral Music—6 symphonies; 4 suites; 3 piano concertos; Violin Concerto in D major; Romeo and Juliet; Serenade for Strings; Marche slave; Manfred; The Tempest; Francesca da Rimini; Variations on a Rococo Theme, for cello and orchestra; Capriccio italien; Ouverture solennelle, 1812; Hamlet.

Piano Music—Sonata in G major; Souvenir de Hapsal; The Months; Twelve Characteristic Pieces; Twelve Pieces of Moderate Difficulty; Children's Album; 18 Pieces.

Vocal Music—16 Children's Songs; 6 French Songs; numerous songs for voice and piano including Again, as Before, Alone, At the Open Window, A Ballroom Meeting, Disappointment, Don Juan's Serenade, If I Had Only Known, It Was Early Spring, A Legend, Lullaby, Night, None but the Lonely Heart, Not a Word, O My Friend, O Bless You Forests, Only Thou, Pimpinella, So Soon Forgotten, Song of the Gypsy Girl, Was I Not a Little Blade of Grass, We Sat Together, and Why?

About

Abraham, G., Tchaikovsky; Abraham, G. (editor), The Music of Tchaikovsky; Bowen, C. D., and Meck, B., Beloved Friend; Evans, E., Tchaikovsky; Newmarch, R., Tchaikovsky: His Life and Works; Tchaikovsky, M., Life and Letters of Peter Ilich Tchaikovsky; Tchaikovsky, P. I., Diaries; Weinstock, H., Tchaikovsky.

Georg Philipp Telemann *1681-1767*

GEORG PHILIPP TELEMANN was born in Magdeburg, Germany, on March 14, 1681, the son of a clergyman. As a child he revealed a remarkable aptitude for languages as well as a retentive memory for poetry. The only music instruction he ever received came from a local organist. After that, whatever Telemann learned in his art came from the study of textbooks, scores of operas and church music, and by trial and error in playing such instruments as the violin, flute, and zither. He was only twelve when he completed a full-length opera in the style of Lully that was heard in a public presentation. At fourteen he directed a church performance.

After attending school in Zellerfeld, where he attracted considerable attention with the music he wrote for and directed at a festival, he went to Hildesheim for his high-school education. He continued to interest himself in music although in 1700 he entered the University of Leipzig for the study of law and languages. Some of his compositions were now heard at the St. Thomas Church. They made such an impression on the town burgomaster that he commissioned young Telemann to write music regularly for church services. It was largely due to this commission that Telemann finally decided to give up law and concentrate his energies and gifts on music.

In 1704 he was engaged as organist of the Neue Kirche in Leipzig. At the same time he founded the Collegium Musicum, a society giving chamber and chamber-orchestral concerts in various German towns. But he did not remain long in Leipzig. In the same year he proceeded to Sorau where he became the *Kappellmeister* to Prince Promnitz. Four years after that the Prince appointed him *Konzertmeister* of the court orchestra. Since the Prince was partial to French music, Telemann cultivated at this time a French style for his instrumental compositions.

In 1709 Telemann left Sorau for Eisenach, where he became court *Kappellmeister*. It was on this occasion that he became acquainted

Telemann: tā'lĕ-män

with Johann Sebastian Bach, who, from that time on, held Telemann in the highest esteem. In 1714 Bach asked Telemann to serve as the godfather of his son Carl Philipp Emanuel.

In 1712 Telemann held the post of *Kapellmeister* at two churches in Frankfurt am Main, and from 1712 to 1721 he was the *Kapellmeister* to the Prince of Bayreuth. In 1721 he settled in Hamburg and there became the musical director of the city, taking charge of five churches, and cantor of the Johanneum. One year later he was offered the post of cantor at the Thomasschule, a post vacated by Kuhnau's death. Telemann preferred to remain in Hamburg, and the post went to Johann Sebastian Bach.

In Hamburg Telemann became involved in a whirlwind of musical activity. He directed performances at, and wrote music for, the five churches of which he was in charge. He supervised musical education at the city high school and at the Johanneum. He was the conductor of the Hamburg Opera. He founded and directed the Collegium Musicum for the presentation of public concerts, and he published the first music journal to appear in Germany. All this did not keep him from producing an almost incredible quantity of music in every conceivable form.

In 1737 Telemann visited Paris where he stayed eight months and supervised performances of his works besides making a firsthand and intensive study of French music.

Telemann died in Hamburg on June 25, 1767. His post was inherited by his godson, Carl Philipp Emanuel Bach.

Telemann was one of the most highly regarded German composers of his generation. Johann Sebastian Bach prized his work. Handel was of the opinion that Telemann's skill was so great that he could write an eight-part motet as easily as others could a letter. Franz Schubert once referred to Telemann as "that peerless master," and Johann Adolf Scheibe, a distinguished theorist and composer, considered him one of the greatest composers of a generation that produced Bach and Handel. One of Telemann's contemporaries, Mattheson, thus extolled him in verse:

> Lully fame has won;
> Corelli may be praised.
> But Telemann alone,
> Above all praise be raised.

Whether or not Telemann deserved such exalted evaluation is now difficult to say,

GEORG PHILIPP TELEMANN

since only a handful of his works is familiar today: some fantasias for harpsichord, the Suite in A minor for flute and orchestra, the *Don Quichotte Suite* for orchestra, some of his chamber music, and random extracts from his choral compositions. What we know of Telemann's music is only a minute fraction of his entire output, since he was not only the most prolific composer of his age but probably of all time. It would be impossible to estimate the number of his works. The Telemann output includes forty operas, seven hundred church cantatas, forty-four Passions, six hundred orchestral overtures, and innumerable suites and concertos. He was a master of technique, but to it he contributed little that was new or original. The exception was in his chamber music (*Tafelmusik*) where he parts company with Baroque practice by dispensing with the basso continuo, thus carrying chamber music to the threshhold of modernity. "I so contrived," he explained, "that the bass was a natural melody, forming, with the other parts, an appropriate harmony, which developed with each note in such a way that it seemed as though it could not be otherwise. Many sought to persuade me that I had displayed the best of my powers in these compositions."

A good deal of what he wrote—more so in his instrumental music than in his operas and church works—had lyrical freshness and an appealing manner together with a solid technique. "If Telemann had been more careful of his genius," Romain Rolland wrote, "if he had not written so much, accepted so many tasks, his name would perhaps have left a deeper mark on history than that of Gluck."

Chamber Music—Quintets, quartets, trios, sonatas.

Choral Music—700 church cantatas; 44 Passions; oratorios including Der Tag des Gerichts, Die Tageszeiten, Der Tod Jesu, Die Auferstehung Christi; psalms, Services.

Harpsichord Music—Fantasias.

Operas—About 40 operas including Der geduldige Socrates, Der neu-modische Liebhaber Damon, Die ungleiche Heyrath, Miriways, Flavius Bertaridus, König der Longobarden.

Orchestral Music—600 French overtures; numerous concertos; Suites, including Don Quichotte and Suite in A minor, for flute and strings; dances.

Vocal Music—Songs for voice and accompaniment.

ABOUT

Büttner, H., Das Konzert in den Orchestersuiten Georg Philipp Telemanns; Hörner, Hans, G. P. Telemanns Passionsmusiken; Rolland, R., A Musical Tour Through the Land of the Past; Valentin, E., Georg Philipp Telemann.

Ambroise Thomas 1811-1896

CHARLES LOUIS AMBROISE THOMAS, composer of Mignon, was born in Metz, France, on August 5, 1811. His father, a music teacher, gave Ambroise instruction when the child was only four. Within a few years the boy was adept at both piano and violin. In 1828 he entered the Paris Conservatory where his teachers included Zimmermann and Kalkbrenner in piano, Barbereau in harmony, and Lesueur in composition. After receiving first prizes in harmony and piano, he won the Prix de Rome in 1832 for the cantata Hermann et Ketty.

During his stay in Rome, Thomas wrote much chamber music, including a string quartet, a quintet, and a piano trio. Of the last, Robert Schumann said that it was "neither heavy nor light, neither deep nor superficial, not Classical nor Romantic, but always euphonious and in certain parts full of beautiful melody."

In 1836 Thomas returned to Paris. From this point on his main creative interest rested in the theater. His first opera was La Double échelle, produced by the Opéra-Comique in 1837. Berlioz found much to praise including the "grace, fire, finesse of dramatic intentions, and tact in employment of instrumental masses." But the general public was apathetic. In 1838 came a second Thomas opera, Le Perruquier de la régence; in 1839, an opera, Le Panier fleuri, and one act of a ballet, La Gipsy. Between 1840 and 1843 four more operas by Thomas were produced. Not until Mina, on October 10, 1843, did he encounter any measure of success.

During the Revoultion of 1848 Thomas enlisted in the Garde Nationale. He was out of uniform one year when he completed a brilliant comic opera, Le Caïd, which had an Oriental setting and a French adventurer in Egypt as hero. A satire on Italian operas boasting exotic settings, Le Caïd was an outstanding success in 1849.

Two more operas by Thomas were heard in the years 1850-1851. One of these was Raymond, remembered today only for its tuneful overture which is a staple in the light-music repertory. Between 1853 and 1860 five Thomas operas were given. Meanwhile, in 1851, he had been elected to the Institut de France. In 1856 he became professor of composition at the Paris Conservatory, and in 1858 he was made officer of the Legion of Honor.

After 1860 Thomas took a respite from operatic composition that lasted a number of years. Apparently the vacation was most beneficial. When he returned to dramatic writing, he created a masterwork, a monument in the French lyric theater. It was Mignon, based on Goethe's novel Wilhelm Meisters Lehrjahre, performed at the Opéra-Comique on November 17, 1866. Mignon was a sensation in its own day, and has been a durable classic since. In less than a hundred years it has had over two thousand performances at the Opéra-Comique alone. It was also acclaimed in most of the operatic centers of the world. The American première took place at the Academy of Music in New York on November 22, 1871.

"If this opera is successful and popular," wrote Henri de Curzon, "it is because it offers many things to many people: laughter and tears; sincere emotion and frivolity, character and facility. . . . Its banal pages are relieved by an inspiration of exquisite grace. Conventional effects are balanced by the poignant truth of still another effect."

Thomas: tô-mä'

What Eduard Hanslick wrote when *Mignon* was heard for the first time in Germany still holds basically true. He said: "This opera is in no place powerfully striking, and it is not the work of a richly organized, original genius. Rather does it appear to us a work of a sensitive and refined artist, showing the practical ability of a master hand. Occasionally somewhat meager and tawdry . . . the music to *Mignon* is nevertheless mostly dramatic, spirited and graceful, not of deep, but of true, and, in many instances, warm feeling."

Thomas's successor to *Mignon* was *Hamlet,* based on Shakespeare—another monumental success when introduced at the Paris Opéra on March 9, 1868. Where *Mignon* had been essentially lyrical, *Hamlet* was dramatic. The telling moments in the later opera are those charged with theatrical electricity, such as the ghost scene and Hamlet's scene with his mother. *Hamlet* is effective opera if "a modern audience can be persuaded to accept the musical and dramatic idiom," said Martin Cooper, "and not to expect something that Thomas never intended to give—namely either the rich metaphysical overtones of Shakespeare or a stark realistic tragedy in the Mussorgsky manner. Thomas's *Hamlet* is a story of a Second Empire palace revolution, as legitimate an interpretation of the facts as our own Elizabethan version, but quite different." Nevertheless, many audiences outside France have not been willing to accept or even tolerate some of Thomas's questionable practices, such as assigning the principal role to a baritone instead of a tenor; or having Ophelia's mad scene set to music in three-quarter time; or interpolating into the text a drinking song that is out of character with the rest of the play.

The immense success of *Mignon* and *Hamlet* brought Thomas popularity that was second only to that enjoyed by Gounod. Thomas was a favorite at the court of Napoleon III. In 1871 he was made director of the Paris Conservatory in succession to Auber.

His duties at the Conservatory, where he instituted major reforms, were all-absorbing and often kept him from composition. Nevertheless he did manage to complete an ambitious opera, *Françoise de Rimini,* based on Dante, which was a failure when given by the Paris Opéra on April 14, 1882.

AMBROISE THOMAS

Thomas became the first opera composer to live long enough to witness the one-thousandth performance of one of his works. The opera was *Mignon,* and the event took place at the Opéra-Comique on May 13, 1894. The elite of French society and cultural life attended to give the eighty-three-year-old composer a thunderous ovation. The French government honored him on this occasion by conferring on him the grand cordon of the Legion of Honor (he was the first musician thus decorated). One day later, on May 14, the Opéra-Comique again honored Thomas, this time with a gala performance in which several of Thomas's operas were represented by excerpts.

Henri de Curzon described Thomas as a man of excessive timidity and reserve who was usually lost in revery. His face generally had an expression of pain "touched with poetry." Thomas himself once commented on his weakness for lapsing into reveries by saying, "I need to dream just as other people need to sleep and walk." In the last quarter century of his life, Thomas became increasingly withdrawn and self-centered, as the fear of death began to obsess him.

Ambroise Thomas died in Paris on February 12, 1896. The funeral services were highlighted by a eulogy by Massenet. He was buried in Paris, in the cemetery at Montmartre.

PRINCIPAL WORKS

Ballets—Betty; La Tempête.

Chamber Music—String Quintet; String Quartet; Piano Trio.

Choral Music—2 cantatas; Messe solennelle; part songs for men's chorus.

Operas—Le Caïd; Mina; Le Songe d'une nuit d'été; Raymond; Psyché; Le Carnaval de Venise; Mignon; Hamlet; Gille et Gillotin; Françoise de Rimini.

Vocal Music—Songs for voice and piano.

ABOUT

Bacharach, A. L. (editor), The Music Masters, vol. 2; Curzon, H. de, Ambroise Thomas; Hervey, A., Masters of French Music.

Revue de Paris, March-April 1896.

Giuseppe Torelli *1658-1709*

GIUSEPPE TORELLI

G IUSEPPE TORELLI wrote the first *published* violin concertos. He was born in Verona, Italy, on April 22, 1658. Not much is known of his early life beyond the fact that his music study took place in Bologna, that he served as a member of the Accademia Filarmonica in that city, and that from 1686 to 1695 he played the violin in the orchestra of the S. Petronio Church.

In 1686 he published a concerto da camera for two violins and accompaniment (op. 2). This is not the first solo concerto to be written, for Torelli had been preceded in this area by Alessandro Stradella (1642-82), but it was the first such work to be published. The concerto form is here clearly defined and is made ready for the hands of its first master, Corelli.

Upon leaving his church post at S. Petronio, Torelli toured Germany as a concert violinist. For two years after that he served as the *Kapellmeister* to the Margrave of Brandenburg in Ansbach. In 1699 he went to Vienna where he stayed two years and completed the writing of an oratorio. With the turn of the new century, he returned to Bologna, where he remained until his death on February 8, 1709. During the year of his death there was published another monumental opus: a set of concerti grossi for orchestra, op. 8, which includes the *Christmas Eve Concerto* (No. 6) still sometimes performed today, though often in a modern adaptation.

"Torelli," wrote Manfred F. Bukofzer, "cast his concertos at first in the mold of the church and chamber sonata, but soon threw off the shackles of the sonata form and established the typical concerto form, consisting of three movements in the order of Allegro-Adagio-Allegro." A solo performance for the violin was also indicated in some of the brief interludes in Torelli's orchestral concertos, op. 6. "Thus both the concerto grosso and the orchestral concerto laid the ground for the solo concerto."

Discussing Torelli's contribution to the development of the concerto grosso, in his op. 8 set, Bukofzer added that Torelli established "a distinct balance between tutti and solo; the solo ceased to be merely a transitional interlude so that the orchestra and soloist become rivals of equal importance." At the same time a contrast between solo and tutti was emphasized by means of "virtuoso figuration in the solo and a pregnant idea in the tutti." All this, for Bukofzer, represented a "great advance over the primitive organization of Corelli's concertos."

PRINCIPAL WORKS

Chamber Music—Balletti da camera; Concerto da camera; Sinfonie a 2-4 stromenti, Concertino per camera; Sinfonie a 3; Capricci musicali per camera.

Choral Music—Oratorio.

Orchestral Music—Concerti grossi.

ABOUT

Bukofzer, M. F., Music in the Baroque Era; Giegling, F., Giuseppe Torelli: Ein Beitrag zur Entwicklungsgeschichte des italienischen Konzerts.

Sir Francesco Paolo Tosti *1846-1916*

SIR FRANCESCO PAOLO TOSTI, eminent composer of songs, was born in Ortona sul Mare, Abruzzi, on April 9, 1846. In 1858 his parents sent him to the royal college of San Pietro a Maiella in Naples. For the next few years he studied violin there with Pinto, and composition with Conti and Mercadante. Mercadante was so impressed by his talent that he appointed him a pupil teacher.

Poor health compelled Tosti to leave Naples in 1869 and return to his native city, where he was confined to bed for several months of sickness and convalescence. During this period he started writing songs for diversion. He submitted two of these in a competition by a Florentine Art Society, and two to the publishing house of Ricordi. None were accepted. But two of the songs he wrote during this same period became exceedingly popular some years later: "Non n'ama più" and "Lamento d'amore."

After recovering from his prolonged illness, Tosti left Ortona sul Mare for Ancola. His poverty was so great that for weeks at a time he subsisted only on oranges and stale bread. He then went to Rome where he found an ally in Sgambati, the distinguished pianist and teacher. Sgambati arranged for Tosti to give a song recital at the Sala Dante. The concert, which included several of Tosti's own songs, was a great success. Princess Margherita, who had attended the performance, appointed him her singing teacher.

This appointment marked a radical change in his personal fortunes. He sold two songs to Ricordi, both of which enjoyed impressive sheet-music sales. He was also made Keeper of the Musical Archives at court.

In 1875 Tosti paid his first visit to England. He made powerful friends there, through whose influence he was able to penetrate the highest strata of English society. He became a particular favorite at fashionable salons, and began to visit England annually until 1880 when he was made teacher of singing to the royal family. He then established permanent residence in London. His fame as composer of songs soared with such numbers as "For Ever and Ever," introduced by Violet Cameron at the Globe Theatre with sensational results, "At Vespers," and "Goodbye Forever." During the ensuing years he added appreciably to his fame and fortune by writing "Mother," "That Day," "Amore," "Aprile," "Vorrei morire," among many others.

By 1885 he had become the most famous song composer in England, and one of the most successful in all Europe. He was an intimate friend of Italian and English royalty, and a frequent visitor at the palace of Queen Victoria. His success reached such heights that Ricordi gave him a weekly retainer of five hundred dollars a week just to produce a song a month.

In 1894 Tosti became a member of the faculty of the Royal Academy of Music. In 1904 he was made Commander of the Victorian Order and four years later he was knighted by King Edward. The fact that Tosti became an English subject, and a recipient of such high honors in England, created a considerable amount of hostility for him in Italy among many who felt he had renounced his own country for the sake of success.

In 1913, convinced he did not have much longer to live, Tosti returned to Italy, and settled in Rome where he spent his last three years. He died there on December 2, 1916.

Tosti was a glamorous figure in English society, famous for his wit, irony, and personal charm. Despite success, he remained a modest man incapable of overestimating his artistic importance. This was perhaps his most endearing trait. Composing was for him a seasonal affair, usually done in the warm months at the seashore. He preferred devoting wintertime to his many social commitments and responsibilities. He was, however, gathering melodic ideas all the time. It was a familiar sight to see him suddenly jot down hurriedly several bars of music on a scrap of paper and stuff it into his pocket—regardless of where he might be at the time, or with whom.

Tosti created a library of songs to English, French, and Italian texts. Robert Bracco said that Tosti's best songs are distinguished by a "modest simplicity," "an inborn dignity," and "untrammeled elegance." Tosti's songs, he added, have "the imprint of the purest and most traditional forms of Italian music."

PRINCIPAL WORKS

Vocal Music—A library of songs for solo voice and piano including Addio (Goodbye Forever), L'Alba separa dalla luce l'ombra, Aprile, Ave Maria, Dopo!, Ideale (My Ideal), Luna d'estate, Malia (Enchantment), Marechiare, Mattinata, Mélodie, La Mia canzone, My Dreams,

Ninon, Non m'ama più, Parted, Pour un baiser, La Serenata, Sogno, Tristezza, L'Ultima canzone, Vorrei morire, and A Vuchella.

ABOUT

Collins, W. F., Laurel Winners; Marco, E. A., Francesco Paolo Tosti.

Musical Opinion, September 1931; Musical Times, March 1917.

Tschaikovsky, Peter Ilich

see Peter Ilich Tchaikovsky

Orazio Vecchi *1550-1605*

ORAZIO VECCHI was born in Modena, Italy, in 1550. His principal musical training came in Bologna from Salvatore Essenga, a monk who in 1566 published one of Vecchi's madrigals in a collection of his own works. In 1577 Vecchi visited Brescia, but sometime soon after that he settled in Modena as a teacher of music. In 1580 he published his first book—a group of canzonette. From its preface we learn that by this time some of his music (issued under the names of other composers) had been performed and had become known in different parts of Italy. Vecchi had also earned a reputation as a poet, singer, and conversationalist.

Apparently Vecchi's meager income was inadequate to meet his basic needs for in 1584 he appealed to the city authorities for financial assistance. He later took holy orders, though precisely when is not known, and after that held the post of *maestro di cappella* in Reggio Emilia. In 1586 he was appointed canon of the Cathedral of Correggio, where five years later he rose to the post of archdeacon. By this time he had produced a good deal of sacred music which was thought of so highly that in 1591 ecclesiastical authorities selected him (in collaboration with Giovanni Gabrieli and Ludovico Balbi) to revise and prepare a new edition of the church plainsong.

In 1595 Vecchi lost his cathedral office, either because of his persistent and prolonged absences from Coreggio, or because he had become involved in brawls. On two occasions he was stabbed, and once he and the organist of the Sant' Agostino Church engaged in an ugly squabble which interrupted the mass.

Vecchi became *maestro di cappella* at the Cathedral of Modena in 1596. Two years later he also became *maestro* at the royal court and music master to the princes. While holding these posts Vecchi wrote music not only for the church but also for court and public entertainments. His fame was so widespread that at one time he was invited to appear at the court of Emperor Rudolf II and at another he was engaged to write music for the king of Poland.

The loss of his post at the Modena Cathedral in 1604, because he had defied the bishop's restrictions against giving music instruction to nuns, is believed to have seriously affected his health. He died in Modena on February 19, 1605, leaving a considerable fortune and an outstanding collection of books and art works.

As a composer of madrigals, motets, Masses, and hymns, for which he usually provided his own texts, Vecchi was a commanding figure in the Italian polyphonic school. He was a contrapuntist of immense technical skill and invention who created, as Cecil Gray noted, intrinsic beauty . . . as fresh now as the day it was written."

One work of his above others stands out in bold relief: *L'Amfiparnaso,* a remarkable set of fourteen five-part unaccompanied madrigals. Set to a text with characters derived from the commedia dell'arte, and intended for stage presentation (Vecchi described it as a "comedia harmonica" or "comedy in music"), *L'Amfiparnaso* is much more than just a madrigal sequence: It is an important transition from the madrigal and the age of polyphony to the opera and the era of homophony. Yet it would be a mistake to designate *L'Amfiparnaso* as an opera, even a primitive one. Vecchi himself emphasized in his prologue that his work was a "spectacle . . . to be seen through the mind which it enters by the ears and not by the eyes." He meant that *L'Amfiparnaso* was to be listened to as music.

Romain Rolland has presented a strong case for considering *L'Amfiparnaso* a primitive "program symphony." Elaborating on this same point, Edward J. Dent has explained: "For Orazio Vecchi and his contemporaries, the most perfect instrument was the human voice, and the polyphonic madrigal, the style over which they had the greatest mastery. . . . Vecchi set the comedy of masks to music not because he wished to be dramatic, but because music without words

Vecchi: vĕk′-kē

was practically unthinkable. The comedy of masks was familiar to his singers in such a way that his setting became virtually wordless. The characters represented would not be made real to their minds through what they said on one particular occasion; they were not individuals, but eternal types, personifications of phases of character that every hearer could recognize more or less in some aspect of his own personality. Similarly in *Ein Heldenleben,* the 'hero' may be supposed by writers of analytical programs to be the ideal hero, or by facetious critics to be Richard Strauss himself; but it is more reasonable and more poetical to consider the work as the expression of what all of us have at some time thought and suffered. To admit this is to simply recognize that the *L'Amfiparnaso* and the *Heldenleben* are attempts of the remote past and the immediate present to express in music what the classical age expressed in Beethoven's symphonies."

L'Amfiparnaso was written and staged in Modena in 1594, and was published in 1597. In three acts and fourteen scenes (text by Vecchi in various Italian, Spanish, and Hebrew dialects), it is built around two separate stories. The first (described by the composer as *lirico tragico*) engages Lucio and Isabella, who are married after various disturbing and emotionally upsetting developments. The other *(grottesco comico)* employs characters taken from the *commedia dell'arte,* including Old Pantalone, the courtesan Hortensia, and the lovers Lelio and Nisa.

In this monumental work, wrote Alfred Einstein, "the madrigal and the lighter forms of sixteenth-century music have met as if by appointment, and have made merry at one another's expense against what appears to be a background. It is an end." As Einstein concluded: "Vecchi is so gay, so light, so impudent, so fascinating a companion that we prefer to see his work as a golden sunset and not as foreshadowing the coming night. After Vecchi there is plenty of comedy in Italian music, but little gaiety that is as pure as his."

There have been some important revivals of *L'Amfiparnaso* in the twentieth century. The work was heard in an English translation in New York in 1933, in a concert performance by the Dessoff Choirs. In 1938 it received a mimed and sung presentation at the Florence May Music Festival. On the

ORAZIO VECCHI

occasion of Vecchi's four hundredth birthday, *L'Amfiparnaso* was staged in Modena and after that was presented in several other Italian cities, besides being recorded in its entirety. A few years later, *L'Amfiparnaso* was heard in its first stage presentation in the United States at the Berkshire Music Center at Tanglewood, in Lenox, Massachusetts.

PRINCIPAL WORKS

Choral Music—Selva di varia recreatione; L'Amfiparnaso; Il Convito musicale; Le Veglie di Siena; canzonette, hymns, madrigals, Masses, motets.

ABOUT

Einstein, A., The Italian Madrigal; Rolland, R., Les Origines du théâtre lyrique moderne.

Rassegna musicale, April 1929; Rivista musicale italiana, 1949, 1950.

Francesco Veracini *1690-1750*

FRANCESCO MARIA VERACINI, known as "Il Fiorentino," was born in Florence, on February 1, 1690. He studied the violin first with his uncle, Antonio Veracini, a distinguished virtuoso and composer, and subsequently with Gasparini. After his studies ended, Francesco Veracini toured Italy as concert violinist, scoring major successes. In 1714 he went to Venice where for a short period he filled the post of violinist in the orchestra at St. Mark's. That same year he performed in England, where he triumphed at the King's Theatre on January 23.

Veracini: vä-rä-chē'nē

FRANCESCO VERACINI

For about two years he served as the concert-master of the orchestra at the Italian Opera; during this period he made many notable appearances as violin virtuoso both in public concerts and at fashionable salons.

Back in Italy by 1717, he was heard by the Crown Prince of Saxony, who hired him as solo violinist at the court of the Elector of Dresden. He held this appointment five years. In 1722, in a fit of madness, he jumped out of a window and broke his hip and leg; he remained lame for the rest of his life. The circumstances surrounding this attempted suicide have never been adequately explained. Some said it was the result of overwork, fatigue, and depression; others feel it was the consequence of a personal and artistic humiliation inflicted on him by an envious Dresden musician named Pisendel.

Veracini left Dresden in 1723, to go to Prague where he served for a while in the chapel of Count Kinsky. After that for a number of years he engaged in concert work in Italy. In 1735 he was back in England to receive honors as a composer. His opera *Adriano* was introduced at the King's Theatre by royal command on November 25, 1735, and proved so popular that it was given seventeen times that season. His performances as a violinist, however, were received far less favorably, since several brilliant younger violinists (among them Geminiani) had usurped the limelight.

Veracini stayed in England until 1745. En route to Italy he was shipwrecked and

lost all his savings and belongings. His closing years were dismal. As a virtuoso he was now in eclipse, and was incapable of earning a living with his violin. Having lost all his savings, he suffered the most abject poverty. He died near Pisa in 1750.

As a composer of violin sonatas, Veracini was ahead of his time. His influence was felt and absorbed by many of the Italian composers of violin music who followed him. "His bold modulations," wrote Edmund van der Straeten "the wealth of his delicately worked out harmonies, his originality in expressing his conceptions, differed too widely from anything that had been heard before, with the result that, for over a century, his compositions were entirely neglected. Only since the second half of the century, violinists and the music public became aware of their rare beauty. In form they show a progress over their predecessors, but it is especially in thematic material and in its bold harmonic treatment and the characteristic chromatic passages that he appears quite modern. Some of his slow movements are truly enchanting, while his Allegros often fascinate by their brightness and natural flowing form."

PRINCIPAL WORKS

Chamber Music—24 violin sonatas; sonatas for violin and flute.

Choral Music—Nice e Tirsi; Parla al ritratto dell'amante.

Operas—Adriano; La Clemenza di Tito; Roselinda; Partenio; L'Errore di Salomone.

Orchestral Music—Symphonies; violin concertos.

ABOUT

Phipson, T. L., Biographical Sketches of Celebrated Violinists; Pincherle, M., Les Violinistes; Straeten, E. van der, The History of the Violin.

Giuseppe Verdi *1813-1901*

FORTUNIO GIUSEPPE FRANCESCO VERDI, Italy's foremost composer of operas, was born on October 10, 1813, in Le Roncole, a town near Busseto in the duchy of Parma. His father was an innkeeper of peasant stock. As a child Giuseppe showed great interest in all kinds of music-making, whether at church or in the streets. Noticing this, his father bought a spinet which became the child's favorite plaything. "One day," recalled a friend of

Verdi's father, "the boy was found in the greatest delight at having found the major third and fifth of the key of C. The next day, however, he could not find the chord again. He fell into such a temper that he seized a hammer and proceeded to break the spinet into pieces."

Verdi's first music teacher was Baistrocchi, the village organist. After a few lessons, Verdi began to substitute for his teacher at church services. When his teacher resigned, the boy was hired as the official church organist at a regular salary. But Verdi's father wisely realized that Verdi needed more training. For this purpose he sent him to Busseto when he was twelve. There Verdi aroused the interest, and acquired the support, of a wealthy merchant, Antonio Barezzi, president of the local orchestra and an excellent musical amateur. Through Barezzi, Verdi became a pupil of Ferdinando Provesi. During the four-year period that Verdi studied with Provesi he became involved in various musical activities. At times he played the organ in the Busseto church; occasionally he assisted Provesi in conducting the town orchestra; in addition, he was writing a considerable amount of music. One of his orchestral pieces was used in 1828 as an overture to a performance of *The Barber of Seville;* other compositions were played by the local band.

The townspeople, headed by Barezzi, created a fund to send Verdi to Milan to study at the famous Conservatory. In 1832 Verdi applied for admission. Because he was older than the required age, he was compelled to take entrance examinations. His piano playing was found faulty; and though his compositions were judged to have some merit, they were regarded as technically deficient. *"Privo di talento musicale"*—lacking in musical talent"—was the final verdict. Denied entrance to the Conservatory, Verdi had to seek out a private teacher and found him in Vincenzo Lavigna, from whom he received a thorough grounding in counterpoint, fugue, and dramatic composition. Lavigna recognized the innate gifts of his pupil. "He is a fine young man," he said, "discreet, studious and intelligent, and will prove a great honor to me and to our country."

In the summer of 1834 Verdi returned to Busseto, where he became municipal music director. He stayed there only half a year, then resumed his music study with Lavigna

GIUSEPPE VERDI

in Milan. But from the summer of 1835 to September 1838 he resided in Busseto where he directed the local music school and was appointed conductor of the Busseto Philharmonic. During this period, on May 4, 1836, he married Margherita, the daughter of Barezzi. The two children born to them in rapid succession died in infancy. Margherita herself died in 1840.

His most important creative achievement during the three years he spent in Busseto was the completion of his first opera, *Oberto.* After leaving Busseto and settling permanently in Milan in 1838, Verdi submitted his opera to La Scala, which introduced it on November 17, 1839. Though it was heard in only a few performances, *Oberto* made enough of an impression to encourage the publishing house of Ricordi to accept it and to commission the composer to write a new opera.

The new opera was a comedy, *Un Giorno di regno,* presented at La Scala on September 5, 1840. It was a fiasco. Not for half a century would Verdi again try his hand at comedy. Despite the heartbreak and frustrations attending a failure of such proportions, Verdi went to work on a new opera, *Nabucco.* "With this score," Verdi himself said, "my musical career really began." Given at La Scala on March 9, 1848, *Nabucco* proved such a triumph that food, delicacies, clothes, and toys were named after Verdi. A failure as a composer only one day before this première, Verdi suddenly found himself affluent and famous.

An impressive creative spurt, undoubtedly stimulated by this tremendous success, followed at once. During the next decade Verdi completed eleven operas of which the most significant were the following: *I Lombardi,* given at La Scala on February 11, 1843; *Ernani,* introduced in Venice on March 9, 1844; and *Macbeth,* whose première took place on March 14, 1847, in Florence. Besides being given in fifteen Italian theaters, *Ernani* became the first Verdi opera to be mounted in London and New York, in 1845 and 1847 respectively.

By 1850 Verdi was the first man of opera in Italy, and one of the most successful in all Europe. His most impressive achievements, however, were yet to come. With *Rigoletto,* produced in Venice on March 11, 1851, a new creative period unfolded for Verdi in which he completed many of the operas by which he is represented most often in the opera theaters of the world. *Rigoletto* created a sensation when it was first heard, and it has remained one of the most beloved works in the Italian repertory. "We can still sense the extraordinary quality of this music," said Francis Toye, "in which the orchestra and voice alike combine to heighten the poignancy of the situation. . . . There is something somber and rugged in the simplicity of *Rigoletto* which entitles it to be called truly great, and it has always remained one of Verdi's especial favorites." The last-act quartet ("Bella figlia dell'amore") remains to this day a miracle of ensemble writing, in which each of the four characters is sharply delineated in the music. As for the equally popular tenor aria, "La Donna è mobile," the story goes that Verdi himself knew how contagious its appeal would be; rather than permit the melody to become known in Milan before the première, he refused to turn the music over to the leading tenor until the day of the opening-night performance.

Rigoletto first came to the United States on February 19, 1855, staged at the Academy of Music in New York. A quarter of a century later, on November 17, 1883, it became the ninth presentation of the initial season of the Metropolitan Opera. (It was in *Rigoletto* that Enrico Caruso subsequently made his historic American opera debut, on November 24, 1903, the opening night of the 1903-04 season of the Metropolitan Opera.)

Two Verdi masterworks followed *Rigoletto* in quick succession: *Il Trovatore,* in Rome on January 19, 1853, and *La Traviata,* in Venice on March 6, 1853. Like *Rigoletto,* both these operas were seen for the first time in the United States at the Academy of Music—*Il Trovatore* on May 2, 1855, and *La Traviata* on December 3, 1856. Once again, like *Rigoletto,* both operas appeared in the repertory of the Metropolitan Opera during its first season in 1883-1884.

On the day that *Il Trovatore* was introduced to the world, the Tiber in Rome overflowed. Opera-goers had to reach the theater by wading through mud and water. Despite this discomfort, and despite the fact that the audience was often puzzled by an overcomplicated and confused libretto, the opera made an overwhelming impression. "The public listened to every number with religious silence," reported the *Gazzetta musicale,* "and broke out with applause at every interval. The end of the third act, and the whole of the fourth, aroused such enthusiasm that their repetition was demanded."

La Traviata, however, met a far different fate at its world première. Some did not like seeing characters wearing contemporary dress, as the libretto originally demanded. Others were shocked by the immorality of the story. Still others were amused to watch an overweight prima donna seemingly "waste away" with tuberculosis. A poorly prepared presentation did not help matters either. Before the final curtain, the audience expressed its resentment in loud catcalls, hisses, and shouts of indignation. "*La Traviata* last night was a fiasco," Verdi told one of his pupils. "Is the fault mine or the singers'? I don't know at all. Time will decide."

The opera was withdrawn from the repertory for a year while Verdi and his librettist revised it in several important details. Setting and costuming were set back to the period of Louis XIII. Parts of the second act were rewritten. Meticulous attention was then given to the matter of casting and production. Returning to the scene of its disaster—Venice—*La Traviata* rose on the evening of May 6, 1854, from the ashes of its one-time defeat to triumph. It was now speedily given in other major Italian cities, and before the end of 1856 it had been seen in London, Paris, and St. Petersburg as well as in New York. It has never lost its dramatic or emotional appeal, and has remained throughout the world one of the most frequently performed and admired operas.

His success enabled Verdi to achieve a lifelong ambition by acquiring an extensive farm in Sant' Agata where henceforth he spent his summers, while wintering in Genoa. A descendant of peasants, Verdi now returned to the soil, tending to his farmlands, stock, and gardens. He was a simple man who, despite his wealth, enjoyed most the elemental things of life; and he was never happier than at Sant' Agata. "Here," said his librettist Antonio Ghislanzoni, "his prodigious activity of body and mind can find vent more freely than elsewhere. At five o'clock in the morning, he walks through the park, visits the fields and farms, amuses himself rowing on the lake in a little boat, which he manages like a skillful water man. Not a moment of respite. As a rest from music, Verdi has recourse to poetry; to temper the strong emotions of the latter and the former he takes refuge in the history of philosophy. . . .

"The master generally composes in his bedroom—a room situated on the ground floor, spacious, airy, and light, furnished with artistic profusion. The windows and doors also gaze out on the garden. There is a magnificent piano, a bookcase, and an enormous piece of furniture of eccentric shape, which divides the room into two parts, and exhibits a delightful variety of statuettes, vases and artistic fancy. . . . From this room, in the silence of the night, rise the exciting harmonies that spring from the creative brain."

Franz Werfel thus described a routine day at Sant' Agata: "Verdi rises early. Like most Italians he takes nothing but a cup of unsweetened black coffee. Then he goes out on horseback—in later years he has the carriage hitched up—to inspect the work in fields, barnyards, and at the dairy farms; or to call on some of his tenants. . . . Between nine and ten he comes home. Meanwhile the mail has arrived. . . . Some time is spent every day dealing with this. If guests come, they generally arrive at noon. . . . The main meal comes at six in the evening. Verdi has the reputation of a lover and connoisseur of good cooking. . . . He loves the light wine of Italy and heavy Havana cigars, nor does he disdain a game of cards after the evening meal."

His life at Sant' Agata was shared by his second wife, the singer Giuseppina Strepponi, whom he married on August 29, 1859. She had been the prima donna in the première of *Nabucco* in 1842, and after that for many years was one of his most intimate friends. She gave up her own career to tend to Verdi's needs and comforts and to the end remained a devoted, self-sacrificing wife.

For a brief period Verdi invaded the political arena. When in 1863 Cavour inaugurated the first Italian parliament, Verdi was elected a deputy. Though passionately patriotic, Verdi disliked politics intensely and soon withdrew. He never again became involved actively as a politician. When, a decade later, the King of Italy conferred on him the post of senator, he could accept the appointment without qualms, since it was an honorary one which would make no demands on him.

All the while, Verdi continued to produce important operas. *I Vespri siciliani*—or *Les Vêpres siciliennes*—was written in 1855 on a commission from the Paris Opéra. Introduced in Paris on June 13, 1855, it was a modest success. This was followed by *Simon Boccanegra*, first seen in Venice on March 12, 1857, but subsequently revised extensively and reintroduced in its definitive version in 1881 in Milan. With *Un Ballo in maschera*, produced in Rome on February 17, 1859, Verdi came to grips with the censors (though not for the first time). The subject of this opera was the assassination of King Gustavus III during a court ball in 1792. Because an attempt had recently been made on the life of Napoleon III, the censors insisted that Verdi delete all suggestions of regicide from his opera. At first Verdi withdrew his opera completely. But later he decided to shift the setting to colonial America, with the King of Sweden becoming transformed as the governor of Boston. The opera now met with favor, both with the censors and the public. But to many Italian patriots, seeking to unify Italy under the House of Savoy, the opera made Verdi a patriotic symbol; the cry "Viva Verdi!" became the rallying cry of all those in favor of Victor Emmanuel as king.

La Forza del destino was written on a commission from the Imperial Theater of St. Petersburg. When introduced in Russia on November 10, 1862, it was received coldly, partly because many thought the opera too somber, partly because a strong Russian nationalist movement opposed the importation of new Italian operas. Verdi's second and last French opera came soon after: *Don Carlos,* its première taking place at the Paris Opéra on March 11, 1867.

Verdi's second creative period, launched with *Rigoletto,* reached its summit with *Aïda. Aïda* was commissioned by the Khedive of Egypt as the initial attraction of a new theater in Cairo, and as part of the celebration attending the opening of the Suez Canal in 1869. Because Verdi took so long in writing this opera—and because the Franco-Prussian war delayed transportation of scenery and costumes from Paris to Egypt —*Aïda* was not produced until December 24, 1871. No expense had been spared in mounting the new opera. Radames' shield and helmet, for example, were made of solid silver, and the design for the throne in the third act had been copied from a work of art at the Louvre. The second-act triumphal march had a cast of three hundred, including Arabian trumpeters and a Cairo military band. Backdrops were copies of actual Egyptian buildings. Amneris' diadem was pure gold.

Nothing was spared to make the première as gala an event as Egypt had witnessed in many years. The Khedive and his harem occupied three boxes. Dignitaries from all parts of the world were generously distributed throughout the auditorium. Tickets for the performance summoned fabulous prices at the hands of speculators. Anticipation ran high, enthusiasm even higher. There was so much applause and cheering after each number that at one point the conductor had to turn around to the audience and shout angrily: "That isn't done!"

Verdi, who hated sea voyages and detested pomp and ceremony even more, did not go to the première. And he did not hesitate to express his outraged feelings at the way things were going in Cairo. *Aïda* in Cairo, he exclaimed, was "no longer art, but a trade, a pleasure party, a hunt, anything that can be run after, to which it is desired to give, if not success, at least notoriety." He insisted that the way *Aïda* was given in Cairo aroused in him only "disgust and humiliation."

The European première of *Aïda* took place at La Scala on February 8, 1872, presented with the dignity and high artistic purpose Verdi demanded. From there the opera

went on to become, as Prospero Bertini described it, "the world's most popular opera." Combining as it does spectacle with sound theatrical values, successfully blending the soundest dramatic and musical values, *Aïda* never fails to make a shattering impact on audiences. To Ernest Newman, *Aïda* was "the culminating point of the older Italian opera," achieving the "highest possible point of expression." To Dyneley Hussey, *Aïda* more than any other of Verdi's operas "exhibits the composer's inexhaustible melodic inspiration, which was capable of pouring out one great tune after another, without ever repeating ideas already used elsewhere, whatever family likeness there may be between them."

Like so many earlier Verdi masterpieces, *Aïda* first came to the United States by way of the Academy of Music in New York; the date was November 26, 1873. The first production at the Metropolitan Opera took place on November 12, 1886.

In his second creative period, which came to an end with *Aïda,* Verdi did not develop new forms or open up for opera new directions. He was satisfied to enrich both the style and structure of opera as it had previously been developed by Donizetti, Bellini, and Rossini. But he did succeed in carrying over into opera some new dramatic concepts. Convinced that good opera must always be good theater, he was ever concerned with the dramatic qualities of his librettos and with every possible detail of stagecraft. Lyricism was never sacrificed. As H. C. Colles wrote, Verdi demonstrated "an extraordinary power of depicting a graphic situation in vocal melodies." Many of the operas of this second period "have an irresistible grip upon the imagination by their sheer force of melody, and *Aïda* . . . is a unique example of a romantic story told entirely in a series of broad and intensely expressive tunes." Among the greatest of these melodies are Radames' radiant first-act hymn to Aïda, "Celeste Aïda," and Aïda's two unforgettable arias, "Ritorna vincitor!" and "O Patria mia."

After *Aïda,* Verdi took a sixteen-year holiday from writing operas. But creatively he was not completely silent in all that time. In 1873 he wrote a string quartet, one of his rare excursions into instrumental music. A year later he completed his most significant work outside the opera house, the *Man-*

zoni Requiem. The latter was written to honor the memory of Alessandro Manzoni, the distinguished Italian novelist, who died in 1873. "It is my heartfelt impulse," said Verdi, "or rather necessity, which prompts me to do honor as best I can to the great one whom I so much admired as a writer and venerated as a man." When first heard at the San Marco Church in Milan on May 22, 1874, the Requiem was received with almost hysterical enthusiasm. Without further delay it was heard in all parts of Italy, sometimes in unauthorized performances and occasionally in unusual transcriptions. Verdi himself went on a tour of Europe conducting this work. Wherever it was heard it was wildly acclaimed.

The Requiem is one of Verdi's masterworks. Brahms declared that only a genius could have written it. Though it is at times a contradiction between the dramatic and operatic as opposed to the religious and spiritual, the Requiem has an emotional impact that is inescapable. In commenting on what she called the "many-tinted emotion which Verdi permits himself in this Mass for the dead," Rosa Newmarch added, "we must remember, however, that there is an order of sacred music which, although it may be unsuitable for the service of the sanctuary does nevertheless express a loftily religious ideal with a kind of mundane amplitude and a lavish use of technical and emotional display. . . . Verdi, by temperament and practice an operatic composer, could not have written in a mystical or purely edifying spirit. In the Requiem he has created a work which moves in an atmosphere of intense emotion. Not contemplation but action is its ruling motive. Grief, awe, the horrors of Death and Judgment, are depicted here in forcible strokes. But hope and aspiring love are not entirely left out of the picture. . . . We must listen to it as an expression of Southern feeling, unrestrained but by no means irreverent. The melody is always Italian melody; the sentiment that moves at high pressure is Italian too."

During the more than fifteen years that Verdi wrote no operas, he devoted himself to his farm which he made into a highly profitable venture through the introduction of new machinery and other innovations. Though he sometimes spoke of doing an opera on Shakespeare's *King Lear* he probably would never again have written anything for the stage if Arrigo Boito, the eminent composer-librettist, had not brought him a masterly text based upon Shakespeare's *Othello.* Up to this point Verdi felt sure that he had written himself out in opera, that the style and traditions in which he had flourished had become old-fashioned in the face of the new aesthetics pronounced by Wagner, whom he greatly admired. But when he read Boito's libretto his creative impulses were once again stirred—and he went to work.

Otello, which was produced by La Scala on February 5, 1887, attracted world interest. Pilgrims from all parts of Europe came to attend the première. They heard not the work of a declining genius, as many had expected, but that of a genius who in his seventy-third year had scaled new summits. While the work was unquestionably pure Verdi in its lyricism, emotion, and Italian traditions, it also revealed new dramatic powers and uncovered a new gift for characterization. The opera was a sensation. As Blanche Tucker Roosevelt, who was present, recalled: "He was called out twenty times, and at the last recalls, hats and handkerchiefs were waved, and the house rose in a body. The emotion was something indescribable, and many wept. Verdi's carriage was dragged by the citizens to the hotel. He was toasted and serenaded; and at five in the morning . . . the crowds were still shrieking 'Viva Verdi!' "

The Otello in the première at La Scala was Francesco Tamagno, one of the greatest interpreters of the role. Tamagno chose the role when he made his debut at the Metropolitan Opera on March 24, 1891. Meanwhile, the American première of *Otello* had taken place at the Academy of Music in New York on April 16, 1888.

If *Otello* had been a phenomenon, coming as it did in Verdi's old age—and after such a prolonged silence—then the opera that followed it (Verdi's last) proved more amazing still. Once again stimulated by a Boito libretto based on Shakespeare—*Falstaff*— Verdi returned to comedy after half a century. Despite the fact that this was for Verdi a comparatively new area of creative activity, the eighty-year-old master fashioned what is probably his most remarkable stage achievement, a masterwork which must stand as an equal partner to such other monumental comedy operas as Mozart's *Le*

Nozze di Figaro and Wagner's *Die Meistersinger.*

Nevertheless, when first performed at La Scala on February 9, 1893, *Falstaff* did not make the same kind of impression that *Otello* had done. Only the more astute critics and the more discerning musicians perceived a far different Verdi, of incomparable creative powers. R. A. Streatfeild wrote: "*Falstaff* is the very incarnation of youth and high spirits. . . . He has combined a schoolboy's sense of fun with the grace and science of a Mozart. The part-writing is often exceedingly elaborate, but the most complicated concerted pieces flow on as naturally as a ballad. The glorious final fugue is an epitome of the work. It is really a marvel of contrapuntal ingenuity, yet it is so full of bewitching melody and healthy animal spirits that an uncultivated hearer would probably think it nothing but an ordinary jovial finale. In the last act Verdi strikes a deeper note. He has caught the charm and mystery of the sleeping forest with exquisite art. There is an unearthly beauty about this scene, which is new to students of Verdi. In the fairy music, too, he reveals yet another side of his genius. Nothing so delicate nor so rich in imaginative beauty has been written since the days of Weber."

Verdi wrote only one composition after *Falstaff*, the *Quattro pezzi sacri*, which includes an Ave Maria, Stabat Mater, Laudi alla Vergine Maria, and Te Deum for chorus. This work was completed in 1898, a year after the death of his wife. The loneliness that followed her death brought on in Verdi a physical and spiritual decline. He refused to inhabit his beloved Sant' Agata any longer. Instead he took rooms at the Grand Hotel in Milan to "vegetate," as he himself put it. His sight and hearing were beginning to fail. "My limbs no longer obey me," he lamented.

He suffered a paralytic stroke in January 1901, lingered for six days, and then died just before dawn on January 27. He was accorded the funeral of a national hero. A special session of the Senate listened to eulogies; the schools were closed; a quarter of a million Italians crowded the streets of Milan to watch the cortege which moved to the strains of a chorus from *Nabucco* directed by Toscanini. Verdi was buried on the grounds of the Musicians' Home which

he had founded and for whose support he had made adequate provision.

Blanche Roosevelt wrote that Verdi was like "a very good natured peasant, or shopkeeper, or perhaps a commercial traveler. Beyond a certain pontifical dignity of manner, acquired from the composer's position and long habit of ermine of success, Verdi is anything but a striking man. . . . His face is pleasant but rather stolid, his smile develops a certain cunning, faithful replica of what you have previously remarked in his eyes." Antonio Ghislanzoni described Verdi at fifty-five: "Tall in stature, active, vigorous, endowed with an iron constitution and with great energy of character, his vitality seems inexhaustible."

Some biographers have hinted that Verdi was miserly, too concerned with accumulating wealth. But Franz Werfel considered this slander: "Verdi was not avaricious; he was the very opposite—he was thrifty." And he was capable of enormous generosity. When in 1880 Italy went through a serious economic crisis, Verdi launched a program for remodeling his farm and home to provide employment for about two hundred peasants so that they might not suffer want. He never invested in the stock market to pile up gains. He preferred putting his money into his farm, or Italian funds that were "more patriotic than profitable," as Werfel noted. He built a hospital in Villanova and supported it; he provided the funds for an old-age home for musicians in Milan and set up a permanent subsidy for its support; he forgot none of his servants in his will. What he did avoid was to "participate in anything that smelled of 'benevolence,' of 'charity.' . . . If the papers printed a story that Giuseppe Verdi had made a donation for the renovation of the little church in his native village, or that Busseto must have a theater, he would fly into a rage."

In evaluating Verdi's artistic stature, Francis Toye pointed up his "unswerving quest for musical truth" and the "intensity of his musical emotion." Toye said: "The fundamental characteristic of his musical personality changed very little. In a sense we find in the composer of *Nabucco* the same traits of power, intensity, directness, and emotion as we find in the composer of *Otello*. The means by which these were expressed underwent an astonishing development, a radical change; but the characteristic qualities themselves were always there, whether in embryo, childhood, adolescence or maturity."

Tomás Luis de Victoria *1548-1611*

TOMÁS LUIS DE VICTORIA (in Italian, Tommaso Lodovico da Vittoria) was, despite his Spanish birth, one of the pre-eminent members of the Roman polyphonic school, second in importance only to Palestrina. He was born in Ávila about 1548. Little is known of his boyhood or musical education, but there is good reason to believe he was a boy chorister at the Ávila Cathedral, and that his music study took place with Escobedo.

In 1565 Victoria went to Rome to enter the Collegium Germanicum (founded thirteen years earlier by St. Ignatius Loyola), to begin studies for the clergy. He did not abandon music altogether. Soon after entering the Collegium he made several appearances there as a singer. He is believed to have spent some time studying with Palestrina. In any event Victoria was appointed *maestro di cappella* at the Santa Maria di Monserrato in Rome, and in 1571 he succeeded Palestrina as *maestro di cappella* at the Roman seminary.

Victoria's first publication appeared in 1572. This was a volume of thirty-three motets which were strongly influenced by Palestrina and are representative of the finest qualities of the Roman polyphonic school. "This work," according to W. H. Grattan-Flood, "displays the master almost in the plenitude of his powers." One of the motets in this collection, *O Vos omnes* for four voices, is one of his finest.

In 1573 the Collegium Germanicum was reorganized by papal order and endowed as a separate institution. Victoria was appointed its *maestro di cappella*. Two years later on August 28, 1575, Victoria was ordained a priest. After resigning from the Collegium he became chorister of S. Apollinare, holding this post for about four years. Then for seven years he officiated as chaplain of St. Philip Neri's church, S. Girolamo della Carità.

In 1585 Victoria published one of his most significant works, the *Passions in the Office for Holy Week (Officium Hebdomadae sanctae),* music for Palm Sunday and the last three days of Holy Week. Here we find works which, in the opinion of Henri Prunières, "reveal most characteristically the vehement and passionate genius of Victoria. Already, by their vigor and realistic detail, they announce the Passions of Bach, which they often surpass by the intensity of their mystical emotion."

Meanwhile, in 1583, in the preface to a volume of Masses, Victoria expressed a strong wish to return to his native land. That return, however, was delayed for more than a decade. When he did get back, probably in 1594, he became organist and choirmaster of the Descalzas Reales convent in Madrid, and chaplain to the Empress Mother Maria, sister of Philip II. His last composition, written in 1603 but published two years later, was a Requiem Mass (*Officium defunctorum*) in memory of the Empress Maria and was probably sung at her funeral. Many authorities regard this as his masterwork, and one of the supreme achievements in the entire literature of *a cappella* music. He died in Madrid on August 27, 1611.

Victoria produced about 180 works, all of them for the church; he was with Palestrina one of the most outstanding musical voices of the Counter Reformation. To J. B. Trend, Victoria was "the greatest figure in the music of Spanish history." Though strongly influenced in technical methods by the Flemish contrapuntists, and though essentially a product of the Roman polyphonic school, Victoria nevertheless brought to his writing a pronounced Spanish identity—notably in his deep-rooted mysticism, spiritual fervor, religious ecstasy, and asceticism. He has sometimes been identified as the El Greco of music. "Spanish musicians," said Trend, "feel his music to be intensely Spanish; they find in him a peculiar attitude of mind which is immediately tangible and makes them feel that he is one of themselves. He is as unmistakably and inimitably Spanish—Castilian even—as a . . . dusty road in La Manche." Trend then went on to explain: "The gruesome cries of the crowd in his Passions are the musical expression of those characteristic groups of colored wooden statuary, carried in procession through the streets; the sensuous morbidity of motets like *Vere languores* or *Jesu dulcis memoria* is less congenial to him than the swirling rhythms and the flowing contrapuntal texture of those Masses and motets which have their counterpart in the Assumptions and Resurrections of El Greco."

PRINCIPAL WORKS
Choral Music—Antiphons, canticles, hymns, Masses, motets, psalms.

ABOUT
Chase, G., The Music of Spain; Collet, H., Victoria; Reese, G., Music in the Renaissance; May, H. von, Die Kompositionstechnik T. L. de Victorias.

Henri Vieuxtemps *1820-1881*

HENRI VIEUXTEMPS was one of the outstanding violin virtuosos of his time, a founding father of an important French-Belgian school of violin playing. He was also a significant contributor to the violin repertory. He was born in Verviers, Belgium, on February 17, 1820, the son of a piano tuner and instrument maker. From his father Henri received his first lesson on the violin. He was soon turned over to Lecloux, a local teacher. Vieuxtemps was only six when he made his public debut with a concerto by Rode. At seven he toured Belgium. Charles de Bériot, himself a distinguished violinist, was so impressed by Vieuxtemps that he took him under his wing and gave him intensive training for three years. In 1828 Bériot took the boy to Paris, where he gave several praiseworthy concerts.

In 1831 Vieuxtemps left Bériot. He returned to Belgium, and independently continued his studies of the violin and his development of a virtuoso career. Two years

HENRI VIEUXTEMPS

later he toured Austria and Germany. In Vienna, where for a while he studied harmony with Sechter, he was acclaimed for his performance of Beethoven's Violin Concerto and for his uncommon gift for playing at sight. In Germany he aroused the enthusiasm of Schumann, who wrote: "Vieuxtemps is the greatest genius of the young masters. His playing has the brilliancy and the perfume of the flower." Vieuxtemps's first appearances in London followed in the spring of 1834. In the winter of 1835 Vieuxtemps settled for a while in Paris, giving concerts and studying composition with Reicha.

For the next few years his tours of Europe were frequent and extensive. His playing was characterized not only by complete technical assurance but also by nobility of style, an unusual sweetness of tone, and purity of intonation. In 1838 he scored such a triumph in Russia that he was invited to return the following year for numerous other performances. His sensational concerts in Antwerp in 1840 brought him the decoration of the Order of Leopold. In many of these appearances he featured his own compositions, including such important works as the First Violin Concerto in E major and the *Fantaisie-Caprice*. "That Vieuxtemps is the greatest and most masterly of living violinists," Wagner wrote in a Swiss newspaper, "is something I need hardly add on top of the established judgment of all experts. But that in his compositions he contributes a quality wholly unusual, great and stimulat-

Vieuxtemps: vyû-tän'

ing, is something I should like to point out with especial emphasis to all those who revere genuine art."

In 1845 Vieuxtemps married Josephine Elder, a concert pianist. During the previous season he had made his first tour of the United States, where a highlight of some of his concerts was a set of pyrotechnical variations on "Yankee Doodle." Vieuxtemps made two more tours of America after that, in 1857 with Thalberg, and in 1870 with Christine Nilsson.

After his first visit to the United States, Vieuxtemps returned to Russia where he was appointed solo violinist to the Czar and professor of violin at the Conservatory. Concert appearances in Europe, however, were not neglected. The two concertos which are most frequently played today were written for these tours: the Concerto No. 4 in D minor in 1849-50 (the composer's own favorite among his concertos), and the fifth Concerto in A minor in 1858. Berlioz, hearing Vieuxtemps play the D minor concerto, reported that the violinist "showed himself no less remarkable as a composer than he was incomparable as a virtuoso," adding that "there are some talents that disarm envy."

The triumphs of his concert life were tempered by personal tragedy. In 1868 both his wife and his father died. He sought escape from his grief in more extended tours, the last of which took place in 1870-71.

In 1871 Vieuxtemps settled in Brussels to become professor of violin and director of popular concerts at the Conservatory. In 1872 he was elected a member of the Académie Royale of Belgium. He was forced to relinquish his posts in 1873 when he was stricken with a paralysis of his left side. He was visiting Algiers, hoping that the favorable climate would relieve his physical distress, when he died suddenly at Mustapha on June 6, 1881.

Strongly influenced by Paganini, Vieuxtemps filled his violin music with dazzling pyrotechnical effects, and often with the kind of staccato passage work that he excelled in performing. He wrote six violin concertos, and many shorter pieces for the violin, including the *Ballade et polonaise* and the *Fantaisie-Caprice.*

Arthur Hartmann wrote of Vieuxtemps's concertos: "We can search in vain for works which in dramatic intensity, in daring virtu-

osity and effectiveness equal the first, third, fourth and fifth concertos. And when we recall that the first great concerto was written by Vieuxtemps when but eighteen years of age, the case may well stand as being without parallel. To my critical judgment, the fifth concerto represents a unique achievement in violinistic art, and is exemplary for its beautiful symmetry, skill and art of construction and for its wealth of noble and musically dramatic utterances."

PRINCIPAL WORKS

Chamber Music—3 string quartets; violin sonatas; Viola Sonata.

Orchestral Music—6 violin concertos; 2 cello concertos; Fantaisie-Caprice, for violin and orchestra; Souvenirs de Russie, for violin and orchestra; Ballade et polonaise, for violin and orchestra; Fantasia appassionata, for violin and orchestra; Old England, for violin and orchestra.

Violin Music—Reverie; Rondino; Saltarello; Sérénité; Hommage à Paganini; Andante et Rondo; Suite in B minor; Marche funèbre; concert études, fantasies, variations.

ABOUT

Bergmans, P., Henri Vieuxtemps; Kufferath, M., Henri Vieuxtemps; Radoux, J. T., Vieuxtemps, sa vie, ses œuvres.

Giovanni Battista Viotti *1755-1824*

GIOVANNI BATTISTA VIOTTI was born in Fontanetto da Po, in Piedmont, Italy, on May 12, 1755. His father, a blacksmith who played the horn, gave the child his first music lessons. When Viotti was eleven, he received additional instruction from a lute player in Fontanetto for an extended visit.

In 1766 Viotti attracted the interest of Alfonso del Pozzo, Prince of Cisterna, by playing some difficult compositions at sight. The Prince welcomed the young violinist into his household and defrayed the expenses of Viotti's study with Pugnani. "I do not regret the money," the Prince was quoted as saying. "We cannot pay too highly for the existence of such an artist." Besides studying with Pugnani, Viotti started writing music even though he had had no instruction in theory up to this time; he completed his first violin concerto when he was fourteen.

In 1780 Viotti undertook the first of many concert tours through Europe. During the next decade he appeared with increasing

Viotti: vyôt′tē

GIOVANNI BATTISTA VIOTTI

success in Germany, Switzerland, Poland, and Russia. By 1783 he was recognized as one of the foremost violinists of his age. On March 15, 1782, he had created a sensation in Paris with his performance at a Concert Spirituel; one of the French critics included him "among the greatest masters."

At the height of his fame and artistic powers, Viotti suddenly decided in 1783 to withdraw completely from the concert stage. One possible explanation is that he was impatient with audiences who revealed no discrimination in their approbation of his work. From that time, Viotti appeared only in private performances, usually at salons. In 1784 he performed for Marie Antoinette, who engaged him as court violinist. A year later he was also heard frequently at private concerts given at Cherubini's home, where he was then living. Viotti did not, however, discourage the public presentation of his own compositions; his *Symphonies Concertantes,* for two violins and piano, were introduced in Paris in 1787.

In 1788 Viotti became a partner of Léonard, the hairdresser of Marie Antoinette, in managing the Théâtre de Monsieur for the performance of operas. Viotti overhauled this institution radically, instituting many reforms and introducing many new singers. The company might have become a successful fixture in the musical life of Paris but for the Revolution, which compelled Viotti to abandon France in 1792, on the threat of

arrest, and escape to London. His fortune confiscated in Paris, Viotti was now forced to return to his concert work in order to support himself. In 1794 and 1795 he appeared at almost all of the concerts arranged by John Salamon. He also became the conductor of Italian operas at the King's Theatre, where one of his most celebrated songs, "La Polacca," was interpolated into a performance of Paisiello's *La Serva padrona* on May 29, 1794.

Falsely accused of being in league with the revolutionaries in Paris, and of harboring sentiments inimical to the Crown, Viotti was ordered by the authorities to leave England in 1798. He went into voluntary exile in Schönfeld, Germany, near Hamburg, and devoted himself to composing and teaching. In 1801 he was fully cleared and allowed to return to London. Unable now to recapture his former position as a musician in that city, he ventured into the wine business in which he sustained very great losses. These financial involvements compelled him to withdraw more and more from his musical activities. By 1813 Viotti was once again able to associate himself with English music by helping to found the Royal Philharmonic Society, which he occasionally conducted during the next few years, and which performed some of his compositions.

In 1818 he returned to Paris, where he was warmly welcomed by leading French musicians and where he made triumphant returns to the concert hall. He was soon appointed director of the Italian Opera, but there misfortunes plagued him and he found himself on the brink of financial ruin. Broken in spirit, his health shattered, Viotti returned to London in 1822 to spend his last days. He was penniless and burdened by debts he could not hope to repay. He died in London on March 3, 1824, owing one of his friends twenty-four thousand francs. "If I die before I can pay off this debt," he wrote shortly before he died, "I pray that everything I have in the world may be sold off, realized, and sent to Madame Chinnery, or her heirs, praying only that they shall pay to my brother, André Viotti, the sum of eight hundred francs that I owe him." He further expressed the wish that no money be spent on his funeral because "a little earth will suffice for such a miserable creature as myself."

In his prime Viotti was impressive both in appearance and personality. His head was described as "grand and powerful," his features as "expressive, amiable and radiant," and his figure as "well-proportioned and graceful." He was blessed with courtly manners and his conversations were spirited. Women were attracted to him, even though he showed little interest in them and never married. He was fond of science and literature and was a devoted naturalist. "A violet hidden under the leaves," M. Eymar wrote, "transported him with the liveliest of joy. . . . He would spend hours lying on the grass admiring a carnation or breathing the fragrance of a rose."

As a composer, Viotti is today remembered most often for a single work, the Violin Concerto No. 22 in A minor. This is a work remarkable both for its lyrical content and its freshness of thematic development. Written in the late eighteenth century, it is advanced for its time in its development of the classical sonata structure and in its orchestral and harmonic language. Some critics refer to it as one of the first "modern" violin concertos. In 1794 one of Viotti's contemporaries described this masterwork: "His themes are splendid; they are developed with intelligence, tastefully contrasted. . . . His harmonies are rich. . . . His rhythms are marked."

Pierre Baillot, who was also a contemporary, was greatly moved by this and other Viotti concertos because they "exalt the soul. It is impossible not to discover in them a poetic feeling, not to see in them some of the heroes of Homer."

Viotti's seven books of string quartets were unknown to most music lovers and musicologists until the Society for Forgotten Music resurrected two of them (B-flat major and G major) and recorded them. They came from a volume entitled *Trois quatuors concertants,* issued in Paris in 1818. These works reveal the same kind of personal lyricism and distinguished workmanship found in Viotti's best violin concertos. They belong, said Vernon Duke, "in the very first rank of eighteenth-century chamber music... full of sparkling gaiety, vigor, and bright Italian sunshine."

PRINCIPAL WORKS

Chamber Music—56 duos; 36 trios for two violins and bass; 15 divertissements; 9 sonatas; 7 sets of string quartets; 6 string quartets on popular tunes.

Orchestral Music—29 violin concertos; 10 piano concertos; 2 symphonies concertantes.

ABOUT

Giazotto, R., Giovanni Battista Viotti; La Laurencie, L. de, L'École française de violon de Lully à Viotti; Pougin, A., Viotti et l'école moderne de violon.

Ménestral, April 1924; Revue de musicologie, August 1924; Strad, May 1930.

Giovanni Battista Vitali *1644-1692*

GIOVANNI BATTISTA VITALI, an important figure in the Bologna school of violin music, was born in Cremona, Italy, about 1644. He studied counterpoint with Cazzati, the *maestro di cappella* at the San Petronio Church in Bologna. In 1666 he played the viola da braccio in the church orchestra and produced a volume of balletti and dances for two violins and continuo, his first publication. In the preface, Marino Silvani extols the merits of Vitali both as a performer and a composer, pointing up the fact that Vitali already enjoyed a considerable reputation. Vitali's first volume of trio sonatas appeared in 1667, the year he was appointed a member of the Accademia dei Filaschisi and of the Accademia dei Filarmonici in Bologna. Several of his works were given at this time in Bologna, including *L'Alloro trionfante,* a cantata he wrote with Giovanni Paolo, and an orchestral overture.

Vitali's most significant sonatas appeared in his fifth opus, published in 1669. These works were in the sonata da chiesa form (in several movements with continual changes of tempo from fast to slow to fast). Here an idiomatic style for the violin is realized. As Martin F. Bukofzer wrote: "Vitali's intimate knowledge of string technique is unmistakably proven by his themes which, directly inspired by violinistic idioms, were admirably designed, like broad evocative gestures." Vitali's style was contrapuntal, but "he supported the contrapuntal flow of the parts with the impelling force of his directed, if simple, harmonies and, consequently could sustain the movements more firmly than could his predecessors."

On December 1, 1674, Vitali transferred his activities to Modena, where he assumed the post of second *maestro di cappella* at the court of Francesco II. A decade later he became full *maestro di cappella*. Between 1677 and 1692 he issued several more volumes of sonatas, balletti, and dances, as well as concertos. There is good reason to believe that when Purcell wrote his own sonatas "in imitation of the Italian masters," published in 1683, he used the works of Vitali as a model.

Giovanni Battista Vitali died in Modena on October 12, 1692.

The traditions of the Bologna violin school were carried on by his son Tommaso Antonio Vitali (born c. 1665). One of the younger Vitali's compositions is still a favorite in the violin repertory. It is the Chaconne in G minor, for solo violin and figured bass, one of the two most celebrated chaconnes ever written for the violin, the other being that of Johann Sebastian Bach.

PRINCIPAL WORKS

Chamber Music—Balletti, correnti, dances, sonatas, trio-sonatas.

Orchestral Music—Concertos, overtures, sinfonias.

ABOUT

Bukofzer, M., Music in the Baroque Era.

Tommaso Lodovico da Vittoria

see Tomás Luis de Victoria

Antonio Vivaldi *1669-1741*

ANTONIO VIVALDI, one of the masters of the solo concerto and the concerto grosso, was born in Venice. The year of his birth has long been set somewhere between 1675 and 1678, but modern musicological research tends to set the date as 1669, possibly June 11. Vivaldi received intensive training in music from his father, Giovanni Battista, a violinist in the orchestra of St. Mark's cathedral, and later from Giovanni Legrenzi. But Antonio was directed not to music but to the church. He took the tonsure in 1693, and received his holy orders sometime before 1703. During this period he composed a considerable number of works and perfected his violin technique.

In 1703 Vivaldi was engaged as teacher of the violin at the Ospedale della Pietà in Venice where, from 1709 to 1740, he also served as *maestro de' concerti*. The Pietà,

a shelter for about six thousand girls—orphans and illegitimate children—held many concerts for which Vivaldi wrote a great amount of instrumental music. "Each concert," reported a contemporary, "is given by about forty girls. I assure you there is nothing so charming as to see a young and pretty nun in her white robe, with a bouquet of pomegranate flowers in her hair, leading the orchestra and beating time with all the precision imaginable."

Though Vivaldi remained attached to the Ospedale until about 1740, he managed to travel throughout Europe during this period, establishing his reputation everywhere as a violinist of the first order. For a four-year period (probably between 1718 and 1722) he was *maestro di cappella* in Mantua to Prince Philip, Landgrave of Hesse-Darmstadt. After 1735 he stayed mainly in Venice, where he became a dominant figure in its musical life, personally honored by the Pope. He had always been prolific as a composer, but never more so than now. As his contemporary De Brosses said of him: "The old man composes like wildfire. I have heard him boast of being able to compose a concerto, completely in all parts, in less time than it takes a copyist to write it out."

In 1740 Vivaldi left Venice for Vienna where he hoped to find a lucrative post at the court of Charles VI. This opening never materialized. The last months of his life were spent in obscurity and poverty. He died in Vienna in July 1741 and on July 28 he was consigned to a pauper's grave.

Vivaldi's red hair and red clerical garb earned him the nickname of "the red priest," a description that stuck throughout his life. In his memoirs, Carlo Goldoni said that Vivaldi "was much better known by his sobriquet than by his real name." From two contemporary portraits—one by P. L. Ghezzi in 1723, and the other by François Morellon de la Cave in 1725—we further learn that he had long, curly hair (often dressed so neatly that it was taken for a wig). He had a "receding forehead, a prominent arched nose, widely dilated nostrils, a large mouth, and a pointed chin."

He was a man of strange contradictions, as Marc Pincherle noted: "Weak and sickly, yet of a fiery temperament; quick to become irritated, quick to become calm; quick to pass from worldly thoughts to a superstitious piety; tractable when necessary, but persevering; mystical, yet ready to come down to earth again when a specific concern was at issue, and by no means unskillful in handling his affairs."

During most of his life he was in poor health, given to attacks of asthma. But his lively nature and creative fertility were unaffected by his indisposition. He remained to the end a man of great piety who —as Ludwig Gerber said in his *Lexikon* published in 1790—"would not put his rosary aside until he took up the pen to write an opera, which happened frequently."

Vivaldi was an extraordinarily prolific composer. His immense output included about 50 operas, 25 chamber cantatas, 14 Vespers, 73 sonatas, 400 concertos, and sundry other compositions. His operas are completely forgotten, and only occasionally is one of his church compositions revived or recorded. When this happens we realize that this distinguished predecessor of Bach and Handel was a master of the contrapuntal technique, capable of their nobility of thought and grandeur of concept. Among Vivaldi's masterworks to survive through occasional performances and through recordings are the Gloria Mass, which bears a remarkable structural resemblance to the Gloria of Bach's B minor Mass (written later), and an oratorio, *Juditha Triumphans*.

But it is on his instrumental music—and most specifically on his concertos—that Vivaldi's present-day eminence rests. Inheriting the form and techniques of the solo concerto and the concerto grosso from Torelli and Corelli, Vivaldi brought to them such a fresh melodic and rhythmic approach, such variety of mood and nuance, such a majesty of style, such solidity of structure that with him the concerto achieves its most advanced stage of technical development and artistic fulfillment before Johann Sebastian Bach and Handel.

Donald Jay Grout thus described the Vivaldi concerto: "Most of Vivaldi's concertos are in the usual eighteenth-century pattern of three movements: An Allegro, a slow movement in the same key or a closely related one (relative minor, dominant, or subdominant); and a final Allegro somewhat shorter and sprightlier than the first. Though a few movements are found in the older fugal style, the texture is . . . [more] homophonic than contrapuntal—but homophonic in the late Baroque sense, with much

ANTONIO VIVALDI

incidental use of counterpoint and with particular emphasis on the two outer voices. Typical of the late Baroque, also, is Vivaldi's constant use of sequential patterns."

What perhaps most distinguished Vivaldi's concertos from those that preceded him is the deep emotional content, the expressive lyricism, and the poetic thinking he frequently brought to his writing, and particularly so in many of his slow movements. As Henri Prunières wrote: "Some of the slow movements in the concerti and in the violin and cello sonatas are as sublime as anything in music. Utterly unconventional is the plastic beauty of his melodies; they are imbued with pathos, without, however, showing a trace of that lyrical extravagance which will soon undermine the great Italian art."

Vivaldi's first volume of concertos, which appeared about 1712, is entitled *L'Estro armonico (Harmonic Inspiration)*, op. 3. We find here four concertos for a solo instrument or solo instruments and orchestra, and eight concerti grossi. Of the former the most famous is the Violin Concerto in A minor, while the most frequently performed of the eight concerti grossi is that in D minor (the eleventh in the group), in a contemporary adaptation made by Alexander Siloti.

Other concertos appeared in op. 4 (*La Stravaganza*), 6, 7, and in *Il Cimento dell'armonia e dell'invenzione (The Trial of Harmony and Invention)* op. 8. It is in this last volume that we find the four concertos that are most frequently represented today on orchestral programs (usually in an adaptation by Bernardino Molinari). These four concertos are collectively entitled *The Four Seasons (Le quattro stagioni),* each intended as a programmatic description of a different season of the year beginning with Spring. A sonnet (probably written by the composer) appears at the head of each concerto to explain the programmatic content of the music. For further clarification the composer invented a device whereby letters placed over various sentences in the sonnet appear also in music over the passages which describe the sentences. Then the music goes on to an almost literal interpretation of the text. Trills simulate the singing of birds; running figures describe the movement of running fountains; staccato figures depict the chattering of teeth in the winter's cold. The music brings up pictures of a violent storm, a flowery meadow, nymphs and shepherds dancing on the heath, farmers celebrating harvest time, people sitting with contentment at their firesides. The music imitates the cooing of a turtle dove, the song of a cuckoo, and the voice of a goldfinch.

It is impossible to exaggerate the influence Vivaldi had on Johann Sebastian Bach and later composers. We know that as a boy Bach used to copy Vivaldi's music and thus commit it to memory; that in his mature years he transcribed some of Vivaldi's concertos and had them in mind in writing his own works in the concerto form. Bach's Brandenburg Concertos, said Olin Downes, are "unthinkable without Vivaldi's precedent. . . . Vivaldi's solo concertos for violin unquestionably gave J. S. Bach the models for his own solo concertos for the same instrument." And, Downes continued, "His music anticipates the methods and divisions of the classic symphony that came later not only in thematic manipulation in which the Germans far exceeded him but as regards contrasting themes and symphonic sections, and also as concerns the programmatic and coloristic tendencies which so strongly influenced the symphony and symphonic poem."

PRINCIPAL WORKS

Chamber Music—Over 70 sonatas for various solo instruments and accompaniment.

Choral Music—Juditha Triumphans; Moyses Deus Pharaonis; Gloria Mass; cantatas.

Operas—About 50 operas including Nerone fatto Cesare, L'Incoronazione di Dario, Farnace, Montezuma, L'Olimpiade, Griselda, and Feraspe.

Orchestral Music—Over 500 concertos; 23 sinfonias.

Vocal Music—Stabat Mater; 43 arias; secular cantatas.

ABOUT

Bukofzer, M. F., Music in the Baroque Era; Guerrini, G., Vivaldi; Pincherle, M., Vivaldi.

Richard Wagner *1813-1883*

WILHELM RICHARD WAGNER, creator of the music drama, was born in Leipzig, Germany, on May 22, 1813. A considerable amount of evidence, gathered by Ernest Newman and other noted musicologists, indicates that he was the illegitimate son of Ludwig Geyer, an actor, and Johanna Wagner. All his life Wagner himself suspected that this was the case. Richard was six months old when the city police clerk, Karl Friedrich Wagner (long accepted as being Wagner's legitimate father), died. About a year later Johanna Wagner married Geyer. There is no evidence (as was asserted for many years) that Geyer was a Jew.

As a boy Wagner showed considerable aptitude for drama and poetry, probably stimulated by his grandfather, who was a man of exceptional culture. As a pupil at the Kreuzschule in Dresden, which he entered at nine, Wagner was an apt student of Greek, history, and mythology. At fourteen he wrote a long poetic play in the style of Shakespeare, in which forty-two characters died during the course of the tragedy.

His music study was haphazard at best. He took random lessons in violin and piano, showing little enthusiasm for either. Then he received some instruction in theory in Leipzig. He proved hardly more receptive to his academic studies. Because of his indolence and indifference to textbook study, he was expelled from the Thomasschule in Leipzig. While attending the University of Leipzig for a brief period he was more interested in drinking and gambling than in acquiring knowledge.

Music began to dominate his life after he heard parts of Weber's *Der Freischütz* and Beethoven's *Fidelio* and Seventh Symphony. Even without adequate preparation, he now plunged into the composition of several am-

Wagner: väg'nĕr

bitious works, including a piano sonata, a string quartet, and a concert overture for orchestra. The last was performed in Leipzig in 1830. In 1831 he started his most important period of study, taking lessons in composition with Theodor Weinlig; these lasted about six months. When this formal training was over, he never again had another teacher. Whatever else he learned about music came from studying treatises and texts and by making a most painstaking dissection of the Beethoven symphonies, all of which he transcribed for the piano. Influenced by Beethoven, he completed a Symphony in C major which was given in 1833 in Leipzig and Prague. And in 1832 he tried his hand at an opera—*Die Hochzeit,* for which he wrote his own libretto. *Die Hochzeit,* however, remained just sketches.

In 1833 he received his first musical appointment when he was made chorusmaster of the Würzburg Theater. While thus employed in 1834, he composed his first complete opera, *Die Feen,* for which he wrote a text based on a play by Carlo Gozzi. "The music," said Ernest Newman, "is decidedly interesting. . . . The first two acts and the overture are full of striking things. There is no question as to the thorough competence of Wagner's technique at the time: everything flows with the utmost ease and clearness from his pen." *Die Feen* was never produced in Wagner's lifetime; its première took place five years after Wagner's death, in Munich on June 29, 1888.

In 1834 Wagner became the conductor of the Magdeburg Opera, a mediocre and insolvent company whose performances left much to be desired. While in Magdeburg, Wagner completed his second opera, *Das Liebesverbot,* his libretto based on Shakespeare's *Measure for Measure.* Here Wagner made use for the first time of the technique of the *leitmotif* or "leading motive," which was to become basic to his mature style. "There is . . . much in it," Newman pointed out, "that is eloquent of the coming dramatist in music—a surprising quickness of apprehension, a faculty for big picture-building, and above all an irresistible ardor." *Das Liebesverbot* was introduced in Magdeburg under the composer's direction on March 29, 1836. It was a fiasco, and was instrumental in sending the company into bankruptcy.

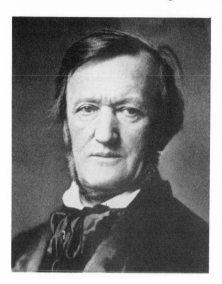

RICHARD WAGNER

Wagner then became the conductor of the Königsberg Opera in East Prussia. There he married Minna Planer, an actress, on November 24, 1836. In 1837 he became the music director of the Riga Opera. For two years he conducted performances of opera and symphonic music; at the same time he completed the libretto and music for two acts of a new opera, *Rienzi.*

Friedrich Pecht, who knew Wagner well in 1838, spoke of Wagner's musical scholarship even during these years of apprenticeship. Pecht wrote in the *Allgemeine musikalische Zeitung:* "His knowledge of the entire musical literature of every epoch was almost inconceivable for such a young man. He was just as familiar with the earlier Italians, Palestrina, Pergolesi, and so forth, as with the older Germans. It was from him that I first gained an idea of Johann Sebastian Bach. Gluck was even then his constant study. Haydn's nature painting; Mozart's genius and the unhappy effects of his position in Salzburg and Vienna; the special characteristics of the French composers Lully, Boieldieu, and Auber; the simple, if popular charms, of his beloved Weber; the figure of Beethoven towering far above them all; Mendelssohn's elegant drawing-room music —every one of them he described to us with such animation and vigor, singing many of the tunes, that they still remain in my memory exactly as he represented them."

By 1839 Wagner had become so hopelessly involved in debt that he lost his position as conductor and was forced to flee in order to evade a prison sentence. Without passports (they had been confiscated) Wagner and his wife were smuggled aboard the *Thetis,* a vessel sailing from the Prussian harbor of Pillau to London. After a particularly stormy voyage which extended an eight-day trip into three and a half weeks, the Wagners arrived in London on August 12, 1839. Five weeks later they arrived in Paris, where Wagner, equipped with letters of introduction to influential French musicians, hoped to make his way with his new opera, *Rienzi.*

He came with high hopes, feeling confident that a city that worshiped Meyerbeer would certainly react favorably to an opera like *Rienzi.* But everywhere he went he met apathy and indifference. *Rienzi* was turned down by the Opéra. To survive, Wagner had to accept all kinds of hack work, and even so there were periods when he and his wife were penniless and hungry. For several weeks in 1840 he was confined to a debtor's prison. It is more than probable that these harrowing years of frustration, humiliation, and suffering in Paris did much to warp Wagner's personality, to make of him an unscrupulous, selfish, and ruthless man. But his creative energy and will were not affected. He completed *Eine Faust Ouvertüre (A Faust Overture),* one of two of his symphonic works that is still played; and he worked passionately on the libretto and score of a new opera, *Der fliegende Holländer (The Flying Dutchman).*

Nobody in Paris was interested in Wagner's music. But the director of the Paris Opéra was willing to buy his libretto of *The Flying Dutchman* for five hundred francs, to be used by another composer. (That other composer was the now forgotten Pierre-Louis-Philippe Dietsch, whose version of *The Flying Dutchman* was produced at the Opéra on November 9, 1842.) With the money acquired from this sale, Wagner was able to sustain himself and his wife for several months. But despite his bargain with the Opéra, Wagner continued to work on his own version of *The Flying Dutchman.* "To compose music," Wagner later revealed in his autobiography, "I needed a piano, for after a nine months' interruption of all kinds of musical production, I had to work myself back to a musical atmosphere. I hired a piano, but when it came I walked

round and round it in an agony of anxiety. I feared to find I was no longer a musician. I began with the 'Sailors' Chorus' and the 'Spinning Song.' Everything went easily, fluently and I actually shouted for joy as I felt through my whole being that I was still an artist. In seven weeks the opera was finished."

The tide began to turn in Wagner's favor in 1842. *Rienzi* was produced at the Dresden Opera on October 20 and proved a tremendous success. This opera, with a libretto by the composer based on Bulwer-Lytton's novel, is the earliest Wagnerian opera still performed. It is, as its composer stated, "on a grand and inspiring scale. . . . I still kept more or less to the . . . operatic standpoint." Lawrence Gilman said of it: "There is no denying the crude vigor of the music; and it has something of the quality which Wagner always possessed, the quality of salient invention."

The Flying Dutchman came to the Dresden Opera on January 2, 1843. In the grand romantic tradition of *Rienzi,* based on an old legend adapted by Heinrich Heine, it also met with considerable public favor. In consequence of the acclaim accorded to both *Rienzi* and *The Flying Dutchman,* Wagner received the important appointment of musical director of the Dresden Opera in 1843. He kept the post for six years. His regime was one of the most important eras in the history of that venerable opera company.

During his regime he introduced another of his operas: *Tannhäuser,* first seen on October 19, 1845. This was a giant stride ahead of both *Rienzi* and *The Flying Dutchman* in originality of conception and homogeneity of style, in the inspiration of its musical material and the skill of the composer's technique. There is a good deal in *Tannhäuser* to foreshadow the fully mature style of the later master, not only in the increasing use of the *leitmotif* technique, but also in the composer's sure dramatic instinct which proved unfailing in his projection of a climactic scene or in portraying character through his music. (The first American performance of *Tannhäuser* took place at the Stadt Theater in New York, on April 4, 1859. Its introduction into the repertory of the Metropolitan Opera took place on the opening night of the 1884-1885 season, November 17, 1884.)

Between 1846 and 1848, Wagner completed *Lohengrin,* with a libretto based on medieval legends. Even more than *Tannhäuser,* the new opera anticipated the artistic directions Wagner would soon take. Romantic in concept and subject matter, *Lohengrin* still clung to some of the old operatic methods. But as William Foster Apthorp noted, "the musical style is distinction itself. Weber almost disappears; what there is left of him is no more than the little occasional touch of Haydn to be found in the works of Beethoven's second period. For the first time, Wagner succeeds in raising his music to the full level of his poetic conception; the vehicle is worthy of the load! The third manner crops up, too, in a far more developed condition in the opening scene of the second act. *Lohengrin* was emphatically Wagner's transition opera; after it, he left the 'opera' entirely for the music drama."

The first performance of *Lohengrin* took place in Weimar on August 28, 1850, under the direction of Franz Liszt. (The American première was at the Stadt Theater in New York on April 3, 1871.) Wagner was not present in Weimar to see his opera performed; indeed, the opera achieved popularity throughout Germany before Wagner was able to attend a presentation. The reason was that by 1850 Wagner had become a political exile. The revolutionary tides that had swept across Europe in 1848 and 1849 had caught Wagner in their undertow. He had become a member of the Vaterlandsverein, a radical political organization. Through it he had become deeply involved in the German revolutionary movement that reached its climax in May of 1849. To avoid arrest, Wagner had fled from Saxony. For a while he found refuge in Weimar with Franz Liszt, whom he had previously met in Paris, who was now an ardent believer in Wagner's genius, and who would soon present *Lohengrin* to the world. But when Wagner discovered that a price had been placed on his head, he escaped from Weimar to Paris. From there he proceeded to Zurich, Switzerland, in May 1849 to establish a residence there that lasted about twelve years.

During a great part of his exile, Wagner dedicated himself to the writing of numerous pamphlets and essays elucidating his ideas about the music drama, and outlining his aesthetic principles as a composer for the theater. In *Die Kunst und die Revolution* (1849), *Das Kunstwerk der Zukunft* (1850), *Kunst und Klima* (1850), and *Oper und Drama* (1851), he forcefully propounded those ideas and theories which he himself would soon put into practice. Music, he maintained, had too long been the end in opera, with drama just the means; the emphasis, he insisted, should be the other way around. Indeed, he felt strongly that opera —or music drama as he now preferred to designate it—should be a synthesis of all the arts. He affirmed that the nineteenth century could produce a theater of its own as majestic as the one the ancient Greeks had created. He wanted a musical theater in which the long-existing and arbitrary distinction between recitative and aria would be eliminated; he wanted music in opera to be a continuous and uninterrupted melody, a melody closer to musical declamation *(Sprechsingen)* than to the old-fashioned aria. Wagner saw the orchestra as a chief protagonist in his musical scheme. He planned the *leitmotif* as the spine and sinew of his musical texture.

Once he had clarified his thinking on what the music drama should be like, Wagner proceeded to follow his principles. While still in Dresden he had become interested in the Teutonic sagas of Scandinavia and Germany. From this material he had prepared a long poem, *Siegfried's Death.* He now sought to adapt this poem into a workable libretto. But as he labored on this text he soon realized that the subject was too vast for a single opera. In 1851 he prefixed to *Siegfried's Death* a second text entitled *Young Siegfried.* But he still felt that too much had been left unsaid. In 1852 Wagner added the poetic drama, *Die Walküre,* and when that was finished he decided to append a short libretto as a prelude to the trilogy; he called the prelude *Das Rheingold.* The text for all four dramas collectively entitled *Der Ring des Nibelungen (The Ring of the Nibelungs)* was completed in 1852, and was published a year later for private distribution.

Now he went to work on his music. Living on the bounty of a wealthy benefactor, Otto Wesendonk—in a small villa, "The Asyl," on the Wesendonk estate—Wagner completed the score of *Das Rheingold* in 1854, and that of *Die Walküre* in 1856. While this Herculean creative effort was going on, Wagner's personal life was becoming turbulent and complicated. He was still living with his wife, Minna, but their marriage had not been going smoothly for several years. They were incompatible in many ways; Wagner's infidelities contributed additional fuel to the combustion of two fiery temperaments. During the period in which he was laboring on the first two dramas of his saga, Wagner was having an illicit affair with Mathilde, the wife of his benefactor. One consequence of this love affair was Wagner's set of love songs to Mathilde Wesendonk's poems, the *Wesendonk Gedichte,* among which is the very popular "Träume" ("Dreams"). Of far greater importance was the completion of his mighty drama of love and death, *Tristan und Isolde.* Did the passions surging through the imperishable love music of the second act come as an immediate result of Wagner's own emotions at the time? Or did Wagner fall in love with Mathilde because his inmost emotions had been aroused by the writing of his music? Ernest Newman inclined to the belief that the latter may very well hold true. In any event, *Tristan und Isolde* was completed in August 1859. The world première took place in Munich on June 10, 1865, Hans von Bülow conducting. In America, the première took place at the Metropolitan Opera on December 1, 1886.

In 1855 Wagner interrupted his creative labors to conduct eight symphony concerts in London and three in Paris. In 1861 he was once again in Paris, this time to help supervise an ambitious production of *Tannhäuser* under the patronage of Princess Metternich, wife of the Austrian Ambassador to France. *Tannhäuser,* with over a hundred and fifty rehearsals, was staged on a very lavish scale. On March 13, 1861, it was finally heard at the Opéra in the French language; it was for this production that Wagner interpolated into his opera the music of the Venusberg scene to cater to the French partiality for ballet sequences. The first performance in Paris went well. But during the second presentation, on March 18, members of the aristocratic Jockey Club of Paris started a riot in a carefully planned maneuver to discredit Wagner and his opera. They succeeded so well that the scheduled fourth and fifth presentations were canceled.

In 1860 Wagner received an amnesty that enabled him to return from exile to any part of Germany but Saxony. Two years later he was also given official sanction to return to Saxony. Although he was active as a conductor, his finances were in such a sorry state that it seemed inevitable that he would again be faced with imprisonment. At this critical juncture, King Ludwig II, who had recently ascended the Bavarian throne, asked Wagner to come to Munich where he stood ready to be his patron. The king promised not only to take care of Wagner's personal needs but to do everything he could to give Wagner's dramas performances meeting his most demanding specifications. Thus in Munich there took place the world première of *Tristan und Isolde* in 1865. This was followed by the premières of *Die Meistersinger (The Mastersingers),* on June 21, 1868, and the first two dramas of *The Ring of the Nibelungs—Das Rheingold (The Rheingold)* on September 22, 1869, and *Die Walküre (The Valkyries)* on June 26, 1870. In the United States, the American premières of *Die Meistersinger* and *Das Rheingold* took place at the Metropolitan Opera, on January 4, 1886, and January 4, 1889, respectively. That of *Die Walküre* was given at the Academy of Music in New York on April 2, 1877.

H. C. Colles described *Tristan* as "coming nearest to the theory of union of the arts" among Wagner's dramas, and *Die Meistersinger* as "the most lovable of Wagner's works." He added: "The natures of the subjects explain both. The delightful character of Hans Sachs, the shoemaker poet at Nürnberg, his genial views of life, his sympathy and unselfishness, make him unique among Wagner's heroes. Almost everywhere else Wagner's heroes are tainted with his own egotism; what they will is right, and they conquer by their self-assertion. Hans Sachs conquers by his humility, he does not champion his own work but another's, and the whole of the music of *Die Meistersinger* is influenced by the character of Sachs. Except for the places where Wagner cannot resist homilies on art and criticism, it is freed from the fetters of his own personality. He is here far more willing to let the listeners take his work in their way rather than in his. One may find in it merely a delightful picture of the old German life of the sixteenth century. The antiquary will find it full of truthful allusions to medieval customs from those of the city guilds to those of musical tablature. The musician can revel in the skill with which three or four melodies develop contrapuntally in the overture; the lover of romance delights equally in the songs of Walther and Eva, the picture of the old street in the moonlight with the watchman droning his call as he goes, and the sunlight festival of St. John's day. The lover of comedy finds satisfaction in the street brawl and Beckmesser's rough handling by the apprentices. . . . All Wagner's means are perfectly at his command; he never wrote a broader or more firmly knit melody than the "Preislied" ("Prize Song") or designed a more vivid and wholly appropriate ensemble than the chorus of the street brawl, or one of greater musical beauty than the quintet."

Lawrence Gilman wrote of *Tristan* that it "soars upward from his [Wagner's] creative history like a pillar of flame, a thing so incandescent and unquenchable that men cannot yet look upon it with untroubled eyes." He then went on to say: *"Tristan* is unique not only among Wagner's works, but among all outgivings of the musical mind, because it is devoted, with an exclusiveness and concentration and intensity beyond comparison, to the rendering of essential experience. Wagner is concerned here not with epic paragons, or elemental beings of fire and of the depths, or gods and goddesses, or a cosmos in distress, or some brilliant and crowded chapter out of a romantic past: but with the inner life of life itself. In this score, he is at the summit of his genius. These passionate transvaluations of love and death have called forth the greatest that he could give; and he has steeped this miraculous music in a beauty that is outside of time."

Wagner's personal life became increasingly difficult. He and his wife Minna finally separated in 1862. By then Wagner was involved with Cosima, daughter of Franz Liszt and the wife of Wagner's devoted disciple and friend, Hans von Bülow. In 1865 Cosima bore Wagner a daughter. Minna Wagner died in 1866. Cosima bore Wagner another daughter in 1866 and in the fall of 1868 Wagner, Cosima, and their two daughters set up home at Triebschen, a village on the Lake of Lucerne in Switzerland.

Hans von Bülow was heartbroken. "If it had been anyone but Wagner, I would have shot him." Franz Liszt was so outraged that for a long time he refused to have anything to do with either Wagner or Cosima. It speaks volumes for the integrity and high musical principles of both these men—Liszt and von Bülow—that despite their deep and bitter resentment against Wagner the man, they never relented in their efforts and dedication in promoting the interests of Wagner the artist.

A son was born to Cosima and Wagner on June 6, 1869. They named him Siegfried. Two and a half months later Richard Wagner and Cosima were married, on August 25, 1870, Cosima's marriage to Hans von Bülow having been annulled. As a birthday gift to Cosima on December 25, 1870, Wagner wrote the *Siegfried Idyll* for string orchestra, and had it performed for her early one morning at their home at Triebschen. Thus Cosima was awakened that day by the strains of what has been described as the most beautiful lullaby ever written.

After completing the writing of *Die Meistersinger,* Wagner resumed work on his monumental *Ring of the Nibelungs.* He finished the third drama, *Siegfried,* in 1869 and the last one, *Die Götterdämmerung (The Twilight of the Gods)* in 1874. But even before he had brought this vast artistic project to its completion, he was fired with a new dream. He now wanted a theater built to his own specifications where his mighty music dramas could be heard in the exacting performances he envisioned, and under ideal conditions. When the city of Bayreuth, in Bavaria, offered him a tract of land on which to build such an auditorium, he determined to raise the money needed for the enterprise. Wagner societies sprang up in different parts of the world to help raise funds. Additional sums came from public subscription. Still more money came from concerts directed by Wagner himself. On Wagner's birthday, in 1872, the cornerstone of his festival theater was laid. On this occasion Wagner conducted a performance of Beethoven's Ninth Symphony.

In supervising the construction of his theater, Wagner applied some of the theories he had long entertained about the nature of an ideal opera house. He wanted orchestra and conductor to be concealed from view, not only for better tone balance, but also to avoid any distraction for the audience from the action on the stage. The auditorium was so constructed that a full view of the stage could be had from every seat. He also insisted that the theater be simple and functional, the stage itself the last word in equipment and facilities.

Other innovations (now basic to the opera house, but revolutionary in the 1870's) were introduced after the theater had opened. No one was to be admitted after the performance had begun; the opening prelude was to be listened to without any interruption; the house was to be completely dark during the performance; there were to be no encores of any kind; applause was not permitted until the final curtain.

Wagner's theater in Bayreuth opened on August 13, 1876, with *Das Rheingold, The Ring of the Nibelungs* being heard in its entirety for the first time. For *Siegfried* and *Die Götterdämmerung* the productions represented world premières—the former on August 16, the latter a day later. Visitors, dignitaries, and famous musicians from all parts of the world attended. "What happened in Bayreuth," reported Tchaikovsky, who was present, "will be remembered by our grandchildren and our great grandchildren." Since then Bayreuth has been a summer festival town for the performance of Wagner's music dramas—a Wagner shrine.

The first time the entire *Ring* cycle was heard in the United States was in 1889 at the Metropolitan Opera House, between March 3 and 11.

W. H. Hadow thus discussed the *Ring* cycle: "*Rhinegold* is undoubtedly the weakest, *Siegfried* undoubtedly the finest. The latter, indeed, is the strongest in construction and the most vigorous in workmanship of all Wagner's creations, and its gold is studded with such gems as the *Schmiedlied,* the *Waldweben,* and the magnificent duet on which the *Siegfried Idyll* was subsequently founded. *The Valkyries* is a very unequal work. It contains, perhaps, as many supremely fine numbers as *Siegfried* itself; but, except for the closing scene, the second act is rather tedious, and some of the other monologues stand in need of judicious curtailment. *The Twilight of the Gods* gives a little the impression that its first two acts were written for the sake of the third. But the whole scene of Siegfried's death, the superb funeral music, in which motif after motif tells the story of the murdered hero, the blazing pyre upon which Brünnhilde

dies amid the wreck of Valhalla, and the overthrow of the very gods themselves, these form a climax of epic grandeur, presented with a vividness of reality which no epic can ever attain."

In 1874 Wagner moved with his family into a new villa in Bayreuth, Wahnfried, which remained his home as long as he lived. (After his death it was the residence of his widow, children, and grandchildren.) His final mighty drama absorbed him—*Parsifal,* a "stage-consecrating festival drama," based upon the theme of the redemption of the Holy Grail and the suffering of Amfortas. *Parsifal* was introduced in Bayreuth on July 26, 1882. Wagner had left specific instructions that he wished *Parsifal* to be performed only in Bayreuth. Despite his wish, when the copyright ran out, *Parsifal* was produced at the Metropolitan Opera in New York on December 24, 1903—the first time it had been played outside Bayreuth.

"There are two reasons," said W. H. Hadow, "why *Parsifal* has a claim to be considered Wagner's masterpiece. In the first place its emotional level is more sublime than that of its predecessors. The central conception of the *Ring* is strength, that of *Tristan* is passion, that of *Parsifal* is goodness. . . . In the second place, it is the most homogeneous of the music dramas; that in which the different elements are most completely fused into unity. . . . In other words, it is the most complete embodiment of Wagner's dramatic theory, and so may be regarded as in a sense the climax of his work."

Shortly after the final performance of *Parsifal* in Bayreuth in 1882, Wagner and Cosima went on a holiday to Venice, where Wagner suffered a heart attack that proved fatal. He died on February 13, 1883. Delegates from Wagner societies throughout Europe escorted his remains from Venice to Bayreuth where Wagner was buried in the garden of Villa Wahnfried to the strains of "Siegfried's Death Music" from *Die Götterdämmerung.*

A police record issued in 1849, shortly after Wagner's escape from Saxony as a political prisoner, provides the following description of the master: "Wagner is . . . of middle height, has brown hair, wears glasses; open forehead; eyebrows brown; eyes gray-blue; nose and mouth well proportioned; chin round. In moving and speaking he is hasty." To this might be added that he had firm lips, prominent chin, and high cheekbones. His eyes had a piercing intensity that electrified those they scrutinized. His large head seemed out of proportion to the rest of his body. His face was deeply lined.

For the most part he was a highly disagreeable man—ruthless, selfish, self-centered, vain, irritable, hypocritical, and with a highly questionable code of behavior. He made enemies more easily than he made friends, and from the latter he demanded unquestioning allegiance to himself, his ideals, his purpose, and his destiny. He brooked no disagreements with what he believed, no differences of opinion even on trivial matters. He had many love affairs, sometimes with the wives of the very men who devoted themselves unsparingly to promoting his art or financing him personally. Pathologically extravagant, he spent lavishly money that had been borrowed and which he never repaid. He knew only one integrity, that to his art. That integrity remained unblemished. However discreditable were his performances as a man, his behavior as an artist was on the highest and most idealistic plane.

The influence of his music and his aesthetics has been immeasurable. As an artist Wagner has been violently attacked and passionately espoused. He has been imitated by some, repudiated by others. But to ignore him was impossible. He changed the format, concepts, and ideology of opera. He evolved his own laws of aesthetics. He introduced a new way of writing for the voice. He brought new dimensions to harmony, orchestration and thematic development. He enriched musical thought. To his technique as composer he brought a mastery rarely equaled. His was, indeed, the "art of the future," the slogan under which his battle was fought in his own time and for some years thereafter.

"All our dreams," said Vincent d'Indy, "even that of composers who most energetically deny the imputation, come from the spring which rises at the feet of the titanic Wagner. Richard Wagner still casts his great shadow over all our musico-dramatic production." And Ernest Newman went on to prophesy that undoubtedly music will undergo a great change in days to come, and some new Wagner will arise to create a new musical art "the nature of which it is impossible to anticipate." That music of the future, Newman continued, will no more resemble Wagner's than Wagner's music resembled Monteverdi's. "But music will still be something different from what it would have been had he never been born; and of only some half dozen composers in the whole history of the art can that be said."

After Wagner's death the Bayreuth Festival was carried on with an autocratic rule by Cosima, who died on April 1, 1930. Since their son, Siegfried, died soon after his mother, on August 4, 1930, the direction of Bayreuth fell to Siegfried's wife, Winifred, whom he had married in 1915. She maintained her control until the beginning of World War II. After the war, the artistic direction passed on to Wagner's grandchildren, Wieland and Wolfgang, who introduced revolutionary new concepts in staging and lighting, and modern approaches to the problems of scenery and costuming.

PRINCIPAL WORKS

Operas—Rienzi; Der fliegende Holländer; Tannhäuser; Lohengrin; Der Ring des Nibelungen: Das Rheingold, Die Walküre, Siegfried, Götterdämmerung; Tristan und Isolde; Die Meistersinger; Parsifal.

Orchestral Music—Eine Faüst Ouvertüre, Siegfried Idyll.

Vocal Music—Fünf Gedichte von Mathilde Wesendonk.

ABOUT

Donington, R., Wagner's Ring and Its Symbols: The Music and the Myth; Finck, H. T., Wagner and His Works; Gilman, L., Wagner's Operas; Hadow, W. H., Richard Wagner; Kapp, J., The Women in Wagner's Life; Krehbiel, H. E., Studies in the Wagnerian Drama; Newman, E., The Life of Richard Wagner; Newman, E., Wagner as Man and Artist; Pourtalès, G. de, Richard Wagner; Shaw, G. B., The Perfect Wagnerite; Turner, W. J., Wagner; Wagner, R., My Life; Wagner, R., Prose Works.

Carl Maria von Weber *1786-1826*

CARL MARIA FRIEDRICH ERNST FREIHERR VON WEBER, who developed German Romantic opera, was born in Eutin, Oldenburg, on November 18, 1786. His father was a former army officer who earned his living as the musical director of a traveling theatrical troupe. Carl Maria was born with a diseased hip that made it impossible for him to walk during the first four years of his life and only with a perceptible limp afterwards. Despite his delicate constitution and physical handicap, the

CARL MARIA VON WEBER

child was taken from town to town by his father. Such a nomadic existence was bad not only for his health but for his education, since any systematic and formal academic training was made impossible by the continual change of scene.

But the child's musical training was not neglected. His father was determined to develop a prodigy like Mozart (who was Carl Maria's first cousin by marriage) and consequently subjected the boy to severe discipline while teaching him singing and piano. When he was ten, Weber started to study piano with Heuschkel in Hildburghausen. One year later he was a pupil of Michael Haydn (Joseph's brother) in Salzburg. Between 1798 and 1800 Weber received additional instruction in singing and composition. While he was no prodigy as a performer, Weber did reveal an exceptional gift for composition. His first published work, a set of six fughettas for piano, appeared when he was twelve. At thirteen he wrote an opera which was never performed. A few days after his fourteenth birthday he attended the première of another of his operas, *Das Waldmädchen*, introduced in Freiberg on November 24, 1800, and later given in Chemnitz and Vienna. Another opera, *Peter Schmoll und seine Nachbarn*, was seen in Augsburg about 1803.

In the fall of 1803 Weber went to Vienna and there studied for two years with the Abbé Vogler, one of the most distinguished theorists of his generation. Vogler recom-

mended him for the post of conductor of the Breslau Opera, which Weber assumed in 1804. This experience was unhappy. Relations between the young conductor and those who worked with him were constantly at the breaking point; and the management resented the way he disregarded budgets in mounting his productions. In 1806 Weber withdrew from Breslau and became the music director for the establishment of Duke Eugene of Württemberg at his palace in Silesia. When the Duke was compelled by financial reverses to give up his orchestra, Weber went to work for Duke Ludwig at Stuttgart as his private secretary and music teacher for his children. There Weber became an innocent victim in a case involving misappropriated funds. Found guilty, he was imprisoned for two weeks, then ordered to leave Stuttgart for good.

All this while he had not been idle as a composer. His opera *Silvana* was heard in Frankfurt am Main on September 16, 1810. And a delightful one-act comic opera, *Abu Hassan*, was given with outstanding success in Munich on June 4, 1811.

Later Weber resumed his former association with Vogler in Darmstadt and also undertook an extensive tour of Germany as concert pianist. Then, in 1813, he was appointed musical director of the Prague Opera. He devoted himself for the next three years to rebuilding the company, which had fallen on evil days, and restoring its former grandeur. Weber's renown as conductor and impresario soon brought him one of the most desirable appointments in Europe. At the invitation of the King of Saxony he became in 1816 the musical director of the German Opera in Dresden. He was an immediate success. Before his first year was over, his appointment in Dresden was confirmed for life. On November 4, 1817, he married Caroline Brandt, a singer, for whom two years later he wrote his most popular composition for the piano, the *Aufforderung zum Tanz (Invitation to the Dance)*, most familiar today in orchestral transcriptions by Berlioz and Felix Weingartner.

His preoccupation with German-language operas in Dresden awakened in him the desire to create a national German opera. One day he happened to pick up a volume of ghost stories edited by Apel and Laun. One of these struck his fancy. He asked

Friedrich Kind to adapt it into an opera libretto. The text went quickly, but it took Weber three years to write his score. The opera was *Der Freischütz*—Weber's masterwork, the first significant German national opera, and the foundation stone on which rest all later German operas.

Der Freischütz was first given in Berlin on June 18, 1821; Weber's wife, Caroline, created the principal role of Agathe. The première aroused considerable anticipation. "Four hours before the opening of the Schauspielhaus," wrote Weber's son in his biography of his father, "crowds were besieging every entrance. To the excellent arrangements of the police it may be thanked that, when the doors opened, clothes alone were torn, and only a few smart bruises given in the fearful rush. The parterre was immediately filled to suffocation, by a compact mass of students, young men of science, artists, officials. . . . Stalls and boxes were filled by members of the high society in Berlin and the leading literary, musical and scientific authorities of the day. . . . All at once applause came from the orchestra. Weber had entered it. And now the whole house with its thousand upon thousand hands, took up the sound and thundered forth its echo. Three times Weber was obliged to let fall his baton and to bow before he could give the signal to begin. In the midst of the storm came suddenly a solemn silence. The magical musical pictures of the overture were now spread forth in all their fullness. The impression was unmistakable. When at last the triumphant finale had blazed forth in all its glory, such a burst of applause broke forth, such a universal shout of 'encore!' that the entire overture had to be repeated, with still greater enthusiasm if possible."

After the final curtain, continued Weber's son, "not a soul left the house. Thunders of applause and thousands of voices summoned the composer before his enraptured audience. At last he appeared, leading Mme. Seidler and Frl. Eunike by the hand. Amid the deafening shouting, flowers and verses were flung from all directions. The success of *Der Freischütz* had been immense—unparalleled!"

A day after the première, as a sentimental gesture, E. T. A. Hoffmann, the German Romantic composer and writer, placed a laurel wreath on Weber—the new Romantic in German music.

During the next year and a half, *Der Freischütz* was performed fifty times in Berlin. The Italian composers—particularly Spontini, who had previously enjoyed such a vogue in Berlin—seemed to lose their appeal for German opera-goers. Musical Berlin responded sensitively and instinctively to an opera whose text had solid Germanic qualities, filled as it was with a love of landscapes and popular superstitions and the supernatural. The Germans expressed their enthusiasm for a work that carried overtones of German folk songs and dances. "Here," as Alfred Einstein wrote, "the musician's art is no longer merely draughtsmanship; it is also coloring. Here the German woodland comes to life with all its magic in the horn music of the huntsmen's choruses and all its eeriness in the evocation of a haunted glen; here a born dramatist breathed abounding life into the girlish figures of Agathe and Aennchen . . . into the weak-willed young huntsman—a truly tragic figure, this—and above all created with a couple of strokes of genius the character of Caspar." The American première of *Der Freischütz* took place in Philadelphia in 1824. It was given a single performance by the Metropolitan Opera during the 1884-1885 season.

In Vienna, as in Berlin, *Der Freischütz* marked the victory of German opera over the Italian; even the great idol of the Viennese public, Rossini, was momentarily overshadowed. Domenico Barbaja, the famous impresario, soon commissioned Weber to write an opera for one of his theaters in the Austrian capital. Weber was partial to this assignment. It provided him with an opportunity to answer those critics who had described *Der Freischütz* as a "Singspiel" instead of an opera because it had spoken dialogue in place of recitatives. Weber now planned a national opera set throughout to music, and Wilhelmina von Chézy (for whose *Rosamunde* Schubert wrote incidental music) provided a text based on a thirteenth-century story by Gilbert de Montreuil. Her libretto turned out to be a silly affair—confused, involved, incredible. Because of that libretto, *Euryanthe* did not have the success previously enjoyed by *Der Freischütz*. When it was seen in Vienna on October 25, 1823, there were many indeed to criticize it most severely, even for its music. Franz Schubert, who attended the performance said: "This is no music. There is no finale;

no concerted piece according to the rules of art. It is all striving after effect. . . . It is utterly dry and dismal."

Yet for all the manifold faults of the text, and in spite of Schubert's low opinion of the music, *Euryanthe* remains an important event in German opera. Since it is set throughout to music, it may be looked upon as one of the earliest German contributions to *opera seria*. It was, as Alfred Einstein noted, the first step "toward the new equilibrium between music and drama which Wagner was to develop to its highest fulfillment."

What is believed to have been the American première of *Euryanthe* took place at Wallack's Theatre in New York in 1863. It was given by the Metropolitan Opera for the first time on December 23, 1887. Since then presentations of this opera have been few and far between. But its overture is an enduring monument in symphonic music, not only for its consistently high level of inspiration, but also because so much of it anticipates Wagner.

The immense success of *Der Freischütz* in London, where it was given simultaneously in three theaters, brought Weber a commission from Covent Garden to write an opera to an English text—*Oberon,* libretto by James Robinson Planché based on an old French romance. Though Weber was already suffering severely from tuberculosis, he accepted this offer. Even before he had finished writing all his music, he went to London (against the advice of his physician) to plunge at once into the task of supervising rehearsals.

Weber himself described the première of *Oberon* on April 12, 1826, as "the greatest success of my life." He added: "When I entered the orchestra, the house, crammed to the roof, burst into a frenzy of applause. Hats and handkerchiefs were waved in the air. The overture had to be played twice, as had also several pieces in the opera itself. At the end of the representation, I was called on the stage by the enthusiastic acclamations of the public, an honor which no composer had ever before obtained in England."

"Oberon," said R. A. Streatfeild, "contains many scenes both powerful and picturesque. . . . The fairy music is exquisite throughout. But the human interest of the story is after all slight, and Weber, on whom the hand of death was heavy as he wrote the score, failed to infuse much individuality into his characters."

Like *Euryanthe, Oberon* today is represented at symphony concerts by its overture, a masterwork. In addition, some of its vocal excerpts, most notably Rezia's magnificent aria, "Ocean, Thou Mighty Monster," are frequently heard at song recitals. But the opera itself is a comparative stranger in the United States where it was heard for the first time at the Park Theater in New York on October 9, 1828.

Though his health was deteriorating alarmingly in London, Weber managed to make several appearances at concerts and in salons following the première of *Oberon.* He was preparing to leave for home, on the night of June 5, 1826, when he died in his sleep. He was buried in Moorfields Chapel in London. Eighteen years later his body was disinterred and returned to Dresden for burial in the family vault. For the occasion Richard Wagner wrote special music and delivered the eulogy.

Weber has been described as a "small, narrow-chested man, with long arms, refined but large hands, thin, pale, irregular face, with brilliant blue eyes flashing through his spectacles; mighty forehead, fringed by a few straggling locks; awkward and clumsy, but charming in spite of all, especially when he smiled." He liked to dress in a long tight blue coat with shining buttons, closely-fitting trousers, Hessian boots with tassels, frilled shirt, yellow cloak with many capes, and a round hat with a broad brim. He had a genial, lovable nature, made many friends, and was very attractive to women. He had wit and a flair for the well-turned phrase. He wrote clever satirical verses. He enjoyed telling naughty stories and singing "rogue songs" to his own guitar accompaniment. Away from music he preferred to discuss politics or at parties to play charades.

Wagner considered Weber the founder of the German Romantic movement in opera, even though elements of German Romanticism had appeared in several works preceding *Der Freischütz.* In discussing Weber, R. A. Streatfeild said: "The genius of Weber was a curious compound of two different types. In essence it was thoroughly German —sane in inspiration and drawing its strength from the homely old Volkslieder, so dear to every true German heart. Yet over this solid foundation there soared an imagination surely more delicate and ethereal than has ever been allotted to mortal musician before or since, by the aid of which Weber was enabled to treat all subjects beneath heaven with equal success. He is equally at home in the eerie horrors of the Wolf's Glen, in the moonlight revels of *Oberon*, and in the knightly pomp and circumstance of the Provençal court. . . . The changes which Weber . . . effected, though less drastic, were in their results fully as important as those of Gluck. In the orchestra as well as on the stage he introduced a new spirit, a new point of view. What modern music owes to him may be summed up in a word. Without Weber, Wagner would have been impossible."

PRINCIPAL WORKS

Chamber Music—6 violin sonatas; Clarinet Quintet in B-flat major; Piano Quartet in B-flat major; Trio in G minor, for flute, cello and piano; Duo Concertant in E-flat major, for clarinet and piano.

Choral Music—Cantatas, Masses, Offertories.

Operas—Abu Hassan; Preciosa; Der Freischütz; Die drei Pintos (completed by Mahler); Euryanthe; Oberon.

Orchestral Music—2 clarinet concertos; Bassoon Concerto in F major; Clarinet Concertino in E-flat major; Concertstück in F minor, for piano and orchestra; Jubel-Ouvertüre.

Piano Music—4 sonatas; Aufforderung zum Tanz (Invitation to the Dance); Rondo brillant in D flat; écossaises, variations, and pieces for piano duet.

Vocal Music—Songs for voice and piano including "Der kleine Fritz" and "Wiegenlied"; songs for several voices; part songs; canons.

ABOUT

Cœuroy, A., Weber; Grüninger, F., Carl Maria von Weber: Leben und Werk; Kapp, J., Carl Maria von Weber; Moser, H. J., Carl Maria von Weber, Leben und Werk; Saunders, W., Weber; Stebbins, L. P., and R. P., Enchanted Wanderer; Weber, M. M. von, Carl Maria von Weber.

Thomas Weelkes *1575-1623*

THOMAS WEELKES, distinguished English composer of madrigals, was born in or about 1575. His birthplace is unknown and nothing has been discovered about his early years. In 1597 his first publication appeared: a set of twenty-four madrigals for from three to six voices. A year later he was in the service of Edward Darcye, Groom of the Privy Chamber, and published a volume of ballets and madrigals. He dedicated this volume to his employer, "the first fruits of my barren ground, unripe of time, unsavory in respect of others. . . . If they offend your stomach, lay them to ripen and you shall prove of my later vintage." Two more volumes of madrigals were issued in 1600, the first in five parts, the second in six.

In 1600 Weelkes was organist at the College of Winchester, and in 1602 he received a Bachelor of Arts degree in music from New College at Oxford. From 1602 on he occupied the posts of organist and chorusmaster at Chichester Cathedral. On February 20, 1603, he married Elizabeth Sandham, by whom he had two daughters and a son. His last publication was a volume of "Ayres," which appeared in 1608.

During the closing years of his life, Weelkes apparently became dissolute in his ways, for in 1617 the Bishop of Chichester removed him from his posts at the Cathedral, describing him as "a common drunkard and a notorious swearer and blasphemer" who spent more time in the "tavern or ale house" than "in the quire." The Bishop, however, allowed Weelkes to continue drawing his salary as organist. Weelkes died in London on November 30, 1623, while visiting a friend. He was buried in the church of St. Bride in Fleet Street on whose walls commemorative tablets were placed in 1923 during the tercentenary celebration of his death.

Though Weelkes produced church music which reveals an extraordinary grasp of the contrapuntal technique, he is best remembered for his madrigals. E. H. Fellowes maintained that "Weelkes certainly surpassed all his contemporaries in the wealth of imagination and originality." Weelkes filled his music with a rich fund of melody. He had a gift for pointing up the context of his poem in his music, and for arriving at dramatic effects. His harmonic writing was frequently characterized by chromatic progressions. Among his finest madrigals are "As Vesta Was from Latmos Hill Descending," which appeared in Thomas Morley's celebrated madrigal collection, *The Triumphs of Oriana;* "O Care, Thou Wilt Despatch Me"; "On the Plains Fairy Trains"; "Hark, All Ye Lovely Saints Above"; and "Sing We at Pleasure."

"No one in any age or country has expressed so many different ideas and moods in pure choral music." wrote Gustav Holst, "and . . . he always expressed them beautifully and well. . . . Weelkes is the true English artist. He is an individualist as opposed to the Latin artist who tends to be a member of a school. . . . There is nothing to suggest that Weelkes hated conventionality. It simply did not exist for him. When his treatment of a subject happened to coincide with the convention of the day, it just coincided, and there is only the superb craftsmanship to show us which is his work. In everything he wrote this craftsmanship enabled him to express all he felt in his own inimitable manner, whether simply or with elaboration, whether in a style that was to vanish from the earth after his day, or in a style similar to that which most people regard as belonging to the twentieth century."

PRINCIPAL WORKS

Chamber Music—Fantasies, pavanes, and other pieces for viols.
Choral Music—Airs, anthems, balletts, madrigals, Services.

ABOUT

Bridge, F., Twelve Good Musicians; Dickinson, A. E. F., Thomas Weelkes; Fellowes, E. H., English Madrigal Composers.

Music and Letters, January 1950; Proceedings of the Musical Association, 1915-1916.

Henri Wieniawski *1835-1880*

H ENRI (HENRYK) WIENIAWSKI, preëminent violin virtuoso and composer of notable violin music, was born in Lublin, Poland, on July 10, 1835. His father was an army surgeon; his mother, Regina Wolff-Wieniawska, an excellent concert pianist. So early did Henri demonstrate an unusual gift for music that as a child he was given formal instruction on the violin by Hornziel and Servacynski. On the counsel of his uncle, Edward Wolff, an important composer and concert pianist who resided in Paris, Henri was sent in 1843 to the French capital where he entered the Paris Conservatory. He made such remarkable progress in his first year under Clavel that he was placed with Massart; Wieniawski then went on to shatter precedent by winning first prize in violin playing at the age of eleven.

Wieniawski's violin study with Massart ended in 1848. On March 31, 1848, Wieniawski made an extraordinarily successful concert debut in St. Petersburg. The boy continued to give performances throughout Russia, Poland, and the Baltic states. Vieuxtemps declared that he had never heard one so young play the violin with such mastery.

In 1849 Wieniawski returned to Paris where he resumed music study with Hippolyte Collet. The pace of his concert tours was constantly accelerated until there was hardly a major city in Europe in which he had not won the approbation of critics, musicians, and audiences. To Anton Rubinstein, young Wieniawski was "without doubt the greatest violinist of our time." Some years later Joachim insisted that anybody who had not heard Wieniawski could not possibly conceive of what the left hand was capable.

From 1860 to 1871 Wieniawski was the solo violinist to the Czar. During this period he was for several years professor of violin at the St. Petersburg Conservatory and a member of the Ernst String Quartet.

His first tour of the United States took place in 1872-73. He made over two hundred appearances from coast to coast (at times in joint recitals with Anton Rubinstein). Most of the money earned from this tour was lost when, during the panic of 1873, a bank in which Wieniawski kept his American funds went bankrupt.

Upon returning to Europe, Wieniawski gave several brilliant joint concerts with Anton Rubinstein in Paris. In 1874 Wieniawski was appointed professor of violin at the Brussels Conservatory, a post vacated by Vieuxtemps. Ill health compelled Wieniawski to give up his teaching chores in 1877 and reduce the number of his concert appearances. During a performance in Berlin on November 11, 1878—when he was scheduled to present the German première of his second violin concerto—he was compelled by a spasm of the heart to leave the stage after playing only the first few bars. Following a brief rest he was seized by a second spasm. Joachim, who was in the audience, leaped to the stage and substituted for Wieniawski by performing the Bach Chaconne.

His health gave way entirely in Odessa, on his way to Moscow. A sentimental need to see for the last time the city in which he had enjoyed some of his greatest

Wieniawski: vyĕ-nyäf'skē

triumphs, made him continue his trip until he reached his destination. He arrived in Moscow with his strength gone, his funds exhausted. All his life a chronic gambler, Wieniawski had lost so much money in gambling and unwise investments that by 1880 he was completely without resources. Mme. von Meck, Tchaikovsky's patroness, provided him with funds, and made him welcome in her home. "Your benevolence to poor, dying Henri Wieniawski," Tchaikovsky wrote his "beloved friend," "touches me deeply. . . . I pity him greatly. In him we shall lose an incomparable violinist and a gifted composer."

Wieniawski died at Mme. von Meck's home in Moscow on March 31, 1880.

Wieniawski was married to Isobel Hampton, an Englishwoman. His love for her had been the inspiration for his *Légende,* one of his most popular violin compositions, which he wrote in Ostend in 1859. One of their children, Irene Regina, or Lady Dean Paul (1880-1932) became popular as a composer of semiclassics under the pseudonym of Poldowski.

Wieniawski was not a prolific composer. He produced fewer than thirty compositions, the best of which are basic to the violin repertory. His Concerto No. 2 in D minor, op. 22, published in 1870, is one of the landmarks in the violin music of the Romantic era. The lyricism throughout is on an exalted plane, and particularly so in the eloquent "Romance" movement which remains a favorite with concert audiences. This concerto as a whole reveals, in the words of Arthur M. Abell, "true inspiration, a most sympathetic . . . melodic invention, brilliant passage work, and an admirable adaptation to the violin."

Among Wieniawski's shorter works are several that make brilliant use of Russian folk melodies. In this category we find the *Souvenirs de Moscou* (a fantasia on two Russian airs, the more important one being "The Red Sarafan") and *Le Carnaval russe.* Some are based on the Polish dance, as for example, the two mazurkas, the *Kujawiak* and the *Polonaise brillante* in D major. Still other pieces are essentially the products of the German Romantic school, and the best of these is the *Légende.*

Wieniawski's brother Joseph (1837-1912) was an eminent concert pianist with whom he sometimes appeared in joint recitals. Joseph Wieniawski was the composer of a

HENRI WIENIAWSKI

fine piano concerto, several piano sonatas, and a string quartet, among other works.

On the occasion of the centenary celebration of Henri Wieniawski's birth, his nephew, Adam, in conjunction with the Chopin School of Music in Warsaw, inaugurated the Wieniawski International Competition for Violinists. The first such competition, held in Warsaw in 1935, attracted one hundred and sixty contestants from twenty-three countries. Ginette Niveau, then sixteen years old, won the first prize.

PRINCIPAL WORKS

Orchestral Music—2 violin concertos; Légende, for violin and orchestra; Souvenirs de Moscou, for violin and orchestra.

Violin Music—2 mazurkas; 2 polonaises; Le Carnaval russe; Kujawiak; Scherzo-Tarantelle in G minor, Capriccio-Valse; Caprice fantastique; Souvenir de Posen; Adagio élégiaque; Romance sans paroles et Rondo élégant; Études-caprices for two violins; gigues.

ABOUT

Desfossez, A., Henri Wieniawski, Esquisse; Reiss, J., Henryk Wieniawski.

Étude, September 1915.

John Wilbye *1574-1638*

JOHN WILBYE, one of England's chief composers of madrigals, was born in Diss, Norfolk, in 1574. He was the son of a prosperous landowner and tanner. Biographical information is meager, but it is known that in 1595 John Wilbye became a resident musician for Sir Thomas and Lady Elizabeth Kytson at their estate, Hengrave Hall, near Bury St. Edmunds. Three years after that he published his first volume of madrigals, thirty in number, for three to six voices. A second volume of thirty madrigals, once again for three to six voices, appeared in 1609. Wilbye also contributed a madrigal, "The Lady Oriana," to *The Triumphs of Oriana*, edited by Morley in 1601, and two motets to Leighton's *Tears or Lamentations* in 1614.

When Lady Elizabeth Kytson died in 1628, Wilbye left Hengrave Hall and became musician to the household of Lady Rivers, the younger daughter of Sir Thomas Kytson, in Colchester. He lived there until his death in September 1638 and was buried at the Holy Trinity in Colchester in an unidentified grave. E. H. Fellowes believed that since Wilbye never married, and so many of his madrigals speak of unrequited love, he was for many years secretly in love with Lady Rivers.

John Wilbye was one of the foremost madrigalists of his age, and there are some who would assign to him a position of first importance in Elizabethan music. Like his celebrated contemporary Thomas Morley, Wilbye could be light and nimble, delicate and gay, charming and graceful—as in madrigals like "Sweet Honeysucking Bees" and "Flora Gave Me Fairest Flowers," two compositions which are still highly popular. "It was . . . the directness and purity of the style," wrote an unidentified critic in the *Musical Times* of London, "the strong sense of beauty in sound, the admirably vocal nature of the part-writing that impressed themselves irresistibly on the mind of the musician."

But Wilbye also had his more serious and sober moods, of which "Adieu Sweet Amaryllis," "Ye Restless Thoughts," "Long Have I Made These Hills and Valleys Weary," "Happy, Oh! Happy He" and "All Pleasure Is of This Condition" are notable examples. "In the serious madrigal," said the *Musical Times,* "Wilbye surpassed all his contemporaries. It afforded him scope not only for the ingenious devices by which he gave dramatic color to his words, as well as for more freedom and sometimes complexity of rhythm, but also for the varied emotional

sentiment which he treated with such depths, although with such true artistic reserve that his work has never been tainted with anything approaching sentimentalism."

"Wilbye is, indeed, often harmonically very daring," commented Ernest Walker, "but he nevertheless always shows a rare instinct for sheer beauty of effect; and however closely he may paint the emotion of individual words, he never sacrifices the broad sweep of his massive structures. Indeed, both as a technical musician and as an expressive artist, Wilbye is one of the very greatest figures in English music; his total output, compared with that of many of his contemporaries, was not large, but its splendid quality places him, along with Purcell, at the head of English secular composers."

PRINCIPAL WORKS

Choral Music—65 madrigals; 2 motets.

ABOUT

Fellowes, E. H., The English Madrigal; Fellowes, E. H., English Madrigal Composers; Walker, E., A History of Music in England.

Musical Times, April 1925; Proceedings of the Musical Association 1914-1915.

Adrian Willaert *1490-1562*

ADRIAN WILLAERT was one of the founders of the Venetian school of polyphony that succeeded the Flemish. He was born in Bruges, Flanders, in 1490, the son of a church musician who hoped to make him a lawyer. In 1514 Willaert was sent to Paris to pursue legal studies, but while there he came under the influence of Jean Mouton, a Flemish composer who had studied with Josquin des Prés and who now served as *maître de chapelle* to Louis XII. Mouton became Willaert's teacher, instilling in the pupil the techniques and styles of the Flemish school. Mouton finally persuaded Willaert to give up law for music. In 1518 Willaert wrote his first three compositions in which the influence of the Flemish school was pronounced.

After paying a return visit to Flanders, Willaert traveled to Italy where, in 1522, he became *maestro di capella* to Alfonso I d'Este, duke of Ferrara. He held this post for three years, then for a brief period served in the musical household of Count Ippolito II d'Este, Archbishop of Milan and brother of the duke.

Willaert: vĭl′ärt

A curious episode occurred in Italy. In Rome he heard one of his own compositions performed in a church as a work by Josquin des Prés. He immediately claimed credit for having written it, whereupon the choir refused to perform it any longer since it had been written by an unknown composer.

On December 12, 1527, Willaert was appointed *maestro di cappella* of St. Mark's Cathedral in Venice. Except for two brief visits to Flanders—the first in 1542, the second fourteen years later—he stayed in Venice for the rest of his life. He helped import to Venice the art of the Flemish composers while adding to it Italian embellishments. He also established in Venice a singing school which helped train a generation of Venetian musicians including Zarlino, Andrea Gabrieli, and Cipriano de Rore.

Willaert enjoyed great honor as organist, composer, teacher, and *maestro di cappella*. He was often honored with celebrations and poems. When, towards the end of his life, Willaert seriously considered returning to his native land, his townspeople in Venice joined forces to prevail upon him to stay with them. He died in Venice on December 8, 1562.

Willaert helped devise an antiphonal style of contrapuntal writing for two choruses which Venetian composers were to use henceforth with extraordinary effect. He designed this method because St. Mark's had two organs and two choirs. His technique was to use the two choruses sometimes alternately (one chorus presenting a musical subject softly, the other replying loudly) and sometimes simultaneously. "As the Venetian painters suffused their work with a transfiguring light," wrote the noted historian Ambros, "so the Venetian composers achieved marvels of lovely sound with the colorful interplay of antiphonal choirs, and later with the mingling of instrumental tones."

Willaert was one of the early masters of the Italian madrigal. "His madrigals," said H. E. Woolridge, "are studiously simple both in form and style of melody." The music follows "the metrical structure closely, yet enriching it . . . with graceful points of imitation and simpler forms of ornamental cadence."

Willaert was also noteworthy for enriching both the style and content of the motet, for dramatizing and helping heighten the

ADRIAN WILLAERT

effect of Masses, for arriving at a harmonic style through the use of chords, and for foreshadowing the use of a recitative style of vocal writing.

PRINCIPAL WORKS

Choral Music—Hymns, madrigals, Masses, motets, psalms.

Instrumental Music—Canzoni, ricercari.

ABOUT

Einstein, Alfred, The Italian Madrigal; Lenaerts, R., Notes sur Adrian Willaert; Reese, G., Music in the Renaissance.

Hugo Wolf *1860-1903*

HUGO PHILIPP JAKOB WOLF, genius of the German art song (lied) was born in Windischgraz, Styria, on March 13, 1860. His father, a currier, was an excellent amateur musician who gave Hugo his first music lessons but who was nevertheless determined from the beginning not to allow his son to become a professional musician. Hugo, however, proved to be such a listless and unresponsive pupil in all subjects other than music at elementary and high schools in Graz and Marburg, that his father finally and reluctantly yielded to his driving ambition to study music seriously. In 1875 Wolf went to Vienna and entered the Vienna Conservatory, where he was a pupil of Robert Fuchs in harmony and Wilhelm Schenner in piano.

Wolf: vōlf

HUGO WOLF

During his first year at the Conservatory, Wolf was decisively influenced by a hearing of Wagner's *Tannhäuser*. The fifteen-year-old boy was shaken by the experience. "I find no words for it," he exclaimed, "and will only tell you that I am an idiot. . . . The music of this great master has taken me out of myself." At that time Wagner was in Vienna conducting performances of some of his operas and was residing at the Hotel Imperial. For hours Wolf haunted the hotel hoping to catch a glimpse of the great man. Finally, with the aid of the hotel manager, Wolf met Wagner and showed him some of his songs. Wagner told him simply: "I cannot give you an opinion of your compositions. . . . I have far too little time. . . . When I was your age and composing music, no one could tell me whether I should ever do anything great. . . . When you are older, and when you have composed bigger works, and by chance I return to Vienna, you will show me what you have done. But that is of no use now; I cannot give you an opinion of them yet." Wolf never again met Wagner. But from that day Wagner was the North Star by which young Wolf guided his own course.

At the Conservatory things were not going well for Wolf. He hated routine, textbook rules, format exercises. He was as ill-tempered as he was undisciplined. He engaged in violent arguments with his teachers. After two years, Wolf was dismissed from the Conservatory, though not through any fault of his own. Somebody had forged Hugo Wolf's name on a threatening letter to the Conservatory director and Wolf was unable to prove his innocence.

He was not sorry to go. He could now plunge into a self-imposed curriculum which suited his temperament far better than his Conservatory schooling. He memorized textbooks on harmony, and he studied the musical scores of the masters. He read poetry voraciously, committing to memory the lyrics of Goethe, Grillparzer, and Mörike among others. He acquired a knowledge of French and English: "Restlessly I am driven to improve my weak talents, to extend my horizon, to endow my thoughts, my actions, my feelings with as ripe an expression as possible." Gluck, Mozart, Beethoven, and Wagner—Wagner most of all—aroused in him an almost religious reverence.

He was miserably poor. He managed to earn a little by teaching, but since he was irritable and abusive he could not hold his pupils for any length of time. He survived mainly through the generosity of his friends. In 1881, however, his appalling poverty was temporarily relieved when he became assistant conductor under Karl Muck in Salzburg. He arrived with a bundle of clothes under one arm and a bust of Wagner under the other. But in Salzburg he was required to work with third-rate music, mostly operettas, and he soon gave up his job to return to Vienna.

The death of Wagner in 1883 affected Wolf deeply. Dr. Heinrich Werner, one of Wolf's friends, described how, upon getting the news, Wolf "without a word, without any notice of us . . . went to the piano and played the funeral music from *Götterdämmerung*. Then he shut down the piano and went—silently as he came. In the evening he reappeared in a subdued and deeply sorrowful mood: 'I have wept like a child,' he told me."

Between 1884 and 1887 Wolf worked as a music critic of the *Salonblatt* in Vienna. Opinionated and outspoken, he made many enemies and some friends. At that time Vienna was divided into two hostile camps: those who favored the abstract music of Brahms and those who regarded Wagner's "art of the future" as the true musical gospel. Some of Vienna's most influential musicians were numbered in the pro-Brahms and anti-Wagner faction. In their hatred of Wagner and their contempt for his ideals and principles, these musicians and critics did not hesitate to destroy anybody who, like young Wolf, was a passionate believer in Wagnerism. It was largely through the influence of some of Brahms' supporters that the Rosé and the Hellmesberger quartets turned down Wolf's Quartet in D minor. When Hans Richter, conductor of the Vienna Philharmonic, offered to perform Wolf's *Penthesilea Overture,* it was only to humiliate the young composer. At the rehearsal, after the orchestra had finished playing, the conductor told his men: "Gentlemen, I would not have played this piece until the end. I was merely interested in knowing the sort of a composer this is who dares write against the master, Brahms."

In the fall of 1887 Wolf's first publications, two volumes of songs, were issued by a minor house through the efforts and subsidy of several friends. The appearance of his music in print seemed to give Wolf new creative resources and to encourage unprecedented activity. In 1888, after giving up his critic's job, he went to live with a friend at his villa in Perchtoldsdorf, a suburb of Vienna. There he unleashed his imagination and creative powers. He himself became awed both by his phenomenal fertility and by the quality of his inspiration. "I am working incessantly with a thousand horsepower from dawn till late at night," he wrote a friend on March 23, 1883. "What I now write, dear friend, I write for posterity, too. They are masterpieces . . . for I have . . . since February 22 composed twenty-five songs of which each one surpasses the others, and about which there is only one opinion among men of musical discernment—that there has been nothing like them since Schubert and Schumann, etc. etc. You may imagine what sort of songs they are." That this was not brash conceit but the conviction of a great creative artist fully conscious of his strength was proved by the masterworks that left his pen before the year 1888 was over: the *Mörike Liederbuch;* the fourteen songs in the *Goethe Liederbuch;* three songs in the *Eichendorff Liederbuch;* six songs after Scheffel, Mörike, Goethe, and Kerner. The mighty torrent swept into 1889 and 1890 with a dozen more Goethe songs, the *Spanisches Liederbuch, Alte Weisen,* and seven songs in the first part of the *Italienisches Liederbuch.* "Am I one who has been called —am I of the elect?" he inquired with amazement in contemplating these achievements.

Then, suddenly and mysteriously, his inspiration ran dry. He turned again and again to writing songs only to find that ideas would not come; the former excitement and vigor had withered. "What a fearful lot for an artist not to have anything new to say," he lamented. By May 1891 he was thoroughly convinced that his career had ended. "I have given up the idea of composing," he wrote. "Heaven knows how things will finish. Pray for my poor soul!"

But his own obituary to his creativity was premature. By the end of 1891 he found a new inner strength and fresh energy. He now wrote fifteen more songs for the *Italienisches Liederbuch* (first part), each a masterpiece. Another period of sterility followed, but it ended in 1895 with the completion of his first opera, *Der Corregidor.* (The text, by Rosa Mayreder, was based on Pedro Antonio de Alarcón's *The Three-Cornered Hat,* which several decades later became a ballet with a score by Manuel de Falla.) In 1896 Wolf wrote the second part of the *Italienisches Liederbuch.* And in 1897 he worked upon a second opera, *Manuel Venegas.*

Though *Der Corregidor* was a failure when produced in Mannheim on June 7, 1896, and though it had been turned down by the Vienna Royal Opera, Hugo Wolf was not without a measure of recognition by this time. He boasted dedicated admirers who promoted his music whenever they could: powerful musicians like Ferdinand Jäger, Franz Schalk, and Ferdinand Löwe. Josef Schalk gave a song recital in Vienna in which he devoted his program to two composers only, Beethoven and Wolf. It is true this concert created a good deal of hostility among the anti-Wagner forces, but in spite of that Wolf's songs made a deep impression. His songs were also heard in other German cities with such mounting appreciation that in 1895 a Hugo Wolf society was formed in Berlin to promote his works further. Meanwhile, several of Wolf's choral works were favorably received in Vienna in 1894. An all-Wolf concert in Vienna in February 1897 proved such a triumph that Wolf's friends easily formed a Hugo Wolf Society in the Austrian capital.

With success at hand, Wolf's health broke. Crushed by the refusal of the Vienna Opera to perform *Der Corregidor,* he began to suffer from insomnia and nightmares. He would wander the streets aimlessly mumbling to himself. Before long he became a victim of delusions, one of which was that he was the director of the Vienna Opera. When he gave way to fits of hysteria he was confined in a sanitarium. He stayed there about a year, profiting sufficiently from the rest cure to be allowed to take a holiday in Italy in 1898. He now even spoke of finishing his opera *Manuel Venegas*. Then, one morning, he tried to commit suicide by plunging into a lake. After that, at his own request, he was committed to the Lower Austrian Mental Hospital. There he was stricken by a paralysis that crippled body and speech. His mind grew more and more confused until he did not know who he was. "If only I were Hugo Wolf," he would exclaim. An attack of peripneumonia proved fatal and he died in the hospital on February 22, 1903.

At his funeral services some of Vienna's leading musicians, including some of his lifelong enemies, came to pay him final homage. Both the Opera (which had refused to perform *Der Corregidor*) and the Conservatory (from which he had been expelled) sent delegations. A chorale by Bruckner accompanied the body to its grave. Soon after the burial of Wolf, the city of Vienna provided the funds for an honorary tomb not far from the graves of Beethoven and Schubert.

In *Musical Vienna,* this editor described Wolf thus: "He was small, of mean build, thin, and undernourished. His eyes looked out starkly. He seemed always on the brink of hysteria. He was wild and excitable in gesture and expression, his heart always pounding—either in admiration or hatred. The small body was an inexhaustible storehouse of energy, or fiercely burning hysterical energy." How excitable he became after reading poetry was described by his friend, the poet Herman Bahr, who found him reacting in the following fashion to some verses by Kleist: "He raved about it; his hands shook if he read only a couple of verses from it; his eyes glittered; he appeared as one transfigured, as though he saw a higher and brighter sphere, whose gates had opened suddenly." Once when Bahr and Wolf were living together, Bahr returned home late at night. Suddenly "the door opened and from the other room appeared . . . Hugo Wolf in a very long shirt, with candle and book in his hand, almost a pale

and fantastic apparition. . . . He laughed a shrill laugh and jeered. . . . Then he came to the middle of the room, waved his candle about . . . and began to read to us, chiefly from *Penthesilea.*"

He was one of the greatest composers of German art songs music has known, a worthy successor of Schubert, Schumann, and Brahms. To lyricism he brought a new dramatic expressiveness, and to piano accompaniments a new independence and richness of thought. Ernest Newman went so far as to rank Wolf above all other song writers because, in his words, Wolf said "a larger number of beautiful things in the lyric, and a greater variety of beautiful things, than any other composer before or since." Then Newman added: "Within the small sphere of the song, Wolf exhibits an architectonic faculty that, I daresay, has not its superior in the whole history of music. No music could be surer in its balance, in the knowledge of when to cease and when to continue; no music conveys more surely the impression that it simply *had* to begin just here and end just there. . . . Equally admirable, equally eloquent . . . is the certainty with which each new touch is introduced here and there in a melody or accompaniment, that seems to flash a momentary . . . light on this word or that, without disturbing the unity and inevitableness of the thematic development."

"His songs," Kurt Pahlen has said "were entirely novel and revolutionary. They went far beyond anything written before. The declamation—in the spirit of Wagner—was dramatically tensed to the utmost. Every word, every thought, had a tonal inflection of its own. The piano accompaniment, already quite independent of the singing voice, depicted moods, at times merely furnished hints, in a manner later adopted by impressionists."

In the entire history of the art song there have been few, if any, other composers so completely and so sensitively attuned to the poems they set as Wolf, who wrote to Engelbert Humperdinck: "Poetry is the true source of music." Elaborating on this theme, James Husst Hall asserted that Wolf gave the poem "first place, and more truly and more fully than any of his predecessors he permitted the poem to shape the song, not only in the large, but particularly in the small details."

PRINCIPAL WORKS

Chamber Music—String Quartet in D minor; Intermezzo in E-flat major, for string quartet; Italian Serenade, for string quartet (also for string orchestra).

Choral Music—Aufblick; Einklang; Letzte Bitte; Christnacht; Elfenlied; Der Feuerreiter; Dem Vaterland; various other compositions for male chorus, mixed chorus, and solo voices and chorus.

Operas—Der Corregidor; Manuel Venegas (unfinished).

Orchestral Music—Penthesilea.

Piano Music—Aus der Kinderzeit; Humoreske; variations.

Vocal Music—Sechs Lieder für eine Frauenstimme; Sechs Gedichte von Scheffel, Mörike, Goethe und Kerner; Mörike Liederbuch; Eichendorff Liederbuch; Goethe Liederbuch; Spanisches Liederbuch; Alte Weisen; Italienisches Liederbuch, two parts; Drei Gedichte von Robert Reinick; Drei Gesänge aus Ibsens Das Fest auf Solhaug; Vier Gedichte nach Heine, Shakespeare und Lord Byron; Drei Gedichte von Michelangelo; numerous other individual songs for voice and piano.

ABOUT

Decsey, E., Hugo Wolf; Ehrmann, A. von, Hugo Wolf: sein Leben in Bildern; Foss, H. J. (editor), The Heritage of Music, vol. 2; Loeser, N., Wolf; Newman, E., Hugo Wolf; Orel, A., Hugo Wolf; Rolland, R., Musicians of Today; Sams, E., The Songs of Hugo Wolf; Walker, F., Hugo Wolf: A Biography.

APPENDIXES

APPENDIX I

A Chronological Listing of Composers

Guillaume de Machaut 1300-1377
John Dunstable 1370-1453
Guillaume Dufay 1400-1474
Johannes Ockeghem 1430-1495
Josquïn des Prés 1450-1521
Jacob Obrecht 1452-1505
Clément Jannequin 1485-1560
Nicolas Gombert 1490-1556
Adrian Willaert 1490-1562
Cristóbal de Morales 1500-1553
Jacob Arcadelt 1505-1560
Claude Goudimel 1505-1572
Thomas Tallis 1505-1585
Andrea Gabrieli 1520-1586
Philippe de Monte 1521-1603
Giovanni Pierluigi da Palestrina 1525-1594
Orlando di Lasso 1532-1594
William Byrd 1543-1623
Giulio Caccini 1546-1618
Tomás Luis de Victoria 1548-1611
Emilio del Cavalieri 1550-1602
Orazio Vecchi 1550-1605
Luca Marenzio 1553-1599
Thomas Morley 1557-1602
Giovanni Gabrieli 1557-1612
Carlo Gesualdo 1560-1613
Jacopo Peri 1561-1633
Jan Sweelinck 1562-1621
John Bull 1562-1628
John Dowland 1563-1626
Hans Leo Hassler 1564-1612
Claudio Monteverdi 1567-1643
John Wilbye 1574-1638
Thomas Weelkes 1575-1623
Orlando Gibbons 1583-1625
Girolamo Frescobaldi 1583-1643
Heinrich Schütz 1585-1672
Johann Hermann Schein 1586-1630
Samuel Scheidt 1587-1654
Francesco Cavalli 1602-1676
Giacomo Carissimi 1605-1674
Andreas Hammerschmidt 1612-1675
Johann Froberger 1616-1667
Marc'Antonio Cesti 1623-1669
Giovanni Legrenzi 1626-1690
Matthew Locke 1630-1677
Jean-Baptiste Lully 1632-1687
Marc-Antoine Charpentier 1634-1704
Dietrich Buxtehude 1637-1707
Giovanni Battista Vitali 1644-1692
John Blow 1649-1708
Johann Pachelbel 1653-1706
Arcangelo Corelli 1653-1713
Giuseppe Torelli 1658-1709

Henry Purcell 1659-1695
Johann Kuhnau 1660-1722
Alessandro Scarlatti 1660-1725
François Couperin 1668-1733
Antonio Vivaldi 1669-1741
Giovanni Battista Bononcini 1670-1747
Reinhard Keiser 1674-1739
Jean-Baptiste Loeillet 1680-1730
Georg Philipp Telemann 1681-1767
Christoph Graupner 1683-1760
Jean Philippe Rameau 1683-1764
Francesco Durante 1684-1755
Johann Sebastian Bach 1685-1750
Domenico Scarlatti 1685-1757
George Frideric Handel 1685-1759
Benedetto Marcello 1686-1739
Francesco Geminiani 1687-1762
Francesco Veracini 1690-1750
Giuseppe Tartini 1692-1770
Leonardo Leo 1694-1744
Pietro Locatelli 1695-1764
Jean Marie Leclair 1697-1764
Giovanni Battista Sammartini 1698-1775
Johann Adolph Hasse 1699-1783
Karl Heinrich Graun 1704-1759
Padre Martini 1706-1784
Baldassare Galuppi 1706-1785
Giovanni Battista Pergolesi 1710-1736
William Boyce 1710-1779
Wilhelm Friedemann Bach 1710-1784
Niccolò Jommelli 1714-1774
Christoph Willibald Gluck 1714-1787
Carl Philipp Emanuel Bach 1714-1788
Johann Stamitz 1717-1757
Pietro Nardini 1722-1793
François André Philidor 1726-1795
Niccolò Piccini 1728-1800
Johann Adam Hiller 1728-1804
Pierre-Alexandre Monsigny 1729-1817
Joseph Haydn 1732-1809
François Gossec 1734-1829
John Christian Bach 1735-1782
Karl von Dittersdorf 1739-1799
Giovanni Paisiello 1740-1816
André Modeste Grétry 1741-1813
Luigi Boccherini 1743-1805
Domenico Cimarosa 1749-1801
Muzio Clementi 1752-1832
Giovanni Battista Viotti 1755-1824
Wolfgang Amadeus Mozart 1756-1791
Jan Dussek 1760-1812
Jean François Lesueur 1760-1837
Luigi Cherubini 1760-1842
Étienne Nicolas Méhul 1763-1817
Ludwig van Beethoven 1770-1827

Pierre Rode 1774-1830
Gasparo Spontini 1774-1851
François Boieldieu 1775-1834
Johann Hummel 1778-1837
John Field 1782-1837
Niccolò Paganini 1782-1840
Daniel François Auber 1782-1871
Louis Spohr 1784-1859
Carl Maria von Weber 1786-1826
Friedrich Kuhlau 1786-1832
Ferdinand Herold 1791-1833
Karl Czerny 1791-1857
Giacomo Meyerbeer 1791-1864
Gioacchino Rossini 1792-1868
Karl Loewe 1796-1869
Franz Schubert 1797-1828
Gaetano Donizetti 1797-1848
Jacques Halévy 1799-1862
Vincenzo Bellini 1801-1835
Albert Lortzing 1801-1851
Adolphe Adam 1803-1856
Hector Berlioz 1803-1869
Mikhail Glinka 1804-1857
Felix Mendelssohn 1809-1847
Frédéric Chopin 1810-1849
Otto Nicolai 1810-1849
Robert Schumann 1810-1856
Franz Liszt 1811-1886
Ambroise Thomas 1811-1896
Friedrich von Flotow 1812-1883
Richard Wagner 1813-1883
Giuseppe Verdi 1813-1901
Robert Franz 1815-1892
Niels Gade 1817-1890
Charles Gounod 1818-1893
Stanislaus Moniuszko 1819-1872
Jacques Offenbach 1819-1880
Franz von Suppé 1819-1895
Henri Vieuxtemps 1820-1881
Joachim Raff 1822-1882
César Franck 1822-1890
Édouard Lalo 1823-1892
Ernest Reyer 1823-1909
Peter Cornelius 1824-1874
Bedřich Smetana 1824-1884

Anton Bruckner 1824-1896
Johann Strauss II 1825-1899
Anton Rubinstein 1829-1894
Karl Goldmark 1830-1915
Alexander Borodin 1833-1887
Johannes Brahms 1833-1897
Amilcare Ponchielli 1834-1886
Henri Wieniawski 1835-1880
César Cui 1835-1918
Camille Saint-Saëns 1835-1921
Léo Delibes 1836-1891
Mily Balakirev 1837-1910
Georges Bizet 1838-1875
Max Bruch 1838-1920
Modest Mussorgsky 1839-1881
Josef Rheinberger 1839-1901
Peter Ilich Tchaikovsky 1840-1893
Johan Svendsen .1840-1911
Emmanuel Chabrier 1841-1894
Felipe Pedrell 1841-1922
Antonín Dvořák 1841-1904
Giovanni Sgambati 1841-1914
Sir Arthur Sullivan 1842-1900
Jules Massenet 1842-1912
Arrigo Boito 1842-1918
Edvard Grieg 1843-1907
Nikolai Rimsky-Korsakov 1844-1908
Pablo de Sarasate 1844-1908
Sir Francesco Paolo Tosti 1846-1916
Henri Duparc 1848-1933
Zdeněk Fibich 1850-1900
Alfredo Catalani 1854-1893
Engelbert Humperdinck 1854-1921
Moritz Moszkowski 1854-1925
Ernest Chausson 1855-1899
Sergei Taneiev 1856-1915
Ruggiero Leoncavallo 1858-1919
Hugo Wolf 1860-1903
Isaac Albéniz 1860-1909
Gustav Mahler 1860-1911
Anton Arensky 1861-1906
Edward MacDowell 1861-1908
Vassili Kalinnikov 1866-1901
Guillaume Lekeu 1870-1894

APPENDIX II

Composers Grouped by Nationality

American
Edward MacDowell, b. New York City

Austrian
Anton Bruckner, b. Ansfelden
Karl Czerny, b. Vienna
Karl von Dittersdorf, b. Vienna
Joseph Haydn. b. Rohrau
Gustav Mahler, b. Kalischt, Bohemia
Wolfgang Amadeus Mozart, b. Salzburg
Franz Schubert, b. Vienna
Johann Strauss II, b. Vienna
Franz von Suppé, b. Spalato, Dalmatia
Hugo Wolf, b. Windischgraz

Czech (Bohemian)
Jan Dussek, b. Čáslav
Antonín Dvořák, b. Nelahozeves
Zdeněk Fibich, b. Šebořice
Andreas Hammerschmidt, b. Brüx
Bedřich Smetana, b. Leitomischl
Johann Stamitz, b. Deutschbrod

Danish
Niels Gade, b. Copenhagen

English
John Blow, b. Newark-on-Trent
William Boyce, b. London
John Bull, b. Somersetshire
William Byrd, b. Lincolnshire
John Dunstable. b. probably Dunstable
Orlando Gibbons, b. Oxford
Matthew Locke, b. Exeter
Thomas Morley, place of birth unknown
Henry Purcell, b. London
Sir Arthur Sullivan, b. London
Thomas Tallis, b. probably Leicestershire
Thomas Weelkes, place of birth unknown
Thomas Wilbye, b. Diss

French
Adolphe Adam, b. Paris
Daniel François Auber, b. Caen
Hector Berlioz, b. La Côte-Saint-André
Georges Bizet, b. Paris
François Boieldieu, b. Rouen
Emmanuel Chabrier, b. Ambert
Marc-Antoine Charpentier, b. Paris
Ernest Chausson, b. Paris
François Couperin, b. Paris
Léo Delibes, b. Saint-Germain-du-Val
Henri Duparc, b. Paris
Claude Goudimel. b. Besançon
Charles Gounod, b. Paris
Jacques Halévy, b. Paris
Ferdinand Herold, b. Paris
Clément Jannequin, b. Châtellerault
Édouard Lalo, b. Lille
Jean Marie Leclair, b. Lyons
Jean-François Lesueur. b. Drucat-Plessiel
Guillaume de Machaut, b. probably in diocese of Rheims
Jules Massenet, b. Montaud
Étienne Nicolas Méhul, b. Givet
Pierre-Alexandre Monsigny, b. Fauquembergues
François André Philidor, b. Dreux
Jean Philippe Rameau, b. Dijon
Ernest Reyer. b. Marseilles
Pierre Rode, b. Bordeaux
Camille Saint-Saëns, b. Paris
Ambroise Thomas, b. Metz

German
Carl Philipp Emanuel Bach, b. Weimar
Johann Sebastian Bach, b. Eisenach
John Christian Bach, b. Leipzig
Wilhelm Friedemann Bach, b. Weimar
Ludwig van Beethoven, b. Bonn
Johannes Brahms, b. Hamburg
Max Bruch, b. Cologne
Peter Cornelius, b. Mayence
Friedrich von Flotow, b. Teutendorf
Robert Franz, b. Halle
Johann Froberger, b. Stuttgart
Christoph Willibald Gluck, b. Erasbach
Karl Heinrich Graun, b. Wahrenbrück
Christoph Graupner, b. Hartmannsdorf
George Frideric Handel, b. Halle
Johann Adolph Hasse, b. Bergedorf
Hans Leo Hassler, b. Nuremberg
Johann Adam Hiller, b. Wendisch-Ossig
Engelbert Humperdinck, b. Siegburg
Reinhard Keiser, b. Teuchern
Friedrich Kuhlau, b. Ülzen
Johann Kuhnau, b. Geising
Karl Loewe, b. Löbejün
Albert Lortzing, b. Berlin
Felix Mendelssohn, b. Hamburg
Giacomo Meyerbeer, b. Berlin
Moritz Moszkowski, b. Breslau
Otto Nicolai, b. Königsberg
Jacques Offenbach, b. Cologne

Johann Pachelbel, b. Nuremberg
Josef Rheinberger, b. Vaduz, Liechtenstein
Samuel Scheidt, b. Halle
Johann Hermann Schein, b. Grünhain
Robert Schumann, b. Zwickau
Heinrich Schütz, b. Köstritz
Louis Spohr, b. Brunswick
Georg Philipp Telemann, b. Magdeburg
Richard Wagner, b. Leipzig
Carl Maria von Weber, b. Eutin

Hungarian

Karl Goldmark, b. Keszthely
Johann Hummel, b. Pressburg
Franz Liszt, b. Raiding

Irish

John Dowland, b. probably Dalkey, near Dublin
John Field, b. Dublin

Italian

Vincenzo Bellini, b. Catania, Sicily
Luigi Boccherini, b. Lucca
Arrigo Boito, b. Padua
Giovanni Battista Bononcini, b. Modena
Giulio Caccini, b. Rome
Giacomo Carissimi, b. Marino
Alfredo Catalani, b. Lucca
Emilio del Cavalieri, birthplace unknown
Francesco Cavalli, b. Crema
Marc'Antonio Cesti, b. Arezzo
Luigi Cherubini, b. Florence
Domenico Cimarosa, b. Aversa
Muzio Clementi, b. Rome
Arcangelo Corelli, b. Fusignano
Gaetano Donizetti, b. Bergamo
Francesco Durante, b. Frattamaggiore
Girolamo Frescobaldi, b. Ferrara
Andrea Gabrieli, b. Venice
Giovanni Gabrieli, b. Venice
Baldassaro Galuppi, b. Burano
Francesco Geminiani, b. Lucca
Carlo Gesualdo, b. Naples
Niccolò Jommelli, b. Aversa
Giovanni Legrenzi, b. Clusone
Leonardo Leo, b. San Vito degli Schiavi
Ruggiero Leoncavallo, b. Naples
Pietro Locatelli, b. Bergamo
Jean-Baptiste Lully, b. Florence
Benedetto Marcello, b. Venice
Luca Marenzio, b. Coccaglio
Padre Martini, b. Bologna
Claudio Monteverdi, b. Cremona
Pietro Nardini, b. Leghorn
Niccolò Paganini, b. Genoa
Giovanni Paisiello, b. Taranto
Giovanni Pierluigi da Palestrina, b. Palestrina
Giovanni Battista Pergolesi, b. Jesi
Jacopo Peri, b. Florence

Niccolò Piccini, b. Bari
Amilcare Ponchielli, b. Paderno Fasolaro
Gioacchino Rossini, b. Pesaro
Giovanni Battista Sammartini, b. Milan
Alessandro Scarlatti, b. Palermo, Sicily
Domenico Scarlatti, b. Naples
Giovanni Sgambati, b. Rome
Gasparo Spontini, b. Majolati
Giuseppe Tartini, b. Pirano
Giuseppe Torelli, b. Verona
Sir Francesco Paolo Tosti, b. Ortona sul Mare
Orazio Vecchi, b. Modena
Francesco Veracini, b. Florence
Giuseppe Verdi, b. Le Roncole
Giovanni Battista Viotti, b. Fontanetto da Po
Giovanni Battista Vitali, b. Cremona
Antonio Vivaldi, b. Venice

The Low Countries (Belgian, Flemish, Dutch)

Jacob Arcadelt, b. Liège
Guillaume Dufay, b. Hainaut
César Franck, b. Liège
Nicolas Gombert, b. probably Bruges
François Gossec, b. Vergnies
André Modeste Grétry, b. Liège
Josquin des Prés, b. Hainaut
Orlando di Lasso, b. Mons
Guillaume Lekeu, b. Verviers
Jean-Baptiste Loeillet, b. Ghent
Philippe de Monte, b. Malines
Jacob Obrecht, b. Berg-op-Zoom
Johannes Ockeghem, b. probably Ockeghem
Jan Sweelinck, b. Amsterdam
Henri Vieuxtemps, b. Verviers
Adrian Willaert, b. Bruges

Norwegian

Edvard Grieg, b. Bergen
Johan Svendsen, b. Christiania

Polish

Frédéric Chopin, b. Zelazowa Wola
Stanislaus Moniuszko, b. Ubiel
Henri Wieniawski, b. Lublin

Russian

Anton Arensky, b. Novgorod
Mily Balakirev, b. Nijny-Novgorod
Alexander Borodin, b. St. Petersburg
César Cui, b. Vilna
Mikhail Glinka, b. Novospasskoi
Vassili Kalinnikov, b. Voin
Modest Mussorgsky, b. Karevo
Nikolai Rimsky-Korsakov, b. Tikhvin
Anton Rubinstein, b. Vykhvatinetz
Sergei Taneiev, b. Vladimir
Peter Ilich Tchaikovsky, b. Votkinsk

Spanish

Isaac Albéniz, b. Camprodón
Cristóbal de Morales, b. Seville
Felipe Pedrell, b. Tortosa
Pablo de Sarasate, b. Pamplona
Tomás Luis de Victoria, b. Ávila

Swedish

Dietrich Buxtehude, b. Helsingör

Swiss

Joachim Raff, b. Lachen